SAVING THE ANIMALS

ARMANDO ANG

Copyright 1998

Copyright © 1998 by Armando A. Ang

Published by: Armando A. Ang

Printed in the Philippines by:
BOOKMAN PRINTING HOUSE, INC.
373 Quezon Avenue
Quezon City

Printed on recycled paper. Twenty percent proceeds from the sale of this book will go to the protection of animals.

ISBN No. 1500254347

DEDICATION

This book is dedicated to all the animal-rights activists and their efforts in giving dignity to animals that share this living planet. They are a truly rare breed that we should all encourage to save the animals from further cruelties, unwanted and unwarranted deaths.

Unless a person is an animal activist or a bookworm, there is little opportunity to read about the abuses humans have done animals. Cruelties to animals have been going on for centuries. It is only the enlightenment brought about by many environmental organizations and the publications of books and magazines that people are becoming aware of the problem. Even then, little is being done about the abuses because of these sporadic reports.

Most people have little regard for the lesser creatures. Unless they are quality animals kept as pets or can command a good price in the market, they are seldom treated humanely. In the Philippines, stray dogs are often starved, killed and made into appetizers. Chicken sold in the wet market are killed by slitting their throat and thrown into the boiling water. Most animals meant for human consumption are killed without stunning them.

All these abuses are about to change as the Animal Welfare Act was recently signed by President Fidel V. Ramos on February 11, 1998. While some people may find the law wanting, it is an important first step toward saving the animals in the wild from extinction and putting an end to the cruel treatments of domestic animals and pets.

I tried to compile the abuses in one book form some of the most cruel and ongoing abuses experienced by the helpless animals inflicted by the greatest predators, the human beings. Hopefully, anybody who read this book will be enlightened and touched into doing something for the animals, creatures that play a vital role in the ecosystem and not meant for abuse by people. Human beings can be the greatest threat or the greatest savior to the survival of animals. Let us all do our share in this endeavor in *Saving the Animals*.

Armando Ang

FOREWORD

Mankind and animals have populated the Earth for thousands of years. From the sabre-tooth tigers that threatened the cavemen to the coral reefs that seem to pose nothing more than glorified undersea museums for today's divers: the millions of species of animals have brought both pleasure and survival lo mankind since time immemorial. But today, in a world of rapidly advancing industrialization and massive ecosvstem destruction, these very animals that sustain us are to be lost through the hazards of extinction.

A Japanese author once said: *I believe all animals were provided by God to help keep man alive.* Nothing can be truer than that tiny proverb proclaimed years before the threat of progress began destabilizing our ecosystems. We must open our eyes and realize the value these animals bring to our daily living, to the minute joys they bring to our lives. These animals have gone hand in hand with the greatest animal of all, *homo sapiens sapiens.*

With the threat encompassing even the archipelago of the Philippines, now is not a time sooner for all of us to get our acts together in saving the biodiversity that inhabits this Earth. This hook is one way we can all clear up the false vision that fogs up our sense of humanity. The author has worked rigorously in preparing this humble book that presents itself as a collection of facts that may prove both startling set pacifying Here he acquaints us with the multitude of cruel practices conducted worldwide that lead to the deaths and suffering of countless animals; usually to no humanitarian benefit Me enriches us with facts that are too fascinating to be believed. From the mating habits to wonderful stories of animal rescues, he manages to enlighten us all to this world of animals we usually take for granted. Finally, he presents clear options for us on how to join this worldwide bandwagon to save the precious animals we have and how to protect them from the juggernaut we call progress.

Written in a concise and entertaining manner; this book will no doubt provide hours of pleasurable relaxation. In addition, we receive the benefit of hours and hours of meticulous research that imparts to us a renewed sense of responsibility we all share in preserving Mother Nature.

I hope you enjoyed and learned from this book as much as I did. I 'm off to do my pawikan research. Maybe I can still save them from extinction. Let's all do our part.

Enjoy reading.

Michael Ang
BS-Environmental Science
Ateneo de Manila University

ACKNOWLEDGEMENTS

This is a complement to my other book, *SAVING THE TREES*. With this book, the protection on wildlife comes in full circle. Although this book was written singlehanded, it was well supported by many writers and reporters who wrote or reported about events concerning animals in books, magazines, newspapers, and other media forum. I wish to acknowledge their untiring efforts in fringing the plight of the animals into focus and inviting the attention of government agencies, NGOs and concerned individuals.

Some of the magazines consulted include *Sierra, Audubon, Birder's World. Wildlife Conservation, Discover, Animals, Environment, National Geographic, Popular Science, Scientific American, E Magazine, Bear Magazine, Reptiles, Earth, Dog Fancy, Cat Fancy, Horses, Cats, E Magazine,* and others. My apology to any book or periodicals I failed to mention. A bibliography of books can be found at the end of the book. To them, I salute their efforts in trying to save the animals from suffering and death.

This book would not have been written without the computer at my disposal. It is to the credit of my son, David who helped me overcome many problems I encountered using it.

Table of Contents

Schombungk's Duck * Stellar's Sea Cows * Stephen's Island Wrens * Tasmanian Tigers * Tecopa Pupfish * Wake Island Rails * Wallaby (Toolache) Wapitis or Easter Elks * Warrahs or Antarctic Wolf

Agriculture * Atmospheric Habitat * Bioinvasion * Coastal Areas * Coral Reefs Damming * Deforestation * Dredging * Drought * Fires * Floods and Typhoons Forest Fragmentation * Human Settlement * Inventory and Monitoring of Species * Land Degradations * Mangroves * Mining Radioactivity * Rainforests Ranching * Roadways * Volcanic Eruptions * Wars

Bowhunting * Firearms * Furs * Harpoon and Other Innovations * Ivory Trade Lead Pellets * Leathers * Leghold Traps * Military Hunting * Museums * Safaris Smuggling * Sporting Clays * Sportsmen * Trophies and Curios

Alternative Tests * Animal-Free Products * Animals in Combat * Cages * Case Against Animal Testings * Circus * Cruel-Free Products * Dog-Eating * Draize Test * Drug Connections * Exotic Foods * Lethal Dose 50 * Military * Tests Oddities * Rituals and Traditions * Seafoods * Silkworms * Sports Cruelty Vivisection * Wildlife Collection * Zoos

Acid Rain * Air Pollution * Balloon * Endocrine Disrupters * Eutrophication Global Warming * Heavy Metals * International Agreement * Land Reclamation Marine Vessels * Mining * Noise Pollution * Oil Pollution * Ozone Depletion PCBs * Pesticides * Plastics * Recycling * Red Tide * River Pollution * Sewage Sludge * Thermal Pollution * Trash

Animal Welfare Law * Anti-Poaching * Boycott * Captive Breeding * CITIES Cloning * Conservation at Home * Conserving Food Resources * Ecotourism Education * Endangered Species Act * Environmental Organizations * Fund Raising * Individual Actions * Letter Writing * Marine Sanctuaries * National Totem * Other Conservation Measures * Regional Agreement * Reward Systems Stamps * Telemetry * Wildlife Parks * Zoological Parks

Did you know that........

In 1988. two million signature seals (*hankos*) made from ivory were produced by the Japanese Elephants were killed by both sides during the Vietnam War to deprive the enemy of arms transport.

Between forty and fifty million fur-bearing animals are killed annually in the U.S. alone. A coat made from the fur of chinchilla at one time can fetch S100,000.

Lead pellets poisoned 1.5 to 3 million waterfowls in the U.S. annually.

The South Koreans eat two million dogs annually in one of the most sadistic ways. The dog is hanged, then electrocuted with a metal rod inserted into its mouth, and finally singed its entire body of fur, and all the time the animal is kept alive while it secretes adrenaline, used for soup.

CITES 1995 figures estimated that 600 million fishes, 15 million reptile skins, 5 million birds, 15 million mammals, and 30,000 monkeys were illegally traded worldwide.

It took less than 50 years to reduce the six billion passenger pigeons to extinction in the U.S., making it the single greatest massacre ever known.

In the 1970s, chimpanzees were used for car crash tests. NIH scientists even had pistons driven into the heads of unanesthesized animals only to discover that the experiments were useless because of their stronger and heavier skulls.

Baby crocodile heads have been made into keychains; gorilla's hands into ash tray; elephant's feet into seats; and caiman skin into shoes.

Zoos in the early days are nothing but caged prisons for kidnapped animals from the wild.

In one experiment, the eyes of scores of snakes were removed to determine if they will eat when blind. In India, lorises' eyes are plucked out and used as folk medicine. They are later returned to the wild because religion forbids the natives to kill the blind animals.

Dogs, cats, chimpanzees, blowfly, and even goldfish have been subjected to alcohol tests in order to gather knowledge for human medication.

Bird flu of 1997 in Hong Kong has resulted in the death of 1.3 million poultry, mostly chicken.

The beluga whales of St. Lawrence River were used for target practice by the Canadian Air Force during World War II.

Cats were mummified by the millions as offerings and buried in tombs along with the Egyptian pharaohs. In the 19th century, so many were exhumed by archaeologists that they were shipped to Britain as ballast then grounded into fertilizer.

During WW I 5,000 dogs were killed as a messenger between troops at the war front and the commanders at the rear. In WW II Germany had an army of 200.000 trained German shepherds guarding concentration camps. The Red Army went one step further by equipping the dogs with TNT charges and an antenna that will trigger the explosives once it touched the metal of the tank.

Unanesthesized dogs have been put under microwave blasts to learn the effect of temperature increase on their bodies. Dogs have been bred to be hairless for people allergic to their hair or fleas. In Taiwan, stray dogs are disposed in landfills and buried alive with the garbage.

Of the two million crocodilian skins traded each year, three-quarters came from spectacled caiman and the Yacare caiman. Most are send to and processed in Italy.

To produce a kilo of musk oil, it will need to kill at least 50 male musk deer. Substitutes are available, but some perfume makers still insist on using it.

During the Vietnam War, dolphins were trained to search mines and guard against saboteurs. The dolphins were equipped with large hypodermic needle attached to high-pressured carbon dioxide cylinders and taped to their frontal head. Anybody struck with the needle is injected with carbon dioxide that causes the body to explode.

Bears are trained to dance by putting them on a hot plate, forcing them to jump from one fool to another while the tambourine is played. Every time the music is played, they dance automatically to the tune. Their teeth are hammered out while young to give courage to the trainers.

More than 10 million Galapagos giant tortoises were taken during the early whaling days. The tortoise can live for months without food.

Traveling showmen use grotesque animals to attract people. Animals are deliberately mutilated, the more grotesque the better for business. A foot is sometimes removed lo display three-footed animals.

Snake charmers use cobras with their fangs forcibly yanked out after they bite a piece of cloth. The snakes often died of starvation while waiting for the jaws to heal.

The USDA used to require cattle coming from Mexico be branded on their face. The cow's head is immobilized by steel pinchers as red hot iron is pressed into its face as the steer bellows and eyes bulge as its flesh burn.

The Exxon Valdez oil spill killed an estimated 580,000 seabirds, 200 to 900 endangered bald eagles, 22 whales, and over 5,000 sea otters.

About 500 lions are raised and butchered for their meat in the U.S. annually.

In Asia drug smugglers use cages and crates made of wood laminated with heroin and exported with the jungle cats. In Afghanistan they use wood laminated with hashish and caged with wolfhounds. Snakes are forced-fed with indigestible packets of drugs before shipment. Crocodiles are killed and sprayed with cocaine powder passed off as white preservative.

Calves raised for veal are subject to toxic chemicals, kept in stalls without room for movement to prevent them from developing muscle and refused iron supplement to make them anemic so as to produce pale, lean and tender meat.

Two million birds died from ingesting plastics thinking they were jellyfishes while another 100,000 mammals either ingested or get entangled in them annually.

Lobsters are eaten alive using chopsticks in some Chinese restaurants.

Bear paws are made into stew and soup in the Orient. Restaurants pay as much as $200 for each paw and sold to groumets for as much as $850 a bowl of bear-paw soup. The left paw is regarded as the sweetest because it is used by bears for collecting honey.

It was the fur trade around the world that is responsible for the colonization of the New World in the 17th century U.S.

Acid rain has rendered more than 14,000 lakes in Canada and 4,000 in Sweden fishless.

In the 1957 atomic bomb experiment, 58 rhesus macaques were put inside tubes and placed at varying distances from Ground Zero. The mokeys near the flashpoint were fried and the rest often died of cancer.

In UK, over one million toads and 200,000 rabbits are run over by automobile each year; 500,000 hedgehogs in Germany.

Augustus Caesar allowed the killing of 3,500 wild cats including a 25-foot snake during his reign. Nero once set a company of horsemen against a collection of 400 bears and 300 lions.

Trajan, after conquering Dacia in 106 A.D. celebrated for four months. Gladiators in Colosseum were forced to fight wild cats in the arena. As many as 10.000 gladiators died together with II,000 animals during the celebration.

In a restaurant in Australia, prawns are cooked in a way known as "drunken or screaming prawns." These are live prawns soaked in alcohol and set on fire. It is so named after the noise they make when they are fried alive.

In 1986 El Salvador exported 134,000 caiman skins although it has only 10,000 of them in the wild. The rest came from Panama and Colombia where it is also a protected species.

The most exploited cat today is the ocelot. Their rarity has pushed the cost of its coat to $40,000.

The legal fur markets of Europe handle 700,000 pelts from wild animals each year. Two-thirds are from the skins of small spotted cats. Traders have discovered ways and means of concealing the sources and destinations of illegal skins by channeling them through third party countries where they acquired legal international trade documents.

During the 1970s, Zaire was the biggest source of ivory because four members of the ruling party and a member of President Mobutu's family were involved in smuggling. A Cl30 cargo plane was flying monthly to South Africa loaded with ivory.

The leghold traps have been banned in more than 70 countries worldwide, but less than a dozen states in the U.S. have adopted the measures banning this tortous machines.

Museums in the past have been responsible for some extinction of mammals and vertebrates.

All swifts and swiftlets use a substance secreted from a pair of enlarged salivary glands beneath their tongues to glue their nests together. The saliva is the principal ingredient made into a gelatinous soup, which is essentially a protein-sugar solution, and eaten by the Chinese for some 1,500 years. Hong Kong imported 8 million of these nests annually.

In 1947, the harvest of sharks together with skates and rays was about 220,000 tons worldwide. By 1994 the amount has risen to 800,000 tons, accounting for for about 200 million sharks. This unprecedented increase is due to the decimation of other species.

Eagles are killed for sports and shooting practices. Rival armies in Lebanon used the eagles as target practice whenever they are not shooting one another.

During the 19th century, the feathers of egret were more expenssive than gold, at $38.

The bullfrog is the mainstay of the market for its edible legs. The worldwide harvest for its legs was estimated at 200 million bullfrogs annually. The huge demand came fron Europe and the U.S. and they are mostly imported from India and Bangladesh. Some 80 million are collected from the rice fields of Bangladesh alone.

The caviar is the most expensive fish dish in the world. A female sturgeon caught in the Tikhaya Sosna River in 1924 weighed 1,277 kgs and yielded 245 kgs of quality caviar and is worth more than $350,000 today.

Papua New Guinea is the only tropical country to have a constitution specifying insects as a natural resource and a government agency dedicated solely to the insect trade,

The fruit growers of California regularly hire beekeepers to pollinate the almonds seasonally.

In China pigs in the rural areas are raised underneath the home of the farmers. A hole is provided that allows the farmer to pour anything edible to the pigs. Wastewater, chicken feathers, fruit peelings, etc. are given. But the worse is yet to come. Every time someone need to go to the comfort room, all he does is crouched on the hole and send his intestinal waste to the pig below.

The ancient Hebrews hated cats because they reminded them of their captivity among the cat-loving Egyptians. St. Augustine, who took the view that man should dominate all animals on the planet has been adopted by many for centuries and resulted in the extinction of many species.

In a span of seven years, a cat can produce as many as 420,000 kittens or more than one million during her lifetime. A dog can have as many as 67,000 puppies In a span of six years.

Roadkill is the number one cause of wildlife deaths in the U.S.

Napoleon Bonaparte had been reduced to a quivering wreck in the presence of cats. One night an aide heard him screaming and lunging his sword to ward off a kitten in his chamber.

SAVING THE ANIMALS

CHAPTER 1

BENEFITS FROM THE ANIMAL KINGDOM

Animals can be found throughout the world. They are so varied and numerous that only about 5% to 10% have been classified by scientists. From the Arctic to the Antarctic regions, deserts to the highest mountains, in the air and under the deepest seas, in the cities and under the ground, animals of different species can be found. They come in all sizes and shapes and range from the largest blue whale which weighs up to 150 tons to the microscopic one-celled amoeba that can only be seen under the high-powered microscope.

The animal kingdom is a complex system of biodiversity that consists of an estimated 10 to 30 million species of organisms. Only 1.7 million species have been classified, out of which 1.5 million species are found in the developed countries. Many unclassified species will probably be extinct before they are even discovered and tested for their possible benefits to mankind. Besides being the source of our food, chemicals and medicine, the animal kingdom provides us pets for companionship and enjoyment for those who study their behavior. They also help us regulate the cycle of life sustaining elements that make life possible on earth. All we need to continue enjoying these benefits is to make sure that they are well conserved and sustainably used.

Animals have special characteristics that set them apart from plants, bacteria and fungi. Except for a few pests, most of the animals have benefited humans in more ways than one. Insects such as bees, beetles, and butterflies have made the proliferation of plants possible and kept the planet alive in preparation for the time mankind would walk on this earth. While they continue to keep the planet teeming with life, it is up to us to harness them for our own benefits. From the animals we can find other benefits that only they can supply. Medicines, therapies, entertainments, waste decomposers, food, draught animals are just some of the many things they do for us.

Animals have also been a source of inspiration for many. Nature lovers continue to find many fascinating facts about animals in the wild. There are a lot more potential benefits we can gather from these animals if we only learn how to treat them more humanely.

ANIMAL BEHAVIORS

Humans can learn many things by studying animals and their behavior. Examples of animal's emotions have been well-documented. In their book, *When Elephants Weep*, the authors documented many instances of the emotional lives of animals. It is also difficult to understand that animals do not do things just by instinct, but have the intelligence to learn.

Mountain goat nannies try to prevent their kids from falling off the mountain by staying on the downhill side, away from the cliff. On one occasion, when a baby goat fell off the mountain, the nanny rushed over to lick and nuzzle the baby goat. A peregrine falcon father taught their offspring not to approach human observers by attacking them until they changed their behavior.

A very interesting behavior is practiced by sea lions after giving birth to baby pups. The moment the pup is born, the mother will raise her high up in the beach and drop her into the rocks until it cries; just like humans slap the baby to make it cry. The procedure will be repeated as often as necessary. Afterwards, the mother sea lion will sniff her pup and listen intently to its voice, which will serve as an identification mark for the rest of their lives. This is important because sea lions are very selfish and will destroy other pups intruding into their close quarters.

Animals have been taught to talk or communicate with sign language. Some chimpanzees have an IQ comparable to children. Parrots are especially easy to teach if we have the patience to teach them. Sparkie, an Australian budgerigar (parakeet) had a vocabulary of 531 words and could speak 354 sentences. He could construct his own sentences and even greet his owner's friends by name. He even went to the extent of teaching other parakeets to talk. The African grey parrot (*Psiitacus erithacus*) named Prudle won twelve consecutive titles (1965-1976) as the best talking bird at the annual Animal National Cage and Aviary Bird Show in London. She had a vocabulary of 800 words. She retired undefeated and was still talking two days before her death on July 13, 1994. However, the record holder is another budgerigar (*Melopsiitacus undulaius*) called Puck owned by Camille Jordan of California, which had a vocabulary of about 1,728 words on January 31, 1993. Because of their talking abilities, many of the African grey parrots have been taken from the wild and exported as pets. During the period 1983-1989, more than 346,000 were exported from 20 African countries.

Unlike birds, some animals, because of the difference in their vocal cords can not speak out but are able to communicate with people using sign language. A famous gorilla, Koko, in a span of two decades was able to learn about 900 different signs. She can even show her emotions by pinpointing to the mate she wanted for a companion. Unfortunately, the owner of the male gorilla refused to give him up.

A lowland gorilla known throughout the world, she recently made her first TV commercial aimed at raising funds for the Gorilla Foundation, a nonprofit research organization that currently cares for Koko and two other gorillas in Woodside, California.

There is a plan to move to a 70-acre preserve in Maui, Hawaii. The move will enable them to expand operations which include monitoring the progress of gorillas around the world and conducting research on *Koko, Michael*, and *Ndume*, her current suitor. The new site will also provide a refuge for captive gorillas stressed out by zoo life, as well as wild gorillas whose lives have been disrupted by civil strife in Rwanda.

We have not learned the meaning of their sound system, but some chimpanzees and other primates have learned hundreds of words of the American Sign Language. Kami, a bonono chimp is able to understand and respond to complex spoken English sentences. He can also produce three-letter sentences using symbols from a computer keyboard. Alex, an African grey parrot, understands the meaning of the words he speaks. Trained by a psychologist, Irene Pepperleng, he knows the names of fifty objects, seven colors and five shapes.

While animals do not seem to have speech that humans understand, there are many instances where they are able to communicate their feelings toward each other. They make sounds to communicate with their own species that we humans do not understand. Animals communicate information through gestures, posturing, sounding, and actions that their own species understand. They are sometimes more efficient at understanding body language than humans are able to understand theirs.

It is difficult for us to accept the fact that animals have strong emotions like companionship and love. Two circus horses, Ackerman and Alle were deeply attached to one another. When Ackerman died unexpectedly, the other refused to eat or sleep. Even when a new horse was brought in to share her companionship, she still refused to eat or sleep, although she was not ill. Within two months, Alle died of starvation.

On the other hand, two Pacific dolphins in a marine park in Hawaii, Kiko and Hoku were devoted to each other for years. When Kiko died prematurely, Hoku refused to eat and-always swam with his eyes closed. He was given a new companion, Kolohi, who swam beside him and caressed him. After a while, he opened his eyes and started to cat again.

Elephants have feelings that are reasonably the same as humans. When a matriarch elephant died, the other elephants clustered around her trying to get her up. One tried to give her food while another tried to raise her up with his tusks. After a while the group left but a female and her calf remained, trying to revive her.

Animals can also feel the loneliness of isolation. One beaver who was without a companion just sat down, refused to eat until he died of starvation. Loneliness could be the cause of many unwarranted deaths among animals. Animals caught from the wild, transported long distances, and that remain captive alone do not live very long. Other emotions such as shame, blushing, embarrassment, modesty, and guilt are also exhibited by animals, though not to the same degree for each animal. These are just a few of the instances of parallelism in human and animal behaviors found by researchers.

Studying animal behavior can be lifesaving. There are roughly 400 species of marine fish worldwide that can be toxic to humans. Ciguatera affects 50,000 people annually. It is a serious, sometimes lethal form of poisoning. The cause may be toxins produced by seaweed dwelling dinoflagellates that travel up the food chain. By observing fishes in the clear waters off St. John, Virgin Islands, doctors from the Southern Illinois University at Carbondale, hope to clarity how ciguatera travels through the food chain. They hope to compare how fish behave when grazing in seaweed full of dinoflagellates and those that roam around seaweed-free environment. They will collect seaweed samples in different habitats; identify, calculate densities and map distributions of dinofiagellates by seaweed species and sites to determine where and what seafoods to avoid.

The more than on hundred pelicans and Brandt's cormorants that went berserk in Sept 1991 off the coast of Santa Cruz, California, lead biologists from the University of California, Santa Cruz to research into its cause. The birds' stomachs were analyzed and found to contain anchovies and a toxin called domoic acid produced by the algae. *Pstudonitzschia australis* feeding on the plankton. Four people died in Canada in 1987. This important discovery lead to the periodic monitoring.

Some 2.000 years ago, Aristotle (384-322 B.C.) had observed the strange behavior of some female spider species allowing themselves to be eaten by their spiderlings without struggle. The mother spider must have known that once she lay her eggs she can no longer reproduce again. To ensure that all her spiderlings survive to adulthood, she fattens herself with insects up to ten times her own weight. The rich nutrients are stored in unfertilized eggs in her ovaries. When foods are scarce, she will allow her body to be sucked by her babies for the needed nutrients until the whole body is consumed completely. It is one way to ensure that her offspring do not eat one another and most of them will survive for the next generation.

The praying mantis is another insect that is willing to sacrifice its life to copulate the female to ensure the survival of his generations. Although the female does not always eat her mates, the risk is always there. To the praying mantis, the survival of future generations seems to be his only goal in life. It is amazing that the male will initiate copulation even after his head and brain are gone. His ultimate goal is to inseminate his mate even after she had eaten most of his body. Nothing seems to deter him from his goal. He becomes a meal that will help her to survive until she has laid the eggs that will become his offspring. Other insects such as the hangingflies will hunt first another insect to present to the female as her food before copulation to ensure his own survival.

Parapsychologists have long been fascinated with the sixth sense that animals possess. They have documented many cases of animals perceiving danger that warn their owner of impending danger. Dogs and other animals make abnormally noisy sounds whenever danger lurks. In China, people have been trained to observe abnormal behavior among the livestock such as chicken and pigs. A pet that insists on going out may be sensing an upcoming danger before it happens. They are particularly keen in detecting signs of earthquake. Even rats will emerge from their hiding places without fear of people. Others refuse to take any food given to them.

During the Second World War in London, a Pekingese named Winky used to follow her master to the market every Saturday. One Saturday, she refused to go along, yelping, screaming and trembling when she was forced to go to the market. The following Saturday, a V2 missile fell on the market place killing 105 people. Another incident during the same period saved the lives of a family when the dog "persuaded" the owners to hide in the cellar after an air raid warning instead of under the dining table where they used to crouch. A bomb exploded at the exact place they earlier intended to hide.

Some horses are more sensitive than others. King Cassius, a racehorse refused to be transported with four other horses in a horse carriage in 1972. No matter how they tried to load him into the carriage, nothing could persuade him to enter the carriage. It left without him and along the road met an accident, injuring the two drivers; one horse was badly injured while another suffered a broken jaw.

Sometimes, animals seem to bring bad omens to the owners. A cock that crows three times in a row could be a warning sign that death is near. Numerous cases have been documented. There was a recorded case of a perfectly healthy man who went out to investigate why the cock crowed three times in a row and died the next day of heart attack. Another whose mongrel dog howled incessantly died of an asthmatic attack. Parapsychologists theorized that some animals may be able to see the impending death due to the loss of aura of a person. It has been known that people who can visualize aura can indeed know the health of a person.

ANIMAL EXPERIMENTATIONS

Medicines from the animal kingdom may not be as plentiful as those coming from the plants, but they play an even more important role as a surrogate for humans. Many discoveries, inventions, and manufacturing of drugs have been made using them. Nearly all advances in the fight against human diseases have been done using animals. Vitamins, drugs, hormones, vaccines, cancer treatments, development of surgical operations have been based on animal experiments. Testing of drugs on animals are necessary to determine their toxicity before they are administered to human beings. The potential for causing cancer and other diseases and possible harm to pregnant women and the fetuses are important considerations that must be taken into account. In the U.S. alone, more than 20 million mammals are used annually for research work. Rodents, mostly mice and rats, comprise about 90% of all mammals used. Cats and dogs comprise a very important 1%. Dogs are essential for heart and artery diseases while cats are used to study vision and hearing as well as brain functions. Rabbits and primates are used in another 1% each. Most of these animals are usually genetically raised for specific purposes.

Galen (130 -200 A.D.) was a Greek physician who was the first to study physiology through the use of animal experimentation. His work were the basis of the evolution of modern medicine, although he never studied human anatomy directly. He dissected and experimented with different animals, especially the tailless monkey called the Barbary ape. He was the first to recognize the automatic heartbeat and the first myogenic theory of heart action. He demonstrated the relationship of blood flow and the aeration of blood through the lungs, the gills of fishes, and the placenta in animals.

Marcello Malpighi (1628-1694), an Italian physician and anatomist, was the founder of microscopic anatomy. In 1661, his examination of the lungs of a frog led to his discovery of how oxygen and carbon dioxide made exchanges in the alveoli ox air sacs during respiration. Subsequently he discovered tiny tubes called capillaries from the lung tissues of frogs which connect the smallest artery and vein systems. The following year, he identified the red corpuscles of the blood and the Malpighian corpuscles of the kidney and spleen.

Most of the scientists and at least 40 Nobel Prize winners in medicine and physiology succeeded because of work done through animal experiments. William Harvey (1578-1657), an English scientist, published his monograph. *Anatomical Exercise on the Motion of the Heart and Blood*, describing the circulation of the blood based on observations made on a variety of the living heart and moving blood in the arteries and veins of laboratory animals and embryos.

In 1733, Stephen Hales (1677-1761), an English clergyman and physiologist, made the first measurement of blood pressure, using a mare as the experimental animal for his cumbersome apparatus. It took a century later for the French physiologist, Jean Poiseuille to invent a mercury manometer that eventually made blood-pressure measurements feasible in clinical practice, using dogs as his experimental subjects.

Claude Bernard (1813-1878), a French physiologist made several important discoveries using dissected animals. He discovered the action of pancreatic juice in digestion and the ability of the body to build up complex substances such as glycogen. The famous Louis Pasteur (1822-1895), a French chemist who founded the science of immunology made several great contributions. One of them that bears his name is the process of pasteurization, a procedure in processing milk and other fermenting foods. Another is the prevention of anthrax, a deadly infectious disease that kills livestock and wild carnivores including people. It was the first micro-organism proven to be the cause of a disease and the first diseases prevented by a vaccine. His accidental observation of earthworms flanging up soil and transporting spores from buried animals to the surface and infecting animals led to the control of the disease by requiring farmers to burn rather than bury all diseased cattle. Another cure he discovered came from his observation that birds infected with old cultures of chicken cholera were resistant to infection with other highly virulent cultures. From this observation was born the science of immunization when he succeeded in attenuating microbes used in immunization. It also led to the cure of smallpox by injection of cowpox vaccine. He developed a technique to attenuate the virulent rabies virus from the spinal cord of infected rabbits and proved that the material so obtained could be used to vaccinate dogs against the disease and finally treat human being bitten by rabid dogs.

In the early 20th century the British physiologist Ernest Starling (1866-1927) devised a heart-lung preparation in dogs to study the mechanics of heart contractions and showed that the energy of contraction is a function of muscle fiber length. Numerous animal experiments such as these demonstrated the mechanisms underlying the symptoms of heart disease. In the 1950's animal studies made it possible to develop the pump-oxygenation, used to support circulation while the heart is stopped for major heart surgery. All organ transplantation techniques have been developed with animal subjects. Similarly, the development of the artificial heart has required years of experiments, using large animals such as calves because of the large size of most of the artificial hearts. Heart transplants were first attempted with laboratory dogs at Stanford in the late 1950s. Researchers used dogs and other animals to develop drugs to prevent the body from rejecting a donated organ.

The Belgian scientist Corneille Heymans (1892-1968), received the 1938 Nobel Prize for medicine for his discovery of the role of carotid sinus played in regulating blood pressure and the rate of respiration. He was able to show that stimulating or cutting nerve pathways in the neck and aorta of dogs affected the

Respiratory and blood circulation. The Argentinian physiologist Bernardo Houssay (1887-1971) was honored with the 1947 prize for demonstrating in dogs the role of the pituitary gland in regulating carbohydrate metabolism.

Animals also provide models for the study of human disease. Strain, of genetically programmed rodents with hereditary diabetes, hypertension and atherosclerosis have yielded information of great value in understanding its effects on human beings. Disease-causing agents that were intentionally infected on animals were isolated and studied, and this has led to the development of vaccines for smallpox, polio, diphtheria, mumps, measles, rubella, etc. All new surgical procedures and medical devices are first tested on animals before they are used on people.

Diabetes is a deadly disease if left untreated. In 1980 an experiment by J. von Mehring and O. Minkowski showed that removal of the pancreas in experimental animals caused a form of diabetes. It was believed that the pancreas produced a hormone, but all effects to isolate it had failed. In 1922 two Canadian physiologists, Frederick Grant Banting (1891-1941) and his assistant, Charles Herbert Best (1899-1978) succeeded in extracting the hormone insulin from the pancreas thus prolonging the lives of many victims. Banting and Best, a medical student, tied off the pancreatic ducts of experimental dogs for a period of seven weeks. Although the pancreas became useless, the islets of Langerhaus remained intact. A solution was extracted from these cells and injected into the diabetic dogs. It restored their health and later proved to be effective on humans.

At the Emory University's Yerkes Center, researchers have been experimenting on the rhesus monkey to find the best surgical therapy for children affected with cataract. The monkey has also been responsible for the discovery of the Rh blood factor in some people. It was discovered in 1940 by Karl Landsteiner (1868-1943) and Alexander Weiner.

Today we are still plagued with many diseases such as cancer, heart disease, arthritis, brain disorder. AIDS and others that can only be cured or alleviated through animal testings. Neurological diseases involving the brain cells have been a challenging experience for researchers. Monkeys were used to study multiple sclerosis. Mice were used to study brain abscesses and rabbits were experimented on for the treatment of meningitis.

The benefits of animal experimentations have also helped in the advancement of animal health. Vaccines against rabies, distemper, and parvovirus in dogs came from our research of human diseases. Much of the researches used in humans has benefitted animals as well, especially in the fields of surgery and drugs since all these have been done first on them in the pursuit of cures for humans.

The Nov. 6, 1995 issue of Time magazine shows a mouse with a human car attached to it. It was a new line of research aimed at replacing human body parts. This mark a new milestone in our search for solutions to replacing human body parts.

Biologists at the Anti-Cancer Inc., are experimenting with gene therapy using mice. Robert Hoffman and Lingnai Li. have successfully implanted a gene in the cells of the hair follicle of mice, an important consideration toward the full-fledged gene therapy for the treatment of baldness.

Rats are also used to test the effect of pesticides on humans. Research undertaken at the University of Alabama at Birmingham may shed new light on whether pollutants that mimic sex hormones like estrogen can affect breast cancer rates in women. They went about by studying the effect of such hormones on the breast tissue of female rats. As in humans, female rats' immature breast tissue is composed of Mbulb-shaped terminal ends, under the direction of female sex hormones, branch out and differentiate into tree of lobules" that produce milk. Since the lobules are less likely to become cancerous than the end buds, early maturation could potentially lower the overall risk of breast cancer. Rats given DDT, diethylstilbestrol or genistein showed maturation, with decreased proportion of end buds and an increased share of lobules. However, rats given tetrachlorodibenzo-p-dioxin (TCDD), a potent dioxin, exhibited retarded mammary tissue maturation. The change could be an indirect contribution to breast cancer.

ANIMAL TRIVIA

The animal kingdom is host to many mind-boggling statistics and records that will surely provide countless hours for those who like trivia. Some of the interesting records are:

African snakes have loose jaws allowing it to swallow food bigger than its head.

Albatross has the largest wingspan at 3.7 meters.

Anaconda is the heaviest snake, weighing nearly 230 kg.

Anemone is the longest living ocean animal in the world.

Anteaters eat up to 30,000 ants and termites every day.

Armadillos can dig very fast before anyone can notice them.

Arrow poison frogs of Cuba are the smallest amphibians in the world.

Axolotl is a salamander which looks like an overgrown tadpole.

Bat-eared fox has a keen ear that can hear insects moving around the grass.

Bee hummingbird is the smallest bird in the world.

Beetles are the largest group of insects, numbering over 300,000 species.

Birds can navigate long distances using the heavenly stars and the earth's magnetic field.

Black cats crave water and have been known to gnaw through lead pipes.

Black rat snake gives off a fluid to help them separate the old and new skins.

Black-tailed prairie dogs are squirrels but they bark like dogs in case of danger.

Bluefin tuna is one of the fastest swimming ocean fishes.

Bowerbirds find the color blue irresistible and will collect anything blue during mating.

Buffalo often use trees as an opponent when it's mock-sparring or play-fighting.

Butterfly wings have thousands of tiny, overlapping scales that gives its color patterns.

California grey whale has the largest migration of any mammals, at 20,500 kilometers.

Camel humps are used as storage for fats which they use in times of scarcity.

Capybara is the largest rodent in the world and can stay underwater for up to 5 minutes

Civet cat has special surface at the back of its eyes that reflects light, causing it to shine.

Cormorant a bird, has been used for fishing for centuries by some countries.

Cone shell has powerful and deadly nerve poison that can kill human beings.

Crested newt starts off with gills and develop lungs as it changes into an adult.

Cuckoo lays eggs on the wagtail nest while replacing the latter eggs for her own.

Darwin s frog carries her tadpoles in its vocal sacs.

Dali's sheep sheds its thick winter coat with shorter summer coat.

Deer coming from the forests of Indonesia are the smallest.

Dugongs and manatees are related more to elephants than to seals.

Earthworms from Africa are the largest at seven meters.

Electric eel has an electric organ that can generate over 500 watts.

Elephant eats about 140 kg of plants and drinks about 40 gallons of water daily.

Elephant's sole has ridges to give it good grip against slipping.

Elephant's trunk contains at least 60.000 muscles.

Elephants of the female sex are in charge of the herd.

Elk or moose are the largest deer in the world.

European penguin lays a single egg that is incubated by the male on its feet for 64 days.

Female crocodiles carry their young inside their mouth.

Female elephant is pregnant for two years, the longest pregnancy in the world.

Fleas living on rats carry the bacteria that caused the bubonic plague from 1346 to 1349.

Fish eyes can see in all directions.

Fish obtain oxygen by passing water through their gills.

Flies are found everywhere with 90,000 recorded species.

Flamingo eats a lot of food containing carotenoid that turn their feathers to pink.

Fly defecates every four and a half minutes as it wanders across foods.

Fly's hairs on its legs act as sense organs and has buds in its feet.

Flying squirrels have large skin flaps that enable them to glide between trees.

Frogs are the most successful amphibians.

Gaboon viper of Africa has the longest fangs measuring up to five centimeters.

Giant anteater can flick their 2-ft tongue in and out of termite mound 150 times a minute.

Giant clam can grow up to 1.3 meter across.

Giraffe strangest feature is that it is almost completely silent.

Giraffe was once thought to be a cross between a camel and a leopard called cameleopard.

Giraffe weevil has an unusual habit of rolling the edges of leaves to hide its eggs

Goby fish from Japan can change sex back and forth when situation permit.

Golden hamsters have enormous pouches on their cheek that allow them to store food.

Golden poison frog has the most active poison known to man.

Goliath beetle from west Africa is the heaviest insect in the world, weighing 100 grams.

Gorillas are the largest primates and use their hands knuckles for walking.

Great white sharks rarely kill humans despite its bad reputation.

Gulls feed on mollusc and oyster by dropping them to break the shell before eating.

Hairy-eared dwarf lemur from Madagascar are the rarest primates.

Harlequin tuskfish have strange blue teeth that can crush crabs and shellfish.

Hatchet fish has organs on the side that give out light.

Heaviside's dolphins are probably the smallest cetacean , at 1-1/2 meters in length.

Hermit crabs' soft bodies make them seek protection inside mollusc shells.

Honeybee regurgitated stomach contents are used to make honey.

Honeybees travel to 10 million flowers to make one kilo of honey.

Howler monkeys are the noisiest monkeys, and can be heard 5 kms away.

Hummingbird can flap its wings 80 times per second and is seen as a blur in the air.

Humpback whale has a brain five times bigger than that of a human being.

Humpback whale has a song recorded and placed on the spaceship Voyager.

Hyenas have the most powerful jaws of all the carnivores.

Insects may number 10 quintillion individually on earth.

Insects regularly eaten by some people around the world number about 500.

Jackson chameleon has a tongue as long as itself and can catch its prey in a split second.

Jaguars are the good swimmers from the cat family.

Japanese macaques are the only monkeys that live in the cold, snowy mountains of Japan.

Jellyfish is 94% water.

Jumping spiders have four pairs of eyes with each pair seeing different images.

Katydid are so-called because some males mating call sound just like it.

Killer whales are the fastest swimmers in the world.

King cobra is the longest and largest venomous snake in the world.

Kitti's hog-nosed bat is the lightest mammal in the world weighing around 2 grams.

Kokoi frogs (male) carry their tadpoles on their back.

Krills are the largest crustaceans and are eaten by penguins, seabirds, and baleen whales.

Leafcutter ant compost plant parts to grow a special type of fungus that they like to eat.

Leech often sucks blood from the skin without anyone knowing it by anaesthetizing it.

Lemmings are forced from their home due to overpopulation.

Leopard cones (molluscs) are aggressive hunters by poisoning their prey.

Lionfish has needle sharp spines that give off poison.

Lions of the female sex do most of the hunting.

Lions always kill the cubs of the defeated lion when he takes over the pride.

Lions are the only cats that have a social life and family of up to 30 animals.

Locust swarm can cover 4,000 square kilometers and number up to 4 billion.

Manta ray is so strong that when caught, it can tow a boat for hours.

Manta ray is a flattened relative of the sharks and the largest of the skates and rays.

Marine iguana of Galapagos is the only lizard that is truly at home in the sea.

Marine iguanas love to swim in the water and bask in the sun.

Megaspira ruschenbergiana, the snail with the longest shell lives in the forests of Brazil.

Millipede has a maximum of 115 pairs of legs.

Mole rats live permanently underground in an elaborate and extensive maze of burrows.

Moose are found only in North America and are the largest members of the deer family.

Mouthbrooder (fish) carries its developing eggs in its mouth until they hatch.

Mudskipper is a small fish that can walk on its front fins and climb up mangrove roots.

Mudskipper can get oxygen from both air and water.

Mulberry silkworm saliva is used in making silk.

Musk-oxen under wolf attack will form circle to protect themselves and their offspring.

Narwhal tusk is formed by the spiral growth of the left tooth and can reach 3 meters long.

Opossum can fake death with its tongue hanging out when threatened.

Octopus color can change according to its surrounding and "mood."

Octopus has 240 suckers on each of its 8 arms and has full control of it at all times.

Octopus is the most intelligent of the invertebrates, with eyes similar to people's eyes.

Ostrich is the largest bird and its egg is the largest in the world.

Otter eats while laying on its back in the water and using its chest as a table.

Owl arches its back to look bigger and ward off the enemy.

Oxpeckers or tickbirds keep the hippopotamus free of annoying insects.

Pacific salmon returns to their place of origin to mate by the sense of smell.

Pangolin sharp-edged scales are actually modified hair.

Parrots are the longest lived birds.

Pen-tailed shrew is the smallest primate in the world.

Peregrine falcons are the fastest animals in the world, flying at 350 kph.

Pipistrelle bat can eat up to 3,500 insects in a single night.

Piranha can tear all the flesh off large animals in minutes, leaving only bones behind.

Pirarucu found in Amazon is the largest freshwater fish, measuring up to four meters.

Platypus' bill is actually a snout used to probe into mud and gravel for its prey

Polar bear looks white because their colorless hair reflects all wavelength of light.

Proboscis monkey makes a loud honking noise with its big snout that attracts females.

Pufferfish, a poisonous fish can inflate themselves with water to discourage predators.

Puffins can hold on to several fish at a time.

Quetzal has a tail that drops off at the end of each breeding and regrows the next year.

Raccoons are probably the most mischievous animals in the world.

Rat has been know to eat unusual things such as candles and soaps.

Rat is alert, intelligent and learns quickly to exploit new sources of food and shelter.

Rats produce a pungent odor to mark out its territory and will defend it to the death.

Rat's whiskers are sensitive to touch and help the animal to feel its way around the dark.

Rattlesnakes can feel vibrations but cannot hear sound.

Red crossbill has crisscross bill used to pry and hold open pinecone scales.

Reticulated python of Asia is the longest snake and can swallow a small deer or pig.

Sand tiger shark is fierce and often hunts in a pack like wolves.

Scallops have eyes around the edge of their shells.

Seabird droppings called guano are rich in phosphates and are mined for fertilizer.

Sea horse, the male rather than the female looks after the young in its pouch.

Sharks are unable to float unless they are swimming.

Sharks can go for months without eating, living off the oil stored in their liver.

Sharks may have up to 3,000 teeth in their mouth at any one time.

Sidewinder travels sideways.

Sifaka, a type of lemur, leaps upright, landing feet first instead of hands first.

Sloth sleeps 15 hours each day and doesn't move around very much.

Snails, many of them are hermaphrodites, have both male and female sex organs.

Snail, the largest of which weigh 900 grams, was found in Sierra Leone in 1976.

Snail's foot contains several organs, including parts of the gut.

Spiders found in Brazil are the heaviest and weigh nearly 85 grams.

Spiny lobsters migrate in single file using their antennae to touch the other's abdomen.

Starfish can push its stomach out of its mouth as it digests the prey.

Surinam toad is tongueless and their eggs are embedded in the females's back.

Swamp spider breathe underwater thru a thin coat of tightly connected air bubbles.

Swifts spends most of their lives in the air. eating and sleeping up to three years.

Turbot is a flat fish which swims on its side.

Two-toed sloth from South America is the world's slowest-moving land animal.

Uakaris is a bright red face and head monkey of South America.

Vampire bat can painlessly cut through flesh with their small razor-sharp teeth.

Vipers and rattlesnakes fold back their fangs against the roof of their mouth.

Vultures eat dead animals so much that sometimes they cannot fly off.

Walrus has thicker blubber than the whale to keep out the cold.

Walrus tusks are modified teeth that they use to pull itself out of an ice floe.

Warthog has three pairs of large warts on their faces around its tusks and eyes.

Weddell seal holds the seal diving record at 610 meters for over an hour.

Weevil has tiny pits, ridges, and notches all over its body that bounce light.

Whales have no fin but blubber under the skin, which can be as thick as 50 cm.

Wrasses act as "cleaners" for larger fish

Zebras at night will assign one or more to stand guard against enemy.

ARTS

Since the prehistoric times, people have used animals in art. Cavemen have carved animals inside the walls of the caves, giving us a glimpse of how our ancestors lived during that critical period of survival.

In ancient times, with the advent of metal sculptures, many of the arts were well-preserved for our appreciation. Most of them can be found in museums throughout the world. One of the finest Sumerian sculptures depict the well known goat and tree which is made of wood, gold and lapis lazuli. An Assyrian sculpture from the 9th century B.C. portrays a winged lion made from alabaster. It was used then as a guard and placed in front of a gate. A display can be seen in the Metropolitan Museum of Art. Known for humane treatment of animals, the Assyrians glorify them with sculptures of horses and lions, represented with grace and strength.

The Persians, who came after the Assyrians and Babylonians built enormous palaces with columns topped by bulls arranged back to back. The Scythians who are animal lovers have all their portable metal objects such as weapons, harnesses and ornaments made with animal specimens. The Egyptian art of ancient history represents the pharaoh as a lion to express his strength and his divine power. He is commonly depicted as the Sphinx. The most famous and oldest of them is the Great Sphinx at Giza, dating back to the 26th century B.C. It is a monumental sculpture carved from a natural bluff of rock. It is a mammoth work of art measuring 21 meters in height.

Even China, where sculptures are far in between has produced sonic small-scale representations of animals made of bronze drinking vessels, marble or jade carvings. Dragons, tigers, lions, and horses are often represented. Large scale sculptures of the Han dynasty (200 B.C. - 200 A.D.) were discovered with carvings of horses. They were clay grave figures that were placed in the tombs to accompany the dead to the spirit world where they are supposedly able to use them in the afterlife.

The earliest surviving paintings can be found in the Lascaux Cave, in Dordogne, France which date back to the Stone Age. Large and realistic representations of animals were drawn over the walls and ceilings of caves. Another famous series of cave paintings can be found in Altamira, in northern Spain. It depicts animals howling in agony and another collapsing. The animals represented are the horse, bison, mammoth and ibex. At later periods (600 - 300 B.C.), most of the mudbrick houses were painted with hunting of animals scenes and vultures attacking humans.

Today most of the artwork depicting animals are found in canvas paintings using oil, watercolour, charcoal, and crayons. These are used as decorations for walls, partitions, clothings, wallpaper designs and almost anything the mind can imagine. Many of the modem paintings of nature have animals displayed prominently. In this period of environmental awareness, nature paintings are in great demand. Not only the big animals are used in many of the paintings, the proliferation of the small insects have been used in artwork since the medieval times. At the time, most of the large wildlife were unknown and insects were often the organisms used. They served as decorative objects such as rings, coins, pendants, and pins. Many nature painters always depict animals because they seem to play an important role in nature. Flowers are often depicted with insects to brighten the painting. They are also used as the basis for the creation of some mystical animals.

BALANCE OF NATURE

The intervention of humans on the natural world often led to an upset of the local ecology. The loss of a species can trigger an unexpected, harmful and destructive ecology. The chain of events can take a deadly turn for some species. The relationship between mongoose, snakes and rats is often mentioned. The introduction of mongoose to exterminate the poisonous fer-de-lance, a pit viper with two fangs which fold away when not in use, led to the explosion of the rat colonies. Initially the mongoose took over the role of the snake in controlling the rat populations, but the intelligent rats soon developed a different lifestyle. They adopted a tree-dwelling instead of ground-based living and night instead of day hunting. Instead of hunting rats for their meal, the mongoose were forced to hunt for chicken to feed themselves. In France, the extermination of the wolf and lynx led to the proliferation of the deer which made extensive damage to the forest trees. The disappearance of the mountain lions in North American led to the rapid destruction of vegetation by the deer.

When the jaguars, pumas and harpy eagles were removed from Barro Colorado island, the ground nesting birds began to disappear due to the proliferation of the monkeys and coati mundis whose population was once under check by the large predators. The same scenario happened in San Diego, California, when the loss of coyotes that helped to keep foxes and cats in check multiplied and preyed on the birds.

In the wild savannas of Africa, the loss of the big cats could lead to the overpopulation of the deer. Because they can reproduce very fast, it could lead to the high consumption of grass that could lead to starvation of other species.

In the wilds where the human hand is not at work, there are many instances of balance of nature at work. It is the reason why no species dominates another species without they themselves being controlled by nature. It could be another animal or the human predators and even the supply of food they need. Insects, the most dominant species on earth, could have taken over the planet had it not been because of the predators that kept their population in check. Only the human beings are proliferating and upsetting the balance of nature.

BIOLOGICAL CONTROL

Not all animals and insects are wanted by human beings nor the surroundings where they are found. However, efforts to remove these unwanted pests are difficult and often unsuccessful. One of these animals is the rabbit. Not only do they grow and proliferate rapidly in the wild, they are also voracious eaters of the vegetation wherever they are found. Human attempts to limit their population have repeatedly failed. In the wilds, predators such as foxes and birds of prey eat the rabbits because, being commoner, they can catch them easier. This helps keep the rabbit populations in check and balance.

The balance of nature in the world is due to the presence of predators. This leads biologists to make use of insects to control other destructive pests. The destructive coconut moth of Fiji was controlled with the introduction of tachinid flies, a natural parasite of the moth. Vedalia beetles were used in California in the 1880s to control a pest that almost destroyed the citrus groves, the cottony-cushion scale.

The use of biological control of unwanted insects and other creatures have been in use for a long time. For centuries, the Chinese have encouraged ants to control pests of citrus fruits and during the Victorian period, gardeners often kept a toad in the greenhouse to deal with insects. A ladybird bug from Australia was successfully introduced to California citrus orchards to control cotton pests.

The importation of the prickly pear cactus to Australia in the 18th century went awry after its seed escaped from its cultivated field. By 1925, it had covered 94,000 square miles of field needed by livestock. It took a South America moth, whose caterpillar was able to eat the dense prickly pear cactus which is considered a pesty plant for encroaching on large areas of Queensland.

Biological control has taken another step further with the help of biotechnology and genetic engineering. The advantage of biological control is that it is not polluting the environment with poisonous chemicals that often cause more harm in the long run than benefits.

Another modern method of controlling certain insect pests is done through the biological sterilization of the male species of certain destructive pests. This is accomplished by releasing into the population very large numbers of males which have been sterilized by gamma ray radiation. When the males mate with the females, the eggs are not fertilized. As the old generations die out, the insect population will gradually fall. This first successful use of this method was the control of screwworm, a livestock pest in the U.S. Millions of male screwworms were sterilized and released to the infested area. The sterile insect technique was developed by Edward Knipling and Raymond Bushland of the USDA. They later received the $200,000 World Food Prize for its development. It was first effectively used in the island of Curacao in 1953. The melon fly, a pest of the vegetables in Guam, was successfully eradicated by this method.

Tampa. Florida has been fighting medflies infestation for more than 40 years. It is threatening their $7 billion citrus fruit industry. The bugs used the fruits such as oranges as breeding ground for their larvae. They served as food for the maggots as they grow. More than 600 million sterile bugs have been imported from Guatemala where the pupae have been zapped with radiation to sterilize the infant insects. The bugs are then painted with orange dye to show that they have been sterilized before releasing them to the wild. Hopefully, this type of biological control will prove successful again instead of using the deadly melathion pesticide that has proved to be hazardous to people.

Like all other biological control agents, it is important to do research work before these agents are introduced into the field. The cane toads were introduced from South America in 1935 to eradicate a beetle plague destroying sugar cane crops in Cairns, Queensland, Australia. Without a natural predator, the toads have proliferated and gone awry. The adult toads, measuring a foot across and weighing up to 2.7 kilos have been spitting poison in many parts of Australia. They devour everything in their path including mice, rodents, snakes, dogs, and even children.

An unwelcome visitor from New Zealand has colonised Northern Ireland and is killing off the native earthworms that are essential to soil fertility. This visitor is a flatworm called Artioposthia triangulata, which can grow up to six inches long and weigh two grams. It can eat a whole earthworm in 30 minutes. The killer worm has been found in every Ulster county and, according to the Department of Agriculture, the only check to its increasing numbers appears to be the availability of food. This could mean that the only way to destroy these killers worm is to starve them to death at the expense of the earthworms.

CYCLE OF LIFE

There is a close and important relationship between plants and animals in the world. The existence of some plants depends on the existence of some animals and vice versa. The leaves and fruits of many plants provide the animals with the food they need to survive. On the other hand, we are familiar with the pollination done by bees, butterflies, bats, and other animals. In as much as there are different plants with different reproductive natures, there is also a need for different kinds of pollinators. This diverse group of more than 100,000 species of animals are found throughout the world. About 90% of the world's flowering plant species, including at least 800 species consumed by people depend on animal pollinators. In moth-pollinated flowers such as jasmine and gardenia, the nectar is often located at the bottom of a tube and out of reach of most insects. Moths with their long tongues can reach the end of the tube. They are also responsible for pollinating a species of night-blooming cacti such as the Amazon moonflower whose flowers open only once a year.

The only way the Galapagos tomato seed can germinate is to pass through the gut of a great Galapagos tortoise. A large proportion of the proliferation and dispersal of plants has been accomplished by animals. The seed of the wild strawberry is often eaten by birds and excreted on a wide area. During winter, squirrels bury acorns and afterwards forget about it, allowing the acorns to grow into oak trees.

All organisms on this planet have a role to play in the life cycle of living things. Even those we consider harmful have an important role to play. The eggs and larvae of mosquitoes are an important food source for fish. The flying insects can be food for birds and other insects. Snakes control rodents and rats wherever they can be found, even to the end of the hiding places deep in the burrows. There is an important relationship between plants, animals and the existence of human beings. With the help of air, soil, and sunlight, they form a complete cycle that keeps the planet teeming with life. Plants are nourished through the process of photosynthesis using the power of the sunlight to produce food. They are in turn consumed by humans and animals. Insects often fall prey to the spider which are themselves eaten by the birds and wasps. They are in turn eaten by higher forms of life and ultimately mankind.

Even in death, the cycle continues. Dead and decaying plants and animals are consumed by scavenging mites, insects, worms, bacteria and fungi which undergo composting that return the nutrients to the soil. Earthworms are great decomposers, consuming dead organic matter in the soil while bacteria and fungi in the soil break down all dead tissues wherever they are.

Some important elements such as carbon, calcium and nitrogen are recycled with the help of animals. Green plants absorb carbon dioxide from the air during photosynthesis and use the carbon as food for their growth. They are in turn eaten by animals which release the carbon dioxide back to the atmosphere; and so the cycle continues. On the other hand calcium does not pass through the atmosphere but is taken in though the plant roots. It is returned to the soil and to water when animals and plants die and decompose.

Another important element is nitrogen. Nitrogen is important to all animals and even man because it is a constituent of protein and therefore essential to growth. There are three ways by which nitrates are formed. Nitrifying bacterias use ammonia and release it into the soil when plants and animals decompose. Blue-green algae and nitrogen fixing bacteria which are abundant in soil form nitrates from atmospheric nitrogen and lastly, lightning can cause the atmospheric nitrogen to form into nitrates.

DRUG MANUFACTURING

The 1962 tragedy of many European women who took the drug thalidomide during early pregnancy has made it necessary for pharmaceuticals to test and screen drugs more vigorously than before. It has become more necessary to test the drug on animals despite the many differences between humans and animals, especially those in the lower order. In fact many drugs have effects on humans different from that of animals. The drug penicillin .s one of the least toxic substances that is fatal to guinea pigs even in small doses. A dose of morphine is used to anaesthetize a dog but it could be fatal lo a human. All these effects on animals differ due to the differences in the chemistry of the human bodies.

The ailments closely striking humans and animals are the infectious diseases. Therefore the efficacy of drugs tested on animals can very well be used on humans. Even then, the procedures undertaken before it can be used on people are numerous and stringent.

Testing new drugs involves several steps and years of experimenting. All these important steps must be taken before the government regulating body will approve their use or before the doctors will be allowed to prescribe them. Despite all these, there are still many restrictions on their use.

Before a drug can be tested on animals, it is necessary to infect the animal with the disease. Doctors will try to infect the laboratory animal that best mimics human physiology. Once a drug has been developed, it is tested on animals such as mice and rabbits to determine the toxicity, effective dose, absorption and excretion rate, and tolerance level. Another test is made on pregnant animals to determine its effect on their offspring. If no ill effects are shown, the dosage is usually increased gradually until the lethal dose is established.

Once its effectiveness on animals has been established, the drugs are then used on volunteers such as prisoners. Identical procedures are used on adults, pregnant mothers, and even children to confirm their effectiveness, dosage and side effects. All these procedures take several years and millions of dollars to produce before they are ready for marketing.

Sometimes drugs and vaccines are even produced from the animals themselves. Numerous drugs have been extracted from the blood of animals. Even the eggs of animals can be used to develop vaccines. In the development of the influenza vaccine, eggs are injected daily with weakened influenza virus. After 48 hours, the eggs' contents are harvested, treated, and mixed with other substances to produce a final vaccine.

Gelatin is a colorless or yellowish protein obtained from collagen. Collagen is in turn produced by boiling the bones and skins of animals with connective tissues in water. It has been used as food and ingredients for candies and ice creams. But it is an important ingredient in the manufacturing of capsules for drugs.

It is an ideal container because of its inertness and its ability to dissolve readily inside the body. It can also be tinted to any of the more than 80.000 different colors to guard against deterioration by light and for identifying purposes.

Every year, billions of gelatin capsules are needed to contain the powdered drugs that cannot be compressed into tablets needed for medication. So important are these capsules that it has become an important industry in the medical field.

screen drugs more vigorously than before. It has become more necessary to test the drug on animals despite the many differences between humans and animals especially those in the lower order. In fact many drugs have effects on humans quite different from that of animals. The drug penicillin is one of the least toxic substances that is fatal to guinea pigs even in small doses. A dose of morphine is used to anaesthetize a dog but it could be fatal to a human. All these effects on animals differ due to the differences in the chemistry of the human bodies.

The ailments closely striking humans and animals are the infectious diseases. Therefore the efficacy of drugs tested on animals can very well be used on humans. Even then, the procedures undertaken before it can be used on people are numerous and stringent.

Testing new drugs involves several steps and years of experimenting. All these important steps must be taken before the government regulating body will approve their use or before the doctors will be allowed to prescribe them. Despite all these, there are still many restrictions on their use.

Before a drug can be tested on animals, it is necessary to infect the animal with the disease. Doctors will try to infect the laboratory animal that best mimics human physiology. Once a drug has been developed, it is tested on animals such as mice and rabbits to determine the toxicity, effective dose, absorption and excretion rate, and tolerance level. Another test is made on pregnant animals to determine its effect on their offspring. If no ill effects are shown, the dosage is usually increased gradually until the lethal dose is established.

Once its effectiveness on animals has been established, the drugs are then used on volunteers such as prisoners. Identical procedures are used on adults, pregnant mothers, and even children to confirm their effectiveness, dosage and side effects. All these procedures take several years and millions of dollars to produce before they are ready for marketing.

Sometimes drugs and vaccines are even produced from the animals themselves. Numerous drugs have been extracted from the blood of animals. Even the eggs of animals can be used to develop vaccines. In the development of the influenza vaccine, eggs are injected daily with weakened influenza virus. After 48 hours, the eggs' contents are harvested, treated, and mixed with other substances to produce a final vaccinc.

Gelatin is a colorless or yellowish protein obtained from collagen. Collagen is in turn produced by boiling the bones and skins of animals with connective tissues in water. It has been used as food and ingredients for candies and ice creams. But it is an important ingredient in the manufacturing of capsules for drugs.

It is an ideal container because of its inertness and its ability to dissolve readily inside the body. It can also be tinted to any of the more than 80,000 different colors to guard against deterioration by light and for identifying purposes.

Every year, billions of gelatin capsules are needed to contain the powdered drugs that cannot be compressed into tablets needed for medication. So important are these capsules that it has become an important industry in the medical field.

1994 smash hit, *The Lion King*, was the top-grosser of the year. Other full-length features include 101 Dalmatians, Swan Princess, Beauty and the Beast. Live animal shows such as Lassie and Rin Tin Tin, Beethoven, and Benji provide countless hours of entertainment. Rin Tin Tin was credited to save Warner Brothers from bankruptcy in the 1920s. The owner insured him for $100,000 and he was given his own valet, chef, limousine and chauffeur. Other features include disaster movies such as King Kong and Swarm

Horses are used in many films involving the animals. All western movies have horses that serve as transportation. It would not be surprising if some movies have horses as heroes. Movies like Black Beauty, has been used by the Humane Society to counter cruelty to horses. Several versions were filmed and it even had a TV series of the same title. The story is told from the horse's point of view and injustice is magnified. The 1979 movie, Black Stallion and its sequel, The Black Stallion Returns are first rate entertainment for family viewing. Other famous horses are Trigger of the Roy Rogers TV series and Silver of The Lone Ranger series.

The most famous dog of them all is Lassie. Movies and TV series have been made of her. She is a collie played by several dogs. Since its first ddbut in Lassie Come Home, filmed in 1943, there were several other movies made and a TV series was first broadcast in 1954 until 1971. In the series, she was always the heroine, protecting her masters against all evil adversaries and helping others in times of danger or disaster. She was also credited with saving her producer from bankruptcy. Another parallel TV scries was the other famous dog, Rin Tin Tin. It was broadcast for 5 seasons from 1954 to 1959. In fact the first feature was made in 1922. Three different German shepherds filled the role in the TV series, two of them descendants of the original Rimy of the 1922 film. The other is the offspring of another movie canine, *Flame. Jr.*

There was even a popular wildlife documentary series produced by Time-Life Films, The Wild Wild World of Animals. The Discovery Channel also produces or broadcasts several series on wildlife. Many of them are very informative, like Those Incredible Animals, Mac and Mutley, Hunters, Wildlife Nature, Nature Watch. Wildlife Chronicles. Wild Discovery, Wild Life, In Care of Nature, ZooLife, Profiles of Nature, Born Among Wild Animals, Lost Animals of the 20th Century, and many others.

Walt Disney, more than anybody else probably, made animals famous with some of his creation. Before his theme parks were constructed, he produced a TV series called Disneyland, many featuring nonhuman stars, such as "Sammy the Way of the Seal." "Greta, the Misfit Greyhound." "Ida, the Offbeat Eagle," "Joker the amiable Ocelot," "Inky the Crow," "The Horse with the Flying Tale," "The Hound That Thought He Was a Raccoon," and many others. Disney also created and made into TV features such characters as Mickey Mouse, Donald Duck, Pluto, and Goofy. Since then many animal characters have been added. Other creators of animal characters are Walter Lantz of Woody Woodpecker, William Hanna and Joseph Barberra of Tom and Jerry and Huckleberry Hound. Fritz Freleng of Tweety Pie and Silvester and many others.

Science fictions and horror movies have also been made using animals as predators. Movies depicting environmental pollution can be seen in movies like "Barracuda, Prophecy," "Congo, The Fly" its remake and a sequel. "King Kong" and a remake. Then there is the 1954 movie about mutant giant ants out to conquer the world. "Them!"

Several movies have been done about dinosaurs Movies like "One Million Years B.C.." which catapulted Raquel Welch to stardom. The best of them is the recent blockbuster. "Jurassic Park." about a modem dinosaur park in which the dinosaurs were genetically recreated from fossil genes found in the jungle of South America. The dinosaurs managed to break out of their confines to bring terror to scientists and children alike. There is an earlier blockbuster. "Jaws" which is about shark attacks and scaring tourists in a New England town. Three sequels were made after this blockbuster. Other animals featured in movies are piranhas, killer whales, cobras, primates, bears and more recently a giant "Anaconda."

Spiders have also been featured in several movies. "The Spider Women" featuring Sherlock Holmes trying to figure out why victims were driven to suicide (after being bitten by poisonous spiders). "The Spider" is about a giant spider terrorizing a high school community. "Tarantulas" is about spiders created by supergrowth formula, and *"Tarantulas - The Deadly Cargo."* another arachnid terrorizing a small town. Probably the more famous movie is "Arachnophobia." about a South American killer spider transported to the U.S. and producing a lot of deadly offspring. Rats have also been featured in films such as "Willard" and "Ben. " Even Alfred Hitchcock the famous director of suspense movies found time to direct a blockbuster involving "The Birds " There are hundreds more of this type of movies that will amuse audience interested in this genre.

Comics often feature animals cither as wise thinkers or heroes, *Garfield. Heathcliff, Baby Huey. Tom and Jerry. Snoopy, Mickey Mouse, Mighty Mouse, Daisy Duck, Scooby Doo,* are some of the well known figures. They have also made the creator of these animals wealthy.

Other comic characters have animal names attached to them. Some of them are made into cartoon strips. TV cartoons and TV series, and even movies. Characters include Batman, Spiderman, and Green Hornet, to name a few.

Animals can also be educational since children find them more appealing than the inanimate objects. The most popular educational show for children is probably Sesame Street It features animals such as Big Bird and Cookie Monster. Coloring books, story books, and stuffed toys often feature them.

FOOD SOURCES

Many tropical countries are endowed with many different wild animals that provide a major proportion of dietary protein. Most of the hunted animals for food are the deer, pigs, birds, frogs and eggs of wild animals. Many invertebrates such as grasshoppers, locusts, termites, beetles, larvae of the large palm weevil, collected from the wild sago stumps are commonly seen in the market. In fact, more than 500 different types of insects are edible for consumption.

Foods hunted from the wild are often safer than those raised on farming factories. For many in the rural areas and jungles of the tropical forests, hunting for deer provides the needed protein; it is a matter of economic survival. In the U.S., game eating is becoming a trend with venison consumption doubling nationwide in the last four years. Many of the Midwest's upscale restaurants are featuring American cuisine using regional foods, including game and with good reason. Game meat is lower in fat, with a four-ounce serving of venison containing only four grams of fat as opposed to an equal serving of beef with 17 grams of fat. A deer has only 5% body fat compared to 25% for domestic animals because game animals are always on the run. Some of the fat is the highly unsaturated omega-3 type, originally thought to be found only in fish.

Venison is also a high-protein meat, containing iron, zinc, and many B vitamins rural people need. They are also free of the injected growth hormones, antibiotics, and dyes. Finally the best part is the flavor. We've domesticated the flavor right out of our meat, but not the animals in the wild.

The bison is another animal that has the same qualifications as the deer in the forests. The millions of bison killed in the last two centuries has been a waste of food protein that could have fed millions of people for years.

HAIR

Unlike the small fur-bearing mammals in the wild, many ruminants and other animals have been domesticated and bred for work, transportation, and other uses while at the same time the hair on their skins is used as an important source of raw materials for the clothing industry. Unlike furs, the hair can be obtained periodically during the animal's entire lifetime. When the raw materials are more valuable than the other by-products, These animals become the main reason for their breeding. Examples are the Merino sheep for wool, Karakul sheep for pelts, Kashmir goats for Kashmir, Cashmere goats for cashmere. Angora rabbits for angora. Alpaca for alpaca wool, and Angora goats for mohair. Other animals are the camel, yak, vicuna, and llama.

Wool, the world's largest source of hair, comes mostly from the merino sheep, whose fleece consists of non-medullated hair of equal diameter. This homogenous fleece allows a particularly efficient production and shearing technique as well as processing technique. A drug has even been produced that allows the sheep to shed its hair or wool without shearing. Once the sheep has been injected with the drug and before releasing it, it is clothed with leather to prevent the wool from falling off.

Cashmere must be combed in a very labor-intensive process at the lime of moulting, or it must be sorted after shearing. Only a few goats endemic to Central Asia produce significant quantities of underhair to make the labor worthwhile. Traditionally, cashmere is a by-product of subsistence-oriented meat and milk production. Crossbreedings with the Turkish angora goats have taken place to increase the yield of underhair.

The angora goat is well adapted to the arid climate conditions and poor soils of some countries. It is a very useful ruminant for the poor people. They not only produce the highly demanded mohair, but they can be used to supply meat and milk.

Mohair is the hair of the angora goat, which is a strong and resilient fiber and has none of the crimp found in other wool. Its smooth surface is more resistant to dust and more lustrous than wool. The most important member of the group of wool-producing fibers, the Angora goat, is native to Asia Minor but is also bred in Argentina, Turkey, South Africa, and the United States with Texas as the lead producing state. More than 30,000 tons are produced annually throughout the world.

The mohair production of South African and North American angora goats is about twice that of the Turkish goats. A breeding strategy between the Turkish and North American goats was performed to increase the mohair production. The result has been very satisfactory; the fibers produced were longer, finer and the quantity is at least 15% more.

What may seem to be a waste product has also been valuable to mankind. The hairs of goats have been used for making carpets, ribbons, ropes, insulation materials, and felt for filters. Even the camel (*Camelus bactrianus*) provides a valuable wool with its typical sandy color. In an elaborate procedure, the wool is plucked after spring moulting, then it is combed, collected and sorted according to quality.

Among the camelids of the New World, the alpaca is of major significance. Its fluff obtained by shearing is largely exported as a raw material, but increasingly in processed form as well, and constitutes a major source of foreign currency for producing countries. The llama produces coarser wool which for the most part remains in the producer country. The wild vicuna has extremely fine hair in its thick fleece, but in very small quantities.

The angora rabbit, a bred of the domestic rabbit, has unusually long and very fine fluff hair. The particularly lightness and the good thermal properties of angoral wool are due to the air chambers contained in the hair.

INCOME SOURCES

Animals have been used for different purposes by different people as they learn more about them. Today, the biggest use for wildlife may be in the entertainment industry. They are taken from the wild and put in zoos and parks for people to enjoy. Billions of dollars are spent every year as more people visit these places.

Insects can be a source of income. The bees producing honey and wax were probably the earliest use of insects for commercial purposes. The Egyptians were the first to domesticate the bees in ancient history. Not until the 16th century with the discovery of sugar cane, did honey take second place. Until then it was the only source of sweetness. Beside its sweetness, honey is full of vitamins and minerals in sufficient amounts that are useful to consumers. It has other uses because of its antibacterial properties. The Egyptians used them as embalming fluid and the Roman soldiers brought it along when they went to battle. The Egyptians even went so far as to use honey in fermenting an alcoholic beverage called mead before the use of grapes for making wine was discovered.

The wax they produced for building the comb has many uses in the household and cosmetic industry. It is used as polishes, candles and crayons. The beeswax because of its low melting temperature has other uses. The U.S. produces 3 to 4 metric tons annually for mildew prevention, waterproofing, adhesives, paints, and other uses. At one time the Catholic Church used beeswax entirely for its candles. Today, the candle contains only 25% beeswax. The list of uses is endless. It is also used in works of art such as wax figures and sculptures. Despite the availability of the substitute, paraffin, beeswax is still in demand.

Many people have taken into farming animals for the income they can generate Butterflies, reptiles, birds, frogs, horses, dogs, and almost all kinds of animals that can generate income for businessmen have been bred and sold for profit.

INDUSTRIAL PRODUCTS

Although not plentiful compared to the plant kingdom, the animals have also contributed a small share to the industrial products we use. Algin from brown seaweed is used in paints, lubricants and coolants in oil drilling, cosmetics, shampoos and soaps. Fireflies have helped scientists produce a light that gives off neither heat nor spark which could be useful for mining and other industries, and in some situations where explosions may be a problem.

Unlike most mammals of the poles that made use of their thick blubber to survive the harsh winters, the bears make use of their hair. The hair of polar bears is an efficient heat absorber that could be used for manufacturing cold-weather clothing. Plans for using it as solar energy collectors is underway.

Cockroaches, crabs and spiders have two things in common. They are all arthropods and they have organs in their exoskeletons that act as strain gauges they use to move their limbs. These natural sensors are the envy of many human engineers. The legs of these arthropods can detect small deformations or strains in their exoskeleton. These so-called biological strain gauges both measure strain and exert control that regulates the creature's movements. Studying the strain gauges of arthropods provides important clues for the science of robotics. To build machines that could navigate rough terrain on Earth or even on the moon or Mars, roboticists have leaned toward crafting insectlike automatons.

Perhaps the most famous such robot is Dante, the eight-legged mobile robot that descended into volcanic craters in Antarctica and Alaska in the early 1990s. Yet that robot, which lipped over and suffered other mechanical trouble, never came close to matching the grace and agility of a spider. The natural strain gauges of arthropods, coupled with other aspects of their locomotion, such as gait and body posture, could be a key to building a more nimble automaton. In fact, Sony Corporation has come out with robot pets that can act like the real thing. The robot will react to patting and other gestures. It can even lie down to sleep.

The strain gauge is a relatively new tool in science and engineering. But arthropods have used comparable devices for more than 300 million years. Each of the three main arthropod groups, insects, arachnids and crustaceans have their own version of a sense organ for detecting deformations or strain in the cuticle or exoskeletal material. Strain gauges have widespread industrial application; they can be used to test the structural integrity of buildings, bridges, automobiles and aircraft. They would also be ideally suited to move over dangerous and treacherous terrain where wheeled vehicles would not stand a chance. Investigation of toxic-waste sites and of craters on Earth, and the moon are among the most frequently mentioned possibilities. The recent Mars landing of the Pathfinder, a robot, was able to bring back photos of Mars and even analyze the soil on Mars. The U.S. Navy has invented a robot using the cockroaches design to find and blow up mines around beaches.

It will be a while before a robot arthropod will be as quick-footed as the real thing. These invertebrates have evolved sensors that take advantage of the laws of mechanics in ways we are only beginning to understand.

Sewage is eliminated by the anaerobic bacteria that gives off methane gas. Known also as biogas, it burns well and is used as a fuel in a number of developing countries. Some bacteria can produce alcohol which is used as a fuel for cars in some countries. Brazil produces about 10 billion liters of alcohol as fuel for cars. The sugar is obtained from sugar cane plantations, and fermentation by micro-organisms is carried out in special factories situated close by.

LIFESAVERS

The proliferation of pets and farm animals and the close interactions between man and animals have given rise to many eventful lifesaving acts on the part of animals. Many of these animals have done it beyond the call of duty.

Pelorous Jack was a fourteen-foot Risso's dolphin who had been guiding steamships off New Zealand through very perilous waters in the latter part of the 19th century. He seems to have made it his duty to guide the ships going his way. After getting one ship safety across, he would return and wait for another ship. He even understood that faster steamships should have priority and always guided them safely across when two ships would appear simultaneously. In 1904, he was granted full protection from harm by the government of New Zealand.

His intelligence cannot be underestimated. When a drunk sailor on the S.S. Penguin tried to shoot him with a rifle, he never bothered to guide the ship again as if he could read the name on the hull. The ship was wrecked in 1909 killing 75 persons in the same place where he used to guide other steamships across.

More than any other animal in the world, dogs have rescued more people than all the other animals combined. Barry (1800-1814), a well known St. Bernard, in his short life span of 14 years had saved more than 40 people in his hometown of Switzerland. He seemed to have a special sixth sense that enabled him to predict upcoming avalanches. Travelers who were unfortunate enough to be buried during an avalanche had Barry to be thankful for. He would lead the monks to where the victims could be found. After his death, he was immortalized by the National Museum in Bern. Switzerland.

Since 1954 Ken-L Ration has been honoring canines with the Dog Hero of the Year for saving life or property beyond the call of duty. In a span of 20 years, all the honored dogs have saved a total of 290 humans and 300 animals. These are just a small list of how animals have helped people in distress

The first awardee was a collie named Tang(1954) who had saved at least five youngsters from vehicular accidents. On another occasion, a two-year-old stowaway would have fallen to the pavement had he not planted himself under a truck and kept on barking and howling until the driver noticed the problem.

Other honorees include Tabby (1956), a cocker spaniel for saving the three-year-old son of the owner Ringo (1968) who saved a two-year-old from being hit by traffic on a busy road Top (1969), a Great Dane, saved two children from death or severe injury on different occasions drizzly Bear (1970), a St Bernard saved her master from a grizzly bear attack Mimi (1972), a poodle saved eight members of a family one early morning by rousing all members of the family during a big fire that completely destroyed the home. Another St. Bernard, Budweiser (1973) saved a four-year-old girl and returned to save a second child from a house on fire.

Under great odds, Balto, a husky, risked his life in leading his master across hundreds of miles of minus 50 degree temperature and an 80 mph gale to bring a much needed diphtheria vaccine to the city of Nome. Alaska to prevent an epidemic. He was rewarded with a statue ten years later, erected at the entrance of New York's Central Park in 1915.

We have often thought of mammals as the only animals capable of saving human lives. Even reptiles like turtles have been known to save lives. Mrs Candelaria Villanueva jumped ship after the one she was traveling on went down somewhere in the Visayas in the Philippines Fortunately two giant turtles were on hand to help her One kept her afloat in the water for thirty- six hours while the other kept her awake. The turtle would climb on her back and nip at her car every time she fell asleep.

In the U.S and elsewhere, dogs are trained for rescue works. In Colorado, the Search and Rescue Dogs of Colorado (SARDOC) periodically train dogs to track and find lost children and adults, dead bodies and locate people buried under avalanches, debris, etc They have to undergo at least nine months of training before certificates can be given. Dogs that underwent specialized training for water and avalanche rescues, and cadaver searches are given special certification by the Federal Emergency Management Agency, the highest certification available Dogs of all kinds can be trained from pound mutts to standard poodles. The idea of dog searching is made possible by the tens of thousands of skin cells human shed every minute. These dead cells, along with the sweat and other body secretions are constantly being broken down into their chemical constituents by bacteria. The gases exuded during those reactions are what give each human a unique scent Dogs are particularly well suited to detect these scents because of their keen scent-detecting receptor cells (Smithsonian. August 1997).

MEDIC AL POTENTIALS

Many of the discoveries made by science and medicine come from the studies of animal behavior, chemicals excreted from their bodies, and experiments done on them. Scientists at Australia's University of Queensland are try ing to find a cure for hearing loss possibly caused by prescription drugs that can destroy hair cells within the ear. They believe that birds and reptiles hold the key to reversing such damage due to their ability to regenerate the hair cells automatically. This is made possible by the presence of certain polypeptides, chains of amino acids that enable hair cells to grow back. They are now working to find out how the process occurs and how it could be used to help humans

In newspaper and television reports back in Nov 1995, a mouse can be seen with a human ear on its back. It was a dramatic experiment on how tissue engineering had progressed to help human replace lost body parts to disease or accident. The idea behind tissue engineering is to trick the body into regenerating its missing parts To make the mouse's third ear, scientists fashioned a precision mold out of porous, biodegradable polymer, seeded it with human cartilage cells, then tucked the structure under the skin of a mouse bred without an immune system to prevent rejection. Nourished by mouse blood, the cartilage cells multiplied, taking the shape of the dissolving polymer scaffold and creating a perfectly formed human ear. The success of this feat could help doctors regenerate organs using parts of the recipient cells so as not to cause any rejection in animals before transplanting them to the patient.

More than three million people suffered from chronic pain every day. But help is on the way from an unlikely source, the venom of the cone snail. The experimental drug SNX-111 has been used for testing very tough and severe pain in seven cases. Five cases had terminal cancers and two had spinal cord injuries. The strongest opiates had since become ineffective. After testing the new drug, five of the patients had their pain disappeared. And the only side effects were mild eye jitters and a slight drop in blood pressure. There are also no sign of addiction or intolerance of the drug. The cost of medication is only a fraction of that of other drugs.

Cancer is one of the dreaded disease that scientists have been looking for a cure. Their exhaustive researches have brought them to the deep seas in search of a cure. Many sea creatures have not been tested for their anti-cancer potentials. One of this is the sea mat - marine animals that mimic plants - has anti-cancer compound called bryostatin L. Experiments have shown signs of killing cancerous cells. Test on mice with leukemia and lymphoma have shown that it doubles their lifespan and stops the growth of melanoma cells.

Researchers at the Harvard Medical School have been studying the problem of sleep in human beings. In correlation with the problem they found that the cat, the best sleeper of the animal world has a higher level of a brain chemical called adenosine when they' are kept awake. As soon as they fell asleep, the amount of adenosine dropped. Other organs such as the liver can also produce the adenosine and it will be only a matter of time before pharmaceutical companies start marketing adenosine preparations commercially once they know what manipulating levels would do the trick.

Researchers studying the sudden infant deaths syndrome (SIDS), a leading cause of one year old and below babies are looking to the elephant seal pups for some kinds of solution. Pup seals have erratic heartbeats for at least six months before they stabilize during apnea, or breath holding while sleeping. This symptom is also experienced by healthy human infants. By studying and monitoring the pup seals, scientists hope to find the solution.

The need to mass produce drugs can be a daunting task using the low-yield, painstaking and time-consuming cultivation of laboratory cell cultures. Scientists are experimenting with the Alpine goats to develop large amounts of life-saving drugs Massachusetts-based researchers are farming animals from New Zealand to produce specific drugs for diseases such as cancer and haemophilia. The goats have been bio-engineered to contain a human gene. This way it can produce up to ten times the normal amount of disease-fighting proteins in their milk for a tenth of the cost.

Dead corals have other uses beside their decorative property for aquarium. They contained minerals like the human bones that made them ideal substitutes to replace damaged bones in reconstructive surgery. Instead of taking bones from other parts of the human body which can be very painful and possibly open to infection, corals are being used today. The interconnected pores of corals allow adjacent living bones to send new blood vessels and bone tissue into the coral maze. A strong new bond is created without the body rejecting the new implant after the coral is first heat-treated to convert it to the same minerals as bone.

Frogs have been known to produce poison to protect themselves against predators. Out of the I3S species of poison-dart frogs, only 55 are known to secrete poison. These toxic frogs have bright neon colors that also served as warnings to predators. More than 300 alkaloid compounds have been recognized. Many of their toxins have medical potentials. One frog, *Phyllomedusa bicolor*, produces the mucus that Indians used in hunting and treating bums. Scientists studying the mucus found that it contains a peptide that enhances the action of adenosine, a brain chemical that reduces the effects of strokes and perhaps Alzheimer's disease and depression. They hope to produce a refined drug for possible use by humans. The pumiliotoxin secreted by *Dendobates auratus* has potential use as a cardiac stimulant for heart attack patients. The Epipdebates tricolor of Ecuador exudes a chemical called epibatidine that is 200 times more powerful than morphine and can be used as painkiller for those that do not respond to plants' alkaloids.

The search for a cure for AIDS has been carried to all kinds of testing for vectors even in animals. The virus causing the pox for canaries is being tested for humans. The pox which is harmless to humans has shown promise in blocking infection by the human immunodeficiency virus (HIV) that causes AIDS. The vaccine has been injected into a group of healthy volunteers and found to cause a powerful increase of killer T-cells, which can protect the body against HIV. When the manipulated canary virus was injected into the body, the immune system responded with the production of T-cells that attack the infected cells. The immune system also detected the HIV genes and made killer T-cells that attacked those genes too.

MEDICINES FROM THE ANIMALS

Animals have provided us with some important drugs. Compared to plants, it may be a minor source of drugs but nevertheless an important one. They supply us with about 3% of the drugs we use today.

Ancrod from the Malayan pit viper is used as an anticoagulant in the of heart attacks.

Alantoin from the blowfly larvae for deep-wound healing.

Ara-A from Caribbean sponge for the treatment of herpes encephalitis.

Ara-C also from another Caribbean sponge used for the treatment of several cancers including leukemia.

Bee venom from the honeybees used for the treatment of arthritis.

Blowfly larvae are used to promote healing

Cantharidin from the European blister beetle is used to treat certain urogenital conditions.

Capybara blood contains compounds that combat leukemia.

Clupeine from salmon is used to check hemorrhaging.

Cod liver oil for vitamins A & D and treatment of wounds and burns.

Cytarabine from marine sponges is used to treat leukemia and herpes infection.

Gamma globulin for hepatitis treatment comes from human placenta.

Halibut liver oil is also used for vitamins A & D.

Polio vaccine discovered after testing on the rhesus monkeys is used in the prevention of poliomyelitis and infantile paralysis.

Rhinoceros "horn" has antipyretic and anti-haemorrhagic properties.

Scorpion venom is being tested for numerous human ailments.

Sea wasp poison is being experimented on for a muscle relaxant.

Tetanus serum comes from horse blood.

Toxin from the crown-of-thorns starfish is used to treat tumors.

Animals produce important enzymes we use every day. One of the attributes of some kinds of bacteria is that they can respire anaerobically. This enables them to ferment sugar with varying results. Some produce alcohol, others lactic acid. Those that produce lactic acid are used for making butter, yoghurt and cheese from milk. Certain bacteria turn lactic acid into acetic acid used for making vinegar. Maggots can shrink the sizes of wound by as much as 25% in a week. By devouring only dead tissue, they can clean wounds while leaving healthy skin and muscle alone. The Maggot Therapy Project of the University of California, Irvine is selling medicinal maggots for use in curing wounds.

NATIONAL SYMBOLS

The importance of animals and the value we attach to them can be found in many of the things we do. Pictures of animals can be found in stamps heraldry and paper currency. Some countries have animals on their flags. As early as the time of Vikings, they used bird designs on their flag. California has had a bear on its state flag since 1846; they even called the state Bear Flag Republic. China, during the Ch'ing dynasty (19th century) had a dragon with yellow background on it. Countries like Uganda, Zimbabwe, Zambia, and Papua New Guinea have birds on their flags. The eagle is particularly popular in the U.S.; Illinois, Iowa, Louisiana, North Dakota, Pennsylvania, and Utah have an eagle embossed on their flags. In Wyoming, the state seal appears on the ribs of the bison. Most of the federal departments and agencies,

Treasury, Health, Energy, U.S. Air Force, U.S. Coast Guard. U.S.. Marine Corps, all have eagles in their flags. The eagle can be found in the seal of the President, Vice President, secretary of State, Defense and Attorney General.

Animals have always been depicted in coins and paper currencies throughout the world. Coins around the world have images of reptiles and amphibians. In a 1995 survey. David Chiszar and Hobart Smith found 1.539 coins from 80 different countries which contain such images. Dragons and other mythological creatures are depicted in more than half of these coins and extinct reptiles are found in another 58.

South African currency has five wild animals on one side. In Rwanda the government puts the gorillas on the banknotes as a sign of their importance due to the successful gorilla tourism that is one of the foreign exchange earners for the country. In Zaire, the 50.000 banknote has Mahashe, an impressive silverback gorilla in Kahuzi-Biega National Park featured on it. He is probably the most famous gorillas due to his size, strength and gentle disposition. The monkey-eating eagle is the national bird of the Philippines just as the bald eagle is to the U.S. It used to be found in 50 centavo coins. The Philippines used to have the one-peso coin embossed with the tamaraw, the national animal.

The quetzal (*Pharomachrus mocinno*) is a magnificent bird of the Trogon family; they inhabit the hilly rainforests from Mexico to Costa Rica at altitudes of up to 9.000 feet. The male can measure up to a meter from the tip of the bill to the end of the tail. Their beautiful colored feathers and breathtaking beauty endeared them to the Aztecs and Mayas who revered it as a god of the air. They are often seen in their art and never killed nor caged the bird. They are only caught for gathering the long tail plumes for ceremonial purposes and released afterwards. Today, it is the national symbol of Guatemala and appears on that country's postage stamps and coins. In fact, the currency of the country is quetzal. But like most rainforest species, the bird is becoming rarer as its forest home is destroyed. Many are also kept in cages as pets.

PEARLS

The pearl is a valuable gem made of calcium carbonate produced by certain mollusks. They can come in varying colors. Pearls are produced when foreign objects such as a grain of sand or parasitic worm, the usual irritants, are lodged between the shell and a sheet of flesh called the mantle. The irritation causes the mantle to secrete layers of nacre around the irritating object.

Cultured pearls are made by deliberately inserting particles of nacre taken from the shell of freshwater clams into the mantle of certain species of oysters or clams. They are then allowed to continue their secretion of nacre for years to increase the size of the pearl. A cultured pearl is just as real or genuine as the natural pearl harvested from the wild.

A Japanese, Baron Kokichi Mikimoto was able to produce spherical pearls using oysters. The irritant uses small nacre wrapped in a piece of mantle cut from the freshly opened pearl oyster. The oysters are kept on suspended baskets in quiet bays until they are ready for harvesting. The resulting finished pearls are difficult to differentiate from the true pearl of the wild. Since the 1970s, the Japanese have been producing smaller, irregular pearls using freshwater mussels for the cheaper market. Both pearls are widely distributed in the market.

PLANKTONS

Plankton is the collective name for minuscule plants and animals organisms that populate the seas and other water bodies of the world. They are divided into either phytoplankton, the plants or zooplankton. the animals. Bacteria and fungi which are neither plant nor animal are included. They are the basic building blocks of all marine animals. It provides food for most sea organisms such as turtles to the biggest whales. Although not easily seen with the naked eye, their absence could mean the extinction of most species living in the waters of the world.

Planktons also produce a lot of oxygen. Pollution of the ocean by hydrocarbons is covering the ocean with a thin film of hydrocarbon that can insulate the atmosphere from the oxygen producers. The role of planktons is becoming more important in the light of the unprecedented destruction of the rainforests.

POLLUTION DETECTORS

Many animals, because of their sensitivity have been employed by people as detectors. Very often, they are used in experimental water pollution to determine the toxicity of the water against the numerous chemicals and pesticides that are coming into the market.

In coal mining, canaries (Serinus canjriu) were used by the 19th century British miners to detect the presence of the poison gas methane that can kill human but affects the birds first. During the First World War, canaries were kept along with the soldiers to give warning of gas attacks.

Rabbits are employed by the U.S. Army to check chemical weapons for possible leaks. They also travel with the gas cylinders being transported to other localities. Fireflies are also used by reading the electric pulse they emit.

In West Germany, goldfish are used to detect water pollution. The goldfish emit constant electrical pulses that slow down when the pollution levels rise. On the other hand, the Japanese have kept goldfish as pets to help them detect an impending earthquake. Once it detects impending vibrations, it will swim frantically inside the fish bowl.

The presence or absence of certain freshwater organisms is often used as a gauge as to the state of the water ecosystem. Freshwater mussels are excellent indicators of habitat and water quality since they can live for 40 years in the seabed without moving from the same spot. All throughout the years, they function as a filter, taking in vast quantities of water and as in the case of the zebra mussels even acted as an absorbent of pollutants. Each mussel species has a particular fish species that it depends on for its reproductive cycle. The absence of this fish will be the doom of the mussels. The absence of the mussels, which can tolerate high toxicity is a vital sign of an impure and toxic water.

SCAVENGERS AND DECOMPOSERS

All living things grow, multiply and die. But these dead plants and carcasses slowly disappear from the environment because of the presence of scavengers and decomposers all around us. Without them we would all be buried under this organic trash. Scavengers feed off the carcasses of animals while decomposers break down the remaining organic matter into even smaller nutrients and minerals that are then recycled back to continue the cycle. Without them the world would run out of nutrients and minerals to continue the cycle of life.

Hyenas and jackals often feed on the animals that are already dead due to old age or diseases. Vultures cat only dead meat. Beetles, the most numerous of insects, are good scavengers. They dig the soil below the corpses to form a pit into which the meat falls, then they lay their eggs into the dead meat. The eggs hatch into grubs which feed on the corpse. Dung beetles decompose human and animal dung. They are particularly interesting because they bury the dung first by making it into a large ball bigger than themselves. In one night, they can bury several dung balls. They also spread the dung throughout the rangeland where they are found. In the Serengeti National Park, they decomposed an estimated eight million pounds of dung in a year, spreading the dung throughout the region fertilizing the soil and making grass grow for the wild animals. The pesty flies lay their eggs in corpses and dungs. The maggots then feed on the dead meat and dung. Some moth larvae can even digest the horn of dead animals. Termites feed on dead wood. Slugs, snails, millipede and most worms feed on dead and decaying organic matter in the soil.

In the ocean, seagulls are good scavengers for food near the sea shore and wastes thrown overboard by ships. Crabs too like to scavenge along the shores and the seabeds. Some fishes such as the hagfish eat other dead fish.

SOIL ENRICHMENT

Earthworms are indispensable to the maintenance of a rich soil structure. They are great decomposers of dead material through their chewing and distributing the dead leaves and food to another locality while ploughing and working on the soil. One well known species, *Lumbricus lerretris* will drag dead leaves and twigs to their burrow for consumption, Unlike most animals, earthworms can digest cellulose, the stuff of plant cell walls as food while the excesses are left to improve the soil. The burrowing of earthworms aerates soil and enhances drainage and so improves the soil condition for plants and other microorganisms. Earthworms are likened to excavators, burrowing by sucking soil through their mouths, digesting much of its organic component and excreting a mixture of soil, leaf fragments and mucus known as worm casts.

THERAPY ANIMALS

Patients, whether children or adults seem to have a certain affinity for small animals. The Devereux Foundation Treatment Center for deficit disorder and hyperactivity uses small animals to treat children with hyperactivity. Some suffer from aggressive disorder that results in quick outbursts One boy had to be restrained 40 times within a span of six months until he was given a chinchilla as a pet From then on his condition improved.

A part-time maternity nurse at Temple University Hospital in Philadelphia takes her Vietnamese pot-bellied pig named Petunia, on therapy visits to a nursing and rehabilitation center in Philadelphia to cheer up all the patients The pig was a favorite of the patients Two adult-llamas used to visit a Colorado nursing home for people suffering from depression and Alzheimer's disease As soon as the animals arrived, they would suddenly come out of their rooms with smiles on their faces upon seeing the animals.

Dolphins are always used in therapy for people under life-threatening diseases This is because the mammal is always smiling and can easily cheer up patients People with Down's syndrome, autism, brain damage, cancer and other ailments find relief whenever they swim along with dolphins In Israel, a former cancer patient Helen Davis, credited the dolphins for her remission.

Even watching animals can have a therapeutic effect on patients about to go for root-canal surgery. A study made at the University of Pennsylvania showed that dental patients were more relaxed before surgery after looking at a tank full of fishes for 30 minutes before surgery.

Animal therapy is very effective for people suffering from motion problems. They can recovery faster by stroking domestic cats and other animals People recovering from strokes are often required to lift dumbbells to recover strength of their limbs. Usually they don't find the workout interesting. Some patients have resorted to throwing a tennis ball for a dog that doesn't complain at all.

Pets are also effective companions for people suffering from heart problems. In one study, only three people out of 58 patients with pets as a companion died compared to eleven out of eighteen who died without pet companionship Even people who live alone with pets as companions live longer than those without pets at home. They help reduce stress and lower blood pressure. This has been found to be true in studies made in Australia

Rabbits are good pain-relieving companions People who underwent surgery for cancer or heart disease experienced relief from anxiety and reduced blood pressure by stroking the animal Arthritis patients are particularly affected by rabbit therapy as they are increasingly used in nursing homes for people undergoing arthritis therapy. Most patients would rather groom the rabbit than do finger exercises. Together with dogs and cats, they are sometimes used to bring back people suffering from comatose.

Horseback riding is one of the best therapy around Disabled individuals can develop self-awareness and self-discipline while it improves confidence and concentration It helps to improve posture, balance, strength, flexibility and eye-to-hand coordination The horse movement helps all parts of the human body to receive exercise that is difficult to achieve under clinical setting Writing dating back to the 17th century had shown the benefits that can be derived from horseback riding However, therapists started to recognize its advantages when Liz Hartel, a polio rider from Denmark won a silver medal for dressage at the 1952

Helsinki Olympic Games. Since then, therapeutic riding has grown through the western world as a form of therapy for the physically and mentally disabled persons.

WORKING ANIMALS

Animals have long been used to help mankind in more ways than one. Probably the first animal to be domesticated and most useful is the dog. It has helped in hunting in the old days as they do today. Many have been trained for other duties. Their keen sense of hearing and smell have been put to use by people. In Canada's Imperial Oil Resources Limited, they use more than a dozen Labrador retrievers to check tiny leaks in oil pipelines that could pollute the groundwater. By injecting a foul-smelling chemical, the dogs can sniff out the leaking chemical as deep as 18 feet. Even under six feet of water, it can smell the leaking chemical. In 136 leaks, the dogs have failed only twice.

The next useful working animal is probably the horse. It was the fastest form of transportation for centuries, before the car was invented. It was at one time used as a draught animal in the field. Cattle are mostly used in the Third World as working animals in place of the horse.

Riding horse-drawn carriages can be dangerous. The horse drawn *calesa* used in Chinatown in the Philippines are particularly risky. The center of gravity is very high and any untoward incident can be dangerous. First, the horses are often small in comparison to the weight they carry and are unsuited to travel along the cement roads. There is not even a law restricting the maximum weight they should carry.

The horses are forced to work for 16 hours or more without rest and little amount of food and water. This is to reduce the amount of excrement. In some European countries, horses are used to deliver wine and milk the traditional way, an easy excuse that has no place in this age of enlightenment. The hoof of the horses traveling for hours on heated pavement can cause them to collapse. Some have been noted to die from heat exhaustion. Any backfire from the automobile can cause them to panic and run wild. Horses are often subjected to whipping when they find it difficult to overcome an obstruction. The presence of uneven pavement and bridges can only double their difficulty in transporting people.

Animals, especially dogs have long been used for guard duties. Other animals such as crocodiles and big cats have also been used for the same purpose. A news dispatch from Jakarta reported in the April 1, 1997 *Manila Bulletin* came out with a report that the military authorities in the Indonesian city of Semarang planned to deploy scores of pythons and snake charmers to assist them in safeguarding the May 29 general election. At least 20 pythons and scores of snake charmers will be deployed to discourage anti-government demonstrators from disrupting the election in Semarang, the capital of Central Java. The pythons would be about six meters long and weighed about 15 kilograms. The newspaper did not say how the snakes would be used. Police in Bekasi were also considering using cobras to handle mass demonstrations.

Elephants of the Asian continent have always played a working role in the economy of the country. They are tourist attraction in many places and "workers" in others. As early as the 3rd century B.C. elephants were used in the building of temples. In the forests, they worked as log haulers using their tusks and long nose to balance and carry the logs around. The use of working elephants in the teak forests of mainland Asia began as early as the 17th century and reached its peak in the late 19th century. The Myanmar Timber Enterprise kept more than 3,000 elephants to help in their logging. They worked for about six hours a day, three to six days a week.

In the desert where roads are unavailable, the dromedary or one-humped camels (Camelus dromedarius) have served as "ships of the desert" transporting people and goods and making desert habitable for people. The two-humped camel (Camelus bactrianus) found mostly in Mongolia and western China have served as domestic animals.

In this mechanized world where abundant forms of transportation are available, there are still those who resort to using horses for transportation. It is excusable for poor people who use them, but it should no longer be used where cars are plentiful such as in the cities. Traveling along the streets with automobiles can be very unhealthy for the horse. They are always the recipient of the toxic fumes coming from tailpipes that cause respiratory problems.

CHAPTER 2

ARTHROPODS

The arthropods come from the largest phylum in the animal kingdom. Beside insects, they include scorpions, spiders, ticks, mites, crustaceans, millipedes, centipedes and many other unclassified or undiscovered species. They have well-developed organs, cuticular exoskeletons used for protection to compensate for their small sizes.

They have been around for 400 million years, far longer than many other living or extinct creatures. They are the most successful animals ever to evolve and their fate will probably last long after man has become extinct. Their reproductive capabilities, diversity, and their ability to adapt to environmental changes and cunning ways to cope with pesticides, pollutions, loss of habitats ensure their survival for a long time. Small and adaptable, their species can be found almost everywhere even in places too inhospitable for humans.

The arthropods lie at the heart of our rich ecosystems. Without them, the world would be very different from what we know today. Many animals in the jungles would not have survived for long due to lack of food. In fact, the evolution of higher forms of animals was made possible only because of the abundance of insects for food. Birds, reptiles, amphibians, and other insect-eaters would not have evolved without them. Many plants would have become extinct without the insects producing food through plant pollination for the more plentiful plant-eating animals.

The interdependency of plants and animals greatly revolve around the relationships between plants and insects. About 80% of the flowering plants are partially or wholly dependent on the insects to carry the pollen from one plant to another. Bees, wasps, butterflies, and many others help pollinate flowers as they travel from tree to tree gathering pollen and other food. Plants on the other hand provide nectar, leaves, and other sugars needed by other insects. They also serve as homes to many insects, birds, reptiles, and other tree-dwelling animals.

The roles played by arthropods for the benefits of the human population are numerous. They are an important link in the chain of food that leads to the humans. Their large diversity makes it possible to control the populations of other insects as well as the human populations with some deadly insects in our midst.

Another important role of arthropods are as good scavengers in the ecology. The bugs are helping us breakdown and recycle unwanted waste and clean up the environment. Without them, the earth will be filled with carcasses and other wastes that could contaminate the various ecosystems vital to human survival. Without them around, the world would have been buried under piles of garbage, dung, and other wastes that cannot be utilized by plants for growing and animals as feed. In return, we can help them by keeping their natural habitat intact. In denuded areas we can plant trees, flowers and shrubs that can be the source of food and shelter for them.

Probably less than 2% of the arthropods species in the world are harmful to mankind due to their ability to transmit diseases and destroy our crops. But as a group, they are becoming more essential as our populations continue to grow without end.

Arthropods are an indispensable part of all ecosystems that make life possible. There are still millions more, maybe up to nine millions and as much as 30 million that are yet undiscovered or unclassified. The majority of them are found in the tropical forests around the world.

BEES

Bees are social animals that live in colonies and are the greatest pollinators, accounting for more than half of the pollination. Because of the social life they lead, they are required to gather nectar for the nests and feed the growing young bees. Each bee makes an average of 60,000 trips to flowers just to make a teaspoon of honey. Throughout the years, they are in constant motion, picking up pollen and transferring it to other flowers for fertilization. The pollens are inadvertently attached to almost all parts of the insect's body and transferred to their next stop which is often the same species of plant. Other pollinators are the hoverfly, butterfly and moth, bats and other flying insects and birds.

The red clover is an important food source of livestock. Without the bumble bees to pollinate the plants, it is almost impossible to produce seeds. When the red clover was first imported to New Zealand, they found it difficult to produce seeds by the native insects, even the hardworking honey bees. In 1885, they introduced the bumble bees and ushered in a new era of abundance.

There is great potential in beekeeping. The investment is small but the return is great. What is needed are bee cages and lots of flowers, and the bees will do the rest of the work. The honey bees (*Xylocopa laticeps*) are great producers of honey and comb. For thousands of years, mankind has harvested the honey from the wild and even domesticated them to produce honey. The combs, with cells full of honey, are often eaten as a delicacy.

Beekeepers in the U.S. have found a gold mine in renting out their bee hives to farmers. About half of the 2,000 commercial beekeepers from the U.S. regularly move their bee hives in trucks to places where there are plenty of flowers for the food of bees. Not only are these hardworking bees getting their share of food while pollinating flowers, the owners are getting paid for a fee. The fruit growers of California, with its huge and densely planted trees that wild pollinators cannot do a complete job, regularly hire beekeepers to pollinate the almond crops during the flowering season. It would require 500,000 hives and each acre would require two hives that cost S32 per hives.

During the past three years, beekeepers in the U.S. have lost half of their hives to a lethal combination of pesticides, two types of parasitic mites, and harsh winter weather. Wild honeybees have fared even worse, an estimated 90% have died. {Popular Science, November 1997) The loss of bees, the chief pollinator for the food industry could spell big trouble for mankind. Pennsylvania's sizable apple industry couldn't get enough commercial bees last year leading to a 40% drop in yield. The cost of pollination fees have doubled in the past ten years.

BEETLES

Of all the insects, the beetles are probably the most successful among them. There are more than 300.000 species of them, the largest group of any species. They can be found in muddy ponds, arid deserts and high up in the mountains. The beetles have a cunning ability to produce and provide for their young and protect themselves against predators. Certain scarab beetles use large moist dung pats of livestock as food for themselves and their youngs. The dung is rolled into a ball and buried in the soil along with its eggs. The newly hatched eggs are then provided with enough food after they are hatched.

Besides being harvested as ornamental jewelry from their many beautiful bodies and eaten by some local inhabitants, some beetles play an even more important role of cleaning up the environment of organic wastes. The scarabs of Australia have long been coping with the small dry pellets of kangaroos. However, they were incapable of decomposing cow dung. The problem was resolved by importing several species of scarabs from Europe and Africa to tackle the problem and they did it with flying colors. The resolution of the problem saved the land from soil pollution badly needed for growing the grass needed by the livestock. There are probably thousands of beneficial actions being accomplished that we are still unaware of.

In parts of the New World women catch some of the more attractive species of beetle, pull off the iridescent wing cover and thread them onto strings as necklaces. In Mexico there is a species of beetle know n locally as the jewel beetle, which is a fairly close relative of the common mealworm beetle. These poor little animals are captured and pieces of colored glass and beads are glued to their backs and a short length of chain is also glued to the animals, which is then pinned to the lapel of a lady's dress as a fashion accessory.

BIOLUMINESCENT INSECTS

Fireflies, lightningbugs, true bugs, and maggots of some flies have special properties not found in other insects. They are able to produce a light by biochemical means. This feature has long fascinated scientists. The light emitted does not produce any heat and can be useful in areas where the absence of heat is an important safety factor. Other animals with this ability include jellyfish, squids, deep-sea fish and even the single-celled organism such as the infamous red tide.

The fireflies are the more familiar insects we can see in the rural areas. The ability to emit brief coded flashes has several purposes. They are used to attract mates or to herald the birth of an offspring. The different characteristics of flashes could convey the sender's specific sex and species that other fireflies recognize.

In India, the insects were once caught and enclosed in gauze and attached to the hair of ladies when they went out for their evening walk. Others make use of their flashes like Christmas lights and placed them in jars for ornamental reasons. Before the introduction of electricity, some poor rural people of Cuba and other West Indies islanders used to catch 20 to 30 of these luminous fireflies and placed them inside transparent jars to help illuminate the home.

BIONIC INSECTS

In 1989, Martin Lindauer, together with several ethologists were able to devise a peppermint-scented robot that can mimic the dancing and buzzing of the honey bees. They were able to entice many bees some distance from other hive where the robot bait is placed. This simple accomplishment could lead to many other uses for many other insects and animals. Luring harmful insects for destruction is one good example.

Kitchen pests such as cockroaches are being turned into bionic sources of information by Japanese researchers. A plastic cage in a laboratory in the heart of Tokyo is crawling with these creatures. They are not the average kitchen vermin - but real bionic roaches, their wings dipped off and replaced with miniature electronic circuits.

These hapless creatures are part of an experiment led by Isao Shimoyama, a mechanical engineer at the University of Tokyo. By electrically stimulating its nervous system using tiny electrodes, Mr. Shimoyama and his colleagues have created "RoboRoach", a cockroach which turns left or right and darts forward on command. They hope that robotic insects will one day led swarms of insects to crops that need pollinating, or lure away plague-carrying insects. Their ultimate goal is to learn from insects' anatomy and build entire micromachines modelled on nature's ingenious designs.

Mr. Shimoyama had been trying to design micromachines for four years before he realized that insects have perfected what he has been trying to do. Insects can move in a far more sophisticated way than any tiny mechanical device ever made. They have evolved through natural selection so that they have suitable mechanisms and structures that are very simple compared to mammals. It is this simplicity that makes insects easy to control. They typically have around 10,000 to one million nerve cells in total, compared with the 10 billion that humans carry around in their brains alone. And unlike humans, insects have a very simple command-response system. Insects only react in one way to a given stimulus, and that makes their responses to artificial stimuli predictable.

The researchers are also studying the silk worm moth's sensory systems in the hope that they might one day be useful in industry - perhaps to detect escaping gases. Conventional gas detectors are much less sensitive than the moth's sensors, which can respond to a single molecule of the pheromone. The researchers hope to pin down the way their sensors work and mimic them in the artificial "noses" of future micromachines.

The researchers have taken insect control a step further using sweet potato moths. They attached a radio transmitter to a moth and measured the electrical signals reaching its muscles during flight. They can now control the fight of the insect by feeding the signals back using a remote-control system consisting of an electronic backpack strapped to the insect. Cockroaches are especially ideal because they have been well studied. They can also walk on any terrain, eat anything and they live a long time for insects, about a year.

By controlling some social insects, it is possible to lead the entire insect group into a net or to pollinate flowers. A handful of bionic locusts might be used to lure a swarm of locusts into a trap And perhaps the dance of a bionic bee could be choreographed to encourage its hive mates to fly to field of crops and pollinate them But whether this will work is a big gamble The researchers warn that it may not be possible to manipulate whole swarms simply by controlling a few individuals.

The team also has an artificial eye on the drawing board, modelled on the compound eyes of insects, that will allow a miniature robot to steer between obstacles The idea is that signals from the artificial eye, corresponding to an object in front, will be converted into signals in the electronic nervous system that directs the robot to the left or right. The compound eye of a fly is very lightweight, but by comparison the images in adjacent lenses, the fly is extremely good at detecting motion and shape Mr. Shimoyama believes a "techno fly eye could function as a camera. That will be useful for inspection work inside pipes.

Press speculation is rife that real insects equipped with miniature cameras can locate people trapped under rubber after earthquakes It may also be used on spying missions. Terrorists holed up inside a building might never notice the odd-looking cockroach scuttling across the floor, its miniature camera relaying pictures

BUTTERFLIES AND MOTHS

Butterflies and moths are under tremendous pressure from eradication like the beautiful and exotic animals found throughout the world. They are even more vulnerable to changes in the environment. The destruction of the forests and grasslands throughout the world have endangered many species to the point that many are listed in the Red Data Book of International Union for the Conservation of Nature (IUCN). Human encroachment of their once pristine habitats with housing and development has also been responsible for some extinction in the past The California's Xerces Blue (*Glauscopsyche xerces*) has become extinct in 1941 due to development. In fact a worldwide conservation group was named after it called the Xerces Society.

There are about 200,000 species of butterflies and moths in the world Out of these numbers, about 180,000 of them are moths. Butterfly and moth collecting is an important hobby for some collectors because of the different and beautiful designs on their wings It has great potential because of the well-established market throughout the world The market once estimated at more than $200 million in 198$ has grown tremendously through the years.

Butterflies can easily be bred by providing a habitat where they can propagate prolifically But many of their habitats have been destroyed and overcollection has forced governments to impose protection One of the most beautiful moths, the Spanish moon moth (*Craellsia Isabellae*) has been under government protection for years Other species placed under protection are the Essex Emerald moth (*Thelidia smaragdaria*), the Philippine swallowtail butterfly (*Papilio chikae*) and the large Homerus swallowfly butterfly (*Papilo homerus*) of Jamaica Protecting their habitat is one way of saving the butterflies and moths but also other organisms that reside within Their chief enemy in this case is the loss of habitat or at least their specific plants. Each species has a preferred food plant for its caterpillar and they will only lay eggs on them. By planting certain species in small plots in the forest, many more butterflies can be raised without affecting the populations.

Papua New Guinea is the only tropical country to have a constitution specifying insects as a natural resources and to have a government agency dedicated solely to the insect trade. The protection accorded the butterflies has also led to the protection of other species such as moths, katydids, some of the longest walkingsticks and most beautiful weevils. Out of the 900 species of butterflies, the most spectacular is the birdwing. In 1966, a collector paid $1,785 for a specimen Troides allortei from the Solomon Islands A single perfect birdwing in PNG can fetch $150 to $1,500. The Insect Trading and Farming Agency buys insects for export from village collectors all over PNG. Since it was established in 1978, its initial export was $250,000 a year, and has gradually increased through the years.

Strict enforcement of protection laws is important if we are to help many threatened species from recovery. Some butterfly species are protected under the Endangered Species Act. When three poachers in the U.S. were captured for illegally trading in butterflies caught from natural parks and forests in California, the confiscated 23,375 specimens was estimated to be valued at $307,642.

Unless butterfly farms are established, there will be a continuing decline in their numbers. Of the 700 species of butterflies and moths in the U.S., 100 of them are listed in the Red Data Book as threatened species due to pesticides, habitat destructions, and climatic changes. Collectors have been responsible for acquiring and mounting large numbers of butterflies, some of them illegally from the endangered species

In Florida, the schaus swallowtail lives mostly in southern part of Florida. Pesticides used to combat mosquitoes are also killing them. In 1991, less damaging pesticides was introduced allowing them to recover. However, the devastating Hurricane Andrew killed the butterflies to near extinction, and the remaining butterflies were captured for captive breeding It is a cruel act no matter how some people view it if we kill the butterflies or for that matter any animal prematurely for the sake of owning their body parts for collection or medicine. In their short lifespan, it is always possible to wait until they die a natural death in order to obtain an important product from their bodies. But that is not the case. Butterflies are often killed to decorate the hair of ladies in the old days and furniture and other households items nowadays.

Some entrepreneurs have taken the steps to make butterfly viewing a tourist attraction Inside the Butterfly Pavilion and Insect Center in Westminster, Colorado is a glass-enclosed pavilion, containing as many as 1,200 tropical butterflies Delicate lacewings from the Philippines, brilliant blue morphos from Costa Rica striped zebra longwings from South America, showy spicebush swallowtails from Florida are some of the butterflies flying and flirting through the thickly man-made rainforest habitat. Winding paths through this lush jungle are constructed where visitors of all ages can have a closeup view of the butterflies.

Most of the butterflies were imported while they were still pupae While they were still in their early life cycle, the pupae were wrapped in cotton to ensure safe passage and shipped from their native lands. It takes a week to 10 days for the pupae to metamorphose into colorful winged adults. This transformation can be seen behind glass in the pavilion's aptly named Emergence Center.

Each butterfly gets a few hours to recuperate from the skin splitting ordeal. Then it is turned loose and allowed to explore its indoor home. Feeding on flower nectar and overly ripe fruit, the butterfly leads a short but sweet life - anywhere from a week to two months, depending on the species and time of year.

The dazzling diversity of butterflies and the dramatic inescapable metaphorical transition from drab pupa to elegant adult are both powerful tourist attractions. In its first year of operation, nearly twice the expected number of visitors visited the pavilion. Such whopping attendance is not just restricted to the Westminster site. Butterfly houses throughout North America and at well-visited locales such as Singapore's Sentosa Island and Australia Butterfly Sanctuary are also attracting record crowds. Today, around 130 butterfly houses exist worldwide, with 20 of them in the U.S. and at least 35 in Britain.

CARING FOR THE OFFSPRING

The ability of the insects to survive in this planet is not confined to their ability to reproduce in large numbers, but also their ability to care for their offspring by providing all the necessary food for them to grow or survive on their own. How they accomplished this responsibility is the envy of many higher forms of animals.

The sacred scarab beetles (Scarabaeus sacer) of ancient Egypt are very efficient providers for their offspring. They lay their eggs in nests and provide the offspring with the necessary food for survival. Before the female is ready to reproduce, she will prepare a cow dung, roll it into a ball and bury it in one of the holes in the soil prepared for the occasion. The cow pat is usually larger than she is and help is often provided by another beetle. Only one egg will be deposited within the dung. This will ensure the hatched larvae will have no competition for the available food.

Many insects make elaborate homes for their young. The honey bees not only provide homes during the early stages of life, but also after their death. Like the ants and termites, they are called social insects. They live in groups numbering from a few dozens to a million or more depending on the species. They cooperate to raise the young within the colony. Each insect seems to know what to do within the organization. One special feature of social insects is that only one queen per colony exists with the help of many nonproducing caste of female workers.

A few insects provide for the young like mammals do. The eggs are retained within the body until fully developed before they give birth to the young. Others produce their larvae and place them as parasites in other animal's bodies such as livestock. The parasitic cuckoo wasp using ovipositor inject their eggs into the body of the host. Parasitic tachinid flies spends its larval existence glued to the skin of the cecropia caterpillar. While still others lay their eggs where it is hidden from outside view; other plant-eating insects lay their eggs among plants where the newly hatched offspring can start feasting.

EXTINCTION

Out of the possible 30 million arthropods around the world, many have become extinct because of human activities. Many of these species, unclassifed and undiscovered, are found in the rainforests of the tropical countries. These important ecosystems are being destroyed and converted to other uses that are neither productive or whose productivity will be exhausted after a few years. The continuing destruction of their habitats will leave myriad of insects without sources of food and poor breeding ground. Many species of animals can only survive on certain plants or animals and the extinction of one can lead to the extinction of another.

In the U.S. alone, about 700 species are cither in the endangered or threatened list. If a country with one of the stringiest laws on conservation is having problems saving some insects.. other countries specially in the tropics may be grappling with a bigger problem caused by the extinction of species.

Unlike the larger animals, insects are small and can easily adapt to any changes in the environment. This is probably the reason why conservationists do not take serious efforts to preserve them. However, most of the insects are found in the tropical countries, and the destruction of the rainforests is causing more extinction of insects than any other animal in the world.

FOOD SOURCES

There are more than one million species of insects throughout the world. They can be found almost everywhere. Their large number is a guarantee that predators will have a good time feeding on them. They are an important source of food for animals such as birds, reptiles, amphibians and mammals. In some parts of Asia, South American and other regions, consuming insects is an integral part of the diet. Water beetles, ants, termites, worms, grasshoppers and the juicy caterpillars and grubs of some of these insects are some of the delicacies. The people of Africa and Mideast harvested the protein rich locusts that overran their land.

The U.S. Food and Drug Administration (FDA) sanctions the consumption of insects by allowing a tolerable level of insects in the food sold to the public. There is nothing abhorrent in eating insects if we consider that most of the food we consume have made insects a part of their food chain. The protein contained in insects is higher than those of plant proteins. They are also rich in vitamins and minerals and often free from insecticides and other chemicals used in breeding farm animals.

Grasshoppers have been eaten by native inhabitants of North America and Mexicans. It contains more calories than beef. Eating locusts is even permissible under Moslem customs. The Romans found the caterpillar a delicacy after being fed with flour. In Africa locusts, termites, ants, grubs, different kinds of caterpillars, larvae etc are eaten by different tribesmen. In Asia, water bugs are sold in market and silkworm are sold in Japan. The ricehoppers are mass produced for the gourmets.

Cicadas often emergy in millions at each outbreak. One outbreak in Chicago in 1990 sent the Chicago Tribute to publish recipies for cooking cicada as part of the daily food and even cicada eating contests were held in bars around the city. Other enterprising jewelers make jewelry out of the cicadas for sale.

FORENSIC ENTOMOLOGY

In the Septermber, 1997 issue of Popular Science, it was reported that the first time an insect was used to solve a crime happened in 1235 in China. It occurred when a dead body was found hacked to death with a rice sickle. During the course of the investigation, the mayor called all the farmers to a meeting and to bring along their rice sickle. He had all of them lay down the sickle on the ground and waited. Before long, a swarm of flies gathered around the murder weapon. The murderer confessed to the crime.

It was only in the past two decades that scientists and law enforcement agencies have become interested in the relationships between insects and crimes. The most interesting thing about insects is the possibility of pinpointing the time of death almost to the hour. For outdoor deaths this is done by studying the age of the maggots. Once a person dies, it will attract the flies even if they are several miles away within a few minutes. The flies will immediate lay her eggs in the carrion. The type of insects surrounding the carrion is often attracted at different stages of decay. This could possibly be caused by the decaying carcass emitting different odors that attract different insects. This has led to the solution of crimes such as murders and suicides and even helped determine the veracity of alibis.

In one investigation in the U.S., a lady dead for several weeks was found in a bathtub in her apartment. The only thing left were some insects still eating away at what was left of the body. The insects were gathered together and boiled to extract what was left in their bodies. A high dosage of depressant was found and police were able to determine the cause of death as suicide. Bugs can also help solve the origin of a contraband such a marijuana or cocaine. Forensic entomologists can determine the type of bugs found and pinpoint the origin of the insects.

There are presently about twenty forensic entomologists in the U.S. today. One of them, Bill Bass is pioneering a database through his Body Farm where corpses are being studied in minute details. It will serve as guide for forensic entomologists. Researchers are doing field work to determine the many factors that will be of help in the future. Animal and even human corpses are kept and analyzed for any changes in the state of the corpses and the types of insects that are attracted at each stage of decomposition. This important tool in the fight against crime has been offered as a course in forensic entomology in some universities.

GALL

Many modern washable writing inks are water solutions of dyes that deteriorate when exposed to light and moisture. Writing inks that last very long usually contain iron sulfate and gallic and tannic acids in addition to the dye. The combination of these ingredients have resulted in an ink resistant to both water and light.

Gall is an abnormal knoblike protrusion in plants resulting from the attack of parasites such as insects. They range in size from a few grams to as much as 25 kilos More than 2,000 kinds of insect galls have been identified in American plants alone. Seventy percent of them are the gall wasps and the gall midges Other insects include scale insects, plant lice, beetles, nematode worms, mites, and others.

The gall of certain plant species can produce very rich tannic acid, a mixture of gallic and ellagic acids. One of the properties of tannic acid is that when combined with salt iron it can form an ink that has been in use for four thousand years The durability of written manuscripts with the ink produced from it has been responsible for the preservation of the old books. Because of their durability, it is used for printing currency by the U.S. Treasury, Bank of England, and several other governments. It has other uses such as dyeing of leather, making nontoxic black dyes for hair, and many other cosmetic uses.

HOME GARDEN

There are many things we can do to help the insects and other animals in their search for food. One easy way that not only helps us in fighting the greenhouse effect but can also help insects such as bees, wasps, butterflies, spiders and larger animals such as bats and birds is gardening. The spiders can build their webs among the branches and help us catch the unwanted pests. The birds can take a respite from flying and maybe even build a nest in the trees.

It would be a good idea to choose the kind of plants and flowers for the garden. Different animals have different tastes of flowers Dandelions, thistles, clover, and nettles are particularly attractive to butterflies Honey suckle, lilac, lavender, marigold, and other colorful and aromatic plants are also attractive to butterflies.

INSECTICIDES

Out of sight and out of mind is the best way to describe the manner we use insecticides. Many of these insecticides are carried in the water system that eventually end up in the oceans. The insecticides used for killing flies has active ingredients tetramethrin and phenothrin, both of which are highly toxic to aquatic animals and other beneficial insects that may come across them. Although the WHO considered them to be moderately harmful, nevertheless, it has been known to kill a child with a dose of 0.5 ounces.

Although insecticides have been applied at particular pests, it has often caused unwanted destruction of beneficial insects. Many of the insecticides are meant to disrupt the endocrine glands of insects, but the effect has become counterproductive. All these insecticides somehow end up in the water systems of the world destroying the reproductive system of many animals from the amphibians, avians up to and including humans.

KRILLS

Krills (*Euphasia superba*) are tiny shrimp-like crustaceans that is at the center of the food chain for animals inhabiting the Antarctica. Whales, seals, birds, and

Other fishes consume them in large quantities. However, since the 1980s, the population of the krill has decreased by about 90% Some 300,000 tons are harvested from the ocean annually, with Japan, Russia and Ukraine accounting for 96% of the catch. They used them as feed supplement for chicken, pig, mink cattle and farm fish. Human consumption is also growing in many countries as other sea foods are becoming scarce..

Commercial krill fishing began in the early 1970s in the light of the dwindling of many other fishes for feeding livestock. They are caught by highly sophisticated trawlers complete with freezer and processing plant that can immediately deliver the goods upon port call. Krills are also made into krill butter, cheese spread, Japanese fish sausage, and okean, a Russian flavoring.

The largest harvest of krill may have a domino effect on the food chain and disrupt the marine ecosystem in Antarctica that has existed for millions of years depending on the availability of krill. It could cause starv ation of many species of animals that are already under threat of extinction Blue whales and other baleen whales, penguins, seals, and seabirds are particularly at risk. The baleen whales cat by opening their huge mouth and allowing the krill to pass through their baleen plates that look like slats equipped with bristles to keep the krill in. Every year they consumed from 50-60 million tons.

Penguin populations in Antarctic islands have been reduced by up to 50% because of lack of food. Since 1995, there were persistent reports of penguin chicks dying of starvation near one of Australia's base in the Antarctica because they can't find enough krill to satisfy their need A substitute food for krill is salp, but it has little appeal to the Antarctic mammals.

MEDICINE

Insects, because of their small sizes produced an array of toxins to defend themselves from predators. Some of these toxins have been harnessed by mankind for its curative benefits. Since ancient times, insects have been used to treat all kinds of medical problems ranging from baldness, sore throat, impotency, and deafness. Many of the concoctions do not have any lasting value, but it shows that ancient people have attached important value to the insect's body parts. It will take modern medicine to find these valuable toxins and venoms, and synthesized for our benefits.

One of the earliest medicines used since ancient times is the gall from scale insects. Although they may not have known the presence of the important tannic acid it was nevertheless used for many ailments. Today, tannic acid is used for the treatment of hemorrhage, gastric bleeding and ulcers.

Insects can also be used directly to help patients suffering from wounds in the battlefield. During the Napoleonic Wars and the American Civil War, soldiers with maggot-infested wounds recovered more quickly due to its consumption of necrotic tissue. Maggots also secrete allantoin, a nitrogenous material that sterilizes the tissues.

Sometimes the insects can be used directly. In the jungles of the Amazon and elsewhere in parts of Africa and India, natives use the jaws of army ants to close a wound around the incision. The sharp serrated mandibles, once locked their jaws on the wound, will be impossible to remove.

Before the discovery of antibiotics, people suffering from the incurable syphilis will do anything to ward off the tertiary stage of the disease. Knowing that the agent spirochete cannot survive temperatures over forty degree Centigrade, victims often resorted to having themselves infected with mild form of malaria. Malaria causes very high fever, over 40 degrees that can kill the syphilis pathogens Cockroaches have been used by Chinese medicine in the treatment of many diseases. Even in the old Prussian empire, cockroaches have been used in a number of preparation. In Jamaica, they are used to treat ulcers. It is also used to treat children infected with worms.

Poisons from the bees and w asps have been used in the treatment of numerous ailments. Bee stings have long been used in the treatment of rheumatism by expanding the capillary and allowing blood to flow freely to the afflicted areas. Pollens from the bees have been added to the vitamin supplements to enhance their efficacy.

Spider venoms are widely used in medicine because of the complex mixtures with many specific components which can be extracted for specific ailment. In 1982, one component from the Japanese spider was found to block the action of the glutamate, a neurotransmitter substance. It is involved in the death of nerve cells caused by injury or stroke. Researches are still continuing to find other uses from spider venoms.

PHEROMONES

The pheromone is a hormone secreted by the female insects to attract their male counterparts for mating. It could also work the other way around. Some animals also secrete the hormones through their urine as in the big cats to bring notice to their presence and their territorial rights.

Some parasites and predators have taken advantage of this attraction. They are able to recognize and follow the sex hormone to their hosts Others such as the wasps arc attracted to pheromones secreted by known host animals where they lay their eggs in the tiny bodies of scale insects, where their larval offspring feed and grow as parasites. Some predators of the same order were able to trap their prey by using a synthetic form of the sex attractant.

Insects are particularly adept at using phermones as a sex attractant. It is so potent that even minute quantities can be detected several miles away. This knowledge has made it possible for humans to produce synthetic pheromones for use against unwanted parasites and pesty insects. They are used as baits or traps in monitoring and controlling the pest populations Synthetic hormones have been sprayed in crop field to confuse the targeted insect from copulating.

Pheromones have other uses that can influence the behavior, development and attraction for a member of its own species Fishes, amphibians, reptiles, and mammals are some of the animals that have effectively made full use of this hormone. Animals used the pheromone cither to find mates or to warn others away. It is like a chemical means of communication among many creatures throughout their smell, taste or some other sensing instruments.

Experiments with male house mice with a pheromone carried in the urine showed signs of speeding up the estrus cycle of females A tiny drop of his urine applied to the female's bedding each day is enough to accelerate her estrus cycle. With this knowledge, researchers tried to find a cure for women with irregular menstrual cycles. The pheromone from the males can be extracted with alcohol from the armpits of men. These extracts can be rubbed on the upper lips of women with irregular menstrual cycle for three times within a week. The women under the program were requested not to remove the hormone for six hours. After the experiments, the women were able to report significant regularity' in their menstruation.

POPULATION CONTROL

The myriad insects and other animals around the world make it possible to control the population of each species of insects. Without the varied insects, the animal population in the world would be left unchecked and grow so large it would cover the world and overwhelm the life support system in a short time. Each species of insect has an important role to play in balancing the nature.

Were it not for some of the diseases brought about by insects, our populations today would have long reached the 100 billion mark Billions of people were not born and need not suffer the harshness of the environment. Even before this limit is reached we would have easily overwhelmed the carrying capacity of the planet faster than any animal can do.

SHELLAC

Insects (*Kerra lacca, etc.*) produce various chemicals and products from their body for their own protection. Some of these products are waxes, fluffs, powders, wings, sticky legs, and armor plates. One of the most useful products is the lac and its derivatives that are used in making shellac.

Shellac is produced from lac deposited as a protection for the offspring in thick, hard layers around the branches of certain trees and shrubs. It is made by scale insects which comprise about 2,000 species of insects in which the bodies of adult females such as the fig and banyan are so modified that they bear little resemblance to the original insect. There are two types of scale insects: the soft scale and the armored scale. Only the armored scale insects can make the lac that is of commercial value Propagation of Kerria lacca is done through parthenogenesis, the female produces between 200-1000 small, red larvae, which then attack the young branches of the host trees creating colonies.

The shellac is a chemical mixture of various polyhydroxy acids produced mostly in India, Indochina. Malaysia, Thailand, People's Republic of China, the Philippines, and Sri Lanka. In India the main production state is in Bihar, around the area of Chota Nagpur In China, this 4,000 years of tradition is being extended to the arid Yan Jiang Valley in the province of Yunnan.

They produce an orange-colored resin of stick-lac, which are simply coalesced bodies of breeding females. Huge populations can coat tree limbs with resin up to one-half inch in thickness The stick-lac is grounded into powder then washed and filtered The chemical is then water-cooled to form a thin film which is the resulting shellac.

The shellac has many uses More than 40 million pounds of shellac is produced in India everv year. It is the source of income for the poor people. They come in different colors through the different chemical reactions It is biodegradable and nonpoisonous and therefore ideal for many applications such as electrical insulations, varnish, sealants, and even printing ink. They are also used in billiard balls, mirror baking, record industry, jewelry setting and glossy playing cards New uses have been found over the years. Today, they are used for coating fruit and vegetables, sweets like chewing gum, marzipan and chocolates, and tablets and vitamin components in the pharmaceutical industry.

The shellac is the only commercially used animal-based natural resin that differs substantially from all other natural resins Aside from their biodegradability and nonpoisonous nature, the shellac is tough, glossy, water soluble and has excellent bonding properties that can combine or crosslink with other resins, allowing it a wider range of applications than synthetic resins.

SHRIMP

The shrimp is one of the favorite seafood delicacies that is being raised in shrimp farms in many parts of the world Since the 1980s, it has become a source of income for many entrepreneurs. Thailand is the world's number one shrimp and prawn producer, accounting for 25.6% of the world's production at 721,000 metric tons in 1991. It is its third export item, after textile and computer parts. But the cost lo the environment is now being felt. Shrimp aquaculture consumes a lot of natural resources and causes a lot of pollution that will take decades to regenerate.

The traditional method of shrimp culture produces 100 to 500 kilos of shrimp per hectare. Under the new aquaculture, the yield is from 1,000 to 10,000 kilos per hectare The ponds where they are bred require large amounts of fresh water, feed, seed, and energy. The lifespan of the pond is only 5 to 10 years. Due to the exhaustion of supply of fresh and seawater and the build-up of sediments the ponds will be abandoned, and it will take 20 to 30 years to regenerate.

Intensive shrimp farms, located inland have been developed in many areas. The same problems encountered in mangrove farms are also present. Another added problem is the effect on land use. The sea water needed for the intensive farms is channelled miles inland into the ponds. Freshwater is needed to reduce the salinity and clean the ponds. They are usually pumped from the ground in order to obtain the optimum salt content of 25% needed for shrimp culture Ground water pumping has caused the lowering of the water level in many areas and the intrusion of salt water. The effect of salinity is causing death to livestock which drink them and the watered crops. To raise one metric ton of shrimp on a more or less intensive farm requires 29 to 60 thousand cubic meters of freshwater. Thirty to fifty percent of the water need to be changed daily depending on the intensity of the aquaculture. At least half of the water is used to dilute the salinity of the pond's water.

Habitats located on the seaward side of shrimp farms are in danger from the discharge of polluted water from the production process due to the release of nutrients, metabolic products and chemical, when the ponds are emptied. Water samples taken when the ponds were emptied to harvest the shrimps contained 7 to 10% organic solids. 1900 lo 2600 mg total nitrogen per liter and 40 to 119 mg/l total phosphorous. Untreated household sew age on the other hand contains around 75 mg/l of total nitrogen and roughly 20 mg/l of total phosphorous. Ammonia and carbon dioxide which are toxic to shrimps and fish are amongst the mam metabolites Chemicals get into the water from using fertilizers. They are also used as disinfectants and for water and soil treatment like calcium carbonate, calcium hydroxide, zeolite, calcium carbide and potassium permanganate. Pesticides which are impossible or difficult to break down are used to destroy food competitors and predators. Chemotherapeutic agents are used against fungi, bacteria and microbes. Shrimp culture is endangering the morphological and biological state of the coastline and is damaging the ecology of coastal habitats both inland and seawards. Ecological damage is affecting traditional coastal industries such as rice growing, fishing and mangrove utilization. The damage caused by shrimp culture also gives rise to social conflicts and casts doubt on some of the economic success achieved.

Another problem encountered by shrimp aquaculture is the presence of eutrophication that leads to red tides. All shrimp-producing countries have encountered this problem that also lead to the spread of other diseases lethal to shrimp and other sea organisms. Only a third of the feed given is consume by the shrimp.

By December 1994, approximately one million hectares of shrimp ponds were established throughout the world. Ninety percent of them are located in Asia. These ponds are often cut out from the mangrove forests. In 1993, Thailand earned $2 billion from its shrimp exports, but in less than 15 years, at the rate of increase, they will wipe out their 180.000 hectares of mangrove forests. Between 1961 and 1991, 65 sq km of mangrove forests have been lost. Bangladesh has densely concentrated shrimp farms located in once mangrove swamps. The destruction of the mangroves has enabled natural disasters to destroy thousands of lives and homes due to flooding and tidal waves.

SPERM POUCH

Humans may think that they are at the apex of the evolutionary process, but other animals have the cunning ability to survive and reproduce their own without difficulties In fact many animals can reproduce and their young able to feed and fend for themselves immediately. But nothing can compare with the ability of animals to reproduce their young like that of the insects.

In most insects, the fertilization of an egg proceeds in a more complex fashion than in humans. They can be economical by fertilizing the sperm whenever they want. It is accomplished with the use of a sperm pouch where the sperm travels after copulation. In this receptacle, the sperm can be kept alive for weeks, months, or even years depending on the types of species. This is made possible for some insects to be fertilized for years after one copulation like the female bees and ants In some species, only one sperm is needed for each egg that is to be fertilized.

Only a few vertebrates have the ability to keep the sperm alive for long. Bats can store the sperm in the reproductive tract up to 200 days. Some reptiles, lizards, snakes and turtles also have a receptacle for the sperm. Turtles can store sperm for as long as four years, while snakes can store them for as long as seven years. This is an important ability allowing insects to lay eggs during the most favorable time and place for reproduction.

SPIDERS

Spiders which have eight legs are from the class Arachnida. There are more than 40.000 species scattered worldwide. They can be found everywhere, from the depth of the ocean to the highest mountain, from the polar zones to the jungles. Spiders are timid creatures and most of them are not dangerous to humans Even the fearsome looking tarantulas are not dangerous.

They rarely bite and their bite is not considered serious Only ten species are considered deadly to people The black widow (Latrodectus mactans) and the brown recluse (Laxosceles reclusa) can give severe or even fatal bites. The black widow's bite contains a neurotoxic venom while the toxin of the brown recluse is hemolytic, affecting tissues and skins surrounding the bite. The Australian funnelweb spider can kill a person in less than two hours.

They play an important role in nature by keeping down the populations of insects. It has been estimated that the spiders in England and Wales eat insects that equal the weight of the entire human population of that area annually.

Silk is the strongest of all natural fibers and spiders make them in the abdominal glands near the back of the body, called spinnerets. Silk is a sticky liquid and has to be pulled out of the spinnerets by the spider's legs. The silk is used for building purposes and to make webs by catching prey. Webs being sticky, make escape impossible Other spiders web trapdoors with silk hatch. When a passing insect wanders by and stumbles, a trap door is pulled shut by a silk thread, the hapless insect is confined with no avenue of escape.

Spider venoms have the potential cure for nervous system disorders. A compound from a Japanese spider venom was found to block the action of glutamate which is thought to be involved in nerve cell death after an injury or stroke.

The orb-weaving spider produces one of the world's toughest fibers. Using recombinant DNA technology, DuPont scientists have recreated synthetic spider silk as a model for a new generation of advanced materials. It has been suggested that a single strand of spider silk, thick as a pencil could stop a 747 in flight. Spider silk is so strong it can catch a fly in flight or a small bird entangled in it. In addition, spider silk is very elastic. It is this combination of strength and elasticity that make the energy-to-break of spider silk so high It could be the toughest material known. All these are made possible with the study of how a spider makes its silk with the help of computer simulation techniques to design a molecular model that integrates all the information available to date about the structure of this amazingly strong and clastic fiber.

Some fifteen species of spiders are officially listed under the IUCN as threatened or endangered species. Many species are yet undiscovered and may actually increase their numbers. Two of the most seriously threatened are the tooth cave spider (*Leptoneta myopia*), from the U.S. and the no-eyed big-eyed wolf spider (*Adelocosa anops*), from Hawaii. Although no species of spider is known to have become extinct in recent times, it is believed that many are disappearing before we know of their existence.

WASPS

Wasps, like the bees and ants are social animals. But some are solitary, living alone and laying their eggs in burrow. But all female wasps are very good mothers. To ensure the survival of their offspring, they will kill their prey where the eggs will be laid so that the grubs will have food to cat as they grow up.

Most wasps spend all their lives killing grubs and caterpillars of insects that damage leaves of trees needed for photosynthesis. The tree wasp (Dolichovaspula sylvestris) is very effective against caterpillars found in many farmer s crops. They are also important complimentary pollinators, pollinating flowers that cannot be done by bees. The tarantula hawk (*Pepsis heros*) is the largest wasp in the world.

In tropical countries, the w asps are seldom considered as pests because of the bountiful food in the forests. But in the temperate zone where food is scarce during the autumn and winter months, they will invade households looking for food.

WEEVILS

Many insects have dual role in relationship to mankind. Some insects can be considered a pest in one instance and a benefit for mankind in another. Others have limited benefits and are widely destructive in most instances. One of these insects is the weevil.

The weevil is a small beetle that is responsible for pollinating the oil-palm plantations When the Malaysians first started the oil palm plantations, the pollination was done manually. It was tedious and expensive Inquiries into the native habitat of the oil palm in the Cameroon's forest by researchers discovered that the tiny weevil was responsible for all the pollination going on Stocks of the weevil were imported and released to the plantations. Since then the weevil have been doing the job for the oil palm and saving the owners $140 million annually.

CHAPTER 3

PETS

A pet is any animal, often a dog, cat, bird, fish, or rodent that we keep as a companion to be viewed, played, observed or studied or a combination of the above. Other exotic and wild animals such as reptiles, amphibians, rabbits, hamsters, monkeys, etc. have also been kept as pets. For owners of these pets, they play other important roles besides companionship. The pet can instill discipline and responsibility in children. They have also been useful as therapeutic animals for those suffering from depression or illness. Some pets have been known to be lifesavers while others have been trained as crimefighters..

There is a proliferation of other exotic animals used as pets. Even poisonous snakes have been kept as pets in many developed countries. More often than not, pet owners don't have the knowledge and skill necessary to raise these animals properly. Whether they are domesticated or wild, all of them have attributes similar to human beings. They suffer both physical, mental and emotional problems encountered by humans. Yet many of these animals are not treated humanely nor do most pet owners try to understand them.

The trade in pets has been responsible for many deaths and sufferings. The smugglings of exotic animals have caused the death of millions of animals as they move from one place to another. Even in the domestically bred animals, they are often raised in cramp and dirty surroundings as breeders try to raise them at the least cost to maximize profits.

Not all pets are easy to care for. Some need special attention if they are to be assured of a long and healthy life. It should never be a matter of impulse to acquire any pet unless we can afford the time, money and responsibility to take care of them as long as necessary. Responsibilities include feeding, cleaning, walking, housing and seeing that all veterinary concerns are taken care of. Any prospective buyer should also find out in advance exactly the kind of pet he/she wants to avoid a mismatch that could result in neglect, abandonment and even cruelty towards the animal.

ADOPTING ANIMALS

There are millions of stray dogs and cats roaming the streets searching for food and shelter; an everyday ordeal for these animals. About 14% of the dogs and 9% of the cats will never find a home. We can decrease this percentage by adopting some of their kittens or puppies scattered around our neighbourhood. Adopting some of these animals as pets from animal shelters, pounds, and even veterinary climes where the pet owners left them can go a long way in reducing the hardships they suffer under their present situation. Our failure to help these animals have caused the deaths of between 10 to 20 million of them annually, where most of them are euthanized in the U.S. alone at a cost of roughly $250 million.

Never buy a pet from the pet shop or breeder because it will only perpetuate the evil practice of breeding and selling pet animals under inhumane conditions. The puppy mills are partly responsible for the plight of pets in the animal shelters because more people are buying from the pet shops instead of adopting from the animal shelters. Every year, more than 300,000 pets are bought from shops supplied by mills in the U S alone Another good reason for adopting mixed breed dogs is that they are often genetically healthier. They have less genetic problems associated with pure bred.

AILUROPHILIA

There are people who care for and value the cats. Islamic tradition has it that the prophet Mohammed (570-632) had a white cat named *Muezza* who fell asleep against the sleeve of his robe. Rather than disturb the sleeping cat. he cut off the sleeve of his garment. His favorable outlook for the cat could be the reason why in many Muslim countries, cats are the only animal permitted inside the mosques Cardinal Richelieu (1585-1642) of France was fanatical about kittens. He made one of his rooms into a cattery where the cats are fed twice daily with white chicken meat In his will he left pensions for 14 of his cats with provisions for two paid guardians, Abel and Tcyssandier, to look after them as long as they lived It was during the same period that Louis XIII (1601-1643) of France called a halt to the cruel tradition of burning cats for witchcraft and religious feasts Madame Dupuis, the famous French harpist died in 1678 leaving her fortune to her cats, providing 30 sous a week to be spent on the cats for their wellbeing. Unfortunately, it was questioned by her human heirs and was overturned by the courts.

Some well known cat lovers are also great writers. They prefer cats for companionship then as they are today. The cats are quiet, less demanding, and easy to satisfy and do not cause too much distraction for the owners. They include the German poet Heinrich Heine (1797-1856), English poet Samuel Butler (1612-1680). French poet Michel dc Montaigne (1533-1592), essayist Henry David Thoreau (1817-1862), American writer Matthew Arnold (1822-1888), and the Italian poet Petrarch (1304-1374), who spent the last years of his life with a devoted cat When Petrarch died, the cat was put to death and mummified Jeremy Bentham (1784-1832), British prime minister William Gladstone (1809-1898), the writer and evolutionist Charles Darwin (1809-1882), and novelist and humorist Mark Twain (1835-1910) also had cats for companionships.

Ernest Hemingway (1899-1961) owned 30 cats, yet he always found the time to look after them American novelist Henry James (1843-1916) often wrote with a cat on his shoulder as did Edgar Allan Poe (1809-1849). Edgar and his wife Virginia had a cat named *Catarina*, who went wherever they went Emily Bronte (1818-1848) wrote Wuthering Heights with her inspiring cat, Tiger, at her feet. The French writer Colette (1873-1954) couldn't write without a cat on her desk. Her home had no less than 10 cats at any time Cats from the neighbors and friends were allowed to stay as long as they wanted. In her writing, the cats were featured in several stories including her most famous book La Chatte.

The English lexicographer Samuel Johnson (1709-1714) personally goes to the market to buy his cat, Hodge, his favorite oyster. He is said to fear that the servant might take a dislike foe the cat foe being ordered to do the errand. The artist and author of children's verse, Edward Lear (1812-1888) was devoted and inspired by his own cat, Foss. When he decided to move lo a new house, he had it built as a replica of the old one so that the cat wouldn't get disoriented. Raymond Chandler (1888-1959). the creator of the detective Philip Marlowe, owned a black Persia cat named Taki. He treated her like a secretary because she was always on top of the desk and he often "talked" to her.

Writers are not alone in their appreciation of the sensitivity and complexity of the cat. Two great physicists, Albert Einstein (1879-1955) was a great cat-lover as well as Sir Isaac Newton (1642-1727) who is said to have invented the catflap for his moggies. Albert Schweitzer (1875-1965), the French doctor/missionary, like Mohammed refused to disturb his cat Sizi, who liked to sleep on his left arm Being left handed, he was forced to write out prescriptions with his right hand.

The only known cat-loving pope of modern times is Leo XII (1760-1829). His favorite cat, *Micetto*, was born in the Vatican and raised by him. His robe was especially tailored to allow the cat to live inside the folds.

Actresses like Brigitte Bardot has 60 cats while Doris Day and Kim Basinger each owned ten cats. Kim had a cat-tight with her then estranged husband. Ron Britton, when he tried to sue her for half of her fortune and custody of their ten cats. She parted with some fortune but not the cats.

Caring for cats is an easy task that makes it particularly popular with busy people with little free time. Abraham Lincoln (1809-1865) took in three abandoned kittens he found during the eve of a battle and without hesitation adopted them. Teddy Roosevelt (1858-1919) had a cat named Slippers who was allowed to roam freely around the White House. Sometimes it would disappear for days and weeks at a time and manage to show up just before big state dinners. On one occasion, distinguished guests were forced to step around Slippers who was lying in the middle of the stately hall and refused to budge. Calvin Coolidge (1872-1933), the 30th President, was perhaps one of the most eccentric cat-lovers. At a White House banquet, guests, unsure of the etiquette, copied everything the President did. All went well until coffee time when Coolidge poured half his coffee into his saucer, his visitors followed suit. He then added sugar and milk - so too did his dignitaries. Then he put down the saucer on the floor • for his cat.

When Winston Churchill (1874-1965) became Prime Minister of Great Britain in 1940, he took his black cat. Nelson, with him lo Number Ten Downing Street. Nelson would sleep on the PM's bed. In 1953 a stray kitten turned up on the doorstep and was taken in. That day, Churchill made a speech at a party conference in Margate, and was so pleased with his performance in this place that he decided to name the cat Margate.

On his 88th birthday, knowing Churchill's fondness for cats, a friend gave him a ginger tom named Jock who would be his last cat. He enjoyed having the cat eat with him and would wait for the cat before taking his meal. As with Nelson, the cat often slept in his bed. In his Will, Churchill had stipulated that the cat be provided for life at his country home in Chartwell forever. When his home was opened to the public, the cat was so popular that after he died in 1975. a look-alike adopted his name as well as his home.

To the ancient Egyptians, cats were sacred. They were prohibited from the export market for many years. They were deified as Bast or Bubastis, the goddess of fertility, wisdom, hunting and moonlight. One of the six major cities of Lower Egypt, Bubastis, was dedicated to the cat goddess. According to Herodotus (c. 485-430 B.C.). anyone found guilty of killing a cat even accidentally, was immediately sentenced to death by beheading. When a beloved cat died, the whole family would shave off their eyebrows in mourning, mummified the cat before encasing it in a bejewelled mummy case along with mummified mice for them to munch in the afterlife. A large number of these mummified cats have been discovered at Tel Basta and some of them can be seen in museums in the U.S. and Egypt. As a battle tactic, an ancient King of Persia ordered his soldiers to carry a cat each in their arms, knowing that the warring Egyptians would rather surrender than risk harming the animals.

In ancient Rome the cat was a symbol of liberty and the Goddess of Liberty was represented with a cat at her feet. The Romans adopted the cat for its cleanliness and its ability to catch vermin. The only animal admitted to Roman temples were the cats.

The feline has been a positive feature in many cultures and religions, from the Incas and the Aztecs in South America, to the Buddhists in Thailand who believed that the souls of people who had attained a high spirituality entered the bodies of cats, before they too passed from this life.

AILUROPHOBIA

Ailurophobia is the fear of cats. Many of the people expected to respect the Lord's creatures are the ones who prosecuted the cats. During the Dark Ages (5th - 10th century) the respect for cats gave way to widespread persecution of witchcraft and cats. Witch hunters often put the cats along with their masters for trial. The cats were even tortured to make them "confess" and later burned alive. Cat burning was particularly popular in celebrating religious feast days. Paradoxically, the cats were often sealed alive in the foundation of buildings to ensure good luck. In the early Judaeo-Christian period, people detested the cats and treated them with contempt and cruelty unheard of in the non-Christian world. The cats were linked to the Devil and subjected to torture and cruelty such as burning or drowning them alive. Pope Gregory IX (1170-1241) is thought to have started the persecution of cats in 1233. The purge continued for five centuries until the 17th century. In 1484, Pope Innocent VIII (1432-1492) turned his focus on witches and setup inquisitions to try these women and destroy them along with their cats. Warts, associated with witches, were considered to be nipples from which the sorceress would feed her cat. Elizabeth I (1533-1603) is known in history as a cat hater. She had a straw effigy of the Pope filled with live cats, which she personally set alight.

The unspeakable cruelty to cats were not carried out on religious ground only. The ancient Hebrews hated cats because they reminded them of their captivity among the cat-loving Egyptians. We have been plagued by cat haters throughout the centuries. St. Augustine, who took the view that man should dominate the earth and that all animals on the planet were to serve mankind has been adopted by many for centuries, even today. It has resulted in the extinction of many species and the devastation of the natural environment.

Some great historical personalities are well-known cat haters. One of them is the German composer Johannes Brahms (1833-1897). He used to shoot the neighbor's cats with bow and arrow from his open window. The American dancer Isadora Duncan (1878-1927) and U.S. President Dwight Eisenhower (1890-1969) were also reported to have killed cats. Eisenhower reportedly ordered any stray cat found in the White House ground shot. His hatred for cats is also matched by his hatred for the crows. He is reported to have a readily available shotgun in his home for shooting crows. Other cat haters include William Goldsmith (1809-1898), James Boswell (1740-1795) the biographer of Samuel Johnson (1709-1784) who was the exact opposite of Dr. Johnson, but never expressed his hatred for the cats in his presence. Other prominent figures include the dictator Adolf Hitler (1889-1945), German composer Giacomo Meyerbeer (1791-1864) and many others

Pierre de Ronsard (1524-1585), and William Shakespeare (1564-1616), were considered cat-haters because of their writings about cats. Ronsard, the French poet, wrote of his hatred for cats in his sonnet while Shakespeare did it on his play. Noah Webster (1758-1843), the American lexicographer was branded a cat hater for defining the cat as a deceitful animal and when enraged extremely spiteful. Percy Bysshe Shelley (1792-1822), an English poet, experimented with electricity by tying a cat to the string of a flying kite during a thunderstorm to see its effect on animals.

There is a difference between hating and fearing cats. In some cases a physical fear of cats would distinguish the real ailurophobes from the true cat haters. Some of the most notorious were Alexander the Great (356-323 B.C.), Julius Caesar (100-44 B.C.) and Napoleon Bonaparte (1769-1821) who is said to sweat profusely and had been reduced to a quivering wreck in the presence of cats. Napoleon would go berserk if a cat came anywhere near him. One night an aide heard him screaming, only to discover that a kitten had made its way into the Emperor's chamber and saw Napoleon lunging his sword to ward off the cat. Henry 111(1551-1589), King of France had 30,000 cats executed during his reign because he often fainted upon seeing a cat near him. His brother Charles IX (1550-1574) also suffered from this strange condition.

ANIMAL ABUSES

Just as human beings are subjected to torture and abuse, so are household animals and pets. Most countries already have laws against animal abuses, but it is seldom enforced. The fact is that many pets have undergone abuses under the hands of owners and people to whom they entrusted their lives. More stringent laws are needed to stop animal abuses. In Wisconsin officials have passed legislation making intentional animal abuse a felony. Laws of these types are necessary if we are going to put a stop to abuses done on innocent animals.

A four-month old puppy named Trio was thrown across the room with full force by its owner for messing up his bedroom. It was an unexpected turn of events for a young pup untrained to take care of home furnishing. His body was badly mangled after hitting a cupboard. One of his legs had to be amputated. The owner was prosecuted and given a light sentence He was banned from keeping animals for five years.

Another one-year old pup named Poppy was put inside a drain pipe by his owner in the hope that he will drown and be flushed along with the water to its final destination. But his whimpering alerted the neighbors who called up the Royal Society for the Prevention of Cruelty to Animals (RSPCA) and the fire brigade. After two hours of digging through five feet of earth, they finally reached the drain pipe, rescuing a half-alive pup. Only around the clock devoted care kept him alive. Oliver, a ten-year-old retriever almost died of starvation when his owner locked him in a room for weeks without food His timely rescue saved him from possible death within two days. All three pets were rescued by a dedicated staff from the RSPCA of England.

One of the common abuses done on dogs is to use them as a sport as dogfighting. It is a very brutal sport for the animals. The savagery done by dogs on each other often result in deep wounds and broken jaws. To sec their long mouth and teeth locked in mortal combat is a frightening scene. This type of sport has been outlawed in most countries, but they are still undertaken clandestinely in many places.

Another abuse done on dogs is killing them for food The dogs are often hanged 011 the tree and a steel pipe or baseball-like bat is used to smash their heads until they die. Obviously, this practice of killing an animal is an unacceptable act of cruelty done on some of man's best friends.

Strayed dogs wandering into the beaches of Boracay were reportedly shot to death Some caught alive were reportedly tortured, mutilated and strangled. In either case, it was not a humane way of solving the problem of water pollution. At the very least, the dogs could have been rounded up and put in city pound instead of killing them and turning them into appetizer.

AQUARIUM FISHES

Tropical fishes are very colorful with variable sizes and shapes that are collected by hobbyists. The hobby has been going since the 17th century when it was started in England but the popularity took off in the 1920s. About 1,000 species have been collected but only 200 species have been established for aquarium habitation.

There are many problems dealing with saltwater fishes. Only a small number of aquarium hobbyists are aware of the complicated process by which the majority of saltwater specimens reach the retailer's tanks. Especially for the novice, much of the hobbyists' success may depend upon how the fishes were handled during collection and shipment. The sheer number of marine creatures that enter the U.S. is staggering. In a single day at the Los Angeles International Airport, the U.S. FWS officers inspected consignments totalling more than 20.000 fishes and nearly

5,000 invertebrates. This is just one day at only one of five major ports of entry.

The problem posed by saltwater fishes is the difficulty in rearing the fish under saltwater conditions. Unlike freshwater, seawater deteriorates easily in tanks and fish find it difficult to survive. It is also difficult to gather pure and clean seawater in the light of the pollution going in the surrounding seas. This makes it necessary to reconstitute the chemical composition of the water which is tedious for most hobbyists to do.

Catching the fish from the coral reef where they are often found is also a problem. Most fishermen have resorted to cyanide fishing to catch them after they are knocked down. Every year the Philippines with one of the largest coral reefs in the world, and home to millions of tropical fishes has been exporting between 3 and 3.5 million marine fishes to the worldwide market. Brazil is the largest seller of aquarium fish. Transporting these fishes around the world often result in half of the mortality.

Goldfishes are especially difficult to care for. A small change in temperature may be fatal to them. Just by discharging them from the plastic bag to the tank at home can also be fatal to them. They should be placed in a well-ventilated and large pool that will provide the needed oxygen at all times. The goldfish is best left in the areas where they are found and not moved around. They are always given as prizes in fairs and carnivals. Avoid the games to discourage the exploitation of these fishes.

BIRDS

Birds like parrots and songbirds have been hunted for centuries. Sometimes they are caught by .local people as food, but the high price commanded by pet lovers have made them an important source of income. But unlike dogs and cats, birds are much more difficult to keep as pets unless we are willing to take the time out to learn the many intricacies of caring for birds. If improperly cared for, they can easily fall into sickness and die. It is important to have an ample supply of freshwater and the correct diet for each species. Some birds are seedeaters while others may eat fruits, vegetables or nectars. Some birds like the Peking robin and the Shama thrush eat insects while other birds will eat almost anything.

Birds that are caged need special innovations in their cages. As much as possible, the cage should be large and roomy for the birds to fly around. Canaries get their exercise by flying from one perch to another. It should be kept clean at all times. The location should be draft-free and not too dark nor too sunny. A cover should be provided in the evening to reduce the light penetrating the case. Caees must be made of rustproof material or aluminum- or lead-free if it is painted over Perches should be placed depending on the number and species of birds. A cuttlebone or some hard material is necessary to sharpen its beak. Tiny bits of gravel should be placed inside the cage every once in a while to help the bird digest its food.

Molting is a natural periodic occurrence in birds. But birds sometimes lose their feathers when they are ill. It is important to consult a veterinarian once it occurs because of possible illness that can be fatal to the birds. Some birds will molt more than oncc a year Many species of birds will molt their old plumage during particular season such as after breeding. A few species will retain some of their feathers far longer than a year. The developing feathers control the molting cycle and not the old or the shedding feathers. It is not unusual for a bird to molt when it is under stress or under changing weather. Birds may have abnormal molts due to artificial lighting, disease related stress factors and malnutrition.

Birds and cats do not get together very well Whenever there are cats around the home or in the neighborhood, it will be risky to have birds around. A 1949 study in Michigan revealed that a single well-fed cat brought home 1,600 small mammals and 60 birds in an 18-month period. In another one-year survey from 1981-1982 showed that in an English village, of 1,090 dead animals brought home by cats, a third of them were sparrow s. Pet cats kill more than 70 million animals, including 20 million birds in England annually A 4-ycar study by Stanley Temple and John Coleman estimated that 1.2 million pet cats in Wisconsin killed 400 million animals each year, including at least 7.8 million birds. In 1949, five cats were introduced to Marion Island in the Indian Ocean to control mice at a weather station. By 1975, there were 2.200 cats on the island and killing 600.000 seabirds annually.

Obviously the best solution to the whole bird business is to stop buying them as pets About 24,000 of these birds are illegally imported from South American countries, depleting many species in the wild. For every bird arriving alive at their destination, 80%-90% die before they reach their destination. Even those imported legally are not well taken care of. Overcrowding, inadequate care and ventilation and often lack of food and water are problems they encounter during transport. To make matter worse, the Animal Welfare Act does not apply to birds.

Different birds have different diets and it is important that we know their preferences. Some birds will only cat seeds filled with carbohydrates while others are carnivores. In the wild, some will cat only flowers and fruits. The carnivores will cat insects and other meat such as worms. Each individual species have different preferences that make it possible for them to coexist in the same habitat without affecting the food supply. As much as possible the same natural diet should be provided and if not possible, a good quality mix from commercial feed millers should be given. Dry seeds should be supplemented with vitamins and minerals to ensure a balanced diet.

Animal protein in the form of insects and egg food should be supplied on a regular basis for some species; it is particularly important when they are breeding. Australian finches will do quite well with a good egg food mix A simple way of producing a small amount is to hard boil an egg for 20 minutes Let it cool, and push it through a potato ricer. Then add small amounts of wheat hearts or over-dried shortcake until the mix is crumbly but moist. Nonbreeding pairs receive one teaspoon of food in the morning A small amount of dicalcium phosphate and vitamins are sprinkled on it. Juveniles receive small quantities throughout the day. Live food is offered at the same time, and the amounts are increased when they are feeding the young. Less domesticated species will raise stronger young if provided with insects. Some species will not raise young without live food. Soft-bodied insects for feeding the young is preferable, since hard shelled mealworms can be difficult to digest. Insects that can be offered include fly larva, waxworms, white worms, fruit flies, aphids, and freshly molted mealworms.

Clean water must be available at all times and replenished each day. The water cups should be thoroughly cleaned to prevent bacterial problems. Place food and water containers in positions where they can't be soiled by droppings.

CARE OF THE PETS

Pets at home are often treated more humanely than those kept under animal shelters and pounds Therefore, it is necessary for us to see to it that they don't get lost or worst, stolen for laboratory experiment. We should never allow them to roam outside the residence unsupervised. Once they are lost, it is difficult to find them unless collars or ID tags are placed on them. Even then, it is no guarantee that they will not end up in some unwanted fate such as the hands of the sadistic doctor. Lost dogs may also end up butchered to death for those who find dog meat a delicacy. Many pets wandering aimlessly are killed by automobile accidents.

It is also important not to leave the dogs unattended whether they are placed in our backyard or left in the car during our shopping trips. Dogs tied to these places have been known to be stolen right under our nose and offered for sale to laboratories.

Every pet owner should have routine emergency supplies for their pets. A little thought and preparation before an emergency occurs could spell the difference between life and death for the pet. Healthy diets and sanitation play a big part in avoiding diseases. Accidents will happen, but many can be prevented if the owner is aware of the hazards that exists in any home.

For the elderly people, provision for the pets should be taken. Unless it is done, the fate of the pets may end up in the pound or in unwanted experimental laboratory. The rich elderly people often have provisions in their wills for taking care of their pets after they are gone. After all pet companionship is sometimes better than human companionship.

Caring for pets should extend to keeping them safe from animal thieves. These bunchers, as they are called cruise around the city streets looking for runaway pets or stray animals. The pets are then sold to breeders, laboratories, and faraway pet shops. Even prestigious hospitals and schools have been found buying stray animals for experiments Laboratories and medical schools in the U.S. use more than 300,000 dogs and 100,000 cats for the experiments. In Asia and South America, these animals are bred and sold to restaurants while others are eaten as a delicacy.

It is often not easy to care for pets especially with regards to the food they can and cannot consume. One example is the chocolate It should never be given to dogs, cats and other animals since it contains a chemical called theobromine, which is toxic to them In some animals, it can overstimulate the heart, muscles and nervous system. Baking chocolate contains as much as seven times theobromine than milk chocolate and therefore more toxic. Dogs have been known to die of cacao products with as little as 0.2% theobromine.

People who are really interested in keeping pets should do well to make researches or read books and magazines on pet cares. There are many magazines such as Cat Fancy, All About Cats, Cat World. Dog Fancy, All About Dogs, Reptiles, Horse Illustrated, The Western Horse, Birder's World, Aquarium Fish, etc. As an illustration, when the chinchillas were in big demand for their beautiful furs, many backyard or garage breeders started to keep the animals for profit. It took 100 of these animals to make one coat. Without the knowledge on how to take care of these animals, hundreds of thousands died as a result. These animals with their natural habitat in the cold Andes Mountain cannot tolerate sunlight and need a cool place throughout the years. Other special care include regular dust bath and not water bath. Different pets have different characteristics and behaviors that any pet lover should do well to learn before taking the task to keep the pet.

Before anyone is allowed to own a dog or any pet for that matter, the government could do well to require prospective owners to undergo a seminar on keeping dogs. Subjects should include development of the mind and body of animals, proper training techniques, food for healthy living, and problems and diseases that confront these pets. Most pet shop owners often know nothing more than just feeding them. Animals in their care must be allowed to exercise and fed a minimum diet for health reason.

In England, the Federation of Dog Trainers and Canine Behaviourists(FDTCB) has the seal of approval from the City & Guilds to give courses in canine history, development and care. They give several levels of courses for with new pet owners and advance courses for experience owners.

CRIME FIGHTERS

More than any other animal, pets are easier and safer to train for preventing and fighting crimes. But sometimes it takes more than ordinary pets to do the job. In one African country, a company engaged in crime prevention is using poisonous snakes to guard the premises. They are very sensitive to vibration in the soil and their presence alone is enough to bring fear to the heart of the intruder.

Nothing beats the dogs when it comes to crimefighting. Their sensitive smell and alert cars have been used for tracking runaway or escaped criminals. The U.S. military often uses dogs to guard the military bases because of their ability to hear and move very fast. They are also used in many drug enforcement jobs where they are trained to sniff out prohibited drugs faster than humans can search for it. *Marco*, a Belgian shepherd has sniffed out more than one million kilos of marijuana, and thousands of kilos of cocaine and heroin. The drug cartel even put up a bounty of $25,000 to anyone who can kill him. Two dogs at the Miami International Airport are also the target of the drug cartel. A black female Labrador retriever, Snag was about to be euthanized when she was rescued by the Texas Border Patrol. Snag was recruited to work in the department's drug enforcement unit, sniffing out drugs such as cocaine and marijuana that smugglers attempted to bring from Mexico. Her biggest haul was when she discovered $800 million worth of cocaine in thousands of bags hidden in a propane tanker. She was even featured in the true crime show, "America's Most Wanted."

DISASTER RESCUE

Whenever disaster strikes, emergency crews are always ready to help out in relief efforts. But when it comes to rescuing pet animals, very often, few organizations or individuals are there to help out. However, one NGO has been helping animals in disasters for more than a century. This is the American Humane Association's Emergency Animal Relief Fund and the only one recognized by the American Red Cross. Because they operate wherever and whenever disasters may occur, they are always in need of volunteers and fundings. Donations are badly needed as they operate in all places. Another NGO recently formed as an offshoot of the Hurricane Andrew is the National Pet Disaster Fund It provides emergency on-site disaster relief for pets and animals

Not to be outdone, dogs working for the U.S. Disaster Team Canine Unit are sent anywhere in the world where catastrophy occurs. Their uncanny ability to search for missing persons have been demonstrated time and again. In UK, the dogs were even fitted with video camera on their heads to send live pictures of disaster scenes.

DISTEMPER

Distemper is a contagious disease that affects dogs, cats, horses, and many other animals. They are distributed worldwide There are several forms of distemper caused cither by virus or bacteria. The most common, canine distemper is caused by a virus. As the name implies, it occurs mostly in dogs

The wolves in India are becoming an endangered species. The reason is the disease, canine distemper that is transmitted by the local, semiferal dogs. Earth Watch teams discovered that all the wolf pups born to two packs of wolves had died. Yadvendradev Jhala has undertaken to inoculate the nine pups born to the two packs this season. So far, one pup has been inoculated.

The disease has also killed hundreds of lions in Africa. But they are not confined to the land. In 1987, a distemper virus killed an estimated 10,000 seals in Lake Baikal. The following year, twenty thousand harbor seals perished in the North Sea.

The distemper virus is also responsible for the largest seal die-off in history It happened in 1988 in the northern part of Europe Dead harbor seals and their pups kept washing up near the shores of islands and countries around the North Sea. The estimated number of deaths was about 18,000 seals.

Two years later in early 1990, schools of striped dolphins were also showing up dead in shores along the coasts of Spain, France, Italy and Morocco. For a while the epidemic slowed and finally stopped, but not for long. The following year, the disease broke out again and dolphins were washing up along the shores of Italy and Greece. An estimated 1,100 dolphins died. The suspect again is the distemper virus that became virulent because of the presence of high concentration of PCBs in their bodies.

DOGS

The dog is probably man's first pet since they are the first animal to be domesticated. They have served as man's companion in hunting and scavenging during the primitive period. During the Middle Ages, they were often found beside royalties Henry III (1551-1589) of France, who hated cats was seldom seen without his papillon. The Pekingese was highly honored in the imperial palace in Peking from where it got its name. Even Queen Victoria(1819-1901) had a special fondness of Skye terriers. Pres. Franklin Roosevelt's (1882-194) Scottish terrier Falla was even specially fetched by a ship sent by the President.

The greatest attribute of dogs that made them attractive to man is their loyalty to their masters. They are also much easier to train, especially when training begins early in their life. This is also important if they are not to develop bad habits.

Keeping a dog can be a very demanding job. Unless we are willing to sacrifice time and effort, it would be unwise to keep dog as a pet. Dogs are also gregarious animals and companionship is often necessary. It is a difficult thing to leave the dog at home because they may wreck the furniture. They also require regular walking and training on where to relieve themselves, otherwise, it could create sanitary problems. Bathing need not be very frequent but regular combing is important to relieve them of fleas.

Sometimes we can overdo the ways we treat animals. Dogs such as dobermans often have their tails mutilated to make them more vicious. In other dogs, the ears are cropped to make them look "sharp" and used for beauty contests. All these amputations of body parts have been the subject of many controversies in the treatment of animals. The ears and tails are often chopped off without use of anaesthesia or other sound surgical ways to reduce cost. This practice has been banned in Britain for being brutal and cruel. It will take a to stop this practice. In the meantime, some kennel clubs have taken the unilateral action. Recently (August. 1997) the Hong Kong Kennel Club has banned dogs with cropped cars from entering beauty contests, which it organized annually.

DOMESTIC CATS

The domestic cat is probably the most common pet in the world. Since 1985, cat ownership in the U.S. outstripped dogs as the number one pet. The most popular purebred cat in the U.S. today is the Persian cat, followed by the Siamese. Abyssinian, Marie coon cat and the Burmese. However, most of the cats today are mixed breed or moggies. One expert estimates that 90% of all cats in the U.S. are moggies. Even the First Cat, owned by Chelsea Clinton is a black and a white moggie named Socks.

Keeping a cat as a pet is probably one of the least demanding hobbies. The cats are more independent, playful but sometimes unpredictable than any other pet. It is easier to take care of its needs and comforts and they are not too demanding. They require no special cages and can be free to roam the grounds-Carefully taken care of, they can live as long as 20 years.

As much as possible, cats should not be allowed to wander around the neighborhood to avoid picking up internal and external parasites. During halloween, it is a dangerous time for your black cats to be wandering in the neighborhood People are likely to harm them because of their close association with witches. Combing their hair is important to keep them from swallowing too much hair that will lead to intestinal obstructions.

Kittens should be taken to the veterinarian for their regular check up and deworming. Like humans, they need vaccinations against infectious diseases. Kittens like to play around and they should be given toys to play with such as dangling objects that they like to swat. Many products are manufactured to entertain the cats. Most importantly, they should not be bathed.

EDUCATION

Anybody with money can almost buy any animal as a pet even without training on how to care for them. It is time to require prospective buyers to undergo a seminar on keeping pets. Subjects should include development of the mind and body of the pets, the types of food to be given to a particular pet, health problems and symptoms of diseases that may be encountered should also be addressed. Proper treatment of pets is important.

People in the pet-related industries should also undergo training on how to care for pets under their stewardship Pet shop owners often know nothing more than just feeding them. Animals in their care must be allowed to exorcise and at least given the minimum diet for health reasons.

In England, the Federation of Dog Trainers and Canine Behaviourists (FDTCB) has the seal of approval received from the City & Guilds qualification in Canine Studies to give courses in canine history, development and care. They give several levels of courses dealing with new owners and advanced courses for experienced owners. The pilot course was a big success and new courses are already swamped with applicants.

LOYALTY

Nothing beats the pet animals when it comes to loyalty. All animals reared by humans have been known to be faithful to the very end of their lives. There were numerous recorded cases of dogs waiting for the return of their masters for years after their decease One of the first recorded faithful dog was called She p. His master, a shepherd, when he died was put on a coffin and sent by train to another town for burial. For five and a half years the dog went to the railroad stations waiting for his master to return. He would check on all the disembarking passengers and sec if his master was one of the passengers His faithful vigil ended when he was killed by a train in Montana on January 12, 1942.

Wild cats have also been known to be faithful to their masters. But nothing beats the faithfulness of a wild board under the care of Dr. Albert Schweitzer (1875-1965), the famous German doctor who spent most of his life treating indigenous people deep in the heart of Africa. He was also a great animal lover. One of the animals under his care was a wild boar called Josephine She did nothing except follow her master around wherever he went, even to the Sunday church.

NATIONAL PET WEEK

Pets are some of man's best friends and it is only fair that a day should be set aside to celebrate their role in our lives. There have been splinter groups of animal shows for different occasions and celebrated in different parts of the world. It is time to consolidate all these events into one special pet week.

Not all dogs, cats, or most animals for that matter are fortunate enough to have a good owner. Many stray dogs and cats do not have a place called home, and most of them are cither placed in animal shelters or pounds or worse, killed. A day or week set aside for them will be a great opportunity to bring awareness to people of the plight of the pets and can serve as a day for adopting animals under shelter.

In Singapore the authorities are doing something to help the pets. The Center for Animal Welfare and Control offers a course on responsible pet ownership, targetting school children as well as adults. Its first National Pet Week (1996), showing exhibition and programs at community centers reached a total of 45,000 participants.

OLD PETS

Most pets except some reptiles have a shorter lifespan than human beings. Dogs and cats, are usual pets at home ha\c a lifespan of about 12 to 15 years. When they reach the twilight of these ages, they will need special attention especially on health care. Vaccinations against diseases must be kept up to date. It is important to take note of any change in behavior in eating habits. Common symptoms such as changes in appetite and sudden thirst may be signs of hormonal or metabolic behaviors. Dogs and cats often suffer the same diseases such as distemper, hepatitis, parainfluenza, parvovirus, and respiratory infections. Their penchance for playing in the ground made it necessary to check regularly for any worm infection especially heartworm.

Proper nutrition has become even more important as they grow older. Vitamins, proteins, and minerals must be maintained along with a balanced meal. This will help maintain their health and reduce the onset of old age illnesses. Some of the symptoms they manifest are the same as humans so it is possible for an observant owner to detect them. Exercises are necessary to keep their muscle tone and help maintain their weight.

Dental care is especially important for old pets. They should be given dental care at a young age for these carnivores just like people to avoid problems as they grow old. Loss of teeth will make it difficult to consume meat for these carnivores. Periodontal diseases are common among old pets and tartar accumulation can cause tooth decay that could lead to harmful effects in animals by their refusal to cat. They can also create disturbances for humans caused by their persistent howling Bacteria on the diseased teeth and gums can be swallowed and lead to problems affecting important organs. These have been proven to be fatal for weak immunity due to old age. Repairing cavities can be dangerous if animals have to undergo anesthesia.

Old pets like old people need to have periodic checkups. Veterinarians recommend two checkups per year for old pets without ailments and more often for those suffering from serious disorders affecting the heart, kidney, liver and other vital organs. Blood tests and booster immunization should by given. Common parasites should be checked regularly. As they grow old, they tend to be obese due to lack of exercise. But they should also be examined for possible metabolic disorders. Advances in veterinary medicine has made it possible to cure many diseases even surgery, if needed. But owners must be prepared to spend for the well-being of their pets.

And most important of all, we must continue to show our affections for our pets as we do while they are young and lively. During these hard times, when our pets reach old age, they are most sensitive to our touch and treatment. They will need careful and extra attention. Look for changes in their new activities and try to adopt them for their comforts and well-being. Remember to treat them as if they were still a member of the family.

PEST CONTROL

One of the common problems with household pets is the fleas that infest these animals. There are more than 1,000 different fleas that can be found. But only a few ways are needed to get rid of them. Flea collars and flea powders are often used to kill the fleas. However, many of these pesticides are just as dangerous as the fleas on the health of the animals. Some of the chemicals used for flea collars are suspected carcinogens. Some of the more effective ways are often the best and safest solution to the problem. Give your pets regular baths with soap and water. Try to drown the fleas by letting the pet stay in the water longer than necessary to drown these pests.

Mechanical methods are often very effective. A flea comb can be used. The teeth of the comb are so close together that any flea caught in it will surely be exposed. The fleas can then be drowned in soapy water by dipping the flea in it. Some pet owners swear that cats and dogs fed on garlic have fewer fleas. An innovative chemical-free flea-control product in the U. S. market is the Radio System's Electronic Flea Comb. It safely and effectively removes fleas from your cat or dog as you comb by using an extremely low electric charge (only one milikolon) to shock the fleas it encounters. This kill them outright or electrically stuns and immobilizes them for easy disposal. The best part about the Electronic Flea Comb is that you groom your pet and get rid of fleas at the same time.

Recently, new chemicals are coming out to fight the fleas and ticks. The chemicals are lufenuron, imidacloprid, and fipronil, and marketed under the brand names of Program, Advantage, and Frontline respectively. The introduction of Program two years ago has proven to be effective. It works like a kind of birth control pill for the fleas. It is an insect development inhibitor that suppresses the synthesis or deposition of chitin, a substance fleas need to produce eggs and larval shells. The drug is taken is taken internally and gets into the bloodstream, where it is eaten by adult fleas and becomes incorporated into the eggs. When the eggs are laid the larvae are weaken, so that they cannot hatch without breaking their exoskeleton and dying. It can be used for the dogs and cats and is taken once a month.

Because the drug Program is taken to stop the reproduction of offspring of the fleas, it has no effect on the adult fleas. This is where the other two drugs, Advantage and Frontline come in. Both products are dispersed safely over the entire body through the oils on the animal's skin. They disrupt the flea s central nervous system function, resulting in death. Advantage is a larvicidal, making it useful for environmental control of fleas while Frontline can kill fleas before they bite treated animals, an important benefit for flea-allergic pets..

PET SHOPS

Instead of patronizing pet shops, we should look to the animal shelters or pounds for these animals. These untagged and unclaimed animals are kept for 72 hours by the Humane Society before they are sent away for destruction or worse, used for experimentation. We can also look for them in the classified Ads. Pet shops are not the ideal place for the pets. Dogs are often caged in small aluminum or steel cages measuring about six square feet with two dogs to a cell when there are more animals than cages available. There is little room for exercise. The food fed to them are often unfit for consumption. Very often, they are left without water for days and they often don't get any bath at all.

In the U.S. approximately half a million dogs sold in the pet shops came from "puppy mills." These are the breeding kennels where dogs are breed for the pet shops or sold to private individuals. According to the USDA, an estimated 25% of the 3,500 federally licensed breeding kennels have substandard conditions. Another 1,600 kennels are operating illegally without federal licenses nor have they undergone any inspection. The American Kennel Club, which derives millions of dollars of income each year from registration of dogs bred in puppy mills has virtually done nothing to stop abuses occurring inside these mills.

The most common type of abuse is the unsanitary condition of the breeding ground. The cages are often small and these animals are treated like prisoners. The female dogs are forced to breed continuously, not even allowed to rest between heat cycles. They are killed when their bodies can no longer produce enough litters for the pet shops. Puppy mill dogs frequently suffer from malnutrition, exposed to harsh weather, suffer from genetic disorders such as hip dysplasia because of inadequate veterinary care. Bad personality traits such as biting and howling are perpetuated.

As in all abuses done by people, it is often necessary to pass laws for their protection and mandatory provisions on inspections of these facilities. In 1988, Kansas enacted a law requiring registration and semi-annual inspections of all commercial breeding kennels to ensure that dogs used for breeding have adequate shelter, food and veterinary care. Connecticut. Massachusetts, and New York have enacted a legislation requiring pet stores to guarantee the health of the animals they sell. The Connecticut legislation also requires that animals in pet shops receive veterinary inspections at least every fifteen days.

Exotic animals are animals imported and introduce to a new country. It is one of the biggest businesses in illegal trade next to illegal drugs and arms sales. Many of these animals died enroute to their destination. It is estimated that ten birds die for every one that makes it to the new country. The same is true of other species especially those smuggled out clandestinely. The animals once sold to the hobbyist often live in cages that are not more than a prison cell. Lack of companionship is often the norm. As high as 60% of the animals imported as pets die during their first year.

The exotic animals that are fortunate enough to survive the trip often end up as prisoners in cages while waiting to be sold. In the cages they are susceptible to premature death caused by overcrowdedness, diseases, hunger, illness, etc. Better facilities are not afforded by the owners to minimize expenses and store spaces in order to maximize profits. After being sold to hobbyists, their habitat are not much improved. They are still caged like prisoners, often under the same substandard condition, without a chance to escape.

Another problem often encountered by exotic animals is their inability to adjust to the extreme temperatures of their new environment. These animals that came from the tropics experience only dry and wet seasons in their old habitat. Unless they are big mammals, they cannot easily adjust to the temperature fluctuations.

Never buy animals as gifts, unless we know that the recipient is a pet lover, or we may unwittingly send them to a lonely and dreadful life. Exotic animals should be never be traded. They come from the wild and are best left in the wild. If we patronize stores that sell these animals, it would only encourage poachers to catch more of these animals because of the demand.

Laws are sorely needed for the protection of exotic animals. Not everybody is capable of taking care of exotic animals. Many of these animals die because the owners do not know how to take care of them. A law requiring would-be owners to undergo training must be undertaken. Limiting the number of pet shops for each locality should reduce the number of pet animals for sale under the harsh conditions they are caged in.

PUPPY MILLS

In the U.S., puppy mills are churning out as many as half a million dogs of all breeds every year, according to the Humane Society of the U.S. Not much different from the farming factory, these animals are caged in small quarters and under filthy conditions. The female dogs are treated like machine, continuously forced to breed without letup to maximize their profits. At the end of their useful life when they can no longer breed they are killed. Despite the overpopulation of the animals, nothing is being done to reduce the inhuman proliferation to the puppy mill throughout the world.

Puppies are often separated from their mothers as early as a few weeks from conception and sold to brokers who pack them in crates for transport and resale to pet shops. During the shipping process, puppies frequently receive inadequate food and water for subsistence. Sick animals are shipped out even while ill or injured. Many pets often arrive at their destination sick and dejected. These animals are often drowned in the back room or left to die to economize. The same thing also occurs when they get sick during shipping to cut costs. Those that are too old are often killed by pet shop owners or sold to bunchers for laboratory use. Killing is often done by bashing their heads with a board.

The equivalent of puppy mills for cats are called catteries. Cats are treated no better than the dogs because there is even less regard for the cats.

QUARANTINE

Quarantine is an important function taken by governments to protect the welfare of the people against the spread of other diseases. But some quarantine laws can be considered inhumane and cruel for the animals. One of these laws in Britain is under attack by animal welfare groups. British law requires pets entering the country to spend six months in confinement to stop the spread of rabies in the country. The law has been criticized in recent years due to the death of two dogs a few months ago. Other measures could have been undertaken such as vaccinating them for diseases that can be spread before releasing them to their owners.

Some activists have come up with a pet passport system that can help animals travel with their owners. This could very well replace the quarantine law now enforced in many countries. The passport system would require identifications, blood tests and vaccinations before the animals are issued one.

RABIES

Rabies is an acute infectious disease that is always fatal unless treated before symptoms appear. It is caused by a virus transmitted to human bites, scratches or even the air around areas infected by rabid animals. The virus attacks the central nervous system of warm-blooded animals including humans. It is a widespread disease because it is carried by many wild animals such as skunks, foxes, coyotes, raccoons, and others; and by domestic animals such as dogs, cats, cattle and others that have been bitten by rabid animals. In most developing countries, dogs are the main vectors transmitting this disease. In India alone, more than 25,000 people die of rabies infections every year.

Treatment of rabies can be a painful experience, but prevention can be easily taken. Pets kept at home should be vaccinated against rabies. Stray animals should be impounded to prevent them from spreading the disease. Wild animals should be avoided and never be kept as pets.

STERILIZATION

Dogs and cats are probably the best pets for human companionship. Their numbers are proliferating faster than the human beings. In a span of six years, a dog can have as many as 67,000 puppies while a cat can produce as many as

420.000 kittens in seven years or more than one million during her lifetime. No wonder millions of dogs and cats are without shelter and proper food. There is therefore a need to control their populations to ensure that fewer strayed and unwanted dogs and cats are roaming the streets.

In the U.S. alone, an estimated 3,000 to 5,000 puppies and kittens are born every hour. This is on top of the 80 to 100 million in existence in the U.S. Worldwide, there are about 400 million dogs. This mean that millions of these unwanted animals are left to fend for themselves. Those that are caught by the pound are often euthanized in animal shelters, allowed to starve to death or die from sickness. Sterilization will mean less unwanted animals in the streets and less suffering. When a low-cost spay/neuter clinic was opened in Santa Barbara, California in 1975, the number of unwanted animals destroyed there were reduced by 80 percent. The Animal Protection Institute reports that in Vancouver, B.C., Canada, an amazing reduction was 89% since it opened its low-cost spay/neuter clinic in 1975. For every dog or cat sterilized, it will prevent the possible birth of as many as 100 offspring. In the streets, these animals often die of starvation, disease or death by automobile accident. Sterilization or spaying/neutering, costing about $45 can be done in many of the veterinary clinics throughout the world. Puppies and kittens should be sterilized as soon as possible to prevent unwanted offspring.

Stray dogs are never wanted by those tasked to clean them up. They are cleaned up in some of the most inhumane ways. In Taiwan, they are rounded by garbage collectors and delivered to dump sites. From their "prison" they are either electrocuted or drown. Others are simply dumped into deep pits and suffocated with other rubbish piled on top of them. The same type of treatment is happening to dogs in Bogota, Colombia as late as 1996. In Peru (1995), the campaign to kill 90.000 dogs using strychnine-laced liver has outraged animal activists for being cruel and inhumane. The poison causes a slow, painful death of up to two hours. What makes it more objectionable is that other more humane euthanasia alternatives are available and the government is employing.

One of the problems encountered with stray dogs and even privately owned dogs is the amount of waste they generate. In Paris, the 500,000 dogs produce so much waste that tourists often found themselves stepping on the doggy-do. To make matter worse, the owners do not take personal responsibility for the wastes generated by their dogs. The government spend more than $8 million annually to clean up just a seventh of the wastes. Research has found that in the French capital, some 5,840 metric tons of wastes are generated every year. To help solve the problem, water closets for canines have been installed with distinctive signposts directing owners to where these facilities are located. Initial tests however, have not been encouraging. This problem can also be found in many cities of the world.

In Australia, there was a proposal by a member of Parliament, Richard Evans to kill all of the approximately 18-20 million feral cats to protect native wildlife. It was immediately quashed after a public outcry from animal rights movements. The ferals have been responsible for the extinction of at least 40 natives species, including the Macquarie Island red-fronted parakeet, the pig-footed bandicoot and the rufous hare-wallaby. This is just to show the gravity of the problem of unwanted cats that could bring havoc to the other wildlife. Instead of using feline disease like the white-blindness virus used in the early 1900s to destroy the rabbits, spay/neuter program for pets and unwanted cats will be undertaken to reduce these excess animals.

STRANGE POWERS

Once in a while, we hear of strange powers performed by animals in our midst. In their book, "Strange Powers of Pets," the authors, Brad Steiger and Sherry Hansen Steiger, related many instances of pet powers that saved the lives of their masters and friends. Filmmaker Richard Savage was saved twice by his Capuchin monkey named Sunday. The first time was when Sunday began screeching and clutching his hand when an unseen 700-pound grizzly bear suddenly charged after him from behind some trees to get to the garbage. Another occasion was the loss of brake fluid from the truck braking system. The monkey kept making a whimpering sound until the filmmaker noticed the ripped off brake fluid line of the truck.

In another instance, a small boy was saved by his pet cats when the cats positioned themselves in front of the boy during a thunderstorm. A lightning bolt created a ball lightning that charged through the window of the boy's room. The entire bodies of the cats glowed as the lightning touched them, but fortunately did not continue to hit the boy. It was also fortunate that the cats survived the ordeal.

A golden Labrador named Toby saved the life of his master, an auto mechanic several miles away. The mechanic accidentally dozed off with his car engine idling while all exhaust systems of the shop were closed. Toby, four miles away from the shop, must have been endowed with some ESP was able to sense the danger that befallen his master. He kept scratching the door where he is staying until the mechanic's mother, along with a neighbor drove to the shop to find his unconscious master.

Even the detested rat can somehow save a friend's life. An elderly coral miner had befriended a rat that inhabited a dark tunnel where he worked. One day, the agitated rat kept scampering up to the miner until he decided to follow the rat around the corner to see for himself the problem agitating the rat. The roof collapsed just as he moved away from the spot where he had been working.

These are only some of the thousands of documented cases of animal-human interactions, that defy scientific explanation. The animals included are not confined to the usual pets we have at homes. Some pets such as Baby the racoon had helped his master in crimefighting. The racoon served as his bodyguard wherever and whenever danger lurks. Then there is Sparky, a beagle with a supernose used by the USDA in ferreting out illegal food stuffs imported from abroad.

THEFT

In the U.S., theft of pets is a very common occurrence because of the high value of many pets. Some are stolen for use in the laboratories of schools and hospitals and biomedical research centers. This is much more rampant because under the Animal Welfare Act, the animals under shelter can not be sold and used for experimentations.

In order to strengthen the drive against theft, it is necessary to impose a stiffer fine or jail term to deter violators. A New York has been filed with one of the toughest penalties in the nation. If it is approved, the penalties for stealing a pet will include $5,000 in fines and four years in jail.

Elsewhere in the Third World, stray dogs often suffer a more miserable fate. Protection is seldom given, and they are often rounded up, killed and turned into a delicacy. Facilities for stray dogs often do not exist.

VIRTUAL PETS

A new invention that has been a craze among children is the "tamagochi." The Japanese invention is an oval shape with a computer video image of animals and other animate object such as E.T., dinosaurs, and even human babies. The object of the toy is to take care of the pet until it grows to an adulthood in about 10 days. The computer pet mimics the real thing in many ways. The owner will have to feed, groom, wash, clean up its droppings, play, and even send for the doctor in case of emergency. All these things can be accomplished with buttons provided at the bottom of the toy. When it first came out in the market, it was selling for more than $420 but is now less than $3 for imitations coming out from China and elsewhere.

People who like to keep pets at home can do so with these virtual pets. Japanese social scientists have speculated that the "pets" fill an emotional needs not easily found in the highly urbanized society. At the very least, it will free up many pets from being owned by people who may not have the time nor the knowhow to care for them, and hopefully dampen the demand for animals from the wild where they belong.

VOLUNTEERS

In many of the animal shelters and pounds around the world, there is a lack of volunteers. These shelters are often set up on a voluntary basis where most of the workers are not getting paid. It is therefore necessary to recruit more volunteers to help in a variety of tasks that lay ahead. Volunteers are often needed to groom the animals inside these shelters and pounds. Instead of being treated like caged prisoners, dogs and cats often would like to savour the outdoor life. Volunteers can walk these animals and let them socialize with other animals. During their outside walks, they may be noticed by would-be adoptees.

Some shelters and other organizations have' outreach programs aimed at helping elderly people with pets at home. Sometimes due to unforeseen neclect, it is necessary to provide food and veterinary assistance for the elderly people.

Volunteers can also assist in the inventory of animals in their locality. This is especially important because the government does not have enough personnel to do the huge task. Inventory of animals is necessarv to pinpoint those under threat or endanger because of human activities. In the U.S., amateur birdwatchers are devoting time and skills to help the government survey birds in the wild, feed bird,

And clean cages at neighboring wildlife centers. Some even go to the extent of cleaning the surroundings of bits and pieces of scraps that birds may mistake for food. There are many other activities that need to be done, except that there are not enough volunteers around, especially in the Third World countries.

WILLS

It has become common practice for rich people to have a part of their fortune bequeathed to their favorite pets. We have read of Cardinal Richelieu who left a pension for his 14 cats in his will. Tobacco heiress Doris Duke set up a $ 100.000 trust fund for her dog. Probably the richest pet is Viking, a German shepherd who inherited an entire block of real estate in Munich in 1971.

More often than not, these types of wills are often contested in courts. To avoid such confusion, it is advisable to find a friend or family member to care for the pet. Bequeathing an outright gift of money on behalf of the dog will be more effective than resorting to trust or will that are often not recognized by courts. Never leave an animal in the care of an NGO or institution without carefully investigating them.

Funds are needed for a successful program. Whether it is an animal shelter for pet animals or to purchase wildlife habitats, funds are needed to buy the necessary shelters or wilderness and to keep the project going. Many wildlife conservation movements and animal welfare organizations will gladly receive whatever help that can be extended.

CHAPTER 4

MAMMALS

Mammals are air-breathing, warm-blooded vertebrates found throughout the world. Most of the large animals on earth today are mammal. There are mammals such as rabbits, bats. dog,, mice, etc. The smallest mammal, the Kitti's hognosed bat, weighs only 15 grams In fact there are about 4.450 species of mammals on the planet Humans are considered as mammals of the highest order. There are many things common among mammals. Their warm-blooded body create their own body heat through the food eaten This enabled it possible them to colonize even very cold regions of the world. Another important characteristic is that the whole body is covered with hair.

One of the most distinctive characteristic found in very few animals except the birds and some reptiles is the care and protection mammals give to their young until they are fully grown. The babies are fed with milk from the mammary glands, from where the word "mammal" came. Mammals have a highly developed placenta from where the young embryo takes its nourishment. They have also the most advance nervous system. Most of all, mammals are the most intelligent of all the animals. They are popularly found in zoos and parks, making them more familiar than any other animal group. Yet more than any other animal, wild mammals are killed and their populations are declining as humans continue to proliferate. Only the cunning rodents, the most numerous, have kept up with the people.

Many mammals are in decline in the wild as their habitats are lost to human encroachment. The pressure is too much for most of these animals. They need large living space to hunt for their needed food to survive and a safe place to mate and breed for future generations. Human disturbances of their habitats have caused a decline in their reproductive rate. The chemical pollutions we emit to the environment is getting into their reproductive system causing the disruption of their hormones.

All the animals mentioned here and in the following chapters are only representative examples of these endangered, threatened, or inhumanely treated. Those that have become extinct are mentioned only insofar as to their causes so that we may learn from the mistakes of the past to save future endangered species.

ARABIAN ORYX

The Arabian oryx is one of the most beautiful antelopes that is hunted for its magnificent horns. They were once almost hunted to near extinction by wealthy Arabs m their desert habitat. The animals were no match for the hunters. Motor vehicles helicopters and even small aircrafts mounted with machine guns were used against these hapless animals. By 1961, there were less than a hundred left in the desert. Still the wealthy Arabs continued with game hunt for the trophy. When another hunting party killed more than half of the herd in the wild, it precipitated the conservationists to undertake a rescue operation to preserve them.

In 1962, the Fauna and Flora Preservation Society of London and the World Wildlife Fund (WWF) launched "Operation Oryx" to save the animal from extinction. Only three surviving oryx were captured in the wild. Together with oryxes from other zoos and private collections, the wild oryxes were put in a special breeding program in the Phoenix Zoo in Arizona. Today, their stock have built up to more than one hundred in captivity. They were reintroduced and dispersed into their old habitats as well as new habitats under strict protection. Today, there are about 1,800 of these animals in the world.

BATS

There are about 1,000 species of bats worldwide, comprising about one-fourth of all the mammals. They are the only flying mammals found in the temperate and tropical regions of the world. Many of them are under threat of extinction. In 1986 only 12 species of bats were listed under IUCN red list, but after a span of only four years, 54 species were listed and four of them had become extinct by 1992. The main cause of their decline is habitat destruction, followed by pesticides, and the shrinking food supply. The encroachment of agriculture into their old habitats has forced many bats to raid agricultural crops to avoid starvation. Farmers are forced to destroy them as pests. Their roost caves are dynamited or sprayed with poison directly.

Bats are voracious eating machines. A single bat can eat as many as 500 insects in an hour. The 20 million Mexican free-tailed bats (Tadarida braziliensis) residing in Bracken Cave, Texas consumed about 250,000 pounds of insects a night. Their absence has permitted the proliferation of harmful insects. Some bats can fly at more than 50 kph. Being social animals, they roost together by the thousands in caves and other sites.

Some bats feed on the pollen of nectars of flowers. In a single night, one short-tailed fruit bat can disperse as many as 60,000 rain forest seeds. A study made by Bat Conservation International (BCI) documented more than 300 plant species in the Old World relying on bats alone for pollination. These flowers will only bloom at night and few insects are active at night. Insects such as bees and wasps gather their nectar during the daytime, but bats do their wonders during the nighttime. In the Pacific Islands, as much as 60% of the trees in the rain forest are pollinated by the flying foxes. Without bats, many of these trees would have long become extinct.

In Africa, the fast declining flying foxes are the only known seed dispersed for the iroko tree, the source of millions of dollars worth of timber annually. The giant baobab tree, an ecologically critical feature of East African savannas, depend on bats to pollinate its flowers, which open only at night. The fruit bats of West Africa disperse nearly all the seeds of "pioneer plants" that start forest growing again on cleared land. In tropical Guam, it is estimated that 40% of the tree species survived only because their seeds are dispersed by flying foxes. Some seeds of tropical fruits need to pass through the digestive tract of fruit bats before they will germinate.

But human intrusion and pollution, especially chemicals and pesticides are rapidly destroying their habitats. Out of the 44 species in North America, six are listed as endangered while another 18 species are threatened. On a worldwide basis, 40% of all the bats are either endangered or threatened.

Besides consuming a lot of insects that destroy plants and spread diseases, bats have other uses. During the American Civil War, a gunpowder factory obtained the important gunpowder ingredient of saltpeter from the bat guano. The Confederates mined the bat guano found in caves in Texas and Tennessee. During the British occupation of Sri Lanka, British soldiers kept the bat caves away from rebels to deter them from obtaining the droppings.

Even the silhouette emblem of the bat had been used for peaceful purposes during the Second World War. From 1940-1942, during the British desert campaign in the Middle East, the army used the emblem of the bat on vehicles to deliver the badly needed blood supply for transfusion to the front line soldiers undergoing surgery. It was also used in the European continent during the same period.

Many endemic species of flying foxes considered a delicacy in tropical islands have became extinct. Some subspecies of the Marianas flying foxes (*Pteropus mariannus*) and the Guam flying fox (*Pteropus tokudae*) have disappeared completely, all consumed by the islanders. Not content with the extinction of their own species, they even imported rare and endangered species from neighboring islands such as the Samoan flying foxes (*Pteropus samoensis*) found only in Samoa and Fiji.

In Southeast Asia, giant fruit-eating bats known as flying foxes are hunted for food, fetching as much as $20 each and $35 in Guam, each huge bat weighing as much as a pound is easy target for hunters with shotguns while they hang in the treetops by the hundreds. A flying fox discovered in the Philippines in the 1960s was extinct by the 1980s. In Thailand the flying foxes (Eonycteris spelaea) are skinned and openly sold in the public markets.

The Rodrigues flying foxes (*Pteropus rodricensis*) of Rodrigues Island were so few in numbers without becoming extinct in 1974 that government took action to protect them. They were greatly decimated due to the destruction of the forest habitat and the fruit trees they needed for nourishment. Realizing the problem, the government took the initiative ot planting more trees for their roosting and fruit trees for their food need. From a lot of less than 80, they have since increase to more than 400 today.

The greater horseshoe bats (*Rhinolophusferrumequinum*) are found throughout Europe, Asia and Africa. Because of the diminishing forest covers, they are forced to roost in the roofs of old buildings. Most of these roofs are treated with wood preservatives that are harmful to the bats. This pollutant has been responsible for their extinction in northwestern Europe.

In some places where vampire bats or other considered pest bats congregate with benevolent bats, eradication campaigns often destroy the unintended bats. The campaign to smoke out the Africa rousette fruit bats (*Rousettus aegyptiacus*) using the poisons, ethylene bidromide and long-lasting lindane backfired. In 15 years, the insect-eating bats were decimated by 90% while the targeted bats migrated elsewhere. As a consequence, several insect species population exploded causing even more destruction to agricultural crops.

Bats are also being destroyed for carrying rabies. But the risk of being bitten by a bat is infinitesimally small and one with rabies is even smaller since the virus has been found in less than one-half of one percent of bats tested. Only the common vampire bats (Desmodus roiundus) of South America have been noted for carrying rabies. They feed only on blood of mammals usually livestock and seldom people..

Mexican long-nosed bats are responsible for pollinating the flowers of cactuses and the agave plants from which the Mexican tequila industry is based. The free-tailed bats of Brazil in one cave can contain 50,000 to 80,000 individuals. For nearly three hours every night, this cloud of mammals will sweep down the valley and consume about 300 million night flying insects, mostly mosquitoes, gnats, and moths. A farmer, after hearing how bats consume so many insects decided to build bat roost boxes for the bats. In a few weeks, all the bugs disappeared without using any pesticide.

Mining in the mountainous areas can also destroy the habitat of bats. The Australian giant false vampire bat Macroderma gigas is sometime called the ghost bat because of the strange color of its pale fur at night. They were severely threatened by the destruction of their roost caves in Mount Etna, Queensland due to limestone mining. Dynamites were legally used to break the solid rock for easy harvesting. Only a resolution passed by the IUCN board did the Queensland government set aside a 15-hectarc region as their sanctuary. In another site, some 1,500 bats living in an abandoned gold mine is being threatened if the plan to re-open the mine is pushed through.

Many who do not understand the role bats play in the environment have tried to exterminate them from the planet. The range of the Mexican free-tailed bats extend from the U.S. to South America and the Caribbean. In the U.S. alone, there are at least a dozen huge nursery colonics. In Austin, Texas, residents even petitioned the government to exterminate one million free-tailed bats roosting under the reconstructed Congress Avenue Bridge. Instead, the government wisely converted the bridge into the "Bat Capitol of the World." Thousands of tourists flock at dusk to see the largest urban bat population to take off in search of insects. The Texas Department of Transportation has since designed more than 60 bat-friendly bridges.

In the U.S. the federal and state governments are finding new uses for abandoned mines. Throughout the country, those mines are closed for safety reasons are becoming useful again for bat homes. To comply with safety regulations, the entrances to the caves and mines are sealed up using steel bar grating to allow bats to enter while keeping away people. According to Merlin Tuttle, founder and executive director of BCI, more than half of North America bat species are now inhabiting abandoned mines and caves. The France government has also taken steps to protect the bats' habitats by this scheme.

Bats have been persecuted for a long time as they are today. Only a few species such as the vampire bats of Brazil have given bats a bad reputation. They destroyed $50 million worth of livestock annually in South America. Our ignorance of these industrious and invaluable mammals to the planet is often overlooked.

They are often depicted as evil due to their relationship to fictional characters like Dracula and witches. Poison gas are sometimes used to destroy them in caves where they are found. They are blasted with dynamite, suffocated by burning tires and even entombed alive by the millions in caves and mines. In 1926, one of their habitats was invaded by miners out to mine phosphate from their excrement. The miners blasted an entrance tunnel directly into the roosting chamber. Today, cold ammonia-laden air often spouts from the new opening. The disturbances can affect their reproduction and hearing ability because they can only fly with the hearing aid of echolocation.

As recently as 1993, men have been using them as target practice at the Snake Range in Nevada. In 1963 an estimated 30 million bats lived in Arizona's Eagle Creek Cave. Within seven years of human intrusion and target practice, the population is down to only 30,000 today.

Pesticides and wood preservatives can work in several ways in destroying bats. They are also susceptible to prey on animals contaminated with pesticides. Because of the loss of their natural habitats, bats are forced to find refuges in areas inhabited by humans. One of the problems they faced roosting on barns is the spraying of chemical wood preservatives in lumber used for the roofs. Chemicals used as wood preservatives can last for twenty to thirty years affecting several generations of bats. They are taken into the body through their wings and respiratory system, leading to internal organ dysfunction that could mutate after a few generations of breeding. Some endocrine disrupters can lead to sterility and increased mortality. Nearly all are carcinogenic and some can be fatal in small doses. Many have been banned in developed countries but are still used in the developing countries. Dieldrin, lindane, PCP, and TBTO, are some examples. Lindane has been used to kill earwigs. It is a persistent insecticide that has been blamed for the decline of the bat population. It is also blamed for the killing of bats because they cannot dispose of it from their body fast enough to remove the toxins. The Nature Conservancy Council suggests using zinc naphthaenate because of its relatively low toxicity.

Most insecticides are fat soluble which mean they can accumulate in the bodies of mammals like bats for years. But for hibernating bats, it could be fatal sooner than expected. During the winter months, the bats are forced to use their stored fats for nourishment. These toxic concentrates, once they reach the brains could be fatal for the bats. Even the newly born bat is not free of the pollution. The toxins are often transmitted to the offspring during pregnancy and feeding.

Hibernation is an important part of the life cycle of bats in the temperate zones. During this period, they are most vulnerable and disturbances of their habitats can be devastating to the mammals. A disturbance by spelunker entering one of their habitats during these periods can disturb their torpor. By the time they settle back to hibernation, it could cost them 30% or more of their body fat. If the fat runs out before spring time, when foods are available, they could die of starvation, it is important then that during hibernation period, their habitats should be off-limit and seasonal closures banned as practiced in many caves.

BEARS

Bears are found in many continents except Africa and Australia. The extinction of the African species is due to the sport cruelty practiced by the ancient Romans. They vary in sizes even within the same species. Brown bears of southern Europe Ire among the smallest in the world. Those of North America are four t.mes as big. The big grizzly sometimes feed on bison and moose. The grizzly was king of the land before human predators move into the continent. It was the fiercest and most powerful omnivore. It could bring down a buffalo with one swipe of its powerful paw. The grizzly is capable of carrying off the carcass weighing one thousand pounds. They did not have enemies until men came along.

As predators they are no match against the human predators. Both compete for the same prey. While they kill the prey for food, humans have other uses for the prey that the bear eat as food to survive. The bears are good hunters and can charge their prey with speed up to 50 kph. Deer and other domestic animals they kill as food only came about as a result in these preys being hunted and killed by local farmers. Thousands are killed annually until government imposed restriction on harming these animals. Because they are widely dispersed, different countries have different ways of treating them.

The brown and grizzly bears are classified into one species. *Ursus acrtos* because of marked similarities. They are found mostly in North America and Asia. In the whole of Europe there are only 300 left in the wild, with France accounting for 30 of them. In Britain, they were all killed a thousand years ago. Because they need so much space to hunt for food, they often encounter farmers who killed them as pests or hunters who killed them for trophy.

The first description of the grizzly bear was not made until the Lewis-Clark expedition of 1804-1806. Forty-three bears were killed by members of the party during the journey across the continent toward the Pacific Ocean. After this expedition, people started to settle the land westward. Lands were staked out and farms were erected. Towns and cities began to sprout out of these wilderness. Along came the roads connecting these towns and railroads were laid. The grizzly bears were pushed farther and farther back into the dwindling wilderness Those left behind were killed. The proliferation of the firearms killed many bears for food and sport. Others were treated like pests and poisoned for destroying livestock.

At one time there may have been more than 10,000 grizzly bears, the largest of them all, weighing as much as 1,000 pounds, in the state of California alone. Today, there are less than 1,000 in the lower 48 states. However, they are still common in Alaska and Canada. The first to become extinct were those from the plains, in the 1880s. Those in California disappeared by 1924, followed by those in the southwestern U.S. in the 1930s. Today, thy are found only in the area adjoining the three states of Montana, Idaho and Wyoming, an area covering about 2 million hectares and in Glacier National Park covering an area of about 1.5 million hectares.

The Wilderness Act of 1964, was partly responsible for protecting the bears from extinction in the lower 48 states by setting millions of hectares of land as natural habitats for many wild animals. This was followed by the listing of the grizzly bears as a threatened species, protecting them within these protected regions.

The brown bears from Kodiak Island are the heaviest of all meat-eaters. In the South American mountains from Colombia to Chile are the bears called the rare spectacled bear. It has rings of white fur around its eyes from which its name was derived. Today there are only 2,000 lefi in the world. They climb trees in search of fruits and often sleep high up in the trees, the only bear to do so.

There are three types of tropical bears in Asia. They are the shaggy sloth bear (Melursus ursinus), the small sun bear (Helarctos malayanus) and the stocky Asian bear (Ursus ihibelanus). The sloth bears were once common in India and Sri Lanka until as recent as 20 years ago. They too are hunted for their gall bladders and fat for medical use. Increasing human populations and encroachment on their habitats are making it difficult for these shy and unadaptable bears to breed under such conditions. The destruction of termite mounds to provide the fine soil used in tennis courts are also reducing its most important diet - the termite - which could lead to their starvation.

The bears in the Asian mainland especially in China are hunted or farmed for medical purposes since the 6th century. The gall bladders which contain the bile salts are used to reduce high fever and used in the treatment of liver disorder. The Japanese use the bear-gall preparations for people suffering from liver, stomach, and intestinal disorders. The South Korean use the purified blood of bears to reduce inflammation. In 1983, at a public auction in South Korea, a gall bladder was sold for $55,000.

A coalition of conservation groups filed a petition with the U.S. Interior Secretary requesting for trade sanctions against South Korea for violating international treaty banning the trafficking of bear parts. Instead of just extracting the gall bladder biles from the bears, the South Korean often kill the bears for other body parts for the gourmet markets. They have wiped out most of the Asian bear population because of the high prices hunters get and the high demand placed on the bear parts. Illegal hunters are now threatening the black bears in the U.S as supplies from Asia is becoming rare. The illegal trade in California alone is estimated at $00 million a year. When the gall bladder bile is extracted and dried into granules, it could be worth $12,000 on the street, which is worth more than cocaine, ounce for ounce.

There is almost an endless use for gall bladders. This is made possible that an active ingredient in the gall bladder contain a bile called ursodeoxycholic acid (UDCA) which has been proven to have medicinal properties for dissolving kidney stones and treating cirrhosis of the liver. However, UDCA can be synthesized from cow bile which should help reduce the demand for bears' gall bladders. But this was not the case. The traditional users believed that those coming from the bears to be naturally diluted and buffered to the proper strength and to exist in the most suitable medium for assimilation by the human body.

In Pakistan the bears are forced to fight pitbulls as a form of entertainment, while in Italy and other East European countries, the bears are forced to dance for the benefit of tourists. This practice has been going on for centuries, first initiated by the gypsies. The cubs are forcibly taken from the mother bear which are usually killed by the poachers. The cubs are sold to the gypsies where their noses are immediately pierced and inserted with a steel ring without anesthesia to keep them from running away. The painful experience was just the beginning of subduing the bear to obedience. In the streets of Istanbul, Turkey, it used to be a common sight to see dancing bears. The bear's mouth is strapped with leather to prevent them from frightening tourists although the teeth have been deliberately broken off with a hammer. Many are suffering from starvation, diseases and blindness and are not being taken care of properly. The owners are not willing to keep them well fed because of their huge appetite and the small income they generate. Fortunately, there is one NGO dedicated solely to stopping the suffering of bears worldwide. The Libearty (sic) Campaign and the World Society for the Protection of Animals (WSPA) of UK has made it their duty to stop all kinds of abuses on the bears. Many bears have been rescued from gypsy camps. In one raid. 12 bears chained to trees in a park in Istanbul were rescued and returned to a sanctuary set up for these bears.

The spectacled bear (Tremarctos ornatus) of South America got its name from the white marks that rings its eyes. They live in the high country of the Andes Mountain. The increasing human population is taking its toll of the bears. Forests are being felled to give way to farmland. This forced the bears to raid corn crops and attack livestock, forcing farmers to kill them as pests. They are also being hunted by the natives as sport.

The polar bears (Ursus maritimus) are the largest living carnivores on Earth. They will travel long distances in search of food. The bears depend completely on the diminishing seals of the Arctic seas for its food. Hunting of these magnificent animals is regulated by the International Agreement on Conservation of Polar Bears. First introduced in 1973 under the auspices of the IUCN, it was renewed in 1981. Under the agreement, the former USSR and Norway will completely halt hunting. Canada, the U.S., Greenland and Denmark will allow hunting by local inhabitants as they did for centuries. It also requires the signatories to protect their habitats and their food supply. This cooperation is expected to ensure their survival for generations. However, the 25,000 strong polar bears are suffering from weight loss, according to Ian Stirling of the Canadian Wildlife Service The survival rate of one-year bears have also declined from 75% to 50% since the 1980s. Several plausible reasons were given. The first reason is global warming. It causes the ice to melt earlier and provided less opportunity for hunting seals. This could lead to starvation and forces the bear to use up their stores of fats

Even if there are ample ringed seals to provide the necessary food for the polar bears, there is another far more subtle and long term effect on the population of the po ar bears. All the seals found in the Arctic are contaminated with high levels of toxic chemicals especially PCBs and chlordane in their blubber and fats. The chemicals are finding their way to the milk of the lactating females and passing on to newborn bears. The PCBs are suspected hormone disrupters that will disrupt the reproductive organs of the bears as they grow. The newborns are particularly vulnerable due to the magnification of these toxic chemicals as they continue to grow and consume more of these toxins.

In Canada and the U.S., there is an open season every year to reduce the population of black bears to manageable level. Hunters have been responsible for the death of 3,600 bears a year in Canada alone. The Federation of Ontario Naturalists and WWF/Canada are asking the Canadian government to cancel the annual spring black bear hunt. Black bears have one of the lowest reproductive rates among land mammals in North America. Females mature until they are 5-7 years old and then only produce litters of two or three cubs once every three years.

Under the law it is illegal to hunt female bears with young offspring, but at night, it is almost impossible to differentiate the sex of the animals and whether they have cubs to nurture. The trial and error method has resulted in unwanted deaths. John Lounds, executive director of the naturalist federation, says that about one-third of the bears killed during the spring hunt are female and 80% of the orphaned cubs do not survive.

In the U.S. black bears are hunted and killed annually just for the trophies to be displayed in living rooms. In 1989, 21,000 black bears were killed legally and poachers killed a few thousands more. The grizzly bear is now an endangered species. Banning their killing will also help control if not eliminate poaching and reduce excessive killing. In a recent sting operation in the U.S., 2,700 grams of bears' gall bladders were sold for $11,000. The same amount is sold in South Korea for $715,000. The more than sixty times rate of return only encourages their poaching.

In Colorado, bears have a bad habit of searching food around homes in the vicinity. Even if they were relocated to other places, as far as 100 miles away, their homing instinct can lead them back to the same locality. Since 1994, the Colorado Division of Wildlife decided that a problem bear can be relocated only once and on the second offense, the bear will be destroyed. Within four months of the implementation of this new policy, 33 bears were killed. It is obvious that the solution lie in the way people dispose of their garbage. People should understand that if they are living in wildlife territories, they should be wary of hungry bears searching for food. If there is any reason why bears cannot find the food they need to survive, it is often the fault of people who compete and hunt their sources of food.

BISON

The white men had begun to hunt the American bison (Bison bison) as early as 1540. It didn't make a dent on their population. Still in 1871 the animals were fairly abundant in most parts of the West. With the introduction of the railroad came large numbers of people including hunters. The railroad industry even went so far as to advertise hunting the buffalo in the safety of the railroad cars. The bisons were no match for the wanton slaughter.

The bison was hunted for food by the Indians in times of famine and for their tongues in times of plenty. They were also hunted as sport by the white man and hides by others. After the introduction of firearms, it became fashionable for anyone to shoot a bison on sight. In less than twenty years, the greatest destruction of land mammals ever known reduced the population to less than 1,000 from a high of sixty millions. In trying to control the Indians, the military also killed as many bisons as possible to deny the Indians an important source of food. Due to the wanton killing of bison, the U.S. Congress in 1874 voted to end all slaughter in federal land but President Ulysses S. Grant vetoed the bill. It was a time when the U.S. Calvary was losing 25 soldiers for every Indian killed.

In the period between 1872-1874, 3.7 million bisons where slaughtered. William Cody, better known as Buffalo Bill, once boasted that he slaughtered 4,280 bisons in eighteen months working as a railroad hunter. Bisons were to feed the hungry workers laying railroad tracks crossing the huge distances through the wild country. The skins were left on the spot and picked up later when they were clean and the bones were grounded into fertilizer.

The killing of the buffalos in a short time is one of the greatest disasters in terms of human food consumption. It was only matched by the killing of the passenger pigeons. The Indians ate bison meat for the protein and the skins were used to make tents and clothing. Other uses include materials such as rugs, coverings, rope, and water vessels. Even the bones were used to make tools like knives, needles and toys. They could have fed millions of people then, and even more today have they been harnessed for commercial meat production. They are easier to breed, with leaner meat, and at a lesser cost. I hey can breed in poor land and provide 50% more meat than cattle. Their meat are 25% higher in protein and 20% less cholesterol. Bison meat do not cause allergy and they don't contract cancer like cattle which can pass on to humans. Antibiotics are not required and they can proliferate without human interventions. Unfortunately, the buffalos were often killed and left to rot.

New tanning techniques has made the buffalo hide commercially valuable. The hides were tanned with fur and made into coats, robes, and other apparels. Shoes are also made from their hides because of its durability. They are also made into belts for machinery and padding and cover for furniture and carriages. The horns and hoofs are made into combs, buttons, knife handles and glues. Even the bones scattered throughout the prairie became a source of income for some scavengers. The bones were sent cast and grounded into phosphorus for use as fertilizer. Newer bones were made into bone char to remove the brown coloration of sugar.

They once numbered more than the U.S. population, at 60 to 100 million before white men arrived at the New World. They were cut down to less than 1,000 at one time. At present they have repopulated to about 250,000 throughout the U.S. and Canada. In 1877 the governor of the Northwest Territory passed a law prohibiting the killing of the buffalo, but it was only in 1897 that the enforcement was relegated to the Northwest Mounted Police. By that time the plain buffalo has become extinct while the wood buffalos are nearly gone.

The bison in the Yellowstone National Park are faced with a new and deadlier opponents: the brutal winter and government sanctioned slaughter. The AUDUBON magazine called it the Yellowstone Massacre in its June 1997 issue. Beside the harsh winter that had killed hundreds by starvation as the buffalo find it difficult to hunt for food under the impenetrable layer of ice. Those that headed out of their territorial confinement in search of food were either shot on the spot or shipped to slaughterhouses. The slaughter was due to a disease called brucellosis caused by the contagious *Brucella abortus* bacterium that can cause spontaneous abortion in domestic livestock. Fear of spread of the disease by cattlemen from Montana forced the government to act on their request. Yet there has never been a recorded case of contamination.

The plight of the bison of Yellowstone started way back in 1985 when the state of Montana started killing bison leaving the Park for fear of contaminating their cattle. Only a public outcry brought a stop to the killing in 1991. But the killings continued by state agents and for the next five years about 400 animals were killed annually. In 1996, a lawsuit brought about by the state on Montana forced the National Park Service and the USDA's Department of Livestock to renew slaughter under an agreement known as the Interim Bison Management Plan. Only pregnant females capable of aborting fetuses on the range were supposed to be killed, yet most of those shot or shipped were bulls, nonpregnant females and calves which posed no risk to the cattle.

Road networks and the mechanically hardened snowmobile trails throughout the Yellowstone National Park have made it possible for the bisons to travel outside of their confinement and into the hands of agents assigned to kill or bring them to the slaughterhouses. Indiscriminate shooting of bisons may have killed about 40% that may be free of the disease. The proposal of the American Indian tribes to quarantine bison tested negative for the disease went unheeded.

Cattle ranching is big agribusiness even the federal government find it hard to go against. Despite findings that there is a remote possibility of infection and the low numbers of infected bison, the state of Montana, together with the cattlemen, opted to destroy all the bison within the Park. In one laboratory report of the C&C Meats slaughterhouse, only 2 of the more than 200 bison killed there were tested positive for brucellosis. That is far less than the 50% rate insisted by the state of Montana to justify the killing spree.

Elk, about 120,000 strong in Yellowstone, are also carriers of brucellosis. Some 30,000 elks outside the Park suffer from abortion but are never shot. Yet Montana has no culling program for elk, a popular game animal that brings to the region more than SI00 million in hunting-related revenues. Instead of meeting a bullet the moment they step outside the park, elk are permitted to wander at will, even though they pose the same risk of brucellosis transmission as bison. (Animals September/October 1997)

Even a New Age religious order, the Church Universal and Triumphant, which is expected to be more enlightened, also wanted the bison entering their rangeland killed. Hundreds of these bisons were killed on their 12,000-acre ranch.

The plight of the European bison (*Bison bonasus*) is not as well publicized as their cousin across the Atlantic Ocean, but they are in even worst strait. Their numbers in the wild were never as numerous and they have been hunted for their meat for a long time. By 1919, there were none left in the wild and only a few remnant found in zoos around Europe. Captive breedings have made it possible to introduce six of them in the wild forest of Bailowieza, Poland. Today, there are more than 250 bison in the wild. Problems may arise from inbreeding.

COYOTES

The coyote (Canis lairans) is another wild dog that closely resembles a small wolf. It is found in many parts of North America because of their adaptability to all kinds of ranges. Their diet consists of small wild mammal, birds and domestic animals. Whenever man intrudes into a locality, all wild animals must retreat or suffer the consequences. Farmers with significant herds of sheep often blame the coyote for any loss of farm animal so they started to poison these coyotes that often lead to unwanted deaths of other wildlife. The measures taken are too drastic considering that a few sheep dogs or even llamas, their natural enemy, are often enough to deter the coyotes from attacking sheep. During the 1980s, farmers have been using llamas imported from the Andes as guards for sheep. Even the wild burros, more than 4,000 of them have been used to guard sheep. Other animals such as the donkeys and ostriches have been employed by shepherds from other countries. This forced U.S. President Nixon to ban the use of poison in 1972.

The Animal Damage Control of the Department of Agriculture (US) is an agency tasked with killing wildlife considered as pests. They can be called upon by any rancher to control any pest free of charge. Public funds are being used to kill wildlife on public land. Between 1990 and 1994, they have killed more than 7.8 million critters which include S00.000 coyotes and 1.228 mountain lions. M-44 Armalites were used to ensure a high kill ratio. The cost to wildlife is tremendous compared to the 2.2% of cattle falling prey to predators.

While the coyotes may seem to be a pest to many farmers, they have an important ecological role to play. They keep the voracious ground squirrels from eating more than their share of the grassland needed by the sheep. Only the coyotes can control their proliferating numbers. Even then the gray squirrels also play an important ecological role in planting millions of nut-bearing trees throughout North America. They do it by burying nuts for later munching and forgot where they hide them. These include hickory, walnut, beechnut, acorn and pecan.

DEER

Deer in the wild are at the center of the food chain. They serve as prey food for the wild cats and mammals, many of them on the endangered list. Indigenous people in the forests also depend on them for protein. Hut in the more affluent countries deer only serves as target practice for hunters. Many are killed for their antler while others such as the musk deer are unfortunate enough to own a gland used for perfume.

Musk deer (Moschus moschiferus) have been hunted for the musk used on perfume. They are found mostly in central and eastern Asia. The musk is secreted by a gland called the musk pod that is found only in the male musk deer. The gland located in the abdomen secretes a semi-solid mass that when processed will yield the important ingredient used in many perfumes. There was a time these animals were so ruthlessly hunted that even today, some species are still having difficulties recovering from extinction.

The pampas deer (Ozotoceros bczoarticus) of South America have long been hunted for food, sport, and its skin for many years. From 1860 to 1879, more than two million skins were exported from just one country. Argentina. The insatiable demand for this deer brought them to the brink of extinction in 1975. Less than a hundred were left by 1975. Careful captive breeding has increased their numbers to a few hundreds, but they are not expected to recover their past glory as their habitats are destroyed to make room for cattle ranching and agricultural farms.

The deer antler is one of the most sought ingredient in traditional Chinese medicine. Most of these animals affected are the caribou, elk, moose and the white-tailed deer. Although deer shed their antlers naturally every year, hunters and poachers usually hunt and kill them to get the antlers. The elk is a preferred target and many farms have been set up to breed elks to collect the antlers for export to China. The antler, boiled and used for treating impotence and blood abnormalities, can fetch up to $200 per pound.

DISEASES

Animals suffered from some of the deadliest and debilitating diseases known to man. Some of these diseases also inflict humans and vice versa. The difficulties in finding a cure or the expensive cost of treatment often result in the slaughters of animals, which is far cheaper than trying to save them. In the South Africa's Kruger National Park, more than 10,000 buffalos are infected with the tuberculosis and are recommended for killing. It is feared that the disease will spread to other rare species. The disease was suspected to be introduced following the introduction of contaminated domestic cattle in 1959. Biologists have found several wild cats and primates to be infected. The 13-year drought that brought many animals to congregate in the few water holes must have abetted the spread of the disease.

Hibernating animals such as bears often suffer from spinal conditions such as inflammation and fusion of vertebrae. Prolonged cave-dwelling during the cold months or keeping them in closed confinement for a long period can hasten these debilitating conditions. They also suffer from at least sixty different internal and external parasites. Ticks, lice, fleas, and different kinds of worms also afflict them. The most important parasite afflicting almost all polar bears and three-quarters of the brown bears is the roundworm Trichinella. The likely source of infection may be the infected seals. Humans who regularly eat raw or poorly cooked bear meat are highly vulnerable to infection.

Anthrax is another dreaded soil-borne disease, the pathogen generally being taken in orally as a spore. It was once very prevalent in Europe and is making a comeback in the game reserves of Africa. There have been repeated epidemics due to the high concentration of susceptible animals and anthrax species. Once a particular site has been infected by the disease, it will be contaminated for decades. In the Luangwa Valley National Park in Zambia, recent losses from anthrax far exceed those killed by poachers. Elephants as well as buffalos, hippos, and antelopes are getting infected and deaths are increasing. There are also sporadic cases of the disease in humans, since the local population are eating the infected meat. The disease can also be transmitted to humans through the use of their body products such as skins and wool.

In 1992, in the Kaokoveld Desert of Namibia where less than a hundred elephants live there, helicopters were used to shoot vaccine-filled darts to immunize the elephants after the game warden found a dead anthrax-stricken elephant. The elephant was probably infected after drinking contaminated water spread by infected animals. In Namibia's Etosha National Park, the disease claimed 20 to 30 elephants annually.

It is only now that an effective vaccine may be possible to immunize the animals susceptible to anthrax. A vaccine from the Sterne spore has achieved virtually 100% immunity in experimental guinea pigs. However, it is necessary to try the vaccine on individual animal species to see if treatment can be effective on them.

Wild animals cannot be immunized as easily as domestic animals. Using darts from helicopters or chasing them by land rovers proved to be too difficult and expensive. For this reason, scientists are trying to produce an oral vaccine that can easily apply to their food sources. Tests on individual animal species is also necessary to determine the optimum dose for maximum efficacy.

ELEPHANTS

The African elephant (Loxodonia africana) is ihe largest terrestrial mammal that measures 3.3 meters tall at the shoulder and weighs 5.6 tons. Numbering about 10 million in the 19th century, the population dropped to about 1.5 million elephants by 1979. Today less than 600,000 are in existence. All this is brought about by the ivory trade and loss of habitats. In Kenya and in many parts of Africa, elephant poachers work in groups of up to 15 men. most of them bearing high-powered firearms and even dynamite to kill the harmless animal and using modem communication and transport vehicles. The elephants are killed by the dozens and their tusks are hacked using axes or chainsaws. The female elephants, as leaders of the herds are also killed to allow poachers to go near the herd to remove the tusks. The killing of these adult animals often leave thousands of calves orphaned. Unless taken care, many of them will die. Between 1980 and 1985, the trade in ivory was about 800 tons each year. To meet this demand some 90,000 elephants must be slaughtered. Most of these ivory are taken to Japan and Hong Kong where they are carved into beautiful ornaments and exported all over the world. Europe and the U.S. are the biggest market in the developed countries. Before Presided George Bush banned the importation of ivory products into the U.S., it was a S2 30 million market. Together with the European Community, they account for 64 of the world's consumption of carved ivory.

Elephant poachers are ruthless gangs who will do anything to get hold o elephant tusks at any cost. An incident in Zaire in 1978 proved this point. with the connivance of corrupt public officials killed more than a thousand elephants by poisoning their waterholes with 22 tons of pesticides. An entire population of elephants including the baby elephants were killed. Even the non-intended animals were killed including some people who ate the contaminated meat of these poisoned animals.

The latest mass killings of 200 elephants occurred only last summer (1996) Wildlife Conservation Society researcher Michael Fay made the startling discovery. What makes it abhorring about this slaughter is that most of the elephants were either pregnant females or juveniles without tusks.

Many elephants in Africa can be found outside the highly protected sanctuaries and reserves. It is necessary to move these animals to protect against poaching for their ivory. Another instance required to spread them to other sanctuaries is to prevent culling due to overpopulation in the region. Their dispersal to lightly populated areas will reduce chances of epidemics that could wipe out the entire herd in a locality.

Since October 1989, the African elephants have been listed in Appendix I of the Convention on International Trade in Endangered Species of Fauna and Flora (CITES) as endangered species that are banned in commercial trade. But some countries refuse to abide by the decision of CITES. This is because there is great profit to be made by the governments or the illegal poachers. A pair of tusks can provide the equivalent of one year's salary.

The elephants in the Okavango Delta. Botswana are earning money for the government through safari trips taken by tourists riding on the elephant's back Each tourist is charged SI,000 for a day's work by the elephant. It is a very safe ride through the wild jungle since elephants do not have any enemy except maybe humans.

The traditional "tying up" system of keeping zoo and circus elephants requires close contact between keepers and elephants. Bull elephants in particular are potentially dangerous. The differences between intensive and extensive caring are numerous. Elephants that are often shackled or living in an enclosed space are more aggressive toward man and than those that can move around. There is no opportunity for socializing and playing for those in intensive systems. Mahouts used in extensive systems are more experienced and better educated than those in intensive systems.

The Asian elephant (Elephas maximus) docs not fare any better. Their population once numbering 200.000 at the turn of the century is down to about 50,000 today. The fragmentation of their habitats is partly to blame. They are losing grounds to the exploding human population. Many are traded in some South Asian countries. About 60% of Kerala's 200 temple elephants are brought to the traditional Sonepur (Bihar) elephant market. Some of them have been poached while others are born under human care. Many calves are illegal caught and offered for sale. In Thailand, many elephants are moved illegally lo tourist centers or brought to Laos and Myanmar borders where timber is still cut down. As many as 15.000 tame elephants live in urban areas under intensive systems.

Reproduction and health care for elephants in confinement are different from those in the wild. It is often the human hands that control their reproduction system. In Assam. Vietnam and Eastern Thailand, elephants caught in the wild are not allow to breed. While the elephants kept in intensive systems sexually mature a year or two earlier, their maximum reproductive period is a little more than ha as long as those in extensive systems. If the infant elephant dies during birth or within the first year of life, the next birth occurs approximately 2.5 years later.

the infant remains with its mother for at least 1.5 years, the next birth occurs about 4.5 years later. This long period can spell the difference should their population continue to decline.

Infant elephants born in the wild have certain advantages not found in intensive systems. "Allomothers", are female elephants, that take care of the calves during their infancy. They ensure the course of the birth, remove the newborn from the embryonic sheet, protect it from possible attacks by the mother, calm the mother and support the calf during its first attempt at walking. Individual cow elephants guard sleeping and playing calves, while their mothers feed, prepare appropriate fodder for the offspring.

The illegal trade in ivory has brought the number of bull elephants to dangerous low level in many parts of Asia. In the Kerala's Parer Tiger Reserve, the 600 elephants include only four adult bulls and the reproduction rate is decreasing.

Elephants has many uses beside their ivory. Tamed and domesticated over 5,000 years ago, elephants still play a fundamental part in the two great religions of India: Brahmanism and Buddhism. They are regarded as the strongest and wisest animals in the world. They have been used for transportation, working in logging, and even military purposes. They were once used as executioners by stomping their huge foot on those convicts sentenced to death.

In case we persist in keeping elephants under human control, it is imperative that we care for them in a humane way. In Germany, UK and the U.S., animal protection societies are fighting against individual keeping and shackling of animals and extreme physical overtaxing circus tricks. In Kerala, national and international animal protection societies are fighting against unnatural keeping conditions and constant physical overtaxing of the animals. In 1993, the mahouts went on strike and tried to fight for better conditions for themselves and their elephants.

FUR FARMS

Because of the demand for fur products, some have resorted to breed fur animals. Most of these fur farms are located in Europe and North America. Finland has more than 6,500 fur farms producing millions of furs annually. These farms contained rows and rows of small cramped cages piled on top of another to save space in disregard of the welfare of the animals. Farmers refuse to allow the free run of the place for fear that the fur will be damaged although animals caged in close confinement are more liable to fighting.

In the U.S. most of the animals bred for furs are the chinchilla, mink, nutria and the silver fox. The animals are kept in small cages and later killed for their furs when they are large enough to make a profit. In order to maximize the profit, the animals are feed garbage that is unfit even for the pet food industry. When they are about five months old are ready for harvesting, the cheapest way is gassing them by attaching their cages to the exhaust of automobiles while the engine is running. This is inefficient because some animals do not die but are awakened during skinning. Other ways of killing animals are through anal electrocution, use of decompression chambers, breaking their necks, and strychnine poisoning. Although less cruel than hunting them by leghold traps, still many believe it to be a cruel business venture.

Most (80%) of today's furs came from fur farms. Modern fur-bearing farms began in 1880 in Canada. But it wasn't until 1940 that the first commercially developed mutation mink, the silver blue, appeared. Further experimentation with mink resulted in other natural colors giving buyers a chance to choose different colors. Other small animals that have made improvements include the foxes chinchillas, and nutria resulting in more animals being farmed. By far the mink is the most favorite because of the declining fur animals in the wild. There are over 4.000 mink farms in the U.S. producing more than 9 million pelts annually. Another 5,000 farms are devoted to breed the chinchillas, producing 75,000 to 100.000 pelts every year. The 2.500 nutria farms produced 3 million furs annually. These animals are killed or skinned while the coats are at its peak of beauty and luxuriance. The imported furs are usually the beaver, fox, mink. Persian lamb, sable and various sheep. Except for the silver and black fox, most are imported duty free. To reduce the commerce for fur, it is therefore necessary to impose a high rate of import duty. A worldwide ban on the commerce of fur will help the animals from suffering and early demise.

Shearing is the removal of the fur with the use of a shearing tool without harming the animal. Long before the Australians started shearing the sheep, the Incas had shear vicuna without killing them. The animals are found in Chile and Peru in great abundance before the arrival of the Spaniards. The vicuna, a type of llama is also rounded up on protected mountain ranches where they are sheared in the traditional way. They were greatly reduced due to hunting by the new invaders who coveted their wool. The shearing could be apply to all other fur animals.

HIPPOPOTAMUSES

Hippopotamuses (Hippopotamus amphibius) are gregarious animal that can grow up to 4.5 meters long and weigh about four tons, making them the second largest terrestrial mammals. They spend most ofthe day in the water and move to land at night to feed on grass. This is necessary because hippos have very thin epidermis making them vulnerable to dehydration under the sun. Sometimes they secrete a pinkish oil from the skin to help them protect against the sunlight.

They once ranged over a wide area from the Middle East to the African continent. Today much of the former ranges have been eliminated and they are now concentrated in east-central and southern Africa. In Biblical times, the hippos were often displayed in circus shows in Rome while their thick hides are often used to make shields for Roman soldiers.

In the 18th century, hippo tusks were used by dentists to make artificial teeth, hey are favored because they do not discolor easily like ivory. Fortunately with the invention of porcelain enamel, the market for hippo tusks has dwindled. But he ban on elephant ivory in 1989 has caused a surge in the demand for hippo tusks. From 1988 to 1991, export of hippo ivory more than quintupled with the corresponding declined in their population. More than 50% drop was noted in Zaire from 1989 to 1994, from a population of 24,000 to 11,000 left. Local people kill the hippos for their low fat meat which they consider very delicious. The hide is cooked into soup which is also a delicacy in some parts of Africa. They are often shot by farmers for stealing grains and other food crops.

The total population of hippos in Africa in the wild is about 150,000, a quarter of that of the elephants. They are just as vulnerable as the elephants because of the loss of grazing land due to human encroachment. These huge mammoths need to eat at least 100 pounds of grass a day to survive.

They play an important role in the ecology of rivers where they dwell. Many of these rivers would be lifeless if not for the dung they produce. It forms the nutrient base of an aquatic food chain that begins with microscopic plants.

The pygmy hippopotamus (Choeropsis liberiensis) found in West Africa is under greater threat than their bigger cousin. These animals which spend most of their time on dry land is hunted for their meat by the local inhabitants. They are also losing their forest habitat due to the intrusion of the increasing human population. Only careful protection under nature reserves will help them survive in the long run.

KANGAROOS

Kangaroos and wallabies are marsupials of the same family with 56 species. They are plant-eating animals that live mainly in the grasslands of Australia, but some may also be found in deserts. They range in size from the rat kangaroos which is about 40 cm long to the largest grey kangaroos. The female kangaroo has a big pouch on the front of her body where her baby grows. The baby called joey born to them one at a time is about the size of a human thumb. It will travel to the pouch on its own and stay there for six months. The joey will continue to nourish until it is one year old.

They feed mainly on grass during the night while they rest during the day. Because of their huge numbers in the wild and the stiff competitions against the more favored grass-eating sheep, they are hunted in areas where sheep are found. At one time, nine sheep owners, within a span of one year, killed 140,000 kangaroos for intruding into the sheep grassland.

Every year two million kangaroos a/e killed in Australia. It is sanctioned by the government as a move to bring down their population to manageable level. Millions of dollars are earned selling their body parts in the international markets. Products such as seat covers, gloves, rugs and toys from their hair and skin bring enormous income to the dealers. Even kangaroo meats are being sold in the market as pet food.

Highway development throughout Australia have also taken its toll on the kangaroos. They often collide with speeding vehicles, killing and maiming them and the car passengers. Another serious problem encountered is the man-made chemicals that is causing widespread depletion of the ozone in the stratosphere in the Antarctic. This has made the ultraviolet ray (UV-B) a major cause of their immune dysfunction The compromised immune system has made some viruses the major cause of blindness in kangaroos in Australia.

One species that is found in the montane forest of New Guinea is the Goodfellow's tree kangaroo (*Dendrnlagus goodfellow*). This marsupial is fairly solitary, but the mother kangaroo and her offspring remain close together for more than a year until the joey is independent enough to separate from the mother. They are mostly arboreal, living on leaves and fruits and moving from tree to tree. Because of the disappearing rainforest and hunting by indigenous people, their numbers have been declining. Their population in the wild is unknown, and without an inventory and protection they may be on the brink of extinction without our knowledge.

KOALAS

The koala (Phascolarclos cinereus) is an Australian marsupial that is a favorite of many animal lovers because of its resemblance to the teddy bear. They are solitary animals, slow moving, and defenceless against predators. Koalas survive completely in an arboreal life on eucalyptus trees. They feed at night on the young leaves and buds while sleeping the whole day for as long as 22 hours a day The koala has a special diet that makes it difficult to rear in captivity. This is due to its inability to eat any other food except the eucalyptus leaves which it eats about 15 kg daily. It will eat only 30 species of eucalyptus out of the more than 600 species available.

One special feature of the pouch of koala is that it is upside down. Instead of having the opening at the top like the rest of the marsupial families, it is located at the bottom. This strange design has baffled biologists until now. The baby which at birth is less than an inch long and weighs 1/100 of an ounce will live within the pouch for seven to eight months.

Another unique feature is that the front feet claws has two thumbs and three fingers. This gives them a powerful grip that helps them live an arboreal life and free from most predators except forest fires which are common occurrences. On the hind foot the second and third toes are joined in a common skin.

Different species of koalas feed on different species of gum trees. Scientists have found that those living in the east coast of Australia feed on the spotted gum and tallow wood while those in Victoria feed on the red gum. At certain times the older leaves and some young leaves at the tip of the branches can release prussic acid, a deadly poison when chewed that could very well kill them.

Before the discovery of Australia by the Englishmen, they could be found in great abundance throughout eastern Australia, except in the coastal regions of Queensland. Numbering more than several millions at the turn of the century, they are now down to about 100,000 today Most of them died because epidemics that swept through their population. Another disease that causes infertility due to the bacterium called *Chlamydia psittaci* affects about 80% of the adult population. This is worrying conservationists because of the declining birth rate.

In spite of their declining numbers, it was a favorite pastime for many to shoot them in their habitat. It would take several shots to kill them and they would often cry like human babies that caused naturalists to condemn the sport. They were also hunted to near extinction for their furs. In 1908 nearly 58.000 koala pelts were sold in Sydney. By 1918, they were completely exterminated in South Central Australia. But the export continues to grow, it gradually increased to more than 200,000 in 1920-1921 and by 1924, more than two million pelts were exported. They are now placed under government protection in their natural habitats.

Koalas are susceptible to fungal infection that also attack humans. That is why cuddling koalas can be risky to them. Very few koalas can be found in the zoos because of the difficulties in keeping up with their diet.

Each koala like the human has a unique "fingerprint" in their hind foot that are different from one another. With this know ledge, the government of Australia has "fingerprinted" all the captive koalas to separate those found in the wild. Poachers who caught these cuddly animals in the wild will have difficulty exporting them without the fingerprint on file, since only captive koalas can be exported.

Like the problem encountered by many endangered species, it is the fragmentation or total loss of their habitats that is causing serious depletion of their numbers. In many areas, eucalyptus forests are being cut down to give way to housing developments and farm lands. Every year about 100,000 hectares of trees are cleared for development. The shrinking and fragmented forest could lead to inbreeding. The koalas are also forced to cross streets that often resulted in their being killed by motor vehicles. Of some 4,000 koalas killed annually, 2,500 died as a result of road accidents. The only remedy is to connect these fragmented areas with corridors, allowing them to travel from one area to another without being molested. NGOs are also working to stop new road developments that traverse their habitats.

In places where they were accorded protection as in some islands, they have proliferated. One of this is the Kangaroo Island. Australian wildlife officials have abandoned a plan to cull the overcrowded koalas after a strong public outcry. Instead they will undertake sterilization of male and female koalas, and relocate hundreds to the mainland in an effort to sustain their population without causing starvation in the future.

PANDAS

The panda (*Ailuropoda melanoleuca*) is rare, large, cuddly-looking, short-tailed black-and-white bearlike animal with a clownish face. They numbered about 1,000 in the world today. Less than a hundred are in zoos in China and another 18 in eight zoos around the world. Despite the world's concern and decades of international conservation works, the animal is still on the brink of extinction. They have been around for 3 million years, but habitat destruction and hunting in the last 2,000 years have reduced their population. Western scientists were unaware that they existed until the French priest, Pere David discovered them on one of his expeditions in 1869. Pandas became the targets for the big game hunters. Their rarity and unusual coats made them desirable targets for hunters. But despite the demand for skins, particularly by the world's museums, very few were killed. Pandas were able to hide in their thick, dense forests.

In 1936, nearly 30 giant pandas were slaughtered for the western collectors. Public appeal for live pandas soon forced the zoos to acquire them for exhibition.

Of the 14 pandas imported by the zoos before 1941, none live long enough to breed in captivity. It was even tested as a source of food by natives, fortunately, its meat was very tough. Today, they survive in 13 panda reserves covering 6,500 sq km in the province of Szechuan. China. They are confined to the bamboo forest, the main source of their food. China considers the panda a national treasure which they give to other countries as a special gesture of friendship.

In 1962 the export of panda skins was banned, but there are demands for ornamental rugs. Today pandas are trapped and often strangled in wire snares placed by poachers intended for other animals.

Pandas eat mostly two types of bamboos called arrow and umbrella bamboos. The arrow bamboo stands one to two meters tall and is found in the lower slope. Logging and farming have removed the umbrella bamboos. They also consume some plants and meat occasionally. Their teeth are especially well adapted to crushing the stems of bamboos. Because of their unique physiology, pandas can only survive where bamboos are plentiful. They have a single stomach and short digestive tract and often leaves and stems pass largely undigested. This can be a big problem for the pandas. They cat 20 to 40 pounds of bamboos a day and because of their thick-walled esophagus they are immune to sharp splinters. A die-off of bamboo in the mid-1970 starved more than 138 pandas in Wolong Natural Reserve leaving around only 145 pandas in 1974.

In May 1983 the arrow bamboo in this reserve mass-flowered and died. It was a year of global concern for pandas. An emergency was called and 4.000 people were mobilized to comb the remote and hard-hit mountains for starving pandas. Rehabilitating stations were erected throughout the reserves. Contribution is an important part of conservation. The WWF-Japan contributed 20 pick-up trucks to haul rescue teams and pandas to the rehabilitation center. In the U.S., children gave five million pennies for Pennies for Pandas Campaign. The Japanese donated $230,000.

In ancient times, when bamboos died in one area, the pandas were able to move somewhere else to find their food. But in recent years farmers have been taking more land for agriculture and gradually pushing the pandas higher up the mountain slopes. In times of food shortage, the pandas have nowhere to go except wait until they starve to death. But the Chinese government, in concert with the WWF, is implementing a ten-year program to increase their food supply. Fourteen new reserves are being set up at a cost of $80 million. Ten thousand loggers and farmers have been paid to move out of these reserves. To generate some of the funds, the pandas will be loaned out to zoos and parks worldwide.

This is not the only ordeal faced by pandas. Local residents and the government have cut down substantial areas of bamboo forests for use in agriculture and firewood. The government has built a power station to prevent the people from gathering bamboos as firewood. The only possible chance for survival is through the help of humans, but humans are often seen competing against them for the arable land for food production and firewood for fuel.

Lack of funds is a major problem that need to be tackled immediately. Researchers at the Qinling Reserve in Shaanzi Province are trying to raise money to relocate the reserve's 2,200 human residents, who have slowly encroached upon the bamboo forests. In Wolong Reserve, new houses have been built for 3,000 residents, but the residents refused to move out unless they are compensated for the loss of income from farming.

The race is on to find a substitute for bamboo. The captive pandas are given diets with rye grass originally from New Zealand II is an important breakthrough because rye grass could be grown alongside bamboo, in the mountains. It could resolve once and for all the bamboo problem So far, the pandas seem to like it.

The concern for the pandas have been manifested in many ways. Even under natural conditions, birth rate is low and infant mortality is high. Veterinarian, have resorted to artificial insemination to reproduce the endangered pandas. Because of the difficulty of breeding pandas in the wild, scientists are hoping to breed pandas from their healthy captives. One of the first baby panda born in captivity is Lan-Tian meaning Blue Sky given to one of the earliest visitors, HRH Prince Philip. Another visitor was the President of WWF. Sadly, she died in the spring of 1989. But today the thinking is different. Panda in zoos have been found to breed poorly. In Chinese zoos, only 2 or 3 cubs are born each year, while in other countries the situation is even worse. Cubs do not survive well in captivity.

As with many wild places where humans coexist, the mountain ranges of the pandas are being cut down for firewood and agriculture. In one of the largest panda reserve at Wolong, 14 sq kms of forests have been cut down by peasants in the last 10 years. The authorities are powerless to slop the destruction. The rate of destruction far outpace reforestation that conservationists believe that it will spell the extinction of the pandas in the wild.

Many mammals on the brink of extinction are largely due to their slow reproductive rate. This is also true with the pandas. The female pandas go on heat for only two days and mate only once a year. Unless done timely, it will be another year of waiting. If they should produce two cubs, only one often survive. Even artificial breeding has not been successful but it may be the only way to delay their extinction. Scientists expect the pandas to become extinct in 40 years, but may delay the process by sixty years with the use of artificial insemination. The success of cloning a sheep in Scotland by inserting genes from a six-year-old ewe into unfertilized eggs drew the attention of those trying to breed the pandas. Now there is a move to use cloning to produce pandas.

Poaching for its pelt is another principal cause of pandas' decline. Unfortunately, anti-poaching patrols are rarely seen as badly needed resources are used elsewhere. Pandas have also been killed by poachers' snares intended for other animals. It is the second biggest cause of panda deaths after habitat destruction. Although protected by law, poachers still hunt them primarily for its pelt Convicted poachers used to receive a 2-year sentence, but since 1987, poachers can be sentenced to death for killing panda Some gangs have already received life imprisonment while another four had received the death penalty. During 1987, 133 poachers have been arrested. Two Chinese seamen heading for Hong Kong with two panda skins were given suspended jail sentences and fined SI 1.000. The local price of panda skin has risen to as much as S20.000. In the race to save the panda they are being caught and fitted with a radio transmitter before releasing to the wild. The radio signals are checked every 15 minutes the whole day round. But the effectiveness of monitoring is useless if the panda had been killed.

Some shops in Thailand, Singapore, Hong Kong have back rooms in which the illegally acquired furs are kept. Some dealers claim they can supply panda skins on demand. Their beautiful skins are always in demand by wealthy collectors. In April 1988, China's Minister of Forestry revealed that 146 panda skins had been discovered in Sichuan Province. That is more than fifteen percent of the total world panda population.

The scarcity of panda means that their skins are very valuable. Their skins are smuggled out from China to traders in Hong Kong. They are then re-exported to Japan and Taiwan for sale. Rewards are high for both the Chinese poachers who risk arrest and imprisonment, and the dealers who may be caught by custom officials. Recently, a pair of panda skins was sold for $200,000. Tempted by the large sums of money, dealers have even offered live animals to private zoos.

Panda is one of the most sought after animal being exhibited in zoos around the world. Zoos around the world have been trying to get them for display and a chance to have them breed in captivity. It can be loaned out for a few months and fetched as much as $50,000 a month. Even circus shows find panda a great attraction. The Shanghai Acrobatic Theatre has a panda named Wei- Wei trained to entertain audience. Breeding and exhibiting do not seem to go together. Their low birth rate in captivity is proof the difficulty of breeding them in captivity when they are also used for exhibition.

PLATYPUS

Platypus (Ornithorhynchus anatinus) is one of only two egg-laying mammals. The other is the spiny anteater. It is a small semi-aquatic, nocturnal, sleek-furred with duck-billed animal found in Australia and Tasmania. Their hind leg is connected to venom glands that can be harmful but not fatal to humans. They are voracious caters, eating more than any other mammal in comparison to its weight. The platypus is a very unique mammal with mammary glands for feeding its young but lays eggs and incubates them. When it was first discovered in 1797, scientists refused to believe an animal with these characteristics exists. The first living platypus was exhibited in 1922 by the New York Zoological Park.

For many years the animals were hunted ruthlessly in Australia for their thick loose skin with dense woolly undercoat very much like the beaver. Many have died trapped in wire cages intended for fish. The introduction of rabbits has also caused the mammals to decline as the rabbits burrow their way into their breeding tunnels.

RHINOCEROS

Rhinoceros have been around for more than 60 million years, but not for long if no drastic measures is taken to protect them in the wild. They are popularly found in Africa as well in the jungles of Indonesia's Udjung Kulon National Park. There are about 50 Javan rhinos, one of the rarest animals in the world. Indonesia is also home of the rare Sumatran rhino, whose population is down to about 800.

They are also found throughout Thailand, Malaysia and Burma.

There are no more than 1,700 Indian or one-homed rhinos, restricted to a few reserves in India and Nepal. They were hunted by sport hunters in the 19th century. Combined with habitat destruction due to agricultural expansion, their numbers have dwindled drastically. Horn from the Indonesian rhinos is more highly regarded by pharmacists than those of the African species. As a result the price is attractive enough to make poaching in the dense jungle where they live worthwhile. Rhinoceros have been hunted for the horns for centuries. Today, the horns are worth more than their weight in gold, fetching as much as $50,000 for a pair of rhino horns in the Middle East. The other buyers are from Asia who use them as medicine.

Because of the highly organized anti-poaching patrols in India, poachers have developed new, silent and grisly methods of killing: electrocution and pitfalls. High voltage wires are strewn along the rhino's path. Once they came into contact with the wires, the animals are electrocuted silently to avoid detection from anti-poachers. On the other hand, pitfalls are lined with sharpened bamboo stakes dug along their routes. Not all animals died immediately, many have to suffer the slow and lingering torture before deaths overcome them. In the 1980s and early 1990s, 700 rhinos were killed for the horn market in India alone and one horn alone was valued at $149,000.

There are also the so-called white rhinos. They are actually grey-brown and they exist in two distinct races. The northern white rhinos number about 23, all living in the Garamba National Park, in Zaire. The more numerous southern white rhinos numbered about 5,000 and live in southern Africa.

The black rhino (*Diceros bicornis*) is one of the rarest animal in Africa. There are about 2,500 left in the whole of Africa compared to an estimated 2 to 3 million at the turn of the century.. EarthCorps workers have helped confirmed the continuing declined. Their reduced number was 65,000 in 1970, 20,000 of them in Kenya alone. Today there are just over 400 of them left in Kenya. Over 90% of them has been wiped out by poachers in less than 20 years. Unless they are well managed and protected, they will be extinct in the wild in less than a decade Special parks and reserves have been set up to protect the rhinos. Roving guards have been hired to protect the rhinos against poachers. In Kenya, surveillance teams make an average of two inventories every day. There is also a standing order of shoot to kill for people found inside the reserve at night. Trade in rhino horns has been banned internationally since the 1970s. But despite all these efforts rhinos are still being killed.

Some African nations have reneged in protecting the rhinos. There is a steady decline in the number of rhinoceros in Tanzania. According to the Tanzanian Rhino Conservation Project in Swara magazine, the rhinos in Ngorongoro crater have dwindled from 108 in the mid-'60s to 10 in 1996. Recently, government officials have confirmed what conservationists long suspected - that most of the rhino poachings in the past were done by the very people responsible for their protection. The low wages and low turnout of tourists have proven disastrous to the rhino population. After poachers killed another rhino last year (1996), authorities turned serious. With help from the Frankfurt Zoological Society, all the rangers were relieved and new equipments were brought to protect the remaining rhinos.

The rhinos from the rest of the country, primarily located in the five-million-hectare Selous National Park was estimated by IUCN at 3,130 black rhinos in 1984 and is down to 132 in 1994. The reason for the decline is that the park is so huge and limited rangers protecting the rhinos against poachers are spread so thinly over its vast territories. Obviously, if the government is serious about protecting the rhinos, they should be adequately protected or else move the rhinos to a smaller area where it can be managed properly.

Ten years ago, Zimbabwe had the largest population of black rhinos in Africa. Today, there are less than 300 of them. The precipitous decline was driven by poachers. All five species are killed for their horns as in all other species. With encouragement from EarthCorps, the Zimbabwe government four years ago set up four Intensive Protection Zones (IPZ) around the country. Each one is adjacent to the country's border, where poachers pose the greatest threat and can operate with impunity. To further save the rhinos against poachers, all the rhinos have been dehorned by the Department of National Parks and Wildlife Management, to remove the incentive for killing them. Many of the rhinos were fitted with radio collars that allow game scouts to track them continuously and which give off a different signal if the animal is killed. The radio collars can be used to study the rhino's behaviors. The area is patrolled by 65 game scouts with automatic rifles and ordered to shoot any unauthorized person carrying a weapon. In the past ten years, 178 poachers have been killed by scouts, while 7 rangers have been killed by poachers. Since the IPZs were set up in 1993, not a single rhino has been lost to poachers.

There are legislations forbidding the importation of rhino horns in places like Singapore and Thailand, yet it is not difficult to find these products in either of these countries. For the Arabs of North and South Yemen, the horns were made into handles for ceremonial daggers as a status symbol. The demand for the Indian rhino (Rhinoceros unicornis) horns is so high that it can fetch up to $62,000 a kilo compared to $ 12,000 for the black rhino's horn. Fortunately, the Yemini government had stopped the buying of rhino horns. Contrary to western belief, the horns of the rhinoceros are not being poached for its non-existence aphrodisiac, but are used as a febrifuge during difficult childbirth and other illnesses such as headaches, polio, lumbago and arthritis. They are bought in Myanmar, Japan, Korea, the two Chinas, and India. Taiwan has the largest market for horns, estimated at 360 kg annually. On May 29,1993, China became the last nation to legislate against domestic trade in rhino horn, but in July of the same year, undercover investigators claimed Chinese state officials had offered to sell them one ton of horn. Taiwan had banned the trade in Nov 1992, yet six months later, 19 out of 24 pharmacies offer rhino horns for sale. A recent survey revealed that 72% of pharmacies in Taiwan possessed rhino horns, despite a price tag of over $80,000 per kilogram and its use being illegal. Stricter penalties are required and tighter controls at the business end of the poaching operations. More financial support and skilled anti-poachers with high-powered guns are needed.

In the 1980s and early 1990s, the horn market has been responsible for the death of 700 rhinos. In 1996, 105 horns from poached white and black rhinos of

Africa, valued at more than $4.7 million were confiscated in London garages. One of the piece was valued at $149,000.

Fragmentation of the rhino populations has lead a number of scientists to suggest transplanting the animals to other areas to avoid inbreeding. They have estimated that mammals need at least a population of 2,000 to maintain a healthy gene pool for any species to avoid genetic bottleneck.

Despite much criticism from western doctors, the horn has been clinically shown to work against some diseases and for enhancing male sexual potency. Substitutes like the saiga antelope horn has also been found to be effective. Unfortunately, they are also threatened with extinction in many places.

Some conservationists are advocating farming the rhino horns for commercial use. Unlike the elephants, rhinos continue to grow their horns after they are cut, replacing them in as little as two years. If the rhinos were farmed and their horn sustainably harvested every two years and sold in Asia in a controlled system, the resulting income would dwarf all the money currently spent on conservation which is less than $1,000,000 worldwide. The amount of horn collected by the government dehorning program in Hwange National Park in 1991 was 360 kg. The potential income from farming rhino horns in Zimbabwe was $50 per hectare compared to cattle ranching at $5 per hectare. Namibia was the first nation to pioneer the dehorning program a few years back. It could be the key to saving the species, but some poachers are still killing these animals out of mistake or out of spite.

Zimbabwe has taken a more drastic step in saving the rhinos from extinction. It is exporting the animals, about 50 of them out of the country, to zoos and sanctuaries in Texas and Australia for safe keeping in captive breeding programs.

First Officer Paul McIntosh, a pilot for Cathay Pacific is the Asia-Pacific coordinator for the Lwewa Wildlife Conservancy (LWC), a Kenya-based nonprofit organization which aggressively supports the effort to avert the extinction of these giant creatures. The interest of one his passengers has recently led to an encouraging development - corporate sponsorship for the next rhino calf born at the conservancy.

Jerry Chamales, CEO of Omni Computer Products, was deeply moved by an article he read in Discovery about McIntosh's efforts to save the rhino. This lead to the creation of the Rhinotek brand of computers, a portion ofthe profit will be used to save the rhinos. The rhino has been chosen as the symbol for the new computers because of its ruggedness, strength and long life. Their joint promotional slogan is "Save the Rhino".

Other fund-raising events in Hong Kong include an annual Chinese New Year cocktail party held at The Ritz-Carlton Hotel, one of the LWC's major supporters in the region. It has also the support of many Hong Kong business communities.

Americans have always been at the forefront in saving endangered species. They have taken the initiative in many ventures, and ways to save their target species. One way is the annual sponsorship made by more than 50 zoo parks in cities across American of the spring bowl-a-thons aimed at raising more than $100,000 for the Ngare Sergoi sanctuary in Kenya, the haven for 25 black rhinos.

Most of the cost of the annual budget goes to security. Over 100 men are employed to protect the preserve's 22,260 hectares from the threat of poaching.

since the project was started in 1983 through the initiative of Englishwoman Anna Merz, not a single animal has been lost. Cathay Pacific is also training staff to identify CITES or IATA-certified endangered species when processing export cargo in Hong Kong. This will make it difficult for poachers to move endangered animals or their parts from one place to another.

Much has been said about the problems of the rhinoceros of Africa, out Asian species is in even worst strait. The Sumatran rhinoceros (Dicerorhinus sumatrrensis) is the smallest, hairiest, and rarest species in the world. The small numbers have been caused by the poaching of their horn for medical uses. They are also faced with the destruction of the forest due to the exploding population growth and transmigration problem. Their natural habitats are cut down to supply the lumbers for new housing development. The fragmentation of their habitats could easily cause inbreeding problems in the future.

The Indian rhinos, although under government protection continue to be endangered as poachers are have developed a new method of killing them One way is through electrocution where high-voltage wires are laid across their paths. Another gruesome old traditional way is setting pit traps lined with sharp bamboo stakes dug across their paths. If the idea is to poach for body parts, it could have been done on a more humane way. Since the rhinos are often in small group or even isolated, a more humane way would have been to tranquilized the animal, cut up its horn and release it.

WOLVES

Wolves are the largest members of the wild dog family. In earlier times, they are also found in almost all continents of the world. These intelligent and clever carnivores, hunt in packs animals that are even bigger than them. In the U.S. they even prey on bison, several times their size and weight. Wherever people intruded into their habitat, they are hunted, trapped, poisoned mercilessly as pest for killing livestock. The gray wolf (Canis lupus) or timber wolf has been killed in huge numbers. In many European countries, they have been hunted to extinction. In Great Britain, they were extinct in the 18th century, followed by some Western European countries. Only about 200 Iberian wolves (Canis lupus signatus) can be found in Portugal. In spite of their low numbers and protected status in 1989, they are still being hunted, poisoned, and their habitats destroyed. About 20 are killed annually. Captive breeding under the Iberian Wolf Recovery and Study Centre hopes to save them from extinction. Across the border in Spain, the wolves are faring better. The presence of more preying deer allows them to hunt in the wild instead of preying on livestock. There are already eight subspecies of wolves that are extinct.

Habitat destruction and overhunting reduced their population to extinction in the 1900s from the Northern Forest of Maine, New York, to Quebec. This leads to the increase in the populations of moose and deer that also cause problems to humans. Most of these problems involve motor vehicle accidents. Those survivals in North America were made possible by the huge wilderness available for them to roam and the supervening conservation movements that lead to their protection.

Today they can be found in only very few places.

With possibly fewer than 2,000 individuals left in the world, the Indian wolf is one of the world's most endangered carnivores, a victim of declining habitat and the wrath of pastoralists out to avenge supposedly wolf-killed livestock. In one of the animals' last stronghold, Yadvendradev Jhala hopes to develop a survival plan based on behavioural, genetic, and biological studies.

ZEBRA

The Grevy's zebra (Equus grevyi) of East Africa has been targeted by hunters because of its beautiful narrow-striped skin used in the fashion industry. They are the largest of the zebra family and are under threat due to the decimation of their population in the wild. Like all mammals, their natural habitats are being destroyed faster than the creation of nature reserves for their protection. Once found roaming in large numbers from Kenya to Ethiopia, they are now fragmented into three isolated areas and numbering only 15,000 today.

CHAPTER 5

WILD CATS

The wild cats are groups of meat-eating mammals which are highly adapted for killing and eating other animals. Forty million years of evolution had made them into one of the killing machines of modem times. All their physical characteristics of long sharp teeth, powerful jaws that can break bones with one bite, sharp an retractable claws, powerful leg muscles that can accelerate and run at high speed in short bursts make them the top predators wherever they are found.

Wild cats are found in all continents except in Australia and the Antarctica. They can be found in the desert to the rainforest and high in the snowy mountains of the world. Most of them live on ground level but some are well adapted living in trees such as the margay, marbled cat, and the clouded leopard.

Cats, whether the domestic or wild ones have always played an important role in the ecology of the planet. Being the top predators, they have been responsible for keeping the rodents and rats that are destroying our food production in check. This is one way of reducing the disease and pestilence brought by these pests.

They are divided into four groups with 37 species of them. One-third of them are under the threatened list while the rest are endangered. The big cats such as lions, leopard, tigers and jaguars are included in the genus *Panthera*. They catch their preys by stalking, leaping, and biting at the neck of the prey. Another characteristic is that they roar although the lion is often the sound we are familiar with. The largest cat can weigh up to 800 pounds like the Siberia tiger. Centuries of unhindered huntings have reduced the populations of many species. The thick and beautiful colors of their skins make all cats the targets of fur hunters. This has lead to extensive poachings in spite of restriction against hunting and protections afforded to these magnificent animals.

The second group is the cheetah which is considered a genus by itself as well as the clouded leopard. The fourth group are the domestic cats, as well as the cougar, ocelot, bobcat, and lynx. These animals have bony connections in their throats and cannot roar but can purr. Most of the wildcat skins come from this group where their fairly large numbers are now hunted in South America. All the Andean mountain cats, such as oncillas, pampas, and ocelots are being hunted for their beautiful marked furs that come in cryptically and mesmerizing patterns of colors, stripes, spots and rosettes. The restriction on hunting the decimated big cats from the wild have made these small wild cats the target of fur hunters.

BOBCATS

Bobcats (Lynx rugus) are medium-sized bobtailed cats inhabiting the southern parts of Canada down to Mexico. They are named for their short stumpy tail. These cats are highly intelligent, and can outsmart hound dogs used by hunters in tracking them down by backtracking over their scented trail without anybody the

Wiser. These fast and fearless cats will stand up against any predator and have been known to hunt prey much bigger than themselves.

Early settlers used to hunt these animals for their furs believing that it can cure wounds by using the fure in poultices. Today they are still hunted for their furs, especially the spotted belly fur. Although the soft fur is not very durable, it is used in making sport jackets and coat trimmings. Every year about 90,000 bobcat and lynx pelts are traded legally. Like all other wild cats, these animals are under tremendous pressures as their habitats are destroyed making them easy prey to hunters.

CARACALS

Caracals (Lynx caracal) are found throughout Africa, Middle East, much of Asia, and some undisturbed parts of Russia and Scandinavia. Taking advantage of their long legs, they often jump to swipe birds in flight. They also feed on rodents and small deer like their big cousins. Because they are expert hunters, they were trained for hunting in ancient Egypt, and by the royalties of India and Iran.

Strong and adaptable to many environments, they have survived in many places where others have become extinct. Although they are hunted for destroying livestock and poultry, still they were able to survive the persecutions.

CHEETAHS

Cheetahs (Acinonyx jubatus) have long association with man for as long as 4,000 years. They are the easiest of the big cats to tame. Ancient Egyptians and Assyrians had tamed them for hunting and made them a part of the household pets. Pictures of cheetah can be found in many Egyptian tombs. For hundreds of years, the Indian maharajahs used to train them to hunt. Kublai Khan (1216-1294) kept thousands of these cats in Mongolia for summer hunting. Akbar the Great (1542-1605) was credited with keeping 9,000 cheetahs during his reign in the 16th century. Even royalties of Europe used to keep them for pets. Charlemagne (742-814) and Haile Selassie (1892-1975) of Ethiopia kept them as pets. Not to be outdone, many movie stars in the U.S. used to have them as pets until the passage of the U.S. Endangered Species Act (ESA) in 1973 prohibiting keeping cheetahs as pets.

The cheetah is the fastest animal on land. A combination of keen senses and powerful muscles make it one of the most skilled hunters among the cats It is capable of running at 70 miles an hour at short burst. The cat is also fast racing toward extinction. Although cheetahs were widely distributed in Africa India and other parts of Asia, today they are found. Only in limited areas of eastern and southern Africa. They once numbered about 100.000 at the turn of the century but less than 15,000 exist throughout the world. They are especially choosy with their prey. The female prefers the Thomson's gazelle for its diet and need to follow the herd around the big range where they travel. Drought can also be a dangerous enemy for these cats.

Namibia has the largest cheetah population in the world. In the past 13 years, it has fallen by half to about 2,500 animals. About 700 are killed by every year. The Cheetah Conservation Fund, headed by husband-and–wife team of Danny and Laurie Marker-Kraus is working closely with local farmers to reverse their natural tendency to shoot the sleek cats, which they considered a killing their livestock. The biologists have discovered to their dismay that virtually all the farmers they interviewed had no idea of the cheetahs' worldwide plight. After learning of the problem, many farmers have opted to stop killing an ins help preserve the animals. Livestock guard-dog and other livestock protection programs have been setup to help keep the cheetahs away.

Another problem has to do with their low reproduction. Scientific research has been going on regarding the genetic diversity of cheetahs. Concerns have been voiced since the 1970s that they were not reproducing well in captivity. Researches into the reproductive physiology of captive and wild cheetahs revealed a large disproportion of sperm abnormalities in male cheetahs, a characteristic loosely associated with inbreeding. Some biologists theorized that the reason for the genetic bottleneck possibly could be climatic changes that destroyed 99% of the cat population in the wild until it loses much of its genetic variation.

The lack of genetic variation has resulted in offspring that are often born dead or infertile. Since they give births to two or three cubs once every two or three years, it is necessary to have as many strong and healthy cubs as possible. Inbreeding could make them susceptible to epidemics that could wipe them out completely. This is an important ground for not reducing their wild population or to try breeding them in confinement unless they are genetically varied.

Another problem that is reducing their population is encountered in the Tanzania's Serengeti National Park. The cheetahs are falling preys to predatory lions, jackals, hyenas and even birds of prey. Ninety to ninety-five percent of the cubs are killed within three months of their births. The rest are left behind by their mothers when local preys are scarce or when danger lurks. The domestic cats in the Serengeti National Park are also infecting the cheetahs with feline immunodeficiency virus that made them vulnerable to diseases much like the AIDS virus that afflict humans.

Captive breeding of cheetahs has not meet with success before 1960 when the first cheetah was born. The Indian princes of old days had failed in breeding cheetahs in captivity. Researchers may have found the reason. In the wild brother cheetahs in group court a female cheetah for days and over long distance. This may be needed to get the female to ovulate or become sexually receptive. Under captive breeding, they don't have the range allowing this elaborate courtship and privacy needed for them to breed.

There is hope as researchers learned to harvest good sperm from caged cheetahs in the American zoos. The Fossil Rim Wildlife Center near Dallas has breed 55 cubs in six years with five adult cheetahs since 1986. Other zoos in America had breed more than sixty-three cubs have been born since the program started in 1986. They made use of artificial insemination.

Wildlife Safari, an open air animal park in southern Oregon was established in 1972. One of its program has to do with studying the behavior of cheetahs and breeding them. From 1972 to 1989, 97 cubs have been born. The survival rate is much higher than the 50% accomplished in the wild. This is mainly due to the lack of predators such as lions and wild dogs. Plenty of food and prompt medical attention is giving the cubs a good chance to survive until adulthood.

In Asia, the cheetahs are well-protected in their natural habitat in Iran. Once common in north and west Africa, they have been hunted to extinction in Ethiopia and Somalia for their skins.

CLOUDED LEOPARDS

The clouded leopard (Neofelis neulosa) which is not a true leopard is also another rare animal found in India, Myanmar. Indochina, and the islands of Sumatra, Borneo, and Taiwan. This animal is also an excellent tree climber. It is so elusive that after 20 years of study, little is known about its habitat and behavior. In spite of their small weight, at 30 pounds, they are able to kill larger prey. It is especially equipped to kill mammals living in trees, even the larger orangutans of Sumatra. They are often hunted by subsistence farmers throughout Asian forests. One of the difficulty in breeding clouded leopard is the high incidence of the males killing the females during captive courtship. This makes them very vulnerable to extinction once their population in the wild is decimated.

COUGARS

They came in different names such as panther and catamount in the east and cougar, puma and mountain lion in the west. But they are not exactly lion that were once widely distributed in the New World. These graceful cats are known for their unearthly caterwauling. They may weigh as much as 200 pounds but are classified together with the smaller lynx and bobcat because of their similar body structures. As soon as the Europeans arrived in the U.S. and settled down to farm ranches and farmlands, the cougars were considered as vermins. Bounty hunting was offered for their demise. In California alone, from 1906 to 1963, with the bounty in place, 12,500 mountain lions were killed. The population started to decline rapidly in the early 1900s when logging devastated vast areas of their habitat east of the Mississippi, while their main source of prey, the white-tailed deer were hunted to near extinction. At present the eastern cougars are not covered under the ESA because they are considered extinct, although there may have been some unconfirmed sightings.

Hunting mountain lions is not a pretty sight to experience. They are tracked and chased by a pack of dogs fitted with radio transmitter in their collar and let lose to hunt. The cat will run until it is exhausted and forced up a tree to wait for its horrible fate, shot at point blank range by the bounty hunter. For the arranged commercial hunting, the cat is often kept at bay for a day or two before the client arrives to pull the trigger and claim his trophy.

Their declining population has forced individual states to pass laws protecting cougars. The western cougars are making a comeback in many western states. There are now about 4,000 to 6,000 of them in the wild. This is renewing the wilh many local communities as human population continue to expand encroach on their natural habitat.

Encroachment on their habitat is the number one threat to the cats. Considered dangerous to man, Florida enacted a law that gave bounty for killing them. By 1887, the bounty had reached $5 per cat, a large sum in those days. As more people migrated to Florida during the 1900s, their favorite wetland habitats were cleared and dredged for development, reducing further their habitats. As a result, many panthers died of starvation in the process of looking for new places and food supply. The declining food supply caused by the hunting of deer which is causing tick infestation of local cattle also lead to starvation of the panthers. Road developments have also been responsible for many accidental deaths, n ten year ending 1989, ten panthers were killed by vehicular accidents during nighttime while crossing the highways.

The Florida panther is a subspecies of cougar that once roamed throughout the southeastern U.S. Today there are only 30 to 50 of these animals living under protected areas in Florida. It is estimated that each panther need about 30,000 hectares with large number of preys to survive. Each cat eats about 35 to 50 deer-sized animals annually. With so much hunting going on, the panthers are finding it difficult to look for food.

Because of the dwindling number of panthers, the same problem encountered by cheetahs due to inbreeding is playing itself with the panthers. Not only do they have difficulty finding mates, many males are found to be less fertile than before. This could be due to pesticides and toxic chemicals that could have disrupted their reproductive system.

The race is on to save the panther from extinction. In 1976, the U.S. FWS formed the Panther Recovery Team. Two years later, the state legislature passed the Florida Panther Act, making it a crime to kill the cat. School children championed a campaign that made the panther a state animal in 1982. The Florida Dept. of Transportation spent millions of dollars to construct underpasses along Alligator Alley, a stretch of Interstate 75 from Fort Lauderdale to Naples, to allow panthers to cross the highway without getting accidentally killed. Fences funnel animals approaching the road into the underpasses. In 1989, the FWS created a 12,000-hectare Florida Panther National Wildlife Refuge as a protected habitat. New lands are being acquired to expand their territory. It will need at least 150,000 hectares or more to sustain them for years to come.

Teams of scientists have been recruited to study the natural behavior of the cats. They are tracked down and tagged with radio transmitter to allow year round observation. This will make it easier to locate the cats for regular vaccination against diseases. A breeding program was also set up in 1990.

GENETIC BOTTLENECK

One problem expected from the declining numbers of animals especially the mammals is the lack of genetic variations. As there are less animals of the same species available for breeding, it is prone to suffer from what scientists called "genetic bottleneck". Baby animals born through inbreeding often have problems with weakened immune and reproductive systems. It could be fatal should an epidemic strike the population. Abnormalities such as low sperm count can be found in many mammals. Offspring of these "abnormal" animals are often born dead or susceptible to diseases. Therefore it is important when breeding animals in captivity to make sure that when they mate, they are as distantly related as possible.

It has become common practice in zoos and wildlife parks for zookeepers to keep a record of all the parents and offspring of animals being bred under captivity. This information is used to coordinate all breeding plans between animals from different zoos and parks to assure their genetic variations. Called the Species Survival Plan (SSP), many animals under the endangered list have all these vital information.

In has been estimated by some biologists that wild animals confined to a limited space should number at least one thousand to reduce the possibility of inbreeding among the animals. Unlike captive breeding, there is no way to keep tract of their genetic variations or breeding mates that it is necessary to have a large population to reduce the risk.

Although the cheetah population is over 15.000 worldwide, careful breeding is necessary to avoid producing genetic disorder cubs. The genetic bottleneck probably occurred ten thousand years ago. when 99% of the cats were wiped out. The small core of cheetahs that survived with their limited stock genetic variations is the source of all future generations of cheetahs Inbreeding leads to smaller sperm count and 75% of their sperm is abnormal.

Because of the endangered status of many of these animals, their importation for exhibition alone has been completely banned. It is important to breed the animals in captivity such that there will always be animals available for display, study, research and for reintroduction into the wild should they become extinct.

Lions, though not endangered, are suffering from inbreeding in some of their habitats. This is causing alarm among biologists. A study made on the lions of Ngorongoro crater revealed that the lions suffer a significant loss of genetic diversity compared with those in the Serengeti. This loss is often associated with a higher degree of reproductive problems, including sperm abnormalities and impaired testicular function. The effect of close inbreeding are cumulative, and their long-term chances of survival are poor unless new blood can somehow be introduced to each population.

The loss of genetic diversity extends to almost all endangered and threatened species. Fragmentation of their habitats reduce the chances of diversified genes that is important for future generations. A small population will lose a large proportion of the genetic variations through genetic drift and inbreeding. Genetic drift is a natural consequence of sexual reproduction caused by random mixing of genes which wild animals do not have any control. Wherever human population caused the isolation of animals from their once contiguous jungle, the separated animals will have lower population and therefore chances of inbreeding will be higher. To combat this risky inbreeding, the South African conservation agencies used to transport wild animals to other faraway reserves.

GOLDEN CATS

There are two species of golden cats depending on the location of their natural habitats. The Asian golden cats (Felis temmincki) are found mostly in Southeast and mainland Asia. They have played an important role in some Asian mythologies. According to traditional Thailand's belief, owning a single stand of this cat's hair is enough to guard against tiger attack which used to roam the ancient land in large numbers. Burning the pelt of this cat will ensure the protection of the whole village while eating all the parts of the cat will ensure a person from all forms of animals attack.

The African golden cats (Felis aurata) are found mostly in West and Central Africa. They inhabit the tropical rain forests of Africa. Like all common wild cats, habitat destruction, persecutions as pest by farmers and hunting for their beautiful furs, are some of the human activities that are reducing their populations.

JAGUARS

The jaguars (Panthera onca) are the third largest cat family after the tigers and the lions. They are good swimmers and enjoy catching fish. They once roamed in abundance from North America down to rainforests of South America. They eat almost anything that move including the armadillo, peccary, deer, paca, tapir, caiman, crocodiles and human beings if other food is not available. They are also scavengers, eating dead carcasses and fish. Human population growth has been responsible for taking a large part of their habitats. Today they can be found only in patches of remaining habitats from South America to as far north as Mexico.

In ancient times, the jaguar is revered as the mysterious God of the Night, sacred ruler of the world. The Aztecs used them to predict omens of drought, war, death and poverty. Their respect for the powerful jaguar restricts the wearing of the jaguar skins to only the bravest warriors among them. The Yanomamo Indians of Valenzuela had their body painted like the spot of the jaguar in order to gain the strength of a warrior. In the Yacutan peninsula at Palengue, the Indians of Colombia respect for the jaguars led to the erection of the Temple of the Jaguar.

During the 1960s, jaguars were hunted so extensively for their furs that many of them were wiped out. Hunters mimic jaguar's guttural grunting to lure the feline within gunshot range. Even with the establishment of wildlife parks, many of them are still in peril because of lack of funds and personnel to guard against poachings. Like the other big cats, farmers are blaming and killing them for the destruction of domestic livestock. The blame should not be squarely on the cats as long as farmers allow their domestic animals to graze openly in the forest.

Another reason for the cats raiding domestic livestock is the fault of the farmers. The ranchers' practice of putting a bounty on jaguars caused more problems than it solved. Hunters using shotguns to hunt them often injured or crippled the cats without killing them. This led the injured animals to turn to livestock which are much easier prey than animals in the wild.

Their habitats in the Amazon basin is being destroyed with the construction of the Trans-Amazonian Highway and its tributaries. Transmigration has made conflict with people more pressing. Minings and oil exploration lead to the construction of airstrip and new road crisscrossing the Amazon basin. All these activities means only more clearing for human settlement and agriculture needed to sustain the new invaders. The accessible roads also enticed hunters and smugglers into the forest to hunt for exotic animals. In addition to the illegal trade of their skins, two of their favorite food, the turtle and the caiman are being killed for their meat, shell and skins. This is jeopardizing their food supply.

Since 1972, the jaguars have been listed as an endangered species under the ESA. They are also listed in the CITES Appendix I making it illegal to trade in jaguars or their body parts. In Nov 1990, the Cockscomb Basin Wildlife Sanctuary in Belize was established for their protection. This 25,000-hectarc reserve is the first one designated in the world. This is a small sanctuary compared to the wide range of habitats that they once roamed throughout South America. Each jaguar needs a home range of 150 to 200 sq km.

The Programme for Belize has bought and paid for 202,000 acres of forest, savannah and wetland in northwestern Belize known as the Rio Bravo Conservation and Management Area. An additional sanctuary of 26,890 acre tract of tropical forest would link together the two existing parcels into one continuous 228,890 acre property. This inestimable value in the ever-critical task of managing and protecting the whole of the Rio Bravo property. The project is supported in part by the Massachusetts Audubon Society. Contributions are welcome. Certificates of appreciation are available for each $50 per acre contribution for individuals or as gifts.

LEOPARDS

The common leopard (Panthera parlus) with 27 subspecies makes them the most widespread big wild cats in the world. This powerful spotted cat is found throughout Asia, Africa, Middle East and Siberia. Unlike the other big cats, the common leopards are expert tree climbers. They are often hunted by man because they kill livestock and even man. Each unique spotted skin is the most beautiful and highly prized by fashion lovers. The claws are made into necklaces by many African leaders including the Zulu king.

Probably the greatest vulnerability of the leopard is that it will not hesitate to eat rotting carrion. It will always return to the carcass even after it was chased away. Hunters take advantage of this weak point in the cat by lacing carcasses with poison. They are often caught in wire snares set to protect livestock along paths that they frequently traveled. Another problem has been the substitute of leopard bones used in place of tiger bones. The exploding human population of Africa is also accelerating the development of the countryside at the expense of the habitats of wild animals.

The Amur leopard, not to be confused with the snow leopard, are native to the forested mountains of Russia. There are less than 50 of them in the wild, making them vulnerable to inbreeding. Persecuted by humans for its skin and killed for destroying domestic animals because of the scarcity of preying deer is leading this predator toward extinction.

The black leopard, commonly known as the black panther are found mostly in the forest of southeast Asia. Their black fur also contains spots that can be seen at close up and under the bright light. They are suffering the same fate that awaits the other cats.

LIONS

The lions were once very common throughout Europe, Middle East, Africa, Asia, and even in Great Britain. They were hunted like pests to extinction in Europe as human population expanded centuries before recorded history. The last surviving lions of North Africa were destroyed within the last hundred years. Today, they are mostly confined in tropical Africa and a small area in the Gir Forest of India.

The Asian lions (Panthera leo persica) can only be found in a small region of the 560-sq-mi Gir Forest on the western India's Saurashtra peninsula in the state of Gujarat. At last count there are about 250 lions under protection. Their decline started in the 19th century mostly due to hunting by British Army officers on horseback. By 1888 the last lion outside the Gir Forest had been shot. The Newab rulers in India's Gujarat state who decreed in 1890 to protect the lions from killing probably saved them from extinction.

In 1947 the Gir forest was declared a reserve and later a wildlife sanctuary in 1975. At the same time, the Gir Lion Sanctuary Project was launched partly to keep cattle out of the sanctuary with the erection of a 400 km of wall one meter high presumably to remove any untoward incident against the local inhabitants.

As with many sanctuaries around the world populated with local inhabitants for centuries, it is almost impossible to change their livelihood. Agriculture, firewood gathering, timber harvesting, and cattle grazing within the sanctuary are allowed. This results in the destruction of their habitat despite its status as a wildlife sanctuary. Lack of wild preys lead the hungry lions to kill cattle. Fortunately, the local inhabitants are compensated by the government for these killings. But more often than not, the lions are chased away after each killing and the poor natives steal the food.

The small number of Asian lions could easily be wiped out in case of disease or natural catastrophe and possibly jeopardized by inbreeding. Biologists are taking steps to introduce some of the animals to the 1,200-sq-mi Kuno Forest Because of the small population of deer for the preying lions, it is necessary to stock the forest with preying animals in order that the lions will survive instead of taking on the livestock of farmers. This could lead to their demise as farmers will hunt them down as pests.

The African lions (Panthera leo) in the wild are easy prey for hunters because they inhabit the open country in groups called pride and their sporadic roars give their location away. This makes it necessary to protect their habitat against poachers, their number one enemy. Since the 1920's they have become endangered species as big game hunters with high-powered rifles were shooting them for "trophy heads" in large numbers. Local tribesmen have also hunted lions for centuries to prove their manhood. Their tribal rulers wear lion skins to show their regal status.

As the human population increases, people are forced to disperse into the countryside. Farmers moving into new territories forced out the lions from their old habitats. The extinction of the Berber or Barbary (Panthera leo leo) and the Cape black-maned (Panthera leo melanochaitus) lions finally forced the government to take actions to protect the rest of the species.

Their appetite for domestic animals and threat to humans have virtually confined them to less than a dozen protected parks and reserves. In the Serengeti National Park, established in 1929, there are as many as 3,000 lions in the 2,330-sq-km habitat that was later expanded to 12,950 sq km. They can also be found in Kruger National Park in South Africa and the Selous in Tanzania.

Male lions are very territorial in their domain. Once they are vanquished by another male lion, the male youngs are often ousted from the pride, while the cubs are killed by the new king of the jungle. This will bring the females into estrus earlier and ensured the new males's genetic legacy. The youngs that left the pride are often forced to hunt for livestock instead of wild animals because they are still unskilled to hunt. This has caused farmers to hunt and kill them. In conjunction, hunters are helping in eliminating young cubs by hunting big male cats for their trophy. Without the father lions, other males will take over and kill the offspring.

Pastoralists do not welcome young lions and try to kill them with carcasses laced with insecticides or other poisons. This tactic was tried out in Amboseli in the early 1990s, that wiped out the entire lion population.

Canine distemper has also been responsible for over one-third of the death of lions in the Serengeti National Park. Tanzania in 1994, Vaccinations of dogs are being carried out to protect the future of the lions. Another disease is brought by the biting fly (Stomoxys calcitrans) that plagued the lions of Ngorongoro Conservation Area. In 1962, only ten lions were left from a population of 70 as they were emaciated and covered with festering sores after the epidemic ends. The decimation ofthe population is currently causing inbreeding problem.

LYNXES

As with all wild cats and fur-bearing animals, the three species of lynxes have been trapped for their furs and the encroachment of humans into their habitats have reduced many to the brink of extinction. The North American lynx (Lynx canadensis) is one ofthe three largest cats in the continent. It is about the size of the bobcat, only taller and had thicker fur, but not as fearless and aggressive. In many of the natural habitat where they used to be found together, they are often driven away by the more aggressive bobcats. It is endowed with very keen eyesight and can spot rabbit a thousand feet away.

In the U. S. about a thousand lynxes are known to inhabit the forest, but the FWS refuses to list them as an endangered species worthy of protection. The cats which used to be found in 12 states from the Alaskan wilderness to the Colorado Rockies and from the Canadian border down to New England are now confined to the old-growth in Washington, Montana, and Maine.

When the northern spotted owls were given a reprieve from the banned logging of the large old growth tracts in the northwest, loggers are moving into the lynx's territory. The U. S. Forest Service planned to log 1,000 acres of forest in the heartland of one of the lynx strong hold in Washington's Okanogan National Forest and another 10,000 acres in Loomis Forest, also in Washington State.

A very peculiar characteristic not found among wild cats is that they would only feed on their favorite food, the snowshoe hare. They would rather starve to death than search for other food. The absence of food often lead to the starvation of the young first, and refusal of the adults to breed for future generations. These double threats could spell their doom m the wild.

Human encroaching on their natural habitat is bringing more hunters deep into the wilderness. Roads had been built making it easier for hunters using vehicles and snowmobiles to set traps in their important habitat.

At present there are two plans being developed to save the lynxes from extinction. One way is to reintroduced the wild cats with two dozen lynx cats imported from the Yukon to their old habitat in the Adirondacks. Another plan advocated by environmentalists is to set aside an area around Okanogan County as a wildlife sanctuary for the remaining lynx populations found there.

The Eurasian lynx (Lynx lynx) is the largest of the lynx family. They can be found in the Scandinavian countries, Russia, the Middle East and have been reintroduced to Western Europe. In Siberia, they are losing ground because of the development projects that are expanding toward their habitats. Hunters in Eastern Europe are killing them for their skins while farmers are destroying them in revenge for the killing of their sheep. In Western Europe, the lynxes are faring better after their reintroduction as some governments have banned their slaughter.

Of the three lynx families, the Spanish lynx (Lynx pardinus) is the most endangered. There are about 100 left in their wild habitats in Spain and Portugal. They were hunted to extinction in many parts of Europe. The Spanish government created the Coto Donana National Park in southwestern Spain to serve as habitat for the lynx and other migratory birds. The 50,000-hectarc served as a good hunting and breeding grounds for the lynxes because of the millions of birds, fowls, ducks, low-flying birds, and rabbits that inhabit part of the wetlands. Their small number will not put a dent on the populations of the birds.

OCELOTS

Ocelots (Felis pardalis) are the most sought after of the South American cats because the fur coat made from their skins that is currently fetching up to $40,000 apiece. They are now under severe pressure from the hunters as their population in the wild are declining rapidly. The ocelots live in the dense forests and feed on rodents, lizard, opossums, and even birds. Another reason is that they reproduce very slowly. In the wild, they start to reproduce when they are two years old and give birth to only one kitten every two years. Compared to a similar sized bobcat which can start breeding after one year with two or three kittens each year, or 30 young in their lifetime compared to five or six for the ocelot. The margay (Felis WMM) and the oncilla (Felis ligrina) or little spotted cat. are closely related to the ocelot and their problems are beginning to be felt as the ocelots are decimated in the wild.

Like all the wild cats of South America, the main reason for their decline is the construction of the Trans-Amazonia Highway and its feeder roads leading deep into the jungle. This made it possible for hunters to travel into the jungle quickly and safely and bring out their preys, dead or alive more efficiently.

The long-haired pampas cats (Felis colocolo) are also hunted for their beautiful coat, which comes in different colors and shades. Occasionally, the tiny kodkod of southern Chile and Argentina and the high-altitude Andean mountain cats are also hunted for their skins.

SERVALS

These beautiful golden fur with black dots servals (Felis servat) are found only in Africa. There are also completely black servals. These cats have long legs and enormous ears that are very keen and helped them enormously in hunting. The golden cats are often hunted for their furs which poachers passed off as leopard or cheetah skins which can command a higher price. Some local tribesmen hunted the servals for food, which they considered a delicacy while other use the fur to make cloak.

Like all cats in Africa that are not protected under wildlife sanctuaries, these animals are being killed for. preying on livestock and has taken its toll on the animals. Other causes of their decline are deforestation and development of agriculture.

SNOW LEOPARDS

The rare and beautiful snow leopard (Paniheria uncia) is one of the most elusive and yet one of the most endangered of the large cats. This first photograph of this elusive animal in the wild was taken by the zoologist George Schallar in 1970. Their thick fur and other physical attributes are well adapted for life high in the rugged mountain reaching up to 20.000 feet. They are found mostly in alpine and subalpine Central Asia. Their numbers in the wild are difficult to estimate because their brown and white skin easily blend with the environment. However, there are probably less than a thousand in the wild. While the snow leopard manages to keep largely out of sight in its Himalayan stronghold, its habitat is being encroached by development, cattlc grazing, firewood gathering and agriculture.

Snow leopards prey on wild sheep, musk deer. ibex, tapir, marmot, wild boars and goats. These diminishing animals are depicted by hunters and local inhabitants forcing the cats to turned to domestic livestock. In retaliation, herders kill the snow leopard and sell their highly prized fur in the tourist markets. A fur coat can command as much as $30,000 in the western black market. Also, the protection accorded the tigers has forced poachers to turn to snow leopard for their body parts and skins as substituted for tiger parts as Asian traditional pharmaceuticals.

Since 1981 the International Snow Leopard Trust, founded by Helen Freeman in Seattle has help saved these endangered cats through research into their hunting and feeding behaviors, public education and the establishment of an international conservation efforts among the twelve nations where the snow leopards inhabit.

TIGERS

There are eight different Asian tigers based on the location of their habitats. These are the South Chinese, Indian or Bengal, Indo-Chinese, Caspian, Sumatran, Javan and Balinese. The Caspian and Balinese species has become extinct while the Chinese and Javan tigers (Panthera tigns sondaica) have been reduced to just a few survivors. Fifty years ago, there were more than 100,000 tigers altogether. Today there are about 5,000 to 7,000, depending on who is doing the counting, left in the wild with two-thirds of them in India. They were at one time very common throughout much of Asia, living in many different habitats from tropical forests to semi-arid desert to as high as 20.000 feet above sea level. Because of their vicious reputations, beautiful skins, and medical value of their bones and other body parts, they were hunted, trapped and poisoned.

Tigers are the largest members of the cat family. Their dwindling numbers have been due to sport hunting and illegal poaching for their skin and other body parts. Some are even poisoned by farmers for raiding farm animals. While there are special laws protecting them and special reserves set aside for them, it was no guarantee of their safety since illegal poaching still abound.

India's Bengal tigers (Panthera tigris tigris) were once hunted to the brink of extinction. They once numbered 40.000 at the beginning of this century and dropped to no more than 1.800 in the early 1970s due to sport huntings made by the maharajahs and their guests. The British together with their hosts are the first persecutors of the tigers. The tigers then were treated as demons and killing them was considered a great service to mankind. To prove their manhood, the maharajahs together with their guests mounted huge elephants on a tiger hunt. When King George V (1865-1936) visited India upon the invitation of the Indian Emperor in 1911, he and his entourage went hunting while mounted at the back of elephants in comparative safety. Drum beaters were used to drive the tigers toward them for the kill. Many British "sportsmen" followed his footstep by making trips to India for tiger hunting. Some tried to make the distinction reputation of killing a hundred tigers.

Not to be outdone, some royalty Indians also made it a point to kill as many tigers as possible. The Maharajah of Surguja boasted that he killed a total of 1, 150 tigers during his lifetime. He was later dethroned and sent to an asylum for the insane. When he was removed in 1950, his regency government took over and continued the insane killing of tigers. Even Prince Philip, together with his party were able to kill two tigers after visiting India in 1961. Other wealthy Americans, Japanese, Germans and the princes of the oil-rich countries of the Middle East joined the safaris to kill tigers before they became extinct.

The Indian government, especially with the active participation of then Prime Minister Indira Gandhi (1917-1984). and with the assistance of WWF acted quickly and declared the great cat a protected species. One of the reserve created by the government is the Ranthambhore, the smallest of the tiger reserves. In 1973, when the reserve was created, there were only 14 tigers left in the wild. Today, the Project Tiger, as it is known, has more than 40 tigers in an area of 392 sq km. Other reserves were set up throughout the regions where tigers existed. In India alone, there are 17 tiger reserves covering a total area of 30,000 sq km.

The large number of tigers can be found in the tidal mangrove forests of Bangladesh and in Sunderbans, India. The muddy tidal landscape made development in these places difficult. With the creation of more national parks in Nepal and India in the 1970s and 1980s by politicians and heads of state and the relocation of entire villages, prey populations rebound and the tiger numbers soared. Since then the tiger population has risen to about 5,000 tiger in the wild. But poachers are still at work. Tiger poaching in India is penalized by a minimum of six month imprisonment. This should be increased to strengthen the law against poaching. Life imprisonment or a twenty years imprisonment at least will lead to more compliance.

Tigers outside of the reserves, numbering about 3,000 are not protected and may be wiped out in a few years. The tigers in Myanmar, Laos, Cambodia, Thailand, and China did not fare as well. Lack of political support was partly responsible. Trapping the tiger's prey could also be responsible for the declining population. Without any prey, the tigers have nothing to eat. The decimation of their prey are forcing many tigers to invade small towns in search of food. The contact with their greatest enemy, the human predators, prove no match for the tigers.

Siberian tigers (Panthera tirgris altaica) have increased their population after the hunting ban was enforced during the 1980s. By 1991, the numbers of Siberian tigers increased to more than 400 in 1991. This is because of the protection accorded by the authoritarian communist regime. But the collapse of the Soviet Union brought widespread poaching of tigers and their preys. Each tiger can fetch as much as ten years of labor for a person. In 1992 alone, 50 Siberian tigers were killed in Russia alone. This led Vladimir Shetinin, head of the anti-poaching brigade, to estimate that the Siberian tigers, mostly confined in Primorye Province, may have lost 40% of its population between 1990 and 1994. The decline is continuing due to new cases of habitat destructions lead by the multinationals.

The Russian move to improve the living standards and pay off some of their huge debts to the international financial institutions has contracted out vast areas of their forested lands to exploitation. These areas ceded to multinationals are the same habitats presently occupied by the Siberian tigers. Korea's Hyundai Corporation and other Japanese companies have contracts to develop the land. Mining and clearing the forest are removing at the rate of 2.5 million hectares annually. The natural resources are sold at bargain prices.

In Manchuria the tigers numbered less than 300 in the wild, most of them belonging to the Siberian species. And their populations are increasing thanks to a certain Mr. Wong. Since 1988 he had bred 54 tiger cubs from caged tigers. By using goats as nanny to the cubs, he was able to allow the tigers to breed earlier than possible.

The Chinese tigers were almost decimated during the Mao Zedong (1893-1976) era. There were wholesale slaughter of tigers during the 1960s and 1970s when the Chinese government decided to establish a huge program to maximize land use for agriculture. Their habitats were destroyed and the tigers were considered as pests to be systematically hunted and killed. From a high of 3,000 a few decades back, they are now reduced to about 50 today and may be on its way to extinction. Not to be outdone, the Soviet army was sent in to help the farmers exterminate the Caspian tigers (Panthera tigris virgata). By 1967, the last Caspian tiger was killed.

Poaching of tigers is not so much for the highly regulated skin trade which can fetch $15,000 apiece but more so for the use of body parts in traditional Chinese medicine. Consumers are not confined to the elite but also the ordinary people who have been following traditions for more than 2,000 years. China, Korea, and Taiwan see traditional medicine as an Asian issue and oppose any move to legislate morality and health-care choices. It is not something that public pressure and a good campaign could easily stop. According to the Wildlife Conservation magazine, China has started to breed tigers in ranches to meet the demand for tiger bones. The bones are used for treating problems from arthritis to ulcer and toothache. In Taiwan, the penises of tigers are cooked into soup and served as an aphrodisiac as a cost of $300 a bowl. However, there are moves especially in Taiwan to find an effective substitute for the tiger bone. But not when the substitute is the snow leopard which is even more endangered than the tigers. Despite the endangered status of these animals, until the middle of 1993, South Korea brazenly imported tiger parts. Both Koreas have longed decimated their tiger population.

Despite the difficulties of changing the tradition of other countries, serious efforts taken by countries with tigers can make a dent on poaching. Well-paid, uniformed guards with a fleet of new vehicles and firearms could virtually end tiger poaching anywhere they are based. But political will, money and international pressure must be put to bear on them.

CHAPTER 6

SEA MAMMALS

The ocean is home to at least 160.000 known marine animal species. Its huge size, covering 71% of the earth with a volume of about 1.4 billion cubic kilometers of water is home to countless billions of sea creatures. Animals eat plants and other animals and are themselves eaten by larger animals. The various species that lies within the oceans are functioned as a cohesive unit that keep the ocean ecology in balance. There is an endless cycle of life going on in the ocean. The ocean has served mankind well since humans learned to hunt the bountiful sea for their food. But we have failed miserably not only in protecting their habitat, but have hunted a few species under very destructive ways that make sustainable use of ocean products unreliable in the future.

The ocean is an ideal place for all aquatic plants and animals. It allows light to penetrate for plants to grow through photosynthesis. There is also an abundance of food for mammals and other sea organisms to grow. The ocean contains vital chemicals and compounds necessary for life to survive for long and its high density enables large mammals to float and survive the harsh environment.

Different mammals have different behavior that we need to respect. Many are quite intelligent and behave like some people. Just as people do not want to be disturbed in their own home, so do mammals. As more people come in contact with mammals, the U.S. Congress passed the Marine Mammal Protection Act (MMPA) of 1972. One of its provisions states that it is illegal to affect the behavior of marine mammals in any way, and lawbreakers can be charged a $10,000 fine. The MMPA dictates that people are required to stay at least 100 yards away from marine animals.

More often than not, it is almost impossible to keep away from the mammals. It is necessary to learn how to interact with them in an ethical and sensible way without causing undue alarm. Education is a necessary part for those who wish to get as close to the mammals as possible. The best way to approach sea lions, dolphins or whales is to go slowly, keep your hands behind your back in an threat-free manner and be patient. Guidebooks and guidelines are available from tour operators.

Sea mammals have also provided us an opportunity to appreciate their intelligence as researchers learn about their behavior. Whale watching has become one of the main tourist attractions in many parts of the world. Whales and other mammals have been trained in captivity for the enjoyment of the public. Some mammals like the dolphins have also saved people in troubled waters.

DOLPHINS

Dolphins are aquatic mammals belonging to the whale family. There are about 37 species found in the seas and oceans of the world. Some can also be found in the large rivers and estuaries. The freshwater dolphins are found in Asia and South America. Dolphins are one of the most intelligent mammals in the world. They can be trained to do many things that are perilous for man and perform acts at marine shows to the delight of the spectators. The most familiar and loved dolphins are the common dolphins (Delphinus delphis), the bottle-nosed dolphins (Tursiops truncal us), and the Pacific white-sided dolphins (Lagerorhynchus obhquidens) commonly seen in California's aquariums.

Researches have shown that dolphins have the ability to communicate by means of a wide range of underwater sounds and pulses that include mating calls, warning of possible dangers, and recognition signals. They can even imitate human speech if only we can understand them. The variety of chirps, squeaks, rattles and other ultra-sounds with frequency of 200.000 vibrations per second are made with the larynx and maybe the melon located at the head. These echo location sounds enable the dolphins to locate objects even if blindfolded. They are able to find the objects in front of them.

The plight of the dolphins in relation to tuna fishing first came into public attention in 1987 when Samuel LaBudde. an American biologist, disguised as a cook on a Panamanian tuna boat was able to secretly film how the yellowfin tuna fishes were caught using dolphins as bait. Huge purse seine nets were set along the path of the common or two species of spotted dolphins because the tuna often swims underneath a school of dolphins. The dolphins are known to help tuna escape the purse seine nets, but still more than seven million dolphins have been drowned or crushed by power blocks as a result of this type of fishing in the last 35 years.

In the small island of Iki, Japan, fishermen routinely kill dolphins on the suspicion that they are responsible for scaring away yellowtail fishes. On February 23, 1978, a fisherman discovered a dolphin following a shoal of yellowtail fish in the water of Tsushina Strait and concluded that the dolphin was responsible for their low turnout. He harpooned a dolphin and the other dolphins came out to help. The fisherman raised the alarm and more than 100 fishing boats closed in on the dolphins and started to drive them toward Iki Island, just off the northern Kyushu. Subsequent slaughters were conducted with military precision. The dolphins were rounded up and forced into a small bay. Once inside the bay, the mouth of the bay was closed with nets to deter any from escaping. The following day as many as one thousand fishermen were on hand with all kinds of weapons to club them to death. Some of the dolphins were even shedding tears, but the fishermen were untouched and continued with the vicious killing of these animals.

A Hawaiian environmentalist, Dexter Cate was astonished with one of these brutal killings of hundreds of dolphins trapped by fishermen in February 1980. He was arrested for freeing 250 dolphins awaiting to be slaughtered. International pressure was brought to bear on his imprisonment and the plight of the dolphins. Because of his action, the merciless slaughter of dolphins ended and he was freed after a few months.

The river dolphins (Lipotes vexillifer) in China are in danger of extinction fewer than 100 are left in their habitat in the Yangtze River of China. They are being destroyed slowly by the noise, pollution, traffic and illegal fishing going on around their habitat. Last January 1996. a female dolphin died of accidental electrocution during an illegal fishing operation.

After the collapse of the anchovy industry in Peru, fishermen were forced to hunt for other sea mammals. The common dolphins and the Burmeister's porpoises were hunted by gill nets, harpoons, purse seines, and in some cases the use of dynamites. The dolphins' meat sold in the market soon found a ready market for diners. This motivated the fishermen to catch the dolphins deliberately. It is estimated that 1,800 husky dolphins are killed annually. Even with the ban passed by government, implementation is not enforced and the illicit fishing continues unabated. The Turks kill more than 100,000 dolphins every year for food.

Volunteers from the EarthCorps working with researcher Wang Ding are trying to rescue the animals from extinction. They are examining two oxbow lakes as a potential sanctuary for the dolphins. The plight of the dolphins spurred China's Fisheries Bureau to host a seminar to strengthen dolphin protection strategies. They have decided to move the dolphins to one of the two sanctuaries. Shishou Baiji Semi-natural Reserve, where the EarthCorps volunteers have worked before. The Fisheries Bureau will oversee the operation to capture and transfer the mammals with full support of the local government.

Diseases often strike when least expected. In 1987-88, bottlenose dolphins from New Jersey down to Florida were dying from an unknown disease that compromised their immune system. Seven hundred dolphins, comprising more than half of its local population wcre found dead. Between 1990 and 1993, more than a thousand striped dolphins were found dead along the shores of the Mediterranean Sea. The same compromised immune system possibly caused by PCBs and other synthetic chemicals may be responsible. Immunological studies of dolphins have found that the immune response dropped as levels of PCBs and DDT increased in their blood. The reproductive system is likewise vulnerable to damage from hormone-disrupting chemicals during parental development and lactating period. The distemper virus could also be an agent.

MANATEES

In the centuries since Christopher Columbus (1451-1506) spotted the first sea cow, manatees have been hunted as a popular food delicacy like their extinct relatives, the Steller's sea cows. Prized for their rich meat and fat that tasted like "sweet almond oil," manatees have been killed by the thousands in the Americas - first by hunters and then by powerboats and other human related activities.

The manatees are also closely related to the threatened dugongs (see Philippine Wildlife). Today, there are no more than 1,500 of them left in the coast of Florida and 3,000 in the world. Around 150 were killed in 1989, 206 in 1990 mostly as a result of collisions with tourist ships and speed boats. In 1991, at least 174 died in Florida, 53 of them due to injuries caused by boats. Although there are laws protecting the manatees such as penalty for boat owners colliding with them, it is difficult to enforce. With more than 8,400 miles of coastline to protect, only 400 officers are assigned. Because of their size and slow movement, they often find themselves on collision course with these fast moving vessels. In 1996, an estimated 415 died prematurely, most of them died from the red tide menace.

Divers and photographers who visit the marinas to interact with these animals are disturbing their habitat unknowingly. The slow reproductive rate and increasing mortality and injury rate could make them extinct in less than a decade. As if all these problems are not enough, they are under new threat caused by a papillomavirus virus that caused skin lesions in two captive manatees. It can interfere with the eyes, nose and genitals of the mammals. A similar virus was responsible for the skin lesion of Keiko, the killer whale featured in the movie "Free Willy." A toxic bloom of red tide killed 151 manatees in Florida in the spring of 1996. It was the largest number of death at one place and one time.

At present the greatest form of protection is to declare their habitats off limit to all tourists and boatings to protect them against collisions and disturbances. So far the only concrete step taken was the new speed zones that went into effect in 1992. Boats near their habitat have been limited in speed and for hundreds of miles around. There is not much to expect if you consider that the boats outnumbered the manatees 500 to 1.

Researchers are studying ways to save the manatees from collision with boats. One manatee in Florida collided with boats at least twelve times. The problem may lie with their hearing. The study involved determining their hearing range, the effect of background noise, and whether they can determine the direction of the noise. Once all these problems can be determined, it might be possible to modify the sounds that boats make to help them avoid these boats.

Many programs have been set up to save the manatees. Some manatees are being fitted with transmitter and monitored by satellite to determine their habitat requirement and behavior. Human activities are banned in some areas where they frequent. Most important of all is the care given to the injured animals. The Lowry Park Zoo, Mote Marine Laboratory, and the FWS are making efforts to rehabilitate injured and sick manatees while monitoring their conditions even after they are released. In 1989, the State of Florida established the Save the Manatee Trust Fund, where voluntary funding can be made through the purchase of special manatee license plates.

MARINE SANCTUARIES

Unless sanctuaries are reserved for the marine animals like what had been done for terrestrial animals, there is no way the marine mammals will find safety anywhere in this world. Sanctuaries designed to protect habitats for marine life must be free from human activities such as oil drilling, dredging, waste dumping, treasure hunting, and restriction on shipping and fishing. Hundreds of ocean and marine sanctuaries have been set up throughout the world. It is still a small area compared to the vast number of species under the threat of extinction.

In July 1994, a 3,139-sq-mi area off the Olympic Peninsula of Washington State was dedicated as the 12th national marine sanctuary. It was eagerly celebrated by scientists and environmentalists alike. The sanctuaries will provide a haven for marine biologists to study the mammals. Although only 12 sanctuaries have been established by the U.S. Congress since 1972, more are expected as funds become available. However, there are always entreprenuers who cam their living from the resources found in the sanctuaries such as oil and gas developers, and treasurers hunters who will fight to exploit these potential sanctuaries.

OTTERS

There are two species of otters, the sea otter of the genus Enhydra, found in the waters of North Pacific Ocean and the common otter distributed widely throughout the world. Both species belong lo the weasel family of Muslelidae. The former is a sturdy, thickset animal that uses its front feet to hold rock for pounding shellfish. It spends almost its entire life offshore in the floating kelp beds of the Pacific Ocean. Cubs born are nursed by the mother otter which floats on her back while the cubs rest, sleep and is breastfed.

Otters are very intelligent mammals. They are often seen in marine shows. The Eurasian otter (Lulra lutrd) has been successfully domesticated and at one time trained to catch fish in Sweden. In India, the otters are trained to chase fish to nets set by fishermen. But more often they are killed for their furs or treated as pests by fishermen. Sea otters of Europe are the largest carnivorous mammals which have been hunted for centuries for fur and as a sport by English royalties. Because of their voracious appetite for fishes and shellfishes, they are often treated as pests to be exterminated. In the 16th century the English officially designated them as pests thought to be harmful to fishes and other sea creatures eaten by people. A breed of dog known as otterhound was trained to hunt them down. They have been hunted to near extinction until the 20th century when laws banning their killing came into force. In England, this came as late as 1978. In Neatherland, hunting and trapping almost decimated their population in the 1940s until it was reversed by a ban. Even then, hunting for their furs continue illegally.

Giant otters (Ptcronura braziliensis) from Venezuela to Argentina are known as water dogs by the local people. The animals feed almost exclusively on fish, mostly cichlids. Fishermen blame them for their poor catches of fish. On the other hand, aquaculture around the coastal area, mangrove forest, and estuary have taken over their habitats making their existence precarious. In California, the sea otters find abalone(a delicious and expensive shellfish for humans, also their delicacy. This led the fishermen to destroy them. The environmentalists formed a group called Friends of the Sea Otter to protect them. The fishermen formed their own organization called Save the Shellfish to counter them.

The overhunting for otter fur is the main reason for the decline of otters in many places. Other causes include disturbances by anglers and tourists, as boating and shipping also affect their breeding. Habitat destruction of coastal areas where trees and its root systems are necessary for them to rest, make nests and burrow are also responsible for their decline. Unless they can settle down without disturbances, they will not propogate. To preserve otters and other sea mammals, it is important to preserve their habitat or return them to their original state before more damage can be done.

Otters' fur cost only S30 each in the market, but some unscrupulous traders can bleach the fur with peroxide and pass them off as albino which can fetch as much a $1,000. The effect of this seemingly innocent way of cheating the rich can lead to increased poaching of this mammal.

PORPOISES

The Japanese have been responsible for killing 70% ofthe Dali's porpoises in a period of three years during the late 1980s. In 1989, they killed 40.000 porpoises and sold the meat in the markets labelled as whale meat. The increased killing of porpoises was an offshoot of the decline in the allowable catch of whales, which is a Japanese delicacy. Pressures from environmental groups forced them to scale down to 18,000 a year. Still the population is declining.

Porpoises are also dying in the high seas, courtesy of driftnets and gill nets with narrow mesh that are meant for smaller sea creatures. In England, fishermen use nets to catch porpoises alarm the environmentalists. More than 8,000 small cetaceans are killed in this way annually worldwide. The conservationists have petitioned the government to designate the area where the mammals are found as sanctuary. Some fishermen joined forces with scientists and engineers to devise an underwater pinger to keep out the porpoises. It has proven to be effective for harbor porpoise (Phococna phococna) in sink gill nets. The pinger is an acoustic alarm that emits a sound with a frequency of 10 Khz and a sound level of 132 dB, all within the hearing range of harbor porpoise and harbor seals, that deter the porpoises from moving closer. These acoustic beacons do not scare away the intended fish.

SEA LIONS

Sea lions are the acrobat performing animals we normally see balancing ball on the tip of their noses. They can also blow musical instruments and clap their flippers together. While they may seem clumsy doing other things, they are one of the best swimming sea mammals.

There are six closely related sea lions in the world. They are mostly confined to their habitats. There are about 50,000 California sea lions, living along the west coast of the North America. They are commonly found in zoos and circuses. Many captives have been trained to do tricks. The Galapagos sea lions are found only in the Galapagos Island. They number about 40.000 today. The most common sea lions are found in South America with about 270,000. Another species, the Steller's sea lions (Eumeiopias jubatus) are found in North Pacific and there are around 250,000 of them. The rarest sea lions are the New Zealand and Australia sea lions, each numbering less the 4,000. New Zealand sea lions have pelts that are valuable for leather and were hunted everywhere they are found until regulations protected them from further decline.

The California sea lions *Zalophus californianus*, inhabiting the waters near the Channel Islands once have DDT and its derivative DDE 100 times the level in their tissues than in 1970. Twenty-seven years ago, their biological systems have an average of 25 pounds of DDT that has significantly affected their breeding. More stillbirths had been noted since 1968. They not only have lower reproductive rate, but nearly half of the pups died of premature birth each season. In 1971, 345 cases had been noted. The source of DDT was the thousands of tons of DDT waste flushed into the ocean over the previous 21 years by the largest DDT producer then, the Montrose Chemical Corporation. Since its cessation of use, the sea lion population has doubled. But there were some stillbirths observed due to the high concentrations of mercury and PCBs in the same animals which have high DDT concentration.

In some places fishermen earn their livelihood by shooting sea lions with firearms. In 1992. a great number of them were washed up in shore of Scotland. The fishermen blamed them for low fish harvest. The same slaughter happened to common seals and gray seals around the coast of Scotland.

SEALS

Seals are aquatic mammals with doglike heads, and streamlined bodies and flippers. They are found in the coastal regions of the world. There are more than 30 species of seals. They have been hunted since the 17th century and some were hunted to near extinction in the 19th century. Some species may have vanished forever by the early 20th century. Like most mammals, they were hunted for their furs and oil by the newly industrialized countries of Europe while other coastal people hunted them for food or culled them as pests for competing against people for food from the sea.

One of the highest slaughters took place on the Juan Fernandez Islands, off the coast of Chile in 1687. For two centuries, the Juan Fernandez fur seals (Arctocephalvs philippii) were hunted until they became extinct. A ship in 1801 carried a cargo of one million skins from the island of Masa Tierra to London. During the period 1817-1824, another three million fur seal skins were taken from the island.

With the discovery of the habitat of northern fur seals (Callorhinus ursinus) on the Pribilof Island of the North Pacific in 1786, more than five million seals inhabiting these islands have been killed since its discovery. Their population had gone below 15,000 before international agreement came into force protecting them from slaughter. Today, these seals are harvested by subsistence hunters under the supervision of the FWS. Some 2,500 are killed annually.

In the San Miguel island off the Santa Barbara coast is the habitat of about one million northern fur seals. The water around the island is 5 to 7 degrees warmer, courtesy of the phenomenon called El Nifto. The effect of the warmer water has caused the disappearance of squids, sardines, herrings, and anchovies, all lifeblood of the seals. It is causing starvation for many young pups as their mother's milk production dried up due to lack of food. Six thousand seals have died since last summer (1997) and the numbers are expected to grow. Experts expect all the young pups to die unless human intervention is taken.

The lucrative commerce in seal fur has been responsible for their decimation. Fur scaling in the Southern Hemisphere began late in the 18th century in the Falkland Islands. It started in 1784 and for the next 15 years, more than a million seals were killed with clubs in small islets where they inhabit. By 1800, the seals of Falkland Islands have become extinct. Other places where seals were once in abundance such as South Africa, Australia. Chile, Antipodes Islands, Kerguelen islands and other places were also hunted to near extinction. The furs then were mostly taken to Canton. China where they were exchanged for teas and silks.

The southern elephant seal (Mirounga Iconina), the largest and heaviest sea in existence was almost hunted to extinction until a ban was imposed in 1964. e northern elephant seals (Callorltinus ursinus) did not fare any better. One hundred years ago, they were almost hunted to extinction. By 1900, there were about one hundred animals left in the world. In 1922 Mexico banned the killing of Guadalupe fur seals (Arctocephalus townsendii) on their last known refuge in the Isla dc Guadalupe, about 120 miles off Baja California. The timely ban and the continuing recovery at the rate of 14% annually for the past five decades have allowed them to increase their population to 150,000 today.

The South Africa fur seals were hunted for their furs until it was regulated. Today, South Africa produces about 20,000 pelts every year under government regulation. On the other side of Africa, 120,000 fur seal pup off Namibia s coast are dying of starvation (1993) caused by stagnant algal blooms that drifted toward their habitat. The disappearing fishes deprive the mother seals of nutrition needed to feed their youngs. At least 55,000 male and pup seals are culled annually to reduce the competition against fishermen. They are killed by clubbing, to protect the pelts that can be sold at higher prices and the genitals as aphrodisiac.

The harp seals (Pagophilus or phoca groenlandisca) are found mostly off the coast of Newfoundland, the Gulf of St. Lawrence and the Arctic waters. Hunting began in the 1750s and continue until today. Their populations declined so rapidly since 1825 when more than half a million seals were harvested annually. By the early 20th century, the catch has fallen to less than 200,000 annually. In the 1950s the government of Canada placed them under protection. The young pups are born with entirely fluffy white furs which are in high demand. They are often killed during the first two weeks of life before the color changes. Animal activists discourage the killing by staining their hides with colored stain to make it worthless for the hunters.

The most recent extinction is the Caribbean monk seal (Monachus tropicalis) of the Bahamas, the Greater and Lesser Antilles and the Yucatan Peninsula. The last sighting was made in 1952. Today, the Mediterranean monk seals (Monachus monachus) are the rarest in the world, numbering about 500 today. They have been killed by hunters and fishermen in large number wherever they can be found. In the Meditcrrenean where they used to loiter, they have been frightened away from the beach by tourists. The Hawaiian monk seal (Monachus schauinslandi) is also very rare, numbering less than 1,500 in the wild and are even more threatened because they are often caught in discarded fishing nets and plastics.

STRANDING

Stranding of whales is a common occurrence in the coastline of many countries around the world. It is a natural phenomenon and has been happening ever since whales were around. Thousands of whales are stranded every year and will die if help is not forthcoming. Some whales deliberately strand themselves due to sickness or injury. But when multiple strandings occur, it must be due to other causes such as disturbances from human activities, pollution, earthquakes or stormy weathers. Another most likely reason for multiple whale strandings is due to their navigational problem. It is postulated that the whales used the earth's magnetic field in navigation that lead them into coastal areas.

Anatomical studies have shown that some whale species such as sperm whales and pilot whales have tiny crystals of magnetite, a substance capable of sensing magnetic field and use it for navigation. In one stranding, research has discovered that in certain areas, whales follow a magnetic field where the lines of equal magnetic field cross the coastline perpendicularly. This could explain why groups of whales refloated back to the sea, repeatedly returned to the same locality.

Whales cannot survive long under the sun. It is therefore imperative to contact the proper authority to act quickly on the problem. Many people are needed to keep the whales cool and moist at all time before high tides allows it easier to refloat them. Seawater soaked cloth should be draped over their entire body to keep them moist and cool. Never cover the blowhole where they breathe.

Other sea creatures have been known to strand in beaches throughout the world. Dolphins have experienced getting stranded in cold areas where they should not be. Turtles have also been stranded In Riverhead. New York, 125 rare sea turtles had washed ashore in 1996. some suffering from comatose from the cold. Many victims are endangered species including loggerhead, green turtles and Kemp's ridley. All were suffering from hypothermia or below normal body temperature. They were brought to hospital and treated with intravenous line to give warm fluids and heart medications. At the Ocean Rescue Foundation, they are appealing for people to walk around the beach in search of stranded turtles, move them to warmer areas or take them to hospital for medications.

WALRUSES

The ivory trade is not confined to the elephants. Other sources of ivory are the teeth of the sperm whales, narwhal (Monodon monoceros), hippopotamus, and warthog (Ohacochoerus aethiopicus). The Arctic narwhal teeth can grow to 18 feet and has two teeth in the upper jaw. The left tusk of the male walrus can grow as long as eight feet.

Walruses (Odobenus rosmurus), the only species of its kind are large pinnipeds with big whiskers and tusks that differentiate them from ordinary seals and sea lions. They use the tusks in cutting and breaking holes in the ice and aid them to pull up from the freezing water to the solid ice. It has other uses such as for defense and for digging up clams, one of their favorite food. Other foods include sea snails, mussels, cockles other shellfishes. The male with the biggest tusk is usually the leader in any group. The whiskers are used to find food in the dark, murky water ocean floor.

Walruses have been hunted by the Eskimo and Chukchee who depended on them for many of their needs as they did for centuries. Commercial hunting on an extensive scale began much earlier than the seals, in the 9th century. The coming of the European hunters in the 15th century ushered in a new era of unrestrained hunting that almost lead lo their extinction. The walrus's habit of congregating together in the beaches or ice floe in massive herds caused their massacre. Many are killed for their ivories while the rest of the carcases are left to rot. They were killed for their oil, tough skin and the ivory from their tusks. Today, there are no more than 25.000 walruses worldwide. In areas where they were found, hunting of walruses are often done until they are extinct from a locality. Like whaling, the walruses are systematically destroyed from one locality to another. Seldom were they given a breathing spell to regenerate. Although the number of walruses killed is unknown, the best estimate puts it at four million of them in the 19th century alone.

Walruses are gregarious animals and often are followers of their leader. In the Togiak National Wildlife Refuge, some walruses have jumped to their death. They made their way up a hill and to the edge of the cliff. One by one, 48 of them toppled to their deaths. A sand dune which used to block passage to the cliff has been removed. The ivory tusks were removed and donated to the Alaska Eskimo Welfare Commission. Some 400 walruses are hunted and killed by the Yupik Eskimos annually to feed the some 5,000 blue foxes managed by the state.

WHALES

Whales are some of the largest and most powerful sea mammals in the world. They spend most of the time under the water and occasionally surface to breathe. The blue whale (Balaenopteru musculus) is the largest animal in the world. It can grow up to 33 meters long and weighs 107 tons. It can survive with only nine heart beats a minute. The newborn calf can be seven meters at birth. Whales take great care of their babies for as long as one year They are also very intelligent, taking care of one another in distress. Some whales have highly developed communication skills, allowing them to communicate with one another over long distances. Humpback whales make songs by humming, moaning, grunting, and squeaking. Every whale's song is different and can last for over half an hour. In fact, a tape recorded song has been send into outer space by NASA for the benefit of any alien that may come across it.

One type ot whales called the killer whales feed on food that are also consumed by people. During the 1980s, in the Gulf of Alaska and Bering Sea, these smart whales wait until the arrival of the fishing vessels before they act. They would gather at the buoy marker and wait for the fishermen to pull up the longlines and start feeding on the black cod caught. At first only a few whales were involved. Gradually, it spreads and increases to many areas. The fishermen initiated many methods to drive them away short of killing them, but to no avail. Later, some whales were killed to put a stop to it.

Fishermen in Newfoundland have been using an alarm invented by Jon Lien for frightening away humpback whales. They are often caught in nets meant for cod. The battery-powered noisemaker, encased in aluminum float, makes sounds like distance hammering on anvil. With the device, there have been less destruction of the nets and drowning of the humpback whales. From 1978 to 1992, more than 650 humpback whales have been saved from disaster. The noisemaker can be modified to other frequency for use with other species.

The most valuable products were the baleen, also called whalebone used to stiffen corsets and the oil derived from blubber. Until kerosene became available in the late 19th century, whale oil was used chiefly for lighting and heat. During the 20th century, whale oil was used in the production of margarine, soaps, lubricants, waxes, explosives, and numerous other products. Sperm whale (Physeter catodon) oil was especially valued as a high-quality lubricant used for automatic gearboxes in cars. By the 1980's artificial substitutes had been found for all whale products. The most important of this is a desert plant native to the southwestern U.S., the jojobo (Simmondsia chinesis), which can provide an economically good substitute for sperm oil which is just as good. Whale meat is still eaten by the people of a few countries, but it is no longer an important part of their diet.

Of all the sea mammals hunted by the human predators, nothing can compare against the rampant attack on the whales. Sustained and systematic killing of whales for centuries have driven many to almost extinction. In this century alone, more than one and a half million whales have been killed. Before commercial whaling came into full force, there were about 250,000 blue whales and as many as 300,000 humpbacks. Today, there are about 4,000 humpback whales alive, many of them still sporting the scars where harpoons that hit them during the savage days of whaling. During the 1930s, the annual killing of whales hover around the 30,000 mark. The number gradually peak in the I960 to around 65,000 mark. By 1972, the number of whales killed had drastically declined to 40,000 a year.

Whales have long been hunted by humans for food and oil for at least a thousand years. The small-scale hunting of yesteryears with small boats and spears have not done any harm to their populations. But modern whaling with fast ships and exploding harpoons is hunting the whales to near extinction. The vicious and inhumane way the whales were killed is made possible because huntings are done far from the public eyes. Only the enlightenment brought by animal activists in the 1960s and 1970s brought whaling to the world's attention.

There are as many varied reasons as species why whales are being hunted. The sperm whales are toothed and prized for the spermaceti found in its head. Most of them are hunted for their oil, normally boiled down from blubber. Although the sperm whale produced less oil than the right whales but its spermaceti could be stored with processing made long voyages economically feasible. Before the advent of the petroleum industry, whale oil provided one of the major sources of lighting. Millions of candles were manufactured from all kinds of whale oil and London even had 5,000 street lamps lit by whale oil in the 1740s. As well as providing virtually the sole source of lubrication for industrial machinery, it is also used to clean coarse woollen cloth. An important supplementary part of the industry was the use of whalebone in corsets, umbrellas, whips, fishing rods and cutlery handles.

The so-called right whale such as the southern, northern and bowhead (Balaena mysticetus) or Greenland species are slow and easy to catch. Because of their slow swimming speed, they are often caught using primitive technology then available. They were chased and harpooned with barbed spears, tied with ropes and hang on for days until the animal died from exhaustion. They are then floated and towed to shore for processing. The right whales had a 12-18 inch layer of blubber, ten times that of the sperm whale, which produced a large quantity of oil and they also produced about a ton of whalebone per animal.

Because of stiff competition between the whalers of the different nations and the fact that they are considered common property makes it extremely vulnerable to exploitation. Every whaler tries to pursue and kill as many before others get to them. It is a free-for-all without letup and mercy just as some species of land animals are also being lead to extinction.

Whales are seldom hunted for their meat except in some established coastal fishery town of Japan where they supply the native with protein because of shortage of domesticated animals. The Faroese people living halfway between Scotland and Iceland have been making headlines for a few days each year. The reason is that they have been killing longfin pilot whales for years in a brutal way. The whales are first chased to shallow waters by motor-powered fishing boats. Then they are hooked, incisions are made on the blowhole and repeatedly stabbed with knives and allowed to linger and bleed to death. According to the Whales and Dolphin Conservation Society, it is an annual ritual of sport and not for subsistence. More than 230,000 of them have been killed in the past 2So years. Other species like dolphins, porpoises and killer whales have not been spared. The killing of these whales are unnecessary because they are seldom eaten by the affluent islanders. It is more a traditional custom they find difficult to stop. Only a boycott of their marine resources called by environmentalists will stop the killings.

As early as the 1930s, it has been recognized that overhunting of whales are taking its tolls. More than 90% of all whaling took place in the Antarctica. The Norwegians were the prime movers in the whaling industry accounting for 60% of the total whales killed. In 1930-31 alone, almost 30,000 blue whales were killed. The bowhead and gray whales (Eschrichtius robusius) were virtually wiped out. The two countries lost their hegemony to Germany, Japan, and later Soviet Union toward the end of the decade. As a consequence, several international agreements were reached, including one sponsored by the League of Nations. The draft was in essence the Norwegian Whaling Act of 1929. Twenty six nations adopted the convention, but Britain delayed ratification delayed the implementation until 1934. Japan refuses to abide by any of them.

After the Second World War, the International Convention for the Regulation of Whaling was adopted in 1946. It also establishes the International Whaling Commission (IWC) the same year with fourteen whaling countries as members with the intention of protecting the great whales from extinction by restricting their harvesting. They meet at the start of each whaling season to determine the quota of whales for the year. But the result was quite the opposite of that intended as each nation tried to harvest as many whales as possible before the end of the hunting season. Many nations ignored the quota altogether. Since 1940, more than 2.2 million whales have been slaughtered.

It was not until 1972 when members of the U.N. agreed that there is a need for moratorium on whaling to be completely stopped in ten years. By 1977, Japan and the Soviet Union controlled 90% of the world's whaling industry. But the IWC voted by a narrow margin to continue commercial whaling until 1982.

In 1982 the IWC adopted a moratorium on commercial whaling to take effect in three years. However, in 1986, Japan, Norway, and the USSR refused to comply with the moratorium and continue whaling. The USSR has since given up whaling. But Japan refuses to honor the moratorium on whale killing and killed more than 10,000 whales as their reply to the moratorium. In 1989, Japan killed 39,000 Dali's porpoises out of an estimated 105,000 worldwide. Their reason was the restriction put on them on whaling.

It was Iceland, using a loophole in the IWC regulations that allowed whales to be killed for scientific research. Japan, Norway and Iceland took advantage of this loophole. In 1989, Iceland announced their cessation of whale killing for scientific research, but Norway and Japan still carrying on with their killings. In 1990, Japan killed 400 minke whales under the guise of scientific research. The minke whales are the smallest of the great whales. It is time to put a stop to "scientific research" on whales. With decades of research on dead whales, the pretext should be stopped altogether.

Public opinion began to change with the actions taken by Greenpeace. News of what this organization is doing to save the whales makes the public aware of the problem. The members of Greenpeace were particularly active. They would sail between the whaling ship and their prey in small rubber boats with camera rolling. Still whales are killed in spite of these actions, but the carnages shown on television were effective in alerting the world to this tragedy.

Norwegian whaling continued until 1987, when scientific uncertainty and political pressures led the government to ban all whaling. However, because of strong evidence of a healthy minke whale stock in the northeast Atlantic, the government unilaterally decided to resume minke whaling as of 1993. The result is that 226 mammals were caught and 69 of which are caught for research. The quota set by the government for the 1994 season was 301 animals, including 110 for research. It is only a smokescreen for the illegal hunting of whales for their meat.

Norway strongly supports continued scientific research and improved hunting methods. Significant improvements have been made. During the 1993 season, there were inspectors aboard each ship to report on hunting methods and number of mammals caught. Compared to the results from the 1985-86 season, the whales were killed substantially more quickly and therefore more humanely.

Norway resumed whaling five years ago in defiance of IWC ban. In the year 1997, Norway's annual whaling season ends with 500 minke whales killed out of the 580 planned but far more than the 381 killed in 1996. There was no active worldwide or even local protests against this violation.

The latest project of the IWC was the creation of the Antarctic Sanctuary for the whales. Together with the Indian Ocean Sanctuary, it will provide about 33% safe haven for whales worldwide. Japan is the only nation objecting towards this effort. It still wants the right to kill 300 whales a year for scientific research. The IWC often gave in to their request, fearful that more drastic actions could mean international repercussion from one of the world's richest nation.

The main reason whaling companies refused to give up their trade is the large investments they have made on whaling ships and other support facilities. The combined production of whale meat actually exceeds the public demand. To protect their investments and to ease the ires of environmentalists, they developed ways to use large amount of whale meat as fish sausages and other products. During the peak of the whaling in the 1950s and 1960s, Japan actually exported several million kilos of low quality whale meat to the U.S. for the pet food industry. The slaughter of endangered and threatened species in order to feed the overpopulated pets and farmed animals reared for their furs.

The Pell Amendment to the Fishermen's Protective Act requires the Secretary of Commerce to notify the president if foreigners are engaged in an activity that diminishes the effectiveness of any international program for endangered or threatened species. The president, in turn, may direct the Secretary of Treasury to prohibit the importation of products from the certified country and shall inform Congress within 60 days of any action taken. The amendment is being used by NGOs in the U.S. to ban import from countries refusing to stop whaling. Another boycott orchestrated by the International Wildlife Coalition, seeks to persuade tourists to shun Caribbean beaches guilty of killing whales. The U.S. Secretary of Commerce has certified Norway for sanction, but the Clinton Administration is reluctant to take action without foolproof evidence and risk alienating a long-standing ally.

Whale watching has come in vogue nowadays. Massachusetts, which had a history of killing whales for profit has turned into a brighter future of watching whales for profit. It brought in more than $75 million a year into the state's economy. Many coastal states had followed suit. In California, a small industry has grown around watching whales. Every year more than 300,000 people watch the migration of the gray whales near San Diego, California. The whales are so friendly you can touch them from the canoe. So many spectators are visiting their breeding lagoon in Baja California that has become a threat to their species. Wherever whales can be found in groups, people visit these places and create a new recreational center just to see these creatures.

Because of the whaling ban. many ex-whalers have found a new occupation as tourist guides for whale watching. In Japan and Norway, although there is still whale hunting, more ex-whalers are in the whale watching business. In some places, boats have been modified to allow scientists to study live whales.

CHAPTER 7

REPTILES AND AMPHIBIANS

There are many similarities and differences among reptiles and amphibians that biologists often lumped them together. Both groups are air-breathing and cold-blooded vertebrates. However, many reptiles can regulate their body temperature by external means. The reptiles have horny scales which is good at keeping body moisture so that they can live on dry land. The amphibians have smooth, scaleless skins although some like the toads have rough skins. The reptiles lay their eggs on land and spend most of their lives in water. On the other hand, amphibians lay their eggs in water and spend most of their lives on land.

Reptiles include the snakes, lizards, worm lizards, the crocodilians, turtles and tortoises, as well as the tuatara. The extinct dinosaurs were also considered reptiles. There are more than 6,000 living species of reptiles worldwide. All are found in the tropical and temperate regions because they depend on the surrounding temperature for the heat. They cannot withstand too much heat and must retreat to a cooler place to avoid upsetting their enzyme systems. Those found in cool climates have adapted to hibernation during the w inter, otherwise they will freeze to death. The female lay eggs and the youngs are born looking like them. However, a few reptiles give birth to live youngs. Being cold-blooded, they do not need to eat to keep warm and can survive for days and months between meals.

Amphibians are divided into three groups: namely frogs and toads; newts, salamanders, and sirens; and the little known worm-like caecilians. They spend part of their lives in water, usually during the early stages of life and partly in land as an adult. Even then they live near ponds and streams to keep their skin smooth and moist and for breeding purposes.

The amphibian's skin has special properties that set them apart from other animals. Besides breathing through their skin, it can take in or lose water, produce colored patterns and markings for defence. Some have poison on their back to protect them against predators. The skin can also secrete mucous to keep it moist or prevent damage. Amphibians are also good indicators of the status of the environment.

Reptiles and amphibians have an important role far beyond giving us food and other body parts for the fashion industry. The crocodilians are important scavengers, cleaning up the carcasses of sea creatures while others consume harmful insects and keep a check on the balance of nature in the wild.

ALLIGATORS

The word "alligator," given by early Spanish explorers in the New World, came from the Spanish word for lizard. Like all the other crocodilians, they keep growing all their life. The females are good mothers and will guard the eggs until they hatch and two more years thereafter.

In many tropical countries, as well as the U.S., they have been hunted for their beautiful hides. Early in the 19th century, the American alligator (Alligator mississippiensis) was the first crocodilian to be widely commercially exploited. They were hunted for the oil to grease the machinery of steams engines and cotton mills. Later as their skins became fashionable in the 1870s, another incentive for killing them began. By 1930, nearly 200,000 Florida alligators were killed in a year. By 1943, they were so rare that the price has increased tenfold. Habitat destruction is also a leading cause of their decline. In the U.S., the F WS classified them as endangered in 1967. By 1977, they have increased in numbers and repopulated many habitats and were reclassified as threatened.

In many parts of the U.S. where they are bred, alligator wrestling is part of the entertainment. They are immobilized by flipping them on the back to cause blood to flow into its small brain.

The Chinese alligators (Alligator sinensis) once found throughout the banks of the Yangtze River is now a rare and endangered species. Some of the alligators have been sent to the U.S. for captive breeding. A joint effort by the New York Zoological Society and the Rockefeller University tried to get them to breed but to no avail. Eventually it was discovered that the body temperature was not conducive to their breeding. It needed to attain a lower temperature enough to chill them into hibernating before they will breed. They were sent to Louisiana because they have the same identical conditions as the Yangtze River.

Although limited to their usefulness as hides for leather and meat for the discriminate diners, they are known to be the saviors of ecosystems during periods of drought. In the Florida Everglades, during periods of drought, alligators will dig water holes with their powerful claws which become sources of water for other animals as well as for themselves.

BREEDING

Many reptiles are in the endangered and threatened list. With the knowledge that the sex of the reptiles are determined by the temperature at which they hatch, scientists are taking advantage of it by producing more females to boost their populations. Warmer temperatures will produce more females and their eggs can be hatched in the laboratory under controlled temperatures. All this is made possible because at high temperatures enzymes produce more female hormones in the embryo.

Now scientists are trying to hatch more females at remote sites without bringing the eggs to the laboratory through the use of the hormone estrogen. By injecting the hormones into the eggs, they prove that it works, although half of the embryo died. A simpler, safer method has been devised by dissolving the estrogen in alcohol and allowing it to be absorbed through the eggshell.

CAIMANS

The spectacled caiman is named for its horny ridge connecting the eye sockets. It resembles the bridge of a pair of spectacles. It feeds on giant aquatic snails, piranha and any animal that stray within its range in their natural habitat in the Amazon and Orinoco river basins. They have a natural lifespan of 70 to 100 years. They usually hunt at night and researchers have found that caiman used the reflections coming to their eyes like a flashlight. This technique has enabled poachers to hunt the caiman easily.

Of the two million crocodilian skins traded each year, three-quarters come from the spectacled caiman (Caiman crocodilus) and the Yacare caiman (Caiman yacare). Another one million are smuggled from Paraguay, Bolivia and Brazil. Most are sent to Italy where they are turned into handbags or expensive wallets.

CHAMELEONS

Chameleons are remarkable animals because of their ability to change color to camouflage against predators and also help them hunt for unsuspecting insects. The skin cells contain pigment-bearing chromatophores, which they use according to the situation. The long tongue and amazing speed make it possible for them to strike at flying insects. Their eyes can move independently of one another allowing them to search for food in the surrounding areas without moving their head.

One of the most beautiful chameleons is the Jackson's chameleon which has three forward facing horns on its head. Others such as panther chameleon, found only in Madagascar, is very colorful and aggressive. The female is normally brownish, and will turn to tawdry orange when they are ready to mate. After mating, it will turn to black with orange spots as a sign that she has mated. In their habitat, the local superstition prevent their being eaten, but the pet trade is taking its toll on the reptiles. Thousands of these beautiful reptiles are shipped to Europe and many died while in transit.

CROCODILES

There are 25 species of crocodilians and they have not changed for the last 100 million years. Crocodiles are the largest reptiles in the world. The saltwater type can grow as long as eight meters long and live for as long as 50 years. Cold-blooded animals require little food to survive which could account for their ability to survive several periods of mass extinctions. They have the uncanny ability to cut the blood supply in their lungs to conserve oxygen, thus allowing them to stay underwater for a very long time with only 3 to 4 heartbeats a minute. Like the alligator, female crocodiles make very good mothers to their offspring. Alter preparing a nest for the eggs, the mother crocodile guard the nest against all predators until they hatch. She carries the young in her mouth until they are too big for comfort.

Crocodilians sometimes feed on carrion which they can detect from a great distance with their sensitive smell. This important role helps clean up rivers and lakes of dead animals that may contaminate the waterways.

Crocodiles have always been hunted by local people on a small scale for the food, clothing, and adornment that they can provide. Crude methods are used an only a small number are killed for the needs. But when commercial hunters moved in to supply the fashion industry, things began to get worse for the crocodilians.

At one time crocodiles were a common sight in the waterways of South America. Nowadays they are much scarcer and are more likely to be seen as handbags in the classy shops of the world's capital cities. The Orinoco crocodile (Crocodylus intermedius) was hunted mercilessly for the fashion industry in the early part of 19th century. In ten years, they were so scarce that hunters shifted to other species. Even without poachers, crocodiles are vulnerable to other predators such as birds, piranhas and other crocodiles. Natives often hunt for their eggs as food while others keep them as pets. All these have put down crocodile population.

In September 1988 it was reported in The Nation, one of Thailand's leading newspaper that the skins of200,00 endangered South American crocodiles estimated to cost $4 million had been tanned in Thailand and exported to Japan. Thai forestry officials were involved in the operation which made it possible. Although Thailand is a signatory to CITES, there is no local law that protects animals imported from foreign countries. Obviously, the government has misinterpreted the provisions of the act. The CITES was created to act as a global protector for endangered animals worldwide or at least to all member countries even if no local laws have been enacted.

Thailand has a large number of crocodile farms engaged in the exportation of their hides. Countries surrounding it used to smuggle young crocodiles there for breeding and subsequent sold for their hides. This has caused a drop in crocodile populations in the neighboring countries. To stem the smuggling, authorities in Thailand require all crocodiles in farms and those returned to the wild to be monitored by means of a computer microchip imbedded into its skin while they are still young. With a simple monitoring device, each microchip will emit their code number which can be checked against the file. All crocodiles without the code are considered coming from an illegal source.

Every year 340,000 crocodiles are killed for their skins out of which expensive shoes, handbags and briefcases are made. Even hatchlings have been killed and turned into keychains. Only a few farms exist, so more crocodiles are captured in the wild in Papua New Guinea, Venezuela and India, and in the Nile and Pacific. The crocodile skin trade is worth more than $100 million annually and one average sized skin is worth about $200. The biggest markets are Japan and France and some other countries to a lesser degree.

One of the vulnerable parts of the wild crocodile is their eyes. It is well adopted for night vision and can reflect light that glow like coals when flashlight is shown on them. Hunters take advantage of this knowledge by sweeping a flashlight over the water. In areas inhabited by humans, hunters have been called to kill these crocodiles. They have been hunted to extinction in many places.

CROCODILES: FARMING

Indonesia has set up a number of crocodile farms located primarily in Irian Jaya. In 1989, more than 19,000 crocodiles are being reared in these farms. Probably the most successful ranching and breeding enterprises in Asia is located in Thailand. The Sumuprakan Crocodile Farm was founded in 1950. Since then it has raised more than 30,000 crocodiles. While the majority of these crocodiles will be used for the skin trade, 4,000 are being kept for breeding. The farm has also become a major tourist attraction since its opening in 1971, attracting one million tourists annually. One of the shows to entertain tourists is crocodile wrestling. It is not difficult to breed crocodiles because they can lay more than a dozen eggs during each ovulation period.

In many parts of the world, crocodiles and alligators are being raised near their natural habitats. In Australia, they have 8 farms, the U.S. has 13 farms with Louisiana harboring more than 20,000 crocodiles with help from the Rockefeller Foundation. Other farms have been set up in Florida and Texas. In Papua New Guinea, crocodile farming began in 1972 with the support of the UN agencies. Government support is an important element in making it a successful enterprise for many. The government even set up a demonstration unit for those interested in this line of business. There are now more than 300 operators.

In addition to the skin business, the meat of the crocodiles is both sold locally and exported. Each crocodile carcass can yield 20 kg of meat, which reduces the need to import and save foreign exchange. The meat is ideal for health conscious people due to its low fat content.

EGGS

Most reptiles lay numerous eggs at one time depending on their size. But some reptiles give birth to live young such as some chameleons, vipers, boas and sea snakes. The eggs come in many different colors, shapes and sizes. The lizards produce eggs with leathery shells except for the geckos. They leave their eggs behind and unless hidden carefully are often taken by predators such as rats and other reptiles. Humans harvest turtle's eggs, a delicacy for many.

There are many interesting ways reptiles lay and hatch their eggs. The Nile monitor lizard likes to lay her eggs on the side of the mounds she tore up. From there she would lay around 50 eggs and expect the heat inside the mound to incubate the eggs, which takes about 10 months. The African chameleon lays its eggs in a burrow to protect against predators. The ground python egg is irregular and elongated, looking like an elongated potato. The common house snake of Africa uses manure heaps to lay her eggs. The caimans and alligators often lay their eggs in mound nests of plant matters and soil. After laying they keep watch over the eggs until they hatch. The matamata turtle has eggs that are very round.

The eggs of reptiles come in different kinds of shells. They are all made of several layers that allow the embryo to breath oxygen through the shell. Inside the shell is a bag of fluid called the amnion where the growing embryo is found. The yolk allows the reptile to feed until they are ready to hatch. One interesting feature of the eggs of crocodiles and turtles is that the sex of these reptiles are determined by the temperature at the time of hatching.

It is worthwhile at this stage to note that eggs are important collector's items that grew in prices as the species became rarer in the wild. To get an idea of the value of the eggs of extinct dinosaurs found in China's Dragon Mountain in 1991, villagers were then selling unknowingly to foreigners for one dollar each. But in the open market of North America, each egg was selling for $1,200. During an auction, a nest of ten eggs was sold for $78,000. After the eggs were declared as a national treasure by the Chinese government, more than 3,000 eggs were confiscated from smugglers in 1993 alone.

FROGS AND TOADS

There are more than 3,400 species of frogs and toads in the world. They can reside in many different kinds of habitats as long as water is available due to the need to breed their young tadpoles in water. Most frogs and toads lay their eggs in water. Each egg is protected by a jelly until they are old enough to become tadpoles. The tadpoles eat plants in the water as they gradually grow and start to eat small animals while the legs begin to grow and the tail gradually disappears.

Frogs have been used in science education, biomedical research, and pregnancy tests for many years until more advance methods were discovered. The seemingly harmless African clawed frog (Xenopus caevis) was imported to the U.S. in the 1940s and used extensively for human pregnancy tests. When more advance methods became available during the 1960s, many of these frogs were turned loose into nearby streams and have since then became a part of the landscape displacing native frogs and fishes and spreading rapidly to other parts of the U.S. They are also voracious eating machines that prey only on living insects and other small animals.

The bullfrog (Rana catesbeiana) is the mainstay of the market for its edible legs. The worldwide harvest for its legs was estimated at 200 million bullfrogs annually. The huge demand comes from Europe and the U.S. and they are mostly imported from India and Bangladesh. Some 80 million are collected from the rice fields of Bangladesh alone. The result is an uncontrolled increase in insect numbers that could further damage the rice production as well as upset the balance of nature. This huge harvest has resulted in a drastic decline of the frog population. Other frogs are also caught for their edible legs. The edible frogs Rana esculenta and the marsh frogs Rana ridibunda are found throughout Europe.

Although about 20 new amphibians are being discovered every year, many more are on the brink of extinction. The declining population since the 1960s caused by habitat destruction however cannot account for the fact that in the pristine forests of many countries, their population are also declining.

In 1964, a biologist discovered the golden toad in Costa Rica which became a leading attraction at the Monteverde Cloud Forest Reserve. In 1987, 5,000 golden toads were seen breeding in this forest. After two years, only one appeared. And now all have disappeared. The same fate also happened to the harlequin frog, which vanished from the same area. The gastric breeding frog of Australia suffered the same fate. Females of this species incubate their eggs by swallowing them, switching off their digestive system and fasting until their offspring hop from their mouth. Discovered in 1973, they have suddenly vanished in 1980.

Experts are speculating that there are several causes. One of the most plausible reasons is the permeatation of the hormone-disrupting chemicals into their body which affected their reproductive organs. The unique physiology of the frogs made them highly vulnerable. Their permeable skin allow the frogs to absorb toxic chemicals much more readily than other animals

As if all these problems have not done enough damage to their population, there is an abnormally high rate of missing legs and other deformities among young toads and frogs in many sites across North America Stanley K. Sessions of Hartwick College, in his North American Amphibian Monitoring Project (NAAMP), theorized argues that the parasitic flatworms known as trematodes is responsible for the limb defects. The outbreak of the flatworms may be caused by human-induced pollutants.

The presence of predators and introduction of exotic species of fishes may also be a possible cause of their decline. The eggs of the frogs and the tadpoles have become part of the food chain of many marine creatures. In some cases, the eggs die from infection of the pathogenic fungus probably caused by the damage to their immune system brought about by the UV-B radiations or chemical toxins Frogs in freshwater are also dying from a certain bacterium that causes "red legs." They are only vulnerable when their immune systems has been compromised and that can only come from being contaminated with toxic chemicals.

The declining populations are not confined to the lowlands Even in high altitude places, the frogs are suffering from diseases brought about by the same chemicals suffered by marine mammals. These chemicals could have been wind blown as they evaporate and recondense in the mountains. Scientists were able to discover all kinds of contaminants on seemingly remote mountains. This theory is boasted by the many studies made on acid rain where all kinds of contaminants are found in remote mountains.

The arrow-poison frogs are so-called because of the powerful poison secreted by the parotid gland located at the back of the frog. The kokoi frog of Colombia has the most powerful poison known among the animal kingdom. The poison called batrachotoxin is ten times more powerful than tetrodotoxin, the poison of the Japanese puffer fish. The poisons are used in arrow-heads by the Central and South American Indians for hunting animals. They collected the poison is one of the most cruel ways inflicted on an animal. To collect the poison they have to pierce the frog with a sharp stick and hold it over a fire like they barbecue meat except this is done while the frogs are alive. The heat forces the frog to release the poison through the skin where it drops into a jar provided

GHARIALS

Gharials (Gavialis gangeticus), also called gavials. are the strangest of all the crocodilians. They have a long narrow snout with small piercing teeth. They are found mostly in the rivers of northern India, Nepal, Pakistan and Bangladesh. The male wards off rivals by a loud buzz made through their gharl on its nose from where they got their name. Even if they may be small in size, they are still hunted and poached for their skins like their bigger cousins.

In the 1970s, there were less than 70 left in the wild. Conservation efforts were immediately taken. Today there are about 1,500 of them after they were reintroduced and more than 500 are in captivity.

IGUANAS

These lizards are found mostly in Central and South America ranging from Mexico to Paraguay or the Lesser Antilles. There are 120 species of them and most of them look like lizards with crest of ridges rising on their back. The largest is the green iguana, reaching up to 1.8 meters long. One kind of iguana called the rhinoceros iguana has two or three hornlike scales on its head.

In many areas their eggs and meat are highly prized as food by local people. Snakes, hawks, rats and other feral animals also find their youngs and eggs a delicacy. The hawks prey on the small iguanas while the boa constrictor has been found to have an adult green iguana inside its stomach. Donkeys and goats destroy their habitats by browsing and trampling on the grass where they hide to breed and raise their young. This is the fate that is awaiting the rhinoceros iguana (Cyclura cornuta) that lives in the Hispaniola and Mona Islands of the West Indies.

The decline of iguanas in the wild has been largely due to the pet trade. They are caught in the wild and sold to the tourists. Some of them are bred in the farms and exported worldwide. Even in the Philippines, iguanas are sold in pet shops for as much as P3.500 for a small one and to P6.000 for a 40-cm long iguana.

The Cayman Island, cast of Mexico is home to one of the near extinct blue rock iguanas. There are less than 150 of these reptiles remaining in the wild. A captive-breeding facility, the National Trust's Blue Iguanas Captive-Breeding Facility has been set up to propagate their population.

The Grand Cayman blue iguana can grow up to five feet in length and weighs 20 pounds. It was originally the largest land animal on Cayman Island without any natural predator. But the hatchlings are often eaten by three species of snakes, and several species of birds. Other predators that are brought into the island by humans are the cats and dogs. They are no match for the dogs, their most dangerous threat, because they have not yet developed a natural fear of dogs, and the food left out for the dogs are inviting the iguanas to feed on it resulting in fatal consequences. Small and medium-sized iguanas are also no match against cats. Although the goats do not eat the iguanas, they destroy huge vegetation needed by the iguanas to hide against other predators.

The land iguanas of the Galapagos Islands are also suffering the same fate. Their population has been declining rapidly as a result of feral dog attacks. The vicious canines attack is motivated by pack frenzy rather than hunger. Sometimes it may be necessary to destroy one species to ensure the survival of another threatened or endangered species. This is the case between the iguanas and the feral dogs. Moves are now underway to poison the dogs with fast-acting poison that would not endanger other non-targeted animals.

Only a fully protected breeding facility offers the best hope for the iguanas to survive and multiply. With their small population, it is important to breed them and set them into the wild as soon as their population increases to a safe level. At the San Diego Zoo's Center for Reproduction of Endangered Species, rock iguanas' eggs from Cuba's Guantanomo Bay, are hatched and given a head start before releasing them to the wild. The Jamaica iguanas have been decimated that it was once thought to be extinct in 1993. However all the fifty adults left are all males. A handful of them were held in captivity for future breeding without fear of predators. At present they are not only hunted by predators, but the iguanas in the wild are often seen basking the warm road surface. Fast moving trucks and automobiles accidentally hitting them is very common.

KOMODO DRAGONS

The Komodo dragon (Varanus komodoensis) is the largest lizard found in the rugged volcanic island of Komodo and the islands of Rintja, Flores, and Padar, all in Indonesia. These islands have been made into national parks especially for the sake of these lizards. An average adult can grow up to 3 meters and weighs 140 kg. Their sensitive tongue is used to feel the air for food. The dragon's saliva is poisonous and can kill a human. There are less than 4,000 left in the world. They are also voracious eater, consuming anything edible, dead or alive, and even its own offspring. A 100-pound meat can be consumed by one dragon in just a few minutes. Long claws and serrated teeth allow them to tear large chunks of meat that it swallows whole. Sometimes it eats so much that it can no longer move and have to wait for several days to digest the food. Local hunters living in these islands have been hunting some of their preys such as deer, boars, and birds. This is causing a real problem and the government often have to bring enormous amounts of meat for their consumption.

The dragons were first seen by a westerner through the eyes of a pilot who landed on the island in 1912. Tales of the viciousness of this dragon was confirmed by Major P. A. Owens, director of the Ouitenzorg Botanical Gardens in Java, who offered skins and photographs as proof of their existence. Soon zoos around the world send hunters to trapped these live specimens for their exhibitions.

After years of breeding in the zoos, only one named Ora, was born outside Indonesia. One of the problems is trying to determine their sex. Ultrasound is used to determine the absence of certain internal structures. Another way is to determine the level of testosterone by blood testings.

LIZARDS

There are 3,000 species of lizards in the world. They have special characteristics that are the envy of other reptiles. To warm themselves they can maneuver their bodies to maximize the absorption of sunlight. Some can even alter the color of their body to absorb more sunlight. Many are collected by hobbyists as pets such as the chameleons, geckos, iguanas, and the small monitor lizards. They have interesting features that make from ideal pels. The mole lizard of South America has a pouch in the throat that can be kept inflated for several hours. They use it to attract a mate or when they are showing signs of aggression. There are also iguanas that can blend with the color of the surroundings just like the chameleons.

Some species of lizards are also parthenogenesis, that is, they can bear offspring without having their eggs fertilized by the males, a rare feat among the vertebrates. The Chihuahuan spotted whiptail (Cnemidophorus exsanguis) of Texas and Mexico is one example. It has an all-female populations.

There are only two species of venomous lizards, the Gila monster (Heloderma suspectum) and the beaded lizard (Helodermahorridum), both found in the deserts of southwestern U.S. and Mexico for the former and west coast of Mexico for the latter. They prey on nestling birds and small rodents. They are capable of fasting for several months without food, living off its fats until the rainy season when food will be abundant.

One of the fascinating lizards is the plum-tree basilisk or Jesus Christ lizard (Basiliscus basiliscus) that can run rapidly across the surface of water without sinking when it senses any danger. Even if it sink, it is a good swimmer.

Geckos have feet that can grip smooth surfaces that other lizards cannot accomplish. Their toes have ridged pads that can attach even to window panes allowing them to walk without difficulty. These tiny reptiles are experts at hunting. In the Mediterranean and the Middle East countries they are kept as pets and let loose to hunt cockroaches and flying insects at rest. Their keen eyesight even at night helps them find pests.

Lizards have very good eyesight and they are good insect hunters. The household lizards are also good insect hunters. They are especially adept at killing flying insects such as mosquitoes that are harmful to humans.

It is sometimes difficult to imagine that lizards which can crawl under crevices can be under threat of extinctions. But that is just the case for a total of about eleven species that have become extinct since the year 1600. Today, South Africa is home to about 25 species of endangered and threatened species, followed by Australia with 22 and Chile with 20 species.

POACHING AND SMUGGLING

The large profits that can be made from the crocodile skin trade, like their counterpart in other species have given rise to illegal poaching and smuggling of the crocodilians and their skins. Poaching is rampant because all that is needed is a small investment. There is more profit to be made from poaching crocodilians in the wild than raising them in farms. It costs more than a S100 to rear a reptile in captivity before they can be sold while the cost of the wild reptile is nil. Prices for crocodilian skins are also very volatile and it could be very expensive to keep them in captivity while waiting for the price to go up. In the 1980s, when the prices tumbled, processed hides from Thailand slumped from $290 to $90 each.

Poaching of crocodilians is made possible by the lax enforcement and penalties imposed for violators in many tropical countries. Many often get away with poaching with a small fine. In Brazil, the fine for poaching is no more than the cost of a speeding ticket. The importing countries like Japan. U.S. and Western Europe should be vigilant against dealing in reptile skins. While it may be difficult to stop poaching altogether, at least a body should be created to monitor the trade and give a seal of approval to any trading.

Smuggling is another problem faced by authorities tasked with controlling these illegal activities Most of the skins come from illegally killed reptiles and smuggled into another country. From there, bogus papers were made to make it appear as legitimate items. With these fake papers, smugglers are able to export the skins almost anywhere in the world without being questioned since under the CITES regulations, the skins are legitimate part of the trade for not being listed on Appendix I.

Another factor that makes it easy to smuggle the skin is the difficulty of differentiating the skin of an endangered species from one that can be traded. Unless a custom official is a specialist, it is almost impossible to tell an illegal skin from a legit. The jacare caiman, a protected species in Brazil is often shipped to the U.S. without the custom officials aware of their endangered status.

Live crocodiles are sometimes smuggled from one country to another. In 1988, a smuggling operation was uncovered when 2,000 live baby crocodiles were shipped from Colombia to Taiwan by way of Panama and Madrid. Only 25% of the reptiles reach their destination alive and the rest are made into curios. In Sarawak, Indonesia, about 200 young crocodiles are caught and smuggled to farms in Singapore each year.

SALAMANDERS AND NEWTS

There are about 330 salamanders and 25 newts in the world. The biggest salamander which also happens to be the largest amphibian is the Chinese giant salamander (Andrias davidianus). It inhabits the mountain streams of northeastern, central and southern China. The average adult can weigh up to 30 kg and 1.1 meters long. However, one species caught in Hunan Province measured 1.8 meters and weighted 65 kg. It is one of the most endangered species because they are hunted by the local people as a great delicacy.

The spotted salamander (Ambystoma maculatum) of eastern North America are under threat of extinction because of acid rain caused by air pollution. They usually mate during spring time, around pools and lay their eggs in the water. Beside acid rain which can kill their eggs in a short time, the young ones are also under tremendous threat of other chemical pollutants.

The olm (Proteus anguinus) found in Yugoslavia and Italy are under threat from several fronts. This strange salamander lives in underground streams and lakes that are becoming polluted in these areas. They are also collected by hobbyists that wherever new habitats are found, they are kept as a guarded secret to prevent their poaching.

The IUCN had listed 39 species of salamanders as threatened or endangered. Although none has become extinct in recent years, five species are feared to become extinct if nothing is done to help them. They are the Abe's salamander (Honeybees abed) and Hokuriku salamander (Hynobius takedai), both of Japan, the desert slender salamander (Batrachoseps aridus), the shenandoah salamander (Plethodon shenandoah) and the Texas blind salamander (Typhlomolge rallibuni), all in the U.S. The great crested newt (Threaders cristatus) is the only newt species considered to be threatened and is now protected the by EC Habitats and Species Directive.

SKIN BUSINESS

The fur industry is often confined to the fur-bearing animals. Some beautiful skin come from the aquatic and reptilian animals. The reptiles include the snakes and crocodilians. Their skin are used for making leather products such as wallets, shoes, watchstraps, purses, handbags, belts, suitcases, and a variety of bags. Crocodilian skins ate particularly beautiful and have been hunted that more than half of the species are under IUCN threatened or endangered list. In fact crocodile farmings have been set up in many places solely for obtaining the highly priced belly and flank skins. The rest of the body is too knobbly. Others obtain their eggs from the wild for breeding in the farms.

Over two million crocodilians were killed for their skin annually. The majority of these reptiles are the spectacled caiman, accounting for about one-half to three-fourth of the total. It has been eliminated from the Atlantic coast of South America where more people live. As the population expand toward the inland, these reptiles are also being killed in the inland rivers.

Beside the skin, some of the reptiles are killed in the most inhumane way. Baby crocodilians are often killed and made into key rings or stuffed toys. Thousands of youngsters are killed and their heads are dried to make key holders. This senseless killing is partly responsible for the decimation of the reptiles in the wild. Others are made into stuffed baby crocodiles and dressed with golfing outfit with one of their front foot holding an umbrella.

The skin of some reptiles like the turtles are commonly known as shells. Most of these shells are made into household items. Sea turtles are sometimes turned into stuffed specimens, combs, cigarette trays, fixtures, and jewelry.

It is almost impossible to control what the indigenous people or illegal poachers will do about these reptiles once they caught them. But consumers can greatly help in reducing their slaughter by refusing to buy any of the products made from their skin.

SNAKES

Snakes have a bad reputation as sly and dangerous, but many of the misguided theories are being disproved only recently. Most snakes do not attack humans unless their habitats are disturbed by intruders. Out of the 2,700 species of snakes found throughout the world except in the polar regions, New Zealand, and some oceanic islands, less than 300 of them are poisonous, and most ot them do not bother people.

Snakes are hunted for centuries because of their bad image and as a vermin to be destroyed. When the Europeans first settled in the American continents, organized snake huntings, dating back to 1680 were undertaken to get rid of the rattlesnakes. During the middle of the 19th century, hunting snakes became a popular festivity. Today more then 50 "Rattlesnake Round-Ups" are held in Texas, Alabama, Georgia, Oklahoma, Pennsylvania and Florida. The largest of these round-up festival is held in Sweetwater, Texas where 35,000 spectators are attracted. As many as 18,000 western diamondbacks (Croialus atrox) are caught every year. Other snakes include the prairie rattlesnakes (Croialus varieties), coachwhips (Masticophis flagellum) and western bull snakes (Pituophis melanoleucus). The snakes are brought to the Nolan County Coliseum, headquarters for the festival where they are weighed and deposited in a snake pit for live demonstrations. They are later butchered and sold to dealers.

In the western part of the U.S., as many as 500.000 snakes, mostly rattlesnakes are round up annually. They are brought to town hall for the festivities such as snake sacking contest. Later the snakes are killed for their body parts. The snakes are blindfolded are slit alive in the belief that the snake bile and blood are more effective as tonic medicine for eye trouble and as aphrodisiac. The head is cut off, packed in transparent boxes and sold for $6. The skins are made into hats and the bodies are chopped and sold at snake meat.

Snakes have a remarkable ability to delay fertilization of the eggs after mating. This ability to control the development of the young can help them to determine the best time or season to bring forth their young. While they do not have ears, they are very keen in detecting vibrations on the ground.

All snakes are carnivorous and they will eat anything from worms and insects to birds and rodents. They have been responsible for keeping a check on the population of rodents that are harmful to humans and their crops. Many farmers in the U.S. keep black rat snakes in their barns to control rats destroying the crops. In fact snakes are better than dogs and cats in killing rats because they can penetrate where others cannot reach. They can enter rat holes and destroy even the young offspring of rats.

Probably the only country that respected the role played by the snakes for the environment is India. In the country teeming with people, the snakes, especially the cobras have been responsible for controlling the population of the rodents that have been reducing their grain production. They are the only reptiles capable of penetrating burrows where rodents breed and kept the stolen grain. The cobra is respected as a god of fertility as in ancient Egypt.

Even in the open grassland, snakes can help reduce the other harmful burrowing animals that destroy crops and vegetations. They can reach into crevices and burrows where others find it difficult to enter. Even water snakes have been found to be effective by eating slow-moving non-game fishes, thus removing them from competing with food fish for the limited food supply. The very venom that makes human fear about snakes is the most valuable product offered by the snake. It is used for the treatment of snake bites as well as some other ailments. Even the bones have been grounded and used for treating arthritis and other pains.

More than any other group of animals, the snakes are being killed in the wild unintentionally. They are often run over by cars along highways passing through their known habitats as they cross the streets. It is therefore important to keep their habitat intact since fragmentation has its danger. Their habitat is their livelihood and without it, they just wither and die. Avoid visiting areas where there are snakes, or we may be disturbing their habitat.

The Milos viper, Macrovipera schweizeri, is a European species endemic to the Greek islands of Milos, Kimolos, Polyaigos and Siphos. Since the 1970s, it has been fully protected along with other Greek reptiles. But in their habitat on the mountain areas are some mining operations that have caused the destruction of their mountain habitat. Mountain tops are sliced off and slopping hillsides are sheered into precipices. Road crisscrossed the island to deliver the gypsum to their harbors. The heavy traffic carrying minerals away from the quarries cause death for large number of snakes. The annual total death could easily ran into several hundreds if not thousands of snakes.

The main reason for their decline is the hunting of snakes for their skin which is used as leather for many products. Major uses are the women's handbags, shoes and other accessories. Southeast Asian countries are the main supplier of snakeskins. The Oriental wart snake (Archrochordus) is specially valuable and sought after. Any snake that is big enough is killed for their skin. Other body parts are also used. They are made into novelties and curios. The liver and fatty tissues are boiled and made into snake oil and used for whatever medical benefits.

Snakes in many isolated islands are constantly under threat of extinction. This is because they have nowhere to hide as their habitat is destroyed. They are open prey to birds of prey and owls that feed on them.

Snakes are also kept as pets in the U.S. and many European countries. Most of these colorful snakes are non-poisonous and some such as the water snakes feed on fishes. As long as food are available, there is no problem to keeping them as pets. However, some basic requirements must be kept. This includes a clean, dry and comfortable place with water all the time. Inside their enclosure must be a place for them to hide. The right kind of food must be given.

TORTOISE VILLAGE

The Tortoise Village is a 2-hectare conservation center founded in 1988. It is especially dedicated to preserving the Hermann's tortoise, France most endangered reptiles and its only native tortoise. Other turtle species also benefit from the village since none of them are ever turned away.

Inside the center is a clinic where sick and injured turtles could receive medical attention. Glassed-in nursery is provided for newly hatched turtles. Enclosures with topped wire mesh netting protects the turtles from airborne predators such as magpies and rooks. Wooden houses and dense underbrush offer refuge from the sun. Another enclosure is provided for reproduction. It is the only area where male and female tortoises live side by side under each own species.

The village was first conceived by Bernard Devaux, a writer and filmmaker in 1985 with David Stubbs, a wildlife ecologists and freelance lecturer Jean-Pierre Pouvreau. They founded SOPTOM, the village's parent organization that leads to its creation.

The Hermann's tortoises have been losing their habitat in France's massif. Roads and developments fragmented their habitat while predators such as badgers, beech martins, foxes, and wild boars often raid their nests. Forest fires claimed hundreds and sometimes thousands of tortoises every year. This is aggravated by the collection of tens of thousands of tortoises by collectors. Their declining numbers made it difficult for the tortoises to repopulate an area.

The village is a self-sustaining conservation center. From the initial contributions made by the British Fauna and Flora Preservation Society and some local NGOs. The village was constructed by Devaux with help from volunteers. Today, the center is financed from the entrance fees paid by visitors, which numbered about 100,000 annually. Other sources of income come from SOPTOM membership fees and sponsors, and sales of souvenirs.

Most of the initial input of turtles and tortoises were donated or contributed from captive -bred turtles. As many as 1.000 sick and dying pet turtles are donated annually. Great pains are taken to prevent the spread of disease. Donated turtles and tortoises are given a health checkup, bathed in disinfectant and then quarantined in small groups until they are deemed healthy enough to join their cousins. Captive-raised specimens are also kept in relatively small groups to keep health problems in check. Since 1992, more than 8.000 Hermann's tortoises have been released back into the wild.

TORTOISES

Turtles are not the only reptiles eaten by people. Tortoises have also been victims of human dietary greed. Because of their ability to live very long even without food and water, sailors often took them along in their long voyages in early times. An estimated 10 million giant tortoises since were taken from the Galapagos Islands by the early whaling fleets. The tortoises of Mascarenas, now extinct were once highly regarded for their liver and the oil that can be taken from their fats. No other part of the body is of any value and are discarded.

As for those people who are only interested in the oil that can be gathered from the fat of the tortoises, a very cruel way had been devised to determine the value of the oil inside the tortoise. A hole is hacked in the shell by an ax big enough to allow a finger to be inserted and to feel if the tortoise is fat enough. Those that did not make it are thrown back into the sea. The mutilation often causes the death of the reptile.

Tortoise shells are also harvested by people because of their beauty. The geometric tortoise (Psammobales geomelricus) is one of the world's rarest chelonian species precisely due to their beautiful shells. The shell of this reptile is marked in a radiating geometric pattern of yellow and black bands. They have been hunted for their shell and only 4,000 are left in the wild. Many of their breeding places have been converted to other uses such as agricultural fields and urban development.

The giant tortoise once roamed this planet in huge numbers. They have remained unchanged for millions of years, but their numbers have declined considerably due to the introduction of predatory animals and humans. Today, there are only two places where the wild adult tortoises can roam freely. The first home for the Aldabra tortoise is in the Seychelles Islands. The other home is the Galapagos Islands, home to the Galapagos tortoise. But the doubling of the human populations in the last ten years and the introduction of cats, rats, and pigs are destroying their habitat and their eggs are being eaten by rats. Goats introduced 50 years ago to the Galapagos outnumbered the estimated 10,000 giant tortoises in the protected islands.

The prolific, tenacious, and voracious goats are the greatest threat to the survival of the giant tortoises. Wherever they are around, they have rapidly defoliated the landscape and driven native populations of tortoises to the verge of extinction. Their latest damage is on the island of Isabela, the largest of the Galapagos islands, where some forty thousand feral goats have crossed a natural barrier from the south end of the island toward the north, reaching a giant tortoise reserve and decimating the plant life that has sustained the tortoises for centuries.

In early April 1994, a reported fire in Isabela Island in the Galapagos destroyed over 20.000 acres and burned for nearly two months. It was probably started carelessly by poachers. The burning of the dense vegetation made poaching possible in their wild habitat. A group of tortoises in Roca Union were found slain by poachers. Helicopters brought in to fight the blaze instead airlifted the endangered species from the hands of the poachers.

Sierra Negra Volcano is one of five volcanos on Isabela Island, and home to four separate groups of Galapagos tortoises. There were originally 80 individuals, but when German Morillo, a Galapagos National Park Service warden went to make an updated census, he discovered more than 30 tortoises killed by machetes. It is believed that local islanders were responsible as they protest against the Ecuadorian government fishing moratorium of harvesting sea cucumber.

The Chaco tortoise (Geochelone chilensis) of Paraguay and Argentina live by chewing fruit, grass and cactus pads. Every year thousands of these beautiful shelled reptiles are caught in the wild and smuggled to the rich countries of the world, especially the U.S. The problem lie mostly in the non-enforcement of conservation laws in countries where they are found. The same is true with this species. The spur-thighed tortoise (Testudo graeca) of the Mediterranean Sea is faced with the same problem.

One interesting thing about the pancake tortoise (Malocochersus lornieri) of Kenya and Tanzania is the soft and flexible shell that it can adopt to its defense against predators. To evade predators, it would crawl into crevices in rocks and expands its body by breathing in large amounts of air. It would be almost impossible for predators to remove them from the hole except against the human predator. The hunters have been responsible for the falling numbers in the wild.

TUATARA

The name of the tuatara (Sphenodon punclalus) came from the native Maori tongue meaning "spine bearer" referring to their crest running down their back. These beaked reptiles were believed to be extinct 180 million years ago until the lizardlike New Zealand was discovered to be part of their group. They look like lizards but are actually the last survivor of an order called Rhynchocephalia. It is a sluggish animal about two feet long and weighing a kilo that feeds on insects and small vertebrates. They have a unique and interesting feature that has fascinated zoologists. They have a third or parietal eye complete with retina, lens, and nerve connected to the brain atop the head, but is not used for seeing. Many other species of lizards have this feature but they are not as developed. It formerly inhabited the main islands of New Zealand but is now found only on some 30 remote small offshore islets off the northeast coast of North Island and in Cook Strait. It is placed under government protection.

Some tuataras in captivity have been noted to live for 75 years. Maori people claim that some live to be 300 years old. The surviving tuatara is a miracle of their survival ability. They are able to survive under very cool weather with little oxygen and food. However, with the arrival of the aborigines, the tuataras have been hunted by rat predators introduced to their habitat. Later, the English migrants brought with them cats and pigs that further reduce their populations.

To save the tuataras from extinction and repopulate the reptiles in the wild, the government of New Zealand are gathering their eggs in the wild and incubating them in the laboratory and later releasing them to the wild. To ensure their survival, periodic checks on the rat populations are taken and people are forbidden from traveling to their island-habitat for fear that boats may carry rats and other predators.

Further researches on the tuatara have revealed that there are actually two surviving species. The individuals living on North Brother Island, in Cook Strait are genetically distinct and now belong to a new species called Brother's Island tuatara (Sphenodon guntheri). The original species, Sphonodon punctalus, is now known as Cook Strait tuatara.

TURTLES

Reptiles with shells are called chelonians. There are between 250 to 300 species of them. Those that spend most of their time in the water are called turtles. The sea turtles have been with us and have changed little for the past 200 millions years. In spite of their restricted anatomical design, they have been able to adapt to many habitats and lifestyles. The leatherback turtle (Dermochelys coriacea), which can grow up to 2.4 meters long is the largest and heaviest of the living turtles. Its shell is made up of immeasurable small bones embedded into the skin. In 1988, one of the enormous turtles weighing 752 kg washed up in a beach in Wales after being entangled in a fisherman's net. They travel throughout the world but always return to the same beaches where they were born. There are those unfortunate enough to find their homes in places where they should never be in the first place. In the 1980s, there were five major nesting beaches in the Irian Jaya. Indonesia. In ten years time, the nesting beaches were down to one. Human encroachment of the beaches was responsible for their decline. Deep inside the hinterland, turtles are killed by loggers using chainsaws. Others are killed by the moving heavy equipment.

Some marine turtles are facing extinction. Their meat is harvested for food including their eggs. The shells are used for ornamental purposes and for fertility potions. Off the east coast of Malaysia, the leatherback turtle nests declined from nearly two thousand in the 1950s to fewer than one hundred in the 1980s. They are now considered an endangered species. The hawksbill turtle (Eretmochelys imbricata) is highly prized for its ornamental shell and are being hunted to near oblivion. The loggerhead turtles are near extinction because of the driftnet and other kinds of nets used in fishing or discarded into the ocean.

The green turtle (Chelonia mydas), the main ingredient for turtle soup, is another turtle on the way to extinction unless they are protected against poachers and gourmets. A few years ago, 5,000 marine turtles were made into 680,000 liters of soup by just one food firm in the Caribbean. In the Grand Cayman Island, a breeding program was set up to save the species. All the three turtles are classified as endangered species by the IUCN. Some are dying of a non-malignant tumor which proves fatal when they grow over the eyes, mouth or internally that could hinder their feeding. Surgery is often the only solution. The main cause is suspected by scientists to be pollution.

Loggerhead turtles (Caretta caretta) like all other turtles spend most of their lives in water. Every year, the female migrates thousands of miles to return to their place of origin to renew the cycle of life. They will look for an ideal place in the sand to lay from 80-110 eggs. They will dig a hole in the beach about one meter in diameter and some 30 centimeters deep and lay the eggs, after which they will covered it again with sand. After seven or eight weeks later, the hatched baby turtles will immediately scurry to the sea. Most will fall prey to fish, birds and other predators. Some will be picked up by tourists. Only a few will make it to adulthood.

In the U.S. the pet trade for box turtles has been increasing since the demand for tortoises from the Mediterranean has been banned by a law passed in 1984. The U.S. exports around 25,000 of them to Europe and Asia. Most of these turtles are caught in the wild by children paid by the U.S. retailers. As in all other reptiles, these animals are often neglected and deprived of food and water during the weeks of transport and delivery. Half of the turtles sent to Europe die within a month. They are very sensitive to climate changes and in places with varied temperature ranges it can be fatal to these animals.

Throughout the world, about 11,000 endangered sea turtles, including the critically endangered Kemp's ridley sea turtles (Lepidochelys kempii) are drowned in funnel-like shrimp fishing nets. Yet a simple device called Turtle Excluder Devices (TED) can deflect turtles during shrimping operations. The U.S. Senate has passed a measure barring import of shrimps from nations whose shrimpers do not use TEDs. Reducing the consumption of shrimps caught from the wild will help reduce their deaths.

The National Audubon Society is urging all Americans to boycott shrimp from the Gulf Coast to force shrimpers to obey federal law by using TEDs on their nets. TEDs are inexpensive and easy to use. However, many shrimpers still refuse to use the devices despite efforts by the Coast Guard to enforce the law. In 1989, they even attacked Coast Guard vessels and blockade ports.

Another reason for their decline is the gathering of their eggs. They are sold in the aphrodisiac markets in Mexico City. In the past huge numbers of female would lay their eggs along the long sandy beach of Rancho Neuvo, Mexico. In 1947, as many as 40,000 can be seen nesting in this area. But the gathering of their eggs has gradually reduced the number of returning turtles. By 1989, less than four hundred can be spotted in the beach. Captive breeding has been initiated in Texas and Mexico. Thousands of these young turtles are being reared to maturity for a better chance of survival once they are released to the wild. The Arrau river turtle (Podocnemis expansa) of Amazon and Orinoco rivers are faced with the same Problems besieging the Kemp's ridley turtles. Millions of their eggs are stolen every year, leaving less and less to breed for the new generation. Now both species are under constant armed patrol.

Another species, the olive ridley (Lepidochelys olivacea) was also hunted for its shell and meat until it was banned by the president of Mexico in 1990. About

75,000 turtles were killed annually. But there was no ban on harvesting their eggs which is the prime reason for their decline today. The eggs are considered as an aphrodisiac and energizing protein by the local people. They are mostly eaten raw in bars found throughout Latin America. Even in Costa Rica, whose government banned the harvesting of egg collection, illegal gathering is still rampant.

Loss of habitat is another important cause of their decline. Many of the beaches the turtles have had to themselves for centuries are now full of people. It is no longer safe to leave the eggs in the sand because people moving around may trample on them. Water skiing and other sea sports involving speed boats add to the many hazards the turtles now have to face. At the very least the natural habitat of any animal should be kept under protection against poachers and commercial trading. Except for the unfortunate animals that went astray, at least those within the protected areas must be free from poachers.

In the Maldives, a group of 1,200 islands located in the Indian Ocean near Sri Lanka, are the nesting sites of sea turtles. In June 1995, the Maldives Ministry of Fisheries instituted a 10-year ban on the trade in sea turtles. The ban encompasses the sale of live turtles and export of turtle products. Before the ban, jewelry made from tortoise and turtle shells was widely sold in the market.

One of the major difficulties in sea turtle conservation is that the animals take no notice of national boundaries. They swim freely from one country to another. Therefore, because different countries have different laws and attitudes toward them, the turtles can be protected in some parts of their range but not in others.

One reason for the decline of the turtles and tortoises throughout the world is due to egg collections. The eggs of the Kemp's ridley are gathered and sold as an aphrodisiac in Mexico City. Ten years ago, the leatherback turtles have lost 90% of their eggs in the black market. This lead to the creation of a national wildlife refuge on St. Croix where they breed.

The black sea turtles (Chelonia agassizi) of Baja California is ruthlessly hunted for its tasty meat, skin, and oil. A close relative of the green turtle, it almost become extinct in the Gulf of California. Illegal poaching and incidental capture in fishnets still threatened the remaining turtles, but the Mexican government has started efforts to save them. It is essential to learn more about its diet, migrations, and use of the bay to maximize the way to save the turtles from extinction.

In Zante, Greece, there is a nesting ground for one of the few remaining population of loggerhead turtles anywhere in Europe. The island is one of the favorite tourist spots and also that of the turtles for centuries. There was a presidential decree in 1986 providing complete protection for the turtles in a large bay and along an important nesting beach. However, developers and others involved in the tourism trade want unrestricted growth in tourism and they completely ignore all the turtle protection laws. They destroyed many turtle nests. Some have built walls, small hotels, restaurants and houses on or close to the nesting grounds. Others have smashed the turtle protection signs and deliberately prevent the turtles from nesting by killing the adults and digging up their nests. The islanders are getting away with all these illegal acts because the turtle protection laws are not being enforced. Unless laws are strictly enforced to the letter, it is inevitable that the turtle will have to look for other places which could face the same difficulties.

Two sandy beaches near Karachi, Pakistan known as the Hawkes Bay and Sandspit, are considered among the top 11 sites for nesting sea anywhere in the world. The green and Pacific ridley turtles are commonly found there, and have been protected since 1982. However, they are still in demand in Pakistan for their shells which are turned into ornaments such as ashtrays, their meat is used to make turtle soup and their eggs are considered by some to be very tasty. Therefore in 1980 renewed efforts were undertaken. Every night, the most important stretch of beach is patrolled by special turtle guards. Whenever they find a female digging a nest they wait patiently nearby and, as soon as she has finished laying, they gather up her eggs, which are then taken to turtle enclosures, that are guarded 24 hours a day. After a few weeks, the tiny turtles are carefully placed in a bucket and carried down to the sea to be released. In one six-year period, no fewer than 185,000 green turtle hatchlings, and 11,400 Pacific ridley hatchlings were released this way. A further 36,000 plus hatchlings were collected on the beach and carried to the sea by hand.

One of the most important aspects of Pakistan's turtle conservation project is to educate people about the existence and value of sea turtles. Guide tours are arranged for visitors to the beaches and many parties of school children have been taken for exciting night-time vigils to watch the animals. The project has been immensely successful. The turtles and their eggs are now well protected, and even the local people have begun to take an interest in the animals welfare. EarthWatch volunteers are especially active in helping protect the Icathcrback sea turtle habitats. Only 20 nesting habitats have remained worldwide. Three of them in Costa Rica are considered the most important. In 1989, Frank Paladino and James Spotila began a long-term effort to seek official protection for the beaches and to learn more about the population dynamics and reproductive biology of female leatherbacks to help in the conservation management plan. In July 1995, the efforts of the principal investigators and their teams paid off. The three beaches became the heart of a new national park, Las Baulas de Guanacaste with the help of a letter from President Bill Clinton to the Costa Rican government.

Before they took the project 13 years ago to protect the leatherback turtles in St. Croix, U.S. Virgin Islands, poachers were taking 95% of all leatherback sea turtle eggs from the beach. But then EarthCorps volunteers began patrolling the beaches and documenting the turtles' nesting habits, today. Since then poaching has ceased and more than 60,000 turtle hatchlings have made it safely to the sea. Volunteers patrol the beach all night, once each hour. When they encounter a nesting female, they will watch her, tag her, and record all vital data, including weight, size and location. Teams will also relocate nests threatened by high tides and help disoriented hatchlings find their way to the ocean. As a result of their work, the site has been declared a National Wildlife Reserve.

They also help patrol the beaches of Sandy Point, U.S. Virgin Islands and Gandoca Beach, Costa Rica. In Sandy Point, they documented 53 leatherbacks laying 325 nests, and rescued 137 nest comprising 6,335 hatchlings by moving the erosion-prone nests elsewhere. In a period from 1982 to 1996, they have saved an estimated 69,420 hatchlings through nest relocation. They also played midwife to

11,851 turtles. In Costa Rica, they helped tag a third of the 932 leatherbacks that nested there. They found more than half the turtles nested only once here and 22 sported tags from elsewhere in the Caribbean. This discovery is an important point that all turtle sanctuaries must be protected to ensure their survival. They also helped set up a national park on the Pacific coast of Costa Rica where it was once a beach full of poachers.

In Sitio do Conde and Arembepe. Bahia. Brazil is a palm-studded, reef* fringed Bahian coast that attract not only fishermen and adventuresome tourists but all five species of Atlantic sea turtles as well. The combination could be a recipe for environmental disaster, but here the turtles have a champion in "Projecto Tamar" - the largest sea-turtle conservation program in the world - which has gained wide publicity for its success in integrating conservation and development. Now in its 16th year, the program mobilizes 250 staff mostly fishermen, who patrol more than 1,000 kilometers of nesting beaches every day and night during the nesting season from September through February, protecting nest sites.

NGOs around the world have drawn up an International Sea Turtle Conservation Strategy to protect the sea turtles. One of the aims of the strategy is to build up sea turtle numbers to their former abundance Nature reserves and marine national parks are being established, there are round-the-clock protection schemes, and many countries are now working to stop international trade of the animals.

Probably the most effective measure that can be taken to increase their number is through captive breeding or at least hatching of their eggs under controlled and protected conditions. In the wild, usually only one makes it to adulthood. The rest are eaten by birds on the beaches, fall prey to fishes at sea or the human predator. At least, in a well-kept hatchery, the turtles can be reared until they are mature enough to survive the sea. At the Rancho Nuevo hatchery in Texas, the eggs gathered from the beaches around the Gulf of Mexico and elsewhere are raised in captivity for ten months before they are released. This will give them a better chance of survival.

CHAPTER 8

PRIMATES

The family of primates consist of about 233 species of mammals. They have several characteristics that set them apart from the other animals. These mammals have relatively larger brains, making them the intellectuals of the animal kingdom. They usually have five fingers hands and feet with flat nails instead of claws. Their hands function very much like humans and their eyes are found in front of their face unlike other animals having eyes on the sides of the face. This enabled them to focus on objects and judge depth and distance. The primates are divided into two groups, the anthropoids, which include the more familiar monkeys, gibbons, gorillas, orangutans, baboons, other apes, and human beings. The less known primitive primates called prosimians include lemurs, bushbabies, pottos, and tarsiers.

Most species are tree-dwellers with dextrous hands that allowed them to move easily from one tree to another. Unlike other mammals with paws or flippers, the primates use the hands to grasp objects, use tools, and seize food. They can also learn new skills simply by observing actions by other people or primates.

The anthropoids are the nearest kin to humans. Scientists have discovered all groups of chimps have the ability to use tools. Along with the orangutans, they know how to use some plants for common ailments. Apes are in some way like humans when it comes to treating their enemy. They are capable of killing wayward chimps that wander off to their territory. Some primates have very strong mother-offspring relationship and on the other extreme capable of committing infanticides. However, their intelligence did not prevent them from being exploited by humans. They are just as exploited as any other animal used in experiments.

Prosimian means "animals that came before the monkey." There are 30 species of prosimian distributed in the tropical forests of the world. The more than twenty species of lemurs are only found in the island of Madagascar, while the five species of loriscs and six species of bushbabies range widely through the tropical forests of Asia and Africa. Most of them live in trees sleeping by day and hunting by night. This may account for the evolution of their large eyes.

BABOONS

Baboon is the common name for eight species of African monkeys. They have pouches on both sides of the cheeks for storing food. The baboons spend most of their time on the ground. The best known species is the hamadryas (Comopiihecus or Papio hamadryas) baboon. These monkeys are now rarely found in the hills of Sudan, Ethiopia, and Middle. In Ancient Egypt, they are worshipped as sacred donkeys, companion to the god of wisdom and magic, Thoth. But they are now extinct in Egypt, a victim of the proliferation of the human population. Being social animals they live in group of as many as 200 individuals headed by a male.

Hamadryas baboons were once trained to harvest fruits from the fig trees be of their lighter weight. They were even kept as pets in ancient Egypt.

One of the large and powerful species of baboons are the mandrills (Papio or Mandrillus sphinx) that are closely related to the drills. They are restricted to the equatorial part of Africa. The mandrills search for food during the day, traveling in troops within their territory. At night they stay up in the trees to protect against leopards and other big cats. They have long been endangered since their populations have never been very large and the continuing conversion of their habitats into agricultural use only heightened the problem.

BONOBOS

Bonobos (Pan paniscus) or pygmy chimpanzees as they were originally known are the last of the four great apes to be identified by scientists in 1933. The name probably came from a town called Bolobo, where specimens were collected in the 1920s for museums interested in their skeleton rather than studying the living apes. These apes are found in the Congo Basin and are about the size of the chimps. They were once thought to be just another ordinary chimpanzee. But unlike the chimps, they spend more time in the trees and form closer social communities where the females play a more dominant role. Bonobos can be distinguished from chimp by their web between the second and third toes. And unlike the chimps, they do not commit infanticide nor do they kill each other. They have very close family ties that last a lifetime. The mothers are very protective of their offspring and will intervene on the son's behalf. They are also under threat of extinction. There are only a few hundreds left in the wild jungle of central Zaire in Africa. Lack of living space caused by logging, agriculture and housing projects have diminished their habitat. They are not expected to survive in the wild into the next century.

The bonobos are the most intelligent of all the animals. Scientists studying their intelligence were able to discover that bonobos can learn communication skills using sign language without being taught. Child psychologists studying their behaviors were able to impart their knowledge of learning to the children with difficulties in communication skill.

Scientists have also found the bonobos are more human-like than any other ape. Two lovers have been found walking arm in arm among the trees. They stopped once along the way so that the male could gently kiss the hand of his beloved. At the top of the trees, they were seen staring at each other eyes intensely, embraced and kissed deeply. Copulation is done not only during optimum breeding cycles as almost all animals do, but whenever the mood suits them.

BUSHBABIES

Bushbabies are also known as galago or night apes and are found mostly in Africa. They are active insect hunters at night. The smallest bushbaby is the Dermidoff's galago, measuring only 4.5 inches from the nose to the tip of the tail. They are agile, moving from branch to branch. With their sensitive hearing and large, keen eyes, they can easily seek their prey under very dim light. The lesser bushbabies (Galago seegalensis) spend the day sleeping but as soon as night falls, start to hunt insects, spiders, lizards, and even nesting eggs. In the absence of these animals, they will feed on fruits, petal and nectar of plants. The bigger bushbabies (Galago crassicaudatus) are physically bigger and have big and strong back legs that help them to leap like monkeys. Like some wild cats, all bushbabies are territorial. They leave their markings on leaves and branches of trees by anointing their hands and feet with their own urine.

CHIMPANZEES

The closest relative to humans are the chimpanzees (Pan troglodytes) of the animal kingdom. Molecular research shows a 98.5% compatibility between the genes in humans and chimpanzees. Next to kinships are the gorillas. But their similarity to humans cannot save them from human exploitation and possible extinction. The common, intelligent and noisy chimp is one of man's best friends from the wild. They are considered as apes and not monkeys. Quick to learn and copy what humans do, some have been taught the sign language used by deft and mute people. The clever chimps can solve problems and use simple tools. Biological researches have also shown that they resemble man even more profound than we had anticipated. The nature of immune responses, the structure of blood proteins, the circuitry of the brain and even the structure of hereditary materials (DNA) of the chimps are closer to man than any other species.

But the similarities did not deter man from killing them. In West and Central Africa, the chimpanzees in the wild are considered common property and are not protected. This leads to harvesting them as food as their meat is a prized delicacy. In Liberia, adult chimps are killed to supply meat for the miners working in the Nimba Range. The young ones are sold to exporters. There are horrifying tales of infant chimps tied up beside the sliced-up bodies of their parents in the meat market. Mother chimps spend six years or more looking after their youngsters and without them a young chimp may not survive in the wild. The small chimps are sold for fattening and future consumption by the protein-starved Africans. Also, chimpanzees are in great demand by the medical research laboratories of Europe and the U.S. To capture these young chimps often entail the killing of their parents. Very often these mortally wounded parents are allowed to die a slow and painful death. The poor babies are tied with wire on their wrists or caged in tiny wooden boxes. It is estimated that for every live infant that arrives in the Western world, an average of six others have lost their lives. Many do not survive past their half lifespan of 40 years in the wild.

The international biomedical establishment has been identified as one of the greatest threats to the animal. The U.S. National Institute of Health (NIH) opposed the reclassification of the animal from threatened to endangered, making them illegal to be exported from Africa. However, chimps are still exported illegally from Africa for medical researches. Others made use of them as props for photography. The animals are either sick or drugged and forced to pose with tourists.

In Spain, for more than a decade, unscrupulous photographers have been capturing these animals in the wilderness in Africa and importing hem illegally. Being illegally imported, these primates are not given the usual checkup for diseases such as rabies and hepatitis that could be transmuted to people. Others come from the Spanish's Canary Island. The primates are dressed up in children's clothes and dragged along to bars, hotels, nightclubs to be photographed with unsuspecting tourists. There are about 200 chimps working as props. They work up to 16 hours a day, eight hours during the daytime in the beach and eight hours in nightclubs and bars.

When they are about two years old, and quite big to handle, the chimps' teeth are knocked out like what they did to bears and are heavily drugged to keep them docile and manageable. The drugs are intended to make them cooperative at the expense of disoriented and frightened apes. When the chimps grow really big and outlive their usefulness, they are either killed by slitting their throat and thrown into the sea, drowned or abandoned.

Several NGOs are working with the government of Spain to stop this business of using chimps for the tourist trade. Under the law it is illegal to use animals for commercial purposes, but the photographers are not about to give up their lucrative venture. They can earn as much as $75,000 a year with minimal investment. Contrary to government's report, chimps are still being exploited by unscrupulous photographers.

In the Canary Islands, the chimps are also exploited by photographers. Just as in Spain, they are also drugged to make them docile. Once they outlive their usefulness, they are sold to the Eastern European medical laboratories. The use of chimps are also used in the beaches of Mexico and Israel.

The chimps played a vital role in making space flights safe for humans. All in all the U.S. Air Force used 41 of these animals as experimental pilots during the early stages of space flights. One hundred thirty one offspring were born and all of them are caged and retired under the auspices of the Air Force or send to biomedical laboratories for experiments. Animal activists are petitioning the U.S. Congress to allow the chimps to be adopted by private individuals or released to the wild. These animals have done a great service to mankind and should be set free. Under confinement their average lifespan in only twenty years compared to forty years in the natural environment.

One tragedy that should never be overlooked is that some scientists are still curious enough to cut up their brain to probe into their inner working. The chimps have their heads broke open while alive to see how it ticks. Those that are unfortunate enough to survive, usually for only two years, will have to undergo the same procedure to determine any damage done due to the loss of memory in the intervening years. All the time, the chimps survive in a pathetic state with broken cheekbones and without the skull to protect them from possible injury. Stuart Zola-Morgan, one of those working on the brain of the monkeys was named by the San Diego Animal Advocates "Vivisector of the Year" three times in a row.

One form of sadistic mental cruelly is to sever the bond of love between mothers and babies. The infants are taken away from their mothers to measure their responses. Different type of isolations, sometimes with the use of restraining device were applied to study their reactions. To maximize the effect of isolation, the mother is separated from the infant with a clear shield between them while the researchers stood and watched the primates rage and scream for their babies. The helpless infant can only huddle the shield with its head. These types of mother-infant separation have been tested for decades, yet new researches are still using these experiments only to confirm what had been known a long time ago. Critics have been right to complain of the uselessness of these experiments. They are cruel and useless to human beings because it does not advance medicine or ease human suffering. If there is anything to learn from all these experiments it is that the primates and humans have almost identical attachment for each other. More than 2,000 chimps have been used for studying the stresses due to separation.

The encroachment of human beings into their habitats are rapidly destroying these animals on an unprecedented scale. There are now an estimated 50,000 left in the wild. Forests are cleared to make room for human use and it reduces the living space allotted for the primates. Moreover, these chimps are susceptible to infectious diseases brought by man. The threat of epidemics caused by human can and will be difficult to control and can devastate the whole population. The chimpanzees and other apes are fighting back with their own deadly diseases such as AIDS and the Ebola virus. But human greed and needs will continue with the destructions.

Many people have taken the cause of the chimpanzees in the wild. The governments of Uganda and Tanzania offer protection to their chimpanzee population. Recent international conservation meeting agreed to put these apes on their list of endangered species needing protection. Programs are being set up in order that chimpanzees needed for research can be established in captivity.

Many zoos today are beginning to display their chimpanzees in groups in fairly spacious enclosures, although there are still many apes imprisoned in the old-fashioned concrete and barred cells. These cages are no more than prison cells for human beings.

The U.S. proposal to change the status of the chimpanzees from threatened to endangered species was accepted under the Endangered Species Act in April 1989. It has made it illegal to import any wild or captive bred chimpanzee from Africa.

EXPERIMENTATIONS

The close affinity of primates to homo sapiens and their long life spans have made them the ideal animals for studies and experimentations. The difference in genes within the cells is about 1.5% from that of human and mostly manifested in the physical appearance. Every year American researchers use some 40,000 monkeys in their laboratories. Although a small number in comparison to the rats and rodents, they are still far too many in the light of the dwindling numbers in the wild. The chimpanzees once numbered 5 million in Africa is down to less than 200,000 by the late 1980s.

Many experiments on primates are worthwhile and useful for mankind. Some powerful and effective drugs were developed and made possible with the help of the primates. Chlorpromazine used to treat mental illness; cyclosporin, an anti-rejection drug used in organ transplants; vaccines against rubella and hepatitis B- and cornea transplant were made possible due to biomedical experiments on them Heart diseases, physical injuries, malaria, Parkinson's disease, vaccine for AIDS and many others are undergoing experiments with the use of primates.

But some can be considered as cruel and uncalled for. At the California Regional Primate Research Center in Sacramento in 1984, scientists were studying the effects of toxic chemicals on the lungs of baby monkeys. The poisons were injected through tubes into the glass cage and the baby primates were observed even in the presence of visitors on how they die of pollution.

One NIH-funded laboratory in Rockville, Maryland called SEMA, Inc. was raided by an underground animal rights group called True Friends. Close to 500 apes and monkeys there were being experimented for AIDS research. All the animals were enclosed in metal cages provided with a small window. Inside the animals are in a pathetic state, ceaselessly rocking back and forth, staring at the walls. Others are starving and too weak to move. Efforts made by Jane Goodall and Roger Fouts with help from PETA, and public pressure finally forced the lab to make changes. The chimps are now isolated in big see-through plexiglass units decorated with jungle scenes.

Last July 31, 1997, the National Health Council has decided that the 1,500 chimpanzees breed for the AIDS research throughout the U.S. have a right to enjoy the rest of their lives under a more humane atmosphere instead of being destroyed under euthanasia, after it was found out that they were very poor models for AIDS research. Many have been given to zoos. Under new guidelines, the monkeys to be given away to zoos must meet at least the vigorous standard used at the Yerkes Primate Research Facility in Atlanta. In this facility, the monkeys are able to enjoy outdoor life every day. The government spent at least $7 million annually to keep these primates.

Because of their unique physiology, testing of drugs for its efficiency and toxicity is often done on the primates. However, one drug that underwent testings on rats and found to be safe turned out to be one of the most notorious and tragic drug ever given to humans. The drug is the thalidomide, where some 4.000 children were born with badly deformed limbs to European mothers. Others were born with missing organs or without normal openings for their gastrointestinal tract. Many deformed babies were deliberately poisoned by their parents who could not tolerate the deformities.

Primate researchers went into actions. They administered the drug to pregnant baboons and the same deformities were discovered. The similarities in the metabolism of drugs between humans and monkeys made the experiments possible. Although the destructive vector of the drug is still unknown, it is unquestionable that some primate experimentations will be needed for years to come.

The monkeys are often used in the study of neuroscience involving the brain. The apes are strapped on the chair and immobilized by restraining devise to keep them still while scientists probe on their brain. To get into their brain, a hole is drilled into their thick skull and a capped tube is inserted into the brain. Through this tube, a needle with a microscopic eye is magnified and used to see the neurons at work. Although the experiment seem to be painless initially because anesthesia was used, the pain will come after the anesthesia wears off. Many conservationists find this type of experiment very revolting since there is nothing to be gained after so many of these experiments have already taken place.

GIBBONS

There are nine types of gibbons and they are known as the lesser apes because of their size. They are small, slender, and most numerous members of the ape family. Gibbons are found only in Asia and spend most of their lives in trees. They have a highly developed brachiating ability to swing rapidly from one branch to another. In Java, the locals called them "wau-wau," meaning "old woman" because of their facial expression.

The pileated gibbons (Hylobates pileatus) once very common throughout Thailand, Laos, and Cambodia have been reduced to remnants in the wild. The main cause of their decline is habitat destruction. Without enough space for breeding, and the rampant hunting for their meat have taken their toll. In Thailand alone, there were more than 2 million of them before logging destroyed their habitats. Now, only about 20,000 are left and their destruction is still going on.

GORILLAS

Gorillas (Gorilla gorilla) are the biggest apes that are closely related to the chimpanzees but are twice as large. They consisted of two races that can only be found in two main areas of West Central Africa. The short-haired lowland gorillas ranges over a vast area comprising the countries of Cameroon, Gabon, Zaire and Tanganyika. They are more numerous with more than ten thousand today. Some were used for scientific research. The rare shaggy-haired mountain gorillas are found in a small area of the great Kayonza Forest and the extinct Viranga Volcano of Rwanda up to a height of about 3,000 meters. A smaller population can be found in Uganda, Burundi, and Tanzania.

Contrary to popular belief, mountain gorillas are gentle animals, which prefer to be left alone. Fighting between two males occurs only when they contend for the right to head a group of females. However, in everything else, they live in harmony and are not bothered by people watching them. Each night they make the nests for themselves in the trees, never staying at the same nest twice.

The first European to see a gorilla was an Englishman named Endrew Battel in 1589 in the jungle of Angola. He was frightened by the big animal because of its size and strength. His exaggerated report of bloody encounters between gorillas and elephants and wild stories of the apes killing the locals led to the gorilla's bad reputation of viciousness and violent temper. But the truth is far from his wild imagination. The only reason the gorillas manifest these reactions was when their family members were wounded or killed without reason by the early explorers. They are fighting in self-defense as people do.

For the 3,000 hours Dian Fossey spent with the mountain gorillas, she had seen one instance of only five minutes of violent behavior. That was when one gorilla killed another in a fight. It was mainly through her efforts and that of Jane Goodall and George Schaller that their vicious reputations have been put to rest and replaced as gentle vegetarians. It was recently demonstrated when a child visiting a zoo in the U.S. felled into the gorilla's den was taken care by the mother gorilla. They are not aggressive apes, but very shy and will avoid contact with people whenever possible.

The combination of loss of habitat, hunting for the trophies, poverty, and the aftermath of the civil war has reduced the population to near extinction. Only about 650 of them are left in the wild, mostly in Rwanda. Their survival owes much to the Rwanda's Mountain Gorilla Project. But in the face of poverty and hunger, these mountain gorillas are being hunted for food by tribesmen who have longed enjoyed eating their meat. The food is to supplement the much needed protein augmented by the sale of their body parts especially the hands, feet and the head. The head and feet are used as trophy and souvenir respectively, while the hands are grounded into powder and sprinkled into baby's bath to make the baby "stronger." Medicines have been made from their bones and brains and are considered great values for renewing vigor and health.

Poachers are always a menace to all wildlife and gorillas. Gorilla poachers are often hired by unscrupulous zoos wanting a gorilla baby, and usually the whole adult group is slaughtered as they will fight to the death to protect their offspring. The fact that gorillas give birth on the average once every four to five years means that even limited poaching can have a disastrous effect on population. While poaching for the gorillas is still a problem in Rwanda, an even greater concern arises when local people, wishing to supplement their protcin-poor diet, attempt to snare some antelope but inadvertently harmed the gorillas. Unfortunate gorilla frequently loses a hand or foot in the trap and often end up dying of gangrene as a result.

Many species of primates such as orangutan, chimpanzee, gibbon and other species are still heavily traded especially for laboratory testings. More than 100.000 primates are imported to the U.S. annually. Dealings in baby primates are often illegal, but they are still being sold clandestinely in hidden compounds of the animal markets throughout Indonesia, Malaysia and Thailand. To capture these baby gorillas often required the killing of the parent gorillas. Therefore the trading of baby gorillas should be totally banned and ownership of these animals should be a prima facie case of illegal trading.

The plight of the gorillas has forced governments in Africa to ban the sale of gorilla's meat as food and body parts as souvenirs. In eastern Cameroon and Congo, hundreds of baby gorillas and chimpanzees are condemned to die after their parents are killed for their meat. Each year an estimated 400-600 gorillas are killed and consumed (1992). The hands are sold illegally at the market. The finger is boiled in water for bathing a newborn human infant to enable the gorilla's strength to confer on the child.

The World Society for the Protection of Animals takes in as many orphans as it possibly can and is leading a campaign to save the primates from extinction. Funds and lack of space are running out, adding to more problems. Even the skull which was used in traditional ceremonies to invoke the Dower of the gorilla by local tribesmen, are made into souvenirs and openly sold in the markets in some African towns and cities.

Logging companies have made poaching possible as they opened up huge tracts of forests that were once impenetrable to hunters and log workers. The gorillas are killed in the mountain, transported to the cities by logging truck drivers and sold to dealers for $30 for a 400 pound male gorilla. The bush meat, as they are called, are then sold in the city at three times the cost of beef. With such a large return and little investment, more of these primates are expected to be killed in the years to come especially when laws banning their sales are not being enforced. The lack of pork and beef in the market is partly responsible for the proliferation of gorillas' meat in the markets.

In the jungle, the only possible enemy beside people is the leopard, but even then it is very rare that they are attacked. The two greatest threats are the loss of habitat and poaching. An internationally sponsored project now pays for guards to patrol their refuge but there simply are not enough guards and there's very little money to provide those already on duty with such basic necessities as guns, ammunition and uniforms.

One way of saving the gorillas is to set up ecotours. Tours that ran along the habitats of the gorillas have proven to be interesting and popular. Tourists are willing to pay nearly $200 each to join the tour in seeing the apes in their habitats. The animals bring in a fair amount of foreign revenue, about $ 10 million annually, and these can be used to protect them and their habitats.

There are about 600 gorillas in zoos around the world. Zoo breeding has not been successful. The mother gorillas find it difficult to breed because of the unnatural conditions of their confinement. Even gorillas reared together in zoos do not breed well and those with babies often fail to rear them properly. Zoos have started gorilla exchange programs with the hope that they will form new social groups and reproduce. Furthermore, the primates are susceptible to diseases that affect humans such as influenza, pneumonia, gastro problems and even bone disease. Recently, some gorillas in zoos are found to be suffering and dying of heart problems. These diseases are rarely found in gorillas in the jungle.

More gorillas have died in captivity than have been born and they have shorter life spans than those found in the wilderness. Facilities that resemble the jungle homes are nowhere to be found in the zoo. They need trees to swing and exercise; they need bamboo, branches, twigs, and straw for building their resting place since they move around a lot and never sleep at the same place twice. By confining them in small open areas is still far from their ideal habitat.

In Africa John Burton of the Flora and Fauna Preservation Society persuaded the local children to design toy rides for gorillas which proved worthwhile in funding gorilla protection. Most people are willing to spend money for the Protection of the wildlife, especially endangered ones.

LEMURS

There are 30 species of lemurs divided into four groups: the true lemurs with 8 species, the indris with 4 species, the dwarf lemurs with six species and the peculiar aye-aye. Most of them are found in the Great Red Island in Madagascar. The smallest lemur and most primitive is the mouse lemur (Microcebus murinus). It is so small it can sit on the palm of a man. On the other hand, indri is the biggest lemur, weighing almost 20 pounds. The ring-tailed lemur is the most attractive of the lemur. It has been copied and made into a delightfully soft toy by a manufacturer. Part of the royalty from the sale of the toys is earmarked toward its conservation.

As with most densely populated countries, their habitats are giving way to agriculture as farmers clear more forest for pastures and farmland. The black lemur, restricted to the Sambirano region of northwest Madagascar are also being invaded by foreign tourists who flock to Nosy Be pristine beaches. Another lemur, the ruffled lemur (Varecia variegata) are sometimes hunted for food by the natives and for the pet trade.

The aye-aye (Daubentonia mudugascanensis) is a unique creature even among lemurs. It has the characteristic traits of many other animals rolled into one. Aye-aye has big ears and large staring eyes. It has also elongated middle finger used to scrape out the inside of sugar cane and dig insects from the bark of trees. Researchers have discovered that they tap on trees and use their keen hearing to locate cavities that may possibly contain insect larvae. Biologists believe they are the only primates to do so. Some hunters hunt for this finger as a magic charm. Others kill them for raiding coconut and sugar cane plantations. Its habitats have been destroyed by slash-and-burn agriculture leaving remnants for the primates. All lemurs endemic to Madagascar are endangered due to the dwindling forest habitats and the growing poor population survive by practicing slash-and-burn agriculture.

However the aye-aye is particularly vulnerable to extinction. The Malagasy tribe of Madagascar consider the aye-aye as harbinger of bad omen. Natives on the island think that these strange-looking animals were the reincarnated spirits of their own dead relatives calling for them. Legend says that should an aye-aye point its elongated middle finger at you, death is swift and horrible. To counter the curse, it became necessary to kill the animal and then place its corpse on a stake at a crossroad, with the hope that a stranger will pass by and absorb the aye-aye's curse.

The only way for the lemurs to survive extinction is to breed them in captivity. This is what the researchers are doing at the Duke University Primate Center. Dr. Elwyn Simons, a primatologist who runs the Center is studying their behavior and hope someday to return them to the wild. The primate center has been successful in breeding at least 400 lemurs from fifteen species kept in large cages or open-air enclosure in the North Carolina woods.

In 1986, Dr. Patricia Wright of the State University of New York, Stony Brook, found a species thought to be extinct, the greater bamboo lemur. Together with a German biologist, Bernhard Meier, they also found an entirely new species, the golden bamboo lemur. Her exhaustive research and conservation efforts led to the creation of a 41,000-hectares park.

LORISES

Lorises are nocturnal, tree-dwelling, tailless primates that are found in Asia. The slow lorises (Nycticebus cuucang and Nycticebus pygmaeus) are found in

Borneo. Java and Sumatra. The slender lorises (Loris lardigradus) are found in India and Ceylon. They are all related to the bushbabies and the pottos. The slow loris is a slow moving animal while slender loris, as the name implies is a slender, more agile animal. They spend most of their time in the trees hanging upside down. They never let go of one tree branch until it has the firm grip of another branch. Feeding on insects, millipedes, fruits, and leaves, they can pounce with amazing speed on target insects. Like the bushbabics, they are territorial animals, urinating on their hands and feet to leave a scent whatever they touch.

Lorises look very much like toys and are in demand as pets throughout the regions where they are found. Many died in captivity because of the difficulties in keeping them. It takes a lot of experience and patience to see them through. They need a constant supply of live insects which many find it difficult to supply.

Lorises in India have a more dreadful fate than death. Their eyes are often removed while alive and conscious and used as folk medicine. Later they are released back to the forest where they are found, completely blind. Although the most humane thing to do is probably to kill the primates, yet the religion of the natives forbade them from killing the primates. These lorises are often starved to death.

MACAQUES

Macaques everywhere are under threat of extinction because of the loss of habitats. Some are under threat from the gourmands. In China, they are a popular choice for stew meat. As with most mammals, they are slow to reproduce, making it doubly difficult to keep them from extinction. The lion-tailed macaque (Macaco silenus) is one example. They are endemic to the south Indian rainforest. Its habitat is now confined to the Western Ghats mountain ranges. Once occupying 5,000 sq km, 60% the area has been fragmented into small patches that makes survival difficult. Since they are social animals living in groups, the fragmented patches of forests cannot support large population.

More than 90% of the existing habitat has been selectively logged in the past few years in spite of the know ledge that it will lead to their extinction. Firewood gathering and other forest products are being harvested in many areas. Conversion of forest to agriculture was a major factor then and now. In Sumatra, 66% of their habitat has been destroyed by the late 1980s; in Bali, 96% was destroyed. Hunting in some areas has reduced their food supply. Planned hydroelectric projects especially in the Kerala region may inundate many parts of their habitat. It is therefore important to have their habitat declared as national park to bring them under protection.

Macaques have always been under threat from biomedical researchers. CITES reported that an annual average of 23,000 crab-eating macaques were exported from Indonesia, Malaysia, and the Philippines in the period of 1980-1985, mostly used for bio-medical research. Of the 20 species of monkeys widely used in biomedical research, rhesus macaques (Macaca mulaiia) head the list, followed by the crab-eating macaques of Indonesia and the pigtail and stumptail macaques. Most of the macaques used in the U.S. are imported from the Philippines.

The rhesus macaques have been used for NASA spaceflight because they one of the toughest monkeys Researchers at NASA-Ames in California had experimented macaques whirling around a centrifuge that would easily sicken the common squirrel monkey (Saimiri sciureus). Their strong survival instinct was their biggest liability, making them ideal candidates for experiments.

A crab-eating macaque named Paul was used in studying the relay system of the brain through the spinal cord to the arm. The nerves in the spinal cord were deliberately severed. Because of its isolation, it began to chew its nerve-dead arm. Its arm was savagely chewed and the bones were cracked under its powerful teeth. The arm was amputated at the elbow, but it didn't stop the mutilation. Finally the whole arm had to be removed along the shoulder because of the gangrene. It died a few weeks later, on August 26, 1989. too weak to support itself and suffering from incurable diarrhea. That was not its only unfortunate ordeal. It was earlier rescue from a Maryland laboratory only to end in a more horrific fate.

One of the greatest contributions of rhesus macaques is the discovery of the "Rh" factor in blood. The discovery was made by the Nobel Prize winner Karl Landsteiner (1868-1943) and his pupil Alexander Wiener in 1940. Because of their discovery, thousands of children are saved today who would otherwise suffer brain damage or die as a result of the incompatibility of the blood between the mother and child. Most of the children in mental hospitals were caused by Rh complications. The discovery later lead to a vaccine

The mobility of the monkeys can be used for other purposes instead of experimentations and entertainments. The pig-tailed macaques of Malaysia have been trained to pick coconuts in Thailand and Malaysia. Their skill are in such demand that in Thailand, a "Monkey Training College" was set up to train the monkey starting at six months old. An expert coconut picker can harvest an many as 800 coconuts a day. They are "paid" very cheaply with bananas.

MANGA BEYS

Mangabeys are large tree-dwelling monkeys found in the rain forests of Central and West Africa. There are several species for which five are well known. They are the white-collared (Cerocebus torquatus), the crested (Cerocebusgalerutus), the gray-checked (Cerocebus albigena), the black (Cerocebus aterrimus) and the sooty macaques (Cerocebus torquatus). They feed on fruits, but deforestations have greatly reduced their food source, destroyed their habitats and brought some species such as the white-collared and crested to the brink of extinction forcing the FWS to place them under the Endangered Species Act, prohibiting their import to the U.S.

Trapping the mangabeys can be dangerous for the primates. Because they spend their sleeping hours high up in the trees, tribesmen used large nets around the tree and set the tree on fire forcing the monkeys to jump to the net. Some died from the flame while others from the fall.

The elusive, rare and endangered mangabeys are not safe from the biomedical researchers who use them for finding a cure for leprosy. A researcher, Robert Gormus, not able to find any mangabey in the U.S. was forced to spend months in

Africa searching for the elusive primates. He was able to find eight live mangabeys abandoned by an animal trader who was frustrated that the animals were not bought promptly from him. The rest of the thirty abandoned mangabeys died of starvation.

MARMOSETS

Marmosets are indigenous to South America. They are among the most beautiful primates, feeding on insects, lizards, frogs, snails, and other creeping animals. Endowed with sharp teeth, they used them to dig into tree barks and lap up the sap. There are several species of marmosets. The tassel-eared marmosets (Callithrix humeralifer) have long bristles on their wrist to help them feel the branches. The pygmy marmosets (Cebuella pygmaea) and the mouse lemur (Microcebus murinus) are the smallest primates. The silvery marmosets (Callithrix argentata), unlike other primates, the father does most of the parenting job except when the mother is suckling the babies.

The common marmoset (Callithrix jacchus) can easily be identified by the two tufts of white hair covering the ears and a white patch on the forehead. Found in the tropical forest of Brazil, these primates live inside the hollows of trees. They feed on insects, fruits, and saps. One unique feature is that only one female in each group can reproduce offspring. The father helps in caring the young.

In the rainforest where these primates are found, vast track of lands are being cleared for plantations and ranchings. Coupled with developmental works and encroachment of humans made possible by the proliferation of roads, could ultimately lead to the extinction of these primates unless sanctuaries are provided while their population are self-sustaining.

MONKEYS

There are more than 200 species of monkeys in the world. They are found in almost all the jungles of the world. They ranged from fairly large one as big as people to the smallest one, the little talapin with their strange bundle of green fur. An interesting monkey is the spider monkey which can hang by its tail from a branch while it picks leaves or fruits to eat. Squirrel monkeys (Salauri oerstedii) are exquisite little mites, through their numbers are declining fast as huge quantities have been exported for research. Their natural habitats in Panama and Costa Rica are also being converted to pasture and farmland as the human population continues to increase.

Another rare monkey found in the rainforests of Amazon is the red uakari (Cacajao calvus) which has a distinctive vermilion face and is completely bald and hairless in the face and part of the forehead. The rest of the body is reddish-brown except for the extremities which are brown. They live in flooded areas but never descend to the ground. They have been overhunted in the wild for the zoos although their survival rate in captivity is very short.

The proboscis monkeys (Nasalis larvatus) are known for their long and bulbous noses. Found only in Borneo, they are falling victims to loggings, forest fires, agriculture and development of new towns. They make their habitats rivers where they are good swimmers, but these places are also coveted by humans. They always lost out to developmental projects unless their habitat is converted to wildlife sanctuary. In Sabah, Malaysia, many monkeys live along the Kinabatangan River which is a proposed wildlife sanctuary. Even then it will have to contend with illegal loggings that have been going on in many areas. They are also hunted for food by natives and for sport. The natives consider their flesh a delicacy and they are hunted wherever they are found. However, successes have been few as these primates have learned to fear and evade humans.

In the densely forested karst spires of Guangxi Province, near the Vietnam border, lives a species of primates found nowhere else in the World: the white-headed langur. Their habitat had shrunk to a mere 200 sq km due to farming and wood gathering. Their population has fallen to roughly 1.400 individuals. Unless both factors are halted, it could lead to their extinction in the wild.

Probably the only monkey killed in vast numbers for its fur is the black-and-white colobus monkey (Colobus guereza) of Central Africa. It was estimated that as many as 2 million of these monkeys were killed for their long, silky and shiny pelts since the 19th century. Many uninformed tourists bought these furs unknowingly. Another species, the black-bearded saki (Chiropoies sonatas) is found in South America. They have a large head with long thick beard. Seldom seen by humans, they are considered rare, but local Indians hunt them for their fur and hair on their tails for decorative use. Their close relative, the langur or more specifically the entellus or Hanuman langur (Presbytis entellus) is considered the sacred monkey of India. These langurs can freely roam and live on the ground of Hindu temples without harm coming to them. They are often found in the cities plundering trees and gardens and stealing food from vendors and vendees.

Like the trapping of many other apes, the mother monkeys are shot first and the babies are caught when the mother falls to the ground. The baby monkeys are easier to handle and transported to their destinations. However, Indonesian animal traders estimate that 32% to 71% of these babies die before they reach their destinations. The culprit is either starvation or disease. On one occasion, during the summer of 1992, an import made by Worldwide Primates of Miami, 110 crab-eating macaques from Indonesia died of stress-induced pneumonia. Twenty of them were still babies.

ORANGUTANS

Orangutans can only be found in the remote forests of Borneo (Pongo pygmaeus pygmaeus) and Sumatra (Pongopygmaeus abeli), Indonesia. There are no more than 2,500 left in their native habitat. As the male grew older, it acquire bulging cheek pads on the face. There are slight differences between the two races and it is important to separate the two during breeding to ensure genetic integrity. They are also known as the "old man of the woods." Orangs travel alone or in groups of twos and do not form a social group like the chimps and gorillas. The native tribesmen used to hunt them for food. When it was first discovered by the outside world, scientists came to the island to study them, not by capturing them but by killing them. They were followed by the hunters in the late 1800s. One of the encounter by Captain Rodney Mundy resulted in the killing of several females trying to rescue their badly wounded youngs. An American hunter hired to collect orangs left with 50 of them, mostly dead. In many areas the orangs became extinct because they could not breed faster than when killed or captured. One of their favorite fruit is the durian that is also harvested by humans. This often lead to unpleasant encounter, leading to the orangs being harmed. Their low birth rate is almost responsible for their decline. The female breeds once every four years or more. This could lead to only a few offspring born in her lifetime.

In the 1900s, zoos were competing for more wild animals and young orangs were in demand. Many wildlife dealers were mobilized because of the high prices offered for these live animals. This lead to another problem more deadly for the orangs. The mother orangs guarding their youngs with their lives will have to be killed to get to the babies. Unfortunately, many babies died because the hunters and their workers do not know how to care for them while they wait for the dealers to pick them up. Many die of hunger and disease without their mothers to care for them. The long voyage by ship claimed even more lives.

Only one out of every five infant orangs captured survive to adulthood. Their slow movement make it easy to capture the animals. Although catching and owning an orangutan is illegal in many areas, poachers continue to hunt and sell young orangs as pets. In Borneo, the Dayak tribesmen have been capturing young orangutans and selling them to wealthy Indonesians for about $320 and to Taiwanese as pets. Inspired by a television show showing orangutans as pets, Taiwanese pay as much as $5,000 to buy smuggled orangs from Indonesia during the 1980s. It was only in 1989 that the practice was outlawed. While baby orangs can be good pets, they become unmanageable as they grow up and are abandoned. They have even found new use for the dead mother carcass, which they used to abandon and left to rot. The head is now decapitated, striped of its flesh, polished and made into carvings and markings to enhance the skull for the tourist markets. Each skull is sold illegally for about $70 to $80. This is made possible because of the lax enforcement of the laws governing endangered species.

In Malaysia, baby orangutans are often abducted from their parents by desperate childless couples. They are then shaved to look like humans and reared for some time. When they grow too old, they are abused by their very owners. Some have been known to be hacked to death for bringing havoc to the family. Although there is a law punishable by five years in jail for owning an orangutan, it is seldom enforced. An average of three to four calls a month have been reported to the government regarding people illegally keeping and abusing apes.

The modern threat to their survival, common for most mammals of the jungle is the loss of habitat. The increasing density of human populations in Indonesia and the on-going loggings in many parts of the country is reducing their habitat and destroying their breeding ground. Unless something drastic is done to reverse the trend, primatologists believe that there will be too few left by the year 2000 and doom them to extinction.

The loss of habitats caused by several months of forest fire in Sumatra and Kalimanta had destroyed more than 100.000 hectares of forest housing millions of animals in Indonesia. Particularly hard hit are the orangutans because of destruction of their tree habitats. Without tree cover, they are easily caught by the human predators who sold them illegally to pet lovers or smuggled them out of the country.

In the U.S. where the law on endangered species is strictly enforced, some legitimate traders have links to illegal trading. The Worldwide Primates owner, Matthew Block was once convicted for illegally smuggling six baby orangs bound for Russia. Four of the six primates died from lack of food and water. They were smuggled using false labels on crates marked "birds."

POLIO VACCINE

Polio is one of the most dreaded diseases to strike humanity. Before the availability of the vaccine, 20,000 people were killed or crippled by the polio virus. With the availability of the rhesus macaques, more than 200,000 of them were imported annually into the U.S. in the 1950s and 100,000 annually during the 1960s. The large demand resulted from the race to find a polio vaccine. Scientists had discovered that the polio virus can grow in monkey cell cultures and medical researchers wanted to use the monkey for experiments. A low estimate had it that more than a million up to five million of these monkeys were sacrificed to develop the vaccine.

There were once more than 5 million macaques in India at their apex. During the late 1950s, the race to find the cure for polio was also the race to slaughter the rhesus macaques of India. The U.S. was importing 200.000 annually of these primates for experiments. In twenty years, the macaque populations fell to less than 200,000 in India. The race to find a cure for AIDS could mean the route for thousands of pigtail macaques. Their numbers were never large in the wild and could easily decimate their population. Fortunately, recent findings show that they are not good candidates for AIDS research.

POTTOS

Potto (Perodictus potto) is the only species of its kind. They are small primates closely related to the loris and are found only in the tropical forests of Africa. Their colors vary with age and sex and ranged from brown to black. They rest by hanging upside down like the sloth. The babies learn to feed on food brought by the mother by pulling it from the mother's mouth. This is how they learned to know what foods are safe to eat. One of their unique features is located in their hands, where the muscular thumb is set across the three large fingers while the index finger is just a vestige. Beside forest destruction, their other enemy is the palm owl. They are rarely seen by humans, therefore little is known about their behavior and breeding habit.

A distant relative, the golden potto or angwantibo (Arctocebus calabarensis) is also the only species of its kind. It is a small primate with a maximum weight of about 465 grams and length of 30.5 cm. The tail is only a protrusion. They are found mostly in Africa where they preferred to reside in areas where trees have been cleared for secondary growth. Their diet consists of insects, caterpillars, and fruits. Loss of habitats has been responsible for their decline and they are sometimes hunted for their meat by the local people.

RUFFIANS

Some animals have been noted for their viciousness in destroying properties. This is especially true of primates. In India where monkeys are considered sacred to the Hindu, they are treated with much respect. Monkeys are associated with Haunuman, the mythical monkey god who was Lord Rama's fearless and loyal assistant in his banle against Ravana, the evil-god king of Lanka (modem Sri Lanka).

Because they don't fear people and are free to roam around, the monkeys have been known to attack people and snatch food. To resolve the problems posed by some of these animals, the primates are jailed behind bars like human beings. In the northern state of Punjab, where there are about 50,000 wild monkeys, ruffians are locked up in a special jail and held until declared fit for release back into society.

One primate at Patiala, north of New Delhi was "arrested" more than a year ago for attacking students and is still being held It has been reported that another pair, arrested for snatching handbags and lunchboxes are being considered for parole.

All life forms must be treated with some reverence and given due respect like the monkeys of India. Most animals have priority over the land people have forcibly taken from them. They have just the same right to co-exist with humans in their own harmonious environment. Should any of them prove to be vicious and brutal, the law should be applied to them humanely instead of killing them. The same should be true of other wild animals. They are victims of our encroachment. Even bears that ransack garbage cans are only trying to survive in the only way they know how.

SLOTHS

Sloths are one of the slowest primates in the wild forests of South America. They spend almost their entire lives hanging upside down the trees, sleeping, breeding, eating, and mating up in the trees. If ever they come down trom the tree, it is only to change venue or drink water. The sedentary life made it difficult for them to walk on their feet and they are forced to drag themselves on their bellies using their hands. The laziness allow green algae to grow on their long thick hair. Another remarkable feature is that their teeth are located in the cheeks that grow continuously throughout their lives.

The seven species of sloths are divided into two groups depending on the number of toes on their feet. The two-toed sloths (Choloepus didactylus), the larger of the groups make their home from Venezuela to Brazil. They survive on a vegetarian diet. The three-toed sloths (Bradypus tridaciylus) are found in the forest of Honduras up to the northern part of Argentina. They feed on a species of trumpetwood leaves and fruits, which they find using their keen sense of smell because they have very poor eyesights. They move slowly among branches and spend many hours hanging in the trunk of trees using the curved claws as hooks.

TAMARINS

Probably the most spectacular prima.es are the various colorful golden lion tamarins (Leontopithecus rosalia), some of wh.ch are completely covered in a long, gold pelt and look like toys. They are very rare these days numbering about 150 and are confined to 5,000 hectares of the Poco das Anas Biological Reserve in Brazil where they are strictly protected. In spite of being well protected, still some of these monkeys found their way in the wildlife markets. People cutting down the forest outside of the protected reserves capture them for sale as pets or for the zoos. Sometimes they are eaten by the local people.

Another interesting primate is the emperor tamarin (Saguinus imperator) of Amazon. It has a distinctive long white mustache. They are all very agile and great leapers. The tamarin comes from the same family as the marmosets of South America where they live mostly in the eastern coastal forest of Brazil near the city of Rio de Janeiro. The loss of their habitat due to logging, charcoal and firewood gathering, ranching and the more recent housing and condominium projects have reduced their habitat to less than 2% of their original forest reserves.

In Brazil in 1974, the tireless efforts of Adelman Coimbra-Filbo, who had toiled heroically for Brazil's wildlife was rewarded by the government with the creation of Poco das Anas Biological Reserve largely devoted to the maintenance of a viable habitat for the golden tamarins. With the help of David Kleiman of the National Zoological Park, the population has grown to more than 370 animals in captivity in 1983. Many zoo-bred tamarins have been released back to their original coastal habitat.

An even rarer species is the golden rumped lion tamarin that is also finding difficulties to survive in the wild. Other species of tamarins are the red-handed tamarins (Saguinus midas) which are completely black except for the hand which is reddish in color, thus giving it their name. The cotton top tamarins (Saguinus oedipus) from Colombia can easily be recognized with its white-crested hair on their head. They are in great demand for the pet trade, causing a decline in their natural habitat. These primates are very sociable and spend most of their time grooming each other.

TARSIERS

Unlike the bushbabies tarsiers are much more efficient and ruthless predators. They hunt at night on bigger insects, birds, and even snakes by killing them with a nip of their sharp teeth. These animals are great leapers, able to leap between trees six meters apart. There are also three species of tarsiers found in the rainforests of Asia. One of their special attributes is their ability to move its head around to the back. This more than makes up for the difficulty seeing sideways. The Philippines is host to one of the species (*Tarsius synchta*). Another species Tarsius bancanus can be found in Borneo while Tarsius spectrum can be found in Celebes and adjacent islands.

CHAPTER 9

BIRDS

Birds are warm-blooded animals with backbones. They lay eggs from which their young hatch. There are more than 9.250 species of birds throughout the world. They can be found as far as the Arctic and in areas as dry as the Sahara Desert. They come in all sizes, shapes, and colors. Their sizes can range from the tiny bee hummingbirds (Mellisuga helenae) of Cuba and the Isle of Pines, to the largest, the ostriches (Siruihio camclus).

Birds have long fascinated human beings throughout history. For millennia, humans have marveled at the flight of birds and hope one day to be able to soar like them. People have also enjoyed viewing the many colorful birds with the unique textures of their feathers. Some birds have become extinct because of feather harvesting.

The birds with their small brains are not stimulating living things, yet many ordinary citizens and the scientific communities have found them fascinating subjects of studies. They make sounds that are distinguished by their own species. Singing, alarm calls, location notes, and other sounds are part of the unique behavior of birds. These various sounds have fascinated ornithologists for a long time. Even their feeding habits with different beaks are adapted for different hunting and gathering of food. The most fascinating characteristic is probably their ability to migrate between far flung places without getting lost.

The birds are the only true flying vertebrates beside the bats. They have feathers throughout their bodies and are designed for flying. The two legs are made of hollow bones to reduce their weight for easy flying. Those that soar high in the sky are hunted with shotguns and are seldom captured alive. More than 20% of the species of birds have become extinct in the past 2,000 years with another 11% on the brink of extinction. Many of these birds are found in islands scattered throughout the world.

Birds also play an important role in gauging the status of our atmosphere. They serve as barometer for air pollution in urban areas. Their presence or absence is a vital sign of the quality of the environment. Some birds played an important role in the ecological balance of the environment. Because they spend a lot of energy flying, they are constantly looking for food to eat. Most birds cat their own weight in insects every day. Their presence in our midst is one way of controlling insects that are harmful to humans.

Probably the most familiar bird of all is the chicken. It provides us with meat and eggs for our consumption. Other domesticated birds are the turkey, duck, geese, ostrich, quail, pigeon, and many others. Some birds are important for the Products they provide. One of the products is guano which is used as fertilizer. They are produced from the droppings of birds such as cormorants and other sea birds in islands off South America and South Africa. Because this important product is supplied to the tune of 300,000 tons annually, the birds in these areas are well protected from human activities.

ALBATROSSES

One of the stronghold of the albatross (Diomedea exulans) is located in Midway. When the island was first discovered in the mid-19th century during a shipwreck, the invaders survived by gathering the eggs of these seabirds. By 1935, people started to colonize the small island and the U.S. Navy started to build a naval base there. On June 4, 1942, the Japanese invaded the surrounding areas and the Battle of Midway ensued. The island was seriously damaged and a heavy casualty of birds were noted. The high mortality is due to one of their peculiar characteristic of staying put in one place even in the presence of danger. Once they have found a breeding ground, they refuse to move even if flooding will cause the death of the chicks.

In 1950, when the Navy decided to construct a $40 million airfield, the albatrosses were all around the island, a million strong. All methods were used to move the animals from their nesting place, but to no avail. Bedsheets were also used to stir the bird to move away. Blank bullets and even smoke bombs were also used. Finally, bulldozers were used to move the birds and more than 59,000 were buried alive and more than 100,000 eggs were destroyed.

The lasting solution was found by paving half of the island with asphalt. The birds don't like the pavement and prefer the grass Half of the island is now paved and the other half reserved for the birds. Today, Midway Island is considered a protected sanctuary under the care of the FWS. The gooney birds mate for life and live for 50 years. More than a million of them nest on the island every year. Other birds have found a sanctuary in this island. Within the 200-mile zone are some endangered monk seals and spinner dolphins. They are well protected by the no nonsense FWS. Fishing is allowed for the first time, but it is a catch-and-release program.

After the ban on the use of driftnets, fishermen have found a new technique of mass fishing. The longline fishing technique uses 2,000 to 3,000 hooks with squids or small fishes as baits intended for the bigger fish. The fish hooks are then laid out in the sea for 20 to 40 miles just like the use of the driftnet. This efficient and indiscriminate fishing method is taking a toll of marine mammals, marine turtles and some seabirds specially the albatrosses. Most vulnerable are the wandering and short-tailed albatross, both under the IUCN's threatened list.

The vulnerability is during the initial setting and the final retrieving of the longline. During the setting of the hook, the birds often follow' the baited hooks into the sea and dive for the baits as they are being laid and getting hooked and drowning. During retrieving, the hooks with their baits or catches are also inviting food for the albatrosses which inadvertently get hooked.

Studies made in 1990 by biologists estimated that Japanese long-liners accidentally hook 44,000 albatrosses a year. Most drownings occur in the southwestern Pacific Ocean where 10 of the 14 species of albatrosses can be found. The short-tailed albatrosses are particularly vulnerable to extinction since only 700 of them remained in the wild. In Hawaii alone, long-liners put out about 12 million hooks each year and drowned as estimated 4.000 black-footed and Laysan albatrosses each year.

To keep the albatrosses away from the hooks, fishermen are thawing the bait so that it will sink faster and using scaring devises such as streamer while the hooks are being laid. Some are adopting this new technique, but most find it a waste of precious time.

BIRD HOUSE

Birds are free-roaming vertebrates and should never be confined. Even in the cities, they are often seen flying from tree to tree in search of food. As more land are put under development, there is dwindling of trees in the cities. We can help the birds find a shelter in our own backyard. By planting trees and setting up a bird house, we can attract birds to our garden. Provide food along with the bird house and in no time, birds will be perching there. Peanuts are especially attractive to birds. Be sure they are fresh peanuts and not those intended for disposal which can be contaminated with aflatoxin. A big birdhouse could also served as a place for birdwatching.

In many places where wetlands and forests have given way to agriculture, farmers are finding it difficult to check the rampaging rodents that destroy the crops. Because the natural food of barn owls are reptiles and rodents, some farmers have resorted to building bird houses throughout the field to attract the owls just as others build them to attract the bats. Both are particularly effective against insect pests which could minimize if not totally remove the use of pesticides that could be harmful to mammals and the environment.

By planting certain plants and shrubs that are attractive to birds, they will be able to build their own nests and find food in the vicinity. Plant trees whenever and wherever possible.

BIRDWATCHING

Birdwatching has been a popular hobby in many countries for many years. Tens of millions are engaged to some degree in this sport. In the U.S., there are more than 7 million birdwatchers. They spent the time watching birds, analyzing their behavior, and taking photographs. Some birdwatchers are willing to pay as much as $15 to watch raptors migrate. Often the difficulties of finding birds in the cities made it necessary for people to venture to the forest or bird sanctuaries to watch these birds. Zoos often have areas set aside for the birds. Aviaries have been set up in the cities for birdwatchers.

Birds are harmless creatures that children can be exposed early in life through birdwatching. It could lay the foundation that will motivate the children to conserve and appreciate the natural world. They will find the experience an enriching and appealing pastime. It is an educational undertaking that could sharpen the senses as we try to learn and identify the different birds. Birdwatching can also be a cheap form of exercise without any of those elaborate setups needed to rear them at home. Teenagers can enjoy the many possibilities and opportunities that come along with birdwatching. Contests have been generated among school children using the birds as objects of studies.

Many of the knowledge gathered about birds have been made through the tireless efforts of birdwatchers. Because of the wide expanse they covered birdwatchers are often called in by government agency to help in any major undertaking. They have been responsible for helping the government determine the status of birds and getting them protected. Even many birds' behavior have been made through the efforts of birdwatchers.

In places where birds naturally habitate, it is important to set these sites as protected reserves. All measures must be taken to stamp out the causes of their decline. Habitat destruction, pollution, poisoning, and hunting are some factors that need to be addressed. The route taken by migrant birds must also be protected from hunting. Once a reserve had been established, it won't be long before people flock to look at the birds bringing with them cameras and binoculars instead of guns. At the Hawk Mountain in the Appalachian Mountains, 40.000 visitors a year watch the birds of prey in this 2.000 acre refuge. These protected reserves are important for their breeding, nesting, and rearing of the youngs.

People who like to watch raptors may find it necessary to travel to high mountains that are difficult to climb. The griffon vulture (Gypsfulvus) found at the 2,500-foot slopes of French Pyrenees is one of them. Instead of disturbing the habitat of these threatened species, a museum was set up in the tiny village of Aste-Beon. It features television monitors showing the birds in all their splendour. Cameras are mounted high in their natural habitat and connected to the museum where the monitors are located. The cameras can be manipulated to show the birds breeding, feeding, and flying without disturbing the vultures.

Augustin Medcvielle, who was a ten-year-old shepherd in 1959 was fascinated by the work of two ornithologists. When he became mayor, he raised $800,000 to build the museum which opened in 1993. In two years time, some 85,000 visitors have visited the place, enjoying the scene without disturbing the birds.

The result of a survey by Penn State University showed that in 1993, visitors at six state natural areas have been w illing to pay more than $1.5 million to enjoy outdoor activities. It is a sign that people are willing to pay for the recreational value of the natural land. This has resulted in a major industry providing binoculars, books, feeding stations, towers, and birds foods. It is a healthy recreation not only for people but also for the birds.

CARING FOR THE BIRDS

Approximately 98% of the health problems seen in pet birds are due to poor nutrition. These are almost total carbohydrates and fat. It's hard to imagine eating nothing but potato chips. Start giving your birds healthy food by providing them the four basic food groups every day. Many birds love peanut butter, tiny pieces of cooked meat, vegetables, and cheese. The fruits and vegetables group is an extremely important part of their diet. Try to feed your bird alfalfa sprout, broccoli, carrots, apples, cherries, and oranges. It is important to be persistent and make any food change gradually. Offer the food in different shapes, sizes and ways. It is difficult to change their junk food mentality, but perseverance will provide a long healthy life.

Birds and cats do not co-exist in harmony. Cats have killed millions of birds every year. Even caged birds have also been killed. If we are to encourage birds into our gardens, we should avoid cats as pets. Even in the wild, birds are vulnerable to preying cats during breeding time. They need to hunt more often and therefore subject themselves to more risk. One way to avoid the cats is either to cage the cats during the breeding season of the birds or putting bells on the collar of the cats to sound off their presence. There are many other things we can do as the situations arise. A little thoughtfulness can lead to satisfying solutions to almost all problems.

CRANES

There are fifteen species of cranes in the world, eight of them are on the brink of extinction. One of them is the Siberian cranes. These migratory birds found mostly in the wetlands between Mongolia and Siberia. The bird measured more than two meters from tip to tip. Many are shot by hunters while others are dying from polluted wetlands. Still others are hunted by local people for food. The desparate move to save them from extinction includes using helicopters to catch the few wild cranes for captive breeding.

The International Crane Foundation in Wisconsin, headed by George Archibald has been working for twenty years trying to save the cranes from extinction. The endangered species are kept in captive breeding. He will often act like the crane itself to induce it to lay eggs for artificial hatchings. Once the young are born, they are fed using the human-masked crane to avoid human imprint and allow the chicks to be able to return to the wild without suffering human "imprint" that made them dependent on humans for life.

The whooping cranes (Grus umertcana) of North America were down to 20 birds more than 50 years ago and has since risen to about 300 birds today. The Asian black-necked cranes which inhabit the Tibetan Plateau number about 6.000. But the changing agricultural practices have removed barley, their staple food, could spell trouble. To dramatize the plight of these two birds, the U.S. and China developed jointly the first stamp depicting these two birds in 1994.

DEFORESTATION

Trees are important habitats for many bird species, more than any other animal in the forest. Trees are being felled in many of their habitats throughout the world. Each tree felled down by the ax is one tree less for birds to build their nest or perch during their long flight. Even dead trees are important haven for birds like parrots which use the hollow trunk for breeding their offspring.

Hidden deep in the jungles of many tropical forests are still many birds waiting to be discovered. They have been well protected by the natural habitat provided by the trees which harbor all kinds of food and materials for birds to make their nests. The trees also provide the birds a safe haven to rear their youngs almost free from predators.

In tropical countries around Asia and Africa, trees are felled and converted into· agricultural field or mono-species of softwood trees. Many of these felled trees have nests built by birds for breeding. Some trees already have eggs which are destroyed during felling. In South America, tropical forests are either burned or logged and converted to cattle ranching. Burning forests could devastate large breeding grounds, destroy eggs and kill young birds that cannot fly away to safety. For those interested in knowing more about deforestation can read my book Saving the Trees, which is available in all National Book Store.

DOVES

The mourning dove (Zenaidura macroura) is a small pigeon found mostly in the U.S. It is also a symbol of peace used by many countries. The bird plays a unique role in the Bible when Noah used the dove to survey the land after the great flood. It has very little meat value, yet every year hunters kill about 50 million of them for no other reason other than that they are flying objects for target practice that so happen to be around at the wrong time and the wrong place. It is one of the most hunted game bird in the world.

The tooth-billed pigeon (Didunculus strigirostris) of western Samoa has a hooked bill similar to the extinct dodo. Although it can fly, it still spends most of the time on the ground, feeding on seeds and berries and making nests on the ground. It has been under threat from introduced animals such as cats and rats. Wild pigs often feed on their nests.

DUCKS

Ducks have always been a favorite hunting preys for hunters. In 1989, more than 5.2 million of just one species in the U.S. were killed. Many of them were illegally killed. In Louisiana, for every duck legally killed, four others are killed illegally.

The large extermination of ducks has been made possible by the use of the illegal baits. Because of the passive nature of the ducks, they often wander into areas with baits where they are blasted away with firearms. The Migratory Bird Treaty Act was promulgated in the U.S. in 1935 outlawing hunting with baits A 1941 survey in Illinois demonstrated that the waterfowls killed annually dropped from one million using baits to less than 175,000 without baits. The same act also makes it illegal to kill migratory birds except during hunting seasons established for a few species.

The provision on baiting is one of the most violated rule of the Act. In spite of this, the hunters want that provision relaxed in order to increase the killing rate. This could further reduce the game bird populations.

To counter the decline of duck population, the U.S. government passed the Federal Duck Stamp Law which requires all duck hunters to purchase. Each year 1.4 million stamps are sold and the funds are used to save their important wetland habitats.

EGG COLLECTIONS

Hunting for wildlife birds often extends to hunting or searching for their eggs. Millions of them are taken from the wild throughout the world every year. The price is often dictated by the supply and rarity of the animal. Every piece of egg taken from a rare species is a move toward the extinction of the species. Collectors are willing to pay high prices for the eggs of fossil species or rare eggs as a collector item with no intention of hatching them. Today, the value of the fossil auk egg is 30 times its weight in gold. With a price like that, no wonder collectors are hunting these rare eggs without regard to the wasteful practice.

When the price is right, people will go to great lengths in gathering these eggs for export and hatching. For the endangered species, it is easier to smuggle out the eggs than the live birds. Egg collectors have been responsible for several extinctions of species in the past.

When a Saudi Arabian learned that a baby gyrfalcon (Falco rusticolus) can sell for up to $80,000 apiece in Saudi Arabia, he undertook to smuggle a dozen eggs out of Canada with a especially made suitcase that also acts as an incubator.

ENDANGERED BIRDS

Many birds are under protection because their numbers have declined to near extinction. Some of them have even been deliberately captured from the wild for breeding in captivity. One of them is the California condor. They have been hunted or killed in the wild in large numbers until they are seldom seen in the sky. Ospreys are also under a 24-hour protection at Loch Garten, Scotland while they are nesting. Hawaiian geese were taken from the wild and have successfully bred in zoos. They have recovered and some have been released back to their island home. There are probably no ivory-billed woodpecker (Campephilus principalis) left in the swamp forests of Louisiana, USA because their habitats have disappeared with the forest clearance. The last sighting was in 1946. Fortunately there are some found in Cuba. Even then only a few remain in a remote forest reserve in eastern Cuba. The red-cockaded woodpecker (Picoides borealis) got a reprieve from a federal judge in 1988 when he ordered the U.S. Forest Service (USFS) to stop clear-cutting within 4,000 feet of the birds' colonies in Texas. Other sites have been included as part of the negotiation between conservationists and the USFS. The rare, grass-eating Cape Barren geese that live on a few islands off the coast of Australia have to compete for food with the sheep brought in from the mainland. Because they have no animal activist to protect their interest, many have been shot by the sheep farmers.

The Great Indian hornbills have been hunted and killed for their meat. The Spanish imperial eagles are also hunted and their homes destroyed due to pesticides. There are only 100 pairs left in the world. The small Galapagos penguins are also in great decline due to hunting and collection of their eggs.

There are thought to be less than 25 Madagascar sea eagles in the wild as well as the limited numbers of Mauritius kestrel, parakeet, pink pigeon and the Puerto Rican parrot. The Jersey Wildlife Preservation Trust which specializes in endangered species has rehabilitated the Mauritius pink pigeon, and some captive birds hav$_t$ been returned to their island home.

Brazil heads the list of countries with the largest number of endangered bird species. At last count it had 34 endangered species. with as many as 150 threatened There are over 10 species in the same situation throughout Asia and Australia and more than 20 in China.

FEATHERS

Birds have different types of feathers that have fascinated different people. The soft fluffy feathers are used to cover their bodies and help them fly. The unique color and shape of their feathers have been responsible for the death of many species of birds. One of the most colorful and amazing bird found in New Guinea is the bird of paradise. Their long and elegant plumes have been hunted by poachers until they are close to extinction. Likewise the Victoria crowned pigeons which can grow up to 84 cm have been hunted for their feathers. One bird that is unfortunate enough to have black feathers with white edges is the black swan. It was imported from Australia to Europe. Many have been killed after successful breeding because of the superstitious belief that they are connected with the devil.

In the old days, the feathers were used as writing implements before the fountain pen was invented. Today, the feathers are being experimented for use in cleaning up oil spills because of their ability to soak up the pollutants effectively without leaving harmful residues to the environment. Hopefully, the feathers will be harvested from dead birds and not plucked from the live birds.

Egrets are herons that are usually white and found throughout the temperate and tropical areas. During the 19th century, their feathers were in great demand for use in ladies' hats. In one season in Florida alone, 130,000 egrets were slaughtered on their nesting sites. The long silky filigress feathers were highly sought after for millinery decoration. The feathers were sold by the ounce and sold for $38 an ounce in the early 20th century. The killing of egrets for their feathers stopped only after Guy Bradley, a wildlife conservationist assigned to protect them was murdered by two hunters. His death caused such a public uproar that led to the passing of a law prohibiting the use of wildlife feathers in New York, the center of this fashion industry.

The spoonbills also went through this holocaust. More than 60 species and subspecies were slaughtered to the brink of extinction, all for the sake of the feathers to adorn women's fashion. Their plumes were sold at $80 an ounce, about three times their weight in gold then. By 1910, all the birds in Texas were exterminated and only two dozen pairs could be found in Florida. Only the timely halt to their slaughter and protection accorded were the birds able to recover slowly.

The huia (Heierolocha aculirostris) is an extinct forest bird found in the southern part of North Island. New Zealand. It was an extraordinary bird with bright orange or blue beaks whose sex can easily be distinguished from the shape of their different beaks. This weak flying bird's difficulty in escaping from people probably caused its extinction. It became extinct by 1907.

The birds were hunted for their white-tip tail feathers which were used in ceremonial headdresses or to adorn the cloaks of tribal high officials of the Maori tribe. When the future King George V (1865-1936) of England made a visit to New Zealand, he was presented with some of these feathers. By sticking one on his hat, he practically invented a new fashion upon returning home. Hunters zoomed down on the birds and slaughtered the remaining ones. The valuable feathers were traded in ornately carved wooden boxes.

Before the arrival of the Europeans, the birds were already in decline, prompting the Maori shamans to restrict their hunt. Once the Europeans set foot on the island, unrestricted hunting began. At one time toward the end of the 19t century, 11 Maori hunters killed 646 huia birds in a single month.

Hawaii is home to about 40 species of extinct and near extinct birds today. They were mostly killed for their feathers. Like the Polynesians who inhabited the other south Pacific islands, they hunted the birds for their feathers. The passerine s feathers were used to make capes and headbands or Used as an ornament for the chiefs helmets. Two other birds, a Hawaii mamos (Drepanis pacifica) and the Giant o-o (moho nobilis), a honeyeater had been reserved for use by the Polynesian chiefs. Although it is forbidden to kill the mamos, and the birds were supposed to be released after plucking the highly prized brilliant yellow feathers, still more than 80,000 mamos died. Few birds were actually released and even then without wings, they were easy prey to predators and many starved to death. They were hunted by the honeycreeper tribe to make the famous cloak worn by Hawaiian monarchs up to the time of Kamchamcha I, the King of Hawaii (1758-1819). Both were hunted to extinction by 1934. There were once 22 species of endemic finches at the turn of the century on the islands of Hawaii. Today, only 13 species are left in the wild.

Birds need not die needlessly for their feathers. In a bid to maximize profits, many farmers have resorted to live-plucking the feathers of birds for sale to fill duvets and beddings. Plucking their feathers can cause pain and open up wounds that can cause infections. Their feathers can be plucked painlessly by cutting off the tip of the feather. But it was not to be. Time is of the essence and businessmen do not have the luxury of saving the birds from pain. One type of feather called the down is used to stuff the inside of pillows. These feathers are plucked from the neck and breast of such animals as ducks and geese. The pain must be intolerable, like plucking out the hair on our head. And the plucking is not done only once, but as many as five times before the birds are slaughtered and sold as food. The live-plucking of geese has become common in Hungary, France, Israel, China, and Poland.

The only bird whose skin can be used as leather is not spared. Because of its particular softness, elasticity, and durability, the ostrich (Struihio camelus) leather is in high demand for use as shoe-upper leather or accessories. Ostriches have been raised for about 100 years on specialized farms in Southern Africa and Australia.

LEGAL AND ILLEGAL TRADE

The trade in exotic birds, whether legal or illegal, has been responsible for decimation of many species. Europe, North America and Japan are the mail importers of these birds. With their wealth, they have encouraged the poor countries to destroy their biodiversity and export them to the developed countries. Every year millions of macaws, parrots, cockatoos, and birds of prey, most of them endangered species are caught and exported. Only 10% of them reached their destinations alive. The rest died on transit from being crammed in cages that are not adequately ventilated, and without food and water. Their own body heat can also suffocate them. Once they arrived at their destination, they still had to be quarantined where many die slowly because caretakers lack the training to care for exotic birds.

Bird tradings in the tropical countries are known for their anomalies. One notorious example is the bird trading of live parrots and birds of paradise from Moluccas and New Guinea. Of the 70.000 birds exported from Moluccas in 1983. only 42,000 were legally documented. Although most countries have restrictions on the export of birds, traders always find ways to export more than they are allowed to. One-quarter of a million exotic birds, many of them endangered are smuggled to the U.S. from developing countries annually. Some species refuted to command as much as $10,000 can only encourage this illegal trade.

Most of the exotic birds smuggled from Mexico to the U.S. died enroute to their destination. The ways they are smuggled are conducive to high mortality. The bird's beak is taped to avoid noise detection. Then they are place in false bottom suitcases, inside coat linings, or in any gap they can fit. Only 10% to 20% of these birds will live long enough to reach their destination. Many birds are young siblings that cannot endure the harshness.

Corruptions are so rampant, it is impossible to stamp the illegal exportation of birds except with the cooperation of the importing countries who have the facilities to check on the birds imported into their country. Yet there are not enough personnel hired to do the job.

MASSACRES

Hunting could have been a nice sport if hunters could only limit the number of preys they kill. Their insatiable drive to kill often leads to the massacre. Hunters have common characteristics of mercilessness and bloodthirstiness toward the animals. American hunters have killed several billions of passenger pigeons in a span of 50 years. The French, the Italians, and the Belgians are also systematic slaughterers. In the Gironde, in a span of two weeks, the French hunters killed about 1.5 million small birds first by trapping them and then clubbing them to death. It was probably cheaper to club them to death than to spend on bullets. In the Landes region, the Belgian hunters shot down hundreds of thousands of ringdoves in one month. Some were shot on the ground at point-blank range. The slaughters are so widespread, yet governments are not taking any action to stop these wanton destruction of animals. It is fairly obvious that the killings are done not for food but for the sheer joy of seeing animals killed. Most hunters are well-to-do people who kill the game animals not for profit but to satisfy their ego.

The red-billed quclea (Quelca quelea) bird is considered the worst pest in the world. With more than a billion of them in Africa, each consuming three grams of seeds every day, it is costing the economy of some African countries more than $200 billion annually. Every year more than 200 million of these birds are slaughtered. Breeding colonies and roosts containing millions of these birds, young and old are slaughtered using flame-throwers, dynamites, and poisons.

Not all birds are fortunate enough to be prolific breeders. The Eskimo curlew (Numenius borealis) once migrated in millions from northern Canada and Alaska to their wintering grounds in South America have been easy target for hunters. Like the extinct passenger pigeons, they have become extinct in many areas. Although presently under protection, the few scattered birds may not be sustained or survived for long in the wild.

OTHER BIRDS

One of the strange looking flightless bird found only in New Zealand is the kiwi. The brown kiwi of North Island's Waitangi Forest has one of the most difficult pregnancy of all birds. The female often carries an egg that weighs up to a pound in its body for more than a month before it is laid. It is one of the largest egg-to-body ratios for any bird. After laying the second egg, the male will do the hatching that lasts for about 90 days, another feat of endurance. In their natural habitats, the kiwis are falling prey to feral dogs that abound on this island. In 1987 astray German shepherd killed 500 kiwis within two months. Fortunately, some of the kiwis are now caught in the wild and transported to other islands where there are no predators.

There are only 22 known species of megapodes in the world and they are mostly found in Asia. They live in moist tropical forests but lay their eggs in the sand near the seashore. Since they breed their eggs in places where people live nearby, their eggs are gathered for home consumption. They are also subjected to human and animal predators in the wild. The Philippines is host to seven subspecies of megapodes. All their populations are in decline because of predators, hunting, gathering of their eggs and loss of habitat. Only a few birds are now in captive breeding.

Migratory birds arc particularly at risk because of the numerous obstacles in their paths. That they breed during summer in the temperate zone and spend winter m the tropical zone pose daunting problems for them. At least 62 million migratory birds in the U.S. are killed annually as they traveled to and from their breeding and resting grounds. Along the route they can encounter transmission towers, aircraft, and even golf balls. Some have to traverse over large expanse of sea powered by a reserve of body fats. Some have died of exhaustion while others died from collision with storms and aircrafts. At their tropical destination, they are often met with rampant deforestation or fragmentation. Fragmentation leaves the birds and their nests more exposed to predators like rats, squirrels, raccoons, snakes, and other birds.

The cheer pheasant (Calreus wallichii) of the Himalayas are under severe threat of extinction. It has already become extinct in Pakistan. They are hunted by the natives for food even inside the nature reserves. Farmers have also set fire on the special grass that they feed on, replacing it with grass meant for the livestock. They are now very rare in their natural habitats.

Many birds make their nests on the field ground that can be easily preyed upon by animals. Others make their nests in farmlands which endangers them. The corncrake (Crex crex) of Europe and Western Asia often makes nests in hayfields that have been destroyed along with the adults and chicks by hay cutting machines.

Birds can be carriers of deadly diseases and spread them through the pet trade. One example is the gouldian finch (Chloebia gouldiae) of northern Australia. Many of these birds have been trapped and died enroute to the pet shops. Those in the wild are suffering from a dangerous parasite that could possibly come from escaped caged birds infested with the disease.

OWLS

There are more than 150 species of owls found throughout the world. They have flat face with large forward looking eyes. Owls can also turn their heads 270 degrees which help them in locating prey noiselessly. Most of them are active at night but a few like the pure white snowy owl hunts during the daytime. They are silent flyers and can surprise their unsuspecting prey. Owls have an acute sense of hearing behind the cover of the feathers and can locate their prey in total darkness. The smallest owl in the world is the North American elf owl (Micrathene whitneyi). The fiercest is the great horned owl (Bubo virginianus), so called because of their two feathery tufts on its head.

Owls are some of the most useful birds of prey because they are excellent hunters of animals that compete with people for food or destroy human vegetation. Unlike other birds of prey that eat fish and other sea creatures that people consume, owls consume mice, rats and voles. It can consume ten mice in a single meal which can save a farmer as much as 360 pounds of vegetation a year. They are effective against nocturnal pests.

One problem causing their decline is the use of pesticides in the farms near their habitats. They are being poisoned directly from the pesticides and the food contaminated with pesticides. Their numbers have also declined dramatically due to the loss of habitat. They need large areas to survive. In many areas that have given way to urban development, the owls have changed their diet of small mammals to small birds such as the sparrous and starlings. The spotted owl (Sinx occidentals caurina), made news in the U.S. bringing their plight to the limelight- A controversy is raging in the northwest between environmentalists and loggers over the destruction of old-growth trees that are home to the owls.

One unique species is the burrowing owl (Athene cunicularia). They live in burrows dug up by other animals and live with them in relative safety. In places where there are no owls, conservationists have constructed elaborate man-made burrows to entice these migratory owls to stay.

PARROTS

The parrot is a group of beautiful birds that include the cockatoos, macaws, parakeets, keas, lories and others. They are most in demand in the pet trade business. Of the 300 species in the world, nearly a quarter is endangered. One-third of all the parrot species in the New World face extinction due to the demand for their feathers and as pets. In the rainforest of south-eastern Brazil there are 115 species of birds of which 94 are endemic. Some of the rarest are the spix macaw (Cyanopsiliu spixii), blue-throated macaw (Ara glaucogularis), and hyacinth macaw (Anodorhynchus hyacinthus) which are highly sought by hobbyists. The spjx's macaw is so rare in the wild that only one survivor was discovered in the remote Tabebuia riverine of Brazil during one search by ornithologists in 1990. It has since been under 24-hour protection. Other highly endangered species are the owl parrot (Strigops habroptilus) and the green-bodied St. Vincent's parrot (Amazona guildingii). They are threatened by a combination of loss of habitat, the illegal trade of these parrots and for their highly prized plumage.

The parrots are essentially social animals. In order to raise a healthy family, young parrots need to undergo training in family groups, where they are trained by the elders. The parents invest a lot of time in raising their offspring which can live as long as humans. This is enough reason why they should not be taken from the wild because they are not meant to be reared in captivity.

All the live parrots and their plumage are destined for the European and American collectors. Each bird can fetched as high as $10,000. The U.S. used to import 500,000 parrots legally every year, most of them caught from the wild. Another 25,000 came into the country illegally from South of the border. The big macaws of South America and the impressive crested cockatoos are prized as status symbols. The macaws also suffered from food hunters. Even dead macaws are valued for their feathers. Other causes include competition with the African killer bees for nesting holes.

There is a need for researchers to study their behavior in the wild. Birdwatchers are needed to observe and document parrots nesting, feeding and socializing life to help in the education efforts of the indigenous people. These birds are in great demand by illegal pet traders because of their uncanny ability to mimic people. The continuing loss of their forest habitat through agriculture and logging have brought many to the brink of extinction and will continue to do so unless conservation measures are enforced.

To protect the wild bird populations from further decimation, the Bush administration passed the Wild Bird Conservation Act (WBCA) in 1992. As a result, only birds reared in captivity abroad can be imported, but this caused the rate of imports to decline dramatically, a sign that most birds imported came from the wild. The action taken by the Bush administration took long in coming. A documented video taken in 1992 by two agents of the Environmental Investigations Agency who went underground made it possible.

They went to Argentina to learn how the parrots numbering between 20,000 and 30,000 were captured by hunters in the wild. The first thing the hunters look for are holes in the trees. Once they are found, the hunter will climb up the tree to listen and check if any bird is inside. If a bird is found, he will reach for the hatchlings with his hand if the hole is not deep. Otherwise, the tree, usually 150 years old, is cut down. Thousands of these ecologically important trees are cut down every year, all for the price of $3 for each hatchlings. It is a cause of deforestation in some locality.

Once the hatchling is caught, this weak and fragile bird is put in a sack and brought to the farm. They are then placed in a wire mesh or wooden cage that are overcrowded with other birds. Each day, they are forced-fed from a food bottle that is squirted into their mouths. Sometimes, this feeding action causes the bird to choke to death. In trying to revive the bird, they try to force out the food by shaking the bird. Needless to say, few if any have been revived this way.

The birds are placed in congested wooden cages once they are ready to be exported to the U.S., Europe, and Japan. At the airport, the export papers are processed expeditiously without anyone taking notice of the birds. Once the hatchlings are loaded into the baggage section of the plane, they are left on their own. Neither additional water nor food is provided for the long journey. There is no ventilation provided which accounts for so many deaths during transit. Due to the campaigns of NGOs against the trade in exotic birds, more than one hundred airlines have made it a policy to refuse to transport wild birds cargoes. The consumers at the destinations are willing to pay as much as $750 for a common parrot made it a lucrative business for the dealers. Probably the only way to stop trading in wild parrots is to stop their importation. The U.S. has done it, and others should follow suit. Only captive birds breed in the local market should be allowed. At least they are treated more humanely by their breeders unlike those caught in the wild.

Some important provisions of the WBCA include the requirement for permit for interstate transport of endangered species; doubling of permit fees and extension of the time period allowed for consideration of a request for permit; and allowing agents to inspect the location and records at any reasonable hour. These rules are closely monitored by the American Federation of Aviculture and the Pet Industry Joint Advisory and Council.

The young parrots are easy prey to other predators such as snakes, hawks and other introduced animals. The kakapo (Slrigops habroptilus) of mainland New Zealand is a flightless bird and has been preyed upon by dogs, cats and rats introduced centuries earlier. This has forced the government to evacuate the 43 birds left in the mainland to outlaying islands that are free of predators.

They can also suffer from natural calamities. In one drought year, half of the yellow-shouldered Amazons (Amazona barbadensis) on Bonaire died of starvation. In Macanao, Venezuela, as many as 100 parrots are deliberately killed by hunters annually as sport or by farmers as an agricultural pests. Conservationists like Kirsten Mariana Silvius, with help from unemployed natives are pre-empting poachers by removing them from the wild before poachers get to them. The birds are usually taken by poachers after the chicks are about one month old. This allows the conservationists to remove them to other places high in the mountain nests unknown to the poachers or to nests where they are under constant patrol.

Habitat destruction, trapping, and hunting are threatening the existence of about 115 species around the world. Their eggs are being eaten by predators. Some parrots are even hunted and killed for the meat by native Indians. Conservationists are organizing and planning to conserve their natural habitats. There have been education and advertising programs aimed at promoting parrot protection in the

Latin American countries through bird's sanctuaries and aviaries. They are a great tourist attractions.

PELICANS

There are eight species of pelicans found in the world. They have long necks and beaks, small heads, with thick plumage. Their most conspicuous feature is the enormous beak that carries a large pouch on the lower part that they effectively use in catching fish. The young pelican cats the fish from the mother's pouch. They are sociable birds and often nest together by the thousands. Most birds breed in isolated island and wetlands while others make their colonies on tall trees.

While the adults have few natural enemies, their youngs have to overcome many obstacles before they are mature enough to go on their own. Many often fall from nesting trees to their death. Others are hopelessly caught in branches unable to get away from their predicament. Some are eaten by the larger birds once they meet accidents and are immobilized. Those nesting on islands are often prey to land predators. Fishermen often blame the birds for their low catch and go to the extent of killing and destroying their nesting grounds.

A few years after the introduction of DDT, the brown pelican was on the verge of extinction. The once common bird of Southern California suffered as a result of eating anchovies contaminated with DDT that caused their eggs' shells to become so thin that they easily crushed during incubation In 1970, some people even wagered whether the pelican will be extinct in both the east and west coasts of the U.S. That year, just one chick on West Anacapa, the primary west coast rookery, survived long enough to leave the nest. Only five chicks survived in Southern California and northern Baja California. The situation was so bad that a public furor helped lead to the ban of DDT in 1972 and the subsequent enactment of the Endangered Species Act of 1973. The timely actions help save them from extinction, but they are still under constant threat.

Disturbances of their breeding grounds often lead to their decline. In Peru, the guano diggers often damage the nests and frighten the parents away leaving the chicks to predators. Today an even worst fate awaits them in many of their feeding grounds. Development projects are draining the wetlands and many lakes are drying up for other large water projects.

The dalmatian pelican (Pelecanus crispus) which inhabits areas from Europe to China are under grave threat of extinction. They often hunt in farm-fish areas provoking the ires of owners who won't hesitate to shoot them because they are very effective in scooping fish with their bill. At one time, millions of pelicans used to nest on the delta of the Danube River before their marshy habitats were drained and converted to other uses. Today, there are less than 50 pairs left.

As if these destructions are not enough, more than 12,000 pelicans died from botulism poisoning outbreak in 1996. Some of these birds are the brown pelican, the most endangered species of the pelicans. It is also the biggest recorded die-off of pelicans in the world.

The pelican was at one time chosen as an emblem for charity and piety in earlier times. This is because of the myth that the bird would pierce its breasts with the tip of her bill until blood flows to feed her young whenever food is not available.

RAPTORS

Eagles, vultures, ospreys, and other birds of prey are large, powerful birds that are at the apex of the food chain. They are the most noble birds that many countries have adopted them as the official emblem or national bird. But this status does not guarantee them safety from persecution. Many of them are subjected to hunting, egg-collecting, pollution, deliberate poisoning and habitat destruction. All these threats have taken toll on their populations in the wild.

The largest decline in their population come with the introduction of DDT in the 1950s. Farmers and householders used them to kill pests not knowing the great harm coming to these birds of prey. The osprey (Pandion haliaetus), a fish eating hawk widely scattered throughout the world except in Antarctica has been decimated in the 1950s and 1960s due to DDT. Their population gradually increased after the ban on the use of DDT in the 1970s. The vulnerability on their fish diet is the first sign of widespread and persistent use of DDT in the environment. The DDT residue is still being felt today, though on a smaller scale. Non-lethal amount of DDT can still be found in the fats of animals which are eaten by mammals and birds. Birds of prey which fed on other small animals contaminated with DDT have been responsible for the thinning of many egg shells that led to easy breakage. It can also be lethal to the birds outright. In 1960 and 1961, thousands of terrestrial birds of prey were found littering the countryside of Great Britain. DDT can also reach the seabirds when they are washed from the soil into the water ecosystems and are taken in by the plankton, worms, and fishes that are eaten by the higher order as it moves along the food chain.

Today, the major cause of decline is the destruction of their habitats. These are caused by logging, ranching, mining, development projects and to some extent transmigration program of government. The Philippine Eagle was particularly hard hit by these factors. Their habitat in Mindanao, once covered 95% of the land mass in 1910 was down to 30% in 1973 and still declining due to legal and illegal logging going on. The Hawk-eagle of Java, living in a tiny island is gradually disappearing as the population increases and pressure on their habitat is reducing the forested areas.

Eagles and other birds of prey are often shot by farmers in the mistaken belief that they are responsible for the deaths of their baby livestock. Because some eagles are scavengers and often seen by farmers feasting on carrion, they immediately blame the birds. In Scotland in the 18th century, farmers shot or poisoned thousands of white-tailed sea eagles to protect their lambs. The birds became extinct by the early 20th century. Poison baits intended for other animals have been responsible for reducing Iceland's 80 pairs of white-tailed sea eagles in 1880 to seven pairs in 1921. In Alaska, between 1915 and 1951, 100,000 bald eagles (Haliaeetus leucocephalus) were slaughtered to protect the salmon stock.

The Mauritius kestrel (Falco punciatus) of Mauritius has returned miraculously from the brink of extinction. In 1986, only six birds were left in the wild forest of one of the mountain slope. They were caught and placed under captive breeding. There are about 200 birds now in the wild.

Other raptors under protection have been killed unintentionally. Soaring high up in the air, it is almost impossible to differentiate an endangered species from one that can be hunted. Therefore, it may be necessary to ban all forms of shooting. According to a wildlife official in South Carolina, random shooting is still the leading cause of mortality for bald eagles in the state. A young eagle was recently killed and there is reward of $5,000 for information leading to the arrest of the person responsible. Only strong arm enforcement of the law will save many endangered species.

Eagles are sometimes killed for sports or shooting practices. Rival armies in Lebanon used the eagles as target practice whenever they are not shooting one another. In Spain, the Imperial Eagle is legally protected, but they are still shot by hunters in remote areas that are not policed by government agents. The only safe haven for the Imperial Eagle can be found in Coto Donana National Park in Andalucia.

The rarity of many eagles and other birds of prey have made them more valuable and therefore subject to poachings. To facilitate the smuggling of these birds, eggs or young birds are taken from the wild illegally and bred in captivity. They are then given false papers showing that they are captive-bred birds and may be traded legally. In the summer of 1976, at least 36 peregrine nests were raided by egg collectors in Britain.

Another threat to the birds of prey are the power poles and transmission lines that have been installed throughout the countryside. According to the National Biological Society Survey report. 25% of reported golden eagle mortality over a 30-year period were caused by electrocution. Of the 1,238 raptors electrocuted in 10 western states between 1982 and 1995, half were golden eagles. It is possible to retrofit the poles so that raptors cannot be electrocuted, but the cost is so high it is seldom undertaken.

Like most animals under threat of extinction, the powerful and leading force that is decimating their population is the loss of habitats. Even if they spend most of the time in the air, they will still need a terrestrial place for rest and breeding. For many birds of prey that are on the brink of extinction, the only solution is probably captive breeding. Successes with the California condors and the bald eagles brought new hope to many endangered birds. At the least, the birds will have enough food in captivity without worrying about being hunted or poisoned by farmers or poachers. The likelihood of survival for their chicks are much better than in the wild. Captive breeding in the U.S. has been well organized. The chicks are first reared at research centers for two weeks before they are distributed around the country and placed in nests of foster or surrogate birds high in the mountains so that they will be familiar with the ways of the wild. This will also allow the mother birds to start breeding at the shortest possible time. Five teams keep tract on the progress of the birds in the wild.

Raptors survive by eating mostly other living animals. It is therefore imperative that their prey be protected. The harpy eagles (Harpia harpyja) of South America are declining due to the declining habitat and the declining monkey populations, their important food source. Sometimes, the birds are themselves considered as vermin and hunted or poisoned by farmers. Because they prey on macaws, pet traders often kill them to reduce competition. In other cases, birds of prey often feast on carrions poisoned by farmers which could be fatal to the raptors.

Birds of prey, being on top of the food chain, often lost out to humans in competition for the same food. This is especially true for sea birds and other fish-eating birds. The striated caracara of the Falkland Islands preys on sea birds that prey on the fishes. The declining fish populations caused a chain reaction that led to the decline of the raptors due to the decline of their prey birds. The loss of an important food source has been the cause of declining populations of many raptors around the world.

ROBINS

The interesting thing about the robin Peiroica traversi of New Zealand is its ability to return from the brink of extinction into one of the most thriving bird despite their inbreeding. These black robins numbered only five in 1980 were found in the Chatham Island. A rescue program was launched to save them from extinction. The eggs were removed from their nests immediately to allow the birds to breed again. They were put into the nests of tomtits for hatching. The tomtits accepted the eggs and went on to raise the chicks as their own. This allowed the robin to breed additional eggs earlier than expected. In one season time, the birds were able to produce three clutches of birds instead of only one. Today there are 200 robins found in two islands in the Chatham Island group.

Scientists using DNA fingerprints from blood samples of their offspring are studying the result of inbreeding. Tests revealed that for the genetic consequences on which the fingerprints were based, the robins appeared genetically identical. Additional tests are being made on the region of the genes called the major histocompatility complex (MHC) which control immune responses. Animals with low diversity of MHC make them susceptible to diseases. So far there are no signs that the robins are suffering from loss of genetic diversity. These findings should quell the anxiety of some conservationists that many endangered species are doomed to extinction from inbreeding.

SWIFTLETS

The most valuable nests in the world belong to several species of cave swiftlets, in particular the white-nest or edible-nest swiftlet (*Aerodramus ficiphagus*), from Southeast Asia. All swifts and swiftlets use a substance secreted from a pair of enlarged salivary glands beneath their tongues to glue their nests together, but in cave swiftlet nests, saliva is the only ingredient. Made into a gelatinous soup, which is essentially a protein-sugar solution, they have been eaten by the Chinese for some 1,500 years. Nowadays they are considered a special delicacy and have become extremely valuable. Collecting this delicacy from the roofs and walls of deep caves can be very hazardous, but the demand and reward are great. Hong Kong, which consumes more than 60% of all the nests taken from the wild, imported some 8 million of them every year. It takes two nests to make one bowl of soup. Because of the raid on their nests, the swiftlets are often required to make three nests before they are able to lay their eggs as two are taken by people.

TREE SNAKES

Bioinvasion of snakes to Guam and Hawaii has decimated the bird population. Scientists agree that the main culprit is the five-foot-long brown tree snake (Boiga irregularis). In Guam, they proliferated so fast that today there are as many as 30,000 snakes per sq mi in some areas. The birds of Guam began to disappear from the island in the early 1960s, which was about the time that the brown tree snakes became common on the island. Some theorized the snakes were introduced there as well as in Hawaii, as stowaways on military transports from the Solomon Islands and New Guinea, where the snakes are endemic. Others think that the snakes in Guam came from stowaways from military ships after the Second World War. At any rate, they are found scattered throughout the 209-sq-mi island. The lean eating machines have wiped out nine of the twelve native birds. The endemic Guam rail and Micronesian kingfisher escaped extinctions only to end up in cages under captive breeding.

A study by ecologist Julie Savidge seemed to confirm the theory that the tree snakes were eating the birds. Six brown snakes have been discovered in Hawaii. They have been found slithering on Hawaiian runways, and scientists speculate that they may be stowaways on planes from Guam. The snake's appearance in Hawaii has spurred research to determine whether the snakes could decimate the Hawaiian bird populations but it is now a foregone conclusion.

Moves have been underway to devise barriers to keep the snakes out of Hawaii. Because of their ability to creep up to the planes, the Honolulu International Airport is being fenced with a barrier made of plastic netting accompanied by an electric fence. Planes from Guam are being searched with specialized snake sniffing dogs. The public is being alerted and educated on the danger of the snake. A Brown Snake Control Act has been signed into law which calls for eradication of the snake.

URBANIZA TION

Urbanization of cities and the increasing presence of garbage dumps is radically changing the behavior of birds in Europe. Storks which used to migrate to tropical Africa now prefer to spend the winters in Spanish cities, feeding off garbage dumps. The two types of seagulls, black-headed gull and lesser black-backed gull, which live by the sea eating fish are also moving inland and scavenging in the dumps. The reason for the new behavior is the availability of food all year round.

The warmth of Senegal or Ethiopia no longer lures the storks. Increasing numbers of white storks no longer bother to fly farther than Spain's southern coast. Some storks have stopped migrating completely, spending the entire year in Madrid and other cities. Storks manage perfectly well in cold temperatures, and now the garbage dumps allow them to eat all year round.

Madrid's huge Valdomingomez dump, which is regularly visited by hundreds of thousands of birds from more than a hundred species is a real birds paradise. The population of black-headed gulls in Madrid has increased sixfold to about 60.000 in 15 years. The lesser black-backed gull population has swollen from 100 or so birds to more than 4.000 in just four years. The same phenomenon has been noted in France, Britain and Germany. Black kites, middle-sized birds of prey which feed on carrion, have made the same discovery as the storks and gulls.

Even if the urban bird has made life easier, it is also fraught with dangers. Their scavenging may reduce the garbage, but some birds confuse plastic tubes, rubber bands and pieces of rope with worms and snakes and eat them They also cut themselves from the sharp edges of open cans.

WETLANDS

The inland water systems such as streams, rivers, marshes, mangroves and lakes are haven to millions of birds, fishes, reptiles, and other mammals. These rich ecosystems, rivaling some rainforests or coral reefs, are rich with plants and animals that attract all kinds of birds. In the U.S., at least 150 species of birds and 200 species of fishes can be found there. They are also home to one-third of the country's endangered and threatened plants and animals. Some birds spent all their lives breeding and feeding in these wetlands. Migratory birds also spend quite a portion of their lives in these areas. Because of the increasing human population, many wetlands have been drained and converted into agricultural land or urban development.

More than half of Asia's wetlands have been lost. In Malaysia and Indonesia, more than half of their mangrove forests have been cut and converted into fish ponds. The situation is even worse in the Philippines where the mangrove trees are harvested for firewood and the devastated areas are converted into fish ponds.

The acceptance of wetlands is now only being appreciated. Government budgets are being allocated to buy back wetlands from private owners in the U.S. However, in tropical countries, wetlands are usually government's properties that private individuals have taken the liberty to convert them into other uses. Privately owned wetlands are drained and converted into developmental projects and even golf courses.

Once wetlands have been degraded, it is difficult, costly, and time-consuming to restore them to their original state. It is therefore important that natural wetlands should remain undisturbed for future generations.

CHAPTER 10

FISHES

Fish is an aquatic vertebrate found throughout the world's fresh and saltwater habitats. It is a cold-blooded animal that breathe air through its gills. With more than 30,000 species, they make up the most numerous vertebrates in the animal kingdom. The smallest fish is the Philippine goby (Pandaka pygmaea) and the largest is the whale shark (Rhinocodon lypus).

Fish plays an important role in the economy of many nations especially the poor Third World countries where they supply most of the protein for the coastal people. The fishing industry provides about 15% of the protein consumed worldwide. Iceland and Japan use up to 50% of the sea resources. However, not all products are used for human consumption. One-fourth of the catch is used for animal feed, fertilizers, oil, soaps and drugs. They provide not only food but also employment and livelihood for millions around the world. In the rich countries, they also serve another purpose - sport and competition fishing.

This is the "International Year of the Ocean." Its importance should never be overlooked. We use the ocean in more ways than one. For centuries it has been used for transportation and source of food for the people. Today, new dimensions are being added that can do more harm to the sea creatures. Ocean floors are exploited for oil and minerals, used as groundwork for the laying of oil pipes and cables. recreation, and worse of all, as a dumping ground for human created wastes, oil spills, and the final repository of chemicals such as pesticides. All these toxic wastes are destroying the marine ecology for many species.

The international problem of fishing rights was partially solved with the implementation of the 200-mile w ide Exclusive Economic Zone (EEZ) But many of these coastal areas have long been fished to near extinction that harvesting has taken to the international waters. Huge and fast ships equipped with the latest sonar and fishing gears have taken over.

The over-exploitation of the marine animals has put many species of fishes under the brink of extinction. Presently, more than 1.000 species were listed in the 1996 Red Data Book of IUCN as threatened or endangered. These include among others, the Atlantic cod, several seahorse species, swordfish, several species of sharks, and the Atlantic bluefin tuna. The problems facing fishes are numerous: overharvesting, destruction of non-target species, cruel harvesting methods, pollution, etc. Because the ocean beyond the territorial limit of two hundred miles has been considered as nobody's sea, there is almost no restriction on the amount of fishes that can be harvested. This has cause many species to be reduced to the point of unsustainable numbers.

ANCHOVY

Anchovy is the name of a family of small fishes that range from 10 to 15 cm in length. They are found in many coastal areas of western Europe, North America China and South Africa. All these areas were the first to be fished out. As if overfishing is not enough, the anchovies of the Black Sea are suffering from contamination of a jelly-like organism that is decimating their population.

In the late 1960s and early 1970s, the anchovy fishery off the coast of Peru was the largest in the world. The total harvest in 1970 was 12 million tons, accounting for about 30% of the country's foreign exchange and 20% of the world's catch. Continued overharvesting reduced the catch to around 4.5 million tons in 1972. 1.8 million tons in 1973 and only 700.000 tons in 1980. Until now it has not recovered from the overharvest of yesteryears.

At the rate they are regularly caught by the poor local people for consumption, it could last them for generations. But others find it more rewarding to make them into feeds for the U.S. poultry and swine industry. The use of these high quality feeds was a wasteful utilization of food that is needed by the poor people. Still others find it cheaper to use as bait for other fishes.

The collapse of the anchovy industry has other repercussions in the ecology of Peru. It resulted in the disappearance of 10 million birds that once feed on the anchovy. Many birds living on offshore rocks starved to death. The loss of the birds also lead to the loss of guano, an important fertilizer industry for Peru.

AQUACULTURE

Aquaculture has been going on since ancient limes. The ancient Egyptians and Chinese had attempted at extensive fish farming centuries before the ancient Romans started to cultivate oysters. Today, it has become an important source of food for the world's increasing population. But unless care is taken, it could cause widespread contamination of the ocean.

The diminishing catches encountered by the fishing industry has led some entrepreneurs to harvest the fishes under the farming method. Aquaculture now produces 12% to 15% of the world's total fish and shellfish. This is doubling every four years as the ocean resources are decimated and demand increases along with the increasing population growth as more people become affluent. Most of these farms are geared toward raising fishes, crustaceans, and molluscs. Each year more than 10 million tons of food has been farmed.

Because of the fast growth of cattle using antibiotics and growth hormones, fish farmers have also adopted the same therapeutic techniques on fishes and shellfishes. Biotechnologists have experimented by injecting the same hormones used on chickens or salmon and found the fish growing up to 50% faster. Now they are mass producing the hormones for salmon. Soon we will be encountering the same problems such as antibiotic resistance as is happening with farmed livestock.

Many fish farms come from important wetland ecosystems. The loss of mangrove forests leads to the destruction of large wetland ecosystem which is rich in marine and terrestrial species. It also restricts or destroys the areas in which young fishes and shrimps and other sea creatures develop. This affects the catchy of the coastal fishing industry. The expansion of shrimp culture has led to reduce shrimps in the wild that could threaten the livelihood of local population. Clearing natural mangrove stocks also means destroying the dynamic of biogenic coastal protection which these forests provide.

Aquaculture farms closely monitored can guarantee safe food free from toxic pollutants. But many enclosed ponds or pens which are located in natural ecosystems or waterways have caused environmental problems. In the Philippines, these fish ponds have been responsible for large scale floodings in their vicinity. It has been responsible for displacing many fisherfolks and peasants from communal foreshore lands and waters by big agribusinesses and landlords. In Negros, big companies have expanded their fishpond and prawn farmings with help from government agency through the Fishpond/Foreshoreland License Agreements (FLAs). These FLAs are leases for 50 to 75 years, giving these companies rights to coastal lands and communal fishing grounds, thus effectively depriving peasants their means of livelihood. Dole Philippines, which controls 143 hectares of prawn farms has expanded its farms to another town to the tune of 400 hectares of rich mangrove lands and displaced hundreds of families.

Other problems include wastes left behind by the fishes. Fecal manure and uneaten feed that settle on the bottom can smother the habitat of benthic creatures and use up the oxygen and other nutrients as they decompose. This could lead to the growth of unwanted weeds and algae. Other wastes include chemicals used in cleaning, pesticides, drug residues used to treat diseases and parasites, as well as soluble products like the ammonia that fish produces through metabolism. The spread of parasites and bacterias that are inherent in hatchery must be guarded.

Single-species aquaculture has the same problems as that encountered with monocrop agriculture or single species timber. It could devastate the fishes in ease of an outbreak of disease. Fish under mono-species can develop diseases easier and pass them on more quickly. Antibiotics are treated on the water and the surrounding areas become contaminated. The dispersal of the unwanted antibiotics to other water ecosystems can reduce the immunity of the wild fishes. Some diseases have become immune to antibiotics treatment, even the full-spectrum types. In Washington State, liver lesions spread quickly among penned Atlantic salmon in 1987 and killed 30,000 salmons. Two years later, officials had to destroy three million young salmons and one million eggs to stop the disease from spreading to the wild stocks. No antibiotics were found to be effective against this unknown disease.

With this knowledge, the Canadian government stopped the use of antibiotics in fishes unless they are suffering from disease. However, there is no technology available for testing fish for residues. The same problems encountered on the cattle and chicken factory farming regarding antibiotics and growth hormones may be replayed with devastating results.

Another problem with fish farming is the possibility of the fishes escaping from their ponds. The genetically engineered salmon from farms, like other over-bred species, can be easy victims of infection and have poor survival rates. This could threaten the survival of wild salmon in the ocean through inbreeding. At least 100,000 fishes from seven farms in the U.S. escaped into the wild after a storm damaged their pens.

BYCATCH

The huge commercial fishing industry has been responsible for catching tens of millions of undersize, juvenile and non-targeted fishes and crustaceans and invertebrates, accounting for about 10% of the total catch. These fishes, called "bycatch" by the fishing industry are thrown back to the sea, but not after some have died. Many of them, rich in nutrients and proteins are discarded even though they are badly needed by those living in coastal areas. They can also be substituted for other animal feeds presently under unsustainable harvesting. To reduce the bycatch, it is necessary to modify the fishing net. Using single layer mesh instead of the conventional two overlapping layers of mesh will allow small fishes to escape.

Other sea animals we take for granted as parasites and useless may have some value after all. The eel-like parasite, the sea lamprey that normally suck the life out of trout and salmon fisheries in the Great Lakes are trapped every year for destruction. The male lampreys are sterilized and released back to the lakes while the females are destroyed to reduce their population. However, in Portugal, these lampreys are considered a delicacy and can feed a lot of people instead of being landfilled. As with products from the rainforests, many tree species people found useless or of no commercial value are often left to rot. But in this world of diminishing return, people are finding some use for these useless species. Many fishes we threw away as garbage may be the hope and survival of others in the poor countries.

Zebra mussels from Europe was first thought to be a plague for Lake Erie in the U.S. when it was first spotted in 1988. In all areas where they inhabit, they clogged water intake system of power plant, boat motors and drinking water facilities. There was great alarm that they would disrupt aquatic ecosystems and crowd out native species. However, the anticipated disaster did not happen. The mussels are good filterers, absorbing a lot of pollutants and storing them in their lipids. They also consume algae, their main food, and large parts of the lake have become cleaner and cleaner. Each adult mussel sucks in about a liter and half of water, retaining the algae and other nutrients including the pollutants. The pollutants are kept in their fatty tissues. As a result, about two dozen plants are now flourishing in Lake Erie, including some that have not been seen there in more than 30 years. Scientists believe that it is the result of the mussels* consuming the algae and other microorganisms. Clearer waters permit more penetration of sunlight, thereby promoting photosynthesis that is essential to plants and increasing the level of oxygen. Both these factors are necessary to increase the aquatic animals because of the available plants for food and the reduction of pollutants.

CAVIAR

Caviar are salted eggs of large fishes coming from the salmon and sturgeon families. It is served as a gourmet dish either whole or pressed and slightly chilled-These colored eggs maybe black, gray or red depending on the species offish. The eggs are taken from the ovaries of female fishes and salted before it is packaged sale. These delicacies are often served in Europe and the U.S. Most of the black caviar entering the U.S. came from Russia.

The beluga sturgeon (Huso huso) can be eight meters long and weighs more than 1,200 kg. It is considered the most valuable fish in the world, mainly because of its caviar, which is the most expensive fish dish in the world. They are considered the finest of the fish eggs and can cost $60 an ounce in respectable restaurants. A female sturgeon caught in the Tikhaya Sosna River in 1924, weighed 1.277 kg and yielded 245 kg of quality caviars worth more than $350,000 in today's value. Most of the caviar came from the Caspian Sea They are caught with gill hooks anchored throughout the width of the sea and down to the sea floor. Because of the high rate of return, the Russian Mafia has joined in this lucrative and illegal business. They have been buying up all the poached caviars and smuggling it out of the country or selling them to foreigners clandestinely.

The declining population of sturgeons throughout their habitat is partly the result of the overharvest of the female species for the gourmet market. Several species are on the brink of extinction. Their ancient breeding grounds in the Caspian Sea were lost when dams along the Volga River dried up the sea's shallow outer rim. Combined with chemical dumping into the Volga, has ruined the commercial fishery. The Aral Sea, another breeding place, has shrunk 40 percent by a disastrous cotton-irrigation scheme that caused the extinction of one species of sturgeon and endangered two other species. In Siberia, plans for logging and further oil and gas development in the rivers of central and northeastern Siberia do not bode well for the future of this venerable fish.

WWF researchers blamed neighboring countries for failing to pass and enforce fishing regulations. Five countries surrounding the Caspian Sea have agreed to restrict fishing and take legal actions against poachers starting in 1997. It is about time to put an end to the consumption of these life-giving fishes especially those that are overharvested or in decline.

With the high price and the Russian caviar industry in disarray due to overfishing, poaching, and pollution, the catches are declining faster than they are being replenished. Unless drastic measures are taken to reverse the trend, there may not be any caviar left for the export market. From 1984 to 1994, the catch has decline by 75%. A 25-year moratorium should be called, allowing enough time for them to recover.

American farmers are cashing in on this industry. It takes twenty years for the beluga sturgeon to produce caviar in the wild. Researchers at the University of California-Davis are trying to speed up the reproduction system of the fish by "leans of biotechnology.

Another species called the common sturgeon (Acipenser sturio) found in several European coastal waters is under several types of threats. Like the salmon, it has to travel more than 300 miles to their birth place to spawn. Dams and embankments have been constructed in many places preventing many from spawning offspring necessary to maintain their population in the wild. Large numbers are also caught for the food and the caviar from the females.

The diminishing caviar from Russia is putting another fish, the paddlefish (Polydon spathula), a relative of sturgeon in the U.S., under tremendous pressure.

It is so called because of its distinctive spatula-like paddle that extends from the snout. The paddlefish can live for 40 years, and starts to breed after ten years. The American paddlefish has declined tremendously in the last few years because of dam construction, pollution, overfishing, and draining and dredging of their habitats. There used to be no limit to the catch anyone can make, but North Dakota and Montana has enforced a quota of one fish per angler after suffering a great decline. There is also a limit to the total state catch of 1,500 fishes annually.

COELACANTH

The coelacanth (Lalimeria chalumnae) is a large deepwater fish thought to be extinct 70 million years ago. The first "living fossil" was accidentally caught on December 22, 1938, in a trawler's net off the coast of South Africa. It was nearly two meters long and died a few hours later. The body was covered with hard bony scales, sharp spines and slimy oil oozing from its skin. Brought to Majorie Courtenay-Latimer, she sent it to London for proper identification. They came back with report that it was supposed to be an extinct species. Leaflets and posters with offer of large reward were distributed among the villagers for another live species. The search took fourteen years before a second fish was caught off the Comoro island of Anjouan, Africa, 1,000 miles away from the first specimen. Soon researchers found that they were not exactly endangered because natives were eating them for generations and using its scaly skin as sandpaper. None of the coelacanth caught has lived more than a few hours.

Today, they are found mostly hundreds of feet below the surface near the Comoro Islands on the Indian Ocean. The fishes are very acrobatic under the sea. They can swim backward, belly up and can stand on their heads and remain vertical for a few minutes at a time. It could be their way of hunting through a special organ on its head that can detect the electrical field that animals produce. Unlike most fishes, it doesn't lay eggs but give births to live youngs.

Since their discovery, an estimated 200 coelacanths have been accidentally captured before restriction was imposed. Some of these fishes were tested for pollutants and have been found positive. At present, the creatures are being threatened by overharvesting due to the sale of its notochordal fluid as a longevity tonic that is valued in Japan on the false assumption that the fluid from such ancient fish must have this property. Tradition is often difficult to overcome even in the face of extinction of such animal. Now fishermen are deliberately capturing them, forcing CITES to classify them under Appendix I that prohibits their capture and trade.

DISEASES

Fishes have been dying by the millions from diseases, parasites, and algae bloom. Our wanton discharge of toxic chemicals has been responsible for most health problems of marine animals. The sudden discharge of cyanide compounds has been responsible for 30 tons of fish kill in the Manila Bay last year. Other toxic chemicals and metals, while it does not cause immediate death can be devastating in the long run. They can cause the disruption of our endocrine gland leading to reproductive problems for people consuming the contaminated animals. The most recent fish kill occurred in four barangays along Marikina River last January 1998 where thousands of freshwater fishes were killed.

The aquatic dinoflagellate *Pfiesteria piscicida* was discovered by researchers at the North Carolina State University College of Veterinary Medicine in 1988. The name literally means fish killer and the toxins produced by this organism affect the nervous sytem, causing disorientation, lethargy and paralysis on the breathing mechanism of fishes. Unless the fish can escape within minutes, it will die of suffocation. Strips of the fish's skin dropped off its body as a result of exposure to the toxins, producing open bleeding ulcers that release blood and tissue on which the Pfiesteria feeds. This vicious circle can only lead to further spread of the toxins.

During the summer of 1996, a record number of fish kills occurred in North Carolina waters. It was also linked to 18 major fish kills in the Neuse and Pamlico estuaries. The culprits have been traced to increase input of the nutrient nitrogen, waste from treatment plants, animal waste lagoons, and farm wastes. Humans who ate the infected fish or worked in Pfiesteria-infested waters have reported lesions, memory loss, nausea, vomitting, eye irritations, numbness of the feet, hands, and lips.

DRIFTNETS

In the race to feed the world's populations with cheap protein available from the ocean, some nations have taken to harvest as much as possible from the sea. To accomplish this, they have taken the liberty to deciminate the sea creatures by all means. One notorious way of harvesting was the use of driftnet. The driftnet is and indiscriminate harvesting equipment for catching sea creatures like squids and tunas. However, more than ever, they catch large quantities of unwanted fish, sometimes accounting for half of the catch and unintended mammals that often died of suffocation. In the last 17 years before its ban, plastic driftnets 30 to 40 miles long had been laid across the North Pacific. After a few years, the fishes caught far outweigh all the other fishing and whaling during the same period elsewhere in the world.

In the past, from May to October each year, more than a thousand fishing vessels were laying these driftnets, 30-45 feet deep and 30 to 40 miles across the North Pacific. It is like clear-cutting done on the rainforests. After each night's work, 85% of the unmarketable fish known as bycatch were thrown away for being useless. But what makes it deplorable is that sea mammals such as dolphins, sharks, and turtles which need open air to breathe were entangled and drowned. In 1990, Japanese fishermen caught 108 million squids along with 26,000 marine mammals, 700,000 sharks, 40 million non-targeted fish and 270,000 seabirds.

Japan, accounting for half of the vessels, Taiwan, and South Korea are the main culprit

A single driftnet can earn as much as $2 million after each port call. That is despite outcries from environmentalists, there seems to be no letup in their use. It was only after a concerted international outcry that lead to its ban in June 1992. The sly Japanese fishermen, the ever selfish destroyer of the ocean ecosystems stopped only at the end of the year. However, there were numerous reports of illegal driftnet fishings still going on. Just this July 1997, a ship was caught in the Pacific Ocean for using this illegal method.

Because of its lightweight, plastics are often used and they can easily be damaged especially by mammals entangled in it. Discarded driftnets have also been responsible for the death of between 500,000 to 750,000 sea birds annually. The driftnets have been banned in all the regions of the Pacific Basin, but wherever there is no legal impediment, it is allowed for use in local coastal areas, on a shorter length.

In the U.S. a law had been passed making driftnet fishing illegal. The Driftnet Impact Monitoring Act was passed by the Congress in 1987, but no funding was given for the enforcement of this law. It is necessary to give teeth to this law if we are to ban driftnet fishing throughout the world. The U.S. with its large and free market has a greater voice than any other country in implementing a law that has worldwide repercussions. With the assistance of the U.S. the South Pacific island nations took the case against driftnet fishing to the U.N. Within a few months, in December 1989, the U.N. passed a resolution banning the use of driftnets in the high seas.

EXCLUSIVE ECONOMIC ZONES

Rampant invasion of the foreign vessels within the 200-mile territorial limit of many countries led to the creation of the exclusive economic zone throughout the world. This has given rise to problems between nations rich in coastal resources and the poor countries with limited coastline. Because of the loss of fishes in many parts of the world, fishing vessels have been intruding into other rich fishing grounds located under the jurisdiction of other countries. In 1995, Canadian gunboats seized a Spanish trawler and destroyed the nets of another, sparkling an international incident with EC which support their member state, Spain. There were also several incidents between Canada and the U.S., and between Britain and Iceland. In the Philippines, foreigners have regularly intruded into the fishing grounds in many areas. Likewise, Filipinos have been detained by Malaysian authorities for alleged illegal fishing.

Another offshoot of the 200-mile exclusive economic zones has presented the nations with coastal and continental shelves an opportunity to harvest a potential wealth of aquatic animals. Instead of careful regulation of these rich ecosystems, governments allowed the unregulated and unrestricted harvest of the coastal resources. This has resulted in the building boom of fishing vessels fueled by cheap loans. The pressure to pay back the loans lead to overexploitation. Large volume of fishes can be caught and transferred to the mother ship while the support ships continue with their harvesting.

Like the rainforests of tropical countries, once these rich ecosystems are opened for exploitation, sustainable use of marine products are no longer enforce Large business enterprises went into action, taking in as much fishes as they can possibly caught. Modern fishing gears, sonars, and even computers are helping them locate these bounties for harvesting.

HOOKS

Millions of people around the world are engaged in fishing as a recreational pastime. In the industrialized countries, license or permit is required before anyone can enjoy the sport. More often than not, regulations that require a limited catch is often ignored. This could lead to serious depiction of many highly desirable species.

The principal way to catch fish as a sport is the use of rod and line with hook at the end. The modern hook is made of steel that originated in Redditch, England in 1560. It was made of steel wire feed in machine that produces the complete hook. Afterward the hook is hardened by heat and tempered on carefully regulated liquid bath. The most popular hook is the "eagle claw" which looks very much like its namesake.

Some environmentalists and animal rights activists have long called for an end to this type of fishing method. They have considered it a very cruel way of inflicting pain on fish unfortunately hooked and its subsequent struggle to free itself often lead to serious injury. Some large fishes have even struggled so hard that part of their brain organs are removed. The pain we feel after a foreign object such as a wood splinter piercing our skin is minor compared to the hook.

OVERFISHING

The world's water bodies composed of 71% of the planet's surface area. Within this massive region, we have harvested its bounty, under an unsustainable rate for many decades. Every year we harvested about 3 million tons of marine plants, mainly giant kelp and large seaweed. The rest are food fishes and many unintended mammals.

Fishes and other marine animals have always been an important and cheap source of protein especially for the coastal inhabitants around the world. As the population increases, so does the exploitation. Until the 16th century, fishing was largely confined to the coastal waters around the world. The unabated harvesting of the sea resources began to be felt around the coastal areas by 1600s. Fishing for herring in the Baltic Sea was the first that almost came to a halt. Within a few decades the same problem was affecting cod fishing off the coast of western Europe. Even then the total stock of fish around the world seemed inexhaustible. The emergence of factory fishing and more mechanized fishing fleets from the major fishing nations of Europe during the latter part of the 19th century marked the beginning of the overfishing industry. Technological advances at the onset of the 1950s further abetted the exploitation of the ocean resources. Coupled with the idea of laissez-faire economics and cut-throat competition, the fishing industry outside the territorial economic zones has become common property where anybody can harvest without limit or regard to sustainable use.

The U.N. Food and Agriculture Organization (FAO) estimated the sustainable catch of global fishing at 100 million tons a year for the 1980s. Yet the commercial catch for 1987 was 91 million tons and another 24 million tons caught by the local fishermen. This could mean that we have been overfishing, way beyond the sustainable level. Today, the catch is down to about 70 million tons and declining faster than we anticipated. Many fishes caught today are smaller and not fully mature which can only lead to further reduction of the stock. The North Sea herring stocks throughout the Northeast Atlantic waters have been decimated and was completely close to fishing from 1977 to 1982 to allow them to recover. There was even a ban on harvesting fishes less than 20 centimeters within the restricted territory. However, unrestricted harvestings have been going beyond the official boundary. It is thus important to place a global ban anywhere once a species has been depleted and considered an endangered or threatened species.

Many nations, especially Japan, Russia, and some European nations are great exploiters of this common property. It is inevitable that the once inexhaustible supply of fishes will decline. According to the 1992 figures, the catches of 18 major species of marine fishes had declined an average of 58% compared to a decade ago. Yet there is little attempt by nations to limit their catches but instead technological advances have made overfishing more rampant and effective. Overfishing caused a decline in areas after areas until the fishermen are forced to catch smaller and immature fishes to augment their catch. This unsustainable way of harvesting the fish can only lead to prolong rehabilitation of the industry if not outright collapse.

The development of canning in 1915 further exacerbated the problem of overfishing. The sardine industry of California is a good example. It expanded and declined rapidly as well. By the 1930s about 600,000 tons of sardines were being caught by especially designed boats known as purse-seiners. Within ten years the industry collapsed because of overfishing. By 1953 there were 10,000 tons caught and in 1967 a ban was imposed by the government. The Japanese catch of chub mackerel in the north west Pacific fell from over one-and-a-half million tons in 1978 to less than half that figure four years later.

Some mammals depend on fishes that are also consumed by people. Any decline in their food resources will ultimately lead to the decline of the mammals populations. The walleye pollocks were once very abundant in the Bering Sea. Since 1986, the annual harvest of 6.6 million tons have gradually declined. It is spelling trouble for the mammals that feed on them. Populations of sea lions, fur seals and some marine birds are on the decline. The Steller's sea lions of Alaska have declined from between 240,000 to 300,000 in 1961 to an estimated 40,000 in 1991. At the Marmot Island, more than 10,000 sea lions used to breed there, with 5,000 pups being born. By 1994, less than 3,000 can be seen each breeding season. The decimation of the blue whale by whalers and the decline of the krill have reduced their population of more than two hundred thousands to the present population of about 14,000. Their decline has led to the upsurge in population of the crabeater seals, minke whales and some penguin species. Now the abundant krills are being harvested by commercial fishermen for human consumption probably made it impossible to replenish the population of the blue whale.

Overharvesting has been responsible for the decline and have been known to change the ocean ecosystem leading to unexpected results. The overhunting of commercial fish in the Black Sea and the North Sea has resulted in the proliferation of the jellyfishes. This led to a competition problem among the fishes and the more numerous jellyfishes for the zooplankton food. The harvest of American lobsters in the eastern seaboard has caused a population explosion of spring sea urchins. The end result is the loss of seaweed beds needed for the protection of the young lobsters.

Much like other industries engaged in the exploitation of natural resources where large financial investments have been undertaken, the fishing industry will overexploit to recover the investment in as little time as possible. Even after the capital investments have long been recovered, they will justify their continued exploitations on other grounds. The whaling industry is one example. Countries such as Norway and Japan still justify their whaling on ground of scientific research and as traditional food for their populations. They have been largely responsible for the near extinction of an intelligent mammal that is the property and heritage of all the people on earth.

Sometimes fish can be overharvested without studying their reproductive behavior. A good example is the halibut. The fishes v. ere unsustainable caught by fishermen since the mid-19th century until it was found that the females became sexually mature at nine or ten years of age. The premature overharvesting of these fishes has resulted in their near extinction. The large appetite for halibut in Boston, where most of the fishes are found can only aggravate the situation.

Well aware of the growing problem of overharvesting of marine animals, the international community had forged several agreements to limit the catches and use less damaging fishing methods as the situation warrants. The driftnets have been banned in the high seas, but it is allowed within the local coastal economic zone. Several agreements have also been made to limit krill fishing in the Antarctica, cod in the North Sea. and salmon in the Atlantic Ocean. Unilateral actions have been taken by governments to protect the catches within their economic zones.

An important factor that drives big time commercial fishing to overharvest is the return in profit they expect to get from their huge investment in ocean-going vessels. Sustainable use of the ocean resources takes a back scat especially when there is practically no regulatory body to control the volume of harvest in the open seas. Attempts have been made to limit the harvesting of seriously depleted ocean resources but there are always a few nations who find it difficult to adhere to the majority's decision.

Businessmen from around the world are always trying to devise ways to make a quick profit the easy and shortest way. They have done that in Asian and African countries using dynamite and cyanide fishing. An almost similar way in the Bahamas makes use of bleaching compounds. Lobster fisherman uses one-gallon plastic container filled with bleach. The fisherman will dive deep down into the ocean with the prohibited "hooker" oxygen supply system driven by a gasoline motor in a small supply boat above.

Down in the water caverns where the lobsters are found, the bleach is squirted into the hiding cavern around the reef, turning it into a gas chamber to force out the lobsters. Those trapped inside will die of asphyxiation. In one such operation, the fisherman can earn thousands of dollars. The reef however, remains burnt, black, and charred for years. It took only a few minutes to destroy thousands of years of works to produce this natural wonder.

Because fishes from the oceans are considered as common property, no nation is willing to reduce their share of fish catches so that the sea creatures can recover. Many important food fishes are vanishing before our eyes all over the world. New Zealand's organ roughy, the Gulf of Mexico's red snapper, bluefin tuna and swordfish from the Atlantic ocean. New England's haddock and flounder, cod from Newfoundland and herring from the North Sea have been virtually wiped out. It took a while before the governments act on the grave situation. Politics of accommodation and greed of businessmen are behind all these problems.

PURSE SEINES

Purse seine is a large net that is set around a school of fish by two ships, each holding one end of the net. As soon as the catch is surrounded, the net is closed. It is very efficient in catching tuna because of their affinity to be around school of dolphins. Purse seine fishing, used for catching tuna have been responsible for millions of dolphins and other creatures killed since 1970.

Recently, the use of this type of fishing method has been brought under control by requiring fishermen to use a redesigned tuna net that allows the dolphins to escape. An escape gap near the top of the net is provided. Despite improvements in the purse seine because of international condemnation and boycott, many have not adopted it as it is still killing large numbers of dolphins. An estimated 100,000 dolphins a year died in this type of fishing. Only the harvesting of tongal and albacore tuna does not threaten dolphins.

Even with improvements the purse seine is still an indiscriminate harvesting method. Many unwanted and unintended fishes are caught beside dolphins. They are thrown back to the sea after harvesting but not until many have died already.

SEAHORSES

There are about 35 species of seahorses found throughout the world. The smallest is the *Hippocampus bargibanti* while the *Hippocampus ingeris* is the longest at 14 inches. The seahorse is a small marine fish whose head look like a horse from where it got its name. It is widely distributed around the tropical and temperate regions of the world. The seahorse lacks a caudal fin, but has all the other small fins. The most important is the prehensile tail which it uses to attach itself to plants for support. It is also capable of changing color to camouflage with the natural surrounding. One unique feature of the seahorse is the presence of the brood pouch in the abdomen of the males. The female seahorse deposits the eggs into the male pouch where it hatches into look-alike offspring. As many as 200 offspring are breed at any time.

It is difficult to raise seahorse in an aquarium because it must be constantly supplied with running sea water. But this is not the number one threat to their existence. Neither are those dried and converted into curios such as key chains, earrings, and broaches. The greatest threat to the seahorses came from the medical use. The Roman naturalist, Pliny the Elder (24-78 A.D), had recommended seahorse ashes mixed with soda and lard from the pig as a cure for baldness.

Since the Ming Dynasty 400 years ago, the Chinese have been using it for curing diseases ranging from the asthma, broken bones, reducing phlegm, arteriosclerosis, skin ailments, heart problems to impotency. As many as 20 million seahorses are used annually for this purpose, according to Dr. Amanda Vincent of the McGill University In Canada, who has been studying the seahorses for ten years now. Demand seems to be increasing at a rate of 10% annually and unless they are drastically reduced, there may not be much left to supply this demand.

Most of the seahorses end up in Hong Kong, for which the Philippines is a major supplier. In the small village of Handumon, Bohol, a local fisherman can earn about P20 ($0.50) for a 4 to 5-inch seahorse, but that same seahorse, after bleaching and dried can command up to $10 apiece. This large profitable rate of return is sure to keep up the demand by pharmacies. The move to use them in grounded powder form will make it possible to use smaller seahorses that could further deplete the population in the wild.

From a high of 40-50 seahorses caught a night by fishermen in Handumon a few years ago. it has declined dramatically by more than 70% to around 15 seahorses. With help from Filipino biologists and Haribon Foundation, Dr. Vincent has set up a conservation effort to stop the depletion. Initial undertaking is to screen all the seahorses intended for export. All pregnant males are kept in cages until they give birth to the offspring. A sanctuary around the reef was also set up to allow the young seahorses to mature without molestation. A more ambitious project is the construction of a seahorse farm in an underwater corral for the seahorse colony. The success of this venture had encouraged people from neighboring villages to follow suit.

More efforts are underway to conserve the seahorses for future generations. Dr. Vincent has joined forces with the Zoological Society of London in launching Project Seahorse. With a contribution of 20 sterling pounds, anybody can adopt a seahorse species for conservation. For more information, they can contact Project Seahorse, c/o London Zoo, Regent's Park, London NW1 4RY. Another center was opened in Exeter, England called the Sea Horse National Aquarium. It hopes to study the problems faced by seahorses and educate the public on how to conserve these threatened animals. A captive breeding program has also been set up.

SHARKS

There are about 375 species of sharks, ranging from the smallest at 16 cm for the dwarf dogshark to over 18 meters long for the whale shark (*Rhmcodon typus*). However, most of them are less than a meter long. They have smooth and streamlined bodies allowing them to swim fast and steady. Sharks have several rows of teeth. When one is worn out or lost, it is immediately replaced with a new one.

Their babies, born live must fend for themselves lest they be eaten by the parent. Only a few shark predators feed on sea mammals such as sea lions, seals, dolphins and other fishes. They also prey on injured and sick animals thus keeping the ocean ecology strong and healthy. However, like their counterparts on land, they are no match for the human predators.

Scientists have been fascinated with sharks for a long time. These creatures are almost free of diseases that commonly afflict mankind. They never contract cancer, eye cataracts and are not affected by toxic chemicals. Chemicals extracted from shark cartilage have shown to kill cancerous tumors in laboratories and their skins are used as artificial skin for burn victims. Their immunity system is being studied for possible protection against AIDS. Their corneas have been transplanted into human eyes. They have the advantage that they do not dilate when the salt content in the surrounding environment varies, unlike those of the bony fishes.

The ingenuity of people have found use for almost all parts of the shark s body. For centuries, sharks have been caught for their teeth to be made into artifacts, tools, knives, jewelry, and other objects. The teeth have been used as weapons because of its sharpness. They have even turned their jaws into souvenirs and trophies, commanding a very high price, while the carcasses are turned into fertilizer. The shark's skin is another prized trophy. It is hard, strong, and durable that they are used to make shoes, sheaths for swords and daggers as in Africa and the Middle East. The denticles are used for making quality shoes and cowboy trousers because it is more elastic than cowhide or pigskin and 150 times more resistant than bovid leather. Before there was industrial sandpaper, the skin of the shark was used for a long time.

There are many things we don't know about sharks. We have only recently discovered that they are physiological more like humans than like other fishes. Studies are being made on how they live and reproduce, and their role as top predator in the hope that a sustainable fishery can be made. Volunteers from EarthWatch are capturing the sharks and fitting them with ultrasonic transmitters before releasing them to study their movements.

Fear of sharks have generated great concerns for swimmers. In South Africa and Australia, nets have been used to separate the sharks from swimmers along the beach. These nets with large mesh holes also trap and kill many harmless sharks, dolphins, mantra rays, turtles, and other large mammals that came across them. The mesh nets are about 100 meters long and 6 meters deep. Mark buoys are used on top to mark their presence and keep them afloat while heavier anchors are used to keep the net vertically erect. In South Africa, around 1,400 sharks along with countless dolphins are killed annually. Divers who persist in swimming in shark infested areas should to well to carry a stick that is very effective in driving away the shark. Bangstick tipped with explosive cartridge often kill the shark by tearing apart their intestines should be banned.

Experiments have been going on to find new ways of keeping the sharks at bay. One way is to use a wall of interlinked chains surrounding the beach. The links have small holes that prevent mammals from being entangled. Although expensive and limited in the area under protection, it affords the best protection without harming the sharks. Cost should never be a hindrance in protecting the animals as well as humans. Chemical repellants have been tried but found ineffective. Cables that emit electrical pulses to deter sharks are also being tested. This could possibly do the job because sharks have an electro-sense that allow them to detect electrical currents that is repulsive to them. The newest product using the sensitivity of shark to electric shock is now on the market in the U.S. (Popular Science. June 1997). The device called Shark Protective Oceanic Device or Shark POD is an electronic shark repellent The device, once activated generates a low-voltage electrical field that extends 12 to 20 feet in radius from the diver Experiments have shown that sharks naturally veer away from the electric field once it is activated, although scientists still do not know whether it is the pores or other sensory system that turn them away The technology is being developed for other uses.

The biggest threat to sharks, like other sea mammals is overfishing accidentally or deliberately. Often sharks are unintentional caught in nets and died of suffocation unless they are freed immediately. Most of them are mutilated of their fins before they are thrown back to the sea. Without their fins, they are unable to navigate properly and may be torn apart by other sharks nearby, caused by the smell of blood from their bleeding body. Shark fins are delicacies of the Chinese restaurants The fins are soaked in brine for two days and dried, packed and sold later. When boiled, the cartilage releases a smooth gelatin which gives body and taste to soups Only the dorsal and pectoral fins are used Because they can be dried and easy to market later in contrast to the shark meats which need to be processed and sold immediately at high cost are often discarded In 1947. the harvest of sharks together with skates and rays was about 220,000 tons worldwide. By 1994, the amount has risen to 800,000 tons, accounting for about 200 million sharks. This unprecedented harvest has led to the near extinction of several species. Other species will soon follow unless drastic measures are taken. Today, an estimated 30 to 100 million sharks are caught, reflecting a sharp decline in their populations

The sharks have been left unmolested by the consumers for centuries But the decimation of many food fishes for human consumptions have lead to the harvesting of sharks' meat. It is now highly sought after in Asia where the Japanese have at least twenty classic ways of preparing it Dried salted shark meat is sold every w here in Mexico. In the U.S., the frozen shark's fillets sold in supermarkets are passed as cod or swordfish meat because of the rarity of these fishes.

Sharks are also killed for their protein by the poor people of the developing countries. The runaway population in the Third World will guarantee that sharks will be hunted for years to come. There are some engaged in killing sharks for the liver oil. Sharks lack swim bladder and most will sink if they stop swimming, but they have oil-rich livers that reduce their weight in water Basking sharks (Cetorhinus maximus), the second largest fish in the world have large livers and are often caught to produce a refined oil called squalene. A single six-ton basking shark can produce 1,000 liters of oil. Shark oil have also been used for a wide range of consumer products such as face creams to prevent wrinkles and signs of aging. Other substitutes from plants and other fishes in abundance are available and just as effective, but human nature is difficult to change.

In Florida and elsewhere, sharks are victims of angling competitions because their big afford a chance to win the competition. Instead of overfishing, some the lemon sharks of Florida are under threat of extinction because of the destruction of their mangrove swamps which are important nurseries of their pups.

SPORT FISHING

Every year more than a billion fishes are captured by American sport fishermen and a few more billions by fishermen around the world to satisfy their urge to cause pain on fishes unconsciously. While they may not be aware of the painful suffering, the fishes do, as they struggle to free themselves from the hooks. The mouth with its tongue and lips is very sensitive to pain and suffering. More than any part of the body, it is the mouth that keeps them alive. Besides gathering food with their mouth, it is used for making nests and sometimes to protect the fingerlings from predators where it is used as a refuge.

Since the 1930s, improvements in underwater equipments have given rise to a new sport in spear hunting. The fisherman used powerful spear guns in hunting large fish such as sharks. Many of these spear guns have explosive charges at the end to make the spear penetrate deeper into the body of the unfortunate victims. Those that do not die immediately and swim away will suffer from a painful and slow death. With fishing clubs sprouting in many areas and tournaments being held for the largest fish caught, more killings can be expected.

The catch-and-release program advocated by some ecologists, while being appreciated by many environmentalists may not vouch well for the fish. It serves no purpose to hook the fish, tear up its mouth, and later release them. Fishing lines are often lost and can entangle birds and even hook them when bait are exposed. If the idea is to catch fish for food, there are other humane ways to accomplish the task.

The whole idea of catch-and-release is to return the fish to the water alive and well. But the fish is often unduly stressed and may not survive for long. Mortality may be as high as 10 percent. The best way to avoid stressing a fish is to release it as soon as possible. Extended struggle promotes lactic acid buildup. Some fishes are so stressed after being landed and handled that their lactic level is so high, their need for oxygen is greatly increased, and require more recovery time before they can swim off on their own. Generally large fish tend to have more difficulties with stress than smaller ones, and often have a higher mortality.

Most sportsmen do not even know the correct way to release the fish. The best way to release a fish is in the water without touching it. But fish that is stressed need to be calmed and receive oxygen. Most instructions on fish revival, if they are read and practice, advise moving the fish back and forth to get the needed oxygen. But in nature a fish takes water into the mouth swimming forward and forces it over the gills and out the external opening to bring oxygen into its blood. It cannot be accomplished by swimming backward or by facing downstream. In fact, a fish held in a strong downstream current would die. But moving a fish forward only is difficult and fishermen seldom bother to do and instead throw the fish back into the water immediately. Mortality is increased.

TRAWLERS

The fishing industry has gradually evolved from the use of spears, fishing hooks, nets to very sophisticated means of fishing methods. Many of the state of the art electronics have been invented to help fishermen locate fish and pinpoint the depth where they are found. Even the fishing vessels have been equipped with refrigeration, allowing them to travel for months harvesting the bounties of the ocean. One of the method employed is trawling.

A trawler is very efficient in catching fish and destroying the seafloor. It uses a large net bag or trawl with its conical-shaped net that is towed through the water as it moves near the bottom seabed. Bottom sea fishes are the target of these trawlers. Many unintended benthic creatures are also dragged along the seabed, leaving behind a widely degraded sea floor. The spawning ground of many fishes are also destroyed.

Once the catches are brought up to the trawler, tons of unwanted or untargeted and young fishes are also harvested. These unwanted fishes take up space and slow down the fishing vessels. They are often thrown back to the sea, but many often die from the trauma.

Intensive trawling in coastal areas is also damaging the seabed, destroying coral reefs, digging up the toxic wastes that lie dormant at the bottom of the sea and spreading them with the ocean current for some time before settling down and disturbing the habitats of many sea organisms.

TUNA

The affluence of some nations have been responsible for the decimation of some species of animals. Whaling and fur hunting have been responsible for the heavy toll on the whales and other large sea mammals. Many large fishes have been caught at unsustainable rate for years or decades. But nothing can match the decline of the giant tuna. The giant bluefin tuna is being hunted to extinction. The population of tuna in the Atlantic coast has declined by 90% since 1975. In the 1970s, the cost of a pound of tuna is just a few cents. Today, with depreciating dollars and high demand, a giant tuna weighing 715 pounds can fetched as much as $90,000 each in the sushi market in Japan. Its high fat meat is in great demand in Japan to the tune of 20,000 tons a year, more than half of the world's catch. This has prompted sport anglers to join commercial fishermen in hunting down these large fishes for the foreign market.

There are two major problems facing the giant tuna. Although an international quota for the bluefins had been imposed more than a decade ago, there are no longer enough tuna in the ocean to make it profitable. In mid-September of 1991, when the tuna season is supposed to be at its peak in Montauk Harbor, the largest giant caught weighs less than 35 kilos. Secondly, the very fishes that are matured enough to spawn are the ones being hunted down by fishermen and eaten by sushi lovers. To compound the problem, the U.S. government, under pressure from the commercial fishing industry voted to increase the allowable catch in spite of the worldwide decline of tuna population. It was also contrary to the U.N. Agreement on Highly Migratory Fish Stocks signed in 1995 and ratified by the U.S. Senate in 1996. The world's most powerful leader should lead by example, obeying international agreements that others may follow. Only a worldwide total ban on harvesting the bluefins can save them from extinction.

CHAPTER 11

PHILIPPINE WILDLIFE

The Philippines is home to a large number of animal species, many endemic to the country. Most of them are small mammals, birds and fishes. The largest endemic animal is the tamaraw, a buffalo-like creature inhabiting the province of Mindoro. Another is the jungle boar called gagil. Other mammals include swamp rats, carabaos, and Palawan mouse deer, the smallest ruminant in the world. There are 56 species of bats and more than 950 species and subspecies of birds, the most famous of them is the Philippine Eagle (Pithecophaga jefferyi). The eagle was once called the monkey-eating eagle, which is actually a small part of its diet. Other birds of prey include the crested lizard hawk (Aviceda jerdoni magnirostris), barred honey buzzard (Pernis celebensis steerei), Asiatic honey buzzard (Pernis apivorousphilippinensis), Philippine falconet (Microhierax erythrogonys), crested goshawk (Accipiter trivirgatus), Philippine hawk eagle (Spizaetus philippinensis), changeable hawk eagle {Spizaetus cirrhalus), Brahminy kite (Haliastus indus), white-billed sea eagle (Haliastiis leucogaster) and serpent eagle (Spilornis holospilus).

There are also 240 species of reptiles such as snakes, crocodilians, turtles, and lizards. Primates include monkeys such as macaques, tarsier, and flying lemurs. Out of all these rich species, some 200 species are under threat of extinction, mostly as a result of habitat destruction and overhunting.

Sea creatures include dugongs, sharks, and at least 2,400 species of fishes. The world's smallest fish, Pondoka pygmaca is also found in the Philippines. Only a few species are edible and the rest are exported as aquarium fishes. There are more than 10,000 different kinds of shells, making us the largest source of seashells in the world. Pearl from the oysters can be found in the Sulu Archipelago, a source of livelihood for many.

Unfortunately, like many island-nations with rich forest ecosystems, pearls are being devastated by greed and poverty in an unprecedented and unsustainable scales. Overfishing has depleted the marine resources and destruction of coral reefs will mean less cheap protein for the large number of coastal people.

BATS

The Philippines is home to 56 species of bats, all of them are either endangered or threatened and some may even be extinct by now. The main reason for their precarious status is destruction of their habitats due to logging, firewood gathering, slash-and-bum cultivation locally known as kaingin, and even devastating typhoons. For every tree cut by loggers, ten other small trees are destroyed as well. Many of these trees harbor insects that served as food for the bats. Other flowering plants serve the nectar-eating herbivorous bats. The indigenous farmers on the other hand are forced by necessity to burn down the trees to get nutrients for their crops. Firewood is used for heating the homes and cooking the meals and are taken from the stems and branches. The small trees are often the target of these gatherers The breakage of these young trees can easily lead to the demise as insects and other organisms are able to penetrate inside the plants and do their damage.

Several species of bats have become extinct as a result of the destruction of their habitats. The Panay fruit bat (Acerodon lucifer) has not been seen since 1988. The bare-backed bat (Dohsonia chapmani) of Negros was only discovered in 1952, but has not been seen since 1964 and is now considered extinct. Also the mountainous region of southern Negros is home to the tube-nosed bat (Nyctimene rabon), first discovered and described in 1983. Only a small remnant can be found and protected under an established preserve, but illegal deforestation, mostly by kaingeros still continue. There were about 150,000 Pleropus vumpyrus in the Philippines in the 1920s, making them the largest group of bats locally. Today, there are a few hundred individuals left as a result of overhunting them for food and deforestation. Unless the bat habitats are vigorously protected, they may soon become extinct.

Just as in many Asian and Pacific island nations, flying foxes are considered a delicacy by some local inhabitants. Furthermore, the demand by other countries for bat meat has spurned a new trend in hunting bats for the international markets. Despite their fast declining populations, the government still allows their exportation. The golden-crowned fruit bat {Acerodon jubatus), the largest endemic fruit bat has been hunted to near extinction.

BIRDS

The once rich ecosystems in many parts of the Philippines have been home to more than 950 species and subspecies of birds. More than any other animal, birds need trees to build their nests for breeding and survival. However, many of them are under constant threat due to deforestation. More than 100 bird species are under threat of extinction, making us one of the countries with the most endangered animals in the world.

There are 27 species of pigeons and doves in the country. Some famous birds include: Mindoro imperial pigeon (Ducula mindorensis), Marche's fruit dove (Ptilinopus marchei), Negros green fruit dove (Ptinopu aucanus), Cebu amethyst dove (Phapitreon amesthystinafrontalis), and bleeding heart pigeon (Gallicolumha luzonica). Birds are good indicators of our environment and their absences can only mean that something is awfully wrong with our environment.

Logging, firewood gathering, kaigin and to a lesser extent, destructions caused by tropical storms that often sweep the country are important factors in their decline. The endemic Philippine kingfisher (Ceyx melamurus), once so common throughout the country, has become so scarce that they are found in a few Pkces in Samar, Leyte, and parts of Luzon and Mindanao. The Sulu hornbills inhabiting the islands around the Sulu Archipelago are hunted by the hungry local inhabitants as food have declined to the brink of extinction. Many other edible big birds are suffering the same fate.

The wattled roadbill and Koch's pitta are rarely seen as well as six species of babblers and couples of species of cuckoo-shrikes. Many birds are restricted to one or two islands without sufficient forest cover for their survival. The black-and-white winged greybirds, Niltava and Vaurie's flycatchers, the short-crested blue monarch, Steere's concul, endemic to the island of Mindoro, and other species are also endangered.

Of the ten endemic species of birds that once inhabit Cebu province, only one the black ghama (Copsychus cebuensis) or locally known as siloy was rediscovered on November 13, 1981. In March 1997, it was reported that the Cebu flowerpecker (Dicaeum quadricolor) locally known aspanagoto, was spotted in five barangays in Balamban town. They were rediscovered in 1992 after an absence of eight years. Their return was made possible because of the availability of a species of trees where they make their nests. The rediscovery, after a long absence, means that they are still very much endangered unless drastic measures are undertaken to ensure their survival and propagation.

The Philippines is home to seven endemic species of owls. While only one species, the Mindoro scops owl (Olus mirus) is listed in the IUCN, all the others are also under threat of extinction as deforestation continues to take its toll on their dwindling habitats and numbers.

More than any other bird of prey, the owls play an important ecological role in maintaining the balance of nature. They are responsible for consuming a lot of terrestrial rodents that destroyed agricultural crops that are difficult for other raptors to catch.

The pet bird trade is becoming a serious threat to the decline of parrots in the wild. Many beautiful parrots like the red-vented and lesser-sulphur crested parrots, cockatoos, racket-tailed parakeets are in great demand and have been hunted from the wild and sold to pet shops. Many of these birds can easily be found in hollow trees. Poachers openly gather these birds because of the lack of enforcement of the law. They are paid about P300.00 each, and can be sold as high as 50 times their value in the international markets. At the rate these young birds are being collected in the wild and exported or sold locally, the future of their generations in the wild is very bleak.

In 1989, the Cincinnati Museum of Natural History and Science and the National Museum of the Philippines began taking an inventory of wildlife in the Philippines. One old species wrongly designated early in the century and rediscovered in 1965 was given the scientific name *Aethopyga linaraborae* in honor of the wife of a Filipino ornithologist who discovered it in 1965. The bird, locally called Lina's Sunbird resembled a hummingbird, but they are not related. The 4 to 41/2 inches long bird weighs about 7 grams.

The British government is also funding a long-term project that is helping Haribon Foundation, an NGO to produce a "Red Book" for Philippines' endangered birds. The book will supply vital information such as description of the birds, where and why they are endangered and what can be done to save them from their present status. The work has been going for over a year and is expected to come out of the press soon. Another book, Philippine Red Data Book, by Wildlife Conservation Society of the Philippines is on the market since 1997.

BUTTERFLIES AND MOTHS

There are roughly five thousand species of butterflies and moths in the Philippines, many of them endemic to the country. Every year new and rare species are being discovered. Some of these new found species are often harvested and lost forever instead of taking chances and allowing them to propagate in the wild. This wasteful practice has been responsible for the loss of many species in the past, not only for insects but also some mammals.

There are many interesting facts about butterflies. The swallowtails (Lapropria mates) is one of the smallest in the world. Some butterflies have interesting behavior. One species would scatter her eggs in different vines to ensure the survival of some offspring. One of the biggest moth in the world is the locally famous mariposa. It has an interesting feature found in very few butterflies and moths in the world. The adult moth does not have any eating organ and it does not eat or pollinate any flower. All the food that it needs had been provided by the caterpillar which took in enough food to feed the moth for the rest of its natural life. Not all butterflies do their feedings during the daytime. Some nocturnal butterflies in the Philippines are becoming very important as nocturnal pollinators since the active night bats are being decimated to near extinction.

One of the havens for butterflies is found in the Quezon National Park, a government forest sanctuary. Some of the beautiful and rare butterflies found there are the Adolias satrapes, Euthaliapanopus, Pachliopta almae, Atrophaneura semperi, Zeucsidia semperi, Plrothoe franckii and Eriboea schereiber luzonmcus. One species, the Papilio chikae, endemic to the Mountain Province is considered an endangered species by IUCN and subject to protection. However, in many places where loggings and minings are going on, their habitats are being destroyed. Some butterflies will only breed on certain plants and failure to stop the destruction of these plants will lead to their demise.

The initial investment in harvesting butterflies is very small compare to its high rate of return. This has been partly responsible for its decimation. Anyone with a small net can catch the easily spotted butterfly which doesn't fly very fast. They can also pick up the caterpillars that are commonly found on leaves. Another common reason is the habitat destruction due to firewood gathering and illegal carabao logging where the timbers are cut and made into flitches and dragged by carabaos to pickup points.

Years ago, people in Antipolo have learned to care for the environment as a result of butterfly farming which is a source of income for many. But human encroachment is diminishing their habitat in the wild. Today, butterfly farming has taken to new heights. There are at least 200 butterfly breeders in the country, mostly concentrated in Marinduque, Mindoro Oriental, Palawan, Cavite, Tarlac, Nueva Ecija, Baguio, Mountain Province, and Surigao. They deal mostly in livestock such as pupae and deadstock, which are papered butterflies used to display in glass. Export markets include the U.S., UK, Switzerland, Hong Kong. Sweden, France, and Italy. The first export of butterfly was made in 1990 with 12 pupae. It increased dramatically in 1993 to 152,864 and over 200,000 in 1994.

The worldwide increase in butterfly collection could doom some endangered species. While they may breed prolifically in undisturbed habitat, there are not many habitats free from human disturbances. People are destroying their breeding plants and overcollecting, leading to deleterious effects on butterfly population.

Sometimes, the pupae are harvested rather than the butterflies because they are easier to "catch." They are either sold to collectors or allow to metamorphose into butterfly. There is an even bigger market for dried butterflies. Museums and collectors often prefer to collect rare butterflies before they are lost forever. Scientists prefer to study them in their laboratories rather than in the wild. There is also a big demand for pupae for propagation abroad. Export of pupae is allowed only on certain species but it still require an export certification issued by PAWB. Every year, thousands of pupae are legally and illegally exported. Dried butterflies are not exempted from certification and thousands have been confiscated due to lack of documentation. Most of these pupae and butterflies came from butterfly farms established around the country.

CARABAOS

The second largest mammal in the Philippines is the carabao (Bubalos bubales), which is an important working animal in the agricultural field. They have been responsible for helping farmers plow their field With increasing mechanization, carabaos are becoming more of a burden to some farmers. These gentle, herbivorous animals used to weigh as much as 350 kg. but have since been reduced to an average weight of 300 kg mainly due to overworking. Beside working in the field, they are also used in transporting people and pulling carts and even help in moving nipa houses.

Like many other animals, it has other uses such as a source of carabeef, which used to supply half the country's beef. The milk is used as part of an ingredient in sweets. Their horns are made into many household articles such as spoons, daggers, ashtrays, trophies, etc. Fortunately these by-products are not the main reasons for killing them. From a high of almost three millions in the 1980s, they have declined to about 2.4 million in 1992. This is because many were slaughtered illegally in spite of the ban against killing male carabaos below seven years and female carabaos below eleven years old. One loophole often taken to go around this ban is to deliberately maim the young carabaos by breaking a bone in their legs.

CONSERVATION

The Philippines is home to a rich source of species. About 960 terrestrial vertebrate species can be found in the Philippines, with more than half of them endemic to the country. There are more than 160 species of mammals. 100 of which are found in the country with 45 of them endemic to single islands within it-Out of the 950 bird species, 395 had their breeding done within the country 183 of these are endemic. There are 253 species of reptiles and amphibians, with 75% of the lizard, 52% of the snake, and as much as 70% of the amphibian endemic to the country. There are probably some more unclassified or yet to be discovered.

But all these species are at risk in one way or another. Natives living deep in the forest are hunting many of these animals for food. Logging, although banned in many areas, have already destroyed a large part of their natural habitats. The high upland population density makes it difficult to stop further destruction of the forests.

One of the richest natural habitats can be found in Mt. Makiling, in southern Luzon. The protection of this sanctuary is typical of what is being done to sanctuaries around the country. In fact, many do not have the blessing of this reserve. Within the confine of this rich ecosystem can be found at least 50 species of mammals and 120 species of birds, and still many unknown groups. The invertebrates include at least 30,000 species of insects, many of them unclassified. In almost all of southern Luzon, there is no longer any refuge for these animals. Illegal loggings sometimes go on within the Makiling Forest Reserve. This could very well spell the end of some species such as the swallow-tail butterfly (Grapophium idaeoides).

First established in 1910 with 44 sq km, it has changed management with different policies on how to preserve the forest. The degree of tolerance for settlers varied over the years until 1993 when it was politically impossible to reverse the influx of farmers. Today, only 20 sq km can be considered intact. The declining areas has led to a decline in species population sizes and possibly reduced genetic variations. Many of the species are thought to be on their way to extinction.

CORAL REEFS

There are several dozen important coral reefs surrounding the Philippines. All of them are important to the livelihood of the people in these areas. But easy means of harvesting, high prices paid by people engaged in the illicit and export markets, and unlimited or unsustainable harvesting have taken its toll in all these sea forests. Before the ban in coral export in 1977 by virtue of PD 129 and PD 1698, the Philippines had been exporting hundreds of tons annually. Some protruding reefs, called atolls are also breeding ground for birds.

The Tubbataha Reefs had been declared by UNESCO as a World Heritage Site in 1994. But this is no guarantee that it will be safe from damages unless people who visit them are careful in following guidelines to protect them. Divers should be careful not to touch these reefs with their hands or feet as they are very fragile and can easily break off.

Located in the middle of the Sulu Sea, 150 kilometers from Puerto Princesa City, it is the Philippines' only national marine park and it seems we can't protect it against destruction unless full time marine guards are in place. It is a sanctuary of many colorful fishes such as the manta rays and green sea turtles as well as many kinds of birds. Its distance is no guarantee against encroachers who go there for scuba diving and collecting corals and fish species. A seaweed farm was even erected there in 1989 by the Shemberg Corporation. The atoll was used as the production platform. Because of the possible damage caused by human activities with this setup it was dismantled by a group of NGOs from Palawan two years later.

Before the government and the NGOs took to protecting the atolls and the coral reefs underneath, it has been subjected to illegal fishing methods such as dynamite and cyanide fishing that has destroyed large parts of the reef. The decline is still going on in spite of efforts to save it. A recent study made by Dr. Alan White of the Coastal Resource Project Management showed that manta rays thrive in only two sites and sea turtles in only five sites compared to 50 sites more than a decade ago. The ban on export of aquatic fishes on March 21, 1997 will go a long way in saving the coral reefs against the use of dynamite and cyanide fishing.

Some of the birds which used to make the atolls their home are the sooty terns, masked and brown boobies and the common hoddy terns. The red-footed bobbies which used to breed there in the thousands can no longer be found. Their eggs and those of the other species have been taken from their nests. Commercial boats used to deliver eggs in 55-gallon drums to Puerto Princesa until the government put a stop to it. Fishermen used to catch lapu-lapu for the gourmet markets in Hong Kong. While staying in the atolls, the fishermen survived by eating fishes and eggs of birds. Hunters used to kill the birds w ith automatic rifles. Even some military men tasked with protecting the place and suffering from boredom used to kill the birds. The disturbances caused by tourists on breeding wildlife, especially those with long breeding periods have been responsible for the declining birds' population. The survival of this reef and all others in the country should be put off limit to people until they are completely rehabilitated.

Sometimes more drastic actions are needed to patrol the coral reefs against illegal harvesting and fishing. Since October 1996, soldiers from the Coast Guard and Western Command have been deployed at the Tubbataha Reef to protect them against illegal activities. It is an expensive and lonely job, but it must be done. Unfortunately, most of the coral reefs are located near inhabited islands and underneath the sea, making it difficult to patrol these waters.

Another important coral reef is located near the Mindoro Island. The state of this coral reef has changed for the worse. The illegal method of fishing called mura ami, and soil erosion had choked the corals to death in many areas. This is aggravated by the deadly crown-of-thorns starfishes that has eaten vast amounts of corals responsible for the formation of the reef. The proliferation of the crown-of-thorns is made possible by people harvesting the conch shell, their natural predator, for the shell market.

In Negros, professional divers are doing something about the problem. They have plucked out more than 6,000 starfishes during a six-day period ending in May 1997. Locally known as salanays, they eat up the corals of the famous Apo Island, where one important reef is located. In this locality, the mass outbreak of the crown-of-thorns may be due to the rampant collection of the Triton snail as well as the overexploitation of the Humphead wrasse and the lapu lapu, are natural enemies of the starfishes.

According to EarthCorps findings at nine sites in Mabini, Batangas, divers and dive operators on these spectacular reefs are being more careful. Coral growth and cover are improving, and there is less damage from anchors and careless divers breaking coral. However, biodiversity continue at low levels, except in two recently established reef sanctuaries. For areas not yet under protection, both food and aquarium fish species have not recovered due to overfishing. Investigators Alan White and Keene Haywood advocated the creation of more reef sanctuaries to help in the breeding.

Another reason for the deteriorating coral reefs has to do with proliferation golf courses. There are already seventy golf courses in the Philippines and ten more are in the planning stage. The corals are harvested and used as filter for sand traps or "bunker" to make the course more challenging. They are used because they do not absorb water like the regular silica sand. In addition, white corals are chosen in contrast to the green landscape. In Zamboanga, coral reefs are collected and used as landfill by farmers evacuees who settled in coastal barangays starting in 1989. Despite the ban against coral reef gathering, the poor fishermen are cashing on the corals at P100.00 per banca load, a small return for the farmers but a giant damage to the reef ecosystem. These corals are sold as decorative items and construction materials. Worldwide, the total trade in corals was estimated at 1.5 million kg, 500,000 kg coming from the Philippines, in spite of the ban against its export, according to the London-based Pan Institute.

Coral reefs and other marine ecosystems are closely related. Reef structures dissipate ocean waves caused by hurricanes and storms and create reef flats and lagoons which permit the growth of seagrasses and mangroves. The new plants serve as food for the fishes and seagrasses are the only food of dugongs while binding the sediments and silts coming from soil erosions caused by farming, deforestation and other development projects that can stir up the soil.

The race to save the environment often starts with a person or a group of activists. This has always been true even with the well-known NGOs of worldwide recognition. They usually start within a small community and gradually expand in area as more members are recruited. In Negros Island, Philippines, Wilson Vailoces, has been the driving force to restore the coastal resources in his community. The wanton destruction of marine habitats is due to soil erosion, overfishing, and illegal fishing. As a fisherman, he knew very well the problems faced by coastal people as the destruction continue unabated unless sustainable development is undertaken before the damage is beyond repair. He plants mangrove trees and builds artificial reefs to save the breeding grounds for marine creatures. He has also recruited 50 volunteers to patrol local water against illegal fishing and poaching. They have apprehended several hundred fishermen for illegal activities. His activities since the mid-1980s land him in the state-of-the-art exhibit called Ocean Planet in the U.S.

Fishermen from Malalison Island in Culasi, Antique are making artificial reefs and deploying these in coastal areas as part of rehabilitation works. It will act as part of the management program of the Southeast Asia Fisheries Development Center Aquaculture Department in Tigbauan, Iloilo.

The continuing destruction of the coral reefs throughout the world have brought together marine scientists, ecologists, biologists, conservationists and other interested parties to declare the year 1997 as the International Year of the Reef. It is hope that this event will bring more awareness to everybody of the important role of the coral reefs.

On July 22, 1997, the Coral Reef Information Network of the Philippines (Philreefs) conferred the Reef Awards to several "reef champions" during the launching of another new program called Adopt-a-Reef as part of the International Year of the Reef. The awardees are business tycoons Jaime Zobel de Ayala and Carlos Soriano for adopting Turtle Island in Sulu and Tubbataha Reef in Palau$_{an}$ respectively. Local rock band Eraserheads was awarded for Acha Reef in Ragay Gulf, Quezon; environmentalist Jun Kalaw of Haribon Foundation for Anilao Reef in Batangas; Philippine Tourism Authority chief Ed Joaquin for Balicasag Reef, also in Palawan; television show host Tessie Tomas and her marine biologist-husband Dr. Roger Pullin for Guiuan Reef in Samar. They were all awarded for adopting an important and fragile reef and soliciting funds and mustering support for the protection and conservation of their respective coral reefs. There are still many coral reefs that are waiting to be adopted. Any individual or group interested in helping save the environment can contact the Foundation for the Philippine Environment.

COWRIES

Cowries are marine molluscs whose shell is mostly made of calcium carbonate. There are at least 77 species of them, and some of the coveted and expensive ones can be found in the Philippines. The main reason for people harvesting the hard tortoise-shaped shells is their beautiful colors and markings. In the past, these shells have been used as amulets, bracelets, necklaces, trinkets, and other body ornaments. Many of the buildings in Metro Manila used cowry shells for decoration. The most famous is probably found in Manila Hotel where dignitaries and tourists have generous praises and good remarks for them.

Two species, the Cypraea aurantium and Cypraea moneia, more commonly known as golden cowry are also found in the Philippines. The same species of shells found elsewhere had been used as currency by the ancient Greek, Nagasof Assam and India. In other places, they are considered as gems and command as much as $500 for a large defectiveless piece.

CROCODILES

The Philippine freshwater crocodile (Crocodylus mindorensis) was once very prevalent in Basunang, Mindoro, Luzon, Mindanao, Samar. Masbate, and Jolo but has become extinct in many of these natural habitats. There are only 500 to 1.000 (1982) crocodiles left in the wild mostly located in the Sulu Archipelago. The decline of the crocodiles is largely due to the demand for its skin which is made into leather products. Another species is the saltwater crocodile. Crocodylus porosus, which is about 4-5 meters long and found mostly in Luzon, Mindanao, Palawan, Bohol, and Negros. In the 1950s, there were about 20,000 of them in the wild but their population in the wild is unknown today. A smaller reptile is the caiman crocodile (Caiman crocodulus) that is so rare, few people know of their existence in our country. They have a better chance of survival since their habitat of saltwater does not easily come into conflict with humans. However, they are still hunted for their skins especially in Mindanao.

The lakes and swamps of the Philippines were once heavily populated with crocodiles just after the turn of the century. The intrusion of people in the lowland forests during the resettlement projects after the Second World War brought many people into conflict with the crocodiles in their natural habitats. Many of their habitats were destroyed or polluted, and wetlands were turned into agricultural fields or housing projects. Mangrove forests, one of their favorite habitats have been converted to fishponds in Mindanao. Trees were cut down and made into charcoal or sold as firewood. Pollution from mine tailings and sedimentation are destroying their habitats.

Because of their bad reputation in connection with corrupt public officials due to their big mouth, and rural folks superstition that crocodiles are bearers of bad omen. Muslim hunters from Mindanao are sometimes recruited to kill them. After killing the crocodiles, their hides are gathered and sold across the strait to Sabah. This has led to an important source of income for Muslims engaged in barter trade with Borneo. To the Muslims, Sabah is considered part of the Sulu Sultanate and to them there is nothing illegal in trading with the people there even in endangered wildlife. Although the trade in crocodile skins is prohibited by law even for those engaged in barter trade across the Sulu Archipelago, the government is either helpless or turns a blind eye to the trade for fear of creating resentment that could lead to a breakdown of peace and order. Obviously, protecting wildlife and stopping their illegal trade is not a priority.

The only way to save them from extinction is a safe captive breeding program. One of them was set up with the help of Silliman University. In 1987, the Philippines requested and got the assistance of the Japanese government to establish a crocodile farming institute for the crocodiles in the country. With an allocation of SI 2.7 million from Japan, the RP-Japan Crocodile Farming Institute (CFI) was formally opened in January 1988 with a ten-hectare land donated by the government in Barangay Irawan, Puerto Princesa, Palawan.

CYANIDE FISHING

Cyanide fishing is very destructive for the corals. It has been in use since the 1960s in the Philippines. Sodium cyanide is squirted on the fishes in the coral reefs which harbor large numbers of fishes. Over 5,000 fishermen practiced this illegal method. A typical trade begins in small fishing town such as Siasi and Pangutaran in Sulu province. Four men climb into a motorized outrigger boat, equipped with food and water for up to two weeks, along with the cyanide provided by the middlemen. When they reach the reef several miles away, a fisherman dives amid the coral, breathing through a crude plastic hose attached to a compressor on the boat. His targets are the groupers, which flit around the reef from 10 to 30 meters under the surface. The fisherman squirts a bottle containing a solution of sodium cyanide and saltwater at passing fishes. Within minutes, several dozen fishes are stunned and netted by the diver. After several operations, the diver surfaces and dumps his catch into a submerged net attached to the skiff. Twenty minutes later, the fishes will recover. Back home, they are placed in holding pens near the fisherman's residence. Within a few weeks, the fishes have expelled the cyanide from their systems and are ready to be hauled to the port of Zamboanga. The constant use of this method on coral reefs have left many coral reefs dying and dead. Because cyanide fishing was made illegal in the Philippines in 1975, the fish are tested in a poison-detection center established a year ago. Only six fishes have tested positive.

After the fisherman squirts the cyanide, the first thing to perish is the reef algae, on which fishes feed. Days later, the living corals start to die. So the reef loses its function as a habitat for the fishes, which eat both the algae and invertebrates that cling to the coral. The reef becomes an underwater graveyard, its skeletal remains brittle, bleached of all color and vulnerable to erosion from the pounding of the waves.

In Indonesia, the trade is typically controlled by the local Chinese restaurants. They outfit the fishermen with boats, foods, nets, and cyanide. When they have caught about five tons, the boats will return to port and to the financing restaurant. The owner of the restaurant takes ownership of the captured fishes and stores them in vast segregated floating cages. Prices are negotiated and a new supply of cyanide is delivered for the future. Cyanide fishing has been outlawed in Indonesia since 1985.

Hong Kong is the regional hub of the trade in exotic fishes. Each large transport vessel carries as much as two tons of fish, worth between $250,000 and $400,000, and its importation into Hong Kong falls under laws written for the aquarium trade. It is exempted from health controls, and doesn't even show up in trade statistics.

In 1995, Philippines' export of marine fish was worth about $7 million and has declined to about $4 million today. The decline was mainly due to the strict implementation against cyanide fishing. All the fishes intended for export are required to get a clearance from the government agency overseeing the export market. The fishes have to undergo testing for cyanide residues. Fishes found with the residues are confiscated. Still cyanide fishing is still in use by fishermen for the local markets which does not undergo cyanide testing. This loophole needs to be remedied. Stricter penalties should also be imposed for those caught using dynamite and cyanide fishing.

Ending the blight of cyanide fishing will not be simple and experts have already concluded that cracking down on the far flung fishermen is futile. The best hope is to police the middlemen and restaurant owners while educating the consumers.

Traditional fishing method for catching grouper are less harmful to the environment. In the Philippine province of Palawan, an NGO, the International Marinelife Alliance has weaned fishermen from cyanide fishing and retaught them the art of fishing with hook and line. In Indonesia's Kei Kecil island chain, 300 households of the Kei tribe refuse to use cyanide or dynamite urged on them by fishing companies.

The ban on cyanide fishing should be rigorously enforced throughout the world in order that there won't be any shift from one locality to another. The fishes caught for export should be tested for cyanide residues such as that practiced in the Philippines. The fishes that passed are issued a cyanide-free certificate and allowed to be exported. But fish merchants in location such as Hong Kong would have to cooperate by purchasing only certified fishes.

DEER

The Philippines harbors several species of deer scattered throughout the country. One of them, the Philippine brown deer (Cervus mariannus or unicolor) is presently under tremendous pressures from hunters. This ruddy-brown deer with whitish chin weighs about 40-60 kg can be found in several provinces in Mindanao, and in Leyte and Catanduanes. It is a favorite prey for hunters since the meat can command P20 to PI00 per kilo while the dried meat can fetch from PI 50 to P200 per kilo. Some are caught alive and sold for at least P2,000. Because of inflation, the prices may have increased.

Other body products from the deer, including the antlers, sinews and hooves can be sold for their medicinal values. The velvet and hardened antlers are sought after by foreigners. Their numbers are declining faster than expected as more people are finding the meat to their taste. It is therefore important to rear them in captivity before they are decimated in the wild.

DEFOREST A TIONS

When an American forester first saw the forests of the Philippines in the early 1900s, he commented that it will take more than a thousand years to harvest the trees in the country. Less than a century later, we have not only removed the forest in many parts of the country but also destroyed the rich ecosystems together with many endemic animals. In spite of this fact, the government still continue to allow our precious forests to be cut down in many areas legally and illegally. Many areas banned from logging are being illegally poached and smuggled out of the country. According to the DENR (January 1997), there are 31 towns all over Mindanao that are still engaged in illegal logging.

Like all old growth virgin forests in tropical countries, we were blessed with numerous wildlife. But we have failed miserably as steward of this unique ecosystem very few island nations are endowed. Logging has many deleterious effects on wildlife. It is the main cause of loss or fragmentation of habitats that could reduce the survival rate of wildlife. The intrusion of logging workers paid with low salaries have forced many workers to hunt and eat wild animals to augment their protein requirement. Roads constructed by loggers have also made it possible for hunters to enter deeper into the forest and hunt animals and birds for stuffed trophies.

Several of the pigeons species, at least four ground doves endemic to the Philippines, and big imperials are endangered or hardly seen for many years. Most of them have been hunted to near extinction by hunters who used tree clearances and roads constructed by loggers to get into their habitats deep in the forest.

DUGONGS

Dugong (Dugong dugon) is a relative of manatees and the extinct Stellar's sea cow. There are between 30,000 and 90,000 of them in the world, most of them are found in Australia. Only about 1,000 are left in Palawan. The only herbivorous sea mammals in the world, they eat seagrasses found in many parts of the Philippines They used to be found in many parts of the country, but catching them for their meat, Oil, and other by-products, despite a ban, have decimated them in many places. They are now confined to Palawan, Isabela-Quezon. and southern Mindanao.

The DENR has collaborated with Toba Aquarium of Japan to help save the sea mammals. There is also the Pawikan Conservation Project. Another NGO called PAMARCON launched a campaign to save the dugongs in Palawan. They were besieged by lack of funds, manpower and technical expertise.

In spite of the DENR Administrative Order # 55 series of 1991, protecting the dugongs, it did not stop the poor fishermen from killing and selling their meat in the public market. As early as 1986 Gregor Hodgson reported that dugongs were slaughtered twice a month by fishermen in Jolo Island. A dugong caught in 1991 was slaughtered and its meat was sold in Pagadian City public market. Another was slaughtered in Basilan in 1994. These are only instances of reported killings, those that went unreported account for even more. As late as 1994, Maurice reported that one or two dugongs in the Green Island Bay in Roxas, Palawan, were killed each month. The local fishermen even fabricated tales that dugongs caught inside fish corrals will not survive and have to be slaughtered. The meat is dried or cooked and eaten as *pulutan*. But all these efforts will prove to be useless as people deliberately killed them for their meat and other body parts. During the 1960s, fishermen used dynamite to hunt down dugongs which was then a major cause of their decline.

Humans always find some applications from the dugongs body parts. In many parts of the Philippines, they considered the flippers to have some medical values. The hair are used to cure indigestion and asthma. The hides and blubbers are used to make candle, oil, scent base, whips, chicharon, soups, and help cure kidney disorder. The bones are used to cure asthma, stomach cramps, indigestion, maternity care and aphrodisiac. But nothing beats the use of the young dugong's tears. To capture the young dugongs, the mothers are often killed for their meat. The pups are kept alive and their tears collected. The liquid is sold to be kept as good luck charm, prosperity and success in love.

D YNAMITE FISHING

For many countries in the Third World who find it difficult to compete against the fishing vessels of the developed world, coupled with the dwindling supply of fish catch, they have resorted to other destructive methods of fishing. Since the 1970s, the Philippines. Indonesia. Vietnam and some African natives have resorted to dynamite explosive to kill fishes, where they are later collected by net as they float to the surface. These explosions also kill many unintended animals and the coral reefs.

Dynamite fishing is probably the most dangerous method of fishing. Those crude bombs have been reported to decapitate the hands of those unfortunate enough to be holding the dynamite when it explode. This is an ominous sign of what could happen to fishes swimming in the vicinity of these exploding dynamites. It is very wasteful because many non-targeted fishes are also killed especially aquarium fish that could be sources of income in the future.

Ramon Tulfo, a columnist with the Philippine Daily Inquirer, reported in his April 1, 1997 column that Mactan, Cebu is abound with corals just 15 meters from the shore. During one of his scuba divings, it was spoiled by the dynamite fishing going on nearby. The dynamites were thrown from a property adjacent to the Coral Reef Hotel. Dynamite fishing is still rampant in Mactan Island because of the teeming fishes surrounding the coral reefs near the seashore. These dynamites thrown from the shores are more dangerous to scuba divers than those thrown from bancas because more people dive in nearby places. If people can practice this nefarious activities from the shore without getting apprehended, what more if they do it kilometers out in the high sea.

The penalty for people caught using dynamite fishing could range from a minimum of ten years imprisonment, but violators don't seem to care. This is partly due to the lax enforcement of the law and even corruption and the reward or return is large.

ECOTOURISM

Ecotourism is becoming a vogue in the Philippines. But there are still very few places in the country where people can visit and spend the days under peace and quiet atmosphere. Many of the nearby and accessible places are under tremendous pressures as more people flock to these places, overcrowding the limited facilities.

Whale and dolphin watching is now a regular and exciting tourist attraction in the Tanon Strait. The Bais City government of Negros Oriental operates four boats for dolphin watching. It started informally in 1994 and is now attracting 2,000 tourists annually. Some 15% of the tourists are foreigners. Mammals that can be seen are bottlenose, Risso's spinner, Franser's pantropical spotted dolphin, short finned pilot, killer whale, and dwarf sperm. All in all there are about 4,000 dolphins and whales that inhabit this area. However, all these tours may be jeopardized by a planned cement plant to be constructed in Looc in Malabuyoc, Cebu, overlooking the dolphin community. Cement plants, one of the most pollutive industry is expected to discharge tons of poisonous waste to the environment. Cargo ships expected to berth near the area are also expected to discharge toxic wastes into the waterways affecting the lives of the mammals.

The Philippine El Nido Marine Conservation Program was chosen the Best Ecotourism Project by the Pacific Asia Travel Association during its annual conference last May 1997. Tourism Secretary Mina Gabor received the award on behalf of the Ten Knots Development Corp., owner and operator of two El Nido Resort in Palawan. The company has spent more than PI.5 million in developing the resort with the intention of preserving the rich ecosystem where numerous seagrasses, corals and a rich variety of aquarium fishes can be found. It is also a rich feeding ground for the dugongs and serves as the nesting site for four species of marine turtles.

ENDANGERED SPECIES

The decades of plunder of our natural resources have left its mark in many parts of the country. The destruction of natural resources found in the forests and surrounding seas has been responsible for the decimation of animal species, many on the brink of extinction in the wild. Some of the species have been considered endangered disallow ing their trade and export under Appendix I of CITES. These species include: Peregrine falcon (Falco peregrinus ernesti), migratory peregrine falcon (Falco peregrinus calidus), Palawan peacock pheasant (Polyphectron emphanum), long-billed curlew (Nemenius madagascariensis), spotted greenshank (Tring guttifera), Mindoro imperial pigeon (Ducula mindorensis), Nicobar pigeon (Calorenas nicobanca), giant scops owl (Otus gurneyi), Koch's pitta or Whiskered pitta (Pitta kochi), tamaraw (Babulus mindorensis), Calamian deer (Axis calamianensis), dugong(dugong dugon), hawksbill turtle (Eretmochelys imbricata), olive-ridley turtle (Lepidochelys ohvaces). green sea turtle (Chelonia mydas), leatherback turtle (Dermochelys coriacea), and the Leyte freshwater turtle (Heosemys leytensis).

Some species have been considered endangered and placed under protection by the Protected Areas and Wildlife Bureau (PAWB). More species should be included in the endangered list but are not. Almost all the birds, owls, and bats are in precarious state and need to be protected as soon as possible. Others include the spotted sambar deer (Cervus alfredi), Philippine deer (Cervus mariannus), Calamian deer (Cervus porcinus), blue-naped parrot (Tanugnalhus lucionensis), spotted greenshank (Tringaguttifera), Philippines monkey (Stacaca fascicularis), leopard cat (Felis mumuta), pygmy curlew (Numenius minuta), bleeding-heart pigeon (Galhcolumba luzonican), rufous hornbill (Buceros hydrocorax), easter sarus crane (Grus antigone sharpii) and many others.

ENDEMISM

While it may be a big pride for a host country like many island-nations to harbor many endemic species of animals, it may not vouch well for the wildlife. Historical records have documented many species of flightless birds and mammals that went extinct because of the presence of predators like cats. dogs. pigs, and other introduced species to the wild for games and meat. These endemic species have nowhere else to run or hide within the island.

Many of our wildlife are endemic to many islands especially in the Visayas. These species can easily be wiped out in case of an outbreak of disease, bioinvasion, deforestation, and hunting by the local inhabitants who often are too hungry to think about saving the animals. The tamaraws of Mindoro are under constant threat of being contaminated with the foot-and-mouth disease. Those under captive farms are not breeding and may not save the species from extinction.

Fortunately, being a nation with many islands, we can save many species from total extinction by dispersing them to other islands after careful studies of their behavior, eating habit, breeding, and ecological effects on the new environment.

FRAGMENTATION

The Philippines is a nation consisting of more than 7,100 islands. This natural fragmentation could have been an ideal situation for wildlife had it not been invaded by animals brought by people and scattered throughout most of the islands. The introduced predators compete with the indigenous wildlife for food, shelter, and sometimes they even preyed on the animals. The native wildlife often cannot move away to save themselves because of the isolation. This is the reason why many mammals and flightless birds are cither extinct and could not proliferate in numbers in the island. Even birds with their short ranged flight cannot escape predators. Historical records have shown that many extinctions occurred on isolated islands.

Our country was once almost covered with forest before the aborigines settled here through the land bridge connecting the mainland Asia. But today, all forests in the country are either logged over and converted to agriculture or human settlements. The rest are patches of forest trees, most of them less than 20% of its original forest cover despite what the government figures show. Fragmented forests can be easy target for further depletion during typhoon season that occurs frequently in the country. Birds' nests and eggs can easily be destroyed under the fury of nature.

LAKES AND BAYS

Manila Bay has been used as human's sewage for centuries. Every year 6.5 million tons of toxic and hazardous wastes are dumped into the esteros carried by Pasig River and ultimately lead to the Manila Bay. Studies made by Philippine International Toxic and Hazardous Congress showed that Metro Manila factories generate about 2,000 cubic meters of solvent waste, 22,000 tons of scrap metals, infectious and biological waste and about 25 million cubic meters of acid and alkaline wastes. Of the 10,000 to 12,000 factories operating around Metro Manila, 315 are considered major polluters from the textile and food industries. Four hundred firms are identified as possible sources of toxic and hazardous wastes. The numerous red tide episodes and fish kill by cyanide poisoning is just some manifestations of the degree of pollution the Bay is constantly facing.

Laguna de Bay, at 90.000 hectares, is the largest freshwater lake in the Philippines. What happened there is typical of what is happening to many lakes surrounded by people and factories throughout the country. It has been undergoing environmental degradation for decades as factories and domestic wastes are discharged into it. Sedimentation has reduced their average depth from seven meters in the late 1970s to a mere 2.7 meters today. The endemic fishes once numbered 23 are now down to 6 varieties today. The 13 species of aquatic plants are now down to the lowly kangkong and the resilient water lily. The livelihood of 75,000 members of fishing families are at risk, not only from reduced catches, but also from eating contaminated food.

Pesticides, heavy metals, and other toxic chemicals have caused the destruction of many fishes that inhabited the lake. The persistent pesticide, DDT, introduced in the Philippines in 1946 and banned later in 1972, is still around and bringing havoc to the Bay and the health of people eating the fishes caught there. It was reported to be present in the milk of lactating mothers. Another chemical that is even more toxic is PCBs. Heavy metals discharged from industrial plants surrounding the bay include chromium, copper, lead, mercury, zinc, and nickel. These toxic metals are taken into the bodies of consumers who ate the fishes contaminated with them. The effects of these toxic metals are well known. Most of them are either mutagenic or carcinogenic.

More than one thousand industries operate around the lakes and only half of those producing toxic chemicals have any treatment plant. Another study made by URS International Trans-Asia Inc. noted that 93-95% of the industries discharge toxic and hazardous substances containing heavy metals into the bay. Other pollutants include fertilizers and pesticides used by farmers from their pig farms. Fertilizers and manure fuel the algae that causes red tide while the pesticides can kill aquatic life gradually. An estimated 100,000 kg of pesticides found their way to the lake every year. The plan to improve the irrigation system can lead to further inflow of fertilizers and pesticides.

Fishes ingested with toxic chemicals, especially DDT and PCBs have disrupted their endocrine glands. They can cause reproductive and developmental defects in animals as well as people. As early as the 1980s some fishes showed signs of suffering from skin cancer while others have deformed bodies and even missing eye. A few years ago, 40 tons of dead fishes worth P20 million were found floating in the lake. This massive fish kill is more due to the one-time discharge of highly poisonous chemicals leach to the lake after a heavy downpour as it did in the recent massive fish kill of 30 tons in Manila Bay.

Aquaculture is also doing its share of damage to the lake. In the 1970s, there were less than 5,000 hectares of fishponds and fishcages. By 1984, half of the lake surface was locked with these ponds and cages. Half of them do not have the permits to operate and most of them are owned by politicians and retired generals. In Taal Lake, more than 5,000 illegal structures were set up along the lake. Most of them are fishcages used in breeding fishes and shrimps ran by Manila-based businessmen. Pollution comes from the unconsumed feeds resulting in the clogging of Pansipit River that causes inundation of the lake during typhoons and heavy rains.

The Philippines uses about 25,000 chemicals in the manufacturing industries, compared to 100,000 chemicals for the industrialized countries. Careless discharge, even in minute amount can easily ruin our rich ecosystem. Republic Act 6969, enacted to regulate the use, manufacture and disposal of hazardous waste, will be updated with a chemical control order (CCO) for new chemicals unforseen before. These chemicals include PCBs, ozone-depleting substances and asbestos. Many of these banned chemicals in industrialized countries still find their way into developing countries.

LEMUR

Asia is home to two species of flying lemurs and one of them is found in the Visayas and Mindanao in the Philippines. Like their nearest cousin, the tarsier, the Philippine flying lemur (Cynocephalus variegatus) habitats are gradually being destroyed by legal and illegal loggings, slash-and-burn agriculture, firewood gathering and hunting. The lemurs live mostly inside the trunks of dead trees during the day, and hunt during the night. They feed on leaves and fruits and occasionally on insects.

The flying lemurs are hunted by smoking them out of their hollow retreat while they sleep. They are eaten by local inhabitants and their furs are made into caps. Because of their small sizes, several specimens are needed to make one cap. Their numbers in the wild have never been plentiful and uncontrolled hunting for food and fur could lead to their extinction.

The continuing destructive forces plaguing the prosimians made it necessary to keep them in captive breeding before they face extinction. As fewer lemurs are found in the wild and the fragmentation of these species, the problem of genetic inbreeding is always a possibility.

MANGROVE FORESTS

The Philippines was once heavily forested with mangroves throughout its coastal regions. From a high of 500,000 hectares early in this century, it has since been cut down to about 38,000 hectares, and continued to be depleted at the rate of 2,000 hectares annually. These habitats are converted to other uses such as aquaculture and beach resorts. In certain areas around Leyte and Bohol, mangrove trees are being destroyed by improper disposal of garbage around mangrove forests. A certain form of microorganisms called Diaptracuprea often accompanied the garbage that feed on the leaves and roots of mangrove tree causing their death.

In a recent study by scientists, they disclosed that the destructions of the mangrove forests and coral reefs are costing the nation an additional 960,000 tons of fish yield every year, enough to provide the protein need of all the rural people. The output of each hectare of mangrove forest is estimated at $11,300 a year. This is because the loss of mangrove also reduces the amount of food for the sea creatures. The common red mangrove (Rhiziphora mangle) sheds more than seven tons of leaves per hectare which are decomposed by fungi and bacteria and later consumed by tiny animals, mostly hematodes and marine worms as well as microscopic crustaceans and later eaten by higher forms of marine life.

People around the tropical countries have long treated the mangrove trees much like they treat the forest trees. The mangroves are harvested and made into charcoal for used as firewood. Waste such as oil, garbage and pesticides are also killing the mangrove trees unintentionally. It is only after the mangroves are seriously depleted does the government and NGOs started to redress the damage. As with all forms of environmental degradations, it is much more expensive to rehabilitate than to maintain these ecosystems in the natural state.

Aquaculture in the Philippines started in the early 1950s with an aggregate area of 88,681 hectares of fish pond reclaimed from mangrove areas. It continued until the early 1980s, reaching 206,525 hectares, according to the DENR's Ecosystems Research and Development Bureau (ERDB). They were used to breed bangus and later shrimp. Others are converted into salt ponds in areas such as Cavite, Bulacan, Pangasinan, and Mindoro.

The DENR has undertook to rehabilitate the mangrove forests in some parts of the country. A 50-hectare mangrove plantation has been set up in the Palaui island.

Another project in Tres Martias Islets in Leyte is under the watchful eye of an NGO.

MINING

Wherever mining occurs in the country, one thing is certain. The landscape will be different even before the cessation of operation. Most of the mines are operated deep in the forest where wildlife abound. The millions of cubic meters of mine wastes extracted from the earth will have to be disposed somewhere in a safe manner. However, no matter how much care is taken, land degradation will occur, otherwise where will the mine wastes go.

The huge volume of earth will cover thousands of hectares of land as the earth is moved from one area to another. There is always the possibility of landslides that could bury whole town and destroy wildlife along its path. Impoundments is no guarantee of its safety as events in the past showed. The spillage of the Marcopper Mining in Boac River in May 1996 destroyed the whole ecosystem of Boac River. Another of their project, the Tapian Open Pit plant in Tapian has been responsible for the siltation of the river killing corals and nesting ground for fishes. Some 145 million metric tons of mine tailings covered more than 50 sq km of sea floor.

Minings near mangrove forests have also been responsible for destroying rich ecosystems. They are concentrated in very few areas such as on Nonoc Island in Surigaodel Norte for mining nickel, and in Semirara Island in Antique where coals are being mined.

MONITOR LIZARDS

The Philippines is home to the Gray's monitor lizard (Varanus gravis), one of the rarest lizard in the world. This five-foot long lizard is considered strange because it eats birds' eggs and fruits and is hunted by local people who considered it a delicacy. This is partly the reason why it has become a rare lizard. The local name given to the lizard is *butuan*.

All monitor lizards are considered endangered due to declining populations caused by habitat destruction. They are cold-blooded animals and are found mostly on the lowland forests which are often the first forests to undergo destruction. The reduced forest cover makes them easy prey to hunters who catch them for pets. In Iloilo, these reptiles are sold for P200 each.

MONKEYS

Businessmen from the Philippines have been supplying primates to laboratories in the West for years. At least 1,500 monkeys worth $400-5500 each is exported annually. These monkeys are either caught in the wild or bred in the farms. There are several breeding centers in the Philippines. There is the Del Mundo Trading in Puerto Galcra, Mindoro Oriental; Scientific Primates Filipinas, Inc in Tanay, Rizal, and Simian Conservation, Breeding and Research Inc. also in Tanay. But news of the contamination of Reston Ebola virus by monkeys from the Ferlite Scientific Research Inc. located in Barangay Banadero, Calamba, Laguna has brought attention to the danger of dealing with diseases harbored by these primates. People contaminated with the Ebola virus often died from haemorrhaging from all body orifices. Mortality is more than 95%. Even the AIDS virus has been traced to the monkeys of Africa.

Not much had been studied about the monkeys in the wild forests where they abound. But one thing is sure, their populations are dropping as people destroyed their habitats and others are caught as pets or exported for the international laboratories for scientific research.

PANAY CLOUDRUNNER

The destruction of the lowland forests has decimated many wildlife throughout the Philippines. Fortunately, there are still some inaccessible areas high in the mountains that harbor some mammals. One of them is the shy and nocturnal Panay cloudrunner (Crateromys heaneyi). The first species was discovered and caught in 1987 by local inhabitants in the Mount Baloy-Mount Madja-as range in western Panay. It is a rodent that looks like a cross between a porcupine and a squirrel, according to knowledgeable sources. The cloudrunner is about 60 cm long with a tail just as long. It has long, soft, and dark brown fur. The head is different from most species of mammals.

After two years of study, it was realized that the species is a new discovery in 1991. An unsuccessful expedition lead by the National Museum of the Philippines and the Cincinnati Museum of Natural History was not able to find any rodent. However, the following year, another rodent was caught by members of the Philippine biodiversity group. Shortly thereafter, five more animals were captured and kept alive. Some of them were brought to Cincinnati Zoo for exhibit, breeding and study of their behavior.

PHILIPPINE EAGLE

The Philippines is host to the second largest and one of the most endangered species of eagle (Pilhecophaga jeffreryi) in the world. It has a wingspan of nearly 2 meters, standing at one meter high and weighs about 7 kg. Each pair needs a habitat of about 60 to 100 sq km to survive. They feed on monkeys, snakes, bats, and other forest animals and it is dwindling as these food resources are also losing ground to loggings, firewood gathering, human settlement and hunting. Today they numbered about 67 in the wild and mostly confined to Samar, Leyte, and parts of Luzon and Mindanao.

There are about 19 eagles in captivity and only two of them are born in captivity, namely: Pagasa and Pagkakaisa. One of the problem with endangered species is often the difficulties encountered in breeding them because of their low reproductive rate. The eagle can only lay one egg atop the tallest tree and the hatched bird will take two years of care before the mother will breed again. In all three precious years will elapse before breeding takes place. To facilitate the breeding, artificial insemination is resorted to. The success of the first cpti»e. bred Philippine eagle. *Pagasa*, was a hopeful sign But it took another 14 years before scientists a. the Philippine Eagle Conservation Foundation (PECF) m Davao finally produced a second eaglet on January 199: named *Pagkakaisa*. Both birds were developed at PECF through artificial inseminations.

Habitat destruction is the number one threat to their existence followed by hunting for trophy in the old days Lack of an effective conservation program is hindering their numbers from increasing Mount Apo National Park, where they once roam is so devastated by logging and firewood gathering that it can only support two or three pairs of eagles. Low productivity, they lay one egg at most every two years is partly responsible for their low numbers in the wild. In captivity, breeding is even more difficult because of the unnatural conditions in a confined area.

The status of the bird as an endangered species was first brought to the attention of the government by Prof. Discoro S. Rabor who spent most of his time in the forest studying wildlife of the Philippines. Efforts to save it started in 1965 by Jesus Alvarez, then director of the autonomous Park and Wildlife Office and Prof. Rabor, a founding member of the Philippines conservation efforts, who took it upon themselves to bring the problem to world's attention Prof. Rabor fought for the listing of the eagle as an endangered species in the IUCN list during one of its meeting.

Soon after the plight of the eagle came to international attention, the famous aviator, Charles Lindbergh (1902-1974), under the auspices of the W WF, was sent to help conserve and save the eagle from extinction during the years 1969-1972. He helped established the Monkey-Eating Eagle Conservation Program. Since then, some companies once involved in environmental destructions are helping to save the eagle from extinction. Banks which have help finance some of the destructions of their habitat are contributing funds to help conserve their habitats

The spectacularly beautiful and nearly extinct monkey-eating eagle had a new lease of life when it was renamed the Philippine Eagle. As a totem of the country, especial attentions are always given to save them from further harm. Laws were immediately passed for their protection and wildlife refuges were set up for them. A captive breeding program was initiated and fully funded by the government But despite all these attention, the eagles in the wild are still being shot and trapped by natives and unscrupulous hunters.

POVERTY

The Philippines has one of the lowest standard of living in Asia. At least 40% of the population is living under poverty level. Most of them reside in the rural, coastal and deep within the forests. Almost all of them have very limited access to social services that could help uplift their living standard.

Living deep in the forests in many parts of the country are some 15 million indigenous people who live under a state of perpetual poverty. No concrete step has been taken by the government or the NGOs to improve their livelihood. Without money to buy food for survival, they are forced to make full use of what the forest has to offer. This could mean burning some trees to get the nutrients for their crops. Or harvest the forest's flora and fauna in an unsustainable way. The need is always immediate and there is no time nor capital available to grow them on a sustainable basis. Some have resorted to hunting animals such as deer for food, illegal trade in birds for the collectors, slash-and-burn cultivation, and illegal Hitching or carabao logging All these activities contribute to the deterioration of the environment.

The same thing is happening to poor people living in coastal areas. Fishermen are forced to catch more than their share to supply the big demand in the cities in the hope of improving their living standard. With more than ten million people directly and indirectly dependent in the fishing industry, the demand for marine food will continue until it is exhausted. Overfishing for years has caused a decline in the edible fish populations forcing many to go into export business using the illegal dynamite and cyanide fishing methods. These ventures are often financed by middlemen who made most of the profits. The dealers who sell them to the end users are also making profits that kept the illegal activities going on.

The presence of middlemen and loan sharks does not help them in any way. By taking advantage of their destitute situations, the poor are forced to overharvest to repay the loans that can only come from the nature and those found within common property.

TAMARAWS

The tamaraw (Bubalus mindorensis) is a small buffalo that is endemic to Mindoro Island in the Philippines. Its preferred habitat is a mosaic of thick forest and open grazing areas. It has been domesticated and used in agriculture and sometimes eaten by the natives. They were once estimated at 10.000 tamaraws at the start of the century but has dwindled to less than 250 in 1953. The current population is unknown but has probably increased because they have been put under protection. One of their habitats, the Mount Iglit-Baco National Park with an area of about 754 sq km has been put under protection. However, the area is under illegal farming and ranching and patchy destruction has occurred throughout the park. To prevent further decimation of their population, the government had undertook to breed them in captivity. In July 1979 a three-sq-km fenced enclosure was set up to hold as many animals as possible for breeding. The only tamaraw born in captivity in 1990; it died a year later. No other tamaraw was born in captivity since then.

TARSIERS

The Philippine tarsier (Tarsius syrichia) is a primitive primate found in the islands of Bohol, Dinagat, Siargao, Basilan, Samar, Leyte, and parts of Mindanao. Nature hunters of Mindanao used to think that it is a cross between a monkey and a bat. This is not surprising because scientists and taxonomists in earlier times have difficulties classifying this primate. The reddish black or brown mammals feed primarily on insects. Their keen sense of hearing and seeing help them to catch insects at night. They can also turn their heads almost full circle, a convenient trait needed when hunting insects that need silence in the dark.

Tarsiers inhabit patches of secondary and bamboo forests and are active mostly at night. Local people hunt them in the forest and sold them in the cities as house pets. Because of the special conditions needed for their survival, the primates are difficult to care and breed as pets. They need special care and food normally not available for captive tarsiers. This is the reason why many died young after being caught in the wild. The offspring do not live normally and often die at very young age. Even the humidity of air must be controlled at 80%.

Tarsiers are difficult to breed in captivity. Their average lifespan in captivity is only 12 years compared to 20 years in the wild. Only a few of these primates have been successfully bred abroad in captivity at foreign zoos. At least this will ensure their survival in the future, although their survival in the wild forest cannot be assured as their habitats are slowly giving way to other uses.

The government has taken many serious efforts to save them from extinction. A ban on exporting these endemic species from the country has been in place since 1988. Sweden and the U.S. used to be destinations of these exports. But many are still poached and illegally exported abroad which can command a higher price Tarsiers caught in the wild are confiscated from hunters and poachers and placed in captive breeding.

TURTLES

Many species of turtles and tortoises find their home in the Philippine beaches. Among them is the green sea turtle (Cheloma mydas lairielle) which is a delicacy for many restaurants in first class restaurants before their ban. This, together with gathering their eggs for consumption is the main reason why it has become extinct in many areas.

The move to conserve their habitats have been undertaken by the government A Turtle Island in Sulu, Luband Island in Mindoro, and some in the coastal areas of Zamboanga and Palawan were set aside to protect the breeding grounds for turtles. Silliman University is also on the limelight in protecting the turtles. They operate one successful 25-hectare sanctuary in the Sumilon Island.

Turtles in captivity are difficult to breed; therefore it is necessary that these reptiles should be banned from the pet trade. They usually breed during certain seasons and along sands that captive turtles cannot do so. One less turtle in captivity is one more breeding turtle for the wild.

CHAPTER 12

FACTORY FARMING

Factory farming gradually evolved right after the American Civil War. It started with the cmcrgence of businessmen and entrepreneurs in the meat-processing cities of Chicago, St. Louis, Cincinnati and Kansas City. Their first move was to take over the abattoirs, railroad lines and distribution outlets. With the availability of rail refrigeration came a new revolution in the beef industry. However, it was in the slaughterhouse that many of the important innovations leading to the assembly line method of farming livestock came about. The huge packing plants on Chicago's south side dwarfed most of the industrial factories of the day. Companies like Armour and Swift employed thousands of workers to facilitate the killing, dismembering, cleaning and dressing livestock like assembly line production.

Factory farming is a multi-billion dollar business venture in the U.S. It involves the slaughter of eight billion farm animals, mostly chickens, annually in the U.S. alone. Some of these companies that have greatly benefited are Cargill, Swift, Armour, Conagra, Continental Grain, Hudson, Tyson and others. In the quest for more profits and the public's insatiable demand for cheap meat, many animal breeders for food have undertaken measures to increase their profits by subjecting farm animals into meat, egg and milk machines.

These animals are forced to produce more under very harsh conditions. Animals dropping dead because of neglect and inhospitable conditions are considered part of doing business. One environmentalist estimates that 95% of animals suffering can be found in factory farming. Neglect on the welfare of animals is the norm. Government inaction, due to lack of fund and personnel to monitor these factory farms are partly to blame. This could be remedied if animal welfare groups and the media are allowed inside the factory farms to check on the conditions of the animals and media should be allowed to videotape the conditions of the confined animals.

A person's health is greatly affected by consumption of factory farmed products. According to the CDC, estimates of the food-borne illnesses that occur annually in the U.S. range from 6.5 to 8.1 million cases resulting in 9,100 deaths. At least one third of the cases are traced to the livestock industry.

Other problems posed by factory farming are increase in atmospheric methane that aggravates the global warming of the planet and waste of grains that could help alleviate the nutrition of millions of people around the world. Animal excrements have polluted important sources of water badly needed by humans.

ANIMAL HUSBANDRY

Animal farming is an important sector for many regions of the world. In the tropics, livestock play a critical role in agricultural production by providing draft power and manure for fertilizers and fuel. They also serve as a financial reserve during time of difficulties. They provide about two-thirds of the world's livestock, but produce only half of the meat and 20% of the milk.

In many societies, it is traditionally the women who are engaged in livestock husbandry. Although in most cases they only derive direct benefit from small ruminants and poultry, this is a crucial source of income for the women. Accordingly, intensification of animal farming at subsistence level does not only contribute directly to the food supply but also serves to provide needed income, enabling women to use their own financial means to improve social security and food supply for the whole family.

The conversion of plant and kitchen wastes into protein-rich food for human consumption is another function justifying animal husbandry. These animals are free from antibiotics and hormones that make them safer for human consumption. Economic development in the tropics has made many people affluent that they can afford to consume more animal products such as meat and milk which cannot be met by local producers. Since the 1990s, the import of milk products by developing countries is worth about $40 billion annually.

The increasing number of livestock must be safeguarded against environmental degradation. According to the World Watch (1991), over 20 million hectares of moist tropical forest were cleared in the two previous decades and converted into cattle pastures. Of these areas, the Amazon region alone accounts for 10 million hectares and Mexico about 5.5 million hectares. The subsequent grazing lead to the complete degradation of these areas within a few years. According to the World Resources Institute (1992), some 25% of the surface area in Africa, the American continent and Asia, have been severely damaged by agricultural use, overgrazing being regarded as the main cause of deterioration of about a third of the degraded area. Only 2% of the grain is used to feed livestock in the tropics compared to 57% for EU countries and 70% for the U.S. The low number of livestock used by rural farmers is very small compared to the large-scale cattle ranchers. This alone is sufficient ground to allow rural farmers continued use of livestock.

The interaction of crop and livestock plays a key role in achieving ecological sustainability led by intensifying nutrient and energy cycles. Crops residues are important sources for livestock feed in small-scale farming system. Livestock herdsmen and small-scale farmers can mutually benefit from a close cooperation. In Africa, livestock herders provide manure for farmer's fields and in return receive watering and land use rights, crop residues and feed supplements for their animals. Small livestock farms provide food security through diversification. They serve as a kind of savings account, with the offspring as interest. An animal can be slaughtered for home consumption or sold for cash to buy food when crops yield is low or for other purposes.

On the other hand, large scale ranching should be limited in scope and area of coverage. Not only do they compete for grain with humans, but they also add to the growing problem of greenhouse warming and water pollution. Cattle produce a lot of methane gas which is four times more effective in trapping the heat from the sun.

ANTIBIOTICS

In the late 1950s, Thomas Jukes of Berkeley University discovered that the antibiotic tetracycline at a low dosage of 50 ppm can significantly increase the weight of livestock. Subsequent tests confirmed that other antibiotics such as chlortetracycline, erythromycin, etc. are also effective as growth factors. This led to their rampant use in the cattle industry.

Antibiotics are chemical substances produced by microorganisms that can inhibit or destroy bacterias and other organisms. Some have remarkable chemotherapeutic potentials that are used in the control of infectious diseases in man and animals. Its impact on medical sciences and human health is tremendous. It has been used to treat pneumonia, dysentery, typhoid and typhus fevers, tuberculosis, cholera, plague and other infectious diseases caused by bacteria, fungi, and protozoa. More than a hundred antibiotics are commonly used. But the careless use and continued contact by bacteria may result in the development of resistant bacteria. Many of the drugs used for treating people are almost similar to those used on animals.

The spectre of a pre-penicillin era because of the resistance to bacterial disease may be just around the corner. There are emerging strains of bacteria infecting humans that are resisting treatment by antibiotics. Many blame antibiotic resistance to doctors for overprescribing the drugs, and patients for not completing the regimen required. The other likely reason often overlooked is that antibiotics are used routinely in animal feeds. More than one half of the antibiotics produced are added to livestock feeds to prevent contagious infection due to overcrowding and stress. The stressful conditions of farm animals in confinement prevent them from growing as fast as those in the field and therefore require antibiotics and hormones to compensate. Some of these drugs may cause allergic reactions in sensitive people.

Congressional testimony by the FDA revealed that of the 20,000 different animal drugs in use. 90% have not been found to be safe and effective. Many of these drugs are still given to livestock that eventually end up in our dinner table. It has been known for quite some time that repeated exposure to these antibiotics can contribute to antibiotic resistance. Meat consumers have no way of knowing if any substance is hazardous to them. A 1989 investigation study by the Wall Street Journal found that 20-38% of retail milk contained antibiotic residues.

The problem of antibiotic resistance has been studied for well over 40 years. The repeated exposures of bacteria to the antibiotics have been found to alter their genetic makeup, making them resistant. A Cornell University study also showed that infectious drug resistance can transfer from animals to humans. A whole range of antibiotics could be at risk of becoming useless in our fight against infectious diseases that regularly afflict mankind.

Animals raised in a free-range, sustainable manner do not require antibiotics for growth promotion or disease prevention. Several European nations banned the use of antibiotics in animal feed, which led to a significant reduction of antibiotic-resistant bacteria. We could reverse this dangerous situation of antibiotic resistance by pursuing legislative action and making responsible consumer choices.

BRANDING

Branding of animals especially cattle to designate ownership was practiced widely in the wild west decades ago, but this has changed owing to successful pressures brought about by the Belgian-born Henry Spira. He has chosen battles he believed to be winnable by carrying out carefully modulated campaigns beginning with attempts to establish dialogue with the opposing camp. If rebuffed, he is ready to move to the next stage, which usually means full-page newspaper ads designed to foment public outrage.

Spira has done this with virtually no organization backing, while remaining focused strictly on the goal of each individual campaign, and avoiding bureaucratic and fundraising distractions which preoccupy many not-for-profit groups.

In branding, the terrorized steer is first trapped between bars. Then its head is immobilized with steel pincers painfully clamped on to the nostrils and pulled on one side. If that's not enough, the cowboy steps on the steer's face with his boot. As the red hot iron is pressed onto its face, the steer bellows, eyes bulge as its flesh burn. The U.S. Department of Agriculture (USDA) halted the practice of requiring the face branding of Mexican cattle imported into the U.S.

There are far less painful ways of satisfying the USDA's desire to trace Mexican cattle. Experts say face branding is not only barbaric but unnecessary. Far more humane alternatives have been suggested including punching a distinctive symbol in the car, notching the car or branding near the edge of the hide of the rear.

BREEDING

In order to keep up the supply of farm animals, it is necessary to breed them as fast as they are being slaughtered. Pigs, chickens, and cattle are the most persecuted animals in the world. Their big sizes and early domestication have subjected them to much abuse under the hands of men. Every year several billions of these animals are slaughtered worldwide. This has been made possible because the female species have been treated like breeding machines, constantly making babies for the factory.

In the U.S. about a hundred million pigs are slaughtered every year for food. Most people are not aware of the dreadful fate in breeding these gentle animals for our palates. These sows are given hormones and fertilized in "rape racks" where they are forced upon by boars. Others are fertilized by artificial inseminations. Once they are pregnant, the sow is chained, confined in a stall and fed once every two to three days for the next 15 weeks. After they give birth, the litters are taken away within three weeks time and the mothers are ready for breeding again.

The piglets are taken away from their mother for fattening at a factory. They are placed in confined cages stacked at several levels to reduce the space they occupied. Their tails are cut off to prevent the pigs from biting them as many animals in confinement do. All the males are castrated to make them grow faster. The pigs are bred to produce as much meat with as little feed in as little time as possible. Without any exercise in their confined cage, many cannot stand long enough to support their own weight. Under these poor living conditions, as many as 30% of them die before reaching the slaughter age of twenty weeks in the. Another 5% die on the way to the slaughterhouse. Most of the deaths are due to respiratory diseases caused by overcrowding. Another problem dealing with congestion is the spread of the parasite causing toxoplasmosis that can be transmitted to humans that are found in 30% of all pork products.

Natural breeding of farm animals has produced some of the most grotesque looking animals in the world. One of this is the Chinese Meishan pig. The pig grows slowly but produce so much fat that it looks so old and ugly with its flesh so loose covering the eyes and its long cars dropping down the sides. It is so fertile, it can start to produce litter after three months, producing 15 to 25 compared to the 8-12 litters by ordinary pig.

CATTLE

Greed is the word that best describes the way domestic animals are raised for our food. The animals are treated like meat machine, fattening them without regard to their well-being. They are being injected with all kinds of chemicals, hormones and antibiotics to fatten them at the least time, and with the least cost to maximize profit.

There are two reasons why it is not advisable to raise so much cattle in our midst. The first has to do with how the animals are treated as cattlemen try to maximize profit. Cattle consume about 70% of all the grain produced in the U.S. This is a waste of good grain that could be used to feed the hungry and malnourished millions throughout the world. To produce a kilo of beef, 8 to 16 kilos of grains are needed. A quarter of all land surface on Earth has been used for grazing or growing grain while only 11% is used for growing food crops.

The increasing availability of cattle has been brought about by scientific approach to breeding calves. Researchers have developed estrus-synchronizing drugs that are injected into the cows so that they all come into heat simultaneously to increase the chances of getting pregnant through artificial insemination.

After the birth of the calves, the males are castrated to make them grow faster and improve the quality of the beef. The castration is a painful process that is done without anesthesia. The scrotum is stretched and a knife is used to cut the sacs open and the testicles are pulled out using a cord.

The calves are allowed to graze for a few months, usually from six to twelve months before they are confined to the farm factory. Because of congestion, the animals are sometimes dehorned to prevent them from fighting and injuring each other. For the very young, a chemical paste is used to burn the root of their horns before it springs out. In older calves, an electronic dehorner is used to cauterize the horn tissue. Saws are used on the older steers. The horns and the roots are cut off without the use of anesthetics.

Since farm animals are in the highest food chain, their bodies are often the storehouse of pesticides, herbicides and other toxic chemicals that are routinely applied to the grass and grain gathered for their consumption. These are not the only risks humans get from eating cattle meat. Farm animals are also regularly treated with antibiotics or sulfa drugs mixed with the feed to combat diseases caused by unsanitary conditions and overcrowding.

Cattle in the U.S. are given growth hormones to increase and speed up their growth and at the same time produce leaner meat. These hormones, mostly estrogen and androgen can cause cancer in humans. Ranchers often purchase these hormones without prescription and therefore could be indiscriminately administered. More than 70% of the cattle raised for the meat have been given growth hormones.

Cattlemen are always finding ways to produce more beef at less cost. Paper products and sawdust are sometime grounded with the feed and given to the cattle. Manure from chickens and pigs are mixed with feeds and fed to the animals. Even industrial wastes and oil are often mixed with feed by some cattlemen. Plastics made of ethylene and propylene as a form of cheap roughage is undergoing experimental use to fatten the cattle. The USDA is even studying the use of cement dust as feed supplement because it can produce 30% more weight than ordinary cattle feed.

Calves raised for veal are subjected to extensive toxic chemicals to produce pale and tender meat. The calves are kept chained in stalls without room for movement to prevent them from developing muscle and gaining weight and are refused iron to make them anemic so as to produce leaner meat. Besides, the treatment of calves is exceedingly cruel. They are kept in total darkness and under wood slated floors without straw cover that cause leg injuries as they fell into the slat. Antibiotics and sulfa drugs are given regularly and they are denied solid food and drinking water.

A recent broadcast by CNN (August 27, 1997) from Germany shows that every year about one million unwanted calves, many a few weeks old, are exported from Germany to France via Spain because of the restriction in direct export. The live calves are forced to travel over thousands of kilometers under very cruel conditions. The export papers claim that they are exported for breeding purposes, but in actuality are killed for their meat. Those that are killed locally are done in one of the most inhumane way. Axes are used because it is cheaper to hack them on the head. Most of the calves do not die immediately and are allowed to be transported alive while they bleed to dead enroute to the slaughterhouse. Complaints from the Catholic Church and NGOs have not stopped the inhumane treatment. Although the farmers claimed that most of these calves were unwanted in Germany, the truth is that the profit motive is behind the continuing breeding of these "unwanted" calves. The cows can easily be refrained from breeding by separating them from the bulls.

This is not the end of the ordeal once they are fat enough to be slaughtered. To move them to the slaughterhouse which is often located a great distance away, the cattle are cramped into giant truck trailers so tightly that there is no room for them to move around. During the long and rough journey, the animals are neither fed nor given any water until they reach their destination. Animals often fall down due to exhaustion and are trampled by other cattle and end up with broken legs and pelvises.

The fate of future cattle is not expected to improve because more people are expected to join the ranks of the beef eaters. Beef is big business for the cattlemen and they are not about to change. The Americans are the leading beef eaters and they slaughter 100.000 cattle every day. In Australia, Argentina, Brazil, Uruguay, and Paraguay, the population of cattle equals or exceeds their respective populations. As more people become affluent, beef consumption is expected to increase without letup. In almost all countries, beef consumption is expected to double in the next ten years.

CATTLE: DAIRY

More than 5.5 million cows in the U.S. are bred to produce milk. As mother cows, they are not treated more humanely than those meant to be slaughtered for Beef. They are also subjected to hormone treatments to increase their milk output One synthetic hormone, dicthylstiIbetrol (DES) has been banned since the late 1970s for being carcinogen It has also caused children two or three years told to experience early puberty earlier after drinking milk contaminated with it.

Other hormones have made their udders heavy and swollen that they have difficulties standing up. Hormones are also given to decrease the time between pregnancy so that they can produce more milk and calves at the least time.

CATTLE: RANCHING

A quarter pounder hamburger is responsible for the destruction of about 5 sq meters of rainforests while releasing 200 kilos of carbon to the environment. The water spent is about 5.500 gallons or equivalent to the amount of water used by a family of four for a month. Half of all the water used in the U.S. is spent on livestock raising. Each adult cow also produces 40 kg of methane gas every year. Cattle are major producers of methane which is a more potent gas than carbon dioxide in causing global warming. Each molecule of methane gas is 20 to 25 times more effective in absorbing heat than carbon dioxide. So it pays to reduce the volume of methane emitted by reducing the number of livestock. Methane is also a suspected gas that is contributing to the destruction of the ozone layer.

To reduce the number of cattle is to reduce their impact on the fragile environment. With about 1.5 billion of them roaming every part of the world, it is abetting and accelerating the destruction of the planet. Many of the destructions are well documented. Cattle ranching in South America has been responsible for the burning of the tropical forests teeming with biodiversity. In many grasslands, desertification has set in due to overgrazing in places as diverse as Africa, U.S. and Australia. The organic runoff from feedlots and manure which they produce are contaminating the groundwater, an important source of water for many areas. Runoffs to the ocean have been responsible for the algae bloom.

Cattle ranching in South America is also perpetuating the poverty of the indigenous people With their wealth the ranchers have taken over large tracts of land that poor people could have used for their livelihood. Instead, these people are forced to hunt deep in the forests for wildlife or burn down forests to get the nutrients needed for their crops. Either way, there is loss of biodiversity.

Half of all the deforestation in South America can be attributed to cattle ranching. The stripping of the Amazonia could doom at least 500.000 species in the next two decades. In the U.S. alone, livestock eat 80% of the corn produced and as much as 95% of the oats. All these feeds have been responsible for the largest soil erosion in the U.S.

A kilo of beef will provide about 1,100 calories for people but uses 44.000 calories of fossil fuels. Several estimates have been made on the amount of grain that would have been fed to starving humans. The 130 million tons of grain given to livestock in the U.S. could have been enough to feed about 400 million people. Another estimate (1991) puts one-third of the 1.7 billion tons of worldwide grain could feed one billion people.

CHICKEN

Over 90% of the chickens and eggs are produced in crowded, windowless buildings, each holding as many as 100,000 animals. Chickens are by far the most prolific breeders and therefore the most maltreated livestock ever known. In the U.S. alone, at least six billion of these birds are slaughtered annually. Because their meat is cheaper than beef or pork, many developing countries have started large-scale breeding. Many of these birds have been genetically altered in the U.S. and exported to developing countries.

Chickens are genetically manipulated to increase their egg laying or fatten their meat as soon as possible. Broiler chickens are treated more like a meat factory. At seven to eight weeks, the chickens are slaughtered by stunning them with electricity and their throats are automatically cut. Chicken processing in a large plant can also waste 100 million gallons of water in a single day. Cutting down chicken consumption will reduce the number of chickens brought up in these cruel and inhumane ways.

The treatment of farm chickens in factories is no better than those for cattle or swine. They are also regularly treated with chemicals to increase their yield. The EEC has guidelines recommending that each hen have at least 70 square inches of space. The U.S. egg-industry groups have held out for 48 square inches as a practical minimum in favor of more profit. The male layer chickens are destroyed by suffocation after they are hatched. Sometimes they are crushed to death and turned into feed for the other chickens or made into fertilizer.

Perdue chicken is under boycott called by Animal Rights International. The chickens are treated in very inhumane conditions. The chicks have their beaks burned off with a hot knife at birth to avoid perking one another because of the overcrowded conditions of their farm. Each bird is allowed a one square foot of living space for its entire life. Such stressful overcrowding results in cannibalism, diseases, epidemics, and a high mortality rate. When they are due for slaughter, the chickens are killed as if on an assembly line. The chickens are pinned upside down before their throats are slitted.

The live chickens sold at the wet market are delivered and caged in wire cages less than eight inches high, forcing the chicken to squat on the wire floor until death releases them from inhumanity. Once sold, the chickens are often slit on the neck and allowed to bleed to death. Others have their neck wrung until they die of asphyxiation. In the Mountain Province, a live chicken has its head firmly keeled under the wing. Then using a bamboo slick, the chicken is beaten all over the body until it dies of haemorrhage.

DISEASES: CATTLE

Because of the overcrowding of most animals bred under factory farming, diseases are easily spread to other animals. One of the most cosily diseases common to cattle is mastitis. It is particularly serious in dairy herds because it affects the udder and sharply reduces milk production. Mastitis may be caused by several bacteria including E Coli. Nearly 20% of cows in the U.S. has mastitis once a year. The two forms of mastitis are acute and chronic. In both forms, the mammary cells are replaced with fibrous tissue, and in advance cases the udder becomes useless. In acute cases, milk secretion stops completely. Fever, dullness, and loss of appetite may also occur. Once these animals cannot produce milk, they are useless to the farmers and are killed immediately to save on feeds. In the acute form, the udder may appear normal but flakes and clots may appear in the milk. The butter and protein content of the milk is usually reduced, and the salt content increases.

During birth, calves can suffer from a destructive disease called calf scours. The typical symptom is diarrhea. The most fatal form of the disease appears at birth within three days. They are often dead in a few days Sometimes, however, newborn calves may have mild diarrhea for up to a month and then recover with little assistance. However some calves luve stunted growth and are susceptible to pneumonia. Other diseases include screw worm infection, brucellosis, milk fever, ketosis, pinkeye, anaplasmosis, tuberculosis, tick fever, and pleuropneumonia. Most of these diseases can be reduced through better nutrition, sanitation and immunization. (Encylopedia Americana, 1989 cd . vol. 6, p. 80-81)

DISEASES: E. COLI

There have been several reported cases of E Coli poisoning in the newspaper recently, but probably more went unreported. Last year (1997) thousands of kilos of ground beef meant for the hamburger markets were recalled in the U.S. Illness and sometimes deaths caused by E Coli contamination of food, fruits, ice cream, hamburgers have been noted in the past. Humans contaminated with E Coli suffered bloody diarrhea, with 5% of the cases progressing to kidney failure resulting in death unless treatment is undertaken immediately. In 1993, undercooked hamburgers containing E Coli killed four people and downed hundreds in Washington state.

Infections usually occur from eating contaminated and undercooked food. Other sources include contaminated water, vegetables using cow manure as fertilizer, and fecal matter from other infected persons. Cattle are particularly susceptible to E. Coli contamination. Studies made by the Animal and Plant Health Inspection Service found that about 1.5% of all herds are contaminated with this parasite.

DISEASES: FLU

Diseases affecting animals that inflict humans can be devastating to the animals concerned. The "bird flu** virus named H5NI that finally killed six people in Hong Kong triggered fears of a worldwide epidemic. Drastic actions were taken and more than one million chickens and other poultry in Hong Kong were slaughtered in a few days.

In markets and farms across the territory, about 1.000 government workers descended on 160 chicken farms, 39 mixed poultry farms, and two wholesale markets to gas 1.3 million chickens, and unaccounted numbers of ducks, geese, quails and pigeons that might harbor the virus responsible for infecting humans with a disease previously thought to affect only birds. The workers bundle the birds in plastic containers, kill them by pumping in carbon dioxide and sterilizing the remains before dumping them in landfill sites. The cost was estimated at US5.17 million.

DISEASES: FOOT-AND-MOUTH

Foot-and-mouth is one of the most dreaded disease against livestock, affecting mostly cloven-hoofed mammals. It is a highly infectious disease caused by virus that affects sheep, cattle and pigs. Initial symptoms include blisters in the mouth, udder and the legs. The animal may become lame, lose weight and milk production is greatly reduced. Later on, blood begins to ooze from their snouts and hooves and can result in death. The disease is not harmful to humans and is still prevalent in Asia, Africa, Europe and South America. A few years ago, it hit the Philippines causing an economic dislocation for many small farmers. In Taiwan, last March 1997, the FMD epidemic cost the economy about $3 billion, half of it from export sales, and 50,000 jobs. As many as 1.6 million out of the 11 million hogs have been exposed and had to be destroyed. Soldiers were called in to destroy the infected animals. Wearing biohazard suits, they zap each animal with electrified metal hooks, then toss the stunted beast into incinerators or bury them alive.

DISEASES: SALMONELLA

Salmonella is perhaps the single most infamous zoonosis, a disease that is transmitted from animals to people. Salmonella is a major cause of food poisoning caused by eating contaminated meat from factory farm livestock. Each year millions of people are contaminated by salmonella poisoning. Salmonellosis begins as a mild diarrhea and abdominal cramps one to three days after eating contaminated food. Healthy people may not experience the poisoning, but infants before two years old and old people are susceptible and likely to die unless treated immediately.

In the U.S. in the early 1940s, only 4 in 100,000 persons suffered from nontyphoid salmonellosis, caused by eating the contaminated flesh of warm-blooded animals. By 1983, the number had increased to nearly 20 per 100.000 persons.

The increase in animal-related salmonellosis parallel the rise in the use of antibiotics in farm animals. The increasing use of filthy slaughterhouses also contributes to the increase in contamination of meat with salmonella. The bacteria in our meat has become far more deadly as a result of widespread use of antibiotic medications in livestock feed and has inadvertently breed antibiotic-resistant salmonella. An FDA study of healthy chickens, cattle, and swine from 1978 to 1981 were analyzed to see what percent were resistant to anti-microbial drugs. The results found that 61% of salmonella were resistant to sulfadiazine; 56% to streptomycin; 33% to tetracyclines; 5% resistant to kanamycin and carbenicillin; and 3% to ampicillin.

For decades, chloramphenicol has been the drug of choice for treating complications associated with salmonellosis. However, throughout the mid-1980s, the drug was widely used on cattle and hogs. It could very well cause the ineffectiveness of the drugs used in treating people suffering from salmonellosis. When 1,000 persons were infected with *Salmonella newport*, in California in 1985, this strain was resistant to chloramphenicol. Instead those who used the chloramphenicol suffered a rare form of human bone marrow disease, aplastic anemia, which is almost always fatal.

A scandal in UK in 1988 almost caused the collapse of the egg industry. Hundreds of thousands of hens were destroyed because their eggs were contaminated with salmonella bacteria. The hens were being fed with grounded dead chicken and contaminated food stuffs. Range-free chickens do not have the same problems encountered as in caged chickens.

Reptiles and amphibians are also carriers of salmonella. More than 200 different types of salmonellas have been isolated from them. Every type of salmonella found in reptiles is considered dangerous to people.

Salmonella is best diagnosed by a veterinarian. Microbiological culture of animal's feces, cloaca or blood may identify the organism. In the early 1970s, it was estimated that 280,000 cases of human salmonellosis were contracted from pet turtles in the U.S. There is no proven treatment for reptiles, and it was suggested that animals be euthanized to protect people and other household pets. Children are susceptible to contracting salmonella from parents who own reptiles.

DISEASES: SCREWWORMS

One of the most serious pests of domestic animals is the infestation of screwworms. When the larvae of adult flies invade the wound of healthy tissues, it creates a foul-smelling, bleeding wound. The odor attracts other flies that could lead to more infestation and severity of the wound. Unless treated, the victim will undergo a tortuous existence finally leading to death within ten days. Death is due either to the maggots or the introduction of pathogenic organisms. During the severe outbreak of screwworms in the U.S. in 1935, 1.2 million cases of infected livestock resulted in 180,000 deaths.

FROGS

Frogs play an important role in nature. They consume a lot of water borne pests that destroy crops. Due to the difficulties of catching frogs from the wild for human consumption, they are now being bred in private farms. Out of the whole frog, only the legs are considered edible for human consumption.

Bullfrogs in Bangladesh, India, and Indonesia are caught from the wild and are considered food delicacies. They are exported throughout the world. The annual export to France of about 3,000 to 4,000 metric tons of Indian bullfrog legs is only a fraction of the market. Since only the legs are considered valuable, they are chopped off from the frog, and the live torso of the animal is allowed to crawl away. Their numbers are dwindling in the wild and may cause environmental problems.

In April 1997, more than two hundred toad corpses were found along a half mile stretch of the river Esk in Scotland. The abdomens were cut open and the back legs had been turned inside out and removed leaving only the skin. Autopsy shows that the legs were extracted while the toads were still alive. Although they are rarely eaten in restaurants in Great Britain, the cruel treatments should be a ground for banning the frogs as a delicacy for human consumption.

As if they have not suffered enough, the frog populations in many parts of the world are declining rapidly. Even undisturbed and pristine forests in Costa Rica and in most of the remotest places in Australia, the frogs are vanishing. Many species of frogs and toads have either declined or disappeared in Brazil, Puerto Rico, Ecuador, Venezuela, India, Bangladesh, Norway, and the U.S.

In 1964 a biologist discovered the golden toad in Costa Rica which became a leading attraction at the Monteverde Cloud Forest Reserve. In 1987, 1,500 golden toads were seen breeding. After two years, only one appeared. Today none can be seen. The same fate also happened to the harlequin frog, which vanished from the same area. The gastric breeding frog of Australia had suffered the same fate. Females of this species turn her stomach into a womb to incubate the eggs she swallows, switching off their digestive system and fasted until their offspring hopped from their mouth. Discovered in 1973, it has suddenly vanished in 1980.

Experts are speculating several causes for their decline. One of the most plausible reasons is the permeation of the hormone-disrupting chemicals throughout the world which is also affecting the reproductive organs of the frogs. The unique physiology of the frogs makes them highly vulnerable. Their permeable skin allow the frogs to absorb toxic chemicals much more readily than other animals. The abnormally high rate of missing legs and other deformities among young toads and frogs in many sites across North America lends credence to this theory.

Alarming deformities of the frogs in the U.S. and Canada have been noted by researchers. In Minnesota, mutations have been found in more than a hundred places. Frogs with four legs growing out of its stomach or neck have been found. Another has its eye inside its mouth. Suspect: a parasite fluke.

The presence of predators and introduction of exotic species of fishes may also be a possible cause of their decline. The eggs of the frogs and the tadpoles have become a food of many other marine creatures. In some cases, the eggs die from infection of the pathogenic fungus probably caused by the damage to their immune system brought about by the ultraviolet B-ray caused by the loss of ozone layer.

The declining populations are not confined to the lowlands. Even at high altitudes, the frogs are suffering from diseases brought about by the same hormone-disrupting chemicals suffered by marine mammals. The chemicals could have been wind-blown as the chemicals evaporate and recondense in the mountains. This theory is supported by many studies on acid rain where all kinds of contaminants are found in remote mountainsides.

Frogs are also dying from a certain bacterium that causes "red legs." They are only vulnerable when their immune system has been compromised and that can only come from being contaminated with toxic chemicals.

HAMBURGERS

German merchants from Hamburg first adopted the raw beef seasoned with salt, pepper and onion juice from medieval Tartars. After grounding them into patties and broiling them, the modem hamburger was born. When German immigrants brought the new preparation to the U.S. in the late 19th century, it took several years, before it finally took off at the St. Louis World's Fair in 1904. It became very popular because it is fast, efficient and convenient way for hungry people on the move.

But it was to the credit of Ray Kroc who organized the first hamburger chain. He noticed the McDonald brothers, Mac and Dick selling hamburgers briskly in a small town restaurant in San Bernardino, California. He got a franchise from the brothers to open branches that lead to the biggest food chain in the world. Today, the food chain has about 10,000 restaurants in the U.S. and 5,000 restaurants in 65 countries abroad. It is increasing by 200 and 500 restaurants a year, respectively. Since its founding in 1955, it has sold more than 80 billion burgers worldwide. From his success has sprout many imitations that have also become successful. All these enterprises could only mean more demand for cattle beef that could lead to more cruel infliction on the hapless animals. Every year, millions of these cattle are slaughtered for the hamburger business as demand for beefs continue to rise.

HORMONES

Bovine somatotropin or more commonly known as bovine growth hormones (BGHs) are administered to animals to make them grow faster with less feed. While it is produced naturally in the body of cattle for milk production, it is being supplemented to cattle to produce more milk. This will enable them to produce 25% more milk with the same amount of feed. However, it was discovered that children who ate a lot of the treated meat developed premature sexual development. While there are laws regulating their use, it is difficult to enforce and occasional spot checks are not enough. A withdrawal period that required the animals to abstain for a few weeks before milking or slaughter is often ignored.

Synthetic BGH is produced by using harmless bacteria and genetically-altered to produce hormones, which are being injected into dairy cows to increase their milk production. The drug always finds its way to the milk and there is no way of removing it. Many scientists, animal right activists, and consumers are up in arms against their use. One reason for their actions is that there is already a surplus of milk in the market. Other groups oppose its use on the ground that it increases the stress on the overworked dairy cows and predisposes them to illness.

The only effective solution is to ban the use of growth hormones on all animals. In 1986, the EEC banned the use of hormones among member nations and disallowed the importation of hormone-treated meat in 1989. This will greatly reduce the consumption of hormone treated meat, but to be fully effective, manufacturing of growth hormones for animals should be banned.

HUMAN HEALTH

Many studies have been made on the health of people consuming beef especially in the affluent West. In one study made in 1990, the relationship between animal fat intake, cholesterol, and human disease was made. In the study of the eating habits of 8,000 Chinese people randomly selected in China, the people consumed 20% more calories than Americans, but the Americans were 25% fatter. This is because most of the calories came from fat, 37% compared to 15% for the Chinese diet. There is a high correlation between meat consumption and incidence of heart disease and cancer. The researchers found that increasing meat consumption also increase the cases of heart disease by fifty fold. Colon cancer also increases proportionately. Reducing the fat intake to less than 10% will reduce the risk of breast cancer in postmenstrual women by 10%.

Many of the food necessary for a healthy body can be metabolized from food coming from plants and vegetables. Soybean, for example, is rich in protein with less contaminants than those coming from animals. Even animals caught in the wild have high levels of pollutants in the fats and tissues of animals. People hunting in the North Pole who regularly eat meat coming from contaminated mammals are suffering from hormone disrupters.

There are nearly 30,000 drugs routinely given to livestock, many of them untested for their long term effect. In fact, many of them have not been approved by the government. Because they are taken by animals, the governments are more lenient with their applications. Some potential human carcinogens include ipronidazole, carbadox, and dimetridazole.

Starvation is a common problem in many poor countries. More than a billion people worldwide live in absolute poverty, but many rich people continue to consume more than their share of calories. Over 15 million children are dying every year due to diseases brought about by malnutrition. Many more go to bed with a hungry stomach. The livestock populations, less than half of the U.S. population, consume twice the amount of grain compared to the people.

LEGISLATION

Legislation is an important route to free farm animals from their cruel ordeal. The strong and powerful agribusiness is not going to change unless they are forced by a law to mend their ways. Legislation has been resorted to in many states in the U.S. as more animal right groups are lobbying for more humane treatment of farm animals.

Sweden had passed an animal bill of rights in 1988, the world's most sweeping, stringent set of protection laws pertaining to farm animals. Cattle are now required to graze, and pigs are no longer confined nor tied down. They are also allowed to bed and feed in separate places. Both cattle and pigs must have access to straw and litter. Chickens must be allowed to roam and peck for grub and not confined to cages all their lives. The use of subtherapeutic doses of antibiotics and hormones is strictly forbidden.

Although cattle, swine and chicken are the animals often mentioned and rightfully so because of their large numbers, many other less well-known animals are also being farmed. These include ostriches, ducks, geese, bisons, kangaroos, sheep, goats, etc. Little is known about how these animals are treated by their owners, but some of them suffer the same fate as the three main factory animals.

The Philippines' Animal Welfare Act of 1998 was finally enacted into law last February 11, 1998. It is a legislative milestone that will go a long way in protecting the lesser creatures from cruelties and inhumane treatments that only the human species is capable of inflicting.

The law mentioned several animals that humans can consume. Two of them, the deer and the crocodiles were included in the list. In the wild, these species are endangered of extinction because of hunting. One species, the caiman crocodile was so rare, not many people know about its existence. The only reason the endemic crocodilians were included for human consumption is probably to tone down objections from our Muslim brothers who kill these reptiles for their hides. At the very least, protect these reptiles found in non-Muslim areas.

There is as yet no reliable inventory of the deer in the wild. The Calamian hog-deer (Axiscalamianensis), Visayan spotted deer (Cervus alfredi), and the Philippine brown deer (Cervus mariannus) are considered endangered due to overhunting, according to the Wildlife Conservation Society of the Philippines. All huntings in the wild should be banned and only those breed in captivity should be allowed for consumption.

Livestock and poultry are often caged together in huge numbers without room for movement. With the mandate given by the law, this is a good opportunity for government tasked to regulate these animals to require a minimum size of cage for each animal raised in farmed factory, sold in pet shops, transported in transit cages, and even sold in the wet market. Chickens being transported should not be forced to squat in cages only 8 inches high. Neither should the cages be stacked in several open layers that allow urine and feces to drop to animals below. The same is true in stacking swine cages.

The law also requires livestock to be fed and given water at least once every 12 hours during transit. Swine and cattle are often raised in outlaying areas, far from the consuming public. Because they are often transported long distances, under filthy and unsanitary conditions, the number of hours between feeding time should be reduced. The crude way they are killed should end. The modern and humane way is to stun them into unconsciousness before they are killed. At least let them die with dignity, not wailing and struggling.

MANURE

Animal factories are the biggest contributors to polluted rivers and streams. This is because the wastes they create are not properly disposed. They are kept in lagoons waiting for the rain or flash floods to discharge them to the river or to seep slowly to the groundwater.

The amount of waste produced by animal farms is enormous. According to a 1994 EPA report, they are the biggest polluters, bigger than storm sewers and all industrial sources combined. Ten thousand egg-laying hens can produce 14 tons of manure every week while 10,000 hogs in a factory can produce 6,000 tons of manure a week. All in all, American farm animals produce about 2 billion tons of manure each year. All these manure could have been scattered in the field if the animals were allowed out of their cages. In one accident, 25 million gallons of hog waste spilled into the New River in Haw Branch, North Carolina, causing serious pollution and killed countless fish.

Factory farming is also a waste of nutrients, vitamins and minerals that is often added to farm animals. All these can be returned to the pasture if the animals are allowed to graze the land. Only about 20% of the ingredients added to farm animals are absorbed and the rest are lost in the manure. These rich ingredients contain nitrates, phosphates, and other minerals that when discharged to freshwater, causes algae growth and uses up oxygen that will kill the fish and other lifeforms in the water bodies.

The 550 million chickens in factories surrounding the Chesapeake Bay contributes heavily to nitrate pollution of the area's soils and waters. Manure from New York state dairies pollutes the watershed for cities' drinking water. Cow manure in Wisconsin carried the microorganism, Cryptosporidium that wound up in Milwaukee's water supply, causing death and widespread dysentery in 1993.

MARKET FORCES

Consumers are partly to be blamed for the suffering of many animals bred for human consumption. Our demand for low cost meat has enabled greedy breeders to try to raise animals under the least cost which is often cruel for the animals.
Like all commodities on sale, the law of supply and demand plays an important role. So long as there are consumers demanding low cost meat, there will be livestock being bred and fattened at very unsatisfactory conditions. Consumers are often unwilling to pay a higher price for farm animals to be bred under better living conditions. Until people are aware of the dreadful conditions these livestock are raised, they will continue to patronage the farmed animals and keep up the demand. But once enlightened, people attitudes will change.

SWINE

Hogs are bred in overcrowded barns built with slatted floors for the feces and urine to fall through and collected for use in the Held as fertilizers. These feces are good sources of groundwater contamination. The wastes are not regularly collected and produce methane gas that is toxic to the swine. Those that live on concrete floors are lying on their own excrement since there is little room for them to move. Unless it is cleaned regularly, disease can easily breed and contaminate other pigs around.

Pigs raised for breeding do not fare any better. They are often chained or tied up that they cannot move at all. This will allow them to grow faster. The piglets born to these sows are taken away after two weeks of suckling. And the inhumane cycle of raising pigs continue unabated. The only solution to minimize animals being treated for human consumption is to eliminate them from our diets. Some supermarkets have been vocal about how the meats of animals they sell are being treated, but there is no better substitute than to avoid eating these meats.

At the slaughtering plant, the treatment of swine is often done under inhumane conditions affecting both employees and animals. According to the union of the United Food and Commerce Workers, the company, John Morrel & Co. has speeded up the assembly-line slaughtering to increase profits. As a result, employees are having accidents and the animals suffering needlessly.

In their Iowa plant, pigs are supposed to be rendered unconscious by an electric stunner before they are slaughtered. However, because the company fears the pig's meat will be damaged, the management ordered the voltage lowered on the stunners. This routinely results in fully-conscious pigs being hoisted upside down and their throats slit, and then being tossed under a conscious state into caldrons of scalding water to prepare them for the dehairing machine.

In the developing countries, pigs fare even worse. Some small farmers cage their swine underneath the chickens being raised. The waste from these chickens are used to feed the swine. Because of their voracious appetite, the pigs do not discriminate against whatever food given them. In China, pigs in the rural areas are raised underneath the home of the farmers. A hole is provided that allows the farmer to pour anything edible to the pig. Wastewater, chicken feathers, fruit peelings, etc. are given. But the worse is yet to come. Everytime someone needed to go to the toilet, all he does is crouch on the hole and send his intestinal wastes to the pigs below.

The U.S. government has found that pork delivered to the market have consistently elevated residues of sulfamethazine, a suspected human carcinogen and other sulfa drugs. These drugs are necessary to prevent bacteria from reproducing and are brought about by overcrowding of animals. A larger accommodation will reduce the use of sulfa drugs. Although these drugs are restricted by regulators, there are not enough watchdogs to check on their use.

In connection with swine raising is the problem of emission of the ammonia. It is a major component of wastes generated from pig farms. Most of the wastes are often left untreated and allow to runoff to streams that can cause acidification. The problem has lead the Dutch government to restrict the expanding of livestock farming. This could lead to fewer animals being bred and subjected to cruelty.

VEGETARIAN

The demand for factory animals is fueled by our insatiable desire for meat. This has been responsible for the billions of animals treated under the most inhumane conditions. We can change all this by shifting to a vegetarian diet. All the proteins, vitamins, and minerals needed by our body can be gathered from the vegetable and fruits we eat. In contrast to animal meat, organic food has less residue of pesticides and other pollutants unlike animals where these chemicals have a tendency to accumulate in the fats. It is also lower in fat content and have less harmful plasma cholesterol that has been responsible for many modern diseases like cancers and heart ailments. Vegetarians tend to have lower blood pressure because they are likely to be less overweight. People suffering from diabetes can benefit greatly from a vegetarian diet because it is rich in complex carbohydrates and fiber. We don't even have to feel a sense of guilt knowing how these animals are treated in order to serve our food need.

A study by Dr. Takeshi Hirayama shows that women eating meat daily are more likely to suffer from breast cancer than vegetarians. Prostate cancers strike three times more meat-eaters than vegetarians.

Sometimes we can force our employees on vegetarian diets through catering. Paul McCartney even went one step further by bringing his own chef and requiring all employees on a vegetarian diet or risk dismissal. McDonald in India, in conformity with the custom of the place served purely vegetarian food in all its outlets.

The one billion hungry people around the world can greatly benefit from our shift to vegetarian diet. The feed conversion for cattle can ranged from eight to sixteen kilos for every kilo of beef produced. In effect, we can feed at least eight people from our change in eating habit while improving our health.

WATER FACTOR

Fresh water is becoming very scarce even in some developed countries. This is because of the competition posed by livestock as we try to feed the overpopulated livestock. Lands have been placed under irrigation to increase the yield of the grain. As much as seventy percent of the water is used to grow food and feed. It is unfortunate that most of the feeds are used for livestock raising instead of crop production. To produce just a pound of grain-fed beef requires hundreds of gallons of precious water that could be used for human needs. One estimate puts it that to produce a kilo of beef protein will require 15 times more water than to produce a kilo of plant protein.

Another problem has to do with the organic wastes produced by livestock. The cattle in the U.S. alone produced nearly one billion tons each year, much of it will find their way to the groundwater and the river ecosystems throughout the country. The nitrogen from cattle waste is converted into ammonia and nitrates that leach into the aquatic systems polluting everything it came into contact.

At the American Association for the Advancement of Science annual meeting in Atlanta three years ago, experts said that by the year 2050, we have to reduce consumption of animal products by half because of increasing population and depletion of resources like water.

Their chief concern and that of all conservationists is clean water. It is being threatened by these mega-factory farms. Even the *Wall Street Journal* has run major stories about the environmental problems they cause particularly the enormous manure lagoons built by corporations that don't give a damn about either the environment or animals.

Another problem is the huge amount of water use by farm animals. Instead of having the animals roam around the field, fertilizing the soil with their manure, water are regularly use to clean their stall.

CHAPTER 13

EXTINCTION OF SPECIES

Extinction is a natural process of evolution. The average lifespan of a species is about 4 million years, according to fossil records. Well over 90% of all life forms have become extinct because of massive natural disasters such as sudden changes in sea level, volcanic activities, climatic changes and possibly comet impact that occurred millions of years ago. There were in fact five such mass extinctions that occurred as far back as 570 million years ago and as late as 38 million years ago.

Human caused extinction is believed to have started about 11,000 years ago. More than 1,000 species and subspecies of birds and mammals had disappeared forever. Mammoths and their relative the mastodons, saber-toothed cats and the giant ground sloths were some noteworthy animals. Since 1600, 58 mammals and 115 birds, most of them found on small islands had become extinct. But today, with the unceasing proliferation of the predatory human species, the main cause of extinction of species, has become faster than the natural processes.

There are several reasons for the extinction. Overkill due to hunting for food and other body parts of animals is the primary cause of extinction during the early recorded history. Hunting has resulted in the extinction of the Steller's sea cow in 1767, New England sea mink in 1880, Caribbean monk seal in 1952, quagga in 1883, Burchell's zebra in 1910, Schomburgk's deer in 1932, and the Gray's wallabee in 1940, just to name a few. By far the greatest extinctions affected the bird with more than 170 species and subspecies attributed to overkill. Some of these species are the great auk in 1844, the passenger pigeon in 1914 and the Arabian ostrich in 1941. Other species include the urus, Asian and North African lion, Carolina parakeet, gray goose, gray headed Assam duck, Asian cheetah, and so on. It is also responsible for the near extinction of many species on land and in the water.

Today it has been taken over by habitat destruction with hunting still running a close second. During the early 20th century, roughly one species is lost every year, but today the extinction process is occurring at 10 to 1,000 times faster, mostly due to habitat destruction and hunting. By the year 2050, more than half the species will become extinct if the trend continues.

Other activities such as the use of pesticides, volcanic activities, wars, forest fires, peripheral development, and fragmentation of their natural habitats are causes of alarm. Other ecological factors make some species more vulnerable than others. The rarity of a species and their inability to replenish faster than they are being killed in the wild is one important cause of their extinction. High mortality and low longevity of some species makes them more vulnerable to changes and disturbances of their natural habitat. The concentration of a species in one area can easily lead to their extinction due to hunting, diseases, climatic disturbances, or forest fires.

The 1995 Global Biodiversity Assessment estimates that the number of species endangered and threatened with extinction numbered at least 5,366 animals known to man. Those unknown or as of yet unclassified are not included in the list. The breakdown includes 533 mammals. 862 birds, 257 reptiles, 133 amphibians, 934 fishes and 2,647 invertebrates.

In the past, studies made on known extinct animals, showed that the major factors involved in their extinctions were 39% for bioinvasion; 36% for habitat destructions and 33% caused by over-exploitation for food, trophies and other body parts.

ARIZONA JAGUARS

The Arizona jaguar (Felis onca arizonensis) was once confined to Arizona, Texas and New Mexico. They are solitary animals that can run and climb trees. One of the critical ingredients in their diet is fish for which they are adept at catching. When humans started to colonize their habitats, these big cats found themselves with new preys that are protected by humans. This spelled their doom. They were shot, trapped, and poisoned until the last one was killed in 1905. Bounties were offered to eliminate them in the wild.

The cruel way they were exterminated was very much like the mountain lions of California. Dogs were set loose to track them down. As soon as they fled to the trees after tiring of running, the hunters moved in for the kill. They are shot at the head. Their highly prized skins was only incidental to the farmers hatred for killing their livestock.

BALI TIGERS

The Bali tiger is the smallest of all the tigers. In their small habitat in Bali, they are in constant conflict with the local inhabitants. They were kings of the jungle as they hunt people beside animals as part of their diet. Hunters were called in to destroy them wherever they are found. Later, with the new market for their skin in the offing, they were vigorously hunted for their skins for the new lady's fashion. This last tiger was killed on September 27, 1937.

BARBARY LIONS

The Barbary lion (Panthera leo leo) was the largest of the lions which used to be found in the forested areas of North Africa. They are closely related to the lions of Africa, with a large mane that covered half of their body. With the expansion of the Roman Empire southward, the lions were trapped and brought back to Rome for the amusement of the dictators. Julius Caesar used to own more than 100 of these lions. They were used to make martyrs out of Christians and also forced to fight gladiators in the Roman Colosseum during festivities. Nero and other emperors used them to terrorize Christians for several centuries.

During the early colonization of Africa by European powers in the 18th century, the Barbary lions were already scattered throughout Tunisia, Morocco,

Algeria, and Libya. In time they were exterminated from one country to another. Those found in Libya were the first to go in 1700. They were followed by those in Algeria and Tunisia in 1891. Over the years, their diminishing numbers and the gradual encroachment of desert forced the wild lions into their last stronghold in the woodlands of the Atlas Mountains in Morocco. The lions were hunted by the local inhabitants and their colonial power to the very end. In Morocco, two tribal groups were given bounties and tax exemptions by General Maguerite for killing them. The last cat was shot to death in 1922.

Another close relative, the Cape black-maned lion (Panlhera leomelanochaiius) became extinct much earlier. They were hunted by the ruthless English and Afrikaan hunters who were also responsible for the extinction of the blue buck and the quagga. The last lion was shot by General Bisset in Natal in 1865.

BLUE BUCKS

The blue buck antelope (Hippoiragus leucophaeus) was a close relative of the roan and sable antelopes found in the Zwellendam province of the old Cape colony. The first settlers called them blue goat because of their distinctive blue-gray coat, seasonal beard and curved horns. They were probably the first African species to be hunted by white settlers to extinction in 1799. Their very nature made them easy prey because they were too trusting of the cunning hunters and can easily be approached. They were hunted for their beautiful skins which were exported to Europe. The meat from these animals were thrown away or given to the dogs.

BURCHELL'S ZEBRAS

Burchell's zebra (Equm burchelli) was cousin to another extinct species of zebra, the quagga. But unlike the quagga they were hunted more for their skins. During the 1850s, a way was found to strip the entire hide by chemical process which lead to more killing of this animal until the last zebra in captivity died in 1910.

CARIBBEAN MONK SEALS

The Caribbean monk seal (Monachus iropicalis) was once very common throughout the Caribbean. However, because of the available oil in their fats and their furs, they were hunted late in the 17th century along with the whales and other seals. During the 18th and 19th century, their skin became fashionable adding a new dimension to their harvesting. Slow moving and friendly, they were easy prey to the human predators.

In 1911, a group of Mexican fishermen falsely blamed them for their low fish catch. The Mexicans invaded their last habitat on Triangle Keys just off Yucatan Peninsula and killed the remaining 200 seals. A small colony was sighted in 1952 but they disappeared soon after. One relative, the Mediterranean monk seal has fewer than 500 left in the ocean while the Hawaiian monk seals number over 2,000 today.

CAROLINA PARAKEETS

The only native parrot found in the U.S., the Carolina parakeet was once very common in the deciduous forests of eastern and the southern U.S. Like all colorful birds, parrots are caught in the wild and sold to bird lovers. With the growing population, trees are cut down to make way for settlements and agriculture. The planting of orchards and grain added a new woeful dimension to their existence. Like all birds, they started to feed on the seeds of the fruits of the orchards and the com planted on the field Even a few of them can ruin a large area of farmland Sensing their livelihood about to be eaten away by the parakeet, the farmers started to shoot them wherever they are found. They can easily be spotted because they fly in groups.

Loyalty among animals is not uncommon. Like the Stellar's sea cows, they are all ready to flock around a wounded bird. This allows the birds to be killed on a larger scale. The last bird in the wild was killed in a Florida field. A captive bird "Inca" died on February 21, 1918 at the Cincinnati Zoo. His mate of 30 years "Lady Jane**" died a year earlier.

DODO

The dodo (Didus inepius or Raphus cucullatus) was perhaps the most famous extinct animal to disappear during the modern times. It once inhabited the islands of Mauritius, Reunion, and Rodriquez in the Indian Ocean. The dodo was a large and heavily-built bird, but it could not fly away in the presence of danger. When the Portuguese discovered Mauritius in 1507, there was no record whether they hunted or ever saw the birds. But it didn't take long before they were rediscovered. In 1598, Dutch sailors caught these birds by breaking the leg of one bird, forcing several dozen around the wounded bird and making them easy prey to the hungry sailors. Forty to fifty of the birds are taken on board as food everyday. A Dutch admiral, Jacob Corneliszoon van Neck brought back two live birds in 1598. Soon more expeditions followed. Dutch settlers started to occupy the land with their dogs, monkeys, goats, pigs and the ever present rats that came along with the ships.

The gentle birds had almost no means of defending itself against predators. The adult birds were hunted by humans for its meat. Their eggs and babies were preyed upon by the exotic animals. Partly responsible was the loss of their forest habitat when the early settlers felled large areas of forest for human settlement. They had no place to hide and the last dodo on the island was eaten in 1681.

eastern cougar

The eastern cougar once ranged from eastern Canada to the Carolinas. They were exterminated because of their habit of preying on livestock. Several states offered bounties for killing them. By 1946 they were declared extinct. However several reports of sighting forced the U.S. Department of the Interior to upgrade their status from extinct to endangered in 1973. For 17 years, none of the big cat was ever captured nor proof of their existence available forcing the government to declare the animal extinct in 1990. Sightings have been made even today, yet proof of their existence is still in doubt.

GREAT AUKS

The Great Auk (Pinguins impennis), a flightless bird was the original "penguin". They were once widely distributed in North America, Greenland, Europe and Russia. The earliest known record was made in 1538 by the explorer, Jacques Cartier. Since the 16th century when its existence and hiding place was first recorded until its extinction in 1844, they had been hunted for their meat, feathers, fat and eggs. Seafarers have been hunting the bird for its soft, downy feathers as well as a source of food. Their fatty tissues also served as fuel for the human inhabitants. Because it can be kept fresh by salting the meat, mass slaughter began and allowed hunters to bring home the birds for home consumption. As early as 1590, a shipload of dead auks was brought back by an Icelander.

As time went by, new uses for the body parts were found. The feathers were stuffed into beds and pillows and their collarbones were used as fishhooks while the meat is sometimes used as fish bait.

A large colony of the auk was discovered on Funk Island, just off Newfoundland. A Norwegian named Stuwitz, after arriving in 1841 went on a rampage and exterminated millions of these tame birds in a span of three years.

Their number continued to fall rapidly that by the mid-1700s, hunters were no longer interested in hunting them. Instead local inhabitants were gathering their eggs for sale and consumption. Continued hunting by local inhabitants and natural disasters finally wiped them out completely. The last pair of the Great Auk was discovered on June 3, 1844, on the island of Eldez, off the extreme southwest coast of Iceland. Three fishermen were hired by a bird collector named Carl Siemsen to look for the birds for his collection. They found the last breeding pair with a single egg among countless different seabirds. Jon Brandson cornered one of the bird and Sigourer Isleffson caught the other one on the edge of the precipice. They later killed the two adult birds with clubs while Ketil Ketilsson smashed the egg with his boot.

HEATH HEN

These light brown plump game birds with black barrings were commonly found in the northeast coast of the U.S. from Maine to the Carolinas. The arrival of the first Europeans to the New World spelled their doom. They were immediately hunted for their meat. Still there are so many around, that servants in Boston sometimes had a stipulation in their contract that the birds should not be served more than a few times a week. It was a slow extinction. Unable to fly predators, they were also killed by cats and other domestic animals. Hunters can easily hunt them down without using firearms by dusting their nests with ashes. Once they started to beat their wings, the stirred up ashes will temporarily blind them and the hunters were able to beat them with sticks.

The transformation of their prairie habitat into farmland makes them even more vulnerable to the human predators. The hunting of these defenseless birds went on that by 1791, there were attempts to stop their hunting. The New York legislature was considering a law against the killing of these and other game birds. By 1880, the bird had completely vanished from the mainland. A group of 200 hens were found on the island off Massachusetts in Martha's Vineyard. A brush fire destroyed much of their breeding ground, followed by a harsh and brutal winter and the invasion of other animal predators such as the cats and the goshawks. The unexplained sterility on the males and females of the species finally killed off the last bird. The last bird became a tourist attraction and survived until 1932 at the age of 8.

JAPANESE WOLF

The Japanese wolf is only 35 cm high and found in Honshu and several other places before their extinction. The Japanese once revered them as howling gods, even erecting a shrine on their behalf, but it does not ensure their survival. They were poisoned by hunters for their fur. During the 19th century there was a great commercial demand for their skins. As the population kept growing, their habitat were being encroached until they came into conflict with the human predators. They are considered as pests and a bounty was offered for their destruction. The last wolf was shot in 1905.

MEXICAN SILVER GRIZZLIES

The Mexican silver grizzly is a solitary animal standing up to six feet and weighs 700 pounds, making it the largest animal in Mexico. They were also found in many parts of southern U.S., but hunting, poison used by farmers, and loss of habitat destroyed all the grizzly bears in the U.S. Hunters hunt them for their meat and skin. By the 1930s the only remaining bears can be found in the remote Sierra del Nido mountain in Chihuahua. Mexico. By 1960 only thirty silver grizzlies remained in the wild. Because they were intruding into the habitats of people, the local ranchers started an eradication program by poisoning them until all were killed in 1964.

MOAS

In many islands in the Pacific Ocean, rats and cats introduced by man have been responsible for exterminating a large number of birds. Of all the known genus of imperial pigeon, the Dacula david is the largest of them all. Found in the Wallis Island, they were hunted to extinction by the Tongans and other Polynesians. But nothing beats the giant moas killed by the Polynesians. There were more than 19 species of moas that lived on the South and North Islands of New Zealand. They are flightless birds that look very much like the ostrich. They ranged in size from the giant moa, *Dinornis maximus* that can be three meters high and weigh 250 kg to the smallest dwarf moa. *Megalapleryx heciori*, about the size of a turkey.

When the Moaris, a Polynesian people discovered New Zealand in the 12th century they found the bird plentiful and hunted them for food without even thinking of domesticating them For six hundred years they ate the birds without letup until they became extinct by the 1800s.

PALESTINIAN PAINTED FROG

The Palestinian painted frog (Discoglossus nigriventer) as its name aptly implied is found only on the swampy shore of Hula Lake on the Israeli-Syrian border. Two tadpoles were first discovered in 1940 and put in a terrarium. As they grew up, one of them ate the other one. In 1955 a female adult specimen was captured by collector M. Costa, who observed and recorded its habits until it died. A land reclamation project in 1956 destroyed its habitat and they were never seen again.

PASSENGER PIGEONS

The slaughter of the North American passenger pigeons (Ectopistes migratorious) is the most notorious case of overkill ever known. Until the 19th century there were huge flocks of passenger pigeons throughout most of North America. It was estimated that as many as ten billion pigeons existed during the first half of the 19th century. John James Audubon (1785-1851) described a flock he witnessed in Kentucky in 1813 which took three days to pass

By 1885 it was known that if nothing is done to protect the birds, it is a matter of time before it became extinct. Yet the hunters refused to give up their hunting. The pigeons were shot, trapped, and netted by hunters who sold them cheaply to the market while farmers poisoned them. Hunting competitions were organized in which more than 30,000 dead birds were needed to claim a prize. Other causes included habitat destruction and forest fragmentation. In the 1890s, a few states passed laws to protect the birds, but it was too late. The last passenger pigeon in the wild was killed by a young boy in Ohio on March 24, 1900. The last captive bird named "Marsha" died on September 1, 1914 in Cincinnati Zoo, USA.

PREDATORS

Predators introduced by humans around the world have resulted in the deaths and extinctions of many birds. Cats are the most destructive toward the birds. Their most notorious victim was the Stephens Island wren (*Xenicus lyalli*) where one cat alone exterminated all the birds in a space of a few months in 1894. The Guadalupe Island storm petrel (*Oceanodroma macrodaciyta*) became extinct by 1911 when all their chicks were eaten by cats while still nesting. The rest of the adult birds died a natural death. The Choiseul Island crested pigeons were exterminated by the cats in 1910. An endemic parrot (*Cyanoramphusnovaezelandiae erythrotis*) of Macquarie Island of Australia, makes their nest under the tufts of grass. This short-sightedness was partly blamed as cats took to feast on their eggs and chicks. Two endemic Hawaiian birds, the Oahu o-o (Moho apical is) became extinct in 1837 and the Bishop's o-o (*Moho bishopi*) in 1904.

Another predators are the stowaway rats scattered all over the world through ships. Five species of birds were killed on Lord Howe Island shortly after rats arrived with a ship in 1918. Four species of birds, a bat and numerous invertebrates were decimated after rats arrived on New Zealand's Big South Cape Island in 1964. A starling, *Aplonis corvina*, endemic to the Kausif Island in the Carolina Islands was also eliminated by rats.

The sandwich rail, Porzana sandwichensis became extinct in 1884. Most of the birds were killed by rats introduced to the islands. They have a bad habit of taking refuge in burrows dug by rats which lead to their early extinction. Another endemic rail, Porana palmeri that lived on Laysan Island became extinct on the island in 1920 after rabbits were introduced in 1930 that went on a rampage destroying the rail's habitat. Some birds survived on two neighboring islands. However, a ship wrecked in 1943 carrying rats invaded the two islands. By June 1944 all the remaining birds were dead.

QUAGGAS

The quagga (Equus quagga) was a subspecies of the zebra that was once very common more than a century ago in South Africa. They are very aggressive and are often used as guards by farmers to protect cattle. The zebra closely resembled the Burchett's zebra, another extinct species. The Boers or early white Dutch settlers in South Africa hunted the quaggas for their meat to feed the servants and workers in the field. They were hunted in waves of wagons bearing firearms that kill anything that moves. The wagons were later filled to capacity while the rest are left to rot. Injured animals are also left to die of starvation. The massacres were repeated throughout the ranges of the quaggas. The exterminators went on a rampage killing these animals without being aware of their endangered status until the last wild one was shot in 1878. The only captive quagga in Amsterdam Zoo died in 1883.

QUELILI

Quelili or Guadalupe caracara (Polyborus lutosus) was a large flightless brown hawk with a black head and gray striped wings, found in the Pacific island of Guadelupe, off the coast of Baja California. It is the only bird of prey to become extinct in the last 400 years. It feeds on carrion, rodents, insects and worms. However, it ran afoul of local farmers who accused the birds of attacking newborn and baby goats. Using rifles and poison, the farmers hunted the birds mercilessly until they were almost eliminated by the 1860s. Once word of its scarcity got out, collectors moved in to finish the job.

In 1897 an adventurer named Harry Drent captured four quelili and put them on display in a large cage in San Diego. Without knowing how to breed the birds, he also refused to release them or sell them at a lower price, always insisting that he be paid $1 SO. The Smithsonian Institution initially offered to pay $100 each and later relented to pay the $150 asked for. He took some time to decide and within a month all the four birds died.

Unaware of its rarity, a fisherman who caught a quelili also tried to sell it for $150 in San Diego. Unable to sell the bird, he killed the bird, cut off its wings and threw its body into the ocean. A taxidermist retrieved the wings, reassembled them, but unfortunately, his workshop was destroyed by fire.

On the afternoon of December 1. 1900, Rollo Beck, an ornithologist and collector, spotted eleven quelili flying toward him. He shot and killed nine of them, while the other two were never seen again.

SCHOMBURGK'S DEER

Schomburgk's deer (*Cervus schomburgki*) endemic to Thailand became extinct in 1932, before any Western scientist was able to study them in their natural habitat. A single live specimen was shown to the public in 1867 in France. Nearly 200 were killed for their skins and velvets which the Chinese regarded as having medical values. People even hunted them using boats as they spent most of their time near water.

The exploding population of poor people in Thailand hunted them for the meat. Coupled with the rampant conversion of their marsh habitat into agriculture and infrastructural development reduces their habitat that made them easy target to human predators.

SPECTACLED CORMORANT

The discovery of the Steller's sea cows in the Bering Island was also the time the spectacled cormorants were discovered. It was also first described by the young naturalist, Georg Wilhelm Steller in 1741. The birds feed on fish and was at one time plentiful. When the shipwrecked Saint Pierre landed on the island, the birds were hunted as food by the starving crew. By 1850, the bird was extinct. The only specimen was collected by a museum in 1837.

STELLER'S SEA COWS

Steller's sea cow (Hydrodamalis gigas) was first recorded by a German physician-naturalist Georg Wilhem Steller in the Bering Sea in 1741. It was big, growing up to 9 meters in length and weighing nearly 6 tons. Dugongs and manatees, their closest relatives are also called sea cows.

When their ship, the St. Peter was shipwrecked on their way home, the surviving crew were forced to survive on the sea otters found near the Bering Sea. The migration of the sea otters during the spring left the sea cows the only source of food. The sea cows provided a tasty red meat that tasted like beef. The 4-inch thick fat had the flavor of sweet almond oil. It can burn with a sweet, odorless, and smokeless flame. Coupled with their heavy weight of fourteen thousand pounds and loyalty to one another made them vulnerable to hunting.

When the sailors returned home with the skins of the sea otters they have eaten earlier, the fur traders found a new source of fur for the international markets. More expeditions were organized to the Bering to hunt for the sea otters while the sea cows served as provisions for food. Their numbers were never large. less than 2,000 at any time. This easily dwindled and by 1767, they were extinct.

STEPHEN ISLAND WRENS

The Stephen Island wren (Traversia lyalli or Xenicus lyalli) could only be found in a small New Zealand island appropriately named. It was the smallest flightless bird measuring only 10 cm in length. This small island is home to a few dozen of these rare birds. When D. Lyall was assigned in 1894 to take over the operation of a lighthouse located on this island, he bought with him a cat. In a few weeks time, the cat killed all the birds found on the island. The extinction was so swift that the British public learned of its existence and extinction at the same lime. The only fortunate thing was that the cat was generous enough not to eat the little birds, leaving behind 16 specimens.

TASMANIAN TIGERS

Tasmanian tigers or thylacines (Thylacinus cynocephaus) were also called Tasmanian wolves because of their wolf-life features. It had a yellow-brown coat marked with 16-18 distinctive stripes on the back of their rump. They were once found throughout mainland Australia and Tasmania. The spread of the dingos in the mainland forced them to retreat to Tasmania where they became the main predators. Their powerful hinged jaws allow them to open their mouth wider than other animals can. They were the last of the largest living carnivore marsupials in the world before their extinction. The last captive thylacine died in 1936 in Hobart Zoo, Tasmania.

They live on kangaroos, wallabies, and ground birds. After the invasion of farmers to Tasmania, they found themselves with more livestock to feast on, inviting the ires of the farmers. They would cat almost anything with four feet including those trapped by hunters. This forced the trappers to set poison traps to destroy them. From 1888 to 1914, bounties were offered by the government and the Van Diemen's Land Co. to exterminate them from the island. More than 2,200 Tasmanian tigers were killed. The slaughter was so successful that the price of bounty was lowered. A distemper-like epidemic that ran through their population in 1910 also helped reduce their population to dangerous levels.

From 1938, they were protected by law, but it was too late. Expeditions were undertaken to find them in the wild for protection, but all efforts proved fruitless. Although there were numerous reports of their sightings, many naturalists do not believe the veracity of the reports.

TECOPA PUPFISH

The tecopa pupfish (Cyprinodon nevadensis calldae) is just one of the 12 varieties found in the salty pools and thermal springs near Death Valley National Monument in eastern California. During the 1940s the North and South Tecopa Hot Springs were channeled by the builders of a bathhouse. The swift-flowing river is not conducive to the pupfish which they find difficult to adapt. This was later compounded with the introduction of the mosquito fish. Not only were these new fishes competing with their food sources, they themselves fell victim to the exotic fish. By 1970 they were all eliminated from their only habitat.

WAKE ISLAND RAILS

The rail (Gallirallus wakensis) is a small and flightless bird that knows no predators in their habitat on Wake Island, north of the Marshall Islands. Towards the end of the Second World War, the Japanese took over the island. Before the Americans decided to take over the island, the rails were still in relative safety. But as the war went on, the Japanese garrison in the island was cut off from supplies. The starving Japanese were forced to kill the rail to survive until all the birds were killed and consumed.

WALLABY (TOOLACHE)

The toolache or Grey's Wallaby (Macropus greyi) is one of the fastest and most beautiful members of the kangaroo family. The aborigines hunted them for food. The speed at which they were able to elude predators made them an ideal target for hunters who found them a big challenge Others hunted them down for their furs. The government of Australia aggravated the situation by offering sixpence for any dead marsupial during the early twentieth century. The hard economic situation led many poor people to hunt down the kangaroos.

By 1923, only fourteen were left in a ranch near Robe. Efforts to save the kangaroos were disastrous. They ran themselves to death trying to elude their captors out to save them from extinction. When news got out that the rare wallaby was endangered, hunters were attracted to the few remaining species. They were hunted until they became extinct in 1940. The last captive one died a few years later in the Adelaide Zoo.

WAPITI OR EASTERN ELK

They are sometimes called the Merriam's wapiti. They were hunted by members of an American fraternal lodge of the "Order of the Elks" for the animal's decorative upper canine teeth used as an engraved watch chain fad. As their population decreased, prices for the elks started to increase leading to more hunting. They once roamed in Arizona and New Mexico, numbering over 10 millions at their peak. The last elk was killed in 1906.

WARRAH OR ANTARCTIC WOLF

The warrah (Dusicyon australis) was found only in Falkland Islands just off Argentina. It is neither a wolf nor a fox, but its wolfish head probably gave it the name Antarctic wolf. In the isolated island, they were the only predators until the arrival of the more ruthless human predators. The warrah survives on mice and birds and their eggs. The settlers brought with them livestock which added more preys for the warrahs. This forced the sheep and cattle farmers to kill the warrachs. As news of their existence spread throughout the world, trappers came to hunt them for their skins as furs and as collector's item Zoos and museums compete to supply their establishments with live animals or for their natural history museums.

When Charles Darwin visited the island, there were only a few killings, possibly out of respect for him. After Darwin left the island, the colonial government set a bounty on the warrahs that lead to their extinction. By 1839, the Antarctic wolf was so rare that the demand increased, resulting in the skyrocketing of prices.

CHAPTER 14

HABITAT DESTRUCTION

Next to clean and uncontaminated food and water, habitat is the next most important element in the survival of any species. Like humans, animals need shelter to survive the harsh environment. Even with all the anti-hunting and protection laws in the world, wildlife has no chance of survival if it has nowhere to live. The proliferation and intrusion of people is the single most important cause of habitat destructions. People destroy wildlife habitats in as many ways as the animals lived. Not only do we encroach on their habitat for development and extraction of natural resources, we have also hunted the wildlife and brought many animals to the brink of extinction. Wildlife habitats are not confined in the rainforests, oceans, and savannas, but include mangrove forests, estuaries, coral reefs and even surrounding air.

Greed is the main motive that drives man to destroy important habitats. The tropical and temperate forests where most of the animals live are being destroyed at an unprecedented scale. Along with their destruction is an estimated extinction of 50 to 100 species of plants and animals every day. Destructions of rainforests with its rich biodiversity is now the leading cause of the extinction of species.

Conversion of forests to agriculture, logging, and mining for minerals is an important cause of deforestation. Such habitat destruction need not be total in order to destroy the species. Fragmentation of their habitat, reduction of their breeding and feeding grounds could push the population size below the survival rate that made them impossible to rehabilitate. Island birds are specially vulnerable to forest clearing. In the Cebu Island, Philippines, logging drove all 10 endemic bird species into extinction. On St. Helena, clearing caused the extinction of three of its four native birds while the clearing of Mauritius and Rodriquez in the Indian Ocean resulted in the extinction of at least 12 species of birds.

Many developmental projects located in rainforests such as big dams for power generation and irrigation can destroy the ecosystem while killing animals by inundation. Roads that are regularly constructed through their natural habitats have resulted in the accidental death of animals. Other forms of habitat destructions may not be immediately apparent, but can be quite devastating in the long run They may include pollution, radioactive emission, oil spills, discharges of untreated wastes, wars, and natural calamities.

More than any ecosystem in the world, the ocean is the last destination of most of our waste discharges to the environment. When the world's population was small, the ocean was capable of absorbing and dispersing the wastes. But the continuing degradation from human discharges, runoff of pesticides and other chemicals, oil spills, and many other human activities are aiding and abetting the destruction of the ocean throughout the world.

The oceans of the world produce an amount of plant and animal products almost equal to that produced on land, and producing them at no cost to mankind.

It js therefore safe to say that protecting these vital ecosystems will assure us a continued supply of food for future generations.

AGRICULTURE

The need to feed the growing populations has remarkably changed the landscape of the whole world. Agricultural activities have resulted not only in the reduction and loss of habitats for wildlife, it has also been responsible for massive soil erosion, runoffs for organic and inorganic wastes, fertilizers, and chemicals such as pesticides and herbicides, many of which prove to be toxic to animals and humans as well.

Other agricultural improvements such as irrigation and channelization are cutting deep into the slopes that are affecting the aquatic systems in many areas. Topsoil is easily carricd away along with the water used in irrigation.

For many indigenous people where slash-and-bum agriculture is the preferred method of cultivation, it has caused the fragmentation of natural habitats for animals. By burning the trees for use as agricultural fertilizer, it has often resulted to widespread fire destroying more forest than is necessary.

Agriculture is the single most important cause of habitat destructions. Since the Neolithic revolution 10.000 years ago, more forests have given way to farms and pastures than any other use. The spread of agriculture is still going on in spite of the fact that governments are aware of the destruction of forest ecosystems and its natural repercussion brought about by natural forces. Deforestation is very common in the tropical countries due to their high birth rates, population density and growing affluence, with increasing need for food and fuel to feed the teeming populations. Before 2000 B.C., men have started to deplete the forests in Europe The natural forest once stood at 95% of the land mass in Europe. By the end of the medieval period, the forest cover was down to 20% and along with it the extinction of countless animals. Swidden agriculture was practiced even as late as the 19th century in many parts of Sweden and Finland. Trees were burned down and replaced with crops for four to six years and then allowing the land to revert to scrub and woodland.

Today the tropical countrics arc still facing thc samc problcms oncc faccd by their ancestors. Crops as food is the driving force behind the conversion of forests into farmlands. The high population growth in many countries will only lead to more deforestations. People need to be fed, sheltered and kept warm and the upland dwellers are mostly too poor to afford all these necessities. Governments are too slow to help them and they have to fend for themselves by the only means they know.

Slash-and-burn agriculture was once feasible in areas where the population is small. It can support crops for a few seasons before they are left to fallow. The fields are generally excellent the first year, dropping by 30% the second and 50% by the third year due to the loss of many nutrients through leaching by the tropical rains and the removal of others in the harvested crops. An essential factor to continued fertility in any shifting cultivation system is an adequate fallow period on a relatively small area to enable the soil to replenish its nutrients. It will take from six to twenty years to regenerate the soil. With population increases and the migration of landless lowlanders to the forests, there won't be time for fallowing and the fields are permanently changed to shrub which cannot support humans and most wildlife.

Modern agriculture has been responsible for large scale deforestation in many Third World countries. As the population in the tropics kept growing, the need to increase food production becomes more vital. This is often achieved not by increasing yield but by expanding arable land or increasing the size of farm animals. Many multi-national companies are engaged in cash crop plantations. Even local companies find it rewarding to go into this line of business in cooperation with or as contractors to the multinational companies.

Some Central American countries are called "banana republic." because thousands of banana trees were planted in previously forested areas. Although the soil is not conducive to cash crops because of its lack of nutrients, the use of imported fertilizers is common place. These nutrients once washed away by rain have been responsible for large scale algae growth in the water ecosystem.

Almost all tropical countries once with rich rainforest have fallen prey to planting cash crops for export. Cash crops such as tobacco, cassava, copra, maize, pepper, sugar, coffee, rubber, and oil palm are often planted in the once rich ecosystem. The tropical countries are ideal for these crops due to the ideal temperature, soil conditions, and cheap labor As early as the colonial times, many countries were colonized to supply these cash crops for home consumption of the colonizers. Governments also encourage local landowners to plant these crops for export to earn foreign exchange.

During the early Spanish era, about 90% of the Philippines was covered by forest. The development of sugar plantations resulted in extensive deforestation to provide land for sugar cane and firewood for sugar processing. Rice farming and livestock ranching also contribute a significant part of deforestation.

In northeast Thailand, the area devoted to the production of cassava increased from 20.000 hectares in 1970 to 674,000 hectares in 1978, all coming from the once forested area. The cassava was used to feed the voracious pigs of Europe.

In fifty years between 1870 and 1920, in the western part of India, land cultivated for cotton was increased four times, all at the expense of large-scale forest clearances. In Algeria, after the French conquest and expropriation of land for European settlements, the local inhabitants had to move into new areas and clear the forests to provide enough land for food production. An area about 500.000 hectares was destroyed. These are just a few examples of forest clearances that are destroying the habitats once occupied by other creatures.

ATMOSPHERIC HABITAT

When we talk about habitats, we often refer to the land and sea habitats, but the atmosphere can be just as important habitat for the birds. This is especially true for migratory birds which often fly long distances at very high altitudes and some birds that stay in the air most of their life. In the air, the main problem encountered by birds has to do with the aircrafts, especially jet planes that fly at low altitudes during practice.

The U.S. Air Force jets run into the birds about 100 times a day every year. The result is often fatal for the birds, but sometimes it could also be fatal for the pilots and crew. From 1987 to 1993, seven planes went down killing six crew members in the U.S. To resolve the problem, the Air Force has organized a Bird Aircraft Strike Hazard (BASH) to develop a computerized Bird Avoidance Model (BAM) which depict bird migration routes in the U.S. This will help pilots avoid the paths taken by migratory birds. The project is expected to expand and incorporate other critical areas around the world.

BIOINVASION

The introduction of alien species without their natural predator and competitors is a common cause of loss of species in the world. They are either deliberately or accidentally introduced. In UK, some 20 out of the 67 wild mammals were deliberately introduced into the country. Some have become useful components of the ecosystem, but most alien species are detrimental to the ecology. The impact may be immediate or delayed. The consequences can result in serious environmental, economic and social upheavals.

Exotic species may proliferate very fast because there is an imbalance of nature. The new species often have voracious appetites and breed very fast. They compete against other species for the available food and breeding ground for the offspring. Some organisms may introduce unknown disease to their new habitat that native species are not immune.

Terrestrial animals can also be an important factor in the decline of native species. House cats, black and brown rats introduced into New Zealand have resulted in the decline of huge bird populations in New Zealand. Snakes introduced in Guam from Papua New Guinea have driven nine out of the eighteen bird species, some lizards, and bats into extinction.

The introduction of the flatworm Arhoposlhia iriangulaia from New Zealand to Northern Ireland, is causing serious changes to soil fertility. They prey on earthworms responsible for soil fertility, will affect agriculture for years to come.

European settlers of Western Australia brought not just their families but their pets and livestock. Many of these non-native creatures, including rabbits, foxes, and domestic cats, have run wild, driving many native species to near-extinction or seek refuge on offshore islands. Bettong and bandicoots, a burrowing rat-kangaroo and a small marsupial, respectively, have been decimated in these areas.

When Thomas Austin of Victoria. Australia introduced a few rabbits, Oryciolagus cuniculus, from Europe for game in 1859, the unexpected happened. Known for fast breeding and voracious appetite and with no natural predator, they were soon overgrazing the grass used for sheep raising, devastating crops and plants over a wide area. Large scale eradication campaigns had little effect. The introduction of the disease myxomatosis from Brazil was able to eradicate 99.8% of the animal. But those immune to the disease soon continued to breed and the rabbit population exploded again. By 1953, approximately 300 million hectares were inhabited by over one million rabbits scattered throughout the country. The same problem can be found in New Zealand and Hawaii.

When rabbits were introduced to Laysan Island in Hawaii, the rabbits ravaged the vegetation, reduced the twenty-six species of plants to only four, and the disappearance of several bird species. Laysan was turned into a desert in a short time. The same breed of rabbits soon took over Lasianski Island, also in Hawaii, and devastated all the vegetation until they starved to death. Other native herbivores starved along with them. Other islands such as the Falkland, Macquarie Island, lie St. Paul, lies Kerguelen, lies Crozet and Auckland Island also suffered severe damage from introduced rabbits. Other predators such as rats, goats, sheep, reindeer and cattle have directly and indirectly caused the extinction of native animals.

The domestic cat. a favorite pet of many people has also been responsible for the deaths of many small marsupials in Australia. The cat together with the fox have exterminated 90% of all the small marsupials in the Australian continent.

A giant snail (Achalina fulica) was introduced to Hawaii in 1936. Since then it has been destroying the native snails and causing considerable damage to plants. In 1956. the escape of the African killer bees {Apis mellifera seutellata), led to their interbreeding with Latin American bees and are on their way to northern U.S. The cross-bred bees have largely replaced native colonies and are more aggressive and yield less honey.

The accidental introduction of the zebra mussels from the Caspian Sea into the Great Lake in 1988 has spread to many major lakes and rivers throughout the U.S. They formed dense colonies taking over breeding grounds of native mussels and spawning grounds of fishes while consuming all the plankton the other species need to survive. Intake and outlet pipes of power plants are clogged with them. There is still no solution to the problem and it will cost billions of dollars every year to contain them.

The Nile perch is also destroying the ecosystem of Victoria Lake in Africa. The introduction of the perch into the Lake in 1954 was to increase the fishing industry for the 30 million inhabitants there. Instead it led to the virtual elimination of the once rich fish species of the lake where people depended for their protein. The predator can weigh as much as 200 pounds and consume vast quantities of native fishes. An estimated 200 out of 300 native species of fishes have been wiped out in the past 30 years.

Sometimes new species have been accidentally introduced into the new habitat with devastating results. The San Francisco Bay alone suffers from more than 200 marine creatures brought by ships from other ports. Microorganisms are sometimes involved. The amoeba-like marine creature such as the Trochammania hadai is brought into the bay and discharged wherever the freighter goes. The organism is stored away in the ballast water used to stabilize the large seagoing vessels. The water is pumped out at each port of call as new crates are loaded. The introduction of the European starling (Slurnus vulgaris) into Central Park. New York by a visiting ornithologist in 1890 has allowed it to spread throughout North America to the detriment and loss of the native birds such as the bluebirds and other songbirds and the destruction of billions of dollars worth of crops annually. His idea was to populate all the birds mentioned in Shakespeare plays as a tribute to the great writer.

COASTAL AREAS

An impoverishment of the animal and plant populations in the vicinity of coastal cities is being reported all over the world. The disappearance in the Adriatic Sea of the brown algae is noticeable. In the Norwegian fjords, seaweeds are disappearing from the areas near towns. In their place, other algae are spreading. The causes are overfishing, pollution, and urban development. In the U.S. coastal waters, nearly one third of all species have declined in the last decades.

The mixture of domestic and industrial effluents introduced into the sea by many coastal towns, can have various effects: the water is warmer, contain suspensions which settle on the bottom; the oxygen balance is upset and trace elements can have a direct and poisonous effect. The effect may not be immediately apparent. It can be circuitous; the flora of microscopically small algae may bloom causing red tide or parasite attack may be facilitated.

The coasts of the world's continents and islands together add up to approximately 1.5 to 2.0 million km, depending on how precisely the curves in the coastline is followed. In these shallow zones human activities hae increased tremendously. Aquaculture is fostered through fish ponds and fishpens construction. Swimming and beach activity is expanding along sandy beaches. Divers frequent rocky coasts and coral reefs. A piece of coral which took many years to grow large and conspicuous is easily injured or killed. In the Mediterranean, the Caribbean, and other places where spear fishing has not been regulated, large fishes have become a rare sight for skin divers. Low lying stretches of land, like the northwest European marshes, are protected against storm flooding by dikes, in the process by which the original saltmarsh is destroyed. Construction of dams, harbors, and piers contribute to the deterioration of our natural environment. It is necessary to restrict human activities in coastal area to maintain the natural landscape for future generations. Coastal natural reserves are also used as feeding grounds for migratory birds.

Damage to fisheries and coral reefs caused by sedimentation is well documented around the world. The harvesting of timber worth only $14 million from the drainage of the South Fork of the Salmon River in central Idaho in the mid 60s caused an estimated $100 million in damage to the river's Chinook salmon fishery. That industry still has not recovered. Fisheries in Bacuit Bay near Palawan, Philippines were depleted after sediments from logging operations started in 1985 in surrounding hillsides. Uncontrolled flow of sediments into the bay killed up to half of the living corals that supported fish and thus deprived local villagers of their only source of protein.

CORAL REEFS

Corals are anemone-like invertebrates that flourishes in the continental shelves of the tropical and some temperate regions. They have existed continuously for 70 million years, living in colonies that spend their entire life rooted on the reefs' surface, using stinging tentacles to feed on plankton. There are two types of corals.

Those that produce hard calcareous shells and those that produce soft proteinaceous skeletons. It is the former that eventually produce the coral reefs. Corals art subject to many problems. The ultraviolet radiation caused by the presence of the ozone hole had caused corals to "bleach." Other contributing factors may be global warming and the effect of El Niño.

Bleaching can be fatal to corals, reaching as far down as 25 meters under the sea. The coral looses living cells, becomes contaminated with dead algae and plankton, and turns pale. After repeated episodes of bleaching, the diverse and productive marine plants and animals disintegrate, forcing molluscs and fishes to search elsewhere for their food. The large amount of nutrients from sewage disposed threatens the survival of the corals. They thrive in sparsely contaminated water and are very sensitive even to low level contaminations. Bleaching can also occur when environmental stress forces the corals to expel the algae that give reefs their colors and accounts for half the tissue mass. This leads to reduce carbon fixation and skeletal growth.

Corals are also sensitive to sea temperature increases and there are fears that global warming might destroy many coral reefs. Classic experiments over 50 years ago established that corals respond to an increase in temperature "bleaching." the loss of pigmentation due to its expulsion from the host of zooxanthellae. The zooxanthellae obtain energy through photosynthesis. The algae benefit from the safe shelter, carbon dioxide, and waste products corals give off. In return the zooxanthellae provide the oxygen, food and the different colors of the reefs. A sustained increase in sea temperature for a few days of 4 degrees C above normal can produce mass bleaching, followed by as high as 95% coral mortality. In the Java Sea, the 3-4% degrees C rise on seawater temperature resulted in 80-90% of the corals dying after massive bleaching.

The corals build hard calcareous shells by absorbing calcium and carbon dioxide from seawater and produce the hard calcium carbonate skeletons to protect their soft bodies. They live and die in colonies for millions of years, forming the colorful reef as we know it today. The largest coral reef, the Great Barrier Reef, of Australia extends for almost 20.000 kilometers.

Australian researchers have estimated the total coral reefs around the world at 732.000 sq km. containing about 900 million tons of calcium carbonate. The calcium carbonate contains about 11 million tons of carbon, an element that once emitted to the atmosphere can cause global warming. Like the trees, their continuing growth will soak up the carbon in the atmosphere.

The coral reefs are castles of rich, colorful and varied marine habitats and they are all in trouble worldwide. A single coral reef can contain as many as 3,000 species comprising about 20 to 40% of the marine organisms. It is the equivalent of the rainforest in the terrestrial world. Like its counterpart, it is one of the most threatened ecosystems of the aquatic world.

The Philippines has one of the largest coral reefs in the world, covering about 33.000 sq km. An estimated 90% are dead or dying and the rest will deteriorate unless protection is urgently undertaken. Every day for the past decades, thousands of fishermen have harvested out in the rich coral reefs carrying nothing but plastic squirt bottles containing diluted sodium cyanide and a small net.

The trade in exotic fishes for the gourmet restaurants is responsible as Asians become more affluent. Cyanide fishing continues to flourish because of the high demand for live fish, dealers' and middlemen's greed for quick profits and the fishermen's need for livelihood.

The cyanide toxin is naturally flushed from a fish's system after a few weeks. But there is no way of purging the cyanide from the water except its eventual dilution in time. But new research shows that the cyanide used to snag fish poisoned the corals immediately. Hundreds of tons of sodium cyanide are being pumped into the coral reefs of Southeast Asia. This illegal method has been going on unnoticed for decades until a comprehensive study of coral reefs was been made. Only then did we realize the gravity and extent of the problem.

The poor people where these precious sea forests are found are cashing in on the bonanza. The alarming rise in cyanide fishing has also been bolstered by the willingness of many hobbyists to pay large sums of money for the aquarium fish. Estimates of the trade on live reef fishes in Asia is between 20,000 to 25,000 tons a year, worth more then one billion dollars, according to Robert Johannes, who has been studying the problem for two years.

Coral reefs are also being damaged because of the tourist trade. Corals are being collected and sold to tourists often at bargain prices. Aquariums, whether big or small are likely to have coral reefs as part of the seascape. Tourist divers enjoying the beauty of the coral reefs are brought to the sites by ships. The anchors are particularly damaging to the reefs as they are often dragged along the sea bed. A comprehensive survey of the extent of the coral reefs will help in their conservation. The whole area can then be sealed off against the intrusions of marine vessels to avoid their anchoring within the fragile ecosystem.

Organic nutrients in sewage contribute to the growth of algae which which can be harmful to the corals. The algae can reduce the sunlight penetrating the seawater that will lead to a reduction in coral growth. Corals grow twice as fast on a sunny day than on a cloudy day. They are also threatened by pesticides, silt, exploitation of coral rocks for building decoration. and lime production for cement manufacturing and building stones. In Hong Kong in the 1960s, coral was used in lime burning and for making cement. Many developing countries still mine corals for cement and building materials. Limestones were deposited millions of years ago by the remains of calcareous animals such as corals and shellfish.

Nothing beats the destructive force of harvesting the corals and mining the coral sand as is happening in Mauritius and other parts of East Africa. Every year, Mauritius excavates half a million tons of sand for the construction industry.

Dredging can stir up the silt, including the dormant heavy metals under the sea bottom and can cover the coral reefs that will lead to the suffocation of the corals and poisoning of their inhabitants. In more than 50 countries around the world silt-laden river runoff is suffocating the reefs. Coral reefs are often damaged by hurricanes and storms that break coral branches and topple whole colonies.

Artificial reefs can be created where none is in existence. The first step is to put up scraps of steels that can be the basis of growth for corals. The U.S. Army disposed of their old battle tanks in the coastal areas to serve as new sites for coral reefs.

DAMMING

Dams are constructed for the hydroelectric generation and irrigation purposes. It is very expensive not only in financial cost but also in terms of environmental degradation. Not only are whole landscapes drowned in water, it also displaces people and kills wildlife. Inundation of dams has been responsible for the destruction of millions of animals wherever they are constructed. There are now more than 38,000 dams worldwide and constructions are going on at the rate of about 170 dams a year.

Hydroelectric plants are attractive to dam builders in forested areas due to the small local opposition and the high rainfall available. But the usual floodings have destroyed large tracts of ecosystem. The Kariba Dam in Pakistan and the Volta Dam in Ghana each flooded about a million hectares of some of the wildest natural settings for rhinoceros and elephants. Brazil has plans for several large dams which will surely destroy more animals than anywhere else because of its dense biodiversity.

One of the developments done along estuaries and rivers is the harnessing of the freshwater flowing to the sea by damming along its mouth. The water is used for power generation, irrigation, and for human consumption. The withholding of the freshwater increases the salinity of the estuary that made it impossible for sea animals such as shrimps, oysters, mussels and some fishes to survive the high salinity water.

In James Bay, Quebec, Canada is a wilderness of 6.000 square miles used as hunting ground by the Cree Indians who have lived and hunted there for the last five thousand years. It will soon be Hooded for a hydroelectric power plant. It is a natural habitat of ancient forest and home to migratory birds, beluga whales, and other animals. The flooding will also release mercury from the James Bay soil into the food chain and contaminate the trout and pike populations around the lakes. An earlier flooding under Phase I of the project drowned more than a thousand caribou. The animals were not even removed before the flooding was unleashed.

DEFORESTATION

The tropical rainforests which covers 6% of the total land is haven to possibly as many as 30 million species of animals, mostly insects. Their survival depend on an intact forest. But with so many activities going on within the rainforests of the world, it is doubtful if the rainforests will survive for another century.

Deforestation comes in many forms. The need of people for lumber, mining, oil exploration, land for agriculture and expansion of human habitat often lead to the felling of trees in an unsustainable way. As an important source of foreign exchange for many tropical countries, logging has become an important factor in deforestation.

The timber industry plays an important part in the economics of all countries endowed with trees. It has been the chief dollar earner for many tropical countries as well as the U.S., Canada and Russia. In many parts of the world, trees are harvested beyond their capacity to regenerate. Once they are destroyed, the organisms that live within are also destroyed unless it can find another area suitable for them.

The ecosystem of the tropical forests, which comprise about 6% of the land surface are very different from the temperate forest. They contain more species than in temperate forests. It is almost impossible to regenerate a tropical forest once it has been deforested. The richness of the forests lie not in the soil but within the trees themselves. Once the trees are removed, the nutrients contained in the trees are taken away, leaving the soil to erode down the slope until it reaches the water ecosystems that can cause siltation and eventual death of bottom creatures by smothering.

In many Asian countries, many protected and endangered animals are caught during logging operations. The felling of the trees also lead to the falling off of the animals from the high trees where they are in relative safety. They are then placed in bamboo or wire cages and brought to the city market for sale. On one occasion in Thailand, as many as 300 birds and mammals listed as protected species in Thailand were confiscated from dealers in Bangkok. For every animal confiscated, there are at least ten more sold illegally. Many of these endangered animals are kept in the backroom away from the eyes of the public.

In the thick forest of Amazon, hunting is almost impossible except by the indigenous people living there. However, with the logging roads in place, hunters and poachers have been provided a way to hunt some of the rare species of birds and animals found deep in the jungle.

Temperate forests are not exempted from environmental degradation that causes deaths to animals and destruction of their habitats. Canada is coming under international pressure to protect its forests and minimize pollution by its $43 billion wood industry. The clear-cutting is destroying the habitats of many land mammals while poisoning the rivers and lakes and polluting the air with effluents from its 145 paper pulp mills. Each year 10 million hectares of forests are felled and within these ecosystem are the systematic destruction of wildlife habitats.

DREDGING

At the bottom of the oceans lay some of the most valuable materials needed by people. If what is happening to all the natural habitats taken over by people is a guide, the ocean floor won't be harvested without some form of degradation. Dredging stirs up the muddy soil while dumping of the mud farther from the shore only aggravates the situation. The muddy soil can suffocate fishes by blocking their gills. Inability of sunlight to penetrate the turbid water reduces photosynthesis that affects the food sources of herbivores.

Dredging can also destroy benthic marine life as well as their breeding bed. Plants and animals are uprooted. Deep sea mining of minerals such as nickel cobalt, copper and manganese are gathered to ocean platform, processed and the rest of the muddy soil is dumped back as waste. The pollution caused is often accompanied by heavy metals that can be consumed by marine animals with detrimental effects to their health.

DROUGHT

Droughts are often caused by the prolonged absence of rainfall. It is often compounded by the lack of forest cover. These forests are efficient in capturing, retaining and recycling water. Forests act like a gigantic sponge, soaking up water during rainfalls, then releasing it slowly and steadily for creatures living thousands of kilometers away all year round They reduce flooding and mitigate the effect of droughts In some areas where deforestations have greatly reduced the amount of rainfall, damage to animal health has happened when they are forced to drink from polluted streams Continuous droughts and food shortages that once inflicted Ethiopia claimed the lives of thousands of people as well as the extinction of many local species, particularly the migratory birds that usually wintered there. Animals are often the first to go, either dying of starvation or serving as food for the people In the Transcaucasus area of Russia, droughts had caused the disappearance of the mole and vole.

Many problems encountered by people during droughts are also experienced by animals. African savannas are very vulnerable to droughts. Very few animals can survive without water as long as they have food to eat because they can get the liquid from the food they cat. but most cannot survive the ordeal. Sometimes the drought can last for years but most animals cannot last that long.

The sub-Saharan African drought of 1991 - 1992 was called the "drought of the century." It has taken its toll on human lives and wildlife, especially in parts of Zimbabwe and South Africa. In Gonarezhou National Park in southeastern Zimbabwe, carcasses of Cape buffalo and zebra lie scattered on the parched ground, and elephants are devastating the remaining woodlands in a desperate search for food. In South Africa's Kruger National Park, the corpses of hippo, crocodile, and baboon can be found along the now-dry Luvuvhu River. Thousands of animals, including 2.000 elephants were deliberately killed to distribute the meat to the hungry villagers. The more endangered animals - rhino, sable, roan antelope, kudu, and nyala - are transported to nearby game ranches.

The 1944-45 drought of Australia brought about a disastrous harvest and more than one-third of the sheep died. It took ten years before the sheep population recovered. The Africa drought of 1995 caused the death of thousands of large mammals in the Hwange National Park of Zimbabwe, one of the world's largest wildlife park It was the worst drought in more than 70 years. During this calamitous events, conservationists were fearful for the animals since most of them would congregate around a few waterholes, making it easy for poachers to find them. The young animals are more vulnerable because they cannot travel fast enough to find new watering holes. Elephants are particularly hard hit because they require more water than other animals.

The Big Heat of June 1980 in the U.S. mid-West and southern states caused a drought that in a short time many cattle had to be slaughtered prematurely. This is mainly due to loss of grazing grass and the skyrocketing price of hay. Corns, soy beans, vegetables, and fruits were ruined. In Arkansas, the main producer of chickens, the birds perished in the sizzling heat and thousands had to be slaughtered.

Today, we are faced with a more ominous phenomenal problem of El Nino. It is a meteorological disturbance that occurs initially in the Pacific Ocean around South America near Peru. It is characterized by long drought in some regions of the world and strong wind and flooding in others. Events in the past have shown that the first victims are the wildlife and livestock. With diminished grain for human consumption, livestock are forced to eat low quality food. Many pigs and poultry suffer from poor living conditions such as low water supply, uncleanliness, and heat stress. For those who cannot afford the high cost of feeding the livestock, many are killed prematuredly.

One of the worst effects occurred in 1982-83 which costs the lives of several thousands of people and the economic loss of several billions of dollars worldwide. In Australia, the episode killed thousands of wildlife as bush fires erupted in many parts of the country due to the drought. In Western Europe and the U.S., flooding caused the death of countless animals.

Another manifestation of the El Nino around the site of occurrence is the warming of water that forces the fishes to migrate elsewhere. Off the coast of California, sea lions are dying of starvation.

ESTUARIES

The importance of estuaries can be glimpsed from the number of people living within its vicinity. Over one-third of the U.S. population live and work close to the estuaries. Seventy percent of the world's population live adjacent to estuaries and other water bodies. Cities have developed on estuaries because of their role as natural transportation centers. Harbors, quays, and wharfs have been built along its banks. Increasing numbers of large ships and other transports that require constant dredgings disturb the sea animal habitats.

Estuaries are the feeding grounds for many species of birds such as flamingos, geese, ducks, and migratory birds because of the abundance of food fishes and other organisms. Biologists claimed that these are the most extensive natural habitats in the world are well founded because they served as nursing ground for two-thirds of all marine animals. It is here where young fishes migrate to grow in safety. The muddy bottom is an ideal location for clams, oysters, mussels and some types of shrimp because of the ideal depth where their sources of food are within reach.

The mixture of salt and fresh water present challenges to the physiology of the animals which were able to adapt to them. But the discharge of pollutants from industrial processes and domestic wastes are adding tremendous pressure to their survival. These areas are also the prime targets of development as they are reclaimed for residential, industrial, commercial, recreation and agriculture uses.

In the U.S. where estuaries or wetlands as they are usually called are mostly owned privately, an estimated 117,000 hectares are being converted to other uses annually. To date half of the nation's wetlands have been drained and filled up with projects intended for people. Conversion to agriculture, development projects such a hotels, housings, harbors and recreational areas have effectively destroyed the estuarial system and denied the sea creatures and the migratory birds their rights to the habitats. As a result, the migratory birds have declined by 62% on the average Even the amphibians such as the frogs have declined dramatically.

Along with the use of estuaries for navigation and harbors has been industrial development. Large-scale industries such as steel works, oil refineries, or chemical works need a combination of flat land and good transportation. Since the land supply of flat land is finite, the increased demand of industry are often met by reclaiming the estuarine mudflat. Farms have been expanded at the expense of reclaimed estuarial salt marshes. To prevent against flood damage, whole estuaries may be shut off the from the sea as had happened in the Netherlands with the closing of the saline Zuider Zee, to become the freshwater Ijselmeer.

To generate electricity required for a modern city requires the construction and operation of large power stations. These are ideally located near the estuary because of the availability of large volumes of water, used for heating steam turbines and for cooling. Many power stations have been built on the banks of estuaries, and the large volume of water used generates large volumes of waste water. If coal is the fuel used, then the ash produced must be disposed of, and on several occasions, ash disposal units have been erected in reclaimed estuary. If nuclear fuel is used, concern may be expressed about any radioactivity in the waste water discharged. Oilfields and storage facilities are now commonly found in estuaries where supertankers are serving.

FIRES

We are aware of the effect of fires on urban lives. In nature, fires could even be more devastating. Forest fires are particularly destructive to wildlife for several reasons. Terrestrial animals often cannot run fast enough to get away from the fire and are roasted to death. Even those that were able to escape the holocaust will find it difficult to adjust and survive in the charred remains of the forest. There is a drastic change in the ecology of the environment. It will take some time before the forest is regenerated and by then, the animals would have starved to death.

In many tropical areas, people are changing the landscape by burning down the forests In Brazil. Indonesia, and Malaysia, forests are being burned down and replaced with agricultural or other projects. In Australia where bushfires are common, fires have devastated large habitats and killed many wild animals. The koalas are particularly vulnerable because their only source of food came from the eucalyptus tree. Endemic species located in small islands are often eliminated by fire. Wildfire can also destroy the food resources of animals feeding on grass.

One significant result of forest clearing by burning is the emission of carbon dioxide to the atmosphere In Brazil, an area of about 20 million hectares of forests went up in smoke The fire sent up more than 500 million tons of carbon, 44 million tons of carbon monoxide, 6 million tons of particles, and 5 million tons of methane besides millions of tons of ozone, nitrous oxide and others pollutants. Most of these chemicals can exacerbate the greenhouse effect that will affect all living organisms for years to come.

Drought can affect rainforests and cause large scale fire either by deliberate burnings or natural causes During the 1980s, when the temperature was particularly high, there have been large and extensive fires in the Dominican Republic. Haiti, East Kalimantan, and Borneo destroying 35,000 sq km. A fire in the moist forest around Cancun, Mexico lasted over 5 months. In 1987, a fire destroyed one million hectares of forest in northeast China.

During the medieval and colonial times, forests are burned down to clear land for housing and agriculture. Today, the tropical countries are also burning the forests for the same purposes Plants and animals are often the first victims of forest fires. Trees often can regenerate itself if the fire is small and isolated, but animals once killed is gone forever.

In the urban areas, caged wild animals in zoos are difficult to rescue in case of fire. This is because it is sometimes dangerous and almost impossible to move the caged animals. This is what happened at the Philadelphia Zoo on Dec. 24, 1995. Twenty-three primates, most of them endangered species were killed during an early morning fire. The primates were caged in a primate house and there was no time to move them away to safety.

One of the biggest fires to dale is the forest fire of Sumatra and Kalimanta in Indonesia. The fire which started in August 1997 devastated more than one million hectares. The main cause is the uncontrolled burning intended for plantations. The delayed rainfall expected to stop the fire is blamed on the effect of El Nino Hundreds of thousands of animals have been burned to death while others are suffering from the drought Orangutans are particularly hard hit by the twin activities of fire and hunting.

FLOODS AND TYPHOONS

Floods and typhoons are common occurrences during the rainy seasons. In the wild, where animals are plenty and free to roam around, they can be subjected to the nature s fury. The great hurricane of February 1760 in the Mascarene Islands resulted in the serious depletion of the bird populations. Storms accompanied by a strong wind is capable of removing the feathers of birds making them vulnerable to land predators. Nests have toppled been toppled destroying chicks or breeding eggs.

During high floods, animals are forced to fend for themselves. Many have drowned because of their inability to swim to safety. In 1993, a flash flood in northern China killed 15,000 livestock. The periodic flooding in India and Bangladesh killed more livestock annually than any other cause. In 1991, a cyclone hit Bangladesh with its 20-foot storm surge that left 139,000 people and nearly half a million animals dead. The loll is often followed by epidemics that could claim even more lives.

The most recent flood (1997) in Central Europe destroyed hundreds of thousands of livestock and washed away topsoil It could mean more deaths even after the flood had receded. Sickness and diseases will continue to take its toll after the flood. Marine animals may be washed inland and left behind after the flood recedes. Unless picked up and returned to the sea, they may suffer a more severe fate of being eaten by people or dying of dehydration.

When Hurricane Andrew tore through the heart of the Everglade in 1992, it ripped off large areas of mangrove forests and 90% of the trees in many areas. The nesting sites of the wood stork were destroyed, leaving only 25 breeding pairs compared to 4,000 in the 1930s. The damaged done to the nesting sites for the red-cockaded woodpecker has delayed plans to reintroduce the birds to their old habitat. Even coral reefs in the Biscayne National Park were destroyed to the tune of more than 30%.

When Hurricane Fran went through North Carolina in 1996, the Neuse River was flooded and overflowed. Sewage treatment plants, overwhelmed by the rains, dumped millions of gallons of untreated waste into the rivers. Several hog waste ponds and junkyards were also inundated. The hog wastes containing organic runoff choked the river, depleting oxygen supply while the toxic oil and grease from the leaking junk killed aquatic life.

FOREST FRAGMENTATION

The human encroachment of natural habitats has resulted in their fragmentation. The fragmented forest increases the outer rim areas making animal-to-human contacts increasingly likely. Most destructions have been caused by logging, housing development, and roadworks passing through the natural habitat. The latter has been the cause of many vehicular accidents involving animals. In Florida, one rare panther is killed every year crossing the Alligator Alley Highway. This has forced the state government to build 36 underpasses funneling the panthers to these crosswalks. Near Orlando, Florida, the State Road 46 had claimed 15 of the more than 300 bears killed from 1976 to 1993. An eight-foot tall tunnel and fences on both sides running for a mile in both directions has been constructed to funnel the bear into it.

In a study in New Jersey, researchers found that 71% of the forest in the rural highlands consisted of patches of forest with 20 hectares or less. These habitat fragmentation divide previously contiguous populations of species into small subpopulations which enhance inbreeding.

All fragmented habitats often have roadways crisscrossing around the habitat. This adds up to additional stress for the environment in general and the animals in particular. In a study of an 80-mile corridor for motor vehicles, besides acid rain, leaches of heavy metals such as lead, nickel, copper from the disturbed soil, and disruption of the forest by arson, trampling and vandalism were present. Fires are frequently set and have resulted in animals dying and breeding places destroyed.

Cattlemen in the U.S. have been putting up barbed-wire fences to keep in their livetock. These obstacles are also fragmenting the once contiguous land. The pronghorn antelope of Wyoming's Great Divide Basin are experiencing another type of fragmentation that block their winter migration to the southern grasslands. In 1983, during the fierce winter, more than half of the pronghorn died of cold and starvation, unable to cross to the south because of the fences erected to keep in the livestock. Some antelopes have died trying to jump over the barbed-wire fences by getting hooked on the wires.

The only remedy short of restoring the habitat to its original state is by providing wildlife corridors linking up all these separate habitats for the benefit of the animals. One of these well developed corridor is the Greenways located in the

U.S. This corridor consists of well protected open spaces, following natural contours and river systems. Outdoor recreational areas are provided in places that do not disturb wildlife and to raise income for use in the maintenance of the corridor.

HUMAN SETTLEMENT

Since the advent of agriculture, mankind has started to settle down in the lowland areas. As the population increases, the need for more land to settle the increasing population led to the destruction of upland areas inhabited by wild animals. Most of the desert lands were once forested, but human activities often led to land degradation.

Not only is it necessarv for the animals to move elsewhere, they are often hunted to extinction as a form of protection against their intrusion into our homes. Studies on two species of warblers in the U.S. found that as a result of steady encroachment of suburban development, their numbers are declining because of the disturbances on their breeding.

One common problem is the presence of domestic predators brought by the owners. To determine the extent and type of predation on songbird nests, scientists set up automatic cameras overlooking artificial warbler nests with eggs. The eggs were raided constantly by a dozen types of predators. They included domestic and feral cats, raccoons, squirrels, chipmunks, skunks, blue jays and even black bears.

Many highly populated countries are using transmigration to disperse people to less crowded areas. All the countries that practice transmigration are in the tropical countries with rich biodiversity. Brazil, Indonesia, Thailand, Malaysia and the Philippines during the early 1950s, made it a government policy to repopulate the people to sparsely inhabited lands. These areas are often found deep in the forest. Swathes of forests are often cut from the jungle to provide living space and agricultural land for farming. Incentives are often given such as a year's supply of food ration and tools and seeds for farming.

In Brazil, transmigration to the Amazonia w ith massive ad campaigns promised $30 subsidies to each family for the first six to eight months, and guaranteed crop financing for workers. Once the farmers ran out of financial aids and fertilizer supply, they were often forced to burn down the forest. Uncontrolled fires destroyed more land than necessary and with it the animals that reside within.

Transmigration has been made possible by the constructions of roadways leading to these rich ecosystems. As the family of these transmigrants increased, some were forced into hunting to augment their income. This is where exotic animals were caught for the middlemen. They hue these jobless people to destroy their own ecosystem by removing exotic animals for the rich American, European and Japanese hobbyists.

The destruction of habitats by developers can be mitigated as long as there is a law that requires them to do so. In the U.S., the Clean Water Act requires property developers to replace any wetland or estuary they destroy. It is supervised by the U.S. Army Corps of Engineers under guidelines set by the Environmental Protection Agency. To be successful, it is necessary that enforcement and long-term monitoring are constantly updated

A new institutional arrangement called mitigation banking may make all the difference. Under this scheme, government agencies or private firms create wetlands as compensation to meet mitigation requirements. The value of the credits is determined by an appraiser and depends on the particular services that each wetland provides. After the credits are transferred, third parties such as conservation groups can manage the restored areas. The Environmental Law Institute estimates that in 1992 there were only 46 such banks in the U.S., and they were concentrated in rapidly growing states with suitable mitigation sites, such as Florida and California.

INVENTORY AND MONITORING OF SPECIES

There is no country on this planet that has a complete inventory of biodiversity. Few countries have the expertise and money to conduct this huge undertaking. Inventory of rare and endemic species of animals is important if we want to place them under the protection for endangered species. Although these large animals compose a small proportion of the population, they are nevertheless important. Experts from the University of the Philippines are undertaking an inventory of rare and endangered species at the 53,000-hectare Mt. Malindang National Park following the discovery of wild plants species there for medical purposes. This should not be the only reason for taking the inventory. Inventories should be taken to determine the status of any animals before they are lost forever. This will give rare species a chance to survive while under protection.

Cincinnati Museum Center research scientists identified a new mammal on the island of Panay in the central Philippines. The fourth-known species of the tree-dwelling mammals, Panay cloudrunner is a nocturnal rodent, first discovered in 1987 by Panay residents and identified in 1992 by museum center scientists. The cloudrunner, which resembles a squirrel, weighs 4.5 kilograms and is about two feet long from head to tail. They rarely come out of their dens in holes of large trees during the day.

Scientists have discovered (1997) a tiny bat and two new rodents species in the 11,000-hectare rainforest inside the Subic Bay Freeport. The finger-sized bat, about 60 millimeters tall, belongs to the *Tyonycteris pachypus* or Lesser Flat-headed bats. One of the rodents belongs to the *Chrolomys* family while the other one belongs to the *Phloemys pallidus* family. The discovery was made under a state-sponsored biodiversity project at the Subic naval base.

The WWF has been active in many countries in helping the host countries inventory their biodiversity and hotspots. In one site in Madagascar they found 51 reptile species, one of the highest density. This fact alone could help in the creation of a proposed reserve in Madagascar. The survey also led the investigators into a previously unknown patch of rain forest, possibly left over from the Pleistocene Period.

The Vu Quang area along the Laos border and the Yok Don region along Cambodia's border have made the environmental headlines the past three years with three major discoveries of new mammals species: soala (Pseudoryx nghetinhensis). giant muntjac (Megamuntiacus vuquangensis), and quang khem, a slow running deer. These animals have been living in unique pockets of ecologically and climatically stable regions for millions of years.

Several international monitoring centers have been set up to inventory and monitor biodiversity. The IUCN's Species Survival Commission (SSC) was established in 1949 to promote actions to stop the loss of biodiversity and restore them to their safe reproductive population levels. The SSC has approximately 3,500 members in 135 countries. It is divided into some 104 Specialists Groups, covering different taxonomic groups and geographical areas. It inventories, monitors and helps produce action plans for effective long-term conservation.

The World Conservation Monitoring Centre (WCMC) was founded jointly by IUCN, UNEP, and WWF to provide information and technical services for conservation and sustainable use of species. They have databases on national parks and protected areas, threatened plants and animals that conservationists can use. They keep track of endangered species and the trade in their products.

The IUCN Red Data Book which monitor the trading in wildlife are produced by the collaboration between the SSC and WCMC. The species are divided into taxonomic or geographical basis for which information regarding status, distribution, population, habitat and other pertinent data are listed. Together with the BirdLife International, they also publish the Red Lists for threatened animals, updated every two years. The Red Data List contains information on nearly 6,000 endangered and threatened animals. Both books provide a useful method for monitoring the threatened status of species.

LAND DEGRADATIONS

Land degradation comes in many forms, including surface and subsurface mining, paved land, logging, housing, pollution and many others. Their impact on wildlife often goes unnoticed. Soil erosion can easily wash many creatures living underneath the soil to less hospitable sites. It could exterminate many life forms found beneath the surface that serves as food for creatures above ground.

For mammals, the displacement from their natural habitats can be a traumatic experience. Their movement to other areas can easily disturb the habitat of the native wildlife. Deliberate introduction of new species often caused unexpected results.

The Chernobyl nuclear accident displaced 100,000 people who won't be able to return for generations. The war in the Persian Gulf made many parts of this small state uninhabitable by the burning of more than 600 oilfields after the Iraqi retreat. The devastation brought about by volcanic eruptions such as the Mount Pinatubo in the Philippines in 1991 displaced hundreds of thousands of people and the problems has not yet been resolved. All degradations are expected to reduce the habitats for animals.

The threat of starvation in the African countries of Ethiopia, Somalia, and the Sudan hangs over their heads as thousands of people are forced to look for water and food for their survival. After years of degrading the land, nature is fighting back with a vengeance.

Soil contamination and pollution have made many areas loo toxic to be inhabited. All the loss of human habitation can be only be replaced with new lands. Our dwindling land resources lead many to colonize new lands currently occupied by the wild species and indigenous people. Our modification of and while it may be an improvement for human occupation, is often a bane for the wildlife.

It is not necessary to destroy whole ecosystem in order to cause extinction. By degrading the habitat, it is possible to destroy animals which cannot adjust to the new environment. In the Columbia River, U.S. salmon and steelhead trout once harvested 19,500 tons in the 1880s had dropped dramatically to 50 tons in the 1980s. The Nature Conservancy reported drastic drops in the harvest of mussels by 67%, gray fishes by 64%, fishes by 36%, and amphibians by 36% throughout the country.

MANGROVES

Mangroves are trees that can tolerate salt water. Their roots are especially adapted to obtain oxygen from the air. They are often found in swamps and coastal areas and they provide shelter for the nursery of young fishes and prawns.

There are several similarities between natural forests being converted to plantations and mangrove swamps being converted to fish ponds. Both the natural forests and the mangroves are cut down for the timber, fuelwood and wood chips and later planted with single or two species of tree plants for the forests while the mangrove swamps are converted to raise a few species of commercial sea creatures. The biodiversity and habitats of both areas are destroyed.

The high cost of land in many urban cities have forced many land developers to reclaim areas once part of the ecological balance and well-being of the environment. Estuaries and coastal areas encompassing the continental shelves are being destroyed in the name of progress. The Sheraton Hotel in Nadi. Fiji is destroying the mangroves to build golf courses intended for their customers. In the Philippines, hundreds of hectares of continental shelves that were once the breeding ground for fish and other organisms have been reclaimed for housing and marina projects.

Attempts are being made to restore the badly damaged mangrove forests. This is done by planting small seedlings in the mud of the affected areas. This is a folly attempt to restore the mangrove swamps when we continue to destroy what's left instead of conserving it. After the mangrove forests are cut. it may be difficult if not impossible to recover because irreversible changes in the fundamental structure of the ecosystem are ensured once the trees are destroyed. This will give rise to other shrubs that can tolerate high salinity, thus reducing the space available for the slow-growing mangrove trees. Soil erosion can then easily drive new seedlings to the sea before they can be anchored on the sea bed.

MINING

Mining has always been with us for a long time. Whether it is for gravel, limestone, ferrous or non-ferrous minerals and coal, there is the problem of mine tailings that could kill organisms. A problem with surface mining is the overburden. If a mined area is to be rehabilitated, then storage practice is crucial. It may be necessary to separate topsoil and subsoil to ensure the former is not compacted, buried or in any way damaged. Even with the best storage, organisms like earthworms and other burrowing animals suffer. Once the soil is disturbed, even revegetation is difficult to return and it will be a loss of food resources for grazing animals.

Hydraulic mining, the extraction of sediments such as sand and gravel from the river bed or the bank and then the washing the material produces a lot of waste silt or tailings. This material can cause flooding and siltation problems. Floodings can kill terrestrial animals while siltation can suffocate seabed organisms.

Mining wastes, chemical and pesticide contaminations may make it difficult to revegetate the affected lands. Tailing into the river and coastal environments can kill fisheries or at least contaminate the fish which are the food of the rural people.

Cyanide and mercury contamination is becoming a serious problem in the Amazonia and the Philippines, where many small gold miners use them for processing and simply discharge the residues into the rivers. They are very toxic to aquatic animals and people who consume these animals are liable to suffer food poisoning. The Ok Tedi Copper Mine in Papua New Guinea has caused considerable damage with it tailings and pollutants and generated much social unrest. The culprit is "red mud" left after processing bauxite to alumina for making aluminum. It is very alkaline and has a high content of sodium hydroxide or sodium chloride. Once it escapes into stream and rivers, it could cause considerable damage to the aquatic ecosystems.

Some regions that are naturally rich in heavy metals like nickel, cobalt or iron such as California and Zimbabwe can cause cattle that graze over such land develop "blind taggers" due to the poison accumulated from the forage. In some areas, like the Okavango Delta in Botswana, home to many wild animals, a planned diamond mine is threatening to disrupt the jungle and the rich water ecosystem in the region.

The sea and sea bed is home to billions of tons of minerals, mostly manganese, copper, cobalt, and nickel. All these minerals are not in short supply now or in the foreseeable future. But greed is forcing some people to take the bounty before others get to it. Advances in oceanology and technology have made it possible to mine some minerals from the seabed. In the 1960s, there were 80 separate explorations going on. Lime shells are mined as raw material for Portland cement. Other heavy metals such as magnesium can be found in abundance. All these activities not only destroy the seabed and spawning grounds for many sea organisms, but the sediment disturbances can clog gills and suffocate sea organisms.

RADIOACTIVITY

During the latter part of the 20th century, additional radioactive materials which have been added to sea waters from the fallout of atmospheric bomb testings by the U.S., France and Great Britain in the South Pacific Ocean have contaminated vast areas of the ocean and displaced thousands of people. The French government testings of nuclear weapons on the atoll of the French Polynesian ended in 1996. The waste discharge from nuclear power plants and reprocessing plants, and from the use of radioactive materials in nuclear-powered submarines have added another dimension to pollution. Some eight submarines using nuclear-powered reactors are now confined in the ocean floor waiting to release their deadly cargoes of radioactive elements on the unsuspecting sea organisms.

The Chernobyl nuclear power station was the worst accident that occurred in 1986. It contaminated large areas of grazing and disrupted livestock production as far away as Wales and parts of Germany, Norway, and Sweden. Contaminated meat were buried in trenches three meters deep. Reindeer have been contaminated enough to make it necessary to ban their meat for consumption. The reindeer's staple food, the lichen is sensitive to air pollution. The lichen had absorbed the radioactive matter Caesium 137 from the fallout.

Livestock within a one-thousand sq km have experienced deformities in their offspring. While more than 100,000 people were evacuated, the animals were left behind. Their extended stay and diet of contaminated food have caused many grotesque deformities. Elsewhere in Western Europe, many contaminated animals have been destroyed. More than 100,000 reindeers were slaughtered.

Another problem has to do with the disposal of the radioactive waste. In 1957, in the Kyshtm area of the Urals (formerly USSR), a radioactive waste dump is believed to have exploded, contaminating hundreds of sq km of lands. Several villages were permanently evacuated and wetlands and streams were affected. The number of people and livestock involved were not reported. It will be centuries before the areas can be rehabilitated.

Researchers at the University of Leeds have found that feeding citric acid mycelium, a by-product of soft drink manufacturing to radioactive sheep can reduce the amount of caesium-137 in the sheep's bodies and block the isotope's absorption from contaminated fodder. Many European countries have faced the problem of radioactive sheep and other animals since the fallout of the Chernobyl nuclear accident in 1986 contaminated the soil with caesium-137. The element is absorbed from the soil by grass, which is eaten by the sheep. The researchers hope that farmers may be able to decontaminate their sheep by feeding the mycelium because the isotope has a half life of 30 years compared to centuries for the caesium to decay to an insignificant level (New Scientist. April 16. 1994).

RAINFORESTS

The rainforests comprises about 6% of the world's land surface but they are home to more than one half of the world's living animals. Most of these animals have not been catalogued and will become extinct even before they are discovered. The reasons are numerous and they all have to do with human activities. The demand for rainforest products especially logs has a great impact on it. Continued population growth has forced people to migrate to the forests in search of food, shelter and livelihood bringing havocs to wildlife in many ways. The conversion of land into agriculture by the harmful slash-and-bum method destroys more forests than is necessary. In parts of South America, forests are being cut down or burned to give way to cattle ranching.

Loss of habitats is the number one cause of extinction in the rainforests and it is imperative that people take a more direct hand in protecting the forests from farther destructions. We must stop subsidizing companies that are destroying the rainforests by boycotting their products. Stop eating hamburgers with beef coming from South America.　　　　.

Hunting and illegal poaching, together is the second cause of extinction. Very often, the animal traders engage the local inhabitants in hunting and poaching. These indigenous people are often too willing to sacrifice their own ecosystems for their survival.

RANCHING

Cattle ranching have been responsible for widespread destruction of rainforests in South America. Very much like shifting cultivation, cattle ranching is not sustainable for more than 5 years after which the cattle have to move to newer pastures. During the past 35 years, cattle has denuded wide areas in South America because of special tax credit given by governments in Central America and Brazil, and aid grants from WB. In Brazil 70% of deforestation is tied to cattle ranching. From 1960 to 1980, the combined herd of four Central American countries doubled to 9.5 million cattle at the expense of a quarter of the forest lands denuded.

Cattle raising in Brazil is a quick, cheap and easy use of raw land. Incentives such as tax holidays and duty free exemption are given but with a catch: the forest must be cleared within a certain period of time. The easiest way was to burn it, sow grass seeds and wait for the highway to pass through and sell the lot for a high profit. Cattle raising in Amazon is one of the most cynical land scams. The cattle ranch is just a smoke screen for land speculation.

ROADWAYS

The once pristine natural habitats of many terrestrial animals have been invaded by people from all walks of life. This is made possible by roads leading or passing through their natural habitats, usually following contours convenient for the motorists even if it passes through the wildlife habitats. With more than 22 million kilometers of roads and highways crisscrossing the world, and thousands of kilometers of roads being paved over annually, death and destruction to the animals naturally follow.

Road networks are a necessary part of human settlement. In the U.S. where more than 150,000 sq km were under all kinds of transportation uses, roads have caused a lot of destruction to animal habitat and their migration. The buffalo during the 19th century were hunted to almost extinction by railroad owners who hired hunters to kill them due to their migration that often damaged the railway.

Military considerations are often behind the decisions to develop forests in many tropical countries. In the Amazonian, road buildings are promoted to encourage local inhabitants to populate the jungles to set a foothold over the land surrounding the boundary of slates.

Anybody with an automobile who drives recklessly can be a hunter without using a firearm. In the U.S. alone, six limes more deer are killed by the automobiles than those killed by hunters. In UK. 200.000 rabbits and hedgehogs and over one million toads are run over by automobiles each year. Even birds are not spared, as 5,000 bam owls are killed annually in UK.

In Germany, over 500,000 hedgehogs are ran over by vehicles every year. In order to minimize the problem of dying animals, the German Hedgehog Association sets up more than 200 emergency stations throughout Germany to treat and take care of animals accidentally rolled over by the automobile.

In 1987, Roger Knutson, an American expert on roadkill wrote a book titled. Flattened Fauna, where he documented roadkill of wildlife in the U.S. According to his research, the most frequent cause of wildlife death is the accidental runover by automobiles passing through the woods. The roadkill varies from 0.429 to 4.10 animals per mile. In one 500-mile trip, a driver listed nine reptiles, 58 birds, and 161 dead mammals. But nothing beats the 598 dead rabbits in a 50-mile stretch near Boise, Idaho.

Some inventors have tried to invent devices to minimize roadway accidents. The League Against Cruel Sports of UK is marketing a device called Animal Warning Device that emits two high-frequency sounds once the speedometer hits 48 kph. It is supposed to alert the animals of an incoming vehicle nearby. It is set at the front of the car to give animals enough time to get off the road. The First American Trading Co., of California is also marketing a device called Bug-A-Way that is attached to windshield wipers that cut down insect splatters by as much as 70%.

Sometimes more direct actions are needed. In England, an estimated 20 tons of toads are run over annually during the rainy season. To reduce the accidental killings, road signs are being put up in areas where they abound. Toad tunnels have also been constructed underground. Tom Langton, organizer of Toads on Roads, together with volunteers have built six of these tunnels. In other places, volunteers have been scooping up live toads and carrying them to their breeding ponds since 1984. In 1991 alone, 8,000 volunteers relocated 200,000 toads to their ponds.

VOLCANIC ERUPTIONS

The harm caused by volcanic eruptions may be on a local basis, but sometimes it could be devastating to the endemic species. Many of these volcanoes are found in islands along the tropical countries where endemic species are often present. The low number of endemic species makes any natural catastrophy dangerous to the animals. The eruption of Mt. Pelee in 1902 caused the death of the last surviving West Indian muskrat (Megalomys dermarestii). Most islands with rich and endemic species of animals have been created by volcanic activities millions of years ago. Fortunately most of these volcanoes are extinct.

Volcanic eruptions can eject into the atmosphere vast quantities of ash and dust that are contain mostly heavy metals and soil. Once it falls down to earth and ocean, these fine particles act as pollutants that can limit sunlight penetration, taken into the bodies of marine life and block the gills of fishes. In the air, the birds unfortunate enough to fly in the path of the eruption can suck in some of these toxic ash into the bodies.

The millions of cubic meters of lahar covered large portions of the once rich agricultural lands and burying all living things in its path. The flow of lahar to the rivers, lakes and eventually to the sea will cover large portions of the sea bottom affecting the breeding places of many marine animals and possibly choke some of the corals in the vicinity. Local wildlife fortunate enough to survive the initial disaster may not be actually fortunate enough to survive its aftermath possibly from starvation or being eaten by the hungry inhabitants. The 15 to 30 million tons of sulfur dioxide emitted to the air will increase the acidity of many water systems throughout the world as it travels for thousand of miles before settling down.

WARS

In any land war, the animals are always some of the first victims to go. They are killed by the hungry soldiers and sometimes used as target practice by bored soldiers. The Arabian oryx was one example of this carnage when the Turks occupied their habitat in World War I. The Scimitar-horned oryx was wiped out from its last stronghold in the Sahel by the war in Chad. The last Pere David's deer in China was eaten during the Boxer uprising. Elephants were deliberately killed by both sides of the army during the Vietnam War to deprive the enemies of a source of arms transport. The last Syrian ostrich was killed in 1944 by hungry soldiers.

Since the end of the Second World War, there has been more than 150 wars or armed conflicts, mostly in the developing nations. These wars have caused a lot of destruction especially on the livestock. In the African continent were most of the affected people are poor, they have resorted to hunting wild animals to survive.

There are also problems with unexploded munitions in many parts of the world. In parts of North Africa, mines placed there during the Second World War numbering more than 9 millions are still a threat to humans and animals alike. So are the sites of the Egypt-Israel War of 1967 and 1973. In Falkland Island, Afghanistan, Iran, Mozambique, Angola, Cambodia, Laos, Vietnam, Korea, etc. there are mines and other munitions that have maimed peasants and livestock. In Indochina, there are over 2 million mines and 23 million unexploded artillery shells scattered over the countryside. Many of the mines are difficult to detect because plastic casings have been used. All these bombs and mines will kill indiscriminately for decades.

Poison gases such as chlorine and mustard gas (phosgene) were used in Europe during the First World War. In recent conflicts in the Middle East and Africa, it was suspected to have been used. Nine million tear gas canisters were used by the U.S. in Vietnam and they have serious effects on animals.

The Vietnam War ushered in a new era of warfare, the use of chemicals to destroy the trees harboring the enemies and depriving the enemies of food crops. Agent Orange, as the herbicide is commonly known was sprayed from aircraft over 4.5 million hectares of forest, mangrove and agricultural lands. It will take years for the land to heal.

The persistent poison can be toxic to animals and may cause mutation. Mangrove forests were specially badly affected. Norman Myers estimated that about 36% of the 7,200 sq km that had been sprayed are dead. Defoliation has also removed many of the food needed by the animals. Those that ate the affected grass and leaves either died or underwent mutation. Once the land has been treated with Agent Orange, there is little value for grazing and cultivation.

The destruction of these important ecosystems not only deprived the people of much needed food, but also destroyed or contaminated the food supply of the animals. Many local populations of valuable species of primates have been poisoned by the herbicides while other starved to death. Vietnam, which has 11 species of primates including the gibbons, macaques, and the rare Douc langur have disappeared or scattered that it may be difficult to replenish the populations.

Between 1965-1973, the U.S. bombed Laos with more than 2 million tons of bombs in a vain attempt to stop the supply lines of food and arms to the Vietcongs. The preferred weapon was the cluster bomb, a large metal container that explodes in midair and sprews 650 bomblets - small bombs - across the countryside. Each of these bombs are no larger than a tennis ball, but they kill and maim humans and animals. About a third fail to explode when they hit the earth. Each bomblet contains 85 grams of cyclotol, an explosive that bursts their metal shells into sharp slivers that can fly up to 500 meters.

The Persian Gulf has been polluted by an average of 250.000 barrels of oil annually. The Gulf War of 1990 added a new dimension to the pollution. Another environmental disaster that was deliberately instigated by the Iraqi dictator spilled six million barrels of oil. Oil was released on the western coast of the Persian Gulf smothering the rich underwater ecosystems such as coral reefs, mangrove areas and spawning and nesting grounds for many important species. Thousands of marine mammals and sea birds were also killed by the oil spill covering 600 sq miles of sea and 300 miles of coastline. The burning of the more than 600 oil wells also did its share of wrecking havoc on the environment. Animals in the zoos were killed for food while those spared are left with contaminated food and water. Grass was stained with oil, and milking cows were contaminated with chemicals from the burning oil.

The recent civil war in Rwanda caused thousands of Rwandan refugees fleeing the war to intrude into the Karisoke Reserve, home to 300 mountain gorillas. The refugees are cutting down trees to hack an escape route to Zaire. There is a big possibility that human diseases such as tuberculosis, dysentery, cholera, and flu can be transmitted to these gorillas.

Zaire is home to four UN World Heritage Sites, the Garamba, Virunga, Kahuzi-Biega National Parks and the Okapi Fauna Reserve. Fightings between the forces of deposed president Mobuto Sese Seko and new president Laurent Kabila are raging inside these parks. Equipments, anti-poaching vehicles, radios needed for the protecting the wildlife were looted in many parks. The wildlife affected includes 29 dead elephants, 24 buffalos. 16 hippos, possibly seven white rhinos, found freshly killed in Garamba National Park. The 30,000 local hippo populations ten years ago have decimated to only about 3.000 in 1996.

In Virunga National Park, the oldest park in Congo, bordering with Rwanda and Uganda, militia groups were still active and heavy poaching was still going on as the anti-poaching units protecting the park is in a state of collapse. In the last two years. 44 guards had died and twelve of the highly endangered mountain gorillas had been killed.

Ammunition dumping has been done by several countries in the ocean. Defective, obsolete, and surplus ammunitions are deliberately dumped in the ocean to reduce cost and possible accident when done on land. Warship losses during wartime also contribute a lot of munitions in the ocean. It is a major hazard on marine creatures. The ingredients used in the making of these ammunitions may be released to the surroundings. Chemical agents have been known to cause injuries to divers once they are release through the corrosion of their storage tanks.

CHAPTER 15

HUNTING

Hunting has always been a part of the heritage of people Since the early days of civilization, primitive people have engaged in hunting for food to survive, as many still do today. They killed wild animals for the food, skin for the clothings and other useful products but never as a sport. Killing is often done when the need arises because there is no way then to preserve the meat for long. Coupled with the small human population and unlimited wildlife, it didn't make a dent on the animal populations.

All these have changed as civilization flourishes and affluence of the modem world is exported to the tropical countries. Rich people go hunting and killing wildlife in the wilderness wherever they can be found. The animals are killed for the pleasure of owning a trophy and not the profits that they can get out of it. In fact many rich people spend more money than they get out of hunting. In the developed world, mammals and birds are being slaughtered by the millions. The meat of these dead animals are seldom eaten making it doubly wasteful. In the U.S., more than 200 million animals are killed by hunters annually And for every animal killed, twice that number are seriously injured and left to die slowly and painfully. A great majority killed are birds (50 million mourning doves, and 10 million ducks) which are now in dangerously low numbers.

Human beings are the worst predators. Unlike the wild animals which kill for survival, we often kill for the sake of sports and for profits. As the human population proliferates throughout the world, we are encroaching in areas that once belong to wildlife animals of the jungle and all other living inhabitants.

The shift to modern hunting gradually developed as some animals are domesticated for food and the advent of agriculture did a lot to reduce the need for hunting wildlife for survival. Some carnivores were hunted down because they are considered as vermin for killing livestock. Bounties were paid to hunters to destroy these livestock predators. Modern hunting has taken a new form as sport and done for the excitement and joy of outwitting the hapless quarry. In the U.S., even children as young as six years old can obtain license to hunt in most states. In Pennsylvania, children assist in the annual Hegins pigeon shoot, in which captive birds are freed and immediately shot. The kids' job is to wring the necks of the injured. Many methods are utilized in hunting. Sonic of the means can be considered very sadistic. Trapping and using snares can be very painful to the victims.

The other type of hunters are those engaged for the profit in endangered species. Although many animals are protected under the law or at least free from seasonal hunting, poachers kill the animals illegally and sell them for enormous profit in the black market. In the Third World countries, it is so prevalent that governments do not have the resources to police the forests against poachers Poaching can be risky, but the lucrative return could spell the doom for many mammals. As the intended target becomes rarer, the price goes up. Many poachings are done by the local inhabitants with rich middlemen financing their illegal ventures. The poaching of a rare and endangered species could mean income for the poacher for years to come.

Some animals are especially targeted for their trophy such as the horned animals. Others are killed for their beautiful furs and skins. Probably the most difficult to control are those killed for their body parts and used as medicine. This is because of the high demand and difficulties of finding a substitute and changing the old traditions.

BOWHUNTING

Bow hunting is one of the more primitive ways of hunting that has been greatly refined for modern hunters. It is use by those who prefer this type of engagement against the tame and hapless animals. Most mammals are fairly large targets. This is a cruel form of hunting because the prey is often left to suffer a slow and painful death. The animal is seldom killed instantaneously. Unless the prey is found and killed immediately, it may take hours or even days before the animal die of bleeding and infections.

In many parts of the developed countries, bowhunting is being encouraged. Contests to hunt for the biggest target is often undertaken In fact several magazines in the U.S. such as Full Draw Bow hunting. Bowhunting and Bowhunters are advocating this type of sport. Fortunately, very few people really take the time to develop the skill needed to be a good bowhunter. It has been estimated that experienced bowhunters injured more animals than the inexperienced hunters because they have far fewer misses. It will take years of experience in the field to hone the skill to really make a kill.

FIREARMS

The development of weapons of destruction has made it possible to eliminate many species in a short time. The use of firearms encourages people to be hunters. It produces less frustration in hunting as more animals can be killed at the least time by poachers and hunters. It took less than 50 years to reduce the six billion passenger pigeons in the U.S. to extinction in the wild. The same was true of the wild bisons. Fortunately and unlike the passenger pigeons, they were able to make a comeback.

The invention of firearms was the first major step in the rapid decline of many species of animals. As early as the 17th century, firearms have been in used in hunting all kinds of game animals. Improvements in the mechanisms, power and accuracy of firearms deployed against the animals abetted the killings. The saving in time and effort of loading mean more efficient killing. Powerful firearms with telescopic lens can kill an animal almost a kilometer away with increase accuracy and kill ratio. A charging elephant could be stopped on its track with a single bullet. This has also made it possible for the cowards and would-be hunters to join the craze of hunting wildlife safe from any danger. The automatic weapons used by the military are sometimes used to improve the killing machine.

The rifle has become an efficient killing weapon that render the birds as vulnerable as any land animals. They are much more visible when they are flying unaware that human predators can shoot them down.

FURS

Fur is the soft, thick, and hairy coat or skin of mammals. It is used by people as protection against the forces of nature and for decorative purposes. Almost all fur-bearing animals have a potential usefulness. Even the seemingly ugly fur can be turn into beautiful objects through the science of chemical manipulations of colors and textures.

The fur industry probably started with the primitive people who used the pelts from the animals they killed for clothing to keep warm. As the years went by, they learned to find new uses such as tents and leather bags for containing water. As early as 1.500 B.C. the Chinese were using sable skins while in India, the ermine was in demand There were few substitutes for clothing then The pharaohs and high priests of early Egypt used lion and leopard skins for ceremonial dresses and ornaments. But the commercial trading of furs probably began during the time of the Roman Empire. Merchants from Western Europe were obtaining furs from as far as Russia During the Middle Ages, furs reach their highest point of popularity. They were sought not just for clothing, but as a status symbol of the upper classmen.

Most of the products such as wallets, belts, purses, good luck rabbit tails, etc. are made of fur at a fraction of the animal's skin However, coat, wardrobe and other suitings are made from tens or hundreds if not thousands of small mammals such as muskrats, rabbits, voles, or raccoons furs. In the early days of nobility in England, the killing of fur-bearing animals were limited by royal decree to the noblemen. King Henry VIII (1491-1547) had several gowns made from sable pelts, one of them came from 350 sable pelts. Edward 1 (1239-1307) bought about half a million squirrel pelts between 1285-1288. During the 1390s Richard II (1367-1400) bought more than 100.000 pelts annually for several years.

In Russia and western Europe during the 13th and 14th centuries the fur-bearing animals in the wild were treated like common property as they are today in many countries. Hundreds of millions of animals were killed at an unsustainable rate As early as 1240. all fur-bearing animals were hunted to extinction around Kiev and Novgorod, the original centers of the trade. Hunters were forced to go beyond the cast of the Urals to find new supplies. Still the size of the Russia medieval fur trade was huge. In 1393 one ship left Novgorod for England carrying 225,000 furs. By the 1460s imports by London merchants from Novgorod had fallen to 200,000 skins a year, half of what it used to be. By the early 15th century, prices everywhere had gone up as demand increased and supply of furred animal populations declined. Throughout Europe, the fur-bearing animals were nearly extinct. The main source of beaver furs in Spain had dried up and substituted with low quality rabbit skins. By the 16th century the beaver was virtually extinct in southern Europe.

Trading in animal skins has always been big business. Once confined within each country, it quickly expanded to other countries as the animals were hunted to extinction locally. English merchants were forced to buy furs from Scotland and Ireland and later across the English Channel to Italy, Spain, Burgundy and Germany. Even with the diminishing animals, the killings continued for centuries. In the 19th century market, Scotland still managed to trap 70,000 hare and 200.000 rabbits a year.

Fur trading has given rise to the establishment of several cities that once served as outpost or trading center. Novgorod in Western Russia is one of them. The value of lands, rentals and supplies were computed in terms of the number of pelts. People in Venice bought 266,000 skins from the Hanseatic merchants in 1409. At the height of the squirrel trade Novgorod was exporting 400,000 to 500,000 skins a year to western Europe while Moscow and Kazan were selling 40,000 sable skins, beside other animal skins a year just to the traders of the Ottoman Empire.

Fur was made an important medium of payment during colonial times in the New World. England, France, Spain and Russia vied for territorial expansion to continue to fur trade. It was the fur traders in the 17th century who help populate large portions of the American continent. Competitions between England and France led to the set up of outposts along the Atlantic seaboards. Trading with the Indians for fur became a lucrative business. With the establishment in 1670 of the Hudson's Bay company, it became the greatest fur trading company in North America.

The fur business is a multi-billion dollar industry today. It is a very profitable business if you consider the number of animals killed for their furs annually. Each fur coat will need up to 15 beavers, 25 foxes, or 50 muskrats. Between forty and fifty million fur-bearing animals are killed annually in the U.S. for the fur industry. This is more than twice the number used for animal testing. The tiny chinchillas, rabbits, beavers, minks, raccoons, foxes, lynxes, otters, opossums, coyotes, and other small animals are the primary victims. Sea creatures such as minke, seals, sea lions, etc have not been spared. Almost all animals with furs are not safe from the traders. This is because they are cheaper to hunt legally or illegally. Farm breeding required capital outlay and in order to be profitable the animals have to be bred under very cheap and cruel environment.

Chinchilla are rodents found originally in South America. They grow a remarkably long, silky and soft fur which is considered the densest and thinnest in the world. They are highly priced, commanding as much as $100,000 per coat at one time. At the height of its great demand, as many as 200.000 pelts were exported from South America in a single year. This led to their extinction in Peru, and near extinction in Argentina and Chile. They are now protected by law and farms were set up to save them from extinction. The first farm was set up in 1924 in Argentina. It was unsuccessful and led to another farm being set up in California the following year. This time it was so successful, that it became the largest chinchilla farm in the world. It is from this farm that all chinchillas were exported to other parts of North America and Europe.

Germany, followed by U.S. and Japan are the three leading buyers of furs. It is a S2 billion industry in the U.S. despite the anti-fur campaigns waged against its use for decades. In these countries, the fur traders are determined to protect their interests against government regulation. In Japan, despite the ban on fur sale for many years, department stores still openly display and sold wildcat coats in the 1980s. In Germany, in 1977, a fur dealer imported 75,000 endangered wildcat skins from Brazil using a false license and another company imported 400.000 skins. Corruptions in the Third World have made all these illegal trade and smuggling possible. It is up to consumers to put a stop to this illegal trade by boycotting these furs and the stores that deal in them.

The gracefulness and majestic of big cats, with their beautiful skins, make them highly sought after by status seekers and self-conscious individuals. Wardrobes and apparels made from the big cat skins are very expensive and these animals are dangerous to trap, but the demand is there. In 1968 and 1969 alone, more than 300,000 big cat skins were imported legally into the U.S. for the clothing industry. In 1973, when the ESA took effect, the U.S. Customs exposed a massive smuggling ring caught with 250.000 skins of animals on the endangered list. Tiger skins are in demand because of its beauty and radiance. Less than 5,000 of them are left in the wild and everyday an average of one tiger is poached.

The most exploited cat today is the ocelot, found mostly in South American tropical forests. It is listed in the U.S. ESA. After years of exploitation their numbers have declined. Its rarity has pushed the cost of a coat from its skin to as high as $40,000. Nevertheless more skins are still traded than one might suppose. Many ocelot skins were exported from Paraguay, although it has been illegal for some time. It is thought that most of them had been brought illegally to Paraguay from Brazil, which also forbids their export.

Humans have high regard for babies and children, but not when they are baby animals which can be a source of large profit. The baby harp seal is one animal unfortunate enough to be blessed with a highly prized white coat for several weeks after birth. The fur coat is used for the lining of jackets and gloves which is hidden from public view. Another use made from the fur is for stuffed toys, a non-essential item for which substitutes are available.

To take advantage of the white coat, Canadians and Norwegian hunters clubbed tens of thousands of these hapless baby harp seals annually just off the Magdalene Islands and the coast of Newfoundland. Sometimes the harp seals are skinned alive. As many as 180,000 seals were killed in one year before it was banned. Only a public outcry in 1968 forced the European Economic Council (EEC) to ban the import of seal skins that effectively reduced the killing and marketing for seal furs. In 1972 the U.S. followed suit with the passage of the Marine Mammal Protection Act (MMPA), which banned the importation of seal skins into the country. However, violations are still rampant. During the year 1996, an undercover videotape exposed 144 possible violations of the Canada's Marine Mammal Regulations.

The 10-hour videotape taken over a period of eight days was released by the International Fund for Animal Welfare (IFAW). It featured seals being skinned alive, the use of hooks to catch live seals, the clubbing of seals with a boat hook, and other abuses. More than 250.000 seals were killed by hunters and fishermen. The fishermen blamed them for the declining fish catches while the hunters slaughtered them for their furs. The Canadian authority indicted 101 scalers for trying to sell 25,000 skins of protected harp seal pups and hooded pups. One of the rare antelopes strictly protected by the government is the chiru found in Tibet. Their horns are sold as traditional medicine, and their wool, known as shatoosh is highly prized in the international market. Shatoosh is also known as king of the wool, being one the finest and most expensive animal fiber in the world. Scarves of woven shatoosh come from two dead chiru have retailed between $2,500 to $3,500 at high-fashioned houses in London, Paris, and New York. The larger shawl can fetch as much as $8,500 apiece. The skins are sold to middlemen who pluck the wool and smuggle it through Nepal to Kashmir in India, where skilled weavers work the fine fibers into finished fabric, sometimes mixed with goat cashmere. In 1992, according to news account, the wools of at least 13,000 chirus were confiscated in India. CITES, together with the Chinese and Indian governments have recently began to crack down on poachers and wool dealers. Consumers need to know that shatoosh products are illegally sold in the market and must avoid them to reduce demand.

Demand for a product is the motivating factor that leads to killing endangered animals. By boycotting these products, we can send a clear message to the retailers and manufacturers that these products do not deserve our patronage. Hopefully this will inspire them to do something about the problem. Dozens of big stores such as Sears, K Mart, Harrods, etc. are no longer selling fur coats. Consumers* power have been effective in bringing this about. Fashion magazine publishers can also help by refusing to accept fur advertisements in order to reduce the market for these products.

Game shows often have fur coats as part of the advertisements or prizes. By putting pressures on TV stations, we can effectively end the awarding of fur products as prizes. Boycotting the concerned stations or the producers of the shows can be a potent weapon. Conscientious actors often have the final words on their sponsorship. Actor Peter Falk refuses to have any fur coat seen on his ABC TV series, Columbo.

Famous people and celebrities, by making known their stand against wearing fur, can induce their followers to do the same. Personalities like Clint Eastwood, Ann-Margret, Jack Lemmon. Paul Newman. Doris Day. Bo Derek. Brooke Shields, and the late Princess Diana of Wales, have been influential. Famous designers such as Bill Blass, Carolina Herrera, Oleg Cassini, and Norma Kamali, are no longer designing fur coats. The Franklin Mint had stopped trimming its dolls in real fur after briefly being the target of letter-writing and phone-in campaigns. When a group of students heard that a fur display is going to take place in their school in Fairfield County, Connecticut, four hundred students signed and circulated a petition against this wanton display. Result: the display was cancelled.

To dramatize action in a public forum against the wearing of fur coats can be a very effective. The refusal of Angela Visser of the Netherlands, winner of the 1989 Miss Universe, to accept the gift of a fur coat was seen by millions Worldwide. This is one way of bringing the plight of the fur animals into worldwide attention. Lisa Verch, a member of Students for the Ethical Treatment Animals let the organizers of the Miss Oregon contest know her refusal to accept a fur coat if she won. even though a mink coat has been part of the reward for twenty-eight years.

We can even go one step further by boycotting products made of animal skins like stuffed toys and curios. Avoid them and we will reduce their demand. Other products such as jackets, vests, and gloves are either made entirely of fur or trimmed with it. Substitutes such as fiberfill and Thinsulate are available. These materials are even warmer than those made of animal furs and have been worn in the Antarctic and Mount Everest expeditions.

People for the Ethical Treatment of Animals (PETA) based in Washington. D.C., is giving out free cards that explain why fur production is cruel to animals. These cards can be placed in coats for sale in the department stores. Prospective customers will be turned off from buying these products once they read the card. The Humane Society of the United States (HSUS), is marketing "Fur Shame" buttons and stickers. It has a poster that reads "You Should Be Ashamed to Wear Fur" as well as other information. Even designer Giorgio Armani has taken one step further by decorating the linings of his faux fur coats with an animal rights statement.

The biggest manufacturing firm of leg hold traps in the U.S. is the Wood stream Corporation, a subsidiary of Ekco Group. Inc. Boycott of their products is often the most effective weapon against big companies It is necessary to let them know the reason behind the action in order that they may change their policy.

Animal Rights Mobilization has established a Fur Free Friday that is scheduled on Friday following the Thanksgiving Day. It has become an important rallying point for anti-fur movements. It gets TV and media coverage regarding the issue of exploitation of fur animals. PETA has also set aside a day for demonstrations against Jindo's fur stores. The event occurs every Halloween night on October 31. A candlelight vigil to protest the beginning of the furbcarer killing season at Jindo's huge Korean fur farm is held in Los Angeles. San Francisco. Miami, Atlanta, New Orleans, and other cities throughout the country. In Canada, the Canadian Anti-Fur Alliance, a project of the Toronto Humane Society periodically scheduled activities on behalf of the animal rights.

Protests against the manufacture, sale and public display of fur products have been successfully waged in Western Europe. In Holland, sales of this product have dropped 80% since animal rights activists took up the cause of fur-bearing animals. In the U.S. radical groups have broken the law to release minks and foxes from their confinement. Women wearing fur garments have been targeted in Great Britain.

A problem often encountered by law enforcers against fur trading is the rampant illegal acts taken during the grace period given to fur traders. To discourage this practice, a ban should be put into effect immediately without waiting for the old stocks to be sold off. Otherwise, poachers will take advantage of the grace period to slaughter the animals and sell the illegal acquired pelts along with the legitimate ones. Furs are often smuggled to areas where enforcement is lax. In the Himalayas, nomadic tribesmen illegally hunted the rare and elusive snow leopard, smuggled them to Kashmir where they are sold alongside legally acquired skins or smuggled to Europe or Japan. One year after the ban on the export of spotted cat skins from Paraguay to West Germany, 95,000 pelts were traded. Despite the protected status of many cats are still readily available in fashion stores in Munich and Tokyo.

The legal fur markets of Europe handle 700,000 pelts from wild animals each year. Two-thirds are from the skins of small spotted cats. The illegal trade may be even greater. Traders and their suppliers have discovered ways and means of concealing the sources and destinations of illegal skins by channeling them through third party countries where they acquire legal international trade documents.

Cheating the system includes giving false declarations of species names, country of origin and purpose of import. A few years ago, a large shipment of cheetah skins was intercepted at Hong Kong's Kai Tak airport on a flight from Switzerland. The consignment was labeled Italian mink.

Furlike fabrics made from various natural and synthetic fibers can be made to resemble the genuine products. Whatever types of pelts, even from the exotic cats can be imitated. The House of Fake Furs in Paris sells many items made of fake furs and skin of endangered animals. The imitation is so good it could fool almost anybody. Some of these fabrics are acrylic, modacrylic and rayon.

To help reduce the demand, conscientious fur owners can donate fur coats to the McCrory Bears where they recycle furs into teddy bears and return a portion of their profits to the Kidney Foundation. The fur coats can be donated to animal rights movements for use in teaching others on how these fur coats are made and the cruelty it inflicts on animals. They can also be donated to orphanages for the use of poor children. There are also markets for recycled furs. These furs are either repaired or made into a variety of smaller products such as carmuffs, headbands, hats, collars, gloves, and other useful items.

HARPOON AND OTHER INNOVATIONS

The harpoon is a spearlike weapon with a line attached to the pole. It has been in use for hunting mammals and other sea creatures since the primitive times. The Eskimos are especially adept at using harpoons in hunting whales, walruses, seals, and polar bears.

The harpoon used by European whalers in the 17th century had a double-barbed head, a shaft, and a wooden pole set into a socket in the shaft. This was the standard design until about 1848, when Lewis Temple, a Negro blacksmith from Brew Bedford, adapted the design of the Eskimo harpoon, which had a bone head that became detached from the pole after harpooning. Unlike the Eskimo harpoon, however, the American designed head does not dislodge.

The first harpoon gun was invented in England in the early decades of the 18th century. Subsequent improvements made by an American, Captain Eben Pierce, revolutionized such weapons with his darting gun, first introduced in the Arctic whaling in 1865. When the harpoon was thrust into the whale, the wire was shoved back, setting off the gun trigger and firing a bomb lance that exploded after entering the whale.

In the last quarter of the 19th century the whaling industry was in severe decline because of the decimation of the slow moving whales. 1870, Svend Foyn, a Norwegian, invented a harpoon that when shot into a whale from a cannon, the barbs crushed a glass tube filled with sulfuric acid, igniting a fuse that explodes gunpowder in the harpoon tip. The gun required a stable platform provided in the form of an engine-powered catcher boat fast enough to catch the fastest whales and sturdy enough to recover them after the kill. Together, the gun and boat made it possible to hunt for the first time the rorquals, including the bluewhales and finwhales, the two largest animals ever to inhabit the earth Rorquals were once too fast and too strong to be caught with open boats and hand harpoons. Even if caught, they usually sank when they were killed and could not be recovered and towed back to the mother ship by an open boat. Another technology that provided the incentive for renewed whaling is hydrogenation, developed by in Germany in 1902. Hydrogenation removed the fishy flavor from whale oil and transformed it into a solid fat suitable for margarine, thus opening up an entirely new market for the oil. These technological innovations ushered in the era of modern whaling.

The last innovation was another Norwegian invention, the floating factory ship. This led to the greatest expansion in the history of w haling and later adopted for other sea creatures. The factory had a stern slipway through which an entire whale could be dragged on deck for quick and efficient processing Virtually all parts of the whale were used: meat for human consumption; oil for margarine, soap, specialized lubricants; bone meal for livestock fodder, fertilizers, organs for vitamins, and waxes for cosmetics.

IVORY TRADE

Ivory is a hard, creamy white material that comes from the tusks and teeth of certain mammals. It has been in use for thousands of years Furniture with ivory were found in Mesopotamia dating back to the 2nd millennium B.C. Other carvings have been dug up from ancient civilizations. The ivories used for commercial purposes today came mostly from the African elephants. They are the ideal animals because of their huge tusks. The ivory from these mammals could be six feet long and weigh from 50 to 200 pounds. For many years, elephant ivory was used extensively in the manufacturing of piano keys, but since the 1950s it has been largely replaced by synthetic materials. Today, ivory is used for hairbrushes and ornamental purposes such as figurines, objects of art and as signature seals.

The East was once supplied with ivory from the Soviet Union with its huge supply of mammoths ivory. It was estimated that between 1860 and 1900, as much as 50 tons of ivory were sold annually. From 1905 to 1914 with the completion of the Trans-Siberian Railway, at least 2,000 tons of mammoth ivory passed through Yakutsk alone The Soviet Union has gradually ban the official export, especially since World War II which caused the price of ivory to jump and made the elephant killing rampant. Even without the ban, the supply of fossil ivory could not keep up with the demand.

The history of the ivory trade is a history of deaths and sufferings of epic proportions. More human lives have been lost protecting the elephants than any other endangered species. People had been enslaved to carry the tusks to the port and later sold as slaves to Europe or the New World In his book. In Darkest Africa, Harry Morton Stanley (1841-1904) wrote of an encounter where all the adult males were massacred and the strong women and children were chained together and forced to carry elephant tusks.

In the 1980s Hong Kong was the center of a global market for ivory, importing 500 tons a year. Today, seven years after the global ban. the business has dwindled to almost nil. But the demand for signature seals - known as hankos in Japan - helps keep the ivory trade going and encourage smuggling, according to a report by TRAFFIC. Japan is the world's largest consumer of ivory today. The wealthy Japanese are particularly choosy about using ivory even though substitutes are available In 1988 alone. 2 million signature seals were used by the Japanese. Today, about a million hankos is still traded every year, coming from 96 tons of raw tusks illegally taken from 9.000 elephants.

TRAFFIC has identified serious flaws in Japan's existing ivory market. Lax control of trade in semi-finished products such as hankos allows illegal ivory to enter the market. Hong Kong still plays a pivotal role in supplying this trade by smuggling ivory to Japan via mail and couriers using a loophole in the law. Traders abuse the rule which exempts Hong Kong residents from requiring a permit to export less than five kg of ivory personal effects. That amount is equivalent to 200 finished seals. In Hong Kong, TRAFFIC investigators posing as buyers were told they could pocket small pieces or pay up to $3,500 per kg for ivory to be delivered to Japan or Taiwan. Since the 1989 ban as much as 177 tons may have been smuggled out of the territory. Stockpiles of ivory in Hong Kong have dwindled from 463 tons in 1990 to 286 tons in 1997.

Last Nov. 1996, agents of the DENR conducted a buy-bust operation against a jewelry store located in Tandang Sora, Quezon City. Philippines. It was the first seizure of ivory tusks in the Philippines. The raw ivory has an estimated value of P200.000 in the black market, and once turned into jewelry, the cost could be worth ten times.

The fate of the elephants is often tied to the economic and political stability of the nation. Idi Amin of Uganda and the Emperor Bakasso of the Central African Republic virtually exterminated the elephants within their boundary. Other corrupt politicians use ivory as a hedge against inflation. During the 1970s, Zaire was the biggest source of ivory because four members of the ruling party and a member of President Mobutu's family were involved in smuggling. A Cl30 cargo plane was flying monthly to South Africa loaded with ivory.

The importance of ivory as a currency has been recognized by governments of the African states. It was used to purchase arms and ammunitions and finance some of the revolutions and dictatorships in Africa. It is through the efforts of many NGOs especially the Environmental Investigations Agency sustained campaigns that brought a moratorium to the ivory trade.

A good substitute for ivory is the vegetable ivory found in the ivory nut. the seed of a South American palm. Vegetable ivory is used as a substitute for the manufacture of buttons and other small objects. Imitations made of hard plastics or marbles have been made without anyone aware of the difference.

Because of the high cost of ivory products, it is often the rich who can afford to buy them. The government of the rich nations of the world should sec to it that these objects of art and beauty are banned from their country and treated like illegal drugs worthy of harsh punishment. Punishment should extend to imprisonment beside confiscation. Consumers demand is often the driving force behind trade in wildlife and their body parts. It is therefore the consumers that can help put an end to the demand.

Other parts of the elephant bodies have been used to make objects for the household use. The large ear of the elephant has been made into coffee tables, the feet into umbrellas and the head stuffed for display. Other objects include belt buckle and musical instruments. The demand by China and Japan was responsible for the upsurge of ivory in 1960 that precipitated the slaughter of 100,000 elephants annually until it was banned in 1990.

As all living creatures will soon die of old age, it would be a wise move to allow the elephants to live out their entire lives. The tusks then are particularly large, and can be harvested for the benefit of the guards or owners. This is a common practice in many Africa countries because of their huge elephant population.

In Asia, many elephants often have the tips of their tusks sawn off. a practice that prevents accidents, injuries or skirmishes when they came into musth. It also helps make the main part of the tusk bigger and stronger. Whole tusk can even be removed on a fairly routine surgical procedure without killing them.

While Asia may be the market of most of our curios and jewelry products made from ivory, some African countries have also started making their own ivory products. Raw ivory tusks are polished and other carved into statues and are sold in some shops in Gabon, West Africa and probably elsewhere.

The greatest thing anyone can do for the elephants is to avoid buying ivory products. Some products may contain ivory we may not be aware of, so it is prudent to ask if any ivory has been used. The effective weapon against importers of these ivory products is the consumers' power to boycott. Refuse to accept gifts made of ivory. Be forceful and let the giver know your reasons behind your decision.

The elephants were given a reprieve on January 18, 1990 when the CITES imposed a total ban on ivory trade. The cost of ivory immediately plummeted. But recently, the meeting in Harare, Zimbabwe allowing three African countries to start selling their stockpile of ivory to the Japanese. It is fear that this action could lead to illegal poaching to complement the release of the ivory. Most of the money derived from ivory sales before, whether legal or illegal often end up in the hands of smugglers, dealers, and corrupt officials. Little is left for animal conservation or local villagers where the animals forage.

LEAD PELLETS

Lead is a naturally occurring metallic element whose toxicity is well-established. It is a cumulative poison that builds up over repeated exposures and never leaves the body. Because it is an element, it never decomposes into another substance tolerable to the body. Damage from consistent lead exposure is usually irreversible.

Children are particularly susceptible. Early symptoms of lead poisoning include abdominal pains, loss of appetite, constipation, muscle pain, weakness, a metallic taste in the mouth, excessive thirst, nausea and vomiting, headache, insomnia, depression and lethargy. Repeated low-level exposure has been found to produce anemia, stomach ailments, and permanent neuropsychological defects and behavior disorders in children, including noticeable learning difficulties, poor IQ and development tests, and short attention spans. In very high doses, lead can cause brain damage, nervous system disorders, and even death. There is no safe level for lead.

Firearms used in hunting today often use lead pellets. Before the move to ban the use of lead pellets, hunters in the U.S. have been spending 30 billion pellets annually in the wetlands. The spent lead bullets from shotguns killed 1.5 to 3 million waterfowls annually through ingestion alone, according to the U.S. Fish and Wildlife Service (FWS). These waterfowls often make the fatal mistake of eating pellets as food or pebbles used for digestion. Unlike other animals, birds do not have stomachs; instead they have gizzards that simulate the function of the stomach. Ingested food is ground up by the action of pebbles that accompany the food the bird consumes. Consequently, waterfowls that frequent shallow areas are in danger of consuming lead shots. These are then ground up in their gizzards and dissolved by digestive juices. The lead is then distributed throughout the bird's bloodstream. Many birds died of lead poisoning while others are chocked to death. The millions of tons still left in the fields will continue to kill and poison the birds for decades to come.

The FWS has finally come to grip with the problem. In the 1996-97 hunting season, it required the use of nontoxic pellets for hunting in certain designated areas of 51 the national wildlife refuges. The FWS hopes this ban will help reduce the incidental poisoning that occurs when birds pick up spent pellets. The nontoxic shot requirement will be enforced around wetlands and seasonally flooded lands where biologists believe spent lead shots pose the greatest risk to birds. Even then, this will only solve half the problem. Birds will still be ingesting pellets that can still choke them to death.

The lead poisoning of the waterfowl may not be immediately fatal to the birds. Like pesticides, it may slowly accumulate in their body. There is the possibility that humans feeding on these birds will be poisoned. In connection with lead poisoning, more than 5.000 sea birds are poisoned by lead weight discarded by anglers into the waterways. Tungsten polymer or tin rubber polymer alternatives can be used instead.

LEATHERS

We slaughter cows and pigs by the billions every year. There are ample supplies of their hides to go around for our needs. But the fashion industry fueled by customers' demand are never satisfied. They have to slaughter other animals such as snakes, crocodiles, kangaroos, caimans, lizards to supplement the supply. Some of this trade comes from legal sources, but like the illegal fur trade, much of it comes from endangered species. In 1986, El Salvador exported 134.000 caiman skins, although they have only 10.000 of them in the wild. The rest came from countries like Panama and Colombia where the caiman is also a protected species.

Beside caiman, ocelot is specially targeted in South America. Professional sharpshooters are hired for the job. Because these animals usually prowl during the night, helicopter gunships are used, flying over jungles at night in search of ocelots. Powerful searchlights are used to locate these animals. The stunned cats are shot between the eyes to avoid damaging the skins. The next morning, a party arrives to recover the bodies. The government is no match for the highly organized and mobile illegal poachers.

Shark skins are in great demand because it is one of the toughest in the market. Mexican fishermen are noted for catching sharks for their leather. The dried skins are sent to the U.S. for tanning and later made into quality shoes and cowboy boots. Because there is no ban yet on hunting sharks, it won't be long before some of the sharks will be on the endangered list.

One problem with trying to restrict trade in reptile skins is that the consuming countries in effect have formed a silent pact to ignore international controls. The primary importers of reptile skins, such as France, Japan, Italy, and Germany receive millions of hides each year, mostly from Asia and South America. Italy re-exports 90% of its tanned hides, mostly to the U.S.

Some countries have introduced crocodile farming to meet the demand for crocodile leather goods. But conservationists argue that the trade encourages illegal killing in the wild as well. When it comes to monitoring the trade, there is no way anybody can distinguish a farmed skin from a poached one. Papua New Guinea's answer is to tag the farmed skins.

The skins of monitor lizards are in great demand for making handbags. They are smuggled to Japan from Bangladesh, Indonesia and Pakistan. Snake skins are also popular, although the distinct skin patterns of pythons are easily spotted by custom agents.

The farming factory business, not content with inflicting so much suffering on farm animals has extended their business to leather tanneries. This could only lead to more senseless and cruel methods of harvesting and slaughter. Reptiles such as alligators and snakes are often skinned alive because it is cheaper than waiting to stun them into unconsciousness. Young karakul goats are boiled alive to produce tender leather for making kids gloves.

Sheep breed for wool do not fare any better although they are not killed immediately. The Merinos are especially breed to produce more wool have cause them to die of heat exhaustion during the summer months. They are not even spared from the cold of the nights. In the Middle East where the temperature difference is large, about 10% of the sheep die of exposure to the harsh weather. The shearing itself can cut and open up wounds. This is especially prevalent in computer operated shearing machines. A hot tar compound is used to seal the wounds.

LEG HOLD TRAPS

In 1865, the Maswa Game Reserve, an 800-sq-mi acacia woodland near the Serengeti National Park was home to many wildlife including elephants, rhinos, lions, leopards, kudu, and eland. Twenty years after, all the elephants and rhinos

had disappeared. The only lion found was three-legged, the other leg was cut off by a poacher's snare. In one snare line twenty lion skulls was discovered left on the line. These indiscriminate killing tools have been responsible for millions of unnecessary
suffering throughout the world.

Trapping is probably the oldest form of hunting that is still much in use today. Snares, pitfalls and baits are the prime ingredients used in capturing wild animals, dead or alive. Pitfalls are used by luring the quarry toward the traps dug along the pathways of the animals. Baits, usually the favorite diet of the animals are used to lure the quarry toward the trap. If the intended victim is to be caught dead, sharp and pointed twigs, or spears are sometimes placed in the trap to kill or badly maim the mammals. Snares such as leghold or noose are usually used to entangle the quarry. The leg is often the targeted limb for leghold and the noose is used to tighten the the neck or leg.

The steel jaw leghold trap is a hinged trap that slams tightly onto the victim s leg. The pain caused by these traps is unbearable. In their struggle to free themselves, animals bite at the trap often breaking their teeth. The struggle often tears into their flesh, severing tendons and ligaments and breaking bones, leading to serious internal and external haemorrhage.

Leghold traps are used by hunters in trapping game animals for the fur industry because it can preserve the value of the body skin. About 30 million animals are trapped in the U.S. annually, with at least 17 million animals badly mangled, suffered and die in these cruel traps that tear their flesh and break their bones. Not all trapped animals are good for the fur industry. About 25 percent of the animals caught with this method are used in the fur industry while the rest were unintended animals called "trash." Some of these animals are from the endangered species such as the eagles, owls and domestic pets.

Approximately 25% of the trapped animals bite off their own leg to free themselves only to die the slowly and painfully. Those who cannot free themselves from the traps often die of hunger or thirst before being found by the hunter, while those found by the trappers are often clubbed, strangled, drown, or stomped to death.

The European Union (EU) recognizes 14 types of injuries as indicators of poor traps that are banned and outlawed. To determine its humane use, at least 80% of the intended quarries caught in these restraining traps must not show any sign of suffering. Caught by the killer trap, the victim must fall unconscious or die within five minutes to be considered humane. All these restrictions will enable manufacturers to develop the best humane traps.

A law was passed in 1991 by the 15-nations block making it illegal by EU nations to import skins of trapped animals using the cruel leghold traps by January 1995. Protests from the U.S. and Canada led to their postponement for another year. Now it is on hold, fearing that they may lose in the World Trade Organization should the complaint be lodged there. Obviously, economic considerations and politics take precedent over and above animal welfare for most people. However, the EU has made a watered down agreement with Canada and Russia banning leghold traps for 12 species under consideration. Five other species will be outlawed from March 31, 2000, provided the deal is on place before Oct. 1, 1997.

Russia will ban the traps by Dec. 31, 1999, provided they will be given financial help. With these agreements, they hope to entice the U.S. to join in the agreement.

The leghold traps have been banned in more than 70 countries throughout the world. But in the U.S., less than a dozen states have adopted the measures banning the use of these tortuous machines. Some of these states are Rhodes Island. New Jersey, Florida. Hawaii, and Massachusetts. The U.S. government through its Department of the Interior still allows these traps on public land as part of its predator control program which aim to destroy predators considered as threats by livestock ranchers using public lands. Other more humane means of predator control are available, albeit more expensive and therefore seldom used.

Laws against the use of steel-jawed traps are often necessary to stop their use. In the absence of such a law, it is still possible to get the local authorities to order the ban. A report in The Animals' Voice magazine says that. "Los Angeles County Agricultural Commissioner E. Leon Spaugy ordered LA County trappers to stop using the steel-jawed leghold trap after county residents, responded to a report that a coyote in Topango Canyon chewed off its leg to escape from a trap, complained about the cruelty of the device to county supervisors." People in authority often respond to the wishes of their constituents. Nevertheless, actions should be taken even before a pressure point has been established

The gentle beavers were once almost hunted to extinction because of the demand for beaver hats and collars. They are often caught in underwater traps set near the breeding places where they shelter and raise their young. It often takes 20 minutes of fruitless struggle before they drown

MILITARY HUNTING

Many countries with rich wildlife and subjugated by foreign military powers are at the mercy of the military government. The military officials trained to use firearms are often trigger- happy to use them. They often set up their own safaris to hunt in the wild. In India the maharajahs during the colonial days always made it a point to organize a tiger hunt whenever they have visitors from the colonizing power.

The colonial powers in the Asian and African regions have been responsible for the decimation of large numbers of animals. They have treated the colonial countries as if they were their private hunting grounds. Safaris are undertaken by their countrymen in the wild. Sometime the military officers have taken to hunting themselves.

The French army has been ruthless in hunting activities in their colonial territories in Africa. The species were hunted with extensive means of weapons at their disposal. The gazelles of the Sahara region were herded with jeeps and gunned down with automatic weapons. Planes were used in locating the elephants and they were used as target practice with bombs and rockets. The officers did not put up any objection and were probably involved themselves. In Madagascar, soldiers of the engineering corps use dynamite on crocodiles. Fire was used against the millions of birds inhabiting the island.

MUSEUMS

The museums of the past have been responsible for the extinction of some vertebrates. Their endeavor to collect rare and endangered species from the wild only hastened the process of extinction. They often hired hunters to bring back exotic animals dead or alive. On several occasions, news of newly discovered animals often led hunters to bring samples for research or display. When the giant panda was first discovered, scores of museums immediately despatched hunters to collect these rare species for display.

Scientists in the past have made it a point to kill the species and preserve them for future reference and study. The latest example of what museum curators are willing to sacrifice to preserve a specimen for perpetuity was the Bulo Burti boubou. an extremely rare species of shrike previously unknown to Western science. When Edmund Smith caught the bird, he kept it for a year before returning it to the wild, hoping it would propagate its species. But harsh words in letters were written to journals for his actions. Museum systematists and other biologists called it shortsighted and overly sentimental. Their contention was that if scientists do not keep the bird, there will be no specimen left for the future except bits of informations.

In the past, only a few naturalists had taken the time to study the animals in their natural habitat. Most of them preferred to stay in their office studying and analysing the dead carcasses. Even if the animals were taken alive, they seldom survived the long journey. Some animals have even escaped from their confinement and drowned in the sea. Those that survived and reached their destination seldom reproduced enough to sustain the population. The low number of animals taken from the wild for display in the zoos were often not enough to propagate, and if they do, inbreeding can be a problem in the future.

The last half dozen of blue buck, now extinct were hunted down and killed by collectors for a German museum in 1799. A famous New Zealand ornithologist, killed the last 20 New Zealand quails in a single afternoon in 1868. The ivory-billed woodpecker, a rare and beautiful bird was competed by museums for its specimen. Hunters hired by museums around the world compete to see who could bring home the most number of woodpeckers before they became extinct. Every major museum seems to have managed to acquire a considerable number of them Two U.S. museums brought back 140 of them.

Museums seldom bother to make an inventory of a rare species before they start to get dead sample of the animal. The Canada's dwarf caribou, a reindeer became extinct because museums offered large rewards to hunters to track down the reindeer. Because of its rarity, there was a scientific debate on its existence. when a hunter finally killed a specimen, it proved to be the last one alive.

Museums are also responsible for the diminishing numbers of wild animals, he predicament of the California condor, a critically endangered bird was Predetermined by the fact that the museums of the world were paying large sums of money for specimens. Between 1880 and 1910, 288 condors were killed for Museum collections and several hundred eggs were stolen. By 1910 there were less than 60 condors left in the world. In 1989, 27 captive birds were left for breeding and none in the wild.

SAFARIS

Safaris of yesteryears have been responsible for the decimation of many animal species in the Africa and Asia. Today most of the safaris are undertaken under the aegis of ecotourism Instead of guns, cameras and videocams are used. However, modern safaris for killing animals as in the old days are still going on. They are responsible for the continuing decimation of large number of animals to the brink of extinction. Big game hunting has been outfitted in South America. The most desirable species are still the endangered cats. Jaguar, the largest cat in South America is highly coveted.

Hunting can bring in more money from each individual hunter than from non-hunting tourists. According to the director of Tanzania's wildlife department, an average hunter paid $12,327 each to the government during the 1991 season. But the system was so abused that the government banned hunting in 1973 only to reinstate it in 1984. However, hunting for profit should not take precedent over the lives of animals. Hunting healthy animals is the ultimate form of cruelty to animals.

A new development is the occurring for big game hunters. In many African, Asian and South American countries, professional hunters organize trips, complete with the necessary transportation facilities, hunting equipment and trackers. The preys are often indiscrimately killed, resulting in the deaths of endangered species. Many of these would-be hunters do not even recognize a rare species if they see one.

These safaris are not confined to animals in the tropical countries. In Alaska and the Far North organized safaris use airplanes to hunt polar bears. The hunters are not in any danger since they snipe at the animals in the safety of the planes. Bombs and explosives are sometimes used.

SMUGGLINGS

The reason it is difficult to stamp out animals or their body pans from smuggling is the lucrative return involved. There are also people who are willing to take risks for its large return. It is estimated that $20 billion worth of wildlife are smuggled worldwide annually, with the U.S. accounting for one-fourth of it. According to CITES 1995 figures, an estimated 5 million birds, 15 million mammals, 15 million reptile skins. 600 million fishes, and 30.000 monkeys were illegally traded throughout the world. The low figure for the primates was due to their declining numbers in the wild.

Given the current level of inspectors in the U.S., it is impossible to check every shipment and the smugglers know and take advantage of this information. In Miami, there are only four people responsible for spot checking tens of thousands of imports and exports. If an advanced country like the U.S. find it difficult to solve their smuggling problems, what can be expected from the less developed countries.

The illegal trade in animal skins and pelts and other finished products is made possible through ingenious methods used by illegal traders and smugglers. Some of these methods while crude have been found to be effective. Outright bribery is often practiced in the tropical and poor countries with large wildlife populations. Others transport the poached skins to another country where the animal is either not on their endangered list or the custom is known for its lax enforcement of laws.

Misdeclaration is often resorted by smugglers. In a consignment of 400 tins of cashew nuts bound for Singapore from India, only 140 contained nuts while the rest contained snake skins worth $1.6 million. Reusing legitimate documents for illegitimate cargo is rampant. Again bribery is often successfully resorted if other means do not work.

Sometimes it is difficult to differentiate a genuine skin from a man-made fabric. It is therefore necessary for custom officials to be trained in spotting illegal pelts. Even then, most airports do not have the manpower and time to check each incoming or outgoing passenger baggage for possible smuggled items. They are mostly concerned with terrorism. But concern for endangered animals should also be given top priority if we intend to stamp out smuggling.

Dedicated inspectors are needed in the war against smuggling. The FWS even went one step farther in stopping the illegal trade of endangered wildlife. Disregarding his own safety, a FWS agent in Miami jumped off a plane dressed like a gorilla, during one of his night-time sting operation. He surprised the smugglers who thought they were buying a stolen ape. The primate had a badge and a pair of handcuffs.

SPORTING CLAYS

For busy hunters who do not have the time to travel very far can make use of a new sport that is proliferating in many areas. These are open field sporting stations where clay pigeons, rabbits, or other fascinating animals are used. A full course can have as many as 60 stations or more using different designs. A trail weaving around the timbered hillsides, taking potshots from a different platform is sure to keep the hunters busy. According to the National Shooting Sport Foundation, 8,657,000 shooters visited the shooting clay ranges in 1993 and the number of clays shot was estimated at 700 million pieces. Even if only a fraction of these shooters visited the wilderness, it could killed a sizable animals in the wild.

Using a variety of portable sporting traps to release the clay animals, the would-be hunter can practice his skill without need of traveling into the wilderness to locate and kill live animals. These machines can simulate the flying pigeons by throwing it in various directions, speeds and ranges. For the more advance and realistic sporting clays, the hunters can visit private artificial habitats that simulate the wild. They even have covered stands that permit shooting during rain and lighting for night shooting.

SPORTSMEN

They kill for the animal's head as a trophy to be displayed at home or the skin as a souvenir to remind them of the venture they have undertaken. There is a multimillion dollar illegal industry that caters to wealthy sportsmen who wish to hunt the rare and endangered species found anywhere in the world. Many of the sites chosen are situated right inside the protected wildlife sanctuaries. It doesn't take very much for unscrupulous guides to bribe the corrupt guards manning these restricted reserves. No place seems to be safe when corrupt money is involved.

Sportsmen have been responsible for the extinction of several important species of mammals and the decimation of many others. All were done for the sheer joy or proving their manhood and bravery although they are often kept at a distance from their intended quarry.

The Barbary golden lion with its golden mane has been hunted since the days of the ancient Romans The last golden lion was killed in 1922 when the French and Arabian sportsmen invaded their territory.

The same fate awaits the Cape black-maned lion. It was hunted to extinction by the ruthless colonizing power of the British and Afrikaans marksmen who were also responsible for the extinction of the quagga and the blue buck. The last black-maned lion was killed by General Bisset in Natal in 1865.

The Bali tiger has one of the most clearly marked coat of any cat family. Its number delivered sharply between the two world wars when the local inhabitants joined their Dutch colonizers in tiger hunt. The last few tigers were shot at Sumbar Kima, West Bali on September 27, 1937. Since then it was never seen again.

Almost all terrestrial animals are under the mercy of well-to-do hunters. They often use modern automatic and high-powered weapons that animals have no match. Some even hire helicopters to hunt them down and kill them under the safety of their plane. A new law recently (1997) passed in Alaska has prohibited the use of airborne hunting of wolves in the state However, ground hunting is still allowed. The law should be extended to other mammals.

TROPHIES AND CURIOS

The trade in wildlife trophies and curios is big business if you consider that the U.S. alone imports around 30 million legal items a year. The illegal imports seized was valued at more than $7 million but a larger amount went undetected. These products include ivory jewelry and carvings, turtle shells in the form of guitars, corals, raw skins, butterflies, sponges and handbags from endangered species. These are only the tip of an iceberg. More products are traded in the less developed countries where wildlife abound. The illegal trade in wildlife is estimated at several billions of dollars a year worldwide.

One of the main reasons for hunting is for the collection of trophies and other curios that are in demand from many wealthy individuals. In most parts of the world, wild animal products are bought as status symbols for display at home or in the office to impress friends. Some people deliberately seek to possess parts from the most endangered species just as museums used to do decades ago. Others buy them unaware of the cruelty involved before they can get hold of these trophies and curios.

The range of curios can be very bizarre and varied. A gorilla's hand and tiger's skull have been converted into ashtray. An elephant's fool is made into a seat, rabbit's tail made into good luck charm, a wild cat's skin made into a rug, the antler's horn displayed on the wall, big cat and shark teeth made into necklaces, baby crocodile's head made into keychains, shoes made of caiman or snake skins, turtle shells made into spectacles for people supposedly allergic to synthetic products in France. Of a stuffed rare leopard used to cover the coffee table. The long and endless list god on as people try to find new ways to cash in on animal parts.

In many tourist areas, the souvenirs available are mostly animal furs and body parts. It is an endless list of how people will go to great lengths to cash in on animal parts. Iguanas and crocodile, are being slaughtered and made into stuffed animals for the tourists. Small animals such as scorpions are killed for the collectors. Butterflies, moths, beetles etc. are tourist attractions. These animals are killed in numerous ways depending on how the collectors want them. Stuffed animals are preserved in formalin, others are killed with cyanide or drowned in alcohol. Be wary of the things we buy, it may encourage more senseless deaths of animals.

Collectors have been responsible for a good number of species that had become extinct. As the species became rare, it becomes more expensive and the race is on to kill the last of them before someone else had the opportunity to profit from it. Museums in the past hired collectors and hunters lo stuff their institutions with these rare animals.

CHAPTER 16

CRUELTY TOWARDS ANIMALS

The pharmaceutical and cosmetic industries are the biggest users of animal testings. These multi-billion dollar industries have been responsible for the suffering and executions of countless animals worldwide. Every year, more than 14 million animals in the U.S. alone, are used to test products for the possible harmful effects of cosmetics, detergents, shampoos, toothpastes, cleaners, and other products on humans. This is on top of the millions more used in testing drugs for medical purposes. Many of these test results are useless because of the different psychological and physiological structures between people and animals. Animal bodies often respond differently to drugs and other chemical ingredients than human beings. Aspirin used for headaches with very little side effects on human is often fatal to the cats. Penicillin, an antibiotic that helps fight infection in humans, can easily kill guinea pigs.

There is no law requiring that household products be tested for toxicity on animals. Even if toxicity test has been undertaken and the result is unsatisfactory, the products are still produced and sold through the counter yet by warning users of its hazards. The tests are often made to mitigate or absolve them of any liability. Every year tens of thousands of users and children have been injured from contact with household products. There are always substitutes that can be used just as effectively as animal "volunteers."

Cruelties are not confined to the laboratories of the world. Others exploit animals in different ways. Animals are sometimes killed for their body parts or caged in a cruel way by some Chinese traders to extract vital fluids used as medicine. Ordinary people have also found ways to take advantage of animals in making a profit. The use of animals for sports is a multi-billion dollar business for many countries.

Animals have been treated as food in some of the most inhumane method the mind can conceive. Even the dogs which most of us consider as friends do not escape the way it is treated to secure adrenaline from its body. Animals have been used as entertainers in roadshows, circus, and marine parks. They are also kept under isolation in zoos for the pleasure of the viewing public. However, behind the facade, the animals are often inhumanely treated.

ALTERNATIVE TESTS

Paradoxically, neither the Lethal Dose 50 (LD50) nor the Draize test is required by law. However, they continue to use it because manufacturers of cosmetics and household cleaners want to avoid placing warning labels on the toxicity of their products. More accurate methods are available. Many cosmetics manufacturers have phased out animal tests confirming that neither these tests are necessary or the alternatives are just as effective if not better.

The EYTEX System was developed by the National Testing Corporation and is now being used to determine eye irritancy of substances as diverse as toothpaste and paint. The system is rapid, easy to perform, objective, reproducible and inexpensive. It is 90% cheaper than the Draize test and is currently in use by many research and development firms.

There are more than a thousand companies in the U.S. engaged in cosmetic and household products without using animals as guinea pigs. Tests are done through in vitro (test tube) studies with sophisticated computer simulations, cell culture systems, or organ culture tests that use chicken-egg membranes or on cloned human tissues. Furthermore, with more than 600 safe ingredients already available, there may not be the need to produce new ingredients or products for the market.

Another new innovation used to test the safety of plastics and other synthetic materials used in medical devices that come in contact with human (issues is the Agarose Diffusion Method. Heart valves, intravenous and artificial lines, and other products have been tested for irritancy with this method for more than 30 years. Adapted for use on cosmetics, this new method is about 85% to 90% cheaper compared to the Draize test. The test can be run in twenty-four hours, and in any microbiology laboratory with uniform results. The test uses cells that originally came from mice. However, these cells are now obtained from cultured immortal cell lines, so no further animals are required.

It is no longer excusable for cosmetics companies to use animals for testing their products. Avon, the world's largest cosmetics company has stopped the practice since June 1989. The same is true for Marks & Spencer, Body Shop, Nature Clean and more than a thousand manufacturers of cosmetics and household items worldwide. Many of these companies have made it possible because of their contributions to the work of the John Hopkin Center for Alternatives to animal testings in Baltimore, Maryland. The contributors later share in making the cost of product testings inexpensive and safer.

ANIMAL-FREE PRODUCTS

Animals have been with us long before we knew how to appreciate the role they play in our lives. We have used them in many ways that are considered inhumane by today's standard. They have been exploited in many products, processes, and other purposes. Consumers are often at a loss as to what products in the markets are animal-free in their ingredients or animal tested for toxicity. It is therefore imperative to pinpoint these products that we may not patronize them.

Most pesticides used at home are tested on animals. Even if they are not, they are still harmful to the environment and living things. If we are willing to boycott all these harmful products, it would reduce the demand and possibly lead to the end of manufacturing other new products that we can do without.

Protein-rich shampoos and skin creams contain animal by-products such as fetal fluids and glandular extracts. These same ingredients are sometimes used in rejuvenating people or for alleviating chronic diseases. Soap may contain tallow from the fats of farm animals and pets such as cats and dogs.

The shampoos and skin cream we use may affect the behavior of animals. Cats like to lick the hair and skin of the owners after they have used shampoo or skin cream because the active ingredients came from the animals. Dogs have been sexually aroused by certain hand creams. The ingredient in the cream is secreted from female dogs that can cause them sexual arousement.

Some of the active ingredients used in the manufacture of cosmetics and household cleaners come from the bodies of animals. Often these substances can be produced by synthetic means albeit at a higher cost. Environmentalists and conscientious people are always willing to spend more for the protection of the animals. But there are always those minority who would insists on the natural ingredients.

In China and both Koreas, thousands of bears are holed up in cramped cages that are no bigger than their bodies. The considerable stress and immobility cause the muscles and bones to atrophy and degenerate. In China alone, there are already ten thousand bears practically strapped to their cages and the government still hopes to increase their numbers to forty thousand. Everyday biles are extracted from their gall bladder by a catheter which is permanently implanted in the bile duct. It took a lot of pressures from animal welfare groups before some of these animals are allowed into a bigger living space, but many are still caged. Even with so many bears already under cage, wild bears are still being killed to meet the increasing demand and others prefer the bile from the wild bears because they are supposedly superior to farmed bears without exercise.

ANIMALS IN COMBAT

Animals have been used in combat and other related duties since the ancient times. During the First World War, 20,000 carrier pigeons were killed in combat as they served as couriers to deliver information to the Allied forces. They were even made to spy on the enemies by fitting them with miniature cameras. Some European countries still have homing pigeons as part of their war arsenals.

Dogs have been used extensively by the military in time of peace and war. During the First World War, 5,000 dogs were killed as they acted as messengers between the troops at the war front and the commanders at the rear end. In World War li, Germany had an army of 200,000 trained dogs, mostly German shepherds, guarding concentration camps. The Russian Red Army even went one step further by equipping the dogs with TNT charges and an antenna that will trigger the explosives once it touched the metal of the tank.

Some of the dogs used by the U.S. military during the Vietnam War were cruelly destroyed. The dogs were trained for many purposes such as sentry duty, flushing out tunnels used by the enemy, detecting mines, and used for scouting and tracking. After the war, many of these dogs were killed for fear that they may be ill-suited for civilian life. Others were given to the Vietnamese who find no use for them except as food for the hungry stomach.

Elephants have been used in war since ancient time. The Romans first encountered the war elephants in 280 B.C. when Pyrrhus (319-272 B.C.) organized 25,000 troops with 20 elephants to help defend the city of Tarentum in Italy.

Hannibal (247-182 B.C.) of Carthage in his war against Rome used more than 300 elephants carrying arms and supplies while crossing the Alps. After the war, Only one elephant was left standing. The Mogul emperor, Akbar the Great (1542-1605) who kept 6,000 elephants was reported to cross the Ganges with 600 'crack' elephants to conquer Bengal General Sir Robert Napier of the British Empire used 19,000 horses and mules. 8,000 camels, and 44 elephants to transport supplies and troops across vast desert to capture Magdala in order to free a British ambassador and other British subjects whom Emperor Theodore II (1818*1868) of Abyssinia seized. The Japanese in Burma during the Second World War used elephants as pack animals as did the Victcong years later. During the Vietnam War, elephants and water buffalos were killed by U.S. helicopter gunships on suspicion of carry ing arms for the Vietcong. On the other hand, the American military organized an elephant paratrooper division by tranquillizing the pachyderms and dropping them into the combat zone. The elephants were used for carrying supplies. It was a no-win situation for those unfortunate elephants.

Although the elephants are seldom used in combat today because of the sophistication of our weapons of destruction, they are nevertheless made into an important foreign exchange in many African countries undergoing upheaval. The ivories from these animals are used for paving weapons in lieu of hard currency.

Horses have been a part of human history for thousands of years. They have been hunted for food during the early man's history After they were domesticated, they have been used in warfare. More horses have died in war than all other animals combined since history. Starting in the 8th century, they were even fitted with armor for protection and were used for pulling chariots and wagons of supplies. Even today, they were still used as riding horse by commanders and officers.

Horses have made it possible for nomadic people to conquer a large portion of the Earth's land surface. The expansion of the Roman Empire has been made possible because horses then were very common The Huns. Arabs, and the Mongols were able to expand their domain with the use of horses. It was also the main transport used by Napoleon in conquering a large portion of Europe. Twenty five horses were shot from under him.

Animals in combat are not confined to the terrestrial creatures. Sea mammals especially the highly intelligent dolphins have been used for combat duties During the Vietnam War, dolphins were organized to patrol the U.S. licet in the Gulf of Tonkin. They were trained not only to search mines but also to guard against saboteurs. The dolphins were equipped with large hypodermic needles attached to high-pressured carbon dioxide cylinders and taped to their frontal head. Anyone struck with the needle is injected with carbon dioxide that causes (heir body to explode. It is believed that 60 Victcongs were killed by the dolphins Today, the U.S. Navy are still training them to hunt mines, retrieve spent torpedoes and even kill enemies by equipping them with explosive attached to their snouts They are trained to ram the device into the enemies and explode upon impact. Some have been trained as sea guards against seaborne intrusion at the Trident Nuclear Submarine Base at Bango, Washington.

Some animals are gifted with special stings lor protection against predators. The stings can be painful and even deadly. During the Biblical times, hornets

(Exodus 23:28) had been used to drive out enemies. During the medieval times beehives were hurled against enemy invaders sieging the castle. They were often used for dispersing mobs or picket lines even in this century.

CAGES

One contention often brought up by animal activists is the way animals are caged in pet shops, biomedical laboratories, and even private homes as pets. In the case of research laboratories, they are always stingy about the cage sizes because it adds expenses to change the size of cages and takes up additional rooms that may not be available. Some cages packed with monkeys in labs are so small that there is no room for them to turn around. Animals in congested cages are prone to fight and become vicious. There will always be infighting about food and water.

Pet shops often use standard size cage for puppies. The usual size is about 2 by 3 feet and 2 feet high. However, should there be additional puppies, these new dogs are caged together with others increasing the density of the cage. This could lead to more infighting and aggressiveness.

There is no standard size that can be apply for all animals. An ordinary monkey may need about three times its standing area, but others such as the macaques need large areas to roam and run. Many monkeys are arboreal and need trees to swing and exercise. For arboreal animals, cages do not satisfy the provision on psychological well-being demanded by U.S. law.

Pet owners are often unaware of the required size for a species of pet. Others could not afford to enlarge the cage size to make life easier for the pets. It is therefore imperative that the government takes the initiative by passing law specifying the minimum sizes for different species of animals. Compliance is often more effective when there is a law penalizing its noncompliance.

It has been discovered by animal behaviorists that some animals do not breed or care for their offspring once they are confined. In one study, researchers discovered that caged tigers in a zoo were not taking care of their youngs. But when a wooden partition was used to screen them from the eyes of the visitors, the female tigers started to take care of her cubs.

Zoos where animals are kept like prisoners often exhibit hostile, aggressive, withdrawn and other abnormal behaviors unlike those in the wild. This is especially true for highly intelligent animals such as elephants, bears, primates and wild cats. They often eat and sleep too much or starve themselves. Gorillas have been known to eat their own feces more often than their cousins in the wild who do it only during periods of bad weather. Gorillas are known to kill their infants because they never learn the necessary skill in the zoo. Other primates tend to self-mutilate themselves. Bears which are great travelers in the wild often end up with bloody and painful paws due to constant pacing in the small surrounding. Most animals refuse to breed and some have been known to harm their offspring or kill their receptive females like the clouded leopards. In the wild, at least the females can scramble for safety.

A study made by the Born Free Foundation, a British NGO monitoring animals in captivity has found many animals suffering from mental illnesses caused by their isolation. They found among a survey of one hundred zoos several bulumic primates, a psychotic baboon and a bear that kept pulling its hair. Stereotyping is very common among caged animals. The neurotic and repetitive behaviors occurred in almost 60S of captive bears. A polar bear at the Brookfield Zoo keeps pacing back and forth in five steps rhythm over and over again. Elephants swaying and giraffes bobbing their heads are common sights even in a zoo like San Diego that has some of the best facilities for animals. A gorilla in the Bronx Zoo repeatedly regurgitates half-digested food with her hand once a minute and eats it again while shaking its head violently.

Another study made over two years by British ethologist Marthe Kiley-Worthington around fifteen zoos in Britain found that elephants spent 22% of the time head-bobbing and biting bars. The bears spent 30% of the time pacing aimlessly, and camels wagged their tails, stamped their feet and shook their heads just like frustrated human beings. Obviously, the solution to many of these animals suffering from neurological and psychological problems is a change in their environment like those found in the wild.

CASE AGAINST ANIMAL TESTINGS

Animal experimentation is big business Of the more than 20 million animals tested each year in the U.S., 85% of them are rats and mice. Of these, 500.000 to one million are killed simply to test the toxicity of cosmetics and to comply with federal products safety law. but none specifically mandate animal testings.

In 1957 scientists plunged unanesthetized rats into the boiling water in order to measure blood changes. Beside these infamous testings, animals are also subjected to fume inhalation tests and skin reaction tests.

For thirteen years, in one medical experiment on head injury undertaken by students at the University of Pennsylvania's Head Injury Clinical Research Center. The primates were anaesthetized and strapped down and their heads are held tight inside a box opening. The heads were attached to a machine that violently snapped back and forth at sixty degrees to study the effect on their heads and necks The physical and psychological effects on (he baboons could be devastating. But what made these experiments so deplorable was that the researchers laughed at the first sign of the animals' agony. The clinic has since closed down due to public pressure.

Monkeys are sometimes dipped in boiling water to sec their reactions. Others are immersed in water and vibrated to cause damage for further studies. Infant monkeys are deafened to study their social behavior or turned into amphetamine addicts to see what happens to their stress level. The former is a useless experiment while in the latter case, there are already an excess of human addicts that can be studied for that purpose. Baby monkeys have also been isolated for 45 days to sec if they cause psychological damage. After it was found that it does, there were Plans to determine other factors such as chamber sizes, shapes and duration of confinement. Fortunately it did not materialize.

In another experiment, monkeys were deliberately driven to madness and later turned loose on their offspring to see what happened. The mother monkeys crushed their infants' skulls with their teeth All these farfetched events in actual life can only be conceived by minds of merciless people but never in the wild. At the Institute of Behavioral Research in Silent Spring, Md., arm nerves of 17 monkeys were deliberately severed to study how they would use their crippled arms by shocking the arm when they failed in the experiments. The way the experiments were undertaken is very remote to realistic human conditions and the number of monkeys used were too large, Eighty percent of the experiments involved rhesus monkeys.

In the 1970s, chimpanzees were used for testing the effects of car crashes. In 1973, NIH scientists had driven pistons into heads of unanesthetized chimps It was later found to be of little value because the primates have stronger and heavier skulls. Oftentimes, most of these unnecessary experiments are useless duplication of works done before.

Oftentimes, animals are tested in the name of scientific research that are useless and inappropriate. The wings of 74 mallard ducks were deliberately snapped to see whether these crippled birds could survive in the wild. Obviously, those ducks tested were one too many and the confirmation of the test results was worthless informations. The Pasteur Institute of France slaughtered hundreds of thousands of snakes for their venoms in spite of the oversupply of the venom worldwide. Snakes have also been killed to study the content of their stomachs to find out about their diet. In another experiment, scores of snakes were mutilated of their eyesight to determine if they would eat when blind. A simple procedure of taping the eyes should suffice.

Millions of drunkards in this world are available for analysis to study the effects of alcohol on people and their sexual behaviors. There are no better candidates than the drunkards themselves Vet many researchers have resorted to testing animals to find the answer to man-made problems. Dogs are often the first victims to this kind of experiment. They are given milk laced with alcohol to study their sexual reflexes. Rats are also subjected to alcohol to determine if animals in general have hangover problems. Chimpanzees, blowfly and even goldfish have been subjected to alcohol tests. What makes these tests objectionable in spite of its uselessness in relation to human alcoholism in that they are undertaken so often that they become absurd and cruel.

Pigs have been blow-torched and observed to sec how they respond to third-degree burns. No painkillers were used in the experiment. Again we have enough human beings suffering from burns that can be studied. At the onset, we know it is a painful experience for burn victims and no animal tests will help in reducing the pain. Even lizards are heated in the oven to see at what temperature they will die. Dogs have been suspended in hammocks and given shock treatment to study the effect of punishment on their learning ability.

Experiments have been done to determine how long it lakes different animals to drown. Man's favorite pets, the dogs and cats are not spared from these useless experiments. Healthy dogs were deprived of air to sec how long before they die. These same experiments were done on rabbits, cats and guinea pigs to determine which one will die first.

In 1961, researchers studying the effect of microwave blasts noted that unanesthetized dogs began to pant rapidly as radiation increased, their tongues swelled, skin crisped, until each dog died upon reaching 107 degree Fahrenheit in body temperature In 1960, scientists studying muscle atrophy immobilized the hind legs of cats with steel pins for 101 days until the tissues withered. In another experiment of guinea pigs, the noses were immersed in mercury. Another dog was plugged with plaster of Paris. Spiders have been killed with carbon dioxide to see if the smell would have any effect on their mates. Crickets were washed with alcohol and ether for the same purpose.

Even the flatworms are not spared from barbaric experiments. To analyze the memory of worms, experimental psychologists gave the flatworms electric shock, slicing them lengthwise, mincing worms, and feeding them to other worms, all these cruel acts just to established the effects on the memory of the worms. These unrealistic tests have no redeemable value in any scientific research.

Many drugs can be tested on terminally ill patients. People are the ideal model, because they have the same physiology and ability to convey the effectiveness of the drugs being tested on them. After more than fifty years of testing on animals for cancer cure, we still made little headway with the disease. Clinical tests on humans were responsible for the drugs used in chemotherapy treatment. Ten rare cancers can now be cured with drugs de\ eloped from human studies. The National Cancer Institute has tested more than half a million animals with only a success rate of 0.01%. This poor success rate does not justify more killing of these animals.

In this age of biotechnology and computer advances, it is possible to simulate many of the tests done on animals. These animal tests can be considered obsolete as many alternatives become available that are often better than the old animal experimentations. Mathematical and computer models, tissue and bacteria cultures, genetic engineering, eggs and discarded human placenta have been used with successful results.

CIRCUS

Another way of exploiting animals is within the venue of entertainment such as roadshows and circuses. Showmen, gypsies, and peddlers with their exhibits are small scale entertainers, but their sheer numbers add up to many animals on the roads. The animals are often chained like prisoners, mostly through a ring in the nose that is used sadistically to break any resistance. If big cats are involved they are placed in small cages that are worse than those used in the big top to save space and reduce expenses.

One way of drawing crowds used by traveling showmen was to use grotesque animals to attract people. These animals are deliberately mutilated, the more grotesque the better for business. A foot is sometimes removed to display three-footed animals. Different methods of mutilation have been used only a deranged mind can conceive.

Animals used for entertaining people do not enjoy the fun audiences seem to relish. Most of the feats they perform are difficult, uncomfortable, and outright dangerous to their health Snakes that bite are taped on the jaws and occasionally put in the refrigerator from time to time to make them sluggish and easier to handle. Many animals died by being forced to be entertainers. During the course of their lives as entertainers, these animals often travel hundreds or thousands of miles in isolated railway boxes without proper ventilation. Many do not have a chance to breathe fresh air or enjoy sunlight and food is given at sporadic intervals.

Most great shows performed by animals are accomplished after long periods of training. The animals are trained under a forced-labor situation often at the whims of the trainers. Last February 5, 1998, a news report on the local PTV 4 showed circus trainers of wild animals in UK using steel bars beating elephants and camels to move into actions. Wild cats are prodded by long metal stick inside the cage, probably to check on their viciousness.

Many methods and tricks forced on the animals are very crude and cruel. Bears are forced to ride bicycle and sometimes even motorcycle; dogs that walk on tightrope: big cats that jump into rings of fire: elephants that play with balls or forced to stand on two legs and on its head, chimpanzees that are forced to act like humans. These are tricks that are difficult to learn but are forced on them.

The first step in training wild cats is removing their claws. Then a slipknot is tied on its neck to break down their viciousness. Everytime the cat springs at his trainer, he is automatically restrained from attack by the slipknot. After a while, it will get used to the pain on the neck and settle down However, some cats have died because of broken necks with this taming method. Another method used is shock treatment to keep animals from getting too close to the trainers. As with all animals, repeated jolts of electricity will soon tame the animals to adopt to the situation.

Bears are often dressed in costumes and forced to entertain people by walking tightrope and even riding bicycles. Those forced to dance are trained in equally sadistic ways. Training starts at a very young age. First, they are decorated with rings around their noses or lips to subdue their aggressiveness while serving as chains. Then the teeth are smashed with a hammer to give courage to the trainers. After all these, the cubs are placed on a hot metal plate surrounded by attendants and trainers with sticks and electrified pitchforks to prevent them from escaping The iron plate is then heated while tambourine music is played. The heat from the plate forces the bears to jump from one foot to another to avoid getting burned while imitating dancing. After repeated sessions, everytime the bear heard the tambourine music, he will connect the music and dance spontaneously to the tune.

In many countries in Western Europe, bear dancings have been outlawed due to the efforts of animal rights groups, but Bulgaria and Italy still allow them. Greece and Turkey has recently (1997) outlawed bear dancing and even provided them a sanctuary to give these animals a chance to taste freedom they have longed for. Currently ten bears are confined in the two sanctuaries provided by government of Greece. Turkey hoped to save all dancing bears from further cruelly with the available sanctuary.

In some carnivals and fairs, bears are forced to go into a wrestling match against people. After the claws and teeth are removed, they are drugged (o remove their aggressiveness. Another common show found in carnivals is the diving mules. These animals are conditioned to dive head first into pool of water from a height of about thirty feet. Electric shocks were used to force them to take the perilous jump.

Snake charmers treat snakes in very cruel ways. Their poison fangs are yanked out without anesthesia. The fangs are violently torn from the jaws by yanking the cloth bitten earlier by the snake. It is not only very painful but dangerous to the snake for it may starve the animal to death while waiting for the jaws to heal. Thousands of snakes, especially cobras die this way from snake charmers found in Morocco, Egypt, India, Indonesian and China.

After they outlive their usefulness, the animals are often sold to the laboratories for further animal experimentations. In the case of traveling showmen, they dump the animals by chaining them to trees and leaving them to fend for themselves or allowed to starve to death.

Even if the animals were not used in the circus, just importing them from their natural habitats is a cruel way of treating the animals. When the colonial powers of India and Sri Lanka began clearing land for agriculture, elephants were caught in large numbers. At least 50 of them were exported to Europe and the U.S. Since the turn of the century at the latest, herds of 50 animals or more became the status symbol for circuses ran by Kingling, Barnum and Bailey, Kludski, Sarrasani or Krone.

Elephants are often required to do some circus tricks to astonish their audience. The most common trick for them is standing on their front and hind legs. Some of these stereotyped movements are extremely dangerous. Unless elephants are performing at circuses or helping build and remove tents, they are kept chained in the stable for up to 22 hours, with the room barely enough to sway their heads and bodies. Some are chained so close to each other that they are unable to lie down to sleep, even for a brief moment.

Public criticisms over chaining of elephants led all large circuses to introduce the electric fence. These are electrified fenced-in enclosures of various sizes to keep the elephants from moving out. Some, like the Swiss national circus, Bros. Knie, treat its elephants more humanely, without chains even in the stable tent.

Times are changing as animal rights activists are clamoring for better treatment of animals. People have start to realize the cruelty humans have inflicted on circus animals and that they are not exactly safe for people to watch. During the last decade, five performing elephants were put to death because they panicked, injured more than 40 people and killed 14 others. One elephant, Tyk, crushed her trainer to death in 1994 in Hawaii. It took 80 bullets to kill her. As a result, a bill has been filed banning wild animals from entering the state and another bill banning all animal shows. In Quincy, Massachusetts in February 1995, it became the first city in the U.S. lo ban the use of wild animals in circuses on public or private property. The ordinance also prohibits the use of domestic animals in competitive races.

The best alternative to these cruel entertainment is the human circus. The well-known Cirque du Soldi, a Montreal-based circus features only humans, using their acrobatic and other awe-inspiring acts. At least these performers have the free will not accorded the animals.

CRUELTY-FREE PRODUCTS

The cosmetic industry is a multi-billion dollar industry. The perfume sector has an annual $2 billion sale. Every year 50 new products are coming out into the market. Many of the ingredients used are tested on the animals. Make sure that the products are cruel-free before we spend our hard earned money.

Most conscientious people will be turned off knowing the products they use are based on cruel animal tests. As more people demand for cruelty-free tested products, manufacturers are heeding the power of the consumers. Many have stopped experimenting with animals in the production of cosmetics, shampoos, personal care and household products. Some have even extended their efforts in producing environmentally-safe products. Be on guard for the possibility that some manufacturers may resort to animal testings again.

Perfume production depends on certain animal body parts for fixations to retain the scent and for product safety tests. One of the products used is the musk oil. It is taken from the secretion of the gland of the male musk deer and civet cats. To obtain just a kilo of this oil will necessitate the killing of 40 adult male musk deer. The gland is cut out and dried. Beside perfumes, other parts of the gland are used in the treatment of asthma and epilepsy, stimulants for bronchitis and pneumonia and as an aphrodisiac. Traditional doctors in India use it as an effective heart and nerve stimulant and the treatment of snake bites. In 1986, it was estimated that 37,000 of these endangered species were killed illegally worldwide. In spite of the international ban against killing musk deer, France and Japan were still able to import the oil, 80% was said to be illegally obtained.

Other animal products used are the castoreum or civet extracted from the anal sex gland of beavers and civet cats, and ambergris from the intestines of the sperm whale. Civet cats in Ethiopia are kept under deplorable conditions and their anal glands are curetted at periodic intervals to collect the musk oil they secrete. Both the musk deer and the sperm whale are listed as endangered and protected by international agreements. Soon the civet cats and beavers will also be endangered as being the only source of these fixatives if some manufacturers continue using them. Although it is possible to extract without killing the civets, they are often shot or die from mishandling. More than 300 synthetic substitutes were already available in the market.

The bottom line is that we need to avoid all these personal care products when simple, inexpensive, and environmental friendly substitutes are available. Despite undergoing all these cruel animal testings, thousands of people are still being hospitalized after being poisoned or blinded by these products that get into the eye or swallowed.

The cosmetics and personal care industry is one of the least regulated by the government. Often times, we use these products without knowing the active and inert ingredients used. Whether the manufacturers are using the benign substitutes it is difficult for consumers to know since labelling often does not include the ingredients and even if it does most consumers are not aware of what they are Sometimes inert ingredients are not included in the labels although they may even be more toxic than the main ingredients.

Most of the people who use animal tested cosmetics and household cleaners do not know the cruelty inflicted on the animals. It is up to us to disseminate this information to our friends, neighbors, schoolmates, and encourage them to do the same. Unless and until the whole world knows about it, the manufacturers will continue to use animals for testings.

Information drives should include one of the most powerful weapon used by environmentalists - the power of the purse Be ready to launch a boycott of companies whose products continue to use cruel-animal tests. Most high profile companies are always wary of their reputation and will mend their methods as consumers' powers go into actions.

Boycott cruel animal tested products. This should extend to all other products made by the same manufacturers. We must let them know the reason why we are boycotting their products that they may change their mode of testing. Gillette, the maker of razors and blades, PaperMates pens, Oral B toothbrush. Liquid Paper Correction Fluid, and other products has been under attack by pro-animal consumers Despite their claims that it is no longer testing products on animals, an employee in their Rockville, Maryland laboratory was able to smuggle out videos and still photographs in 1985 of how it was still testing toxicity of products using animals. Dandruff shampoos were tested on rabbits until their skin blistered and peeled Rats were killed by forcing them to inhale massive amount of hairsprays and aerosol deodorants. Due to pressures from animal rights groups, the laboratory was closed down, but the same tests were farmed out to other laboratories.

The clothing industry also uses a lot of animal testings. The production and processing of fur, cotton, leather, wool, and the newer synthetic materials are often tested on animals. Many chemicals are used before the final product is brought out into the market. These products such as dyes, bleaches, colorings, and even pesticides need to be tested to determine their toxicity to humans.

The manufacturing processes of many cosmetics and household products in the market are unknown to the general public. Many NGOs have taken the vital step informing the public of cruelty-free products. The Buyer Beware guide is designed for travelers about endangered species that may be made into exotic products and curios. It is made available by WWF/TRAFFIC. The PETA has also come out with a Shopping Guide for Caring Consumers which list companies that refuse to test products on animals. It also published a wallet-sized list of companies that manufacture cruel-free products. Vigan Street has a catalogue of "Cruel-Free and Environmentally Safe Products" that we can avail of. These brochures could help us make intelligent decisions and bring about changes in the ways some companies treat animals. One way of boycott is to patronize other cruel-free Products. There are many other brochures that are given free by other organizations forking on behalf of animals.

DOG-EATING

Many people in the world are shocked when man's best friend, the dog is butchered and eaten by humans. People expect better treatment for the dog, but a few countries in Asia find the dog a delicacy. In the Philippines, dogs are killed not as a main dish for hungry people but as a cocktail dish or puluian The Animal Welfare Act of 1998 prohibits dog-eating, but many people are up in arms against the provision. Those who peddle these animals for slaughter keep the dogs m crammed cages, under the hot sun and left without food or water for five days. The idea is to clean the gastronomical tract of the animals before they are cooked. Many stray dogs in the Philippines are killed without a whimper from NGOs and government agency. Hopefully, all this will change with the enforcement of the new law.

On November 6, 1997, it was reported in the Philippine Inquirer that around 200 dogs in frozen pieces arrived in Manila from Bacolod City, Negros Occidental. The cargo was registered as fresh fish. On November 10, 1997, it was again reported by the same newspaper, datelined Bacolod City that 500 kilos of dog meat were confiscated in the wharf while about to be shipped to Manila, again misdeclared as fresh fish. The meats are sold in restaurants, beer houses, and even marketed in Divisoria. Each kilos is sold for about P80 to PIoo. The smuggling operations is probably run by a syndicate for some time.

Dogs have been raised as delicacy by the Polynesian and the Aztec of Mexico in early times. Today, they are still being raised in some Asian countries as a delicacy. They are often fed on vegetables and garbage like swine. Dog meat is also considered a delicacy in Indonesia, Vietnam and China. Along die Hong Kong-Canton railway line is a big attraction for selling dog meats. The dogs are crammed together in cages unaware of what fate awaits them. When a sale has been made, the dog is openly killed in public using a metal hook applied to the throat or slits with a long knife. Elsewhere, the dogs are butchered with a good bash of the hammer on the head.

One of the most cruel and horrible method ever inflicted on dog is described in the February/March 1997 issue of the magazine COLORS, herein quoted:

> "A dalmatian is dragged out of a cage and into the alley behind Chilsung market in Taegu, South Korea. As a rope tightens around its neck, the dog defecates from shock. A metal rod connected to an
> electric generator is shoved into its mouth, and electricity surges through its frame. The process is repeated several times. Stunned but not dead,, its entire body is scared with a blowtorch to burn off the fur. The whole procedure last an hour. Its purpose is to make the
> dog secrete as much adrenaline as possible at the momemt of death.
> The adrenaline-rich meat is believed to be a powerful aphrodisiac, giving men long-lasting erections. Most of the two million dogs eaten annually in South Korea are roasted or prepared as youngyangiang (healthy soup), and sold for 20,000 won (USS24) per kilogram. While the meat spoils quickly if not refrigerated, the erection, legend has it, can last for hours."

DRAIZE TEST

The Draize Acute Eye-Irritancy Test was developed more than 50 years ago by Dr. John Draize, of the U.S. FDA, as a means of screening substances being considered for chemical warfare during the Second World War. In 1944, it was adopted in the U.S. as the standard test for eye irritancy.

The Draize test is performed almost exclusively on albino rabbits. They are the preferred subjects because they are docile, cheap, and their eyes do not shed tears that will wash away the chemicals. Their clear eyes make it easy to observe destruction of eye tissue and their thin corneal membranes are extremely susceptible to injury.

During each Draize test, 6 to 18 rabbits are immobilized and placed in cages with only their heads protruding. The substance to be tested is placed in the lower lid of one eye of each rabbit. These substances can be anything from liquid, solid, powder or gel. The rabbit's eyes remain clipped open and anaesthesia is rarely administered. These rabbits are then examined at intervals of 1, 24, 48, 72, and 168 hours. Some studies continue for weeks. Reactions, which may range from severe inflammation, swelling, clouding of the cornea, to ulceration and rupture of the eyeball leading to blindness are recorded by technicians. No attempt is made to treat the rabbits or provide medications. Those rabbits who survive the tests are then used as subjects for skin-irritancy tests.

DRUG CONNECTIONS

Illegal trading in prohibited drugs is the most lucrative black market business in the world. It is followed by arms sales and the trade in wildlife. Drugs and illegal wildlife trading make a powerful and deadly combination at the expense of the wildlife. Drug smugglers have resorted to using animals in moving their contrabands across international boundaries. They have devised ingenious ways using animals as dummy. Some birds destined for the U.S. are deliberately killed and stuffed with cocaine or heroin. Because of the usual deaths during transit, custom officials do not find anything wrong and allow their importation. Another way is to conceal the liquid cocaine in bags of tropical fishes.

In Asia, drug smugglers use cages and crates made of laminated wood and heroin to export the jungle cats. Inspection is often not undertaken. In Afghanistan, they use wood laminated with hashish cages in transporting wolfhounds. Snakes are often force-fed with indigestible packets of drugs before shipment. They are later killed at their destination to recover the drugs. Crocodiles are not spared from the illegal drug smugglings. They are killed and sprayed with cocaine power passed off as white preservative. At their destination, the cocaine is simply vacuumed up.

The menace of drug addiction has impoverished a lot of drug users. Some of them have resorted to killing animals for their body parts to perpetuate their habits. In one ease investigated by the FWS in Alaska called Operation Whitecoat, some 80 natives and non-natives were charged for hunting walruses for their tusks. The ivories were then exchanged for marijuana and cocaine.

EXOTIC FOODS

Many people find it repulsive seeing exotic animals eaten as food. In China, over 100,000 exotic and often rare animals are smuggled into Hong Kong each year to treat the more affluent islanders. In certain luxury restaurants in Macao and Hong Kong they even feasted on live monkeys. The young monkey is strapped in a cage, and forced to drink alcohol to make them drowsy, then they are brought to the dining table with its head protruding from the top. A hole is bored into the monkey's head and diners feast on the live brain matter.

Bear paws are made into stew and soup in the Orient. Restaurants pay as much as 5200 for each paw and sold to gourmets for as much as $850 for a bowl of bear-paw soup. The left paw is regarded as the sweetest because it is used for collecting onev. The meat is eaten and said to be good for rheumatism, weakness, and beri-beri. The bones are used for treating rheumatism and nervousness in children. The spinal cord is used in the treatment of deafness and giddiness, promote hair growth and removes dandruff by rubbing it on the scalp.

The giant tarantula (Theraphosa leblondi) of Amazon is eaten by the Piaroa Indians and other tribes. The barbed hair is singed off and the legs and thorax are barbecued. It is supposed to taste like shrimp.

These eating habits are not confined to the East. French restaurants often serve legs cut off from live frogs. The live frogs are then thrown away, possibly thinking that it would be more humane to keep them alive. More than 4,000 tons of frog legs are imported into France annually. In one recent occasion, 20,000 live Yugoslav frogs destined for Italy were intercepted by the Austrian authority.

Whales meat are still in great demand in Japan. Norway, and Iceland as they petition the Whaling Commission to lift the ban on whaling. In fact, Japan continues to hunt for the whales despite a standing ban. Part of the reason is the large investment they poured into the whaling fleets after Great Britain and Denmark sold the fleets together w ith their quota before the ban. The quotas are granted to the ships and not to the country.

Lions are probably the only few wild cat species not on the endangered list. Polarica Inc., of New York is an exotic meats distributor. It will buy injured lions, slaughter and package the meat for sale to local restaurants that serve lion stew on its menu. In fact there are several specialized lion breeders in the U.S. breeding for the restaurants. Around 500 lions a year are raised and butchered for their meat annually.

Canning has made it possible for exotic food to be reserved far longer than refrigeration and exported to the remotest part of the globe. It is also responsible for more slaughter of animals than when they are consumed immediately. In Japan, whale meats are canned and exported abroad despite the ban on whaling. Also in Japan, bee larvae are gathered, seasoned and canned instead of allowing them to mature into bees which are far more beneficial to mankind. Rattlesnakes and elks from the U.S., crocodiles from several countries, seals from Canada, and reindeer from Norway are just some of the exotic animals slaughtered, canned and exported worldwide. Once demand picks up, it could only lead to more killings of these animals. In Germany, it is still possible to find meat coming from wild cats, reptiles, elephants, and bears.

Many animals are slaughtered under very inhumane ways. In Norway, the young reindeer calf is rounded up and slaughtered with a pneumatic hammer pummelled into the head. With mechanical efficiency, the carcass is bled, skinned, dehorned and decapitated, all within two minutes. The antlers and penis are shipped to Asia and sold as aphrodisiacs. The skin is made into seat cover. The prime cuts are sold to classy restaurants while are the rest are hermetically sealed and sterilized, canned and exported worldwide.

There are 14 horse slaughterhouses in the U.S. Each year they slaughtered more than 125,000 horses and export all of the meat to Europe and Asia. The demand for horse meat is up because of fears of mad cow disease. Between 1986 and 1995, 2.5 million horses were slaughtered, and most of them relatively young. A high percentage are racing horses especially breed while the rest are wild mustangs rounded by the Bureau of Land Management.

Birds are not free from human exotic tastes. A French favorite dish called Pate de foie gras is made from swollen livers of the geese. The geese are forced-fed with a funnel forcibly inserted into the throat of the geese to ensure the liver is of the right size and texture. Other delicacies like pickled skylark and thrush pate are in great demand. Another favorite dish is the bird's nest soup. These nests are made from the saliva of cave swift and are supposed to be gathered when the nests are empty. However, collectors often leave the chicks on the cave floor, opened to predation by voracious insects.

More often than not, we are not aware of how the food we consume are made. One of this is the widely sold dessert made by Atlantic Gelatin called Jello-O. Everyday, two million boxes of Jello-O are sold to the unsuspecting public. It may be tasty to the palates but not to the conscience of anyone who knows how it was produced. The ingredient is taken from the six-month-old calf. The slaughter of the calf starts with a jackhammer piston that is punched through the cranium of the calf. A metal rod is rammed into the hole and forced through the spinal column. Then the whole carcass is hoisted by a chain winch where the throat is slit. The fats from the body are gathered and sent to a processing plant where lipsticks and shaving creams are made. The skin is boiled in water, and the residue is filtered, dried, and grounded into powdered gelatin. The powder is then mixed with ingredients such as sugar, adipic acid, fumaric acid, disodium phosphate and other chemicals to come out with the finished product.

LETHAL DOSE 50

Lethal Dose 50 (LD50) is another very cruel test used on animals for testing the toxicity of substances. It is a gauge for determining the lethal dose that will kill half of the test animals in the test group which consists of about 40 to 200 animals. The animals are fed with substances such as toothpaste, lipstick, floor wax, hair dye, facial cream, cleanser, pesticide, and other chemicals. Depending on the type of chemicals to be tested, there are several ways to get the substance into their system. Sometimes the substance is fed through a tube inserted into an incision made in their stomach. The animals involved are mostly beagles, rabbits, and calves. These animals suffer from vomiting, convulsion, paralysis, and respiratory illness. No anaesthesia or pain killers are administered to reduce pain and suffering. These animals are observed for about 2 weeks to determine the percentage of fatality. The dosage is gradually increased until the 50% fatality is obtained to determine the LD50. Sometimes the substances are forced through the sex openings of the animals. Non-oral methods are sometimes employed such as injection for liquid substances, inhalation for gaseous substances, or applying them to the skin directly. Those animals that are fortunate to survive are killed to minimize their sufferings, instead of rehabilitating them.

The controversial LD50 test has been in use for more than 60 years. It has been the subject of attack from ordinary layman, animal activists and even the scientific circles. Its effectiveness as a gauge in determining the effect on humans has been questioned for years. Clinical experiments have shown that the lethal dose for animals often has no relation to the lethal dose applicable to human beings. The test results of LD50 are notoriously difficult to reproduce for verification. This is one reason the federal government of the U.S. does not require the LD50 test to verify product's safety. Furthermore, there are other alternative tests that are available and just as effective in determining a product's toxicity.

MILITARY TESTS

The U.S. military forces have been training animals for military purposes. During the Second World War, the Canadian Air Force had encouraged their trainee pilots to use the beluga whales for target practice. This cruel method of using live mammals for the folly of mankind should never be sanctioned. Homing pigeons were recruited, packed with explosives to act as guides for locating enemy navies and committing kamikaze. Fortunately, sensible military officers stopped the program. Other flying birds such as crows, ducks, geese and even turkeys have been recruited to carry explosive loads.

Mammals such as bats were planned as suicide bombers. The incendiary bomb weighing about an ounce was to be surgically attached to the bat. The idea was to drop these bats over Japanese cities with the fire bomb suture on them. As soon as the bat finds a refuge, usually in the attic of some buildings, it is expected to chew the suture and trigger the fuse to ignite the bomb and destroy the building.

Because of the hearing sensitivity of dogs, there was a plan to use them as guidance systems to pick up the pinging sound of submarines. Fortunately, technological advances made it unnecessary.

The weapon researchers use a lot animals in their experiments. Monkeys are the usual subjects of these lethal experiments because of their close physical anatomy to people. They have been subjected to the effects of nuclear bomb radiation and the toxicity of chemical warfare agents. In the 19S7 atomic bomb experiment, 58 rhesus macaques were put inside tubes and placed at varying distances from Ground Zero during the test. The monkeys near the flashpoint were fried and those that didn't die were returned to their cages and monitored for the after effect of radiation. Cancer is often the result of these atomic radiations. As if unsatisfied with the test result, these barbaric testings continued through the 60s and 70s. About 3,000 monkeys were subjected to 200 times the lethal dose of radiation. As if their suffering had not been enough, they were later forced to move around treadmill by electric shocks to measure their endurance.

People have been shooting one another with different calibers and at various distances. But military researchers have done their share of atrocities. They shot rhesus macaques in the head with rifles held an inch away. Others were shot in the stomach with a cannon impactor traveling at 70 mph to study abdominal trauma Monkeys have also been crippled by having heavy weights dropped on their spines.

Monkeys have been used in testing the different chemicals. Many of these chemicals have undergone similar tests in the private sector Unnecessary duplications were the norm At a government probing ground in Aberdeen. Maryland, monkeys were exposed to chemical and biological warfare agents. Organisms have been injected into their bodies for possible potential use. They have been sprayed with cholera bacterium inside isolated rooms and allowed to undergo ceaseless and draining diarrhea. Probably the deadliest virus of them all, the Ebola viruses were injected on these hapless victims and allowed to die and drown in a pool of blood. All these experiments have no value in helping the monkeys or humans in the future.

Even the pigs have been experimented for war duty. Pigs have even better sniffing ability than dogs, capable of sniffing bombs buried deeper than dogs can sniff out. The scheme was not adopted probably because it was difficult to keep up with the pigs and train them. This was not the end of the story for the pigs. The military took the liberty of surgically opening the bellies of some wild boars and implanted them with objects to determine the carrying capacity of the belly. They are going to be used to carry explosives into enemy territory.

Planned military testings of the Star War missiles on Kauai, a Hawaiian island has caused alarm recently. It is the breeding ground for the endangered monk seals, humpback whales and countless birds and mammals.

ODDITIES

Phineas Taylor Barnum (1810-1891). the fabulous showman made his fortune by displaying all sorts of human oddities during his lifetime. He almost single-handed lifted the circus to what it is today. All his freaks and oddities were work of nature. His most famous animal was Jumbo, the giant elephant he bought from the London Zoo and displayed in the U.S.

As if animals are not suffering enough under the hands of mankind, there are scientists and breeders who have nothing better to do than manipulate the genes of animals to create grotesque and disfigured animals for display or scientific study.

Goldfishes with bubble eyes have been bred for the aquarium trade. Lately, a new bubbled-eyed goldfish was developed by cross-breeding generations of deformed goldfish to produce this unique and ugly feature. The eyes are so large it was several times the size of its head. The reason for producing this grotesque creature was to sell it at premium price because there are some people who patronize them.

Mice are probably the most genetically altered laboratory animals. They have been bred for all kinds of experiments for different medical uses. Many have been developed to harbor human diseases such as Alzheimer's disease or to produce human antibodies. The British company Imutran has engineered pigs with human genes for eventual harvesting for organ transplants. The organs involved are the liver, heart and lungs. One mouse, called the rhino mouse was developed for anti-aging cosmetics. This harmless mouse was genetically manipulated so that its skin became so wrinkled that only a mother can love.

In Israel, they have genetically engineered chickens to grow almost without feathers. According to the scientist, Dr. Reem Yuris, who helped develop the bird, the chick will grow faster by a week than the normal broilers. It will also it make easier to process the featherless chicken.

Some breeders make use of inbreeding to exaggerate and produce genetic mutants. A barb pigeon was produced with cosmetic growth in its beak. Like the old carnival days, it will be shown to the public for its grotesque features and hopefully bring income to the owner.

Rabbits are deliberately bred to have their ears as big as possible. The American Rabbit Breeder's Association even award the "Standard of Excellence" for the rabbit with the biggest lop, bigger than its body. The rabbit was supposed to be a great pet, but this rabbit finds it hard to hop around and keep its head up.

Try to imagine a dog without hair. This is what happened to the Chinese crested dog. It was bred to be hairless along its entire body for its owner who suffered from allergies. Without the hair, there was no shedding and it did not smell nor harbor any flea. But generations of inbreeding produced a weak, feeble and ugly animal.

RITUALS AND TRADITIONS

Animal sacrifice had their origin in Biblical times when Abel sacrificed the first born of his sheep to God. Soon it was followed by the sacrifice of a ram instead of his son Isaac by Abraham in Mt. Moriah as a burnt offering to God. After their exodus from Egypt, animals sacrifices have been used in the cleansing of diseases and penance for their sins. Soon, the Greeks and later the Romans adopted some of these practices to sacrifice to their gods in Olympus. The night sacrifice was given to appease the chthonic powers.

Primitive people used animal sacrifice for the preservation of the life and power of the deities in order to bring abundance and grace to the people. Today, some tribes under the influence of the Iron Age still practice this ritual. Certain animals are hunted by local inhabitants and used for traditional sacrifice and ritual.

The eagles in the American continents are often hunted for their feathers and used to make the headdresses of Indian chiefs. The same practices happened to the Hawaiian Mamo (Drepanis), the New Zealand huia (Heteralocha acutirostris), and the Giant o-o (Molo nobilis). The eastern wapiti was hunted for its teeth and made into necklace.

In the island of Bali, Indonesia, indigenous people still practice animal sacrifices like they did during primitive times. On each occasion, the people gather one of every species of animals on the island, and brought them to a designated spot where the ritual dance is undertaken before the animals are butchered.

In the Mountain Province of the Philippines, ikik is a cultural practice by tribal folks in Sagada. The tribal people hunt the migratory birds from Europe and mainland Asia such as the yellow-brown shrikes, storks and blue birds. The exotic bird is turned into pinikpikan - a native delicacy done by slowly heating the bird like barbecue, singeing its feathers and later boiling it in water. This tradition, called a ritual by some environmentalists is requested to be stopped by animal advocators but to no avail.

The Ainu tribe of Siberia catch a small bear at the end of each winter and feed it for nine months before it is sacrificed. After giving the bear due honor, it is killed in ritual as they dance around the bear and later feast on it. Among the Gilyaks, the bear is sacrificed every time a kin died to send the spirit of the bear. The Todas of South India sacrifice a bull calf every year and the adult men have to eat them in the forest. In many satanic cults in the West, cats and dogs are often stolen from towns and sacrifice.

SEAFOODS

People since prehistoric times have been consuming seafood. As more people are becoming affluent, their tastes for sea creatures also increase along with their wealth. While many animal rights activists have condemned the treatment of livestock to produce cheap meat for the consumers, a lesser known barbaric treatment of sea creatures is being eaten alive in a few Asian restaurants.

The serving of live shellfish especially prawns and lobsters is being condemned by many quarters. Taiwan restaurants are noted for this eating practice. The lobsters are eaten alive usually by the use of chopsticks. Most complaints centered on consumers sticking the chopstick on the live lobster while it tries to crawl off the plate. In one restaurant in Australia, live lobster is served on a plate with its head partially severed and its shell cracked open, allowing diners to pick on the living flesh. Even if they are cooked, lobsters, crabs, and other crustaceans are often steamed or cooked alive.

On the other hand, prawns are eaten in a new way of cooking known as "drunken or screaming prawns." The live prawns are soaked in alcohol and set afire. The "screaming prawns" are so named after the noise they make when they are fried alive.

In many countries, laws against cruelty to animals often do not apply to the treatment received by sea creatures consumed by people. But it has long been established that crustaceans and other shellfishes feel pain and should therefore be included. When any quiet animal starts to "scream," it could only mean that it is feeling the pain of being fried alive.

The state parliament of New South Wales is reportedly set to include all the shellfishes under the law against cruelty towards animals. Under the amendments, Irving live prawns and lobsters will be outlawed and penalties will include a two-year jail sentence and a hefty fine of about $7,500.

The giant clam (Tridacna gigas) is prized by poachers for its shell and by food lovers for the high protein meat in its adductor muscle. Because of their decimation, it has been listed by IUCN as an endangered species. The Australian Navy has stepped in to help prevent its extinction in many South Pacific islands and in the Great Barrier Reef. Many of these 2-foot clams weighing 40 pounds each have transferred to undisclosed places.

Turtles are often caught and turned into soup. Most wild species are under threat as demand continues to rise. Because of the declining population, others have started to rear turtles on farms for their meat and making soup. To keep them fresh before cooking, they found it necessary to leave them on their backs for hours.

SILKWORMS

Just as fur-bearing animals are reared and later killed for their furs, silkworms are also farmed and later killed for their silk. The silk is produced from the salivary gland of some insects and the abdominal gland of spiders. The delicate silk threads are used to weave shelter commonly known as a cocoon to protect the young pupa.

The common caterpillar that is farmed for its silk thread came from the moth Bombyx mari. For 4,000 years, the silkworm moths have been reared in farms to by eggs by the hundreds. Each moth can deposit more than 500 eggs, which can produce the silk in three weeks. The eggs are glued together by a very sticky mucilaginous secretion. Once the caterpillars are hatched, they are placed on mulberry leaves and to consume foliage approximating its own weight. After six weeks and three inches long, they will stop feeding and start spinning silk to form the cocoons. For about five days, it will shake its head about 300,000 times to produce about 600 to 900 meters of silk. Before the hatching, the farmers kill the pupae by boiling, applying acid, gassing or steaming ihem alive before they break the silk threads to ensure the fine yarns of consistency in size and strength.

Their instinct for survival made them spin the cocoon to protect against predators only to be killed under the human hands Like all living animals they too feel pain. Until people have devised a way of harnessing the silk without killing the pupae, they should be left alone.

We can stop buying clothes made of silk if we want to reduce if not totally eliminate the culture of silkworms for the silk. Alternatives to silk include alginate fibers from seaweed, ardil from peanuts, and vicara from maize.

SPORTS CRUELTY

During ancient times and even until the 19th century, some tribes in South America still revered the wild cats. The Egyptians especially revered the big cats in many of their practices. But in a relatively short time, the Roman emperors managed to convert the mysticism and reverence for animals into a blood thirsty appetite for violent sport. Augustus Caesar (63-14 B.C.) allowed the killing of 3,500 wild cats including a snake said to be 25 meters long during his reign. Nero (37-68 A.D.) once set a company of horsemen against a collection of400 bears and 300 lions. The Colosseum was sometimes flooded so that gladiators could kill hippos, crocodiles and seals. Titus (39-81 A.D.) in the three years between 79 and 81 A .D. was responsible for the death of 5,000 animals. Not to be undone, after the conquest of Dacia (Romania) in 106 A .D. Trajan (53-117 A D.) celebrated for four months. Gladiators in Colosseum were forced to fight wild cats in the arena for the entertainment of the elites. As many as 10,000 gladiators died together with 11,000 animals during this celebration.

In Turkey, camels are trained to wrestle one another for human entertainment during the Camel Wrestling Festival. The organizers took advantage of the mating season when the males are especially aggressive and encourage the camels to fight until one crushes the other with its weight. It is difficult to understand how the deranged minds of some people can conceive using the clumsy camels for sport entertainment. In some parts of Asia, the huge elephants have been trained to amuse the people. They are forced by their mahouts to collide head on with each other in a fight until death.

Badgers have been subjected to cruelties in Britain much like the other rodents and foxes that hide in burrows and holes. Until the passage of the Protection of Badgers Act in 1992, they are often dug up in their dens and flush out with hound dogs. Even with the passage of the law banning the practice, they are still being dug up in South Yorkshire and in northern England, and killed as pests. Now, a group of conservationists called Badger Group are building badger bunkers. Pipes are laid in deep trenches leading to chambers of concrete reinforced with steel and concrete on top.

The first attempt to outlaw cruel bloodsport in Britain was made in 1800 when MP Sir William Pulteney introduced a bill banning bull- and bear-baiting with dogs. It was narrowly defeated by two votes. Bear-baiting largely died on its own because of the decimation of the animals in Europe and the high cost of importing them from North America. It was formally outlawed in 1835, thanks to the tireless effort of MP Joseph Pease, a member of the RSPCA committee who introduced the bill. Along with the Act were bans on cockfighting and dogfighting. But the legislation was not fully effective in ending cockfighting until the 1911 Protection of Animals Act made it illegal to keep a place for cockfighting purposes. The law was further strengthened in 1952 with the Cockfighting Act that made it illegal to possess any instrument or appliance that can be adopted for cockfighting.

SPORTS CRUELTY: BEARS

The Ancient Romans were particularly barbarous in their treatment of bears. The brown bears were forced to fight against dogs and gladiators for the amusement of the people. Even the polar bears had been pitted against seals in underwater combat. A wealthy Roman who later became Gordian I (159-238 A.D.) sponsored an event in the Colosseum resulting in the senseless slaughters of more than 1,000 bears by fully armed gladiators. The bears were no match for the gladiators.

Another cruel sport is bear-baiting. It evolved in Europe during the Middle Ages and is still going today in Pakistan as an amusement. It was once very popular for centuries in Europe and continued until it was gradually banned in most countries. In England, it was so popular that even Queen Elizabeth I (1533-1603) was an avid spectator and supporter. The bear used for baiting is first blinded and then chained either by its neck or hind leg and led to the baiting pit where a pack of dogs await it.

The 19th century Californians also find this cruel sport very amusing to their taste. They would arrange prize fights between grizzlies and the Spanish bulls. The reluctant bear was goaded into fighting by sticks with nails at the end. Many bears died as a result of this cruel sport, a major cause of its extinction in California.

SPORTS CRUELTY: BULL

People have always been fascinated at the cruelty some animals can inflict on other animals. In Britain, an eyewitness account reported by Zacharias Conrad von Uffenbach in London, in 1710 depicts the cruel sport of bull-baiting.

"Towards evening we drove to see the bull-baiting, which is held here nearly every Monday in two places. On the morning of the day the bull, or any other creature that is to be baited, is led round. It takes place in a large open space or courtyard, on two sides of which high benches have been made for the spectators.

First a young ox or bull was lead in and fastened by a long rope to an iron ring in the middle of the yard; then about thirty dogs, two or three at a time, were let loose on him, but he made short work of them, goring them and tossing them high in the air above the height of the first storey. Then amid shouts and yells the butchers to whom the dogs belonged sprang forward and caught their beasts right side up to break their fall. They had to keep fast hold of the dogs to hinder them from returning to the attack without barking. Several had such a grip of the bull's throat or ear that their mouths had to be forced open with poles. When the bull had stood it tolerably long, they brought out a small bear and tied him up in the same fashion. As soon as the dogs had at him, he stood up on his hind legs and gave some terrific buffers; but if one of them got at his skin, he rolled about in such a fashion that the dogs thought themselves lucky if they came out safe from beneath him. But the most diverting and worst of all was a little common ass, who was brought out saddled with an ape on his back. As soon as a couple of dogs had been let loose on him he broke into a prodigious gallop - for he was free, not having been tied up like the other beasts - and he stamped and bit all round himself. The ape began to scream most terribly for fear of falling off. If the dogs came too near him, he seized them with his mouth and twirled them round, shaking them so much that they howled prodigiously. Finally another bull appeared, on whom several crackers had been hung: when these were lit and several dogs let loose on him on a sudden, there was a monstrous hurly-burly. And thus was concluded this truly English sport, which vastly delights this nation but to me seemed nothing very special."

From ancient times until as late as the Middle Ages, the bulls have been treated with divinity in many places. The Phoenicians, Indians, and the Romans have established a cult of bull worship. Other used the bull as a form of sacrifice to appease the gods. In Greek mythology, Zeus was considered a bull god while his wife Hera was a cow goddess.

Today, all these have changed to the detriment of the bulls. The bull cults have given way to a new form of public entertainment: bullfighting. The Spanish bull,

especially bred for fighting is no longer a sacrifice to the gods. Like most sports of men pitting against beasts, the encounters often result in the death of the animals. It is a one-way fight to the death for the animal. They are bred to die in gory in the arena for the entertainment of the blood thirsty audience.

The modern bullfighting is probably the most ruthless form of sport cruelty sanctioned by some governments. It started in Crete during the ancient times as an offering to the gods, but humans found the bloody sport interesting enough to adopt it. Modern bullfighting started in Spain in the early 18th century. It was so popular that more than 400 bullrings have been established throughout Spain. It has also been exported to Central and South America, and in European countries like France, Italy, and Portugal. Animal activists were up in arms when it was newly established in Macao, a Portuguese colony last year. The promoters hoped to expand to mainland China in the near future.

Every year about thirty thousand bulls are killed worldwide, half of them in Spain. Before the bulls are released, they are tormented and weakened to reduce their aggressiveness Many attempts are taken to reduce the danger faced by the matador. The eyes of the bulls are smeared with Vaseline to blur their vision, the horns are filed to reduce the sharpness, and cotton is stuffed into the nostrils to shorten their breath.

Along with the bulls are hundreds of horses killed. The horses wore blinders on the side from where the bulls attack. They are often drugged and their vocal cords cut to reduce any possible scream that tourists may hear. Portugal, where the bulls are not killed in the ring, are put under a prolonged and agonizing ritual of healing. It is difficult to stop this type of sport as long as government sanctions them. But we can do our share by refusing to patronize it.

SPORTS CRUELTY: COCK FIGHTING

Cockfighting has been popular in ancient times in India, China, Persia, and other eastern countries. It was exported to Greece during the time of Themistocles (524-459 B.C.) when he first noticed two cocks fighting during a military venture. Upon returning home he honored the victory with cockfighting. From Greece the sport spread to other areas in Europe. It was introduced to England from Rome where the sport is particularly popular among the royalties. Henry VIII (1491-1547) even added a Royal Cockpit to his palace in Whitehall. They even had "battle royal" contests where all the cocks are placed in a pit and allowed to fight until one survivor is left. Other variations include the "Welch Main," where through the process of elimination, starting with eight pairs were allowed to eliminate one another until only one pair is left.

Today, the bloody sport is still common in many countries. The cocks are forced to fight to the death, often fitted with sharp knives or spurs on each leg to facilitate the death ritual. Heavy betting is involved, making it even more interesting to the aficionados.

SPORTS CRUELTY: CRICKETS

Crickets are any of the group of insects known mostly for their chirping noises. Only the male can produce a chirp by elevating their upper pair of wings and rubbing one wing over the other. The sound or song is either made to attract mates for courting or as a fighting song to repel other males. The crickets are so common they are found almost everywhere in the world.

The Chinese have for centuries taken advantage of the cricket fighting spirit. They have been betting on cricket sport which is very popular. Crickets are even trained and selected for their fighting ability. Two male crickets are placed in a small box laid with straw. Being territorial, the cricket will initially sound out his opponent with its antennae. Aggression can be heightened by stroking on their antennae with a fine straw. To facilitate fighting, crickets are sometimes put along a single narrow file surrounded by walls so that there is no way the cricket can move except forward and towards each other. The fight is often to the death and serious injuries for the winner is very common. This is a deadly sport even though the animals involved may be small.

SPORTS CRUELTY: DOGS

Greyhound racing is very prevalent in the U.S. Only five states, Maine, Virginia, Vermont, Idaho, and Washington have laws banning them. Massachusetts may soon follow if the bill is passed. As many as fifty thousand greyhounds are especially bred for this sport, but less than 30% will make it. Those that have no chance of winning are often euthanized or sold to laboratories. Others are sent to Mexico to continue the race until they die. Many greyhounds have a short lifespan. According to the National Greyhound Association, which keeps track of all the records, 12,000 racing greyhounds were killed in 1995 while 16.000 were adopted. Others were sold to laboratories. During their training days, live rabbits or kittens are used as baits and they often end up dead.

Training greyhounds can be very cruel. According to the Animal Protection Institute, more than 100,000 rabbits, chickens, guinea pigs, and even kittens are used as bait annually. Rabbits turn lose in the field can provide a good chase, but to ensure that they do not escape, their hind legs are sometimes broken. Using the illegal baiting method, the preys are attached upside down to mechanical arms that spin around the track at 35 mph. being chased down by the dog. A stop to greyhound racing will put an end to breeding dogs for this cruel sport.

Dogs are also used in sled dog racing through the snow. Because of the rigorous drive undertaken by dogs, it could be fatal to them. In the 1997 Iditarod Trail Sled Dog Race, a distance of 1,161- mile race from Anchorage to Nome in Alaska, five dogs died from the cruel race. In the 25-year history of the race, other causes of deaths wqre drowning, moose attack, and entanglement from leads. Animal welfare groups are requesting for a shortened race, but only a total ban ought to be imposed.

Dog fighting while illegal in almost all countries in the world are also rampant in many places. In all the U.S. states, dogfighting is illegal, but in California this nefarious activity is specially rampant. This clandestine sport is difficult to uncover because it seems to be an exclusive club among aficionados. The ugliness of the sport can be seen when the dogs, with their long protruding mouth are tearing apart with their loeked jaws relentlessly. This has lead some states to consider the cruel sport a felony punishable by imprisonment.

SPORTS CRUELTY: HORSES

Animals have been used for amusement and entertainment in many parts of the world. Horses have been subjected to torturous contests. Not only are they forced to outrun each other. They are sometimes called to do strenuous works or amusement contests. In one county fair in Flora, Illinois, the horses were required to drag a 3-ton concrete block in a contest of power. Several horse-killing-for-profit schemes have been uncovered recently, involving mostly racing horses.

The center piece of any rodeo show is the bucking-bronco act. Sometimes, the domestic animals and not the real wild horses were used. The tame horses are agitated into "wild horses" with the use of bucking straps placed and tightened in the area of the genitalia to agitate them. Horses often end up with broken legs and later slaughtered.

Horse racing is a very popular gambling sport everywhere they are found. The U.S. has far more horses today because of breeding for the race horses. They will not hesitate to destroy the horses that do not perform well because caring for them can be expensive. The fate of the losing horses is one of the cruel act done on the animals. The horses are trucked to Canada and shipped to Europe where they are slaughtered and eaten by those who consider horsemeat a delicacy.

One cruel acts perpetuated on horses as sport is practiced in several towns and cities in Mindanao. There, the horses are enticed to fight with the winning horse getting the mare as a prize. Before the fight began, a mare was brought out and tied in the middle of the ring. A stallion is brought out to smell the mare for about 15 minutes. Another stallion is brought near the mare that causes strong and violent reaction from the first stallion which is claiming the mare, forcing the two stallions to fight with hooves and teeth. The "sport" is perpetuated by gamblers who bet on the horses, although organizers claim it as a cultural show and were even given permit from the local office of the Department of Agriculture. No protective gear is worn by the horses to keep the eyes from injuries as the horses fight until the defeated is subdued or runs away from the fight. It won't be long before some horses suffer broken legs.

VIVISECTION

Vivisection is the dissection of living animals used in experiments in school or for biomedical researches. Since the early days, much have been learned from the experiments done on animals. But today, much of what we have learned are still being done all over again in classrooms and research laboratories despite the liability of computer programs, plastic models with complete anatomy, films, photographic plates that can be reused over and over again.

The prevalence of vivisection actually started in the 19th century because of dances in biomedical sciences and additional fields of studies such as physiology, pharmacology, and pathology. Experiments on live animals to educate and train biologists, medical students, surgeons, veterinarians, and the development of new surgical techniques also help in the proliferation of vivisection.

The explosion of knowledge and increased use of live animals in the laboratories have given rise to rampant abuses and maltreatment of animals. It is only natural that animal liberation groups will sprout out. Unseen from the public eyes, animals are treated in some of the most deplorable and inhumane conditions. Useless experiments have been done on animals without any redeeming value except to satisfy the requirement for getting grants from government and private institutions. Many humane organizations have been established to help researchers establish the most humane procedures and treatment of animals in their custody. Other vocal and radical groups opt for a complete stop to all forms of animal testings.

Anti-vivisection and animal welfare organizations have sprouted throughout the world. In the U.S. alone, there are over 400 such organizations with over 10 million members and contributed about $50 million annually. Every year since the late 19th century, anti-vivisection groups have sponsored bills in the U.S. Congress to stop vivisection, but to no avail. But some have succeeded on a local basis in preventing research laboratories and profession schools from obtaining domestic pets from the animal shelters.

Because of the inability to get reforms from the government, some groups such as the Animal Liberation Front have taken more drastic actions to stop the practice. They can be very dangerous as Professor Colin Blackemore of Oxford University is finding out. In his research on amblyopia, a common form of child blindness where the eyelids of anaesthetized kittens or monkeys are sewed up, anti-vivisection groups have resorted to threat of bodily harm and kidnapping to force him to stop.

Every year in the U.S., more than six million animals are dissected by students in the subject of biology. More than half of these animals are frogs. Other unlikely animals include snakes, sparrows, sharks, and chipmunks. After decades of animal dissections, there are enough documented materials, slides, photographs, computer programs, and plastic models with all the organs intact that can be referred to by students

In California, students in public schools are allowed by law to refrain from dissecting animals. It is only fair that students be allowed to follow the dictates of their conscience. Furthermore, most of the studies done on animal dissection will probably be forgotten in a few years.

Some physicians, even though they would have benefited from vivisection have joined together to put a stop to this practice. Physicians Committee for Responsible Medicine (PCRM) of Washington, D.C. is one of them. They provide support for medical students opposed to animal experimentations. The New England Anti-Vivisection Society (NEAVS) of Boston provides a comprehension book on sources of alternatives such as computer programs, models, and films for high school students forced against their will to dissect animals.

WILDLIFE COLLECTION

There is a $20 billion-dollar black market for exotic animals. As many as 80 to 90% of these exotic animals die within six months of captivity. The deaths are not limited to the difficulty in transporting these live animals, but the buyers at the other end are often ill-equipped to take care of them.

The lucrative business of wildlife trading and the restrictions placed by government regulators have forced some traders to engage in underground and illegal trading. Because of corruption, traders are often allowed to export more than they bargained for. ranging from protected species to overharvesting. These animals are then technically smuggled out of the country with false license and permit. Sometimes, the import papers are furnished by licensed zoos only to be sold to private collectors. Forgery and outright bribery are rampantly used in the Third World.

A problem encountered in wildlife trading is the cruel way in which many animals are trapped. Most baby primates are captured by killing their mothers The monkeys that died along with the mother are slaughtered for their furs. The healthy primates are destined for laboratories throughout the developed world.

Traders of exotic animals will go to great lengths to protect their business. In one instance, an exporter deliberately damaged the testicles of the animal by crushing it with clapboards that made it difficult to detect. The reason behind the dastardly deed was simply to stop the animal from breeding so that importers will continue to order from him.

Wildlife is often killed for its head as a collector's trophy. Because of the rarity of some animals and the obsession to own a trophy, many endangered species have been hunted to extinction. Big cats such as the Bali tiger, black-maned lion and the Arizona jaguar have been hunted to extinction for their heads. Less known animals are not spared.

One problem often encountered by conservationists and ecotourists is the harvesting made by indigenous people who try to sell the animals to them. The animals are sometimes brought to them in poor conditions that people take pity and buy them. This encourages them to catch more of these animals, treat them inhumanely until tourists out of pity buy them. Because of the many conservation restrictions on animals going on, many trappers hired by the big-time traders found themselves jobless. If the animals they caught cannot be exported, or sold in the local market, the local people are forced to eat them.

ZOOS

Zoos can be beneficial or a curse for the animals. They can be prison for animals on display or as breeding grounds for endangered species. But unless carefully monitored, it could lead to mismanagement and plays a "cruelty" role in the treatment of animals. In the early days, zoos were nothing but prisons for animals. Not only do animals need companionship of their own species, they also need large areas to breed, play, and run around. They need to enjoy life as people do. One sure way to know that the animals are unhappy is when the young do not play around and the adults do not breed.

Birds, especially the birds of prey need to soar high into the sky to thrive. For flying high and catching their own food and breeding are the greatest activities of their existence. That is why birds are always ready to escape their confinements.

We are often deceived by zookeepers and maintainers that all is well in the marine parks and oceanariums. The truth is that they have very high death rate in captivity. A pilot whale displayed at one oceanarium was actually thirteen different mammals with the same name. The life expectancy of killer orca is as long as human beings, but at Sea World, in San Diego, they last an average of eleven years, way below their average age living in the ocean.

For animals to enjoy their life, it is important to have freedom. Given an opportunity the animals will try to escape again and again. When the chimpanzees at Arnhem Zoo were allowed out of their caged quarters for the first time, they jumped up and down in exultation. A two-year-old panda exploded with joy by trotting up a hill and somersaulted down several times. It was filled with joy to savor the freedom.

Zoos provide a loophole in the fight against importing endangered species. Some unscrupulous zoo owners import more than they need and sell the excesses to laboratories for experiments. Up to 80% of these animals are dead within six months of their captivity.

Elephant is one of the main attractions in zoos. Beginning in the 1850s, zoos have shown individual elephant in astonishing large cages. But large importation of elephants from Asia necessitate chaining them in small areas around the zoo because of lack of space. Since 1907, when Carl Hagenbeck pioneered the idea of open air enclosures, new problems were created for the animals. They were kept in platforms with deep, sloping ditches. Introduced in 1926 for the first time at the Leipzig Zoo, it has lead to numerous accidents, some resulting in deaths to the animals. To avoid the accidents, the elephants were chained at night.

Elephants kept in zoos around Asia fare no better than prison cells. In the Malaysian state zoo of Kuala Lumpur, four elephants were kept in shackles within an enclosure. Since 1963, six elephants have died in this inadequate facility During Sundays and holidays the elephants were allowed to leave their enclosures to perform circus tricks in a small open arena. Elephants from other parts of Asia rarely report births since most of them do not survive to adulthood under the current situation.

Animal-rights activists have been fighting against the creation of zoos that are unfit for wild animals. Those captured from the wild even though uninjured have to undergo considerable stress. Once they are caged, their behavior change and show signs of psychological damage that make them aggressive and even inflict self-mutilation. Their life expectancies are reduced drastically.

Many zoos are too small to accommodate the living animals and provide them the necessary pastures to roam around. Zoos where animals are on display inside cages or small enclosures should be phased out. Wild animals should be allowed to freely roam in the jungle where they belong. They have a better chance of survival. For people who like to see wildlife, there are many fours organized to see wildlife in their natural habitats.

The zoo in Cairo, Egypt was under fire by two animal activist organizations The recent (1997) visits made by the activists found that many of the animals are not being treated in a proper manner that can be beneficial to them. Elephants are found to be chained up all day. Many of the caged animals live under concrete floor and without water available at all times lo quench their thirst. Polar bears are kept under 100 degree F of heat unlike the cooler climate where they belong. Foods other than fishes are given. Feeding of most animals is given low priority as is their enclosures. Forty two lions were kept in cages instead of roaming freely. Only six wild cats were found to have the open air range. Two cubs born to the wild cats were separated from their mothers and returned only after complaints from the animal activists. While the management complains of lack of funds, yet every year two million tourists visited the zoo. Most of the funds are used to improve the landscape for the benefits of the tourists. The management promise to spend more funds for the improvement of the facilities for the benefit of the animals. The activists are keeping their fingers crossed and promise to keep a watchful eye on the progress being made.

A total worldwide ban on trading in exotic animals should be imposed immediately. Specialized captive breeding for rare species can be conducted in their place of origin to minimize death during transit. The wild animals need not undergo the often fatal way of transporting them halfway around the world It would also eliminate cost.

CHAPTER 17

POLLUTION

Pollution is one tragic creation in our efforts to advance science and improve the well-being of humanity. The drive to a better and convenient life has been accomplished at the expense of the environment. Pollution has penetrated the entire planet's biosphere and is seriously affecting all life forms. From the air we breathe, the water we drink, and the food we eat, pollution is affecting us as well as other wildlife in a number of ways.

The air, land and sea are closely interlinked together, especially with regard to pollution. Most of the land degradation such as soil erosion, sedimentation, pesticides and man-made toxic chemicals eventually find their way to the water system of the world. The ocean is often the recipient of much of our wastes generated from inland homes and industries, due to its vastness and accessibility through tributaries from many inland rivers. Other wastes left on land can be carried by rainfalls and discharges through sewer lines are also carried to the sea and left behind. Centuries of deliberate and unintended dumpings are taking their tolls on marine life.

Pollutants can be subtle and long lasting especially those chemicals considered endocrine disrupters. These hormone-like chemicals have been known to pass from one generation to another, and may have mutagenic and carcinogenic effects on living things.

Water pollution can come from improper dumping of semi-treated and untreated sewage into waterways. Contamination can also come from overfertilized farmlands. The introduction of toxic materials and chemicals can affect aquatic wildlife. Organic wastes use dissolved oxygen making fish and invertebrate organisms difficult to survive. Logging and grazing have resulted in increased runoff, carrying the suspended solids to the streams and rivers. Mining and its tailing runoff are particularly destructive on a local basis. Some of these material formed complex interaction with prolong exposures to wildlife. Soil runoff increases turbidity of the water, reduces the amount of sunlight and oxygen available to aquatic life, and destroys the habitat for many species.

The greatest polluter of them all is the oil. It is released to the environment intentionally from domestic use, cleaning of oil tankers, and sometimes accidentally as in tanker accident. The effects on animals are numerous. It can suffocate sea creatures when garbage are eaten as food, poison them like heavy metals and pesticides, deform, maim, and kill outright in many cases.

ACID RAIN

Acid rain is a general term used to describe the deposition of all atmospheric pollutants of acidic nature as they fell to earth in the form of rain, snow or even m gaseous or solid state. It is produced by the reaction of moisture with sulphur dioxide or sulphate particles and nitrogen oxides and converted into sulfuric acid and nitric acid, respectively. The sulfur dioxide comes primarily from coal- and oil-powered utility plants, furnaces and non-ferrous smelters. Nitrogen oxides, an acrid reddish gas, formed when fuel is burned at high temperature, comes from gasoline and diesel engine exhausts, electric utilities and industrial boilers that burned coal or oil.

Another gas that can cause acidification on a smaller scale is hydrogen chloride. Coal combustion is a major source of this gas followed by waste incinerator. Methane is also growing because of the use of fertilizers to increase food production. The guts of some animals like cattle produced wastes that emit methane. The increasing number of cattle has been responsible.

Once emitted to the atmosphere these gases can travel for thousands of kilometers before they settle down. During the period in the air which usually last for several days, the gases are oxidized and converted into sulfuric and nitric oxides and eventually captured by clouds and fall down to earth as rain or snow. Even though most of the deposition fell on dry soil, the runoff during rainfall often leads to lakes, rivers, and streams. From here, the acid rain is drained to the sea, and diluted in the ocean. However, when the acidity is found in the lakes, there is almost no way to remove the acid except by neutralizing it.

Acidification not only decreases the food available for fish, it can kill the fish outright with its acidity. While some fishes may tolerate high acidity, their sources of food may not and they will starve to death. The fish eggs have difficulties surviving in an acidic condition. Acidification in many European and North American countries caused by acid rain has made tens of thousands of lakes deadly for sea animals. Once the acidity increases to the range of pH 4.0 and below, it will be able to leach toxic aluminum, lead, mercury and cadmium from rocks and soils. Even if some fishes do not die from the acidic water, consumption of these creatures can lead to accumulation of these toxic elements in our body.

Massive fish kills as a result of short, sharp episodes of high acidity during heavy rain or snow have been reported. A pH of 5.1-5.3 for 12 days was responsible for the death of the majority of salmon in the River Viksdalselva. Presence of aluminum compounded the falling pH. Up to 70% of the added acidity was exchanged with aluminum ions on the stream bed, increasing its acidity. Acidification also leads to change in the population of all microorganisms, lower the available plants and aquatic invertebrates that are part of the food chain used at all life stages of fishes. Fingerlings are particularly vulnerable at all stages.

Numerous studies have been made on acid precipitation in Europe and North America. In Lock Fleet, UK, brown trout caught annually has been declining since 1950 until no fish was caught after 1972. In 1971, in the Adirondack fountain of New York, half of the lakes above 610 meters had pH values less than 5.0 and 90% have no fish compared to only 4% in 1930. In Norway, half of the 20,000 sq km of lakes are lifeless while in Sweden, 4,000 lakes have no fish. Canada, even with its sparse population has 14,000 of its lakes devoid of fish. Most of the acid rain comes from the northern U.S. power plants and smelters.

Fish kill is the most visible sign of acid rain. All other organisms have been noted to decline such as insects, frogs, turtles, and salamanders. There are evidences that acid water decreased the diversity of all kinds of plankton and benthic invertebrates. The reduced populations are likely to seriously disrupt the food chain of the fishes. Some crustaceans, molluscs, and mayflies, caddis flies and their nymphs are also vulnerable to acidic conditions. Many lakes used by migratory birds which feed on the fishes and insects have declined.

The need to reduce substantially the emission of sulfur and nitrogen oxides into the atmosphere has been recognized by governments. Virtually all the sulfur in coal can be removed by chemical treatment during coal liquefaction and gasification. Few utilities have these expensive facilities. Only by taxing these harmful emissions will encourage industries to drastically reduce their emissions.

The process of acidification in lakes can be reversed by liming them, but at prohibitive costs compared to other measures that control the undesirable emissions at its source. Not only are lakes the beneficiary, other surrounding ecosystems will benefit as well.

Energy conservation can reduce the demand for electricity and oil and therefore fossil fuel combustion. Other less pollutive form of energy generation are also available. But these alternatives are not expected to help much in the reduction of acid rain in the near future. It is therefore incumbent among us to reduce our use of energy and the automobiles.

AIR POLLUTION

Air pollution is usually confined to urban areas. The main pollutants are sulfur and nitrogen oxides, carbon monoxide, various hydrocarbons and particulates, all coming from the burning of fossil fuels used in power generation and driving the automobiles. All living things are affected in one way or another. Smog is a serious problem arising from the huge volume of fossil fuel burning vehicles and power plants, trapped in a confined space. In some places as in Mexico City, where the smog is highly concentrated, birds are dying in the center of the city in Chapultepec Park. The same tragedy is happening in Athens during summer months.

Several episodes of death due to air pollution occurred in the Meuse Valley of Belgium in 1930 and in Donora, Pennsylvania in 1948. Probably the most notorious smog that killed thousands of people including many pets, livestock, and wildlife was the London fog of 1952.

As early as 19th century it has been known that air pollution from industries has adverse effect on domestic animals and wildlife. Arsenic emissions from silver foundries have killed deer and wild rabbits in Germany. Main song birds died from inhaling sulfur emissions from a pulp mill in Canada. Industrial fluorosis has been found in deer from the U.S. and Canada. Baboons and rodents are dying of asbestosis while living in the vicinity of asbestos mines in South Africa. In the San Bernardino Mountains near Los Angeles, bighorn sheep are suffering blindness caused by oxidants from air pollution.

BALLOON

The innocuous looking balloons may seem harmless to animals, but they often play a role similar to plastics once they are released to the atmosphere and blown hundreds of miles into the oceans They are made of strong and durable materials that do not break down easily. In places surrounded by water, balloons can easily reach the ocean. Once in the ocean, the painted color of the balloon can easily dissolve making them transparent like jellyfish. Sea creatures and birds often mistakenly eat these balloons. Many sea turtles have starved to death because of balloons that blocked their digestive track. Even large mammals such as whales have been known to be killed by balloons that became stuck in their stomach. Some balloons are made of a material called Mylar which is a silver metallic element that can be toxic to the mammals. In July 1985 a one-year-old sperm whale almost died from indigestion when a Mylar balloon lodged in its stomach. Timely human intervention saved it from certain death because there is no way an animal can remove a foreign object once it has been ingested..

ENDOCRINE DISRUPTERS

Hormones are important body's chemical messenger produced by the endocrine glands. Once secreted to the bloodstream in infinitesimal amount they can have profound effect in many aspects of development of the body. Timing of ovulation, fetal and sexual development, growth of vital organs are all linked to the hormones.

Many common pesticides, industrial organochlorine chemicals such as polychlorinated biphenyls (PCBs) and pharmaceutical products such as diethylstilbestrol (DES) can act like the female hormone estrogen. Tests have shown that in excess amount, it can disrupt an animal's endocrine system, impairing both development and reproduction. Researchers have long suspected that many animals have had reproductive failures and deformations in their reproductive organs due to these chemicals. There are growing evidences that the combination of these chemicals have a synergetic effect one thousand times more potent than the individual substance. Tests on turtles confirmed the effect that a mixture of two different PCBs can alter the sex of developing males, but have no effect when taken separately.

School children from Minnesota New County School were the first to find 200 deformed frogs during the month of August 1995. One frog had a twisted hind leg. Others have one leg, another three legs and one even had abnormally high number of twelve legs. Others have misplaced or missing organs. One frog has legs coming out of its stomach, while another has an eye coming out of its neck.

In 1970, Mike Gilbertson, a biologist, visited a gull colony on Near Island Instead of a lively place teeming with birds, he found unhatched eggs and dead chicks everywhere. Those that survived show deformities such as club feet, missing eyes, and twisted bills. Some were suffering from wasting disease.

Scientists studying alligators of Florida have discovered pesticide residues and contaminants from a chemical plant that has closed down more than a decade ago. The pollutant is still bringing havoc to the environment. The male alligator has undersize penis one-fourth its normal size. Blood tests have confirmed a high amount estrogen, a female hormone estrogen and lower testosterone Female alligators have ovaries producing abnormal eggs with multiple nuclei and more than the usual one egg per follicle. Even the plant-eating red-eared turtles are suffering from reproductive difficulties due to the absence of males. Researchers found many females and the rest were neither male or female, their sex orientation were stranded in the gender bending state called intersex.

Oystein Wiig, a polar bear researcher from Oslo. Norway has been tracking more than a dozen bears from Svalbard Archipelago. After a failure of an expected breeding, he had the bears tested and found industrial chemicals and pesticides such as PCBs. DDT in the fats of these bears, although they lived in remote and pristine environment, thousands of miles away from any industrial cities. The fats in these bears carry as much as 90 ppm of pollutants, a potent dose that could reduce immune functions, cause deformities in the uterus and fallopian tube that transport the eggs to the ovaries in female bears.

Endocrine disrupters not only disrupt the normal flow of hormones, it can also destroy the immune system of animals. The 1988 massive harbor seal die-off affecting 18,000 seals has been partly traced to their weakened immune systems caused by PCBs, making them susceptible to phocine distemper virus, a morbillivirus related to canine distemper virus.

Gulls with vestiges of both male and female gonads and fishes that failed to mature sexually have been found to be carrying high amount of synthetic organochlorine chemicals in their bodies. Gulls from the California coast were not breeding and females were nesting with females Dissection of some birds by Michael Fry. an avian toxicologist discovered that some males were functional hermaphrodites with partially formed female sex organs. The culprit: DES.

DES was first synthesized by David Dodds in 1938. Since it was under the auspices of the British Medical Research Council, long-term testing was not undertaken It was widely produced for man> applications such as oral contraceptives, treatment of menopause problem, amenorrhea, and other reproductive problems. In 1942, when it was discovered that experimental rats could grow faster without increase in food intake, farmers started to use it on cattle and poultry.

Probably the deadliest and most toxic chemical on earth is the dioxin or 2,3,7,8-TCDD. Its toxicity is measured not in the ppm or ppb, but in ppt or parts per trillion. It is a by-product of the chemical industry, created during the manufacture of certain chlorine-containing chemicals. Dioxin is also produced by waste incineration, chlorine-bleaching of paper, and burning of fossil fuels.

One problem faced by people contaminated with dioxin is the development of certain types of cancers. But the more insidious effect is on the endocrine glands. Scientific research on rats has discovered that adult rats given dioxin have lower testosterone level and their sex organs also lost weight. But like other endocrine disrupters, the toxicity is most pronounced during pregnancy. The male pups showed reduce sperm count by as much as 56%. Feminizations of the male rats have also been observed.

EUTROPHICATION

Eutrophication is the over-enrichment of any water bodies as organic wastes are degraded by bacteria and stimulating the growth of phytoplankton. When carbon dioxide, nitrogen, phosphorus and other salts conducive to eutrophication. As a result of over-fertilization, an undesirable flora displaces the normal algae flora.

The effects of eutrophication are usually observed in increased green phytoplankton and benthic micro- and macro-algae, leading to decreased transparency in surface waters and oxygen deficiency resulting in high mortality of the bottom fauna and fishes. During eutrophication, the phytoplankton may produce an algal bloom which may be toxic to other organisms but certainly deadly to humans. In 1987, such a red tide bloom forced the closure of 250 km of clam and oyster beds in North Carolina. Other species of algae release toxins that have cause mass deaths in European farmed salmon. Even after the algae died, the toxins are released to the water and are difficult to remove by normal water treatment processes.

Another source of eutrophication comes from nitrogen due to drainage from the fertilizers used in agriculture, and from inland sewage works. Less than half of the fertilizers applied to agricultural crops are absorbed while the rest is lost to rivers, estuaries, bays and to the seas.

Most of the chemicals came from human activities. Studies in Germany show that 40% of the phosphorus came from detergents, 27% from feces, 17% from livestock wastes, and 13% from industrial sources.

Organic compounds produced by people such as untreated and semi-treated human sewage, tannery wastes, runoff from feedlots, food processing industries, cellulose wastes from paper industry and fertilizers constitute nutrients for lakes and streams. The resultant increase in bacterial activity lowers the dissolved oxygen, which makes the water uninhabitable for a number of organisms. This whole process of eutrophication of lakes and estuaries is accelerated by the disposal of organic wastes in excessive quantities.

The enormous growth of algae and aquatic plants may provide a small portion of the food for the fishes and aquatic invertebrates. The deaths of these organisms will accumulate in the sea beds and their decomposition decreases the dissolved oxygen in the wastes that gradually kill the fishes and other invertebrates that need oxygen in the water.

Massive fish kills are common occurrences around the world. The algae bloom in the eastern Mediterranean Sea caused the demise of the sardine industry. In the Albermarle and Pamlico sounds of North Carolina, the slow strangulation has suffocated thousands of basses, crabs, and eels. The Pasig River flowing around Metro Manila was once teeming with fishes is now devoid of them because of the algae bloom caused by the overnutrition of phosphates used in the soap industry, and the soupy toxic chemicals discharged by manufacturing firms throughout the towns and cities surrounding the river.

A massive fish kill in 1976 along the Atlantic coast of the U.S. was carefully studied where fish and shellfish were killed by the thousands. Some 14,700 tons of surf clams were destroyed along with ocean quahogs and sea scallops. Lobster Population was reduced in half. All these creatures were killed due to the deficient oxygen as oxygen were consumed by bacteria hard at work disintegrating the waste produced by people.

The effects of all these various activities are similar, despite differing origins of the organic matter. Organic matter is vital to the functioning of the estuarine ecosystems, as the basis for detritus food chains. A small amount of organic matter, well dispersed, can readily be utilized within the estuarine ecosystem to enhance the levels of biological production Problems arise if a large volume of organic effluent is discharged at a single point. When excess quantities of organic matter are present, then bacteria and other microorganisms which utilize the organic matter will consume all the available oxygen in the water. Such problems may be particularly severe in summertime because of reduced river flow coupled with temperature increases which lead to enhanced bacterial activity, and thus accelerate the depletion of the oxygen content of the water.

The first thing to protect the water ecosystems is to control all effluents All wastes must pass through water treatment plants before they are discharged as wastewater. Reduction in the number of industries discharging their wastes will help reduce the pollution. Reclamation should be avoided if not entirely eliminated. Constant monitoring is necessary- to assure the continuing healthy state of the ecosystem. Actions should be taken at the first sign of pollution because it is always cheaper to clean up at the source than to clean up the water bodies once they are polluted and dispersed.

Wastewater treatment for industries that discharge toxic and organic wastes are needed. In agricultural areas, soil erosion and water runoff control needs to be imposed to minimize their reaching the waterways. All these long-term but expensive solutions need to be taken if we intend to save the water bodies from further degradation. For the immediate action is to remove the unwanted plants and algae wherever they are present.

GLOBAL WARMING

Global warming is caused by the accumulation of carbon dioxide, carbon monoxide, methane, nitrous oxide, CFCs, hydrogen sulphide, and other man-made gases in the atmosphere. Carbon dioxide is at present the main culprit because of the large scale deforestation throughout the world. The carbon dioxide is emitted from burned forests to the tune of 6 billion tons annually. Methane is also a very effective greenhouse gas.

Methane is particularly ominous because it is rising very fast and is about 25 times more effective in blocking the sun's ray. It is produced through biological decomposition
by microorganisms under anaerobic conditions, in swamps, paddy fields, landfills, peaty oils, coal and oil mining accompanied with natural gases, by termites, and guts of livestock. A domestic cow generates about 200 grams of methane a day.

These gases act like glass in a greenhouse, letting the sun's ray through but trapping some of the heat that would otherwise be radiated back to space. This in turn will increase the average temperature of the globe. Some possible consequences of global warming is the increase in sea level, stormy weather, and other atmospheric disturbances.

Global warming can cause the melting of the icecaps in the polar zones, inundating lowlands and islands. Computer model trend predicts a significant melting of icebergs in the 21st century and possibly total loss of ice shelves within 500 years if the trend continues. Ice shelves bordering 44% of the 1.5 million sq km of Antarctica have started to break off and melt. In recent years, huge icebergs have broken off the Larsen ice shelf along the Antarctic Peninsula after sustaining warming of 4.5 degrees Fahrenheit in the last 50 years, according to one report.

The rising sea level could also be the result of our dumping of garbage and the soil erosion that continue to flow into the sea. The rising sea could cause more coastal land to undergo soil erosion. It could render 20% of the cropland useless for food production due to reduced areas and saltwater seepage and salt intrusions into aquifers. This will lead to more deforestation as the need for new croplands arise. The mass resettlement of people will encroach on agricultural land while the poorer people will migrate to the upland, adding more pressure on the forests. Reclamation of coastal areas in many parts of the world is also compressing the ocean and forcing the sea level to rise.

The impact on wildlife is likely to be faster than natural climatic changes. If past events are any indication, the warming after the last ice age killed thousands of species, 32 genera of mammals alone became extinct. The wildlife is less able to adapt to new environmental stresses as humans. Their limited breeding grounds will make them difficult to adapt to the new environment and compete for food. There may be a resurgence of pesty organisms and diseases unknown to mankind. Parasites and pests generally thrive in warmer climates. Locusts, mosquitoes, and other pests proliferate during summer than in winter. The barber worm that infests sheep in Australia reaches epidemic proportion during summer than in the winter. Studies in UK have shown that several insects such as moths, butterflies, crickets, cockroaches, dragonflies, and a dozen more species are invading the northern part of UK. Some native species have been forced out of their old natural habitats by the invasion of new species. The bee wolf (a big wasp), has begun its northern swift, paralyzing the honey bees with their stings and feeding the bees to their grubs.

Scientists agree that warmer weather in the Mediterranean region is the main factor. A tiny difference in average temperature makes a big difference in the insect's chances of survival. In the last 10 years, at least eight summers have been warmer than average. There is reason to believe that warmer weather has led to an increase in the population of rodents in Europe.

Some of the warmest years occurred during the 1980s and early 1990s. The July 1995 heat wave in Chicago and surrounding areas is a harbinger of bad news for people and animals alike. The temperature was 106 degrees Fahrenheit and killed 566 Chicagoans alone and many more elsewhere. Thousands of livestock died, with their bodies swollen and rotting in the field.

HEAVY METALS

Heavy metals are natural constituents of seawater. However, human activities often discharge concentrated amounts into the environment. The intense sedimentation in estuaries, rivers, and other coastal areas trap a large quantity of metals which become adsorbed to sediment particles and carried to the bottom. Sediments in industrialized estuaries with major ports contain the legacy of a century or more of waste discharges. The regular dredging of shipping channels disturbs large quantities of soil heavily contaminated with metals and usually dumped farther out to the sea. Other sources can be direct discharge of industrial and other wastes by pipelines. and in sewage sludge and industrial wastes dumped at sea.

Heavy metals can also come from atmospheric processes. Metals such as aluminum can actually exist as wind-blown dust derived from rocks and shales, and mercury from volcanic activity and degassing of the Earth's crust. Atmospheric contaminants may exist in gaseous forms such as mercury, selenium, and boron or aerosols that become part of the environment.

Heavy metal poisoning may not be immediately apparent for people or mammals eating fishes or other mammals from the oceans. Even fishes consuming trace amounts of heavy metals from the polluted sea may not be immediately fatal. The poisons are often stored in the fats which are later taken in by larger animals in the food chain and ultimately by people.

HEAVY METALS: ALUMINUM

Aluminum is a very common metal in the world Those found in the environment usually come from the leaching caused by the acidity of the soil. Scientists testing fishes in a laboratory show that some fishes can withstand pH 4.5 or less but when aluminum silicates are introduced, the fishes die ot asphyxiation. The cause was due to the fine insoluble aluminum compounds that block the sodium and oxygen exchange sy stem in the gills of fishes resulting in death en at pH of 5.0 to 5.5, aluminum ions can interfere with the calcium of gill permeability or enhance the loss of sodium that cause clogging of the gills with mucus and interferes with their respiration.

Fish fry is particularly susceptible to acidification when aluminum ions are involved because it may interfere with the calcification of their skeleton resulting in stunted growth. This could result in a gradual decline in their population

In July 1988, an accidental introduction of 20 tons of aluminum sulphate to the water supply in Cornwall, UK affected 20.000 people and the livestock there. Mental, neurological, and reproductive problems were found in pigs supplied with the contaminated water. Many died or had to be destroyed.

HEAVY METALS: COPPER

Natural input of copper to the marine environment comes from erosion of mineralized rocks. About 7.5 million tons are discharged as wastes after producing electrical equipments, in alloys, as a chemical catalyst, in anti-fouling paint for ships' hulls, as an algicide, and as a wood preservative. Urban sewage contains a substantial amount of copper. Run-off from mine tailings in tin and copper mining areas results in high copper and zinc concentrations.

Copper in trace amount is an essential element for animals and the highest concentrations are found in decapod, crustaceans, gastropods, and cephalopods, in which the respiratory pigment haemocyanin contains copper. Despite the existence of several detoxifying and storage systems for copper, it is the most toxic metal after mercury and silver for a wide variety of marine life. This is the reason why it is widely used in anti-fouling preparations. The damaging effect is usually in concentrated form. When a quantity of copper sulphate illegally dumped onto the Dutch coast near Noordwijk in 1965, it moved up the coast, causing the deaths of planktons, fishes, and shellfishes

HEAVY METALS: LEAD

The world produced about 45 million tons of lead annually. Much of it is recovered and recycled. However, some are used as additive for gasoline engine and are lost to the atmosphere after burning. Lead aerosols are carried around Earth and widely scattered and often end up in the sea.

Lead in the sea is not particularly toxic to sea organisms even if high concentrations can be accumulated by some animals However, people and wildlife consuming these contaminated organisms are at risk. A rare instance of lead poisoning occurred among shore birds wintering in the Mersey estuary. More than 2.400 birds, mainly dunlin died in 1979 and a smaller number the following year after consuming the contaminated fishes. The dead birds contained more than 10 ppm of lead in their liver, mostly in the form of trialkyl lead.

HEAVY METALS: MERCURY

As with all the other metals, most of the marine mercury came from human activities. A substantial proportion of the annual production of 6.000 tons annually is lost through industrial processes. During the 1950s and 1960s, Finland and Sweden lost about half their mercury from the chloro-alkali industry. Chlorine and caustic soda are manufactured electrolytically using mercury electrodes. In the process, about 150 to 200 grams of mercury per ton of product are lost to the atmosphere and eventually settled in the seas. Other mercury products are used in the lumber and paper industry to prevent fungal growth, anti-fouling paints for ships, pesticides, and seed dressing in agriculture, and the pharmaceutical industry. Other sources include the burning of fossil fuels especially coal. Although it contain very little mercury, the large volume of coals burned make their input to the environment considerable.

Burning wastes by incineration has been responsible for the emission of mercury into the atmosphere. It is easily released from incinerators because a mild rise in temperature is enough to vaporize it. Lingering in the atmosphere for up to two years, it can travel for thousands of miles before dropping to earth. Fortunately, many of the mercury containing products are no longer in use. Agricultural pesticides, pharmaceuticals, timber and paper industry ure no longer using mercury in the U.S. Mercury is prohibited in anti-fouling paints in many countries, including the EU.

Mercury is also released to the environment in the Amazon, in the Philippines, and in places where gold prospectors are found. The mercury is emitted to the atmosphere as well as the river, killing fishes downstream. Organic forms of mercury are more toxic than inorganic salts. A number of mercury compounds can be taken up by algae and invertebrates and these in turn can be eaten by fishes Most species of fishes in ocean water contain 0.15 ppm of mercury in muscles although under contaminated water, the mercury can be as high as 4.9 ppm. The high figure often results from bioaccumulation and biomagnification, since carnivorous fishes are at the top of the food chain. They are very active with a high metabolic rate. They swim continuously with their mouths open, thereby producing a forced flow of water across the gills picking up dissolved metals in the water. Mercury in the ocean is usually transformed into methyl mercury and is difficult to excrete.

Halibut is a long-living fish species that accumulates high concentration of mercury. A big halibut of 300 kg may be 50 years old. In one study, all specimens over 115 kg and half those weighing more than 60 kg have been found to contain over 1 ppm of muscle mercury. As with most fishes, more than 90% of this is in the form of methyl mercury and such fishes are unsuitable for human consumption. One disturbing finding is that acid in lakes and in atmosphere and ozone pollution from cars and power plants can quickly convert the elemental form of mercury into its more toxic form. Some environmental agencies have discovered that the highest level of mercury was found in fishes taken from the most acidified lakes.

Birds tend to accumulate mercury in their liver and feathers. The larger sea birds may live for 20 years or more and those feeding at high tropic level are likely to accumulate mercury. Species that feed on or close to shore are most at risk. In Sweden and Finland, the populations of both osprey s and white-tailed eagles have declined during this century as a result of mercury poisoning. The mercury concentration in feathers of the white-tailed eagle increased from an average of 6.6 ppm between 1880 to 1940 to about 50 ppm in 1964-65. In the mid-1960s, white-tailed eagles are known to have died from mercury poisoning in southwest Finland, and fortunately none of the osprey s died.

Marine mammals accumulate large quantities of mercury from their contaminated food without coming to harm. This may be due to selenium which antagonizes the toxic effects of mercury. In seals, sea lions, and dolphins, there seems to be a balance between selenium concentration in the tissues and mercury.

The first known mercury poisoning affecting humans and animals must be the 1810 mercury poisoning aboard HMS Triumph The ship carried a cargo of 130 tons of mercury salvaged from a wrecked Spanish vessel. The mercury was contained in leather pouches which eventually became damp and rotten, allow ing it to vaporize. Within three weeks all 200 sailors were suffering from symptoms of tremor, paralysis, profuse salivation, diarrhea, all classic symptoms of mercury poisoning. Almost all the cats and rats, a dog and a canary died.

Minamata is a small town in Japan w ith about 50,000 inhabitants who depend mostly on fishing as their livelihood. The rest of the community depends on the Shin Nihon Chisso Hiryo Company, a producer of vinylchloride and acetaldehyde since 1952. Mercury chloride is used as a catalyst in the production of vinylchloride. During the washing process, a small portion of mercury is discharged as waste into the water. When producing acetaldehyde from acetylene, mercuric sulfate with acetylene are used as catalyst. For every ton of acetaldehyde produced, 15 to 50 grams of the poisonous methyl mercury is also produced. Between 1952 and 1960, the industry had discharged the waste of mercury compounds into the Minamata

Bay. Cats were the first to die after eating the fishes in the bay. The accumulation of mercury in the human population was manifested some years later. Deaths and serious injuries soon followed those who have eaten the contaminated fish caught in the bay. More than one hundred people died and over 10,000 suffered gross mental and neurological defects such as blindness, paralysis, deafness, kidney failure and brain damage. New born babies were not spared from brain damage.

Mercury is accumulating in fishes in thousands of lakes across the U.S. an Canada, poisoning wildlife and threatening human health. Governments have warned their citizenry against eating fishes in these highly contaminated lakes. In areas where fishes are contaminated, particularly high concentration of mercury are found in seals and marine birds that feed exclusively on fishes and are the final link in the marine food chain. In the liver of harbor seals caught off the coast of Netherlands. 225-765 mg/kg of mercury was found. Seals from the North Sea coast off Germany have up to 100 mg/kg of mercury. Research has found that even a few months of eating invertebrates on English tidal flats results in elevated mercury concentration in sea birds.

Mercury has been confirmed as the cause of deaths of panthers and loons in Florida and is suspected in the failure to reproduce youngs by eagles, minks, otters and in the Great Lakes regions.

In 1970, toxicologists also found an abnormally high concentration of mercury compounds in freshwater fishes from I ake Brie. The Liverpool Bay in England is also contaminated with mercury as many places around the world where gold prospectors use mercury to separate the gold from the rocks and sediments. A chemical plant on the Adriatic near Ravenna, Italy, which produce acetaldehyde by the same process as in Minamata. Fortunately, the fishes were not eaten because the oil which they absorbed from other effluents ruined their flavor. No technology is available to remove the toxic waste. Once inside the animal or human tissue, mercury interacts with body chemicals. Some of the mercury compounds formed in the body pass readily through membranes, and neurological disorders can result when the compound reaches the brain.

To free the mercury contamination of waterways, additional means would have to be employed beside reducing the mercury discharge from manufacturing processes. Only a complex, costly process, and individual initiative is needed to eliminate all mercury coming from dentistry, chemical laboratories, instrument manufacturing, instrument and fluorescent light bulb breakage, which finds its way to the ocean.

INTERNATIONAL AGREEMENT

The effect of pollution transcends the international boundaries. Japanese scientists have found DDT on Antarctic animals which have never been subjected to this pesticide. The DDTs were used in some Southeast Asian countries that eventually find their way to the ocean. This made it mandatory for all nations to come to an agreement to protect the ocean from the harmful effects of pollution. The current international agreement needs to be expanded to include non-members to bring them under the jurisdiction of the treaty. More teeth for the enforcement of the provision must be undertaken. The 1976 Convention in the Prevention of Marine Pollution by Dumping of Wastes and Other Matter that covered the dumping of industrial and radioactive wastes in the ocean was repeatedly violated by Britain and several European countries. It took Greenpeace several years of lobbying, active blockade of the disposal of drums full of waste, and the persuasion of the British railway unions to refuse to handle any train carrying radioactive wastes for ocean dumping did the illegal dumping stopped.

A comprehensive international agreement covering all nations need to be enacted against local coastal and estuary dumpings of toxic wastes. This will effectively prohibit one country from exporting to another poor Third World country from accepting the toxic wastes and later dumping them in the ocean.

LAND RECLAMATION

In view of the ever increasing number of people and the need to feed the population, continental shelves around water bodies are often reclaimed. Throughout the world, and for many centuries, men have drained and converted salt marshes and estuaries into productive agricultural land, but at great cost to the environment. In India, Bangladesh and other congested countries, governments are reclaiming lands to feed and house their people.

Most industrial development sites are flat lands near transportation centers are no longer available except in reclamation areas along estuary and coastal regions. In the estuaries of eastern Britain, land reclaimed for industrial uses has obliterated over 90% of the Tess estuary. On the Forth estuary approximately half of the intertidal area has been reclaimed in the past 200 years. Recently, more areas have been reclaimed to accommodate industries such as power stations, refuse disposal and fly-ash dumping, all because of the population growth. Within Southampton, coastal reclamation has taken place over many years to meet the needs of new docks, oil refineries, power stations and other industries. The removal of these salt marshes and estuaries has reduced substantially the input of organic detritus needed to feed the sea organisms. As these intertidal areas have been obliterated, the commercial clam harvest has fallen from 100 tons to 60 tons per annum, and the birds feeding in these areas have declined substantially.

MARINE VESSELS

Wastes coming from marine vessels are sources of contamination of the ocean. A major source is the discharge of raw sewage and garbage directly to the sea. The increasing use of private boats discharging wastes into water also contributed their fair share of pollutants. This problem can easily be resolved by having a trash can for waste disposal. Plastics, six-packed rings, discarded fishing lines and nets should be placed where they belong, in the trash can.

Boat motors should be properly serviced and any leak should be repaired before they are launched into the ocean. Avoid using toxic paints on the vessels. During dry dock, the paint remover should be properly disposed of and not down the drain and into the sea.

Shippings also add heavy metal pollution because of the metal lie-based ingredients used in the paint to prevent algae and sessile marine animals like barnacles and mussels from fouling the hull Mercury, cadmium, lead, zinc, tin and copper are some important ingredients. Mercury and lead have long been banned from use. but some developing countries are still using them in paints.

An active and effective ingredient used in painting the bottom of ships and nets offish cages against the barnacles and mussels that foul it is the tributyltin (TBT). Experiments with this chemical have shown that it is a mutagen that can transform the sex of the shellfish dogwhelks in less than 1 part per million (ppm) Other marine life are also affected. Like the pesticides. TBT pollution extends as far into the North Sea and it is a matter of time before the whole ocean is contaminated with it unless a total ban is enforced. The French and English governments have banned their use on small boats but not on the big ships. The ocean-going vessels, with their wider range, can easily spread this deadly chemical.

Marine vessels have been responsible for the death of many sharks, manatees and other sea mammals caused by colliding with fast motor boats or getting entangled with the motor blades Avoid unnecessary use of these boats, especially for pleasure cruise.

MINING

Several problems are brought to mind with regard to mining. Most of them have to do with changes that it provokes in an aquatic ecosystem. Mining wastes such as tailings increased siltation and disturb river and stream sediments. Mining also pollute the ecosystems through the use of mercury, spillage of petroleum oil and the use of detergents. In gold mining, detergents are used to prevent the formation of micro-bubbles in fined-grained gold which might attach themselves to the gold particles and are inadvertently flushed away. Mining done along the river with the widespread use of mechanical crushers disturb the sediments. This increases in turbidity has been responsible for the decline in fish population. In Brazil, this has led to massive fish kill.

One of the best documented cases of fish decline happened in the Gorotire reserve of the Kayapo Indians in the south of Para state. Before the discovery of gold in 1982, the Rio Fresco was a crystalline river where the Kayabo used for fishing and the water for drinking. After the discovery and growth of mining, pollution turned the river opaque and inhibited the growth of fishes leading to their decline. The water is so contaminated that the Indian agency. FUNAI, found it necessary to pipe in water from other sources to the affected villages.

Another more serious problem related to gold mining is the use of mercury for separating the gold from the ores. For the poor miners, there is no cheaper alternative to mercury. After the mercury-gold amalgam is formed, the compound is heated which releases elemental mercury vapour that is a source of contaminated air around the vicinity. The vapour is readily absorbed by inhalation and deposited in vital tissues in the central nervous system and the kidney. The fallout from mercury on the soil is taken by the plants and those on the waterways can be taken by the fishes. In the aquatic environment, methylation of mercury into the more toxic form occurs through microbial action. The toxic methyl mercury can easily enter the food chain by tightly binding proteins, resulting in biomagnification, and eaten by the fish species. The fish eaten by the community can cause a devastating disease called mercury poisoning.

Coal mining is also very pollutive. Acids are often drained to the rivers and streams where fishes abound. Untreated mine water have caused the depletion of sensitive sea organisms by smothering the amount of oxygen and covering the river bed with iron oxides. This in turn destroys the spawning ground for fish breeding by occluding the interstices of the gravel with fine sediment. The low pH (acidity) can be toxic and can cause damage to the fish gills. The acid can react with heavy metals such as aluminum surrounding the rivers and lakes which are also toxic to fishes.

NOISE POLLUTION

Water is a good conductor of sound waves and noise can affect the sea mammals. This is because some mammals such as whales, dolphins, and porpoises use underwater sound to communicate with one another and to hunt for prey. Some of these communications that take place over wide distances can be broken by human interferences. Noise pollution is frequently associated with transport systems and oil and mineral explorations have an insidious effect on wildlife. It could disturb their breeding ground and even cause deafness in some sea mammals. There have been concerns by whale enthusiasts about the possibility that the experiment using underwater sound waves to investigate global warming could deafen marine mammals. The experiment run by the Scripps Institution of Oceanography in La Jolla, California, was supposed to fire sound from underwater speakers across the Pacific Ocean daily for at least a year in the hope of calculating temperature change. Because of the concern, the experimental sounding is done once every four days. If the tests show no significant effect on the mammals after a year, the daily sounding will resume.

The U.S. Navy is preparing a study on the sub-surface noise generated by a new submarine detection program. The Navy hopes to employ a low-frequency active sonar array for a new breed of submarines. These signals will cover vast tract of ocean at 230 decibels, well above the noise level of a jet engine at 120 decibels. Obviously, the sound range is still high, although much lower than the present noise level. Still it is still necessary to make improvements.

Fighter jets from NATO on training in the northern coast of Germany have been causing the disappearance of mother seals in their natural habitats. The flight maneuvers, which happen in the month of June, fly as low as 150 meters with its earsplitting noise have frightened the mother seals into leaving their pups.

Many of the babies are left behind and need to be taken care by people. The National Park Wattenmeer found 16 abandoned baby seals in the past and took them to the seal station for human care. The seals will be kept for three months and released to the North Sea.

The Luke Air Force Base in Arizona has been under fire by the Defenders of Wildlife. The noise and air-to-ground live fires from low-level flight training are threatening the last 100 endangered Sonoran pronghorn antelope. Because of a lawsuit brought by the Defenders of Wildlife, the Air Force has temporarily canceled three scheduled bombings where the antelopes are found. The FWS will determine the fate of the antelope this spring (1997).

Birds are particularly affected by noise pollutions when their habitats are invaded by minings and oil explorations where explosives are often used. This could lead to disturbances most birds cannot withstand. One reason for the decline of the California condors is the oil exploration being made near their habitats that greatly affects their breeding.

OIL POLLUTION: IMPACT ON SEA ORGANISMS

Researches have been going on to find solutions to clean up oil spill at the least time with fewer personnel. But the solution is not forthcoming soon. Concerns will continue as long as oil is being extracted from the ocean floor and transported by sea. As much as 30% of the oil today come from offshore drilling and more than 60% of all oil are transported through the sea lanes

Numerous studies have been conducted to study the toxic effect of oil on marine organisms. It is well-documented that even 1 mg/l (1 ppm) of oil in seawater can harm sensitive organisms. They can impede larvae hatching from eggs, and hatchlings often die immediately. This was the observation when the tanker Argo Merchant with 29.000 tons of fuel oil went aground 29 nautical miles from Cape Cod. Cods and pollacks' eggs were found dead or dying. Some ingredients in the oil interfere with the sex behavior of affected marine animals. Subtle effects can also include the reproduction of organisms. Some crabs exposed to water-soluble extract of crude oil for a day no longer react to the amino acid taurine which usually signal food for them.

Pollution near the coastal areas are the most difficult to clean up. And depending on the nature of the oil, a considerable variety of animals are killed together with their sensitive minute food. Once the oil reached the beaches, cleanup is much more difficult as they adhere to the sand and gravel. Large amount of stranded oil may kill animals by smothering them.

The conspicuous damage on some Cornish beaches following the wreck of the Torrey Canyon was not due to the stranded oil but to the very toxic oil-spill dispersants then in use. The mixture of oil and dispersant proved far more lethal than the oil alone and most organisms on the affected beaches were killed. A 90% mortality of pilchard (Sarda pilchardus) eggs was observed around the sprayed areas and 50% mortality over a much wider area. The limpets Patella were completely wiped out.

One of the more insidious effects of oil pollution are the diseases it may cause. There have been reports of tumors and fin erosion in fishes and precancerous conditions in bivalves from areas chronically polluted by oil. While these pathological states may occur naturally, these incidences are increasing in polluted water. Damage to shellfishes may persist as long as the pollutants remained.

Even small oil spill can be devastating. When the barge Florida ran aground in Sept. 1969 during a storm in Buzzard's Bay, Massachusetts, it spilled 10,000 gallons of diesel fuel. Winds and strong waves drove the oil onto the beaches, churning up bottom sediments and contaminated it with oil before settling down to the bottom. There was an immediate fish kill along the shallow creeks and bays which sheltered juvenile flounders and blue fishes, and even a variety of adult bait fishes. Lobsters, crabs, shrimps, scallops, and bivalves were killed in large numbers by smothering. Effects on crab population were still obvious seven years later. The discharge of 8,000 tons of bunker C from the Arrow, in Chedabucto Bay, Nova Scotia contaminated 240 km of shoreline and the population of the clam Mya arenaria was still adversely affected six years later. Commercial shellfish beds had to be closed to protect the health of the people Five years later, detailed studies showed that subtidal benthic community is still unstable in the most polluted parts of Wild Harbor.

Plankton, food for most fishes living in the upper few centimeters of the water surface are particularly hard hit by oil pollution. Oil and its distillates are toxic to a wide range of planktonic organisms. Plants along the mangroves and salt marshes are likely to suffer as oil adhere to them according to the season. Oil can inhibit flowering for plants in bud. The oiled flowers rarely produce seeds, and the oiled seeds have impaired germination These chain of events could mean less food for the herbivores.

The loss of sea birds to oil pollution is of great concern to environmentalists. In the northeast Atlantic, hundreds of thousands of sea birds are oiled annually since the 1920s when tankers came into use Estimates made in the 1970s showed that 150,000-450.000 birds died each year from small and deliberate discharges of oil in the North Sea and North Atlantic. Major spills are no included and they can kill large numbers in a matter of days. The breakup of Torrey Canyon off the coast of England killed 40.000 to 100,000 birds in a few weeks. The stranding and subsequent leakage of the tanker Gerd Maersk in the Elbe estuaries in 1955 killed an estimated 250.000 to 500,000 birds.

It is feared that sea bird populations have decreased as a result of persistent high mortality. Unlike most organisms in the sea, sea birds are mostly harmed through the physical properties of floating oil and its ingestion. When oil contaminates the bird's plumage, its water-repellent properties are lost, allowing water to penetrate the plumage and displace the air trapped between the feathers and the skin. This important air layer provides buoyancy and thermal insulation for the bird. With the waterlogged plumage, the bird may sink and drown. Even if it survive, the loss of thermal insulation results in a rapid exhaustion of food reserves as it attempts to maintain body temperature, followed by hypothermia and death. Birds attempting to clean their plumage by preening often swallow the oil causing intestinal disorders and renal or liver failure. If death does not ensue, the ingested oil can depress egg-laying and the number of hatched eggs are reduced. If oil penetrates the incubating eggs, the embryos may die prematurely.

OIL POLLUTION: SPILLAGE

Crude oil is probably the most complicated natural mixture on earth. There are thousands of different compounds found in oil. Although primarily composed of hydrocarbons, it also contains elements such as sulfur, vanadium, and nickel, approximately 5 million tons of oil are discharged into the water systems of the world annually. Other sources come from domestic effluents as more people use and discharge used oil and lubricants indiscriminately. Marine transportation and industrial wastes also contribute a significant amount. Much of it end up in the estuaries and coastal areas where they kill sea organisms and those that feed on them including the birds. The oil that sinks to the sea bottom also poisons the sea bed and the creatures living there. The fish and mussel taste oily only after having contact with petroleum.

Our need for oil is bringing us deeper and farther into the ocean with the improvement of technology for deep sea oil drilling. More than 20.000 offshore locations have been drilled between 1950 and 1980 and they are accelerating due to the limited supply of oil on land. In the North Sea alone, more than 1,000 locations have been drilled. These offshore oil explorations had resulted in oil spills on several occasions. Some of the oil spills are natural occurrences in the ocean. Before the Spanish conquistadors came to the coast of California, oil eruptions constantly took place in the Santa Barbara Channel Development only aggravated the problem. In 1969, the blowout of Union Oil off Santa Barbara. California spilled 7.5 million liters of oil in the Santa Barbara Channel while the blowout on June 3, 1979 in Campeche Bay. in the Gulf of Mexico spilled 530 million liters and was on fire. It took nearly 10 months to cap. but not before it killed hundreds of thousands of birds and mammals The hole was closed with a 30 tons concrete top.

The more common oil spill came from shipping accidents often caused by human error at the loading terminal or near the shorelines. Small and outdated tankers have been responsible for most of the oil spill during the early days. These coastal spillages may be devastating to wildlife. The Exxon Valdez spilled II million gallons of crude oil off Alaska in 1990 contaminating 1,600 kilometers of pristine coastline. It took the lives of about 580,000 seabirds, mostly common murres. 200 to 900 endangered bald eagles, 22 whales and over 5,000 sea otters. The herring and salmon populations were still suffering three years after the disaster. Eggs from contaminated species had trouble hatching and yielded some genetic defects: herring with twisted spines and salmon with club tails. More than 1,600 kilometers of pristine coastline was affected. On January 5, 1993, a Liberian-registered tanker, Braer, lost power in the sea off Scotland and lost 85,000 tons of light crude and 5,000 tons of heavy fuel oil. The damage affected mostly farmed salmon. A Greek tanker, the Aegean Sea, grounded during severe weather in the Tower of Hercules, Spain, broke into 2 and ruptured 7 of its tanks, contaminating 52 sq km of the Galicia coast.

The spillage of refined oil accounts for about 200,000 tons annually. These are just as toxic as the crude oil. Some oil spills are deliberately discharged into the oceans by tankers during the course of cleaning their empty tanks. The oil contains many different fractions, some of which are toxic while others are relatively inert. The slick can easily spread to the beach smothering animals in burrows or on rocks, and prevent sunlight from penetrating the sea to allow photosynthesis of Plants The more toxic and volatile water-soluble compounds spilled in American estuaries have devastated commercial shell fisheries. The heavier compounds will tend to sink to the bottom where they undergo microbial decomposition. But this will happen long after the bottom creatures have been devastated.

The Gulf War of 1991 was the scene of one of the world's worst environmental disasters About 6 million barrels of oil were released to the sea. At least 30,000 sea animals such as turtles, sea cows and birds were killed by the oil slicks which also severely damaged reefs and the seabed. Thousands of birds and farm animals also perished from suffocation and poisoning caused by the burning of oil wells as the Iraqi retreated from the occupation of Kuwait.

In the rainforests of Ecuador, Texaco had for 20 years produced one billion barrels of oil. At the same time, it had also polluted the land with 17 million gallons of spilled crude oil, and discharged 20 billion gallons of wastewater containing hydrocarbons, heavy metals, and other toxic chemicals that contaminated the fishing grounds of the indigenous people. The toxic chemicals will develop ailments and diseases for the native inhabitants for decades to come. The road networks built to transport the crude oil also opened up a million hectares of forest land to new migrants for colonization and therefore led to more habitat destruction.

Half of the cutthroat trout exposed to crude oil of 2.4 mg per liter died within 96 hours and this was below the threshold of 10 mg per liter allowed by the oil and gas industry in Wyoming, Colorado and Montana. This reflects the need to impose more stringent standard

Another problem related to offshore oil exploration is the subsurface dumping of drilling mud from oil platforms. Drilling mud fluid is a clay-based fluid used to lubricate the drill bit, circulate the drill cuttings to the surface, help seal the well wall, and control the pressure in the well. Lubricants and other substances are added that include heavy metals such as arsenic, chromium, and mercury, all highly toxic. Somehow, all these elements will find their way to the environment.

Most spillages and wanton discharges of wastes need not happen. Jailing and heavy fines will encourage oil companies to be more vigilant in hiring well-trained personnel, install better navigation system, purchase new or improve the seaworthiness of their tankers. A law requiring the use of double hulls on all tankers visiting the U.S. ports has greatly reduced the accidental oil spills. This law must extend to all countries and to all vessels carrying oil or other toxic chemicals anywhere in the world.

OIL POLLUTION: TANKERS

More than half the crude oil is transported by more than 6,000 tankers worldwide. After the tanker has unloaded its cargo of oil, it has to take on seawater as ballast for the return trip. The ballast compartment is often the same one occupied by the oil. During unloading of the ballast water, some oil, roughly 0.25% is left behind during the delivery. It is discharged later to the sea along with the ballast water. This amounts to about 500 tons for every 200,000-ton tanker. In the old tankers, many still lying inter-island routes, the dirty ballast containing oil are discharged to the sea during the return journey and are responsible for much of the deliberate oil pollution of the world's oceans. However, two techniques have substantially reduced this possibility.

Since oil is lighter than water, the water can be discharged from the bottom while the oil on top is transferred to a slop tank. This is called load-on-top system. The other improved and expensive way is to use different structure for segregated ballasts. The ballast water does not come in contact with the oil so that no oil is lost to the ocean.

During dry docking for servicing and repair, it is essential that oil be removed from the cargo compartments of tankers and other ships, to avoid the risk of explosion from petroleum gases. Slop reception facilities should be provided by all the ship repair yards.

About 75% of tanker accidents are caused by human errors and can result in large spillages. They occur more frequently on tankers registered under cheap flags where safety regulations and crew qualifications are not strict. These ships carrying toxic chemicals should be banned from any port call in the world if found tc be unseaworthy.

OZONE DEPLETION

Ozone depletion is caused by the destruction of the ozone in the stratosphere. It is due to the reaction of chlorine contained in the C'FCs and other gases with the ozone. The two common CFCs used for refrigeration, cleaning solvent, and plastic blower take about two years to reach the stratosphere before they can make any damage. However, once in the atmosphere, it will take the two common ozone depletes 76 and 139 years to disintegrate, Each chlorine gas can interact and destroy about 10,000 molecules of ozone.

Other ozone depleters are halons used in fire extinguishers, methyl chloroform used in correction fluid and carbon tetrachloride used in dry cleaning. Each halon molecule can destroy at least three times the capacity of the chlorine molecule.

Without the protective shield, the UVB radiation can cause unwanted harm. The present holes in the polar regions have reduced the healthy growth of phytoplankton needed by the marine creatures by as much as 20%. It can have a negative effect on the marine biology. There will be reduced plant metabolism affecting the growth of oceanic plankton which is the main source of food for the sea organisms. There may also be mutagenic effect on animals as well as increases in skin cancers and eye cataracts of animals. Their immune systems may become less resistant to diseases. Some animals in Chile are suffering from blindness as are the kangaroos in Australia, all blamed on the UVB.

PCBs

The Hudson River was the dumping ground for PCBs in the 1960s before it was banned in 1976. Introduced in 1929,. the family of 209 chemicals collectively known as PCBs have been found to be useful for many products. Because it is non-flammable and extremely stable, it has been adopted for use as coolant and insulators in transformer, waterproofing and other electrical products. It is also used as lubricants, hydraulic fluid and other sealants. Household products and pesticides have PCBs as one of their ingredients.

Most of the 3.4 billion pounds produced prior to the ban have been scattered worldwide and there is no way of cleaning it up. Birds that feed on fish from contaminated rivers are experiencing reproduction problem and feather development. Fish populations are also affected. From a high of 25,000 sturgeons in 1977 in Hudson Bay, they have declined to about 3,000 in 1996.

PCBs have been found in the tissues of mammals at the top of the food chain. In 1987, hundreds of bottlenose dolphins washed up on the eastern coast of the U.S. This was followed by another batch of hundreds of dolphins on the western coast of France. In 1990, five thousand striped dolphins were stranded on the beaches of the Mediterranean Sea. All of them had high levels of PCBs with depressed or damaged immune systems. Immunological studies have found that the immune response dropped as levels of PCBs and DDT increased in their blood. Their reproductive systems are likewise vulnerable to damage caused by hormone disrupting chemicals during parental development.

PCBs in very low concentration (1 ppb) have been shown to be lethal to estuarine life both in laboratory tests, and in field mortalities around industrial and agricultural discharges containing pesticides. Due to the biomagnification effects of PCBs, top predators such as birds and seals are particularly at risk. Within the Baltic Sea, high levels of PCBs within seals have been held responsible for the failure of reproduction in many female seals.

Ranch mink feeding on fish contaminated with PCBs were dying because of their sensitivity to the toxic chemical. The females failed to reproduce when fed with food containing 0.3 to 5 ppm. Adults animals died at doses of 3.6 to 20 ppm. The same thing happened to the otters during the 1950s in Britain and Europe. The lake trout has become extinct in many places contaminated with PCBs.

Fortunately, PCBs have been found to degrade naturally by certain bacteria found in sediments. The bacteria strip chlorine atoms from PCBs, thus lowering their toxicity. It has less effects on the reproductive cells of experimental mice. But the huge amount already released to the environment will take decades to degrade to a harmless state.

PESTICIDES

Pesticides made of organochlorine and organohalogen compounds pose considerable threats to the environment. Unlike petroleum hydrocarbons, these halogenated hydrocarbons (hydrocarbons containing chlorine, bromine, iodine or fluorine), are not degraded by chemical oxidation or microorganisms. Like metals, these substances are permanent additions to the ecosystem, but compared to metals, even minute quantities of these man-made substances can be hazardous to marine life. The organohalogen compounds include the PCBs (polychlorinated biphenyls), HCB (hexachlolorobcnzcne), HCH (lindane, hexachlorocyclohexane), dieldrin, and DDT (dichloro-diphenyl-trichloroethane). These substances cannot be excreted by any animal once ingested, and they accumulate principally in fatty tissue of its victim. This bioaccumulation leads up through the food chain, and by biomagnification, the top predators have the highest concentration and may suffer most. It is not surprising that pesticides have been responsible for the death of millions of nontargeted animals.

Other compounds used on pesticides, agricultural chemicals, detergents and ingredients in plastics can disrupt the functions of the endocrine glands. Even in minute quantities, they can alter a whole spectrum of morphological and reproductive systems of the organism. Tumors, deformities, reproductive abnormalities are found in some exposed fishes, birds, and mammals.

The Beluga whales in the estuary of the St. Lawrence River in north-eastern America have been the traditional food for indigenous people and later hunted by the European colonizers for their hides and oil. Today, they are fighting a losing battle against a new menace to their survival - pollution. They have lost 90% of their population of about 5,000 at the beginning of the century and are down to about 500 today. It was only in 1979 that the Canadian government granted protection to the white whales through the efforts of ecologist Leone Pippard. Still their population continue to decline. Since 1982, 73 dead belugas have undergone autopsies. DDT and PCBs were discovered in the blubber at the highest level ever recorded for any mammal. The eels upon which they feed have been found to be especially heavily contaminated with PCBs. Autopsies have also indicated that the DDT, PCBs and other chemicals such as Mirex are actively transported from the blubber into the internal tissues. Baby whales suckling from contaminated females may have received massive organochlorine pesticides from their mothers' milk and experienced toxic shock. The health of the beluga served as a good index of the health of the ecosystem where they inhabit.

The belugas suffer from bladder cancer and herpes-viral dermatitis, the first time discovered in cetaceans. They are also suffering from significant incidences of gastric ulcers and tumors. Most of these deadly chemicals have not been in use in recent years, but their continued presence in the bodies of the largest predator in the river estuary demonstrates how pervasive and persistent these poisons are.

No pesticide has been intensively studied than DDT. This synthetic organochlorine is one of the most stable pesticides that does not break down easily and is recycled throughout the food chain, passing from lower form to higher form of animal. It easily accumulated in high concentration in the fatty tissue because it is fat-soluble. Other chemical pesticides include the extremely toxic but less persistent organic phosphates such as parathion, malathion, etc.

Pesticides are often sprayed over large areas, harming birds, mammals, and beneficial insects unintentionally. Use of pesticides to control mosquitoes, gypsy moths, locusts, etc often left behind the pesticides that continue to bring havoc to the environment. Beside, those insects that survived the initial attack develop resistance to chemicals by producing detoxifying enzymes that immunized their offspring. It became necessary to introduce even deadlier toxic chemicals to counter the immunity.

The peregrine falcon is a swift and deadly bird of prey found in the coastal areas of North American and European continents. It feeds mainly on fishes and other sea birds. Biologists started to notice a dramatic decline in their numbers after the Second World War. But it was not until 1958 when a British ornithologist.

Derek Ratcliffe, observed many broken eggs in their nests and the parent birds eating the contents. At first he thought it was a behavioral disorder caused by the pesticides attacking the nervous system of these birds of prey. However, Ratcliffe noted that the decline in the number of peregrines had begun at about the time that DDT and other pesticides were being used. Careful observations lead to new findings. He noticed that the eggs were not deliberately broken, but were crushed during incubation because of their abnormally thin shells. The broken eggs were eaten as a natural response.

The brown pelicans favorite food is the anchovies DDT manufactured from the pesticide plant in Palos Verdes Peninsula was piped miles away into the sea. These are taken in by the anchovies which are later consumed by the brown pelicans. Although the pelicans have regained their population as a result of the ban on DDT, they are faced with a grim future as a result of overfishing.

Many researches have been done about how DDT affects birds. They found it interferes with the hormones that control the deposit of calcium in eggshells. This resulted in thin-shelled and fragile eggs and reduced sex hormone estrogen, resulting in the birds laying fewer eggs than normal.

DDT and other banned pesticides are still in use in some developing countries because it is cheap and effective. These pesticidos are turning up thousands of miles away from where they were used. A group of atmospheric chemists from Indiana University has found 22 heavily chlorinated compounds as far as the polar regions. Cleaner substitutes or alternatives are necessary to replace these toxic pesticides.

Along the coast of Jutland, Denmark, is a chemical plant producing the pesticide parathion. The effluents from this plant is piped to the North Sea since 1961. Dead fishes began to be noted along the mouth of the pipeline in 1964. Lobsters were also dying up to a distance of 60 km along the coast. Test results showed that the soupy effluents even at a dilution of I to 50,000 were fatal to the lobster. The effluents were even found to be more toxic than the pesticide parathion. The plant was required by the government to purify its effluents that allowed guppies to survive at a dilution of 1 to 50.

In 1965, the number of Sterna sandvicensis terns on the island Griend off the coast of the Netherlands decreased dramatically. Only 650 out of 20,000 breeder pairs survived. The dying birds showed definite signs of having been poisoned. The terns were eating fishes poisoned by the effluents of a chemical plant manufacturing the chlorinated hydrocarbon pesticides telodrin, dieldrin, and endrin. Between 1964 and 1967, the females of the Somateria mohssima cider duck were also found dying in large numbers. In 1967, measures were taken so that toxic effluents were no longer discharged. By 1974, the number of terns had risen back up to 5,000 breeder pairs.

PLASTICS

One of the modern conveniences of life has been brought about by the proliferation of the use of plastics. They are light-weight, easy to transport, and transparent. These products are usually made from the non-renewable sources coming from the petro-chemical industry.

The U.S. Office of Technology Assessment reports that millions of tons of plastic improperly discarded each year posed a far greater threat to marine mammals and birds than all the pesticides, oil spills, and contamination run-off from the land. The U.S. National Academy of Science place the number of discarded plastic objects at 640,000 each day. This is on top of the 150,000 tons of fishing gears lost or dumped by the fishing industry each year.

All creatures that inhabit the seas are at risk to plastic pollution. Captain Cline Kelly, an English ecologist and filmmaker, once encountered a dead sea turtle weighing 14 kilos with three kilos of plastic, a balloon, three condoms, four meters of ribbon, plastic bags, etc. in its body.

Thousands of albatrosses are dying in the Pacific Ocean, choking on plastics and other products such as colored caps and even cigarette lighters. These lighter than water objects are often mistaken for food by birds because they have long been eating anything that float on water. If they do not choke to death, the plastic in their stomach makes them feel full and they don't eat anymore, causing them to lose weight leading to their starvation. At other times, the plastics are treated as food and given to their young, causing them the same suffering.

Even animals on land can suffer from plastic ingestion. In India, the sacred cows are dying of starvation caused by eating plastics in garbage dumps. Because of the lack of taste buds, the cattle will cat anything they can scavenge in the garbage dump. One cow had 50 kilos ot plastics surgically removed from its stomach.

Some ingredients used in the making of plastics have been found to mimic hormone-disrupting chemicals. One of the active component in the plastic is p-nonylphenol, commonly added to polystyrene and polyvinyl chlorides (PVCs) to make them more stable and less breakable. Researchers also found that alkylphenol polyethoxylatcs, chemicals found in many detergents, pesticides, and personal-care products, can break down into nonylphenol and other chemicals when they encounter bacteria in animals' bodies. Because of their toxic effect on aquatic life, several European countries had already banned their use in the 1980s. Another estrogen mimic chemical, bisphenol-A, can leach from polycarbonate, another entirely different kind of plastic used in the manufacture of lab flasks, giant jugs used to bottle drinking water and metal canned foods.

One well-known plastic is the six-packed rings used in the beverage industry. Improper disposable of these rings often end up in the rivers, lakes, and oceans around the world. These seemingly innocent packing materials have taken the lives of thousands of birds and sea creatures. These transparent plastic rings are almost invisible to the sea creatures. They are often caught inside the rings that can entangle them causing their drowning. Fish accidentally swimming into these rings have been known to starve to death when the ring that entangled them were themselves entangled. Small fishes caught with the ring can outgrow and tighten around their head and strangle them to death. Today, much fishing is carried out by fishermen using driftnets made of fine plastic that are so huge and transparent that they cannot be seen by diving birds or detected by dolphins with their sonar.

To remedy the situation, petition the manufacturers to stop using these six-packed rings for the beverage industry. No plastic ring means less accidental deaths. Avoid buying drinks that use these rings. Boycotting products using them will send a clear message to the manufacturers and retailers of our abhorrence to this practice. In cases we had occasion to encounter these rings, snip the rings before throwing them to the garbage can. Avoid throwing them into the water.

An innovative cardboard six-packed ring has been manufactured. It disintegrates within two months and their tensile strength decline within 5 days because it uses less glue and thinner than the plastic ones but strong enough to carry a six-pack soda. This will allow any mammal caught by the ring to be able to escape in a short time.

It takes at least four hundred fifty years to degrade, even in saltwater. Two million birds have died for eating plastics thinking they were jellyfishes while another 100.000 mammals either ingested the plastics or entangled in them.

RECYCLING

Recycling is one of the most potent weapons to save the environment from degradation. It is easy to accomplish beside being cheap, and effective in reducing pollution. Many household products that would otherwise end up in the environment can be recycled or reused. Some of these products are toxic and have been tested on animals. Used motor oil, pesticides, household cleaners, radiator water treated with antirust chemicals, are not only toxic to humans but to animals as well.

Plastic packaging, discarded tin cans, razor blades, etc. have been found to be harmful to wildlife that came in contact with them. The millions of birds and sea animals killed annually by plastic discards could have been saved if they were recycled. Animals have been harmed trying to cat the food inside discarded tin cans. The open can sharp edges can cause wound along the neck area. The same is true with razor blades.

The disposal beverage can with the pull are often discarded along the beaches. Heads of small birds may be caught inside these discards and harm the birds. Make it a point to crush the can before disposing them. Better yet. send the cans to the recycling center for recycling. These aluminum cans can be recycled indefinitely at only a fraction of the energy required to make the can from raw material.

RED TIDE

Red tide is caused by any of several species of dinoflagellates. It can either be Gonyaulax, Gymnodmium or Pyrodinium. all of which contain dangerous neurotoxins. The phytoplankton has a potent toxin that causes reddish discoloration of seawater that accumulated in marine animals such as clams, mussels, and oysters without harming them. But they are deadly to people who consume them and to fishes found in their locality. The red tide bloom along the middle section of the Gulf Coast of Texas had killed 40,000 fishes. The algae attacks the nervous system of these fishes such as thread-fin, herring, red snapper and hardhead catfish.

There were several documented cases of people dying after eating contaminated sea food. In Finland, Russia, and the Philippines liver failures resulting in deaths have occurred after eating shellfishes. The disease called paralytic shellfish poisoning which causes symptoms such as nausea, loss of balance, defective vision, convulsion and death, is not a new phenomena. As far back as 1773, a red tide incident killed one person and downed four others. Another incident in 1799 caused the death of one hundred men on a Russian expedition. Today, more incidents of red tide are being reported. In Manila Bay and elsewhere in the coastal city around Metro Manila, incidents of red tide menace have been reported periodically. The accumulation of red tide organisms in the seawater is probably the result of eutrophication compounded by pollution.

RIVER POLLUTION

Human beings first settled down along the coastal areas because of the abundance of sea food available. As the population increased, people were forced to disperse inland, always living near the river networks. The pollution discharged on the waterways did not affect the environment because of the small population and the absence of industrial pollutants. The Industrial Revolution spelled the onset of the pollution of our river system. Toxic metals and chemicals were dumped into the river without treatment. Disturbances from steamships, river engineering works such as port and harbors, dredging, damming have started to damage the ecosystems. This happened to the Rhine River as early as the 18th century as heavy industries were constructed along the river. By 1969, the worst fish kill was recorded in this area. Massive fish kills also occurred in the Dutch Rijn.

Fish kills have also been recorded in the Manila Bay as recently 1996. Thirty tons of fish were killed by cyanide poisoning. Chemical toxins came from some of the factories that discharged their waste into the Pasig River. No one has yet been charged. Pollution has been responsible for the red tide scare that has become a periodic occurrences in the Bay.

The effects of pollution differ in different species of fishes. The salmon find their homes from the Atlantic Ocean by smell. Pollution affecting their sense of smell may thus be harmful. Trout eggs will not survive attack by sewage fungus even under ideal conditions. Pollution also affects the invertebrates, the lowest ranked food chain for fishes and mammals. The ingestion of pollutants by the lower life forms often accumulate in the bodies of the fishes and mammals which are later consumed by people.

Sea birds are not spared from water pollution. They may be affected simply by resting on the water poisoned by surfactants like oil and toxic chemicals. Some birds like swans may eat plants, invertebrates and even gravel which may contain toxins. The lethal lead weights dropped by anglers have been mistaken for gravel. Birds feeding on contaminated fishes will accumulate the toxins. Birds of prey have declined dramatically as a result of ingesting organochlorine insecticides found in their prey, reviving only after the uses of these pesticides dropped.

England has been one of the best habitat for otters as late as 1955. But the introduction of organochlorine insecticides such as dieldrin, aldrin even in degraded forms is no guarantee that it is safe. Their numbers dropped drastically in many parts of the country until these compounds were removed from use. A new type of pesticides called organophosphorus are just as harmful.

The fishes we eat can also contain dangerously high level of heavy metals The most toxic is mercury and the least is sodium Heavy metals are more soluble, therefore more toxic on acidic waters. Lead poisoning can occur in acidic water while becoming less harmful in alkaline ones Fish kills at lower pH may be due to the natural aluminum changing from the insoluble hydroxide to the soluble aluminate. Some species develop tolerance, which is good for the animal but not for their predators.

SEWAGE SLUDGE

Sewage is the primary organic materials often discharged deliberately to the watercourses with only the primary treatment. In early times, the ocean sink is so large compared to the existing human population that its environmental impact is negligible But since the 18th century, the population has increased tremendously that further pollution is detrimental to the sea inhabitants as well as humans who feed on the marine animals.

One of the constituents of sewage is ammonia. It is particularly toxic to fishes and a major source of acidification since it can be oxidized to nitric acid. Ammonia can react with dissolved oxygen causing oxygen deficiency that lower the concentration of hemoglobin in body fluids causing lowered hatching and growth rate of fries.

Sewage is subject to bacterial decay resulting in the oxidation of organic molecules. As a result of this bacterial activity, the oxygen concentration is reduced, leading to the smoothering of many organisms. To avoid tragedy, the sew age is often treated before it is discharged Three stages are necessary if we are to clean the water of sewage toxins.

The primary treatment used to remove large solids is the settlement tank. The large proportion of suspended solids undergo a secondary biological treatment to reduce the biological oxygen demand (BOD) The water is filtered through a bed of 4-15 cm of rocks or coke, with a large surface area for bacteria w hich degrade organic matter in the water as it percolates through the bed. Material settled from the outflow may be disposed of and supernatant liquid discharged to the water system. The tertiary treatment is required for high quality water. The water is retained for further filtration to remove the suspended solids. Nitrates may be removed by algal growth in retaining ponds and phosphates can be removed by electrolytic methods.

Shallow water dumping of sludge have been responsible for toxic metals found in the guts of fishes caught off the Clyde River in Scotland. The British shellfish industry was destroyed due to the introduction of disease-causing agents accompanying the sludge. Britain alone dumped 10 million tons of sludge into the sea each year. Even deep-sea dumping can travel thousands of miles from its source and settle in breeding areas for clams and other molluscs.

As a result of pressure from environmentalists and the European governments. Britain will stop dumping sewage sludge in the North Sea by 1998. The sludge is contaminated with heavy metals, more than normal spores of bacteria and other industrial pollutants. Economics play an important role in their decision to continue dumping at sea in spite of the availability of other forms of disposal including incineration and conversion of sludge into fertilizer.

THERMAL POLLUTION

Marine life can be found in temperature that range from -2 degree Centigrade in the Antarctica up to 50 degrees in tropical shallow waters. However, some marine life in the tropical marine life can be fatal between 32 and 34 degrees Centigrade. In deep ocean water, many animals are subject to a narrow range of cold temperatures. A minimal change can damage plants and animals resulting in fish kills and plankton blooms. Some fish especially in freshwater can tolerate higher change in temperature as long as the change is not sudden allowing them to adapt.

Most of the thermal pollution come from residual heat generated by power plants and industrial plants that has not been cooled down before discharging to the river or ocean. In Britain, all but one of the nuclear power are in the coast to take advantage of the sea water. Water is used in cooling turbines, generators and other equipments is often released into lakes and rivers. The water returned to the ocean is about 10 degrees C higher.

Subtle changes include change in the reproductive biology of aquatic organisms. Thermal pollution often acts synergetically with other forms of pollution. The increase in temperature increases the metabolic rate that could lead to faster growth, but it decreases the solubility of oxygen which could lead to lack of oxygen. Improvements and investments are needed to reduce thermal pollution.

TRASH

The ocean has always been the recipient of human refuse. It is therefore not surprising that each year, billions of kilos of trash are washed into the ocean. Whether these trash are plastics that float or tin cans that settle down to the bottom of the sea, they pose a hazard to all sea organisms. The degradation of some of these products may be poisonous to the sea creatures. It is only a matter of time before the ocean reaches its saturation point. The volume of discharged wastes into the ocean is partly to be blamed for the sea level rising.

Discarded razors and blades, and even broken glasses in the garbage can be dangerous to scavenging animals. Keep these items out of reach of animals. Wastepaper should never be thrown away because they can easily be recycled. In the oceans, they can float and be mistaken for food by some mammals and birds.

The design on some containers made of plastic or cardboard may be hazardous to animals. Squirrels and other small animals have been found dead, their head stuck inside the containers while trying to get the food inside. This is due to the small openings in these containers. Openings in bottles and small cans are the other culprits.

CHAPTER 18

CONSERVATION

The wildlife are important components of the planet's ecology and like the trees are renewable resources that can be utilized for the benefits of all. For centuries, there was no need to set aside wilderness and forests for the preservation of wildlife. It only became necessary as a result of the proliferation of the human species, and the intrusion of people into their natural habitats. Even just keeping the status quo of many of these habitats is no longer enough to save many species from extinction. This is because many habitats are destroyed beyond regeneration and their inhabitants are doomed to extinction unless other drastic measures are taken.

Conservation has taken different forms to different people. Basically it is to protect all living or non-living things from being destroyed or polluted and keep it in a healthy state. Applied to the animal kingdom, it means not only to protect the animals but also the ecosystems where they inhabit in a balance and harmonious state. Others consider conservation to mean setting up wildlife parks in the cities and to help fund and save endangered species. Still some conservationists are considering ways to save them from extinction through scientific methods while under captive breeding.

Wildlife conservation is a complex procedure of evaluating habitats, taking inventory of the stock of each wildlife within the ecosystem, and learning how to conserve and save wildlife. One effective way of conservation for endangered species is to capture and rear the wildlife in parks. It brings together biodiversity of species so low in numbers that there may not be able to propagate in the wild and to prevent inbreeding. As the science of biology continue to gain headway, we have learned to keep eggs and sperms of endangered species in freezer as a hedge against extinction.

Funding is an important component of a successful conservation effort, especially for the poor countries w here wildlife abound. Education is also important if we want to eliminate cruelties on animals. Other important conservation measures include improving facilities of wildlife parks, passage of wildlife protection laws and others. Wildlife conservation has also became high tech. Scientific methods and new technologies have been used to keep track of endangered species through the use of telemetry.

Individual efforts can also be effective in saving wildlife. These may include letter writing, donations, joining the environmental organisations, petitioning our lawmakers, reporting cruelties to proper authorities, and many actions and ideas people can think up.

ANIMAL WELFARE LAWS

Although the first animal welfare legislation was made in 1641 by the Puritans, the war against animal abuses still goes on. The modern fight to improve the welfare of the animals did not really take off until late in the 18th century. Sporadic episodes of war against animal abuses took place through individual efforts. It was an uphill fight and took decades of hard works by dedicated individuals.

In the last 100 years, animal welfare groups have been at the forefront in espousing animal rights. The American Society for the Prevention of Cruelty to Animals (ASPCA) was founded in 1866 and is still active today. After the publication of the book, Animal Liberation by Peter Singer in 1975, a lot of animal rights movements sprouted out. It was through their efforts that new laws have been enacted toward this end at all fronts including Congress. The first humane slaughter bill was presented to Congress by Sen. Hubert Humphrey in 1955. In essence, the law requires all animals to be slaughtered and rendered insensible to pain. It took three years to pass into law and became effective in 1960. The Laboratory Animal Welfare Act took even longer, six years, before it was signed into law in 1966. The opponents were the powerful medical and pharmaceutical interests. An amendment in 1970 requires all experimental animals to undergo anaesthesia whenever it doesn't affect the purpose of the experiment.

All the fights for animal welfare has been uphill and long. It was not until 1985 that more amendments were incorporated into the Animal Welfare Act in the U.S.. This include supply of companion animals as an end to unnecessary isolation, protection and care during transportation, and penalties against sale and use of stolen animals for laboratory experiments. The latest amendments have given rise to the 3 R's espoused by NGOs. They are reduction in the number of test animals used in animal experimentations and unnecessary researches. The law also requires all laboratories to keep a data bank to reduce the duplication of animal experimentations. They are required to set up animal-care committees and submit to annual inspections. Housing facilities for dogs and other primates must provide room for exercise. Animal experiment before it commences must undergo reviews by a committee as to its worthiness before it takes place. Refinement of techniques used in experiments must reduce suffering. Last, but not least, the replacement of live animals with cell cultures or computer models whenever feasible must be employed.

Sweden had passed a law on animal rights in 1988 that is meant to protect farm animals. Under the law, cattle must be allowed to graze in the open land. Pigs may not be confined and must be allowed access to straw for bedding and feed in other places. Chickens must be given opportunity to roam and peck for foods and not kept confined in cages or eat feeds that are highly drugged. Veal calves may roam around pastures and use of sub-therapeutic doses of antibiotics and hormones is strictly prohibited.

Developing countries around the world are slow in enacting laws for the prevention of cruelty to animals. Even if there are laws, enforcement is often neglected. It is obvious that animal welfare are given low priority. Activists and animal welfare organizations must take concerted actions for the enactment of animal welfare laws. After the enactment of the Animal Welfare Act of 1998 on February 11, 1998, some quarters have voiced their objections to certain provisions of the law especially on dog-eating. It has long been considered acts of cruelty to kill man's best friend and the strict enforcement of this provision to the letter seems remote in many places. A full text of the law is provided at the Appendix.

ANTI-POACHING

Poaching is the illegal hunting of wild animals live for the black market or dead for their skin or body parts mainly for profit. The problem is becoming more severe today as the target wildlife becomes depleted and rare and prices soared to new heights. The wildlife poachers are everywhere, but nothing beats poaching in the tropical countries. This is mainly due to the poverty and unemployment problems besieging these countries and the lax enforcement on anti-poaching laws. For the poor poachers, a single kill of an endangered species could mean up to a year's salary looks enticing. Serious efforts must be taken if poaching is to be stop.

Funding is often the first priority for a successful anti-poaching drive. In the 1970s, more than 20,000 rhinos roaming the parks in Kenya were reduced to a few hundreds by poachers. All these unlawful killings were made possible by lack of funds to patrol the parks. In one visit to the Kora National Park by Raymond Bonner, the author of At the Hand of Man, found that the warden tasked with protecting wildlife did not have the resources for an efficient anti-poaching drive. There was no money for equipments and uniforms, salary is low, firearms were old bolt-action rifles pitted against automatic weapons used by poachers and the only patrol car was an old military truck without headlights.

During the year 1989, Kenya was a killing field for elephants. An average two to three elephants were killed by poachers daily. In March 1989, a group of seventeen elephants were found dead in Tsavo National Park and another group of 24 elephants were killed in a privately owned ranch. All these killings were done by professional poachers and not ordinary hungry locals trying to make ends meet.

When news and scenes of gruesome dead elephants began to show up on TV news worldwide, the President of Kenya, Daniel arap Moi was forced to took an uncompromising stand against poachers. He ordered all poachers shot on sight. His paramilitary unit had been deployed at the Kora National Park in an attempt to stop poachings. Eleven suspected poachers were killed before the end of the year 1989. When Richard Leakey took over as director of the Kenya's Wildlife Department, an average of one poacher was killed every four days during his first year in office.

The successful effort in Kenya has persuaded other African nations to adopt the shoot-to-kill policy to stem the tide against poachers. In Zimbabwe, 145 poachers were killed between 1984 and 1991. After the WWF provided Zimbabwe with funds to buy a helicopter for its war against poachers, more than 50 suspected poachers were killed. While the killing of poachers may be condemned by some parties, it could be the only way to stop the extinction of many species in the wild.

BOYCOTT

The boycott is the consumers' most effective weapon against companies engaged in harmful and unwanted environmental degradations. It is even resorted to by countries such as the U.S. and EU. The U.S. threat to invoke sanctions against Japan has led to a Japanese commitment to eliminate importation of Hawksbill turtle shells. Probably the most effective weapon against another country is total embargo, where the government itself takes an active role against the abuses done by another nation.

Boycott may be manifested in other ways. One form is divestment, the cessation of investment in a target company. This has been resorted to by investors who find it difficult to invest in companies that do not give justice to animals or the environment in general.

Media coverage helps to enhance the boycott impacts on targeted companies. Most high profile companies are very sensitive to their reputation and will go all out to cultivate a good relationship with consumers. The threat alone is sometimes effective in bringing about changes in company's policies. Boycott empowered the small people who would otherwise have done nothing. It is direct, easy to organize, few or no debate, and no legislative and bureaucratic red tapes are encountered.

Boycott has always been effective on a local scale because fewer people need to be reached. On a large scale, backing by NGOs is necessary to succeed. The Sea Shepherd Conservation Society of Canada undertook a boycott of Norwegian fish products in protest against the brutal slaughters for sport of thousands of pilot whales by the Faroe Islanders. The whales approaching the shore are stabbed behind the dorsal fin with spears, causing great agony while they beached. The other whales soon follow suit, beaching themselves in the shallow water. The hooks are then sunk into the whales' heads and used to drag them on the beach. A knife is used to cut the whale's spinal marrow, blubber, and blowhole. These painful wounds cause the whale to thrash violently and break its own spinal cord paralysing the entire body.

Another boycott was sponsored by Boycott for the Whales, a coalition of environmental and animal welfare organizations. Japan Air Lines was the target because it was owned by the Japanese government to the tune of 40 percent.

Greenpeace, one of the militant environmental organization, co-sponsored an international boycott of Icelandic fishes due to its scientific research w haling after the establishment of the moratorium on commercial whaling in 1985. The boycott, which lasted until July 1989, were participated by restaurant chains like Long John Silver's, Red Lobster, and Shoney's, plus some schools as well as the City of Boston. Hundreds of demonstrations helped to dramatize the boycott campaigns. It cost the fishing industry of Iceland some $50 million before the boycott was called off after Iceland announced an end to its w haling activities.

In the case of farming factory, it is necessary to boycott the manufacturers and suppliers of these farm products. Insist on buying products from animal range farmers. It will encourage more farmers to raise animals more humanely.

CAPTIVE BREEDING

A large number of animals in the wild are in precarious low numbers and in need of drastic actions to save them from extinction. One effective w ay is through captive breeding where animals are placed under the best care and facilities with the best doctors on hands. They are fed regularly without fear of being stalked by predators. In the absence of poachers and natural threats, these animals improved their chances of survival and were able to breed without fear.

Pere David's deer, Arabian oryx, Hawaiian goose are just a few species that owed their continued existence to captive breeding. Another successful captive breeding is the Przewaslo's horse, the last true wild horse species. They once roamed in the Mongolian steppes for thousands of years before the nomadic tribes settled there with their livestock. They were hunted down as pests until a few were left and had to be rescued before they became extinct. The last wild horse was captured in 1947 and taken to the AskanyaNova in Ukraine. Today more than one thousand wild horses are in captivity. Some have been released to their original habitat.

The careful breeding of cheetahs has made it possible to choose the various genetic variations that could produce a stronger and healthier breed of cheetahs that would one day repopulate the wild without fear of experiencing genetic bottleneck.

Artificial insemination (AI) is an effective weapon used in captive breeding. AI uses the sperm taken from the male species and inserted into the reproductive tract of the female when it is in estrus. The sperm must be fresh and used within a few hours. Improvements have made it possible for the sperm to be stored in liquid nitrogen at -196 degree Centigrade and then thaw before it is used. This is much more effective since the sperm can be gathered from faraway places to avoid inbreeding and kept on hand when needed. Sometimes, it is difficult to determine the period of ovulation and a readily available sperm bank will be handy when needed.

Other advantages include easy transport of sperm instead of the animal for breeding. Frozen sperm is less costly to maintain under a small space than keeping the animals. The sperm can also be kept for perpetuity. AI has also made it possible to use sperm from the wild animals. The animals can be anaesthetized in the wild and the sperm taken from them without need to breed them in captivity. The animals are induced electrically via the rectum to ejaculate. But it does not always work. Rhinos refused to ejaculate when anaesthetized, and if they do, the sperms are of poor quality with low sperm count.

Test tube fertilizations have also been resorted to. Sperm from the male and egg from the female are surgically removed from their respectively sex organs and placed in a petrified dish for fertilization. After a few days, the embryo is placed inside the bodies of a surrogate animal for nourishment until it is born.

Captive breeding can also served as a ground for learning and research into animal behavior. When Bronx Zoo got some gerenuks, a dainty antelopes, from the African savannah for display and breeding, the animals will not breed despite lavish attention. Careful researches and observations led to the discovery that the females need plenty of water. The excreted urine contains a reproductive signal that the female is in estrus. Further observations led to the restructuring of the water supply to optimize the signal to get the males going. The result was a successful breeding program.

The year 1996 was a record year for the Exotic Feline Breeding Compound (EFBC) Feline Conservation Center in California. The Center is devoted to the breeding of endangered species and ihe development of captive breeding techniques. Thai year, their wild cats had produced eleven offspring between May and October. These were three Amur leopard cubs, one jaguar cub, one Northern Chinese leopard cub. two black Asian leopard cubs and four fishing cat kittens The Center is particularly proud of Gigant, a handsome Amur leopard is proving himself to be a great father. It is believed that there are fewer than 100 left.

After years of successfully breeding the rare Chinese leopard (Panthera pardus japonensis), the EFBC began a worldwide, cooperative effort to breed the Amur leopard and increase its captive gene pool The first Amur leopard to arrive was Gigant. from Helsinki Zoo. Finland. In 1995. Gigant reign began when his mate Kuhka gave birth to a cub named Nadia on Ma> 30. 1995. Last year (1997) Kishka and Solstice. both females on loan to the compound from European zoos, have added three bonny cubs to the captive population.

Al has also been used for animals having difficulty to breed in the wild such as the pandas. Because of their declining population, it has become necessary to create a germplasm or sperm bank for the endangered species not only for breeding in the future, but also to reduce the chances of inbreeding. It is important to have separate germplasm banks in different localities as an insurance against natural disasters, diseases outbreak, fires, etc.

Captive breeding has also been responsible lor bringing back several birds from the brink of extinction. The most famous of them is probably the California condor (Gymnogyps californianus). Their numbers have been depopulated by hunters, egg collectors, lead poisoning from hunters, pesticides, and others were killed for perching on high-voltage powerlines. The population was so low in the wild that the U.S. government decided to catch all the condors in the wild for safe-keeping and breeding. By 1987, all the 27 condors were caught and placed in the San Diego Wild Animal Park and Los Angeles Zoo for breeding. By 1994, their population has grown to 75 condors in captivity and some were released into the wild.

Only four Mauritius kestrel (Falco punctatus) were left in the wild in 1973 when the Mauritius Kestrel Conservation Programme was started. Captive breeding was responsible for saving these birds from extinction. There are now more than 300 kestrels in captivity and in the wild. Another bird species that returned from the brink of extinction is the Catham Island black robin (Petroica travtrsi) of New Zealand. By 1976 there were seven birds left. In ten years time, the population has increased to 37 by clever manipulation of the breeding pairs and using cross-fostering to allow them to breed more often. Much of the credit should go to one bird, Old Blue. In 1976 she was one of the two surviving females She began to breed in 1979, at the age of nine, by which time she was the only productive bird. Had she not lived to the grand old age of 13, a rare accomplishment for a black robin, and had she not bred every year until her death, the species would have been extinct then.

CITES

The Convention on International Trade in Endangered Species of Wild Fauna and Mora, better known as CITES was created in Washington in 1973. It came into force in July 1975. after ten years of debate and two years of waiting, with initially

10 nations as members. The agreement was a comprehensive international conservation agreement to protect all fauna and flora. It was prompted by an alarming increase in the trade of wildlife and wildlife products. Before the ban, in one single year, the U.S. imported skins from more than five million crocodiles, 13,000 jaguars, 9,000 leopards, and 1,000 cheetahs.

During the early parts of its organization, several countries took advantage of loopholes in the agreement. Countries not signatory to the agreement were used as conduit for illegal tradings. In the early 1980s, Belgium was used as a base for importing and then exporting 500 tons of ivory tusks. When it joined the CITES, the role was taken over by Singapore which exported 250 tons of ivory in 1985. After Singapore joined CITES in 1987, the conduit shifted to Burundi. Between 1979 and 1987, Burundi exported 1,450 tons of elephant tusks which came mostly from the large elephant population of Zaire and Tanzania. Most of the ivories end up in Japan. The elephant then was listed under Appendix II which allows trading in ivory.

Now there are more than 127 member countries. Since its inception, CITES have been playing a more active role in enforcing its rule on member nations. Offenders are being arrested, fined and sometimes jailed for indiscriminately killing wildlife. In the U.S., in November 1978, three companies were fined $87,500 for shipping 2,500 alligator skins intended for the black market worth more than $1 million for tanning in France. In Hong Kong, in January 1979, a magistrate imposed the maximum fine of $1,000 on the Hong Kong Pur Factory for smuggling 319 cheetah skins worth several hundred thousand dollars from Ethiopia. It is obvious that the penalty is small compared to the destruction brought about the illegal trade and the huge gain made by illegal traders. Governments that use obsolete or lenient laws in applying the penalties do not help deter the illegal trade. CITES should promulgate its own penalties for adoption by all member nations. The penalties should extend not only to the confiscation of the illegal items, the penalty should be several times the cost of the item. But more important, it should sentence violators to jail. Jailing the guilty parties is often more effective than any pecuniary penalty any state can enforced.

CITES has been actively helped by environmentalists. In the tropical countries, they help put up signs in international airports against trading in endangered species. Many countries joined the organization without being serious except as a showpiece to the rest of the world. Some countries passed laws to protect the environment but few really take the initiative to stop illegal logging and trade in wildlife seriously.

The power of CITES over member nations should be strengthened. CITES in trying to regulate international trade need their full cooperation. In turn governments should provide all the necessary personnel and fundings, while development assistance should be provided for those countries who could not afford them. Many Third World countries are too poor to give priority to wildlife protections.

CLONING

The successful sheep cloning at the Scotland's Roslin Institute was an important engineering breakthrough in the history of developmental biology. Its repercussions on biomedical research and conservation of endangered species may not be far behind. By using nucleus from a mammary cell of a six-year-old sheep, the scientists fused this genetic material into an egg cell from another adult sheep produce an exact replica of the donor sheep.

Many endangered mammals that are difficult to breed in captivity using proven techniques may find hope in this new technique. But more researches are necessary to increase the success rate. Pandas, rhinoceros, some big cats are goo candidates for cloning.

CONSERVATION AT HOME

Conservation need not be confined to the wildlife areas. Nor do we need to contribute funds to help in the conservation efforts. We can use our consumer power to save the animals. We can write our supermarkets how we feel about any product they are selling that are made from animal parts or has been produced under cruel circumstances. Boycott these stores unless they heed our warnings. The reduction in demand for these products will help save the animals from further killings. Stop buying things made from ivory, tortoise and turtle shell, corals, furs, products made from the skins of reptiles, stuffed animals and countless other products. Tell our friends to do the same. Encourage them to use animal-free substitutes.

It is important to learn about endangered species so that we can make intelligent buying. Avoid eating seafoods or going to seafood restaurants. Most marine creatures caught as food came from the driftnet and even dynamite fishing. The local lapu-lapu are often caught using cyanide to knock them out before they are netted. Tuna fishes are caught with driftnet along with dolphins, their favorite partners in the ocean. These dolphins often drowned before the tuna are harvested. In recent years, an estimated 6.5 million dolphins have been killed in nets. Dolphins are highly intelligent animals, but fishermen do not have any use for them and are often left to die or mercifully killed. The fishermen often do not have the time to save these mammals.

Do not buy exotic and domestic animals as pets. It can only increase their breeding for the pet trade. We can instead cultivate a new hobby such as building birdhouses for the birds and feeding them if possible. In the garden, plant flowering trees and shrubs to provide a source of food and shelter for the birds, bees and butterflies.

CONSERVING FOOD RESOURCES

Mankind has been facing the problem of feeding its huge population for centuries. To accomplish this goal has been responsible for the loss of many food sources needed by wildlife. Vast lands from the rainforests have been converted into agricultural uses. And there is no end in sight as the population keeps growing. Forests are also cut down to harvest the trees for our shelter and other tree products.

To protect the animals in the wild from extinction, it has become necessary to protect the sources of their food. Big cats are carnivorous animals that feed on other game animals. It is necessary to protect these game animals, otherwise these big cats will starve to death. It is estimated that food for each wild cat will need about ten times its population of game animals.

Sometimes our own survival made it necessary to conserve the animals. Such is the case with most of the sea fishes that we need for our diet. It is important that we never harvest more than they can be replaced by their natural process of reproduction. Unless these food animals can be sustainably developed, it may take decades for them to regenerate. It is just as important to protect the food chains which these animals depend on.

Grassland cover nearly 20% of the earth's surface and they are important for the wildlife found there. In North America, they are referred to as prairies, savannas in Africa and steppes in Russia. These rich ecosystems support thousands of species of animals. The tall grass itself serves as food for the numerous wildlife such as wildebeest, deer and other herbivores. These animals in turn are the food needed by the wildcats to survive

ECOTOURISM

Many poor Third World countries are rich in natural resources. They are often gifted with invaluable rainforests that are home to many wildlife. Most of them are in dire need of funding to help prevent more extinction. One way to capitalize and enjoy these great natural wealth is through ecotourism It will save not only the rainforests with its biodiversity, but a great source of income for the cash-strapped country. A responsible and educational trip to these wild places can help maintain the environment and improve the livelihood of the local dwellers in these places. Worldwide, tourism is a $3 trillion business and ecotourism is taking a big chunk of the business. Many nature reserves have been set up as the main attraction. The potential of ecotourism was an important consideration in the development of Costa Rica's tourism industry. In 1986, Costa Rica earned $138 million. $310 million in 1991, and more than $400 million by 1994. In 1986, Ecuador earned $180 million from the Galapagos Island increasing to $250 in 1994 and Belize earned $95 million in 1991.

Although the initial income from ecotourism is small compared to the one-time logging, it is a self sustaining undertaking that can only grow with time. Kenya has been at the forefront in ecotourism. Safaris can be set up for tourists who enjoy watching wildlife and taking photographs. It earned $424 million for Kenya in 1991 from more than 800,000 tourists, becoming its top foreign exchange earner. Fifty-five thousand people were employed. It has been estimated that elephant viewing in Kenya generates $27 million per year. Share your adventure with friends and encourage them to visit these places.

It is important that ecotourism should not be taken too far from the original goal of saving the environment and its inhabitants. Too much improvement can have a negative effect on wildlife. Hotels, roadworks, and other support facilities should not take precedent over from areas set aside for wildlife. Restrictions should be placed on disturbing the sanctuary of animals to avoid disrupting their breeding and resting time.

The Canary Islands has become a tourist hotspot when more than 7 million people visit the island each year. Harbor and hotel constructions have destroyed fish habitat. Overfishing and raw sewage have directly polluted and threatened fish populations. Surveys made on the fish populations during two years show a big decline in their numbers. The decline is partly due to the widespread use of fish traps, which can wipe off whole pockets of fishes in a few days. EarthCorps volunteers are helping the government form policies to ensure sound coastal development while enriching the qualities that make the island such a popular attraction.

Animal watching has become an important part of ecotourism. Scientific researchers have embarked on trips into wild places to study nature and animals at work. Cameras instead of guns are used. Some even install cameras around breeding ground to minimize disturbing the animals. Several NGOs such as the Audubon Society, Nature Conservancy, Earth Watch and others offer people a chance to visit nature reserves for scientific research or just plain observation, all geared to the benefit of people and wildlife.

However, ecotourism can have a detrimental impact on wildlife unless it is carefully managed. Too many tourists can disturb the hunting made by wildcats. Harassment by tourists taking pictures has caused the reduction of preying animals for the lions in Africa. This could lead to starvation of the cubs. Even the vehicles moving around the sanctuary can scare away prey.

EDUCATION

Education is probably the most important element in protecting the environment and collaterally in protecting many species of fauna and flora. It should start at the young age to encourage children to adopt them as they grow older. Children can be taught early in school not to keep exotic birds since these birds are not supposed to be caged at all. Even the food we eat can serve as ground for learning how to save the animals. Many inhumanely treated animals should not reach our palates to reduce demand. When children are taught early in life the fragility of the environment, they will learn to protect and help solve some of the pressing problems face by animals in the future.

There are many things we can learn to do to help the animals. Keeping plastics away from the river systems can greatly reduced the suffocation of birds and sea animals when they consume these plastics thinking they are jellyfishes. Snipping the six-packed ring that has been responsible for many strangulations is a simple but effective way of learning and keeping the animals, a measure that children can adopt.

Animal rights movements resort to picketing and public speaking to convey across their message on behalf of animal^. This has largely gone unnoticed without media coverage. Today, they are resorting to educating the children in Schools. The battle is now to teach kids over the issues of animal research. Some teachers in the U.S. are even more enthusiastic about teaching the students these important issues. PETA is spending more than $1 million a year for school education. In Defense of Animals has a full time staff going to schools, lecturing and giving away buttons in support of alternative testings. The American Humane Society and the ASPCA have set up educational centers to further their information drives.

ENDANGERED SPECIES ACT

The indiscriminate killing of wildlife and destruction of their habitats by the increasing human population led the U.S. Congress to pass the Endangered Species Act (ESA) in 1973. It was the first comprehensive attempt to preserve and restore the vertebrates. Soon it was followed by the enactment of the CITES by the United Nations. CITES provided for international ban against trading in the rare, threatened, or endangered animals or their body parts. More than 600 plants and animals are included in the list. The Philippines became a member in 1981.

One of the criteria used to classify an animal as endangered is the number of surviving animals in each species. For the vertebrates, the minimum number is 1,075 and 999 for the invertebrates. The relatively large number is necessary to ensure its survival without causing undue problems such as genetic bottleneck and random disaster even on a small scale.

Through the enforcement of the provision of ESA, the habitat of the spotted owls was saved from logging. The same provision also prevented the clearing of land inhabited by the kangaroo rats in Morro Bay. in Southern California. The law is also credited with preserving many species in the U.S. such as the California condor and the San Francisco garter snake.

In the 24 years of its existence, many animal species were rehabilitated. The American alligator, the gray whale, the Arctic peregrine falcon and the brown pelican are some notable species. A further 25 species are approaching recovery goals. The ESA has been instrumental in bringing listed species back to sustainable levels. The western black-footed ferret is one of the rarest animals in the world. It is now reproducing in the wild after a captive breeding and reintroduction program in South Dakota and Montana. The population of the gray wolf is stabilizing after it was reintroduced to the wild. The manatees, Louisiana black bears and sea turtles have come under the protective custody of the ESA.

Critics of the ESA have come to appreciate a provision of the law. More than 4 million residents of San Antonio, Texas, took advantage of the law by forcing city officials to protect the municipal water supply. San Antonio draws its water from the Edwards Aquifer, which flows underground for 175 miles across south-central Texas. Water users from the city are invoking the ESA to regulate groundwater pumping for irrigation purpose. However, under Texas "tight to capture" law, landowners can withdraw as much as they please. In 1993 Sierra Club and the Guadalupe-Blanco River Authority sued the state of Texas for violation of the ESA for overpumping that threatened to destroy the habitats of five species, including the mountain darter, Texas blind salamander, San Marcos gambusia, and Texas wild rice. The court ruled in favor of the plaintiffs and there is a now a limit to how much water can be pumped from the aquifer.

One of the problems encountered by those vested with authority to determine the endangered status of animals is the lack of funds. There are currently more than

3,600 species of plants and animals under consideration for protection. Some of them have become extinct while federal authorities deliberate on their status. The wing maple leaf mussel is one example By the time it was listed as endangered in 1990. only a single population was around and it wasn't even reproducing in the St. Croix River.

ENVIRONMENTAL ORGANIZATIONS

There are more than 10,000 animal-protection groups worldwide and more are being organized. Their activities range from passive letter writings to outright illegal acts to free animals from their detention centers to the bombings of laboratory facilities used for animal testings. In the U.S. where they are very active, animal advocators have sponsored local ballots to regulate the treatment of farm animals and ban the use of animals in product safety tests. They have declared war on the fur industry through picketing and block new constructions of animal research facilities. Scientists have been harassed until they give up their experiments. Groups like the militant Animal Liberation Front have destroyed millions of dollars of laboratory equipments around the country with the use of bombs and explosives.

There is always power in numbers. So joining an organization can be an effective weapon in any undertaking. More people would mean wider coverage and more funding. Rallies need people to be effective.

NGOs have been responsible for bringing not only awareness to the people but persuade government officials to act on behalf of the environment. Many environmental laws in the U.S. for the protection of the environment and wildlife have been lobbied by NGOs. They have also been responsible for the establishment and creation of marine and wildlife parks, sanctuaries, and breeding grounds throughout the world. Once established and well protected, these ecosystems can recover very fast.

One of the earliest organizations to be created for the welfare of the animal is the Royal Society for the Prevention of Cruelty to Animals (RSPCA) which was founded in UK in 1824. This was later adopted by Henry Bergh, who founded the American Society for the Prevention of Cruelty to Animals (ASPCA) in 1866. when it was given the right to enforce the first animal cruelty law . Most of these early statutes involve treatment of work animals, since pets are relatively rare. One of its accomplishments is getting the "swill milk" banned as cruel punishment for the cattle. It prohibits the use of the wastes coming from the brewing industry to feed the animals. Bergh encourages the founding of new ASPCA organizations in many other cities. The ASPCA has for 100 years been responsible for New York City's animal control program, euthanasing millions of unwanted pets. Later, other organizations such as The New England Anti-Vivisection Society (NEAVS) was founded in Boston in 1895 by Philip Peabody and a host of Bostonians. One accomplishment is the repealed in 1983 of the law enabling research laboratories to take animals from shelters.

For more than 25 years, Greenpeace has been at the forefront in the fight against environmental abuses. Their non-violent tactics, direct actions, and uncompromising stand in protecting the environment have been respected and admired worldwide.

The Hunt Saboteurs Association of UK has been trying to end all bloodsports. Volunteers will try to thwart hunters from getting to the prey. They leave false trail for the hounds, stop hunters from digging out foxes from their burrowed holes, and even block the hunters with cars and trucks from pursuing animals.

Another active NGO that has carried out in-depth investigations and documented the environmental abuses is the Environmental Investigation Agency (EIA) of UK. It has played a key role in getting a ban on international trading of ivory products and trading in wild bird in the U.S. The EIA campaigned tirelessly and successfully against the gory slaughter of pilot whales in the Faroe Island to cull their population. It has brought the plight of other small mammals to the attention of the IWC and the European Parliament. One of its accomplishments was to persuade the IWC to pass a resolution requiring Japan to kill fewer porpoises annually. The volunteers even went one step further in protecting animals by taking a direct hand in the prosecution of poachers and dealers. The EIA has detectives working full time, using hidden camera, microphones and tape recorders, and traveling around the globe to collect evidences against people illegally trading in endangered species. One of its greatest detective works is the discovery of the biggest stockpile of illegal rhino horns coming from 300 dead rhinos.

PETA is one of the most active organizations specializing in the animal rights movements. It targets institutions and companies that refuse to give up testing on animals. One of its targets is Gillette, which in 1993. used 2,304 animals to test its toiletries. The organization was organized in 1980 by Alex Pacheco and Ingrid Newkirk and they had fewer than 20 members then. Today it is one of the biggest organizations for the animal rights movements.

In 1981, the 23-year-old college student, Alex Pacheco, applied as volunteer researcher when there was no paying job available at the Institute for Behavioral Research in Silver Spring. Maryland. What he discovered at the laboratory convinced him of the need to take a more active role in protecting animals used by scientists in laboratories worldwide.

Alex was able to convince Edward Taub of his dedication to the job when he requested to work at night. Once alone in the dark, he was able to photograph the monkeys in all their gory states. This convinced the county to close down the laboratory and file 17 charges of animal cruelty against Taub.

The scientist had been experimenting with a group of 17 monkeys: sixteen crab-eating macaques where Paul, mentioned earlier, was one of them and a rhesus monkey. The technique used for studying the sensory nerve is called deafferentation. It requires a doctor to open the spinal cord and probe into individual or group of sensory nerves to study its possible effect when severed. The doctor can select any target limb he wishes for possible study.

During Alex's short stay, eight of the monkeys had all the nerve connections to one arm severed while another had both arms surgically numbed. To force a crippled monkey to use its bad limb, the monkey's good arm is strapped on a straitjacket while leaving the damaged limb alone. Electric shocks are applied to force the monkeys to move their numbed arms. After one year of experimentation, the animals will be cut open to examine the result of the experiments on their spinal cords.

Each monkey is placed in an 18 by 18 inches cage during the studies. Under this deplorable condition, the caged survivors suffered symptoms of stress by spinning themselves around the cage, banging their heads on the cage walls, and chewing their numbed arms leading to infection.

NGOs and animal activists have been responsible for the establishment of national parks and wildlife sanctuaries in the world. One of the biggest, the WWF had supported many national parks and operates in more than a hundred countries. Another project in conjunction with British Overseas Development Agency works to protect a forest in Korup, Cameroon. WWF is also active in Nepal, trying to protect the rhinos and Bengal tigers.

Conservation International has been responsible for the first debt-for-nature swap. The private conservation group bought from Citicorp Investment Bank $650,000 debt of Ecuador for $100,000. In return 1.6 million hectares of forest will be put under preservation. WWF and Nature Conservancy (U.S.) acquired $9 million debt for a little more than one million dollar in another swap. Another creditor, American Express Bank, in January 1989 sold SS.6 million of Costa Rica's debt to Nature Conservancy for $784,000. The Conservancy then traded back the paper to the Costa Rican Central Bank for $1.7 million in local currency bonds, with the interest to be paid to a local conservation group to manage nine environmental projects.

A medical research facility in Rockville, Maryland funded by the National Institute of Health (NIH), was broken into by animal activists. They look photos of the caged chimpanzees used for experiments before freeing the four chimps. With the publicity of the photos, the lab was forced to install room-size enclosures with climbing equipment. This has led others to set up nature-type habitat for the other experimental animals.

FUND RAISING

it is only through the efforts of many environmentalists that the plight of the planet is coming into focus in many places. However, very few of them are capable of facing the challenge on their own. Funds are greatly needed if we are to save the environment and all the creatures living within. There are many methods of fund raising.

Donation is an important part of saving the rainforests, the home to most animal species. Many tropical countries endowed with important rainforests do not have the resources to keep their heritage intact. Often times they have allowed NGOs and private individuals or corporations to take the initiative in saving the rainforests.

In 1989 the Massachusetts Audubon Society formed an alliance with the Belize Audubon Society to save a vulnerable rainforest donated by Coca Cola. The company gave it up after criticisms of its plan to develop the forest land by replacing it with a plantation for citrus fruits. The donation of the rainforest is not enough to save it from destruction. It will still need $6.7 million to manage the forest for perpetuity. At present it has a scheme to save the 42,200-acre reserve including the 210,000 acres adjacent to it. Anybody wishing to help can donate a minimum of 25 pounds or roughly $40 to Programme For Belize. P.O. Box 99, Saxmundham, Suffolk. England IP 12 2LB. Contributors will be given a signed Certificate of Purchase.

Phoenix Zoo's latest exhibit are two spectacled bears from South America. They are kept in a one-hectare recreation of their Andean mountain habitat called the Forest of Uco. A quarter mile trail lined with rocks and trees winds through the man-made forest. It took six years for researchers, biologists, volunteers and designers to recreate the natural habitat. The cost of the $2 million project was raised by the Wildest Club in Town. They did it by selling 17,500 bricks at $50 to $200 apiece which were used to build an entrance bridge to the zoo. Each brick has an inscription from the donor.

We can help fund animal rights organizations directly. One way is to buy some of their fundraising products such as shirts, stickers, buttons, books, pamphlets, etc. Not only will it raise the funds, the merchandises can be a source of inspiration for someone to take actions. Books and pamphlets could be a source of information that could bring attention to the public.

People are always willing to help save the environment and the easiest way for them to part with their money is in small amounts. Taking advantage of this simple generosity, the Center for Ecosystem Survival in cooperation with Rotary Clubs and other NGOs put up "conservation parking meters" around more than 1.600 U.S. and Canadian aquariums, zoos, stores, etc. adorned with live parrots. These look-alike parking meters decorated with pictures of plants and animals allow anybody to deposit his loose change into the slots.

David Shepherd, a well-known British painter has been painting wildlife in Africa and selling them through auctions for the benefit of the wildlife. He had raised millions of dollars through his unique talent. During the 1983 die-off of bamboos, the staple food for pandas. 50 Chinese calligraphers and painters donated their works to the Chinese Wildlife Conservation Association to help raise money for the panda fund drive in China.

The Internet has made it possible to communicate with almost anyone around the world. When part of the 5.000-acre marsh at the mouth of the Loire River in western France was being claimed by the port of Nanteso-St. Nazaire as a potential repository for the muck dredged from the Loire channel to keep it clear for ships, the local inhabitants using the World Wide Web circulated a petition to President Jacques Chirac to protect the whole marsh for the wild birds. More than 3.000 signatures were obtained, some coming from as far as Taiwan and the United Arab Emirates. The petition initiated by Michel Chomienne is raising funds to buy several parcels of marsh land, whose ownership will be transferred to the donors around the world.

INDIVIDUAL ACTIONS

Environmental awareness has made some individuals instant green consumers It has also persuaded companies and traders to change their policy toward the sustainable use of animal resources and for protecting animals against cruelty. The willingness of consumers to join forces is a potent weapon that has forced tuna canners to purchase only tuna caught using dolphin-free fishing. This has led Australian and American fishermen to catch "dolphin-free" tuna and canned their products with label to that effect.

Concerted efforts by individuals can be a very potent weapon. We need not undertake perilous journeys or death defying actions to save the animals. In helping to save the ocean, there are many simple things we can do to accomplish our aims. Joining a cleanup drive along the coasts and beaches of our local community is one way. Disposing properly our toxic wastes is another. Using nontoxic alternatives whenever possible will minimize and discourage the manufacture of these toxic substances. The simple act of not throwing the cigarette butt into the sea will save some marine birds from consuming it as some kind of food. The butt does not break down easily in the sea as they floats on water.

Paul Watson, a Canadian who founded the NGO called Sea Shepherd, has been working to protect the whales. In 1979, he sank the pirate whaler ship. Sierra, by ramming the vessel while it was docked. The high profile action helped bring attention to the plight of wildlife. Last year (1997) he spent most of his time in a Dutch's jail for vandalizing a whaling boat in 1994. Norway sought for his extradition after he was arrested in Neatherland in April. His extradition was rejected, and instead he was held for 80 days, the same penalty he would have gotten in Norway. However, he is still wanted in Norway for another charge of ramming a naval vessel during a whaling protest which could mean a longer jail term.

Henry Spira was credited with persuading Revlon to research alternatives to the Draize test, which entails exposing the eyes of rabbits to products ranging from mascara to household cleaners. When he first approached management about using alternative tests, they just jerked around. He decided to run full-page advertisements with the caption asking "How many rabbits does Revlon blind for beauty's sake?" That finally led Revlon to contract with Rockefeller University for $500,000 over two years to find alternatives to the Draize test.

Turpentine Creek Exotic Wildlife Ranch was the Jackson family pet project. Instead of household pets, they take care of big cats that have been mistreated, abandoned, or given away by circuses or film animals that have outlived their usefulness. The ranch spread over 459 acres of hills, but the animals live in a square compound of about two-and-a-half acres. The animals first arrived in 1977 when Don Jackson took a cute little lion found tied to a cinder block. But the family really started collecting more animals five years ago.

When the family learned of an illegal breeder in McAskill, Arkansas who was abandoning 42 big cats crammed into cattle trailers, they launched their mission to bring the cats to their ranch. It took them one year to move the animals. The latest was a black leopard from Colorado. At last count (1995), there were 53 big cats including lions, tigers, and cougars. Other animals include the bears, foxes, raccoons, deer, exotic birds, a brown capuchin and other monkeys. The ranch provides all the food and veterinary care needed by the animals. Janet Crawford, a veterinarian lives there full time.

The 1996 drought in Texas took its share of toll on wildlife. In Cedar Park, one woman had opened her home to some hungry and thirsty animals that might not otherwise survive. Kay Sones, a licensed animal rehabilitator took in a dozen very young fawns and a baby screech owl, among others. The fawns were then too weak because their mothers were deprived of the moisture needed to create milk for nursing. In addition to dehydration, the animals need medical attention for other drought related problems. One fawn suffered from severe bites of fire ants who were also thirsty and only blood can quench their thirst.

Dale Shields is known as the Pelican Man. He earned the reputation for setting up a sanctuary from his personal fund twenty years ago to help care for injured pelicans. Today, more than 100,000 pelicans and other animals have been helped by the center. Although most of the animals that end up in the shelter are nursed to health and sent back into the wild, some become permanent residents. He seems to have special rapport with all birds in the sanctuary, even teaching one crow to talk. Although he suffered several heart attacks, he managed somehow to keep going, helping raise funds for the center. Today there are more than 20 full-time staff members and 350 volunteers. Most of the annual budget of $600,000 come from donations.

The late Lila Acheson Wallace, co-founder of the Reader's Digest, was largely responsible for bankrolling a biological oasis for the Central Park Zoo in New York. It cost more than $35 million for the benefit of the zoo animals.

Peter Singer is an Australian philosophy professor who wrote the book Animal Liberation in 1975. It was a well-reasoned and persuasive argument against cruelty towards animals on ethical and moral grounds. His argument is based on the pain and suffering that animals experienced like humans and therefore should be treated more humanely.

LETTER WRITING

Letter writing is a very potent weapon to bring awareness to the problems faced by many species of animals. It can easily be harnessed to protect animals against human abuses. Gene Sackett tried to get funding from the NIH for the classical isolation experiment in relation to the study of the self-injurious behavior syndrome in human beings. His proposal was to isolate infant rhesus monkeys for 4 years and to remove their brains to study their effects. He expected some of the monkeys to mutilate themselves in some way. Although the experiment was approved by a vote of 10 to 7, members of the Progressive Animal Welfare Society of Seattle went into action. They held protests and debates and swamped the members of Congress with letters of protest and dismay. The grant was not funded.

In many developed countries, letter writing is usually resorted to by the public. Concern for animal welfare is the third most commonly written problem to members of Congress. Every week more than 70,000 letters have been written to members regarding the treatment of factory farmed animals. But in developing countries like the Philippines, people are voicing their sentiments not to their lawmakers but to the general public.

Letters to newspapers for general public reading can even be more potent especially against private corporations and public officials. Companies are well aware of keeping their important public image and will not antagonize the buying public with negative publicity. Public officials always react to newspaper reports regarding their actuations and public exposures of their activities. Letters against cruelty to animal issues and encourage open debates and hopefully lasting actions.

Animal rights groups have routinely produced postcards with endangered species on its face and sold them to animal lovers or ordinary citizens willing to help save the animals. These cards and letters are ready for signing and can be mailed to public officials with request for supporting a good cause. Letters for Animals, based in Factoryville, Pennsylvania sends out a packet of 20 custom letters and envelopes for $135 annual fee. The letters are complete with sender and recipient names and addresses and ready for mailing. The recipients are mostly important people in the government who can help the animal cause. Others are sent to targeted companies requesting them to stop experimenting with animals.

In Defense of Animals, with 60,000 members is vocal against animal experimentations. They waged letter-writing campaign to Stanford University complaining about the work of one its researcher, Seymour Levine.

It was largely due to the worldwide letter campaigns that so many nations were added to the membership of the IWC in the 1970s and early 1980s that eventually allowed the conservationist nations to achieve the three-quarters majority needed to established the moratorium on commercial whaling.

Personal letters can be very effective than any other form of petition or postcard. Letters must be concise and direct to the point with one subject matter discussed. It must be timely for greater impact especially when it is being discussed in the hall of the legislative body. Be sure to put your name and address because of possible invitation to expound on your meritorious ideas. Substantiate your letter with facts and figures to make a good impression. Make sure to convey your reasons for writing the letter and what you hope it can accomplish. Most important of all, address your letter to the proper individuals with their correct designation. Be respectful.

MARINE SANCTUARIES

There are hundreds of marine sanctuaries scattered throughout the world and mostly located near land masses. Most of them are designed to protect coastal areas where people venture to see the beauty for recreation and for educational purposes. Today, many are being established to protect against killings and destroying marine habitats.

The large expanse of the ocean is no guarantee that people will give way to the ocean creatures. Many mammals survived in small areas they regularly used as breeding or feeding grounds. It is therefore important that these places are placed under protection. Our encroachment has been responsible for the disappearance or decimation of many species. It is a small sacrifice for mankind to give way to the animals.

NATIONAL TOTEM

Conservationists have found an effective way to bring awareness to local inhabitants on a national basis by requesting the host country to adopt any unique animal under threat of extinction as a national totem or state animal. This practice has been adopted by many U.S. states and some tropical countries. The mountain gorillas was adopted as a totem by the Rwandan government that will assure their survival for years to come. In spite of an ongoing civil war a few years ago. none of the mountain gorilla was killed. The Philippine Eagle was adopted as the national bird thereby bringing awareness to the local inhabitants. The government even infused badly needed funds to support its breeding program and habitat protection.

A few years ago, conservationists convinced the state of Connecticut to adopt the sperm whales as its state animal. As a consequence, the state government has taken an active role in saving the sperm whales located throughout the world.

Probably the most famous animal used as a totem or logo is the giant panda of the WWF. This quiet and tame animal is known and loved throughout the world and serve as a reminder of the plight of all animals under siege from the human predators.

OTHER CONSERVATION MEASURES

In conjunction with preservation is conservation. Conservation as the name implies is to conserve species for future generations. Drastic actions are needed to conserve their populations and habitats. Sometimes special steps have to be taken to help endangered species to survive. Such was the case with the Hawaiian goose. These unfortunate birds were shot by hunters and their chicks were preyed upon b> animals introduced by humans. By 1950, they were almost extinct, save for a few that were brought to the Wildfowl Trust Centre at Slimbridge in Gloucestershire. UK. In one of the best-managed semi-natural ecosystems in the world, they were able to breed successfully. In the early 1960s some of them were taken back to Hawaii and released. Since then their numbers have gradually increased. This is a success story in conservation, but sadly there aren't many like it.

Conservation efforts are not confined to land only. Reef Relieve, established in 1986, has installed more than 100 mooring buoys at seven popular offshore coral reefs, discouraging divers and fishermen from dropping anchor on the vulnerable coral reefs. The Key Largo National Marine Sanctuary and adjacent John Pennekamp Coral Reef State Park, named after the determined local newspaper editor who sought its establishment, are world class destinations for scuba and snorkel diving enthusiasts.

The Florida Keys Wild Bird Rehabilitation Center in Tavernier offers visitors a chance to see pelicans, spoonbills, hawks, herons and other magnificent species up close as they recuperate from injuries. Likewise, the Dolphin Research Center at Grass Key near Marathon is one of three Key facilities that aid exhausted and injured dolphins. The Key Deer is home to a herd of pint-sized mammals unique to the region. All six locations are open to visitors.

Another project in the offing is a hospital and rehabilitation center for stranded mammals and reptiles in Bourne, Massachusetts. The location is ideal for many of the stranded whales, dolphins and turtles. The National Marine Life Center is raising $12 million to build surgical suites, diagnostic rooms, and life-support pools to accommodate everything from pilot whales and harbor porpoises to leatherback and ridley sea turtles. It will be staffed by marine scientists and veterinarians Funds are expected to come from government and private contributions. Even the Army Corps of Engineers helped set up the pumping station for sea water needed in the water tanks.

One of the most industrious conservation efforts is the Hidden Harbor Environmental Center, a rehabilitation and research facility for sea turtles affected by a mysterious disease that produces grotesque and fatal tumors. Proprietor Richie Moretti established Hidden Harbor, more commonly known as the Turtle Hospital, with proceeds from his adjoining motel.

Probably the most ambitious plan underway for years is the Species Survival Plan (SSP). It is a joint effort among many zoos throughout the world to ensure the survival of all endangered species of animals Records about sex, age. parents, locations, habits, etc. of endangered species found in zoos and wildlife parks are kept to find the most suitable mate for each other and avoid inbreeding. In conjunction with SSP is the establishment of sperm and egg banks of endangered and threatened species.

What may seem innocuous in the things we do can have a far greater impact on wildlife somewhere else. Our insatiable need for energy has lead oil companies to some of the wilderness and inhospitable places looking for black gold. Deep in the jungles of many tropical countries, oil companies go in search for oil and minerals. Even the continental shelves and other deep seas are subjected to oil exploration. All these places are rich in wildlife and any contamination of these places can be hazardous to the inhabitants.

Demand for natural resources such as minerals, logs, precious stones and metals are found in areas seldom inhabited by people but mostly by wildlife. Forests are cut down and mountains removed and later converted to other uses that are not conducive for wildlife habitats. Even our demand for water made it necessary to take over wild places for impoundment of water leading to the construction of dams that wreaks havoc to large areas. Inundation of dams had been responsible for destruction of many homes of indigenous people and death to wildlife living there.

All these destructions can be reduced if we take practice simple conservation measures. Practicing the three common R's can help reduce demand and wastes. Every time we reuse an inconsumable items such as packaging or bottles, we effective reduce the demand for that item by 100%. Items we don t need can also be reused by others. Selling it to secondhand stores will effectively reduce the demand for raw materials that can only come from wildlife habitats. Reducing our demand for unnecessary items will also help the environment. We can insist on buying goods packed with less materials w ithout compromising safety and sanitation Forty percent of the refuse we throw away came from paper and paper products that are in turn harvested from trees found only in forests of the world.

Recycling is also an important leg in saving the environment. Instead of throwing away used, broken and unwanted things, we can have it recycled into new products that can be useful again. Items like papers and paper products, metallic materials, bottles, aluminum cans can be reused time and again by recycling.

REGIONAL AGREEMENT

Regional agreements are easier to define and provide an effective approach to protecting the ocean against unwanted intrusions. One of this agreement is the Convention for the Protection of the Natural Resources and Natural Environment of the South Pacific (SPREP). It prohibits the dumping and storage of all kind of toxic wastes in the South Pacific. Another pact signed between 22 nations of the region imposed a 200-mile exclusive economic zones against driftnet fishing. It was precipitated by the invasions of a fleet of 200 Asian driftnet fishing vessels.

The prestigious J. Paul Getty Prize with a $50,000 prize was recently awarded jointly to the Pawikan Conservation Project of the DENR and the Malaysian's Sabah Parks for the establishment of a regional sanctuary for turtles. The Turtle Islands Heritage Protected Areas (T1HPA) was the first trans-border protected area for the endangered sea turtles.

Pawikan Conservation Project which helped established the Baguan Turtle Island Marine Sanctuary of the Philippine once convened a symposium on marine turtle conservation that brought together several southeast Asian countries. Malaysian Sabah Parks on the other hand has released to the wild four million turtle hatchlings in the last 15 years. Together the two managed a 4,300-acre marine sanctuary known as Turtle Islands Park, composed of six islands from the Philippines and three islands from Malaysia.

REWARD SYSTEM

The ocean has been abused by humans for centuries. Until laws were passed restricting the dumping of wastes into the oceans, garbage, sludge and other toxic wastes have been dumped deliberately. In just one year in 1968, 14,000 out of the 330,000 tons nationwide of waste matter from pesticide plants along the Mississippi were dumped into the Gulf of Mexico every month.

Other wastes include 560,000 tons from oil refineries, 140,000 tons from the paper industry, 940,000 of various waste matter, 2.7 tons from waste acids, 40 tons of chlorinated hydrocarbons in the same period were dumped into the Atlantic Ocean every month by Germany. In the period from 1963 to 1969, 38,000 barrels containing chlorinated hydrocarbons and 40,000 barrels containing cyanide compounds, arsenic, and other poisons from Great Britain were dumped. It won't be long before all these barrels begin to rust and disperse in the oceans, contaminating everything it touches. During the 1970s as much as 6 million tons of garbage alone were dumped into the seas worldwide.

The environment is an active microcosm that can do without human interference.

Damages made by people have often gotten away because of its passiveness. Help is on the way in individuals through the reward system. The governments in many countries found it necessary to offer rewards for people who risk their life in reporting violators for destroying our environment. The ABS-CBN, a private company has a program called "Bantay Kalikasan" receiving reports of environmental violations.

There are numerous laws enacted by governments around the world against dumping of wastes in the ocean. Reward can be a good motivating force in helping clean up the environment against unwarranted and illegal dumping of wastes. In 1991, Alvin and Marilyn Levett videotaped Regal Princess employees discarding 20 plastic bags of garbage as the ship sailed off the Florida coast. Princess Cruises, Inc., the owner of the ship was fined $500,000, half of which went to the Levetts. Sadly, it was a rare occurrence the violator was caught red-handed.

The reward system can be extended to the violations of laws protecting the animals. Reporting illegal harvesting of wild animals and even timber harvesting can greatly help in protecting the habitats for the wild creatures. Taking photos can be an effective weapon. A picture is worth a thousand words in the fight against illegal activities that harm the animals.

Many U. S. states have laws regulating hunting seasons and reward tipsters for reporting any violation of the law. In Louisiana, rewards of up to $1,000 may be paid to informers depending on the seriousness of the violation and how much the informant contributes to the investigation. To facilitate the conviction of violators, gather as much informations as possible such as names, type of vehicle, plate number, location and time of violation, and other pertinent informations that may be helpful. More than $100,000 have been paid off by the Operation Game Thief as of 1994.

STAMPS

One way of raising funds for the protection and rehabilitation of wildlife can be raised through the issuance of stamps or stamp tax. In the case of ordinary stamps, they should feature some endangered species so that they will bring awareness to people of their status. They are also collector's items that should give countless hours of enthusiastic collection. A portion of the proceeds from the stamps can be allocated for the benefit of the animals.

It is not always easy to get the government to put out stamps. It took the school children from a school in Westfield, Pennsylvania four years of letter writing before the Post Office came out with several 32-ccnt stamps. Some of the stamps featured the black-footed ferret, Hawaiian monk seal. American crocodile, ocelot, Wyoming toads, California condor, gila trout, garter snakes, etc.

In the Philippines, there is an annual anti-TB stamp month where all letters need the special stamp attached for mailing during the month. All the proceeds go to the fight for the eradication of the dreaded disease which kills more than 20,000 people annually. We could repeat this endeavor to raise badly needed funds for protecting the environment and helping save many animals in the country from ultimate fate of extinction.

TELEMETRY

Telemetry or electronic tagging of animals is part of the on-going research to find the best way to preserve endangered species by studying their behavior in the wild. Animals are first caught, and vital statistics such as their weight, size, sex, and the place where they were captured are recorded. Afterward, they are either ordinarily tagged with electronic chips. In ordinary tag, the animal should it be caught in the future can be measured again to determine its growth and habitation pattern. There are several ways of electronically tagging the targeted animals. For snake, a tiny transponder is injected under the skin before it is released. Each chip has a unique code, consisting of two letters and two numbers that can be read electronically using a small portable transmitter/receiver. By these means, many individuals can be identified if it is captured again. New data can be compared against the old data to determine any discrepancy and movements.

For large species, more sophisticated telemetry consisting of a small plastic-covered capsule transmitter is surgically implanted into the skin under anaesthesia. The wound is then sealed with surgical tape. The capsules contain a small battery and an electronic transmitter so that each tagged animal could be located easily in the future. This system allows the animals to be monitored at all times with help from a satellite transmitter. The batteries last for 2 years before replacement becomes necessary.

Electronically tagging of endangered species is important especially for free roaming animals that move a lot. This will enable a patrol guard to keep track of their whereabouts at all times. They can concentrate on each animal instead of wandering endlessly the vast forest in search of them. Once an animal is killed, the patrol can swing into action to find the poachers.

The most recent whale to be tracked by satellite is Duke, a 4-meter great white male whale. A cylindrical capsule was implanted into the whale at the Kamogawa Sea World before he was released to the ocean. Inside the capsule was a generator powered by vibrations and a small wireless transmitter tracked by the satellite. Japanese researchers hope to implant more of these capsules in the blue whales found in the Antarctic Ocean.

WILDLIFE PARKS

The explosive rise in human population has made it necessary to protect important areas against human encroachment that often lead to environmental degradation resulting in the decimation and later extinction of the species. It has become mandatory to set these nature parks and reserves to protect them.

In the U.S. and elsewhere, since the 1970s, people have come to realize the role played by some animals toward the state of the environment. The presence of biodiversity in an ecosystem meant that the environment is a healthy one. A lack of biodiversity often comes to symbolized possible degradations. This has brought about the need for diversity and multiple use approach to wildlife management.

To achieve the goal of multiple-use, wildlife parks are opened to the public to help finance the management of wildlife sanctuary through payment of entrance fees. Wildlife enthusiasts such as bird-watchers, photographers, and their support groups are formed. Boats are charted to see and photograph birds and mammals in the wild. Longer trips are often regularly scheduled for wildlife tours and trips.

The first national park established in Africa in 1925 was the Albert National Park and later renamed the Virunga National Park of Zaire. It is a unique park that no tourists are allowed except scientists who study the gorillas. The next park in Africa to follow is the Kruger National Park of South Africa which was established in 1926. By 1933, there was a momentum to create more national parks in Africa. Ministers and officials from nine countries with colonies in Africa met and signed an agreement on the Convention Relative to the Preservation of Fauna and Flora in their Natural State. Seventeen animals were placed under Class A for protection against their killing. The agreement led to the creation of more national parks for the regulation of wildlife. This also led to the complete ban on hunting of lions at the Serengeti National Park.

The Hluhluwe-Umfolozi Game Reserve, the first one in Africa, located in Natal, South Africa was created in 1895. It was then the only reserve that harbored the only white rhinos left in the world - just 30 to 40 individuals - from which today's 6,000-strong world population emanates. The park has also healthy populations of elephant, buffalo, lion, leopard, and other large African mammals. But the caretakers of Hluhluwe-Umfolozi know better than to be complacent. Every two years, they conduct a census of the park's 20 largest plant-eating species, in a bid to keep track of all w ildlife

At present, many of these wildlife parks in the tropical countries are under siege by local inhabitants. Many government agencies do not have the resources to protect these reserves since they are given a lower priority. Others give only lip service to the creation of wildlife parks in order to get concessions from the rich donors. Real honest to goodness conservation measures are mandatory if we want to save any species from total annihilation.

Various approaches have been undertaken to protect wildlife. The most important form of conservation is probably preservation. Parks and wildlife sanctuaries, usually maintained with little or no changes, are probably the most popular w ay of preserving their habitats. Some of the successful endeavors toward this end are found in the wildlife sanctuaries set up by governments in many tropical countries in Africa, South America, and Asia.

Much of Africa's remaining wildlife live in special parks and wildlife sanctuaries set up to protect them. Among them are the Serengeti and Ngorongoro Crater in Tanzania, the Maasai Mara in Kenya, Luangwa Valley in Zambia. These wilderness are still teeming with wildlife animals like nowhere else in the world.

An important consideration in wildlife parks is the size. Because of the numerous animals in the park, all with different habitats and survival means, it is necessary to ensure that all animals are adequately sheltered and feed. Other factors should be taken into considerations such as environmental changes, climatic upheavals, water sources, the available plants and trees that are necessary for the existence of all animals.

Once a wildlife park has been set up, it is necessary that protections be accorded not only against poachers but also against human activities that are likely to affect the well-being of the animals Nepal's premier nature reserve. Royal Chitwan National Park is home to highly endangered rhinos, tigers, sloth bears and the gharial crocodile. Despite its protected status, the area is undergoing pollution caused by human activities. The Narayani River, which flows along the park's edge, transport undesirable chemicals from farms and factories in the park. Since the river is a major source of drinking water for people and animals alike, it is necessary that the wastewater should be treated before it is discharged to the river.

ZOOLOGICAL PARKS

In the last few decades, ordinary zoos have given way to zoological parks that mimic their natural habitats in the wild. These parks have become important repository for endangered species and almost all animals in general. Large animals such as tigers, elephants, pandas, rhinoceros, etc. need a natural range where they are fed, cared, and allowed to propogate in an undisturbed environment. At the San Diego Zoo, tigers and Malaysian sun boars live in special places that look just like the Asian rainforests where they came from. This is important to minimize neurological and psychological problems.

The Wildlife Center in Central Park, New York which is home to Arctic mammals is currently testing a new electricity-based water treatment system using ozone treatment to kill bacteria, viruses and remove odors from the waterpool used by mammals. The ozone treated water allows fishes, which cannot tolerate chlorine water to be introduced so that mammals like the polar bears can hunt as they did in the wild.

If there is any zoo that takes environmentalism to heart, it is the North Carolina Zoological Park. The $60 million natural habitat facility near Asheboro is designed for animals as well as visitors. It is one of the largest zoos in the U.S., located in a 1,448 acres land. It is also the first American zoo conceived and built using natural habitat which allow' animals to move freely through spacious exhibits that closely resemble their wild environments. The zoo also participates in seven Species Survival Plan breeding and care programs a well as Project ChimpanZoo. a cross-cultural behavior study coordinated with Jane Goodall Institute. The project, which involves 14 U.S. zoos, studies socialization among chimps in captive environment and compares their behaviors to that of w ild chimps observed by Jane Goodall during her studies in Africa. The master plan envision the establishment of seven habitats. North America. Africa, Asia, Europe. South America, Australia, and the World of Seas. So far, North America and Africa are opened to the public. Almost one million visitors visited the park in 1996.

APPENDIX

REPUBLIC ACT NO. 8485

AN ACT TO PROMOTE ANIMAL WELFARE IN THE PHILIPPINES OTHERWISE KNOWN AS "THE ANIMAL WELFARE ACT OF 1998"

Be it enacted by the Senate and House of Representatives of the Philippines in Congress assembled:

SECTION 1. It is the purpose of this Act to protect and promote the welfare of all animals in the Philippines by supervising and regulating the establishment and operations of all facilities utilized for breeding, maintaining, keeping, treating or training of all animals either as objects of trade or as household pets. For purposes of this Act, pet animal shall include birds.

SEC. 2. No person, association, partnership, corporation, cooperative or any government agency or instrumentality including slaughter houses shall establish, maintain and operate any pet shop, kennel, veterinary clinic, veterinary hospital, stockyard, corral, stud farm or stock farm or zoo for the breeding, treatment, sale or trading or training of animals without first securing from the Bureau of Animal Industry a certificate of registration thereof.

The certificate shall be issued upon proof that the facilities of such establishment for animals are adequate, clean and sanitary and will not be used, nor cause pain and/or suffering to the animals. The certificate shall be valid fora period of one(l) year unless earlier cancelled for just cause before the expiration of its term by the Director of the Bureau of Animal Industry and may be renewed from year to year upon compliance with the conditions imposed hereunder. The Bureau shall charge reasonable fees for the issuance or renewal of such certificate.

SEC. 3. The Director of the Bureau of Animal Industry shall supervise and regulate the establishment, operation and maintenance of pet shops, kennels, veterinary clinics, veterinary hospital, stockyards, corrals, stud farms and zoos and any other form or structure for the confinement of animals where they are bred, treated, maintained, or kept either for sale or trade or for training purposes as well as the transport of such animals in any form of public or private transportation facility in order to provide maximum comfort while in transit and minimize, if not totally eradicate, incidence of sickness and death and prevent any cruelty from being inflicted upon the animals.

The Director may call upon any government agency for assistance consistent with its powers, duties, and responsibilities for the purpose of ensuring the effective and efficient implementation of this Act and the rules and regulations promulgated thereunder.

It shall be the duty of such government agency to assist said Director when called upon for assistance using any available fund it is its budget for the purpose.

SEC. 4. It shall be the duty of any owner or operator of any land, air or water public utility transporting pet, wildlife and all other animals to provide in all cases adequate, clean and sanitary facilities for the safe conveyance and delivery thereof to their consignee at the place of consignment. They shall provide sufficient food and water for such animals while in transit for more than twelve (12) hours or whenever necessary.

No public utility shall transport any such animal without a written permit from the Director of the Bureau of Animal Industry or his/her authored No cruel confinement or restraint shall be made on such animals while being transported.

Any form of cruelty shall be penalized even if the transporter has obtained a permit from the Bureau of Animal Industry. Cruelty in transporting includes overcrowding, placing of animals in the trunks or under the hood trunks of the vehicles.

SEC. 5. There is hereby created a Committee on Animal Welfare attached to the Department of Agriculture which shall, subject to the approval of the Secretary of the Department of Agriculture, issue the necessary rules and regulations for the strict implementation of the provisions of this Act, including the setting of safety and sanitary standard, within thirty (30) calendar days following its approval. Such guidelines shall be reviewed by the Committee every three (3) years from its implementation or whenever necessary.

The Committee shall be composed of the official representatives of the following:

(1)   The Department of Interior and Local Government (DILG);

(2)   Department of Education, Culture and Sports (DECS);

(3)   Bureau of Animal Industry (BA1) of the Department of Agriculture (DA);

(4)   Protected Areas and Wildlife Bureau (PAWB) of the Department ol Environment and Natural Resources (DENR);

(5)   National Meat Inspection Commission (NMIC) of the DA;

(6)   Agriculture Training Institute (ATI) of the DA.

(7)   Philippine Veterinary Medical Association (PVMA);

(8)   Veterinary Practitioners Association of the Philippines (VPAP)

(9)   Philippine Animal Hospital Association (PAHA);

(10)   Philippine Animal Welfare Society (PAWS);

(11)   Philippine Society for the Prevention of Cruelty to Animals (PSPCA);

(12)   Philippine Society of Swine Practitioners (PSSP);

(13)   Philippine College of Canine Practitioners (PCCP); and

(14)   Philippine Society of Animal Science (PSAS).

The Committee shall be chaired by a representative coming from the private sector and shall have two (2) vice-chairpersons composed of the representative of the BA I and another from the private sector.

The Committee shall meet quarterly or as often as the need arises. The Committee members shall not receive any compensation but may receive reasonable honoraria from time to time.

SEC. 6. It shall be unlawful for any person to torture any animal, to neglect to provide adequate care, sustenance or shelter, or maltreat any animal or to subject any dog or horse to dogfights or horsefights, kill or cause or procure to be tortured or deprived of adequate care, sustenance or shelter, or maltreat or use the same in research or experiments not expressly authorized by the Committee on Animal Welfare.

The killing of any animal other than cattle, pigs, goats, sheep, poultry, rabbits, carabaos, horses, deer and crocodiles is likewise hereby declared unlawful except in the following instances:

(1)   When it is done as part of the religious rituals of an established religion or
sect or a ritual required by tribal or ethnic custom of indigenous cultural communities; however, leaders shall keep records in cooperation with the Committee on Animal Welfare;.

(2)   When the pet animal is afflicted with an incurable communicable disease
as determined and certified by a duly licensed veterinarian;

(3)   When the killing is deemed necessary to put an end to the misery suffered
by the animal as determined and certified by a duly licensed veterinarian;

(4)   When it is done to prevent an imminent danger to the life or limb of a human being; and

(6)   When the animal is killed after it has been used in authorized research or experiments; and

(7)   Any other ground analogous to the foregoing as determined and certified by a licensed veterinarian

In all the above mentioned cases, including those of cattle, pigs, goats, sheep, poultry, rabbits, carabaos, horses, deer and crocodiles the killing of the animals shall be done through humane procedures at all times.

For this purpose, humane procedures shall mean the use of the most scientific methods available as may be determined and approved by the committee. Only those procedures approved by the Committee shall be used in the killing of animals.

SEC. 7. It shall be the duty of every person to protect the natural habitat of the wildlife. The destruction of said habitat shall be considered as a form of cruelty to animals and its preservation is a way of protecting the animals.

SEC. 8. Any person who violates any of the provisions of this Act shall, upon conviction by final judgment, be punished by imprisonment of not less than six (6) months nor more than two (2) years or a fine of not less than One thousand pesos (P1,000.00) nor more than Five thousand pesos (P5.000 00) or both at the discretion of the Court. If the violation is committed by a juridical person, the officer responsible therefore shall serve the imprisonment when imposed. If the violation is committed by an alien, he or she shall be immediately deported after service of sentence without any further proceedings.

SEC. 9. All laws, acts, decrees, executive orders, rules and regulations inconsistent with the provisions of this Act are hereby repealed or modified accordingly.

SEC. 10. This Act shall take effect fifteen (15) days after its publication in at least two (2) newspapers of general circulation.

Approved,

JOSE DE VENECIA. JR   NEPTALI GONZALES
Speaker of the House   *President of the Senate*
of Representative

Approved: February 11, 1998

FIDEL V. RAMOS
President of the Philippines

BIBLIOGRAPHY

Allen, Robert, How to Save the World, Littlefield, Adams and Co., 1980
Anderson, Stanley, Managing Our Wildlife Resources, Charles Merrill Publishing Co., 1985
Attenborough. David, Life on Earth, Collins, 1979
Arthur, Alex, Shell. Dorling Kindersley Ltd, 1989
Baer-Brown, Leslie and Rhein Bob, Earth Keepers, Mercury House, 1995
Balouet, Jean-Christophe, Extinct Species of the World, Charles Leets, 1990
Banks, Martin, Conserving Rainforests, Wayland, 1989
Barnes, Simon, Tiger!, St. Martin's Press, 1994
Barrow, C.J., Land Degradation, Cambridge University Press, 1991
Bender, Lionel and Gamlin, Linda. The Book of Natural History, Aladdin Books, 1994
Berenbaum, May, Bugs in the System, Addison Wesley, 1995
Blackmore, R. and Reddish, A, editors, Global Environmental Issues, Open University, 1996
Blum. Deborrah, The Monkey Wars. Oxford, 1994
Braus, Judy, etc.. Amazing Animals, Q. & A Book, Wishing Wells Book, 1993
Bright, Michael, Alligators and Crocodiles, Franklin Watts, 1990
Bright, Michael, Eagles. Franklin Watts, 1990
Bright, Michael, Killing for Luxury. Franklin Watts, 1988
Bright, Michael, Saving the Whales, Franklin Watts, 1987
Bright, Michael, The Dying Sea. Franklin Watts, 1988
Brown, Lester, et. al. State of the World (1996), W. W. Norton and Co., 1996
Burnie, David, Bird, Dorling Kindersley Ltd, 1988
Burton, Maurice and Robert, Encyclopedia of the Animal World, Black Cat, 1988
Carey. John, editor. Eyewitness to History, Avon, 1987
Carwardine, Mark, Animals of the World. Horus, 1995
Carwardine, Mark, The Guinness Book of Animal Records, Guinness. 1995
Cherfas, Jeremy, Zoo 2000. British Broadcasting Corp., 1984
Chinnery, Michael, adviser, World of Nature, Rainbow Books, 1991
Clark, R.B., Marine Pollution. Oxford University Press, 1992
Clark, Dr. Barry, Amphibian, Dorling Kindersley Ltd. 1993
Cleave, Andrew, Snakes and Reptiles, Magna, 1994
Colborn, Theo; Dumanoski, Diane; Myers, John, Our Stolen Future, Plume Book, 1997
Coote, Roger. Atlas of the Environment, Wayland, 1991
Craven. John and Carwardine, Mark, Wildlife in the News, Hippo Books, 1990
Croke, Vicky, The Modern Ark. Scribner, 1997
Day, David, Noah's Choice, Viking, 1990
Day, David, Environmental Wars, Ballantine, 1989
DeRose, Chris, In Your Face, Duncan Publishing, 1997

Domalain, Jean-Yves, The Animal Connection, William Morrow and Co. Inc 1977

Earthwork Group, The, 50 Simple Things Kids Can Do to Save the Earth, Andrews and McMeel, 1990

Encyclopedia Americana, 1989 edition

Encylopedia of the Animal Kingdom. Black Cat, 199

Ferguson-Lees, James and Farell, Emma, Endangered Birds, George Philip, 1992

Few, Roger, Children's Guide to Endangered Animals, Macmillan, 1993

Gaski, Andrea and Johnson, Kurt, Prescription for Extinction, Traffic USA, 1994

Goudie, Andrew The Human Impact on the Natural Environment, Blackwell, 1993

Hartston, William, Drunken Goldfish, Fawcett Crest, 1987

Haslam, Sylvia, River Pollution: An Ecological Perspective,

Hamilton, Geoff and Owen, Jennifer, The Lliving Garden, BBC Books, 1992

Hester, R.E. and Harrison, R. M., Mining and its Environmental Impact, Royal Society of Chemistry, 1994

Koebner, Linda, Zoo Book, Forge, 1994

Laidler, Liz and Keith, China's Threatened Wildlife, Blandford, 1996

Lawick-Goodall, Jane van , In the Shadow of Man, Dell Publishing, 1971

Laws, Edward, Aquatic Pollution, John Wiley & Sons, 1993

Legg, Gerald, Amazing Animals, Watts, 1993

Macquitty, Miranda, Amazing Bugs, Dorling Kindersley, 1996

Macquitty, Miranda, Ocean, Dorling Kindersley, 1995

Macquitty, Miranda. Shark, Dorling Kindersley, 1992

Maniguet, Xavier, The Jaws of Death, Crescent Books, 1996

Martin, Dr. Anthony, Fact Finder Whales, Crescent Books, 1990

Martin, James, Living Fossil. Crown, 1997

Mason, B.J., Acid Rain, Oxford University Press, 1992

Matthews, Rupert, The World of Sharks and Whales, Kibworth, 1993

McCarthy, Colin, Reptile. Dorling Kindersley, 1991

McLeigh, Ewan. The Spread of Desert, Wayland, 1989

Miller, G. Tyler, Jr.. Environmental Science. Wadsworth, Inc., 1995

Morris, Desmond, The World of Animals, Viking, 1993

Morris, Desmond, Animal Watching, Jonathan Cape Ltd, 1990

Mound, Laurence, Insect, Dorling Kindersley, 1990

National Georgraphic Society. The Emerald Realm. National Geographic Society, 1990

Newkirk, Ingrid, Kids Can Save the Animals!, Warner Books, 1991

Newkirk, Ingrid, Save the Animals!, Warner Books, 1990

Nichol, John, The Mighty Rainforest, David and Charles, 1990

O'Toole, Christopher, The Encylopedia of Insects, Andromeda Oxford, 1995

Papastaurou, Vassili, W'hale, Dorling Kindersley Ltd, 1993

Parker, Steve, Mammal. Dorling Kindersley Ltd, 1989

Parker, Steve, Pond and River, Dorling Kindersley Ltd. 1988

Penny, Malcolm. Protecting Wildlife. Wayland. 1989
Perucca, Fabien. Pouradier, Gerald, The Rubbish on Our Plates. Prion Books, 1996
Philp, Richard. Environmental Hazards & Human Health, Lewis Publishers, 1995
Pollution Probe Foundation, Can. Green Consumer Guide, McClelland and Steward. 1989
Ponting. Clive, A Green History of the World, Penguin Books, 1991
Porritt, Jonathan, Save the Earth. Dorling Kindersley Ltd., 1991
Redmond. Ian. Elephant, Dorling Kindersley Ltd, 1993
Redmond, Ian, Gorilla, Dorling Kindersley Ltd, 1995
Reid. Struan, Bird World, Hamlyn, 1991
Rifltin, Jeremy, Beyond Beef, Plume Book, 1992
Riflcin, Jeremy, The Green Lifestyle Handbook, Henry Holt, 1990
Richarz, Klaus, Limbrunner, Afred, The World of Bats, T.F.H. Publishing Inc., 1993
Roberts, Michael, The Living World, Thomas Nelson and Sons Ltd, 1991
Rogers, Barbara Radcliffe, Galapagos, Mallard, 1990
Rue III, Leonard Lee, Elephants, Magna, 1994
Scholastic Inc., Animals and Nature, Two-Can Publishing, 1995
Schwartz, Linda, Q & A Book on Save the Earth, Publicatgin International, 1992
Sequoia, Anna, 67 Ways to Save the Animals, Harper Perennial, 1990
Sherrow, Victoria, Endangered Mammals of North America, 21th Century Book, 1995
Sirett, Dawn, The Really Amazing Animal Book, Dorling Kindersley Ltd, 1996
Sleeper, Barb ara. Wild Cats of the World, Crown, 1995
Southwick, Charles, Global Ecology in Human Perspective, Oxford, 1996
Steiger, Brad and Steiger, Sherry Hansen, Strange Powers of Pets, Berkley, 1993
Taylor, Barbara, Arctic and Antarctic, Dorling Kindersley Ltd, 1995
Taylor, Barbara, The Animal Atlas, Dorling Kindersley Ltd, 1992
Taylor, Barbara, Animal Homes, Dorling Kindersley Ltd, 1996
Taylor, Barbara, The Bird Atlas, Dorling Kindersley Ltd, 1993
Touchstone, Save the World. Touchstone Publishing Ltd., 1991
Tudge, Colin, Last Animals at the Zoo, Island Press, 1991
Tulin, Melissa, Aardvarks to Zebras, Citadel Press, 1995
Vallely, Bernadette, 1001 Ways to Save the Planet, Ballentine Books, 1990
Wade, N., Dean, C, Dicke, W., The Book of Science Literary Vol. II, Times Book, 1994
Waldbauer, Gilbert, Insects Through the Season, Harvard, 1996
Wallace, Irving and Amy, Wallechinsky, David. The Book of Lists, Bantam, 1977
Wallace, Irving, Amy and Sylvia, Wallechinsky, David, The Book of Lists H 2, Bantam. 1980
Wallace, Irving and Amy, Wallechinsky, David, The Book of Lists U 3, Bantam, 1983
Wallechinsky, David, Twentieth Century, Little, Brown and Co., 1995

Ward, Paul and Kynaston, Suzanne, Bears of the World. Blandford Book, 1995
Weiner, Jonathan, The Next One Hundred Years. Bantam, 1990
Wells, Susan, Ocean of the World*, Horus, 1995
Whalley, Paul, Butterfly and Moth, Dorling Kindersley Ltd. 1988
Williams, Jeanne, editor. Animal Rights and Welfare, H.W. Wilson Co., 1991
World Conservation Union, The Last Rain Forests. Mitchell Berzlcy, 1990

INDEX

www.ingramcontent.com/pod-product-compliance
Lightning Source LLC
Chambersburg PA
CBHW070102290526
45789CB00005B/1894